MEASURES FOR COMMUNITY AND NEIGHBORHOOD RESEARCH

In memory of my amazing big brother Bob. And, to all the dedicated community people I've worked with, who give meaning to these measures!

Mary L. Ohmer

To my wonderful family, Jim, Hannah, Caitlin, Tim and Theo, and in memory of G. Thomas Kingsley who led the National Neighborhood Indicators Partnership and contributed greatly to the field of community measurement.

Claudia Coulton

To my family (Heath, Miles, and Tate) for their unwavering support and community partners who taught me the meaning and importance of each of the concepts described in this book.

Darcy A. Freedman

To social workers, residents, and students who conduct community and neighborhood research so that we can understand more completely the strengths and challenges of where we live, engage and succeed.

Joanne L. Sobeck

To my mom, Melanie Kent, for her relentless courage and commitment to the truth.

Jaime Booth

MEASURES FOR COMMUNITY AND NEIGHBORHOOD RESEARCH

Mary L. Ohmer
University of Pittsburgh

Claudia Coulton
Case Western Reserve University

Darcy A. Freedman
Case Western Reserve University

Joanne L. Sobeck
Wayne State University

Jamie Booth
University of Pittsburgh

SAGE

Los Angeles | London | New Delhi
Singapore | Washington DC | Melbourne

SAGE

FOR INFORMATION:

SAGE Publications, Inc.
2455 Teller Road
Thousand Oaks, California 91320
E-mail: order@sagepub.com

SAGE Publications Ltd.
1 Oliver's Yard
55 City Road
London, EC1Y 1SP
United Kingdom

SAGE Publications India Pvt. Ltd.
B 1/I 1 Mohan Cooperative Industrial Area
Mathura Road, New Delhi 110 044
India

SAGE Publications Asia-Pacific Pte. Ltd.
3 Church Street
#10-04 Samsung Hub
Singapore 049483

Printed in the United States of America.

Library of Congress Cataloging-in-Publication Data

Names: Ohmer, Mary L.

Title: Measures for community and neighborhood research / Mary L. Ohmer, author.

Description: Thousand Oaks, California : SAGE, [2018] | Includes bibliographical references and index.

Identifiers: LCCN 2018006611 | ISBN 9781483358369 (pbk. : alk. paper)

Subjects: LCSH: Community development—Research—Methodology. | Community organization—Research—Methodology. | Community psychology—Research—Methodology. | Community-based social services—Research—Methodology.

Classification: LCC HN49.C6 O364 2018 | DDC 307.1/4072—dc23 LC record available at https://lccn.loc.gov/2018006611

This book is printed on acid-free paper.

Acquisitions Editor: Joshua Perigo
Editorial Assistant: Sarah Wilson
Production Editor: Andrew Olson
Copy Editor: Karin Rathert
Typesetter: Hurix Digital
Proofreader: Theresa Kay
Indexer: Sheila Bodell
Cover Designer: Janet Kiesel
Marketing Manager: Kara Kindstrom

18 19 20 21 22 10 9 8 7 6 5 4 3 2 1

TABLE OF CONTENTS

Chapter 13 • Community Well-Being and Quality of Life **427**

This chapter covers measures that identify and capture perceptions of community well-being. It also describes indices or indicators of well-being that use existing data sources, including overall quality of life, social and community well-being, and well-being and human development indices.

LIST OF MEASURES AND TABLE NUMBERS

Chapter 6 • Social Connections and Processes in Communities

Chapter 7 • Community Empowerment and Engagement

Chapter 8 • Community Resources and Resident Satisfaction

PREFACE

This book provides a summary and analysis of some of the most widely used community and neighborhood measures. The goal of this book is to help researchers, professors, students, and practitioners better understand and contribute to communities. To our knowledge, this is the first book of its kind to compile, organize, describe, and analyze multiple measures for community and neighborhood research from a broad range of disciplines, including social work, sociology, policy studies, political science, community psychology, community development, urban affairs (e.g., urban studies, planning, and geography), criminology, urban economics, community education, public and community health, prevention science, and so on. Community and neighborhood measurement instruments can come from so many fields, so it's no wonder that few people have attempted to write a book like this! To say it was a bit daunting is an understatement! We are inspired and humbled by the amazing work of the many researchers whose measures we include in this book.

While the term "community" can refer to multiple types of communities (e.g., communities of identity, race, etc.), our book focuses on the geographic places where people live, work, and play. These places can have a tremendous impact on who we are, what we become, and how we interact with one another and the wider community. Based on our inclusion criteria outlined in Chapter 1, we provide a comprehensive analysis of some of the most utilized and empirically, theoretically, and/or conceptually grounded and supported measures that span the following areas: community readiness and capacity for change, strategic collective action, community social connections and processes, community empowerment and engagement, community resources and satisfaction, the built environment influencing healthy living, housing and neighborhood revitalization, community disorder, crime and violence, place-based social exclusion and unequal access to resources, and community well-being and quality of life.

This book is distinct from other measurement books in several ways. The majority of other measurement texts attempt to find and summarize as many instruments as possible within one text. Instead, we focused on finding some of the most widely used and empirically, conceptually, and theoretically based measures in the field. Second, most measurement texts typically provide a very brief introduction to each measurement area and a brief description of each measurement instrument. In this book, each of the measurement chapters includes the definition of the measurement area and its importance to community research and the corresponding theories/conceptual frameworks and relevant research associated with each measurement area. We also provide an analysis of the measures, compare and contrast similar measures, and include the historical development of measurement areas that have emerged over several decades of research. The introductory chapters in this book are also unique in measurement books because we provide our own conceptual framework for community research within which researchers can utilize the measures in the book, examples of how researchers have utilized some of the measures in the book, and a comprehensive analysis of the importance of and methodological issues with community and neighborhood measurement. In short, our book is not simply a dictionary or compendium of measures but a comprehensive guide to measures and measurement in this field.

Each of the measurement chapters was informed by a thorough review of the literature in the substantive area. However, we recommend that this book is just one component or phase of your community research. We strongly encourage readers to explore their focus area further by examining the literature we reviewed for each type of measurement instrument. Moreover, we do not include all of the items for the measures in this book, so we encourage you to review the references for each measure and contact the primary author for more information on the prior research, results, and items for each measurement instrument.

The audience for this book is as broad as the disciplines working and conducting research in communities and neighborhoods. While this is clearly a book that community researchers, professors, and students can use, it can also be helpful to community practitioners working in neighborhoods. I worked for many years as a community organizer/developer prior to getting my PhD in social work and would have found this type of book useful in helping me, as well as the community and grassroots organizations I worked with, better understand and evaluate the impact of our work. Thus, our vision is that this book is used not only by research institutions but also by the numerous community agencies and public and private organizations who work to improve conditions in communities and neighborhoods.

—Mary L. Ohmer, PhD

ACKNOWLEDGMENTS

I could never have written this book without my incredible co-authors! I am especially thankful to Claudia Coulton, who I consider a mentor, friend, and one of the most brilliant community researchers in the field of social work today. Claudia and I began this book together several years ago—her support, dedication, and amazing knowledge about community research helped me to persevere throughout the entire process. This was a daunting task, so a few of the people we started with were not able to finish. Thus, I am incredibly grateful to my co-authors who came on board after the project was already started: Darcy Freedman, Joanne Sobeck, and Jaime Booth. They all provided expertise, enthusiasm, and genuine commitment to completing this book! I am grateful for their contributions and especially their friendship!

I also want to personally thank Nancy Kropf, who was the Director of the School of Social Work at Georgia State University (GSU), where I worked when I began this book. Nancy was incredibly supportive and provided helpful suggestions, feedback, and advice as I began this journey. Nancy also provided support for a graduate research assistant (GRA) who was very helpful: thank you to my former student Allison Hood for lightening the load. I also want to thank two of my colleagues at GSU, Elizabeth Beck and Fred Brooks, who helped to frame this book and contributed to some of the early thinking about the measurement areas we should include. I am also thankful for the support of Tracy Soska at the University of Pittsburgh, School of Social Work, where I currently work, who provided moral support for this project. I am grateful to Dean Larry Davis, who provided support for GRAs who assisted me. Thank you to my former students Megan Bassler and Sore Shields for your contribution to this project. Finally, I want to thank Kassie Graves, former publisher for Human Services for SAGE Publications, who took the risk on producing this book and believed in the project from the get go! I also want to thank Nathan Davidson, former acquisitions editor, and Joshua Perigo, current acquisitions editor, from SAGE Publications, for their support and encouragement.

My co-authors would also like to thank several people. Claudia Coulton would like to acknowledge Youngmin Cho and Jiho Park for their editorial assistance. Darcy Freedman is grateful to Stephanie Pike for her research assistance, her family (Heath, Miles, and Tate) for their unwavering support, and community partners who taught her the meaning and importance of each of the concepts described in this book. Joanne Sobeck would like to thank the Wayne State University Center for Social Work Research for their assistance in gathering articles and organizing the literature for her review of measures. Jaime Booth is grateful for the collaboration with all of the co-authors on this book.

Finally, all of us would like to thank the many reviewers who provided substantive feedback and helpful suggestions throughout the writing of this book. We are grateful to all of the people who reviewed our initial proposal, including Marie Weil, Tracy Soska, Virginia Majewski, Noam Ostrander, R. Maldonado Moore, Richard Smith, Robert Wright, and Tracey Mabrey. We are thankful that our editors at SAGE Publications allowed us to send batches of chapters out for review as we wrote them. This allowed us to incorporate suggestions and changes into future chapters as we were writing them. Therefore, we thank the following reviewers: Debra S. Norris, Packiaraj Arumugham, Patricia M. Henry (first batch); Bonnie Laing, Daniel Brisson, Richard Smith (second batch); and Robert Silverman, Richard Smith, Anna Maria Santiago, John R. Barner, and Douglas Perkins (last batch). We are especially grateful to Richard Smith who not only reviewed our proposal and multiple chapters throughout the writing of this book but provided some of the most substantive and thoughtful feedback, comments, and suggestions not only on SAGE's feedback form but also within the text of several chapters he reviewed.

—Mary L. Ohmer, PhD

ABOUT THE AUTHORS

Mary L. Ohmer, PhD, MSW, MPIA, is an Associate Professor in the Community, Organization, and Social Action Concentration at the School of Social Work at the University of Pittsburgh. Dr. Ohmer has worked extensively as a community organizer/developer and community-based researcher. Her current research and teaching focus on community organization and development and community-based intervention research, fair housing, youth engagement, and international social and community development. A central part of her research focuses on a community level intervention to facilitate collective efficacy to prevent community and youth violence and promote community health. Dr. Ohmer has published in several highly ranked journals and was the lead author of *Consensus Organizing: A Community Development Workbook: A Comprehensive Guide to Designing, Implementing and Evaluating Community Change Initiatives;* and associate editor of *The Handbook of Community Practice, Second Edition.*

Dr. Ohmer is a Board Member of the Association for Community Organization and Social Administration (ACOSA), and she serves as the Co-Chair (with Dr. Joanne Sobeck) of both the Community and Neighborhood Research Special Interest Group and the Conference Cluster for the Society for Social Work and Research (SSWR). She received her doctorate with distinction from the University of Pittsburgh in 2004, was a recipient of Pitt's prestigious Interdisciplinary Fellowship for Community-based Evaluation; and received the *Emerging Scholar Award* from ACOSA. She has also worked internationally, including facilitating study abroad programs in Costa Rica and Cuba, conducting community research in Ghana, and presenting at international conferences in Hong Kong, China and Tokyo, Japan.

Claudia Coulton is Distinguished University Professor and the Lillian F. Harris Professor at Jack, Joseph and Morton Mandel School of Applied Social Sciences, Case Western Reserve University. She is founding director of the Center on Urban Poverty and Community Development. Under her leadership, the Center has built a model capacity to provide data for community initiatives and research, including a dynamic neighborhood indicators portal, a parcel-based data platform for community development collaboration, and a longitudinal multi-agency integrated data system. Coulton is a founder of the National Neighborhood Indicators Partnership and has served as research adviser to many community change programs including Aspen Institute's Roundtable on Comprehensive Community Initiatives, the Annie E. Casey Foundation's Making Connections program, and the Invest in Children initiative. She is currently leading a Grand Challenge for Social Work, Harnessing Technology for Social Good, with a focus on better utilizing information technology to inform social policy and practice. Her research focuses on how neighborhoods and communities affect families and applications of big data and spatial analysis to understand these issues. Her most recent studies focus on the impact of neighborhoods' housing quality and market forces on children's health and development. She is the author of numerous scientific publications and policy reports.

Darcy A. Freedman, PhD, MPH, is Associate Professor of Population and Quantitative Health Sciences at Case Western Reserve University, School of Medicine, where she also serves as Associate Director of the Prevention Research Center for Healthy Neighborhoods. Trained as a community psychologist with a specialization in public health, Dr. Freedman's research and pedagogy are rooted in the concept of community as both a context and process for community health development. This perspective informs her research, which is focused on the influence of community environments on health and wellbeing with an emphasis on strategies to promote health equity. Much of her research examines policy, system, and environmental strategies aimed at improving neighborhood access to healthy foods for chronic disease prevention. In addition to her research in this area, Dr. Freedman is engaged in food policy coalition efforts, serving as the Founding Director of the Food Security Partners of Middle Tennessee, Appointee to the South Carolina Food Policy Council, and Co-Chair of the Cleveland–Cuyahoga County Food Policy Coalition. She received the 2016 Sarah Samuels Memorial Award from the American Public Health Association, Food and Nutrition Section recognizing her outstanding contributions to advocacy, policy, and evaluation for public health nutrition. In 2017, Dr. Freedman was appointed a Standing Member of the Community-level Health Promotion Study Section of the National Institutes of Health. A native of Ohio, after a 15-year experience of working in several southern states, Dr. Freedman returned home and now lives in Shaker Heights with her husband, Heath, and two sons Miles and Tate.

Joanne L. Sobeck, Ph.D., is an Associate Dean for Research and Director of the Center for Social Work Research in the School of Social Work at Wayne State University. In this capacity, she directs strategies for maintaining an infrastructure to support faculty research and community partnerships to develop and evaluate best practices in social work interventions. She has developed a collaborative model for research that leverages university resources and builds capacity of communities and organizations. Because of her efforts, the Center is a working hub of engagement with the community dedicated to solving some of the area's most difficult challenges in improving lives of disadvantaged individuals, families and communities.

Her recent research interests include community capacity building, child welfare workforce development, and health and environmental justice. Dr. Sobeck co-directs a nationally funded child welfare workforce recruitment and retention program. She also collaborates to reduce health disparities by building habits of community engagement for health with citizens, and co-developed a course on community engagement methodologies and practice. Most recently, she has been involved in an inter-disciplinary study to examine the relationship between the Flint water crisis and the outbreak of Legionnaires' disease. Dr. Sobeck has published on predictors of adolescent substance use, child welfare policy, Native American health, capacity building, and sustaining grassroots organizations. Her combined experiences and publications in community-based research, community engagement, and capacity building provide a strong basis for her teaching, mentoring, and commitment to fulfilling her school's urban mission.

Jaime Booth, PhD, is an assistant professor in the University of Pittsburgh's School of Social Work. Dr. Booth's research strives to understand how social factors, such as neighborhoods and acculturation, impact health disparities, with the goal of developing interventions to mitigate their impact. Dr. Booth has published extensively on neighborhood effects on health, acculturation stress among Latino youth and culturally grounded prevention interventions to improve health outcomes. Her work has been recognized by Arizona State Women Faculty Association (2014), the American Public Health Association Latino Caucus (2015), and the Association for Community Organization and Social Administration (2016). Dr. Booth's current funded projects include an exploration of the use of Twitter feeds to understand neighborhood effects, an examination of the role of implicit bias among mortgage brokers and landlords in maintenance of neighborhood segregation, a project engaging youth in the development of a mobile application to create collective efficacy, and a study using visualization and dialogue to understand Latino youths experience of acculturation stress in emerging Latino communities. Dr. Booth also recently received a K01 award from the National Institute of Drug Abuse to investigate the way in which youth in disadvantaged neighborhoods interact with activity spaces and the impact of the interaction on substance use.

Sara Miller McCune founded SAGE Publishing in 1965 to support the dissemination of usable knowledge and educate a global community. SAGE publishes more than 1000 journals and over 800 new books each year, spanning a wide range of subject areas. Our growing selection of library products includes archives, data, case studies and video. SAGE remains majority owned by our founder and after her lifetime will become owned by a charitable trust that secures the company's continued independence.

Los Angeles | London | New Delhi | Singapore | Washington DC | Melbourne

1 INTRODUCTION AND PURPOSE

This book is the first of its kind to organize, describe, and analyze measures for community and neighborhood research in an accessible manner. Our goal is to provide students, professors, researchers, and community-based practitioners with a helpful resource to locate, compare, and utilize community and neighborhood measures. This book can be used by research institutions as well as the numerous nonprofit agencies and other public and private organizations that work to improve conditions in communities and neighborhoods. This chapter provides a discussion of how to define communities and neighborhoods, including their essential components and various ways researchers have defined place. The types of measures in the book are discussed, along with the inclusion criteria we used to select the measures. Finally, the purpose and overall structure of the book are described.

DEFINING COMMUNITIES AND NEIGHBORHOODS

Communities and neighborhoods in this book are defined as identifiable geographic locations or places. Place-based communities have specific geographic, social, and psychological meanings as well as consequences for the people who live and work there (Chaskin, 1999; Coulton, 2005). Sampson (2013) argues that the city is ordered by the spatial logic of neighborhoods that are always changing but have maintained their hierarchy or relative position in the city persistently over time. Even in a society where technology "seduces us to transcend place," the commitment to communities and places continues along with persistent and strong associations with specific places that motivate people to act (Sampson, 2013, p. 2). Research demonstrates that the quality and quantity of human behavior is profoundly impacted by place (Sampson, 2013).

Communities and neighborhoods can be agents of change, targets for change, or the context within which change happens (Coulton, 2005, p. 74). In this book, we present measurement tools to examine the essential components of neighborhoods and communities and the various roles that communities and neighborhoods can play in people's lives. Significant research has been conducted on the essential components of communities and their effects on creating healthy, strong, sustainable, and effective places where people live, work, and play (Coulton, 2005), including the following: social capital (Putnam, 2000), community capacity (Chaskin, 1999; Foster-Fishman, Cantillon, Pierce, & Van Egeren, 2007), collective efficacy and social control (Sampson & Graif, 2009; Sampson, Raudenbush, & Earls, 1997), sense of community (Chavis & Pretty, 1999; Peterson, Speer, & Hughey, 2006), neighboring, and amenities and resources (Grillo, Teixeira, & Wilson, 2010; James, Carswell, & Sweaney, 2009; Sirgy, 2012), collective action, civic participation, engagement, and neighborhood activism (Foster-Fishman et al., 2007; Foster-Fishman, Pierce, &

Van Egeren, 2009; Lenzi et al., 2012), community empowerment (Peterson, Lowe, Hughey, Reid, Zimmerman, & Speer, 2006; Zimmerman & Rappaport, 1988), community well-being (Manderson, 2004; O'Brien, McClendon, & Ahmed, 1989; Pacione, 1982), and neighborhood disorder and safety (Mooney et al., 2014; Ross & Mirowsky, 1999; Skogan, 2015). This book contains measurement tools and instruments that can help practitioners and researchers examine the essential components of communities and their impact on people and their overall quality of life.

The symbolic idea of a neighborhood is also important; "citizens make decisions and render opinions every day based on broad perceptions and imagined neighborhoods, which in turn have real consequences" (Sampson, 2013, p. 8). Sampson (2013) conceptualizes "neighborhood in theoretical terms as a geographic and, hence, ecological section of a larger community or region that usually contains residents or institutions and that has socially distinctive characteristics" (p. 8).

However, scholars have debated extensively over the proper operational definition of neighborhoods and how to study them (Sampson, 2013). Coulton (2005) argues that researchers and practitioners must be clear about how they define community or neighborhood boundaries. Vague, unclear, or arbitrary statistical definitions of neighborhoods that don't represent the importance of place can undermine the authenticity and statistical power of community research (Coulton, 2005). Researchers often define neighborhoods as aggregations of U.S. census tracts, which are small, relatively permanent subdivisions of counties (Azrael et al., 2009). Some scholars have suggested that census tracts may not be a good proxy for how residents experience their neighborhoods (Azrael et al., 2009). School districts and zip codes have also been used to define neighborhood or community boundaries; however, these spaces may not conform to the lives of residents and how they define the boundaries of their communities (Coulton, 2005). Despite these limitations, there are strategies for more clearly defining neighborhoods (Azrael et al., 2009; Coulton, 2005). For example, researchers can use GIS and block-level census data to define community boundaries that are visual representations of residents' perceptions of their neighborhoods (Chow & Crowe, 2005; Coulton, 2005; Ohmer, 2008). Other scholars have used a multi-step process to define neighborhoods, including developing census block group maps, reviewing land use, and conducting field visits and on-site observations in communities to define boundaries (Weiss et al., 2007, as cited in Azrael et al., 2009). The unit of analysis (e.g., small or large; or individual, organizational, neighborhood, or community) will depend on one's research questions (Hipp, 2007, as cited in Sampson, 2013).

In this book, we include community-level measures of larger geographic areas (e.g., cities), measures of smaller geographic areas (e.g., entire neighborhoods or micro areas within neighborhoods, such as block groups or faces), and also individual-level measures that reflect perceptions or observations of place-based communities, including their characteristics, the interactions among people, and the organizations within communities. In Chapter 3, we discuss in greater detail the methodological considerations for community and neighborhood measurement, such as identifying community and neighborhood boundaries, and also the unique challenges when the unit of analysis is the neighborhood or community itself.

OVERVIEW OF MEASUREMENT METHODS AND INCLUSION CRITERIA FOR MEASURES IN THIS BOOK

Monette and colleagues (2011) define measurement as "the process of describing abstract or theoretical concepts in terms of specific indicators by assigning numbers or symbols to these indicators" (p. 104). The process of measurement involves the assessment of "how much, or to what degree, a variable is present" (Monette, Sullivan, & DeJong, 2011, p. 104). There are several techniques for measuring concepts in the social sciences, but the main ones include (1) verbal reports: people being interviewed or people answering questions and responding to verbal statements (e.g., survey research on people's attitudes or perceptions); (2) direct observation of phenomena: directly watching people or making note of phenomena in their setting (e.g., observation of residents' behavior at a community meeting); or (3) archival records: review of available recorded information, such as government records and secondary data sources (e.g., review of neighborhood data from the U.S. Census) (Monette et al., 2011, p. 105). This book includes verbal, self-report or survey instruments, and observational assessments as well as place-based measures that utilize administrative data or neighborhood indicators.

The following **types of measures** are included in this book:

- Individual measures of people's relationship to and/or perception of place, neighborhood, and community (e.g., sense of community, perception of community resources)
- Measures of the social unit of the community, neighborhood, or place as a whole (e.g., collective efficacy, crime, housing vacancy, etc.)
- Measures of the community or place in relationship to the external region of which the community is a part (e.g., transportation access, access to jobs, inequality, etc.)
- Measures of community organizations and institutions (e.g., coalitions, collective action)

This book is not intended to provide a summary of all of the available and current community and neighborhood instruments or measures. The purpose of this book is to provide an analysis and synthesis of some of the more widely used community and neighborhood measures and provide a context and conceptual framework within which researchers can utilize these measures, as well as an analysis of the importance of and methodological issues with community measurement. The measures included in this book were based on the following **inclusion criteria**:

- Measurement instruments or methods that are widely used and distinct, published and/or manualized, and fully documented from the following types of publications:
  - Peer-reviewed publications
  - Government publications
  - Other accessible publications (e.g., articles, reports, etc.)
- Measurement instruments with replicable and discernable measurement methods that can be used by researchers and practitioners
- Where possible, measurement instruments or methods that have demonstrated evidence of reliability and/or validity, including the following:
  - Reliability that is examined using methods that are appropriate for the level of measurement (Note: a brief overview of measurement reliability is discussed below.)
  - Theoretical assessment (e.g., there is a clear conceptual or theoretical rationale or framework that supports the measure)

  - Criterion, construct, or other types of validity (Note: a brief overview of measurement validity is provided below.)
  - Valid data sources (e.g., such as the U.S. Census)

- Published in English: the majority of the instruments were examined and tested in the United States; however, we also include measures from other countries if they are more widely used, available in English, and/or published in English journals or publications.

Measurement Reliability

Reliability is the ability of a measure "to yield consistent results each time it is applied" (Monette et al., 2011, p. 119). Measurement reliability is based on one of the two following principles: (1) stability: "a reliable measure should not change from one application to the next, assuming the concept being measured has not changed"; and (2) equivalence: "all items that make up a measuring instrument should measure the same thing and thus be consistent with one another" (Monette et al., 2011, p. 119).

The measures in this book utilize several different methods for examining reliability based on the unit of analysis and the type of measure. Verbal reports, including survey measures using scaled variables, are typically assessed using psychometric methods of reliability analysis. Measures examining observations of neighborhood phenomena may use traditional psychometric methods of reliability as well as methods that are adapted from psychometric reliability methods. Community- or neighborhood-level measures may examine reliability at the larger geographic level (e.g., entire neighborhood) using a method called ecometrics.

Psychometric methods for examining reliability typically include inter-observer or inter-rater reliability, test–retest reliability (e.g., tests over time), multiple or parallel forms (e.g., different versions of the same test), and most commonly, internal consistency reliability (e.g., a test at one point in time) (Monette et al., 2011). Inter-rater reliability analyzes whether or not different observers of the same phenomena are consistent. The researcher examines the percentage of agreement among raters to determine this type of reliability. This is typically done by calculating a Pearson correlation to determine if the measures by different raters are significantly associated with one another or by computing an intraclass correlation to compare the responses of more than two raters or more that two sets of scores (Monette et al., 2011). Test–retest reliability applies a measurement instrument at repeated times (e.g., at least twice) for the same group of people under the same conditions (Monette et al., 2011). If the scores are stable when the instrument is administered a second or subsequent time, then measure is considered reliable. Typically a correlation between the two measures is calculated to identify their degree of association (note: reliable measures have a high degree of association, e.g., a correlation of .80 or above) (Monette et al., 2011). When two different forms or measures are used to measure the same thing but include different times or questions, then multiple forms reliability can be used. The researcher administers both forms to the same people and computes a correlation between the two forms to determine if they are significantly associated with one another (e.g., .80 or above considered reliable) (Monette et al., 2011). Finally, internal consistency reliability uses a single scale administered to one group of people to develop an estimate of reliability using one of two primary methods: split-half reliability or Cronbach's alpha reliability (Monette et al., 2011). Split-half reliability randomly divides all responses to the instrument into halves, treating each as though it were a separate scale. The researcher then computes the correlation between the two halves (e.g., a correlation of .80 or above demonstrates reliability) (Monette et al., 2011). Cronbach's alpha reliability is by far the most commonly used method of assessing the reliability of psychometric properties. The Cronbach's alpha is the average of all possible split-half correlations (Monette et al., 2011). The following methods are used to calculate the Cronbach's alpha. One method divides the scale into all possible configurations of two halves; a correlation is computed for each possibility, and the average of those correlations is computed to derive the alpha score. Another method is an inter-item correlation where the researcher correlates each item in the scale with every other item and then uses the average of these correlations as the measure of reliability. Measures with Cronbach's alpha scores of .70 and above are considered reliable (Monette et al., 2011).

Neighborhood researchers have adapted reliability methods traditionally used for psychometric measures to examine the reliability of neighborhood-level individual perceptual and observational measures, including social and physical disorder and collective efficacy (e.g., Raudenbush & Sampson, 1999; Sampson & Raudenbush, 1999). This newer method of examining reliability of neighborhood-level phenomena is called *ecometrics* (Raudenbush & Sampson, 1999). Ecometrics is a refinement on psychometric methods that attempts to address the measurement error resulting from aggregating variables measured at the individual level to describe neighborhood or community-level concepts. Sampson and Raudenbush (1999) explain that these methods attempt to address the following measurement error: "(*a*) item inconsistency within a face block, (*b*) face-block variation within larger geographic units, and (*c*) temporal variation" (p. 618). For example, researchers examining observations of physical or social disorder in neighborhoods collect observations that will vary depending on the time of day the observation takes place; therefore, measures need to estimate and adjust for this as well as allow for any randomly missing data (Sampson & Raudenbush, 1999, p. 619). Researchers conduct a three-level hierarchical regression model to calculate reliability of these types of observational measures (Raudenbush & Sampson, 1999; Sampson & Raudenbush, 1999). Results from the analysis determine whether or not the observational variables are reliable at the ecological level (Sampson & Raudenbush, 1999). A more detailed explanation of ecometrics is provided in Chapter 3.

Measurement Validity

A measure may be reliable but not valid; however, it is commonly understood that if a measure is valid, then it is most likely reliable (Monette et al., 2011). Validity refers to the accuracy of a measure, including how well it measures the variable it is intended to measure and whether or not there is a clear and logical relationship between the way a variable is defined and the way it is operationalized (Monette et al., 2011, p. 115). There are two main types of validity: expert judgments and empirical validity. Expert judgment forms of validity include the most basic forms of validity called face validity and content validity (Monette et al., 2011). Face validity is subjective in nature and examines whether a "logical relationship exists between the variable and the proposed measure" (Monette et al., 2011, p. 115). Content validity examines whether the measure covers the full range of meaning as well as a representative sample of all the content, elements, or instances of the phenomena being measured.

Empirical validity can be examined using several methods, including criterion validity and construct validity. Criterion validity "establishes validity by showing a correlation between a measurement device and some other criterion or standard that we know or believe accurately measures the variable under consideration" (Monette et al., 2011, p. 116). One form of criterion validity is concurrent validity, which compares the measurement instrument to some other already existing criterion, such as the results of another measure that has already established validity. In this method, both measures are applied to the same sample and the researchers compare the results by calculating the correlation between the two measures (e.g., a correlation of .50 or above is considered the minimum required for establishing concurrent validity) (Monette et al., 2011, p. 116). Criterion or predictive validity is when a measurement instrument predicts some future condition. The most complex is construct validity, which "involves relating an instrument to an overall theoretical framework to determine whether the instrument is correlated with all the concepts and propositions that comprise the theory" (Monette et al., 2011, p. 117). The measures are assessed as to whether they relate to some criteria or criterion that are derived from the underlying theory. These are the most commonly used methods for examining measurement validity; however, Chapter 3 also includes a discussion of validity when examining neighborhood or community-level measures.

PURPOSE AND STRUCTURE

As researchers, practitioners, trainers, and teachers, we saw the need to provide a resource on community and neighborhood measures for our own projects as well as those of our colleagues. We are not aware of other books that have organized and synthesized the types of measures we are including in this book in one place. There are online and other resources that are very helpful and useful in locating community and neighborhood measures, including the National Neighborhood Indicators Project (see: http://www.neighborhoodindicators.org/), NeighborWorks Success Measures (see: http://www.neighborworks.org/Community/Outcome-Measurement), and resources that provide content specific measures (for example, The Centers for Disease Control and Prevention's compendium of youth violence prevention measures: https://www.cdc.gov/violenceprevention/pdf/yv_compendium.pdf). While these resources are helpful, their focus is more limited, making it challenging for researchers, students, and community practitioners to identify measures addressing multiple community and neighborhood concepts. The purpose of this book is to promote the use of reliable and valid measures that can be used in community and neighborhood research, program evaluation, community-based and community-level intervention research, research on neighborhood effects, and community-based participatory research. The book is also meant to be used by multiple disciplines, including social work, sociology, urban and community development, public health, community psychology, and so forth. This book can also be used to train students as well as staff from community agencies and to promote services, programs, and interventions that benefit community residents and institutions, including neighborhood organizations, community development corporations, foundations, intermediaries, city planning and urban development agencies, social services, and other nonprofit organizations.

Description of Book Chapters

This book consists of two main sections. The first section of this book, including this chapter, provides the rationale, structure, and purpose; our conceptual and theoretical framework; and an analysis of methodological issues in community and neighborhood research. The next section of the book contains 10 chapters that analyze and describe measures for community and neighborhood research. In **Chapter 2**, we illustrate and describe our ecological/conceptual framework for community and neighborhood research, including how the measures in the book fit within this framework. Chapter 2 includes a table with the domains covered in the book and the associated measures. We also discuss in detail the types of measures included in the book (e.g., individual, group, organizational, individuals nested in communities; and structural, process, physical, and dynamic measures). Information is also provided on how readers might use the book and the measures in their own research, including sample research questions, strategies, and illustrations. **Chapter 3** discusses overall methodological issues and considerations for community and neighborhood measurement. The first section of Chapter 3 discusses the unique methodological issues that must be considered when measuring concepts at the neighborhood or community level, including validity and the drawing of inferences with ecological units, such as communities, sampling, and sample size considerations. The second part of the chapter discusses issues that impact the field of community and neighborhood measurement and research more generally, including approaches for defining and specifying the community or neighborhood, specialized approaches to data collection related to community measurement, strategies for engaging community partners in neighborhood research, particularly in selecting measures, as well as using new sources of technology in community measurement.

The next ten chapters synthesize measures for community and neighborhood research and provide tables summarizing each of the highlighted measures. Each chapter defines the measurement area and its importance to community and neighborhood research. Where applicable, theories and conceptual frameworks related to each measurement area are also discussed. This provides readers with the overall context and language used in each area of measurement. Each chapter is then subdivided into the key measures associated with each measurement area. The key measures are discussed, including key findings and analyses conducted on each measure. A table is provided on each measure that includes a description, scoring and measurement methods, assessment (e.g., reliability), a description of the sample(s) and data used in the study, related references where applicable, contact information for the primary author, and any associated websites. The first two chapters discuss measures that help researchers assess capacity for community change and the ability of communities to engage in collection action and collaborative efforts. **Chapter 4** describes a public health model for community readiness and provides an analysis of measures for ***community readiness and capacity for change***, including readiness for change, capacity of community-based health and social initiatives, community and organizational capacity measures, and community ownership and preparedness. **Chapter 5** analyzes and discusses measures and strategies for engaging in ***strategic collective action*** in communities, including examining participation and representation in collective efforts; the contexts affecting community organizing; assessments of community-based participatory research; and measures for examining the activities, functioning, and characteristics of coalitions and partnerships, including power, trust, and leadership.

The next two chapters analyze and describe measures that help researchers examine the nature of social processes and engagement in communities, including the impact on social connections, empowerment, and efficacy. **Chapter 6** describes and analyzes measures of ***social connections and processes in communities and neighborhoods***, including measures that assess the various types of connections among residents and/or their relationships to a neighborhood or place, including sense of community, social capital, social cohesion/ties, and collective efficacy. **Chapter 7** analyzes and discusses measures of ***community empowerment and engagement***, including psychological empowerment among youth and adults, community empowerment, civic engagement, participation in neighborhood and community organizations, neighborhood activism, and sociopolitical control (leadership and political) among both youth and adults.

The next four chapters are focused on community characteristics that are often the focus of community interventions or analysis, including neighborhood resources, community structures—such as parks, grocery stores, and housing—and neighborhood environmental factors—such as poverty, blight, disorder, and crime and safety. **Chapter 8** provides a discussion of measures of ***community resources and satisfaction,*** including observation-based measures of neighborhood resources, survey-based measures of community resources and amenities, and environmental indicators; awareness of and satisfaction with public services and facilities; perceptions of neighborhood quality and neighborhood and community satisfaction. **Chapter 9** discusses measures of the ***built environment influencing healthy living***, including the neighborhood food environment related to nutrition and food access, cost and quality; walkability, pedestrian and cycling assessments; and measures examining neighborhood green spaces, recreation, and physical activity. **Chapter 10** focuses on measures used in ***housing and neighborhood revitalization***, including housing quality, affordability, and market strength; measures of vacancy and blight; residential mobility; and gentrification and displacement. **Chapter 11** focuses on measures of ***community disorder, crime, and violence,*** including observational and survey measures of physical and social disorder, measures of fear of crime and exposure to violence, as well as a discussion of methods and data sources that are often used for indicators of crime and violence in communities.

The final two chapters present and discuss measures that help researchers examine the overall quality, and character of place-based communities, including examining issues of inequality, the unequal distribution of resources in communities, as well as measures of overall quality of life. **Chapter 12** discusses measures of ***place-based social exclusion and unequal access to resources,*** including racial and economic segregation, negative environmental exposures, access to transportation and jobs, and access to services. **Chapter 13** defines and discusses various aspects of ***community well-being and quality of life*** and includes both domestic and international survey measures examining resident perceptions of individual and community well-being as well as indicators of well-being that use existing data sources, such as human development, quality of life, and livability.

CONCLUSION

Many of the measures in this book have a long historical and critical development, with multiple researchers examining and refining the psychometric properties and measurement strategies and methods used to develop sound community and neighborhood instruments. While some of the measures presented in this book are widely used, they vary in terms of their reliability and validity. We provide an analysis of the measures in each chapter that should help the reader understand both the strengths and limitations of each of the measures. With this in mind, we leave it to you, the readers, to discern which measures would be the most useful for your research or practice. We also realize that there are measures that we have not included in this book that you may be currently using. We may not have included areas with limited measurement instruments or that are in their early stages of development. Despite these limitations, we believe this book provides a helpful synthesis of community and neighborhood measures that can be used by researchers and community practitioners. We hope it inspires you to conduct further research using these measures, including engaging in further tests of reliability and validity as well as creating new measures in areas that lack sound community and neighborhood instruments. We hope that this book helps to further research, strategies, and interventions that improve the lives of individuals and families in communities, creates community change, and builds strong, healthy, and sustainable communities.

REFERENCES

Azrael, D., Johnson, R. M., Molnar, B. E., Vriniotis, M., Dunn, E. C., Duncan, D. T., & Hemenway, D. (2009). Creating a youth violence data system for Boston, Massachusetts. *The Australian and New Zealand Journal of Criminology, 42*(3), 406–421.

Chaskin, R. J. (1999). *Defining community capacity: A framework and implications from a comprehensive community initiative.* Retrieved from Chicago: http://www.chapinhall.org/sites/default/files/old_reports/41.pdf

Chavis, D. M., & Pretty, G.M.H. (1999). Sense of community: Advances in measurement and application. *Journal of Community Psychology, 27*, 635–642.

Chipuer, H. M., & Pretty, G. M. H. (1999). A review of the sense of community index: Current uses, factor structure, reliability, and further development. *Journal of Community Psychology, 27*(6), 643–658.

Chow, J. C., & Crowe, K. (2005). Community-based research and methods in community practice. In M. O. Weil (Ed.), *Handbook of community practice* (pp. 604–619). Thousand Oaks, CA: Sage.

Coulton, C. (2005). The place of community in social work practice research: Conceptual and methodological developments. *Social Work Research, 29*(2), 73–86.

Foster-Fishman, P. G., Cantillon, D., Pierce, S. J., & Van Egeren, L. A. (2007). Building an active citizenry: The role of neighborhood problems, readiness, and capacity for change. *American Journal of Community Psychology, 39*(1–2), 91–106.

Foster-Fishman, P. G., Pierce, S. J., & Van Egeren, L. A. (2009). Who participates and why: Building a process model of citizen participation. *Health Education and Behavior, 36*(3), 550–569.

Grillo, M., Teixeira, M., & Wilson, D. (2010). Residential satisfaction and civic engagement: Understanding the causes of community participation. *Social Indicators Research,* 97(3), 451–466.

James, R., III, Carswell, A., & Sweaney, A. (2009). Sources of discontent: Residential satisfaction of tenants from an Internet ratings site. *Environment and Behavior,* 41(1), 43–59.

Lenzi, M., Vieno, A., Perkins, D. D., Santinello, M., Elgar, F. J., Morgan, A., & Mazzardis, S. (2012). Family affluence, school and neighborhood contexts and adolescents' civic engagement: A cross-national study. *American Journal of Community Psychology.* doi: 10.1007/s10464-012-9489-7.

Manderson, L. (2004). Disability, global legislation and human rights. *Development, 47*(2), 29–35.

Monette, D. R., Sullivan, T. J., & DeJong, C. R. (2011). *Applied social research: A tool for the human services* (8th ed.). Pacific Grove, CA: Brooks/Cole.

Mooney, S. J., Bader, M. D. M., Lovasi, G. S., Neckerman, K. M., Teitler, J. O., & Rundle, A. G. (2014). Validity of an ecometric neighborhood physical disorder measure constructed by virtual street audit. *American Journal of Epidemiology, 180*(6), 626–635.

O'Brien, D. J., McClendon, M. J., & Ahmed, A. (1989). Neighborhood community and quality of life. *Community Development, 20*(2), 59–71.

Ohmer, M. L. (2008). Assessing and developing the evidence base of macro practice interventions with a community and neighborhood focus. In M. Roberts-DeGennaro (Ed.), Paradigm of evidence-based macro practice [Special issue]. *Journal of Evidence-Based Social Work, 5*(3/4), 519–547.

Pacione, M. (1982). The use of objective and subjective measures of life quality in human geography. *Progress in Geography, 6*(4), 495–514.

Peterson, N. A., Speer, P. W., & Hughey, J. (2006). Measuring sense of community: A methodological interpretation of the factor structure debate. *Journal of Community Psychology, 34*(4), 453–469.

Peterson, N. A., Speer, P. W., & McMillan, D. W. (2008). Validation of a brief sense of community scale: Confirmation of the principal theory of sense of community. *Journal of Community Psychology, 36*(1), 61–73.

Peterson, N. S., Lowe, J. B., Hughey, J., Reid, R. J., Zimmerman, M. A., & Speer, P. W. (2006). Measuring the intrapersonal component of psychological empowerment: Confirmatory factor analysis of the sociopolitical control scale. *American Journal of Community Psychology, 38,* 287–297.

Putnam, R. D. (2000). *Bowling alone: The collapse and revival of American community.* New York: Simon & Schuster.

Raudenbush, S. W., & Sampson, R. J. (1999). Ecometrics: Toward a science of assessing ecological settings, with application to the systematic social observation of neighborhoods. *Sociological Methodology, 29,* 1–41.

Ross, C. E., & Mirowsky, J. (1999). Disorder and decay: The concept and measurement of perceived neighborhood disorder. *Urban Affairs Review, 34*(3), 412–432.

Sampson, R. (2013). 2012 Presidential Address to the American Society of Criminology: The place of context: A theory and strategy for criminology's hard problems. *Criminology, 5*(1), 1–31.

Sampson, R., & Graif, C. (2009). Neighborhood social capital as differential social organization: Resident and leadership dimensions. *American Behavioral Scientist, 52,* 1579–1605.

Sampson, R. J., & Raudenbush, S. W. (1999). Systematic social observation of public spaces: A new look at disorder in urban neighborhoods. *American Journal of Sociology, 105*(3), 603–651.

Sampson, R. J., Raudenbush, S. W., & Earls, F. (1997). Neighborhoods and violent crime: A multilevel study of collective efficacy. *Science, 277,* 918–924.

Sirgy, M. (2012). *The psychology of quality of life: Hedonic well-being, life satisfaction and eudaimonia* (2nd ed.). Springer: New York.

Skogan, W. (2015). Disorder and decline: The state of research. *Journal of Research in Crime and Delinquency, 52*(4), 464–485.

Zimmerman, M. A., & Rappaport, J. (1988). Citizen participation, perceived control, and psychological empowerment. *American Journal of Community Psychology, 16*(5), 725–750.

2 FRAMEWORK FOR COMMUNITY AND NEIGHBORHOOD MEASUREMENT

The community and neighborhood measures included in this book represent indicators for different levels of influence across the ecological spectrum. Our focus on measuring multiple levels of influence is underpinned in ecological perspectives that contextualize human choices and behaviors within diverse settings (Bronfenbrenner, 1977; Lewin, 1935; Stokols, 1996). Ecological perspectives draw attention to the ways that communities and neighborhoods shape opportunity and emphasize different contexts of influence within individual, collective, community, and societal settings. Applications of ecological perspectives are widespread in community and neighborhood research addressing a range of issues, such as bullying (Hong & Espelage, 2012), sexual health (Baral, Logie, Grosso, Wirtz, & Beyrer, 2013), and physical activity (Fluery & Lee, 2006).

Measures described throughout each chapter of this book represent four ecological settings (individual, collective, community, and societal) that are important for research, policy, and practice focused on communities and neighborhoods. These settings build on prior research highlighting different spheres of influence that have direct and indirect effects on individual and collective well-being (Bronfenbrenner, 1977). Given interactions between settings, researchers and practitioners are encouraged to select measures representing more than one ecological setting. In Chapter 2, we introduce topics that are covered in greater detail in subsequent chapters. These other chapters are denoted throughout to promote linkages for further examination of the topic.

Measures targeting the *individual-level* focus on attitudes, cognitions, skills, and community participation and engagement among adults and youth. These measures may be used to evaluate community engagement initiatives aimed at preparing residents for change (Chapter 4), increasing empowerment among residents to engage in change (Chapter 7), or sociopolitical skills necessary to lead neighborhood change (Chapter 6). Measures targeting the *collective level* provide tools for evaluating actions of collectives, such as coalitions, community organizing groups, neighborhood associations, and grassroots organizations. Collective action is a key strategy in initiating community change, and these measures offer tools for evaluating factors that may facilitate successful coalition functioning and significant indicators of collaboration (Chapter 5).

Within this book, readers will find measures representing *community-level* indicators focusing on four aspects of communities and neighborhoods. First, there are community-level measures of inclusivity that reflect the ways that residents feel connected to both people and places within community boundaries. These indicators may be useful in evaluating how a sense of community (Chapter 6) among residents affects interventions aimed at promoting greater connection. Second, community-level measures assess the availability of resources and amenities accessible to residents. Such observation-based measures are discussed in Chapter 8, which provides methods for assessing resources, such as recreation facilities, stores, and parks. In addition, these measures also assess satisfaction with community resources, therefore offering opportunities to evaluate factors influencing resource utilization and identify targeted approaches for improvement. Third, community-level measures may be used to examine built and natural environments that shape communities and neighborhoods. Built environments include human-made infrastructures, such as housing (Chapter 10) and grocery stores (Chapter 9), while natural environments include green space for recreation (Chapter 9). Fourth, community-level measures assess community safety and security, including indicators about crime and violence within communities and neighborhoods (Chapter 11) as well as exposure to community violence (Chapter 11). Also included in this book are measures of community well-being (Chapter 13).

The fourth setting represents *societal-level* factors that support or hinder communities and neighborhoods. Measures focused on this setting assess the implications of local, state, and federal policies that systematically limit investment and opportunity within certain communities, often along lines defined by social hierarchy. These measures, for instance, may be used to inform and evaluate policy interventions aimed at promoting equitable opportunities for housing and/or employment (Chapter 12).

CONCEPTUAL FRAMEWORK

The conceptual foundation for this book is based on seven domains (individual engagement and efficacy in the community, collective engagement and efficacy in the community, community amenities and resources, community economics, community safety and security, built/natural environment, community inclusivity) that provide a way to organize compatible measures and differentiate those measures to examine interactional processes at multiple levels.

The first domain, *individual engagement and efficacy in the community,* includes a range of activities and involvement in the community that are meant to bolster personal empowerment and skills as a method to shift power and influence from formal or traditional sources to citizens or residents. These measures assess individual-level participation, perceptions, and behaviors related to the processes and/or outcomes of citizen engagement in their neighborhood and/or community.

Collective engagement and efficacy in the community captures processes involving groups, organizations, associations, coalitions, and partnerships, who work together to solve common problems or issues. It includes measures that assess a collective units' (e.g., community, organization, coalition, and partnership) perceptions and behaviors related to the processes and/or outcomes of engagement in a neighborhood and/or community.

The domain of *community amenities and resources* takes a strengths-based approach to community development and can be important for identifying assets and opportunities for change, which in turn may lead to more precise community-level interventions. Instruments are included that assess perceptions and objective measures of community and neighborhood resources and public amenities and services.

Community economics is a concept that encourages the use of economic tools to analyze elements of communities that impact residents' ability to access things such as housing, employment, and public financing. These measures use data to determine economic disparities in communities and neighborhoods because of unequal access to jobs and resources, including housing market strength.

The domain of *community safety and security* represents one of the central concerns in communities and neighborhoods, with an intersection of individual, collective, community, and social contexts as targets for intervention. Community safety measures assess perceptions and objective indicators of crime and violence and residents' fear of crime in their neighborhood.

The *built/natural community environment* refers to the human-made or natural surroundings in a community setting that impact people. Measures comprise the physical capital of neighborhoods and communities, including housing (quality, affordability, vacancy, and blight), access to health food, walkability, resources, and perceived disorder.

Community inclusivity is a concept promoting equality of access to resources, treatment, and opportunity of all people in a community. Measures assess the geospatial distribution of the population and resources across communities and neighborhoods to understand the impacts of social exclusion and segregation and unequal access to resources as well as gentrification and diversity.

Finally, measures of *overall well-being* reflect how well individuals in a neighborhood and the community as a whole are doing in terms of overall quality of life and access to resources and opportunities. This is one of the overarching concepts/emerging properties in our conceptual model, which is discussed next.

The domains reflect a broader conceptual level of thinking that can assist community researchers and practitioners to understand the main purpose behind the measures and to see how they are deeply embedded in complex social structures of community well-being, culture, and power. Our conceptual representation of these factors is presented next (see **Figure 2.1**).

FIGURE 2.1 ■ Conceptual Model for Research With Communities and Neighborhoods

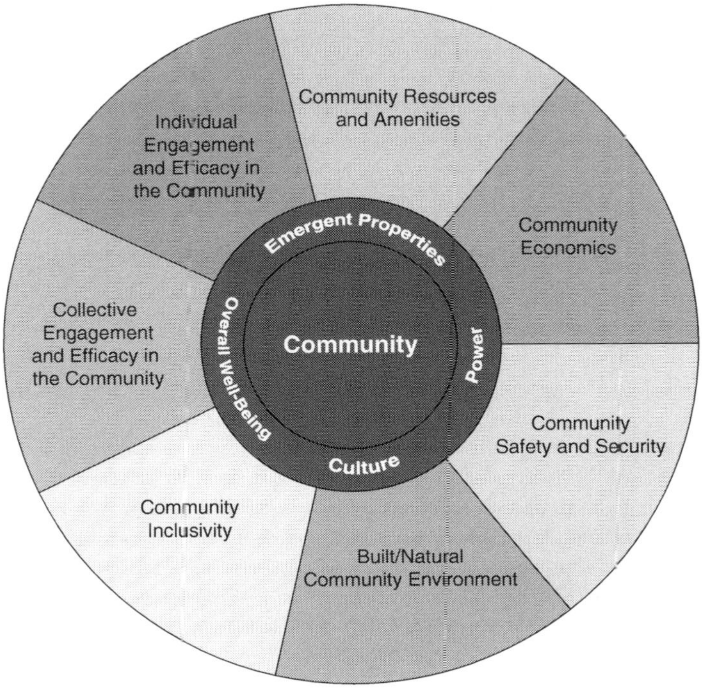

Unique to the complexity of community and neighborhood research is the idea that a set of attributes or traits that make up a community are not always additive or equal to the sum of the various components (or domains) (Checkland & Scholes, 1990). That is, when conceptual components, including individual and collective engagement, community resources, economics and built/natural environment, safety, and community inclusivity are studied together, properties emerge that cannot be predicted by observations and knowledge of these sub-components. These traits represent "emergent properties" that stem from the interaction between components and the environment (Lewin, 1935; Martin, 2001). When the community is the focus of the research, new structures, patterns, and properties, including overall community well-being, culture, and power, are likely to appear. The emergence of these structures in turn influences the various components (domains of community research), which provides a multilevel understanding of transactional causation between various domains. For example, the concept or the action of power emerges out of the complex interactions between collective engagement and community safety and security, which is supplemented by action often bolstering a greater sense of engagement in the community.

Furthermore, we can study communities and neighborhoods as complex systems by creating probes to make the patterns or potential patterns in community more visible before taking action. We can assess the relationships between community capacity and readiness and make sense of data to identify patterns of behavior, conduct analyses to identify the people and other information sources critical to the setting in order to develop the best intervention, and then we can build on what works and dampen down on patterns that are not effective. Below are key emergent properties that are likely to develop out of interactions when conducting community and neighborhood research.

Community well-being is an overarching concept and goal that many community activists and researchers seek to achieve and measure in their work. It is used interchangeably with concepts of community satisfaction, quality of life, and happiness. Research studies may ask: Is the community thriving? Are residents satisfied with their neighbors, amenities, and networks for leading a fulfilled life? Sirgy, Widgery, Lee, and Yu (2010) propose that community well-being is measured as the summation of individual levels of satisfaction with community characteristics. McCrea and colleagues (2014) think that community well-being is best conceptualized as a state, at one point in time. They argue that it is an evaluation of important aspects of community in relation to expectations or standards of comparison. Chapter 13 focuses on community well-being and quality of life and identifies several individual, social, and neighborhood/community-level features to help conceptualize well-being for research on communities and neighborhoods. For the purpose of this chapter, community well-being stems from the interaction between the other conceptual domains described above and may include social (individual and collective), economic, environment, and political processes and specific areas such as safety, health, and employment. Community researchers and practitioners are encouraged to test conceptual links using well-being as a direct outcome or one that transpires as a result of including more than one domain in their study or target of practice. Community well-being, for example, can be studied in relation to an element of community participation such that feeling satisfied with one's participation in a community event or activism (collective efficacy) relates to a positive sense of community well-being. Alternatively, a resident's satisfaction with community functions or resources may be a sufficient measurable outcome but when combined with collective efficacy, global community well-being may emerge.

Culture is a characteristic of societies, communities, and organizations that is defined and used differently in many ways. The traditional anthropological concept of culture is defined as shared assumptions, values, beliefs, rules, and customs of conduct of a group or community of people. In this definition, culture is viewed as omnipresent, meaning culture is present in all places at all times. However, if we think of culture as a meta concept, we have more possibilities for framing neighborhood and community research in a richer context. Meta culture is a dynamic system with its own interactions of structures and patterns that can be differentiated into subcultures that may be appear to be fragmented or complementary to other structures (Patterson, 2014). In community and neighborhood research, culture, for example, embodies the process of individual engagement (collectively made, reproduced, and unevenly shared knowledge) and how that relates to building the physical capital of neighborhoods. It may include the comparison of what people perceive of neighborhood resources to what they actually use. For our framework, culture is an emergent property, interacting with structural forces in constraining and enabling human agency (Patterson, 2014).

The Robert Wood Johnson Foundation (2015) recently launched a Culture of Health Program conceiving of culture as a meta concept. The program is based on ten underlying principles (vision statements) that are used to inspire action to mobilize a "culture of health" and achieve the outcome of improved population health. These principles acknowledge the following: how good health exists across geographic, demographic, and social sectors; how getting healthy is valued by the entire society; that individuals and families have the means and opportunity to make choices that lead to a healthy life; that multiple sectors (individual, business, government, and other organizations) collaborate to build healthy communities and lifestyles; that all of society has access to affordable, quality health care; that health care is efficient and equitable, producing less burden on the economy; that sustaining healthy citizens guides public and private decision-making; and finally, that Americans understand that everyone is in it together. These principles articulate the espoused values and beliefs important for developing a culture of health.

The Robert Wood Johnson Foundation (2015) Culture of Health Program also outlines a set of drivers for making health a shared value. These drivers include the mindset and expectations, sense of community, and civic engagement among citizens. Creating a culture also depends on the number and quality of partnerships, investment in cross-sector collaboration, and policies that support collaboration. Other drivers include the built environment/physical conditions, social and economic environment, policy, and governance. Other causes (drivers) for strengthening the integration of health services and systems focuses on access, consumer experience, quality, balance, and integration of medical treatment, public health, and social services.

Culture as a meta concept helps us to understand the many facets of conducting research with communities and neighborhoods. The assumptions and the drivers for developing a culture of health are similar to the targets when conducting research on communities and neighborhoods. It demonstrates how research and practice in one domain must adapt to new knowledge as it develops in other domains and be able to emphasize its own importance to building the knowledge of the whole. Finally, it provides direction for building hypotheses between individual engagement in community, building partnerships, the physical environment in which residents live, and their influence on community well-being.

Power is a concept that may facilitate or inhibit community development and sustainability, yet it is understudied in community research. Power has both positive and negative aspects (Nelson & Prilleltensky, 2005). On the positive side, power aids in the ability of individuals and communities to achieve goals evidenced through a sense of mastery and control over circumstances. On the negative side, power may be used to inflict harm or maintain inequity. According to Neal and Neal (2011), power can also be conceptualized at multiple levels. At an individual level, power is understood as empowering individuals or facilitating social capital that may be leveraged to promote change. At the group level, power is conceived as the collective capacity for a group to impact community policies and resources. At the structural level, power constructs represent the outer setting or external structure of the community, including political climate, public policies, and economic climate. These structural dimensions of power constrain opportunity and freedom. Social hierarchies shaped by race, class, and gender are a manifestation of structural dimensions of power. In community and neighborhood research, these dimensions of power combine to influence geographic distribution of both benefits, such as access to resources (e.g., supermarkets, high quality schools), and burdens, such as distribution of opportunity (e.g., employment) and well-being. Furthermore, some groups understand power as a dialectical process between the individual and organizational level of analysis (Speer & Hughey, 1995). Within the framework of community and neighborhood research, power can be studied as a process, an end state, or as an emergent property.

Conceptual Domains

The seven conceptual domains of the framework denote the various aspects of research on communities and neighborhoods. In order to encourage further research, we identified several dimensions within each domain that measure a specific element of the concept and the chapter location of each associated set of measures (see **Table 2.1: Measures for Community and Neighborhood Research Associated With Our Conceptual Model**). This table shows that measures from different chapters can fit conceptually together under one domain, demonstrating that some measures may be used for multiple purposes. For example, measures or instruments assessing walkability in a community are compatible with measures assessing housing affordability, vacancy, and abandonment. We also include in the table the measures associated with the overarching concept/emergent property of community well-being from Chapter 13.

The conceptual boundaries of each measurement domain are identifiable based on contextually and pragmatically driven frames of reference. Every research question and study implemented in communities and neighborhoods is being conducted within the context of a certain time and space, which means that the measures included here may not keep pace with the interpretation of these concepts. For example, community building has a long tradition steeped in communal labor, social support, and development of public schools, but our definition of community building has changed dramatically with increased mobility, Internet use, and divisions of status, income, and other differences. The conceptual domains are also identified by the intended use of the measures within and across the domains. Walkability, housing quality, and access to community amenities serve as indicators of the built/natural environment, and the results from these measures have multiple uses. They can help the private sector guide homebuyers on where to live. Government agencies use these measures to develop social policies for community reinvestment. Moreover, these indicators also relate to the health and development of residents and to a sense of community satisfaction and well-being. The conceptual links and multiple levels of association between the domains and among the measures demonstrate the fruitful ground for research on neighborhoods and communities. To inspire further research and methodological development for community and neighborhood research, a few examples from the authors are provided next.

EXAMPLES OF COMMUNITY MEASURES IN RESEARCH AND PRACTICE

Our purpose here is to link the measures contained in this book with the practice of using them in various contexts for application, including access to healthy food, promoting community health, safety, and preventing violence and substance use disorders.

TABLE 2.1 ■ Measures for Community and Neighborhood Research Associated With Our Conceptual Framework

CONCEPTUAL DOMAINS							EMERGENT PROPERTY
Individual Engagement and Efficacy in the Community	**Collective Engagement and Efficacy in the Community**	**Community Amenities and Resources**	**Community Economics**	**Community Safety and Security**	**Built/Natural Community Environment**	**Community Inclusivity**	**Community Well-Being**
Citizen participation (e.g., groups, organizations, coalitions) **CHAPTERS 5 & 7**	Community and organizational capacity and readiness **CHAPTER 4**	Community organizations, services, resources, and amenities **CHAPTER 8**	Housing market strength **CHAPTER 10**	Crime indicators and levels **CHAPTER 11**	Home and community environment **CHAPTER 8**	Network assessment **CHAPTER 5**	Individual well-being **CHAPTER 13**
Civic engagement (duty, skills, connections, participation) **CHAPTER 7**	Community ownership and preparedness **CHAPTER 4**	Access to community resources and services **CHAPTER 8**	Housing cost burden and housing induced poverty **CHAPTER 10**	Exposure to community violence **CHAPTER 11**	Resources (parks and green space) **CHAPTERS 8 & 9**	Residential stability and instability **CHAPTER 10**	Community and neighborhood well-being **CHAPTER 13**
Sociopolitical control (leadership competence, policy control) **CHAPTER 7**	Community organizing (contexts and outcomes) **CHAPTER 5**	Satisfaction with services (e.g., social, government, and health services) **CHAPTER 8**	Deprivation and concentrated disadvantage **CHAPTER 12**	Perceptions of crime (fear, risk) **CHAPTER 11**	Healthy food environment and access to healthy food options (e.g., in neighborhoods, stores, restaurants, etc.) **CHAPTER 9**	Gentrification **CHAPTER 10**	
Psychological empowerment (cognitive, emotional, behavioral) among youth and adults **CHAPTER 7**	Collaboration and coalitions (characteristics, functioning, and processes) **CHAPTER 5**	Community satisfaction and attachment **CHAPTER 8**	Economic segregation **CHAPTER 12**		Healthy physical environment (e.g., walkability, physical activity, recreation) **CHAPTER 9**	Spatial and social isolation **CHAPTER 12**	

(Continued)

TABLE 2.1 ■ (Continued)

CONCEPTUAL DOMAINS							EMERGENT PROPERTY
Individual Engagement and Efficacy in the Community	**Collective Engagement and Efficacy in the Community**	**Community Amenities and Resources**	**Community Economics**	**Community Safety and Security**	**Built/Natural Community Environment**	**Community Inclusivity**	**Community Well-Being**
	Partnership networks, trust, power, and synergy **CHAPTER 5**	Community resource fit **CHAPTER 8**	Income diversity **CHAPTER 12**		Housing quality and affordability **CHAPTER 10**	Racial and ethnic diversity **CHAPTER 12**	
	Neighborhood social processes; collective efficacy **CHAPTER 6**				Community order and disorder (physical and social) **CHAPTER 11**		
	Social capital **CHAPTER 6**						
	Community empowerment **CHAPTER 6**						
	Sense of community **CHAPTER 6**						
	Neighborhood activism and community mobilization **CHAPTER 7**						

Community
(Synergistic and Emergent Properties)

↓ Culture ↓ Community Well-Being ↓ Power

Example Application 1: Improving Access to Healthy Food

There is growing attention focused on inequitable access to healthy foods within rural and urban communities throughout the United States as well as in other countries (Beaulac, Kristjansson, & Cummins, 2009). As a result, numerous calls for action have been made for community-level changes to improve healthy food access (Institute of Medicine, 2012; Khan et al., 2009; U.S. Department of Agriculture, 2014). Measures included in this book provide tools for evaluating the impact of healthy food access interventions, such as the development of farmers' markets or healthy corner stores that sell healthy foods, such as fresh fruits and vegetables in neighborhoods with limited access to supermarkets. A first step to measurement may be the assessment of the food retail environment using measures described in Chapter 9 to determine the availability, price, and quality of healthy foods at retailers located in the community. For example, **Table 9.2, Nutrition Environment Measures Survey in Stores (NEMS-S)** assesses a variety of features of the food retail environment. Other measures in Chapter 9 could be used to assess the impact of the farmers' market or corner store interventions, especially if data were captured before and after the intervention. While this information is necessary, it may not be sufficient to mobilize support for establishing a farmers' market or transforming a corner store to include healthier food options. Therefore, the project might benefit by examining citizen participation in the healthy food access intervention planning and implementation process using tools described in Chapter 5. Given wide variability across neighborhoods, the project may also benefit by including assessments of community readiness and capacity for the intervention using measures described in Chapter 4, such as **Table 4.6, Capacity of Community-Based Health and Social Initiatives.** Together, these measures allow for examination of neighborhood change processes that catalyze or demobilize the healthy food access intervention and allow for assessment of impact.

Example Application 2: Promotion of Community Health

Health disparities and health equity issues continue to burden communities across the world. Excessive rates of diseases and death combined with a lack of access to health care create complex social, cultural, and economic conditions that may benefit from the use of multilevel measures and interventions. To demonstrate how research on communities and neighborhoods can be a dynamic community and data-driven process, we begin with a collective engagement of community agencies and resident members who coalesce together to address health issues that are critical to their own personal and community well-being. Chapter 5 contains measures that can evaluate the characteristics and functioning of a coalition (**Table 5.7, Coalition Characteristics and Impacts**) and suggests instruments that can track participation and representation of its members. Identifying factors that contribute to effective collaboration can help clarify the theoretical linkages between the collective benefit of multimember collaborations and community health. If one of the goals of the coalition is to build leadership competence around health, then measures of sociopolitical skills found in Chapter 7 (**Table 7.6, Sociopolitical Control Scale**) can assess outcomes at an individual level. The health coalition can also benefit from collecting data on the resources available in the community and resident satisfaction with services as suggested in Chapter 8 (**Table 8.6, Perceived Accessibility to Key Resources** and **Table 8.16, Access to and Satisfaction With School and Community Health Services**). Measuring access to resources and services can indicate the services currently being used and can also identify gaps or services that need to be developed. Emerging from these various approaches to health, measures of community well-being (**Chapter 13,**

Table 13.3, Overall Community Well-Being) and general satisfaction (**Chapter 8, Table 8.11, Community Satisfaction**) can aid in assessing the potential impact and outcomes of collaborative work.

Example Application 3: Promoting Community Safety and Preventing Violence

Strategies to promote community safety and prevent violence may focus on community building and organizing with the goal of increasing community engagement. These connections may result in increased collective efficacy and decreased fear among residents, with the ultimate goal of reducing neighborhood crime (Sampson, 2004; Sampson, Raudenbush, & Earls, 1997). This community engaged model for crime prevention—such as the approaches used by Ohmer and colleagues (2016), Beck, Ohmer, and Warner (2012), Smallwood and colleagues (2015), and Zeldin (2004)—may be informed and evaluated using measures described in this book. Efforts may begin by collecting and analyzing data about levels of crime and exposure to violence across different communities. Measures described in Chapter 11 may be used to provide evidence for targeting interventions in a specific context by understanding current crime levels and residents' perceptions of crime and disorder (see measures contained in **Table 11.1, Community Disorder and Fear of Crime**). After one or more communities are identified, then additional information may be collected to better understand existing levels of collective efficacy and engagement within the community by utilizing measures described in Chapters 5 and 6. This type of information may reveal the differences in organizational and community capacity across different communities to mobilize around crime and violence prevention and thus lead to more tailored strategies to build their capacity to achieve the same goals. Within these collectives, information may be gathered to assess resident capacity for leading community change or levels of civic participation among residents. For example, strategies that engage youth can use the measures in Chapter 7 to examine the impact of their efforts on empowering and building their capacity (e.g., leadership and political skills) to prevent youth violence (see **Tables 7.3 and 7.4, Psychological Empowerment Among Urban Youth**). You can also use the measures in this book to examine how community interventions that facilitate collective efficacy (see **Table 6.6, Neighborhood Collective Efficacy**) can prevent crime and violence and promote empowerment among both youth and adults (Beck et al., 2012; Ohmer, 2016; Ohmer et al., 2016). Taken together, these measures focused on individual, collective, and community settings that provide information that helps to identify actions and interventions aimed at curtailing crime and preventing community violence.

Example Application 4: Prevention of Substance Use Disorders

Substance use and substance use disorders, including the recent problem of opioid addiction, represents a target for research and multiple interventions at individual, collective, and community levels. The Strategic Prevention Framework (SPF) developed by SAMSHA is a data-driven, dynamic process focused on population-level change intended to guide prevention efforts of diverse community partners. It uses concepts such as the risk and protective factors associated with substance use to understand the conditions in a community and the needs of a population, including the community's capacity to organize. The framework helps advocates to plan multiple strategies and establish potential outcomes for prevention efforts.

The framework is widely used across the United States. Guided by the SPF, the measures in Chapter 4 are relevant for assessing the readiness of the community in planning prevention strategies (**Table 4.3, Community Readiness for Community-Based Prevention**). For example, collecting data on community leadership, engagement in community decision-making, and the extent of social ties may help to identify geographically based priority areas who are ready for substance abuse prevention. Measuring satisfaction with public services, including substance abuse prevention and treatment (**Chapter 8, Table 8.14, Satisfaction With Community-Based Services**) will indicate the community's preference for and evaluation of the current service network.

CONCLUSION

The measures involved in conducting research in communities and neighborhoods are based on numerous theories and models. Theories, models, or frameworks relating to research on communities and neighborhoods will propose different hypothetical causal pathways for linking concepts like psychological empowerment to indicators of community well-being. Each theory or model may identify a slightly different set of antecedents, moderators, or mediators. Ecological theory offers four different contexts or settings for research on communities and neighborhoods, and the use of any one will draw attention to those constructs and provide a different framework for measurement and intervention. However, research and practice in communities and neighborhoods reveals the need to conduct more multilevel studies, particularly in the area of linking constructs (Altman, Sebert-Kuhlmann, & Galavotti, 2015), such as the link between citizen participation, empowerment, awareness and use of community resources, collective action, and community outcomes—such as safety and community well-being. Using a conceptual model that includes the "emergent properties" of community well-being, culture, and power may yield more robust meaning around the interactions or processes studied in community and neighborhood research.

REFERENCES

Altman, L., Sebert-Kuhlmann, A. K., & Galavotti, C. (2015). Understanding the black box: A systematic review of the measurements of the community mobilization process in evaluations of interventions targeting sexual, reproductive and maternal health. *Evaluation and Program Planning, 49*, 86–97.

Baral, S., Logie, C. H., Grosso, A., Wirtz, A. L., & Beyrer, C. (2013). Modified social ecological model: A tool to guide the assessment of the risks and risk contexts of HIV epidemics. *BMC Public Health, 13*(482). Retrieved from https://bmcpublichealth.biomedcentral.com/articles/10.1186/1471-2458-13-482

Beaulac, J., Kristjansson, E., & Cummins, S. (2009). A systematic review of food deserts, 1966–2007. *Preventing Chronic Disease, 6*(3), 1–10.

Beck, E., Ohmer, M., & Warner, B. (2012). Strategies for preventing neighborhood violence: Toward bringing collective efficacy into social work practice. *Journal of Community Practice, 20*(3), 225–240. doi: 10.1080/10705422.2012.700278

Bronfenbrenner, U. (1977). Toward an experimental ecology of human development. *American Psychologist, 32*(7), 513–531.

Checkland, P., & Scholes, J. (1990). *Soft systems methodology in action*. Hoboken, NJ: John Wiley.

Fluery, J., & Lee, S. M. (2006). The social ecological model and physical activity in African American women. *American Journal of Community Psychology, 37*(1–2), 141–154.

Hong, J. S., & Espelage, D. (2012). A review of research on bullying and peer victimization in school: An ecological system analysis. *Aggression and Violent Behavior, 17*(4), 311–322.

Institute of Medicine. (2012). *Accelerating progress in obesity prevention: Solving the weight of the nation*. Retrieved from Washington, DC.

Khan, L. K., Sobush, K., Keener, D., Goodman, K., Lowry, A., Kakietek, J., & Zaro, S. (2009). Recommended community strategies and measurements to prevent obesity in the United States. *MMWR, 58*(RR07), 1–26.

Lewin, K. (1935). *A dynamic theory of personality*. New York: McGraw-Hill.

Martin, G. G. (2001). *Human ecology—Basic concepts for sustainable development*. London: Earthscan Publications.

McCrea, R., Walton, A., & Leonard, R. (2014). A conceptual framework for investigating community wellbeing and resilience. *Rural Society, 23*(2), 270–282.

Neal, J. W., & Neal, Z. P. (2011). Power as a structural phenomenon. *American Journal of Community Psychology, 48*(3–4), 157–67. doi: 10.1007/s10464-010-9356-3

Nelson, G., & Prilleltensky, I. (Eds.). (2005). *Community psychology: In pursuit of liberation and well-being*. New York: Palgrave.

Ohmer, M. L. (2016). Strategies for preventing youth violence: Facilitating collective efficacy among youth and adults. *Journal of the Society for Social Work and Research, 7*(4), 681–705.

Ohmer, M. L., Teixeira, S., Booth, J., Zuberi, A., & Kolke, D. (2016). Preventing violence in disadvantaged communities: Strategies for building collective efficacy and improving community health. *Journal of Human Behavior in the Social Environment* [Special Issue], *26*(7–8), 608–621.

Patterson, O. (2014). Making sense of culture. *Annual Review of Sociology, 40*, 1–30.

Robert Wood Johnson Foundation. (2015). *From vision to action: A framework and measures to mobilize a culture of health*. https://www.cultureofhealth.org/en/about/how-we-got-here.htm;#twn-underlyingprinciples

Sampson, R. (2004). Neighborhood and community: Collective efficacy and community safety. *New Economy, 11*, 106–113.

Sampson, R. J., Raudenbush, S.W., & Earls, F. (1997). Neighborhoods and violent crime: A multilevel study of collective efficacy. *Science, 277*, 918–924.

Sirgy, M. J., Widgery, R. N., Lee, D. J., & Yu, G. B. (2010). Developing a measure of community wellbeing based on perceptions of impact in various life domains. *Social Indicators Research, 96*(2), 295–311.

Smallwood, S. W., Freedman, D. A., Pitner, R. O., Sharpe, P. A., Cole, J. A., Hastie, S., & Hunter, B. (2015). Implementing a community empowerment center to build capacity for developing, implementing, and sustaining interventions to promote community health. *Journal of Community Health, 40*(6), 1122-1129. doi: 10.1007/s10900-015-0038-9

Speer, P. W., & Hughey, J. (1995). Community organizing: An ecological route to empowerment and power. *American Journal of Community Psychology, 23*(5), 729–748.

Stokols, D. (1996). Translating social ecological theory into guidelines for community health promotion. *American Journal of Health Promotion, 10*(4), 282–298.

U.S. Department of Agriculture. (2014). *Supplemental Nutrition Assistance Program Education Guidance and Templates.* Washington, DC. Retrieved from https://snaped.fns.usda.gov/administration/snap-ed-plan-guidance-and-templates

Zeldin, S. (2004). Preventing youth violence through the promotion of community engagement and membership. *Journal of Community Psychology, 32*(5), 623–641. doi: 10.1002/jcop.20023

3 METHODOLOGICAL CONSIDERATIONS FOR COMMUNITY AND NEIGHBORHOOD MEASUREMENT

Place-based communities or neighborhoods as objects of measurement present some unique conceptual and practical challenges. This chapter discusses several methodological issues that researchers may need to consider when designing their study and selecting their community and neighborhood measures. Methods and measurement decisions will depend on the particular focus of their study and their conceptualization of community. We begin by discussing the unique methodological issues that must be considered when measuring concepts at the neighborhood or community level (e.g., such as collective efficacy). This discussion includes several well-known pitfalls that community researchers should be aware of with respect to validity and the drawing of inferences with ecological units such as communities. Researchers studying neighborhood- or community-level phenomena may also encounter some distinctive problems with regard to sampling and sample size considerations, and these are also discussed.

In the second part of the chapter, we consider issues that impact the field of community and neighborhood measurement and research more generally, including approaches for defining and specifying the community or neighborhood, specialized approaches to data collection related to community measurement, strategies for engaging community partners in neighborhood research, particularly in selecting measures, as well as using new sources of technology in community measurement.

METHODOLOGICAL ISSUES WHEN USING COMMUNITY OR NEIGHBORHOOD-LEVEL MEASURES

Special Problems With Ecological and Geographic Units

There are several problems with interpretation and inference that can be of special concern for neighborhood- and community-level measures. These issues are explained below so that community researchers can consider whether any of these apply to their particular study or situation.

Ecological Fallacy

The ecological fallacy arises when inferences are made about correlations at the individual level based on correlations from aggregated population data (Greenland & Robins, 1994; Openshaw, 1984). For instance, if unemployment rates were found to be correlated with rates of family violence at the county level, it would be unreasonable to infer that individuals who lost their jobs were at higher risk of engaging in family violence than those who remained employed because there are other possible explanations for the observed correlation. Perhaps rising unemployment in their county cut into social connectedness for individuals regardless of their employment status, and the resulting social isolation might be the factor contributing to violence in individual families.

A misunderstanding of the ecological fallacy should not be a reason to focus on individual-level studies and ignore social context (Pearce, 2000). Community researchers are typically more interested in studying the relationships among community-level phenomenon or in evaluating the effects of community attributes on individual outcomes than inferring causality at the individual level. Properly handled, measures of social, physical, and economic environments can be evaluated as contributors to individual behaviors or outcomes with reasonable certainty. Moreover, these collective or ecological phenomenon are important subjects for investigation in their own right and are not in and of themselves subject to the ecological fallacy.

The Modifiable Areal Unit Problem (MAUP)

The specification of the neighborhood unit can affect research findings in part because of what has been termed the modifiable areal unit problem (Fotheringham & Wong, 1991; Heywood, 1998; Haynes, Daras, Reading, & Jones, 2007). If the size or number of geographic units is changed, the relationships among variables measured on the areal units will be affected. Moreover, if the specific locations of the boundaries change, such as when census tracts or other administrative zones are shifted, it introduces a degree of ambiguity into any comparisons. These two aspects of the MOUP are referred to as scale and zone effects. The MOUP can make it difficult to compare the results of studies that are carried out using units that vary in these ways.

One way to address this limitation is to examine the sensitivity of study results to changes in the number and size of units or across time. If the data permit, researchers can examine their models using several different methods of defining neighborhood or community units. Researchers also need to take care when interpreting and comparing the findings of different studies to consider how the number and size of the units may have affected the relationships among variables or the statistical significance of the results, considering the concept and the place rather than arbitrary designations.

Uncertain Geographic Context Problem (UGCoP)

Especially in studies that seek to determine how community attributes affect individuals, there is the problem of knowing whether the areal units that are measured truly represent the relevant context. This is referred to as the uncertain geographic context problem (Kwan, 2012). Unlike the MAUP discussed above, the problem is not mainly because of the possibility of varying the size of the units but rests more on the possibility that the relevant area varies across individuals or differs depending on the community processes or individual outcomes that are being studied. If the community units are not correctly specified, this can contribute to measurement error that is difficult to evaluate. Under such circumstances, a study may fail to uncover a neighborhood effect that exists (i.e., false negative) because of the measurement error introduced by incorrect specification of the area.

To guard against this problem, it is crucial that investigators give careful consideration to their selection of the contextual unit, as discussed in previous sections of this chapter. This selection should be guided by theoretical considerations about how community structure and processes work and how they affect individuals. Where possible, studies should evaluate the sensitivity of their results to alternative specifications of the areal units. Moreover, there is a need for more research on how the placed-based community or neighborhood is differentially experienced according to individual characteristics, regional or cultural factors, or the particular phenomenon that is under consideration. Such information would allow researchers to tailor their specification of the areal unit accordingly.

Violation of the Independence Assumption

When statistical models are applied to data collected in place-based communities or neighborhoods, it is important to pay attention to the independence assumption, which underlies standard statistical tests. This assumption tends to be satisfied when individual elements (e.g., persons, households, properties) are randomly sampled from large populations and there is little possibility that they are related in any way. However, when sampled individual elements are clustered within communities or neighborhoods, they may be related (i.e., correlated) through this shared environment. This relatedness potentially violates the independence assumption.

If the clustering of individuals that are sampled within communities or neighborhoods is ignored, some statistical tests may be invalid. There are a variety of approaches to addressing this problem in clustered data, and there is a rich literature on the topic (Arceneaux & Nickerson, 2009). The method selected has to be driven by the specific research question and hypothesis being tested. Generally speaking, there are a few distinctive strategies. Sometimes the researcher is only interested in analyzing measures at the neighborhood or community level, as for example in a study of the impact of neighborhood crime rates on civic engagement. In that case, the attributes of individuals or events are combined (e.g., summed or averaged) to produce aggregate values for each neighborhood, eliminating the problem of correlated errors at the individual level. Alternatively, in some studies it is only the individuals that are of analytic interest, for instance, when low-income neighborhoods are selected as sites for a study of age differences in digital literacy. The sampling design in such cases can be directly adjusted for by calculating robust standard errors that take the clustering into account (Moulton, 1990). Statistical analysis can proceed as usual using these adjusted standard errors. Finally, it is often the case that researchers are interested in assessing whether community or neighborhood factors affect some outcomes for individuals. In such instances, a multilevel or mixed-modeling approach is preferred. These methods allow the error structures to be modeled correctly at both the within cluster and between cluster levels (Raudenbush & Bryk, 2002).

Another aspect of dependence in the error structure of statistical models can come from geographic proximity of either individuals or neighborhood units. Even within neighborhoods, individuals may be closer or farther away from one another or from specific attributes. Similarly, neighborhoods or place-based communities may be contiguous to one another or located at greater distances. Spatial autocorrelation refers to the degree of geographic contiguity or nearness among individuals, objects, or places. Statistical models should take such contiguity or distance into account when spatial dependencies are a concern, in order to avoid biased estimates. This can be accomplished through estimating spatial errors or spatial lagged models (Anselin, 1988; Banerjee, Carlin, & Gelfand, 2004).

Sampling Considerations When Community Is the Unit of Analysis

Addressing Sparseness Within Neighborhood Samples

A common concern in the measurement of neighborhoods and communities is the problem of reliance on sparse samples in underlying data sources. Community measures are frequently based on information obtained from households or individuals that are then aggregated to form measures of the constructs of interest, typically expressed counts, percentages, means, or medians. For example, neighborhood economic disadvantage may be measured by the poverty rate and the percentage of the population with at least some college coming from the American Community Survey. The amount of violent crime may be based on a crime count for a one-year period. Or the level of physical disorder may be measured using the mean score on a scale derived from a survey of a sample of residents. When neighborhood sample sizes are small, sample-based estimates of neighborhood characteristics will have margins of error (MOE) that may be so large as to be problematic either for descriptive estimates or for use in more complicated analysis.

A simple fix for this problem that is often utilized for neighborhood measurement is to combine several contiguous neighborhood units or several years of data in order to gain sample size and thereby, more precise estimates. However, these aggregations are typically less useful on a practical level and tend to introduce unwelcome heterogeneity because of the fact that there may be variation that is obscured when time points or locales are combined. Moreover, combining units where conditions vary can introduce the modifiable areal unit problem discussed above (MAUP) (Hipp, 2007).

Another option is to leverage spatial correlation in order to improve the reliability of measures. By utilizing information from surrounding areas, the resulting estimates for each place borrow power from the sample in those areas that are nearby. When an unreliable estimate is adjusted based on the estimates in nearby areas, the new quantity is often referred to as a *shrinkage estimate*. This term reflects the reality that the adjusted estimate shifts toward the surrounding values based on the relative degree of unreliability in the estimates. In other words, an estimate for a neighborhood that has a high standard error (because of small sample size and/or large variance) moves closer to estimates from other areas that have less error. Neighborhood estimates that have little error do not "shrink" very much. Because the reliability (or error) of the measures is determined from the data, these are referred to as empirical Bayes estimators (Bingenheimer & Raudenbush, 2004).

When the values on neighborhood indicators are spatially correlated, then taking distance into account may provide a more precise approximation to addressing the problem of unreliability. This was demonstrated in a study that compared survey-based neighborhood measures using empirical Bayes estimates that were nonspatial and those that took spatial contiguity into account (Savitz & Raudenbush, 2009). Using survey data from the Project on Human Development in Chicago Neighborhoods, the researchers selected only a small subsample of the cases in order to simulate a situation of sample sparseness. A first order contiguity matrix was utilized as the model for spatial dependence. Applying a two-level spatial hierarchical linear model to a measure of collective efficacy, they demonstrate that the neighborhood estimates utilizing spatial dependence have less error and more predictive validity than do unadjusted estimates or nonspatial empirical Bayes estimates.

Sampling Neighborhoods or Place-Based Communities

Although the ideal research design might involve a nationwide study of all communities or neighborhoods, this is seldom practical. The exception would be studies using nationally available data sources that have geographic identifiers, such as census surveys or big data generated by social media or other digital platforms. But these data sources can only answer a limited range of questions. Researchers that want to collect original data or use local data sources often focus on neighborhoods or communities within a single region or comparative studies of a few metropolitan areas.

Several widely cited studies have been conducted on representative samples of community areas within a single city that were predefined by researchers based on homogeneity of socioeconomic characteristics and natural boundaries. For example, the Project on Human Development in Chicago Neighborhoods identified over 300 neighborhood clusters and studied a random sample of 80. Such designs have the advantage of yielding large and diverse samples of neighborhoods and generalizability to a known population.

Another option has been to study purposive samples of neighborhoods, such as those that have been part of a program or initiative or are representative of interesting types of areas. The Making Connections program focused research on neighborhoods in ten cities that were part of a community change initiative. Households within these neighborhoods were randomly selected to answer survey questions about their perceptions of neighborhood conditions.

It should be noted that neighborhood studies that rely on individuals to be informants about neighborhood conditions have to address additional sampling considerations. Within neighborhoods, sampling is typically done on housing units (or addresses), and it is necessary to then select the individual(s) that will participate in the survey. To assure representativeness, the individual should be selected at random from among the eligible individuals occupying the housing unit. Otherwise, bias could be introduced into the neighborhood measures because of over-representation of household members that are more likely to be available to answer surveys.

Although much of the literature focuses on predefined neighborhood units as the basis for community measurement, a growing body of work begins with sampling small geographic units, such as blocks or land parcels. Spatial sampling is particularly useful for measurement of the physical and social environment and provides flexibility in crafting environmental measures at various scales (Bader & Ailshire, 2014; Lee, Moudon, & Courbois, 2006). Using GIS tools, these samples allow the relevant community areas to be derived inductively based on spatial patterns. This can be followed by recruiting household samples within selected locales that are representative of the range of environmental conditions of interest to the research.

Sample Power in Multilevel Studies

Studies designed to detect effects of neighborhoods on individuals need to be concerned about sample sizes in a multilevel framework. Statistical power refers to the probability that the null hypothesis will be rejected when it is false, and sample size is one of the key elements of the power calculation. Assuming that the variables are measured without error, the power to detect a neighborhood effect if one is present is affected by the sample sizes at both the neighborhood and individual levels and the variance within and between neighborhoods. However, given the many parameters that are estimated in a multilevel model, there are no simple methods for determining the sample power or the precision of estimates of the various parameters.

A number of simulations have examined how sample size affects the precision of various parameter estimates, including slopes and variances (Scherbaum & Ferreter, 2009). Neighborhood researchers often have a keen interest estimating fixed effects of neighborhood variables at Level 2, in this case at the neighborhood level, along with cross-level interactions with Level 1, in this case, the individual-level covariates, for example. It has generally been shown that these parameters are most affected by sample sizes at Level 2 compared to the sizes of samples within neighborhoods (Level 1). As shown in examples provided by Snijders (2005), the precision of estimates is increased markedly as Level 2 units increase from 30 to 50 holding the number of Level 1 units constant. Although some analysts suggest rules of thumb, such as the minimum 30–30 rule (i.e., 30 units at each level), there are many factors that must be taken into account to develop accurate power or precision estimates for a particular study design. For a program for determining statistical power in two-level designs, see https://www.stats.ox.ac.uk/~snijders/multilevel.htm#progPINT.

Assessing the Reliability of Neighborhood-Level Measures: Ecometrics

The growing interest in using survey or observational data to measure neighborhood concepts has led to some important work on how to evaluate the reliability and validity of such measures. Asking individuals to observe and report neighborhood factors has allowed researchers to measure features such as neighborhood social cohesion and disorganization but introduces new sources of measurement error (Mujahid, Diez Roux, Morenoff, & Raghunathan, 2007). Aggregating variables measured at the individual level to describe larger entities, such as school organizations, or cities, is typical in social science research; however, early studies made no attempt to test the reliability of these measures when aggregated (O'Brien, 1990). Researchers now realize that they cannot simply apply the techniques of psychometrics (tests of psychological measures) that began in the early 20th century and resulted in the development of several standardly employed statistical tests, such as Cronbach alpha and factor analysis. In traditional psychometrics, measures are assessed for variation between items, level one, and between individuals, level two; however, neighborhood-level measures require a third level, variation between neighborhoods. Although some methods developed to test the accuracy of psychological measures can be applied to the development of neighborhood-level measures without modification, such as content and criterion validity, other methods have been refined to match a different set of assumptions and logic (Raudenbush & Sampson, 1999).

The refinement of psychometric methods to fit neighborhood-level measurement has been termed ecometrics (Sampson, 2017). Essential to this discussion is the idea that ecological assessment is more than simply the aggregation of individuals—neighborhood-level measures are assessing phenomena that are conceptually separate and apart from the individuals that inhabit the space. In this context, individuals completing surveys or observations about neighborhoods or communities are simply informants providing information about their neighborhood. Variations in individual perceptions because of individual or contextual factors has the potential to introduce error in measurement that must be assessed and, when possible, controlled for. Researchers developing tests of reliability of neighborhood-level phenomena are, therefore, attempting to maximize the variation in a scale across neighborhoods rather than individuals, despite the fact that the measures originate at the individual level (Raudenbush & Sampson, 1999). Optimally, responses to a neighborhood-level scale would not vary within a neighborhood, assuming that there is a static neighborhood feature that all participants are observing and reporting on. If all residents sampled are in agreement about the presence of a neighborhood feature, then we could say that the measure has good inter-rater reliability. This however is rarely the case because of observer bias or differences in individuals' experiences. It is assumed that given an adequate sample size and a valid measure, individuals' response can be aggregated to understand neighborhood-level phenomena. Aggregating across multiple raters may minimize the error introduced by individuals but has also necessitated the development of measurement tests that were able to assess the reliability of the measure at the neighborhood level. It is also important that neighborhood-level measures distinguish between neighborhood characteristics or are adequately sensitive. If for example a neighborhood measure asked about the presence of roads, this item may not introduce error based in individual bias, but it would also not provide information about variation between neighborhoods. Ecometic tests are, therefore, designed to assess a measures' variation within individuals and between neighborhoods, with the goal of understanding how reliable the measure is assessing a neighborhood-level phenomena.

The methods used to assess the reliability of neighborhood-level measures have evolved over time. The early studies that aggregated individual-level variables to make inferences about neighborhood-level phenomena would simply provide Cronbach's alpha—or reliability of the measures at the individual level before they were aggregated. This method was criticized because it typically over or under estimates aggregate-level coefficients. In one of the first proposed solutions to this problem, O'Brien (1990) suggested that an aggregate-level reliability score be estimated by dividing the universe score variance, variance in neighborhood means, and the expected observed variance, the grand mean across all respondents. In this method, the universe score measured the systematic differences in neighborhood-level means, and the expected observed variance included both the systemic differences between individuals and neighborhoods. By dividing these means, the researcher was able to understand the amount of variance that was occurring at the individual and neighborhood levels. O'Brien (1990) also proposed that internal constancy reliability coefficients for aggregates be calculated by dividing the variance components that make up an aggregate by the number observations used to create it. As the sample size increases, the contribution of each individual to the overall error variance decreases, increasing the reliability of the measure. These basic models can be adjusted to account for error that may be because of variation in interviewer or time of day, addressing issues of generalizability.

Sampson and Raudenbush (1997) applied these concepts in the context of multilevel models using a test that is typically called interclass correlations (ICC). The interclass correlation is essentially the ratio of between neighborhood variance and the total variance. ICCs are used to test inter-rater agreement. The ICC scale ranges from 0 to 1—with a high number indicating that the measure is capturing more neighborhood-level differences than individual—and is therefore a reliable measure of neighborhood-level phenomena. It is, however, rare that neighborhood measures that are assessed using individual surveys have ICCs larger than .5 because of the high level of variation that occurs within individuals (Raudenbush & Sampson, 1999). These small ICCs should not be interpreted as small effect sizes; one does not necessarily indicate the other (Duncan & Raudenbush, 1999). The ICC can then be used to assess the neighborhood-level reliability of a measure with a given number of participants or raters. With an ICC of .36, Raudenbush and Sampson (1999) demonstrated that social disorder could be reliably measured at the neighborhood level (.70 to .90 inter-rater reliability), with a sample of 20 participants per neighborhood. ICCs are now one of the most common measure of reliability for neighborhood level measures that are originally assessed at the individual level.

Refined methods of assessment are also needed to assess the quality of neighborhood-level variables that are measured using systematic social observation rather than surveys. Raudenbush and Sampson (1999) outlined the application of item response theory to indicators of disorder assessed using systemic observation. In this analysis, they attempted to (a) understand how much each item of their measure of disorganization (i.e., needles, graffiti, and condoms) contributes to the larger construct of disorganization, and (b) if an item appears in a consistent pattern across neighborhoods. They were also interested in understanding the level of variation that was happening because of observations taking place at different times during the day (Raudenbush & Sampson, 1999). Accounting for temporal variation was important when the observer was measuring social dynamics that could be drastically different in the morning or evening. In order to assess this, Raudenbush and Sampson (1999) recommend that the reliability of the measure be assessed using three-level measurement model, assessing consistency at the individual, block face, and neighborhood levels, accounting for variation that could be because of individual or temporal differences.

The first level of the model assesses the relative contribution of each item to the overall assessment, a method akin to confirmatory factor analysis. The second level of the model assesses the variation of these scales across blocks, accounting for threats to validity, such as time. The Level-3 models, similar to those used to assess survey items, assess the level of variation at the neighborhood level. Although these tests have not been applied uniformly across neighborhood measurement studies, they are considered the current gold standard (Martin, Inchley, Humphris, & Currie, 2017).

Mujahid and colleagues (2007) applied these methods to their assessment of seven neighborhood measures. In this study, the authors first assessed the measures psychometric properties using the Cronbach's alpha coefficient and a two-week test–retest reliability test. They then estimated a three-level measurement model where level one assessed the amount of variation in item response among individuals, level two assessed the amount of variation in individual responses within a given neighborhood, and level three assessed the amount of variation in the means between neighborhoods. This model was used to calculate the ICCs of each measure and the overall reliability of the measures. This paper provides a good example of how ecometrics can be applied to understand the reliability of neighborhood level measures.

OVERALL METHODOLOGICAL ISSUES FOR COMMUNITY AND NEIGHBORHOOD MEASUREMENT

Specifying Neighborhood as a Social and Geographic Unit

Prior to deciding what measure to use, it is necessary to be clear about what constitutes the unit of analysis to which these measures will be applied. In the case of neighborhoods or place-based communities, this is not simple. Conceptually, these are both geographic and social units, and typically their boundaries are not obvious and may even be contentious (Coulton, 2012; Downey, 2006; Galster, 2001; Gotham, 2003; Nicotera, 2007). Practically, the researcher has to consider the feasibility of collecting data on community or neighborhood units, making considerations such as sampling, ease of observation, or data availability pertinent to the definition. There is considerable debate about how the concept of neighborhood should be operationalized for analysis. However, if the unit as measured is not the neighborhood or community area that is pertinent to the issue under investigation, error or bias can be introduced into the findings. In this section, we discuss several methods of defining neighborhood or community units, including administrative boundaries, resident perceptions, physical and spatial characteristics, and activity spaces.

Administrative Boundaries

The vast majority of studies use administratively defined units as proxies for neighborhoods or place-based communities. However, administrative boundaries are established for statistical or programmatic purposes and do not necessarily coincide with individuals' experience with regard to their neighborhoods. Census tracts are the most commonly chosen units for research because many government agencies report economic, demographic, and housing statistics for these geographic units. Census tract boundaries are redrawn every 10 years. Census tracts have an average population of approximately 4,000 but vary markedly both in terms of population size and area. Census tracts are comprised of several block groups, but less data is available for these smaller units. Researchers occasionally use other administrative units, such as zip codes, school zones, or electoral districts, as proxies for neighborhoods, and special tabulations of some types of data are available for these areas.

A key question in considering the use of such administrative units is the degree to which they fit the purpose of the research and its conceptualization of neighborhood or community. Zip code boundaries, for example, are drawn for mail delivery, not statistical reasons, and end up being quite variable in size and often encompass sub-areas that are quite different in their socioeconomic and physical conditions. Thus, measurements made at the zip code level may reflect averages that are unlikely to represent the actual neighborhood or community experience for most residents. Although census tracts tend to be smaller and more homogeneous than zip codes, there is evidence that they do not necessarily coincide with neighborhoods as perceived by residents. For example, a study of neighborhoods in 10 cities found that the typical resident drew their neighborhood boundaries to incorporate an area of .35 square miles, whereas the typical census tract in these same locales was .51 square miles (Coulton, Jennings, & Chan, 2013). Furthermore, residents living in the same census tracts showed considerable disagreement about the exact locations of neighborhood boundaries (Coulton, Chan, & Mikelbank, 2011).

Resident-Perceived Neighborhoods

Resident perceptions are an alternative basis from which to define neighborhood boundaries that have the advantage of representing the areas that are relevant to their everyday lives (Matthews, 2011). That residents often embrace some of their surrounding space and disavow other parts of it (Entwisle, 2007; Gotham, 2003; Gotham & Brumley, 2002) suggests the value in taking their perceptions into account in measurement. Residents' perceptions of neighborhood boundaries can be used to craft neighborhood units based on consensus. It is also possible to create bespoke neighborhood units that are customized for each individual based on their unique boundary specifications.

A community mapping exercise is one technique that researchers have used to define neighborhood units based on residents' views. An illustration comes from the Annie E. Casey Foundation's Making Connections program, a community change initiative in low-income areas in 10 cities that focused on strengthening families and improving neighborhood conditions. Representative samples of adults in each community were asked to draw the boundaries of their neighborhoods onto GIS-generated cartographic maps. The digitized maps were overlaid and GIS tools were used to identify the blocks that were included in a plurality of resident maps. These contiguous blocks were considered to constitute the neighborhood for the purposes of measurement (Coulton, Chan, & Mikelbank, 2011).

Researchers can also use resident perceptions to create unique neighborhood units for each individual. Vallée, Le Roux, Chaix, Kestens, and Chauvin (2014) asked survey respondents in Paris to identify the streets that bounded their neighborhoods and used GIS tools to draw a polygon for each individual that represented their perceived neighborhood. To examine the validity of this method, they compared measures of health care accessibility for the resident perceived neighborhood units with units based on isotropic circles centered on each study respondent (further discussed in the next section). Residents' estimation of the number of health care providers in their neighborhood more closely matched the number of providers found within the resident-perceived neighborhoods than the count within the boundaries based on isotropic constant size buffers.

Physical and Spatial Characteristics

It is also possible to define neighborhood units using spatial buffers or physical features. As mentioned in the previous section, GIS tools can be used to draw individualized neighborhood boundaries centered on each person's location. Sometimes referred to as egocentric or sliding neighborhoods, buffers of varying sizes can be drawn around each household's location, and neighborhood measures are calculated for these buffers (Chaix, Merlo, Evans, Leal, & Havard, 2009; Guo & Bhat, 2007). The buffer may be specified by distance weights, population size, or some other geographic features (Chaix, Merlo, & Chauvin, 2005). There is evidence that the magnitude of contextual effects on some health outcomes is greater when egocentric or sliding rather than census defined neighborhoods are utilized in statistical models (Chaix, Merlo, Subramanian, Lynch, & Chauvin, 2005).

Another approach to neighborhood boundary definition is to utilize aspects of the built environment that are theorized to structure everyday life. An example of this approach are T-communities defined by the network of streets that pedestrians can traverse without crossing main streets (Grannis, 2005). The boundaries of T-communities are demarcated using street data from the Census Bureau's TIGER line files so that tertiary street networks fall within the area that is bounded by main streets or other physical barriers. GIS tools are used to identify the blocks that fall within these networks of pedestrian streets. The resulting areal units (T-communities) demonstrate predictive validity with respect to various hypotheses about racial segregation and interaction (Grannis, 2005). Moreover, T-communities identified through GIS can be combined with local knowledge to further refine this street-based definition of neighborhood units (Foster & Hipp, 2011).

Finally, sometimes it may be desirable to designate neighborhood units according to specified criteria, such as a specific population and designated size or not crossing certain barriers or landmarks. Automated zone design programs can be utilized to aggregate areas together while optimizing such criteria (Cockings & Martin, 2005). This method of crafting neighborhood units was investigated in Bristol, England, applying constraints with respect to population and housing characteristics, area size, and geographic considerations (Haynes et al., 2007). The resulting neighborhood units were found to be similar to community areas that were designated by local government officers.

Activity Spaces

Another approach to determining the areal unit for community measurement is to base it on areas in which individuals spend time. This method recognizes that as individuals move through their surroundings, they carve their own activity space that does not necessarily map onto their residential neighborhood alone or comport with predetermined geographic boundaries (Sherman, Spencer, Preisser, Gesler, & Arcury, 2005). It also allows for the fact that the attributes of residential neighborhoods are not the only ones that matter and that the nonresidential places that individuals spend time may differ on those attributes (Jones & Pebley, 2014). Once the unique activity space is determined for individuals, it is possible to measure social, physical, and other characteristics of that space.

On a practical level, activity space measurement requires knowing how much time individuals spend in various places, along with data on relevant characteristics of those places. The data are typically weighted by the time spent in each location to obtain the measure of exposure. For example, Sharp, Denney, and Kimbro (2015) used survey data from Los Angeles to determine where, in which census tract, respondents worked, shopped, and participated in a number of other activities. Using census data, they were able to characterize the time-weighted exposure of respondents to concentrated disadvantage in their residential neighborhood and compare it to the concentrated disadvantage in the rest of their activity space. They found that the effects of concentrated disadvantage on health were significant but showed differential effects from the exposure coming from residential as compared to other parts of their activity space.

Considerations in Selecting the Unit of Analysis

All of these alternatives to administratively defined neighborhoods face practical challenges. The availability of data can be a problem. Point level or small aggregations such as blocks are fairly easy to allocate into unique boundaries, but data that are available only for larger geographies (e.g., census tracts) may have to be approximately apportioned to the new units. Moreover, the burden of analytic work required to utilize resident maps, street networks, spatial buffers, and so forth is not trivial. However, when the purpose of a study is to explain how neighborhoods change or affect behavior, such methods hold promise as a way of assuring that the neighborhood is correctly specified for the individuals involved.

Finally, although the above techniques are promising as alternatives to neighborhoods delineated by administrative agencies, it is important to further evaluate them based on a deeper understanding of how people interact with and relate to their place-based communities (Matthews, 2011). The relevant neighborhood unit might differ depending on the phenomenon of interest and by characteristics of individuals (Spielman & Yoo, 2009). For example, a concept that rests upon the direct experience of individuals with their neighbors (e.g., social cohesion) may require a unit of measurement that is closely related to shared perceptions. By contrast, a measure of social structure (e.g., racial segregation) would be theorized to operate at a larger scale. Moreover, it is important to consider the variation within neighborhoods and communities on any particular measure and how the designation of neighborhood units affects the magnitude of that variation (Merlo, Ohlsson, Lynch, Chaix, & Subramanian, 2009).

Objective Versus Subjective Neighborhood Measurement

Another crucial decision for researchers interested in community/neighborhood-level phenomena is whether to use objective or subjective measures to document aspects of the neighborhood/community they are interested in investigating. These decisions are largely dictated by the research questions and the concepts being measured. Additionally, practical logistics of completing a research study such as time, money, and available personnel may also be a factor. Still, it is a worthwhile exercise to consider the optimal method of data collection for a given research/practice question with practical barriers removed. Striving to achieve the best method, given the inevitable restraints, will lead to more rigorous and productive research studies.

In the field of neighborhood measurement, there has been a move to include or favor objective measurements of neighborhood environments. This preference for objective measurements stems from an epidemiological approach to science that strives for unbiased measurement (Veenhoven, 2002). Methods for "objectively" measuring neighborhood environments include administrative data that may provide raw counts of physical characteristics or demographics, systematic observations, and/or social experiments. One of the more common objective measurements used is a single item or index constructed from census data to characterize a concept like disadvantage (Carpiano, 2007; Cummins, Curtis, Diez-Roux, & Macintyre, 2007; Krieger et al., 2003), although it should be recognized that the census is itself based on a resident survey, so individual subjectivity in providing information cannot be ruled out.

Humans are the primary actors in their social environment, and the impact of their environment on individual outcomes is in part dependent on their perception and interpretation of that environment. Subjective measurement, typically derived from survey items that assess individuals' perceptions of their neighborhood, can be influenced by internal processes, such as depression or differing frames of reference. For example, if an individual is experiencing psychological distress, this emotional state may influence their perceptions of potential dangers in their neighborhood. In another case, if an individual who is housebound is asked about the proximity and quality of nearby parks, his or her limitations will influence the responses. Some researchers have argued that subjective measures such as these are really assessing the features of individuals rather than the features of a neighborhood. They may suggest, for example, that the relationship found in several neighborhood studies between neighborhood disorder and depression might only reflect the tendency of individuals experiencing depression to perceive and report disorder rather than a relationship between a neighborhood characteristic and a mental health outcome (Weden, Carpiano, & Robert, 2008). This has been termed *same source bias* (Weden et al., 2008). When aggregated, the means of subjective reports within neighborhoods may control for the noise introduced by individual characteristics and provide insight into neighborhood-level processes. However, in order to aggregate individuals' perceptions of neighborhood-level processes, an adequate sample size (discussed in a previous section of this chapter) is needed to make neighborhood-level inferences and to test the validity and reliability of the measures of neighborhood-level phenomena.

When deciding whether to use objective measurement or subjective measurement of relevant neighborhood attributes, researchers must be clear about what they are trying to understand. While objective measurement is thought of as a more robust measure, subjective perceptions may be more closely related to individuals' behaviors and well-being (Weden et al., 2008). It is also the case that individuals may not be able to perceive and/or report on the structural aspects of their neighborhood that impact their lives. If, for instance, individuals rarely travel outside of their neighborhoods, they may not have the frame of reference necessary to assess such structural factors as levels of poverty. In some instances, the researcher may be interested in the impact of structural neighborhood characteristics, and in others, it may be that individual perceptions are the greater focal point of the investigation.

Matching the form of measurement to the research question is a critical aspect of rigorous research, and the selection of objective or subjective measures is very frequently driven by practical issues. Objective measures of a neighborhood environment typically come from two sources: (1) administrative data, which is inexpensive but may be not address the concepts of interest, or (2) observations, which are costly and labor intensive. Subjective measures are typically assessed using surveys that require an adequate sample size to make neighborhood-level inferences, a labor force to conduct the surveys, and an effort to ensure that the sample survey is adequately representative. In some cases, limited time and resources might require the researcher to rely on data that has already been collected. In other cases, the research team may have resources to conduct a survey on another topic and decide to include questions about respondent's neighborhoods in their survey instrument. When time and resource limitations dictate the decision to use objective or subjective neighborhood-level measurement, it is important that the researcher restrict their inferences to the type of measure employed. Perceptions of disorder, for example, cannot be used to infer crime rates unless prior research has shown that these are measuring the same construct.

Many of the most comprehensive neighborhood studies have addressed the limitations of using a singular measurement approach by including both objective and subjective measures of the phenomena, arguing that both are critical and measure different aspects of the same underlying construct (Weden et al., 2008).

In a study that used census data to measure affluence and disadvantage (objective measures) and surveys to assess perceived neighborhood quality (a subjective measure), both aspects of the neighborhood affected individual health in distinctly different ways. Additionally, the subjective measure of the neighborhood continued to impact health, even after controlling for individual SES and depression (Weden et al., 2008), lending support to arguments that subjective assessments are tapping into aspects of the neighborhood that are apart from the individual's attributes that might be confounding their assessment. When possible, using both objective and subjective measures of neighborhoods provides the most comprehensive assessment of individuals' lived environment.

Engaging Community Partners in the Selection of Measures

Researchers in the social sciences have a long history of conducting research on individuals or communities without gaining their perspective or evaluating the usefulness of the findings to the everyday lives of the participants, a practice that often leads to stigmatized or stereotyped narratives and ineffective interventions (Christopher, Watts, McCormick, & Young, 2008; Duran, Wallerstein, Avila, Lorenda, Minkler, & Foley, 2013). In marginalized communities, this approach to knowledge creation has undermined trust, left communities feeling disempowered, and inhibited their desire to participate in research (Christopher et al., 2008; Schwab & Syme, 1997). In order to address these issues, methods for community-driven research have been advanced (Israel, Schulz, Parker, & Becker, 1998). Although community-driven research has been given several labels, "participatory action research" (Freire, 1987; Smith, Willms, & Johnson, 1997), "participatory research" (Green et al., 1995), "action research" (Stringer, 1996), and "community-based research" (Schulz, Israel et al., 1998), it is generally agreed that community-based participatory research "is a collaborative, partnership approach to research that equitably involves . . . community members in all aspects of the research process" (Israel, Schulz, Parker, & Becker, 2001, p. 184). This includes measurement selection and development.

The positivist paradigm in research has discouraged the inclusion of participants in the research process based on the belief that their inclusion would bias the results, ultimately resulting in poor science (Dean & Fenby, 1989). In the past century, social scientists have increasingly endorsed alternative paradigms that argue no reality exists free of the influence of the historical, social, and political context in which they are situated and that multiple constructions may exist based on differing experiences within these differing contexts (Lincoln, 1994). Therefore, including community partners in the selection and/or refinement of the community/neighborhood-level measures may be essential to accurately capturing the phenomena of interest. Community members may bring unique insight into the acceptability or applicability of some concepts or items to their neighborhood context that is essential to understanding the neighborhood-level mechanisms. While seeking the feedback of community members and modifying measures to fit their context may not be feasible for all research questions or designs, doing so may enhance the accuracy of the measures being used and the validity of the findings.

One of the key challenges in conducting CBPR is maintaining scientific rigor in the research while being responsive to and representing community perspectives (Israel et al., 1998). In the process of developing a research project with a community partner, practical compromises are typically made that, in some cases, jeopardize the rigor of the study, resulting in unreliable results. Measurement is one area of the research design that is vulnerable to compromises that may jeopardize rigor.

In an ideal situation when deciding on measures, a researcher would present the community partner with a variety of strong validated measures that have been develop to assess the phenomena that the community is interested in and the community members would select the one that they believe fits their question and context. Because psychometrically validated measures are typically developed from researchers' perspectives, it is far more common for community partners to assert that none of the measures fit their context completely and that they either want to develop their own measure or modify an existing one (Hausman et al., 2013). This is especially true when working in cross-cultural contexts, where cultural worldviews, expressed in language, may lead to different definitions of constructs and interpretations of concepts (Gonzalez & Trickett, 2014). The likelihood of finding a validated measure that fits the culture and context of a community partner is compounded by the lack of validated neighborhood-level measurement and the variety of context in which these measures are being applied.

Despite the apparent benefits of engaging the community in the development or refinement of measures, extreme caution needs to be taken when refining measures that have been developed and tested for validity and reliability or when developing a new measure from scratch. Changing the language of a measure even slightly may compromise the integrity of the measure. In order to successfully engage a community partner in the selection of measures, there are two essential considerations to take into account when establishing a truly equitable research partnership: (1) how a researcher/community practitioner communicates measurement issues and builds the community partners' capacity to participate in this aspect of the research process, and (2) the necessary steps to modify or develop measures to fit the context of the research study without compromising the validity and reliability of the measure.

Israel and colleagues (1998) argued that community-based participatory research (CBPR) should (a) recognize the community as a unit of identity, (b) build on the strengths and resources within the community, (c) facilitate a collaborative partnership in all phases of research, (d) integrate knowledge and action for the mutual benefit of all partners, and (e) promote colearning and an empowering process that attends to social inequalities. Within this framework, building a community's partners' capacity to engage in research has been an essential part of ensuring an equitable distribution of power and control. Community partners typically come to the research project with limited knowledge of research design and measurement. This deficit must be addressed, or the dynamics may reinforce an existing hierarchy (Israel et al., 1998). Helping the community partner develop the language and skills to fully participate in the selection of measures is essential to a successful CBPR outcome. While some community partners may have limited knowledge about measurement, more often than not, both parties—the research team and the community partner—have to spend time developing a common research language in order to communicate effectively on research decisions. Sometimes this is accomplished through formal training (Nyden & Wiewel, 1992; Schulz et al., 1998); sometimes this is accomplished through the process of conducting the research. Building research capacity and developing measures can take a considerable amount of time, time that often the community partner is not willing to spend on the tasks (Israel et al., 1998). It is possible the community partner may wish to defer to the researcher regarding decisions on research methods, or it may be decided within the partnership that, because of scarce time and resources, it will be best for each party to do what they are experts in. It is important for the researcher to assess if these decisions are simply being agreed to because of the partner's lack of knowledge or if this is, in fact, what the partner wants. Despite the extensive time commitment involving community members in the development of research instruments, the partnership improves the quality of research and the results (Schulz et al., 1998).

When working with community partners to develop or adapt community/neighborhood-level measures, some established steps should be followed to ensure the validity and reliability of the measure. Most of the community and neighborhood measures presented in this book have been developed based on a theoretical framework and rigorously tested to assure they are measuring what the designers intended them to measure. Changes to the measure, even small ones, could potentially threaten the integrity of the measure. It is frequently the case, however, that community partners will report that a certain item or a particular use of language does not apply to their community/neighborhood context or that certain items that may be important to assess are missing. In these cases, researchers typically defer to the community's expertise and modify the measure. Several methods have been employed to integrate community perspective while maintaining a commitment to using reliable and valid measurement.

Two studies that have recently used CBPR methods to develop and refine measurement will be discussed to illustrate some of the methods that have been developed to ensure rigor. In one process implemented by Hausman and colleagues (2013), community members participated in focus groups where they were asked about youth violence in their community. These focus groups were coded, and with the input of community advisors, 43 indicators were identified. The community/academic team then went to a bank of psychometrically validated measures that had been used in a previous round of data collection and attempted to match the constructs identified in the focus groups with the existing measures. In this study, 17 of the 43 indicators were represented in the measures reviewed. The existing data was then used to evaluate the psychometric properties of the new scales that were developed based on the community's definition of factors that are crucial to youth violence. The results of the psychometric tests were then discussed with the community advisory board and further refinements were made.

Similarly, Gonzalez and Trickett (2014) describe a three-year process of measure development and testing that occurred in partnership with two rural Yup'ik communities. In this study, the first year was spent developing a model and gathering and evaluating existing measures that assessed the constructs in the model that were deemed important. In the course of discussions with the community partner, several topics in the models were identified by community members as being too sensitive to discuss and therefore were admitted or modified to fit the context. A final list of important and appropriate validated measures was then created. Each item for every construct was then evaluated by the community/university team to assess its cultural relevance. While the language of most scales was retained, some items had to be extensively modified. After the revision process was completed, the revised scales were piloted, the participants provided feedback on the constructs, and the scales psychometric properties were tested. After further refinement, a four-hour workshop with community members was held to review the measures that had been developed, leading to more refinement and discussions with the community over the length of the survey and the use of first-person language.

In both of these examples, extensive effort was made to involve community perspective and maintain rigor. Both studies started from existing validated measures and tested the validity and reliability of all modifications. Although time intensive, the modification of the community/neighborhood measure to fit the community's cultural constructions and contexts must be done in a scientifically rigorous order to maintain the integrity of the measure.

Using New Technology to Measure Neighborhoods

New technologies are being increasingly harnessed to improve upon the existing methods used to measure neighborhood-level phenomena. The five biggest areas of development relevant to neighborhood measurement are the proliferation of GPS technology in mobile phones, the use of advanced computational methods to analyze large amounts of geo-located data generated in social media, the use of satellite imaging to collect objective measures of neighborhood environments, the use of webcams to capture neighborhood processes, and the proliferation of publicly available administrative data.

GPS tracking data can be integrated with traditional survey methods to provide a richer understanding of an individual's interaction in space and how it impacts their perceptions and well-being (Browning & Soller, 2014). At the most basic level, GPS data can be collected over a given time period, such as a week, and used in interviews to ask participants to discuss where they spend their time. GPS technology is also being paired with Ecological Momentary Assessments (EMA), which are useful for examining daily life and the context in which it occurs (Fritz, Tarraf, Saleh, & Cutchin, 2016). Mobile phones are also being increasingly used to collect relevant spatial survey data in real time. Using the GPS technology currently available on most mobile phones, applications have been developed that will push brief surveys to a user's phone when he or she enters into a given geographical space. In addition to surveys, mobile phones are being used to ask participants to take pictures, video, and audio recordings of their surroundings, providing additional data of their lived experience. Using this technology would allow researchers to obtain more fine-grained information regarding how neighborhood environments are impacting individuals. Although both of these measurement methods are essentially examining individual experiences in neighborhoods, they can be aggregated to observe neighborhood-level processes and mechanisms. This technology would also provide researchers with access to neighborhood-level networks, which are theoretically essential to neighborhood constructs but have until recently been extremely difficult to measure (i.e., collective efficacy). Despite the exciting promise of these methods, collecting such fine-grain, real-time data is still relatively expensive when coupled with survey methods.

Mining geotagged user-generated data, such as that produced on social media sites like Twitter, Facebook, and Instagram, is being discussed as a cost-effective way of collecting enough data to make inferences across neighborhoods (Shelton, Poorthuis, & Zook, 2015). Every day, millions of users are generating text data that can be traced back to a geographical location. The size and scale of this data has made it difficult for researchers to make sense of it, but new methods of big data analysis pioneered in the information sciences are making it more feasible to make inferences about neighborhoods. User-generated data have, for example, been used to understand how individuals move in neighborhoods (Ratti et al., 2010; Reades, Calabrese, & Ratti, 2009). Using this method, studies have demonstrated that individual mobility can be typically characterized by small groups of frequently visited sites that are dynamically close locations (Bagrow & Lin, 2012). The ability to understand mobility patterns using geolocated user-generated data may allow neighborhood researchers and practitioners to more accurately define the concept of "neighborhood" and account for the differences in exposure to stressors and protective factors. For instance, Quercia, Capra, and Crowcroft (2012) investigated the spatial distribution of online social ties. User-generated data also show promise for assessing neighborhood-level rates in well-being. Dodds, Harris, Kloumann, Bliss, and Danforth (2011), for example, have used geolocated Twitter feeds to observe temporal and spatial variations in individuals' happiness. Twitter data also have been mined in real time for geocoded information regarding emergent public health problems (Aramaki, Maskawa, & Morita, 2011). The efficacy of collecting large-scale user-generated data and the ability to account for mobility patterns (instead of relying on residential administrative boundaries) may significantly improve existing neighborhood research methods.

The use of tools like Google Earth to collect systematic social observations is making it more feasible to obtain objective measures of neighborhood environments. To date observations using this technology have been done manually using this technology and the traditional method of systematic social observations (Clarke, Ailshire, Melendez, Bader, & Morenoff, 2010). There has been an effort more recently to automate this process. Commuter algorithms are being designed and tested to identify attributes automatically using machine learning. Naik, Philipoom, Raskar, and Hidalgo (2014) took the first step toward designing an automated process for assessing perceptions of safety. They started by asking a sample to rate their perception of safety for 4,109 images and used that information to create a computer vision algorithm that was used to assess one million images across 21 cities. A computer vision model was also created to assess income and housing prices in New York City, using Google Street View. The researchers discovered that the computer-vision model could accurately predict income but was less precise when it came to housing prices (for details about the methods used, see Glaeser, Kominers, Luca, & Naik, 2016). Although these methods are still in their infancy, they may prove to be very cost-efficient ways of assessing the objective neighborhood environment.

Similarly, webcams are being used to document observable social process, patterns of mobility in neighborhoods, and human interactions with the built-environment (Schootman et al., 2016). If, for example, a researcher was interested in how parks were being used in neighborhoods, webcams could be used to observe the patterns of use. Webcams on wearable technology could also be used to record characteristics of a build environment as participants moved through it. Collection of webcam data is currently underway (AMOS; http://amosweb.cse.wustl.edu/), providing open access to 29,000 webcams across the world. Webcams allow researchers to stream images in real time without the need of extensive personal involvement. They also allow for observations to take place without impacting the environment that is being observed. Although the integration of this technology in neighborhood research holds promise, the acceptability of these methods in neighborhoods and the obligation of researchers to report certain types of crime need to be considered when designing research projects. This is certainly true regarding the implementation of all new technology, but it is especially true for the videotaping of public spaces, an act that could be viewed as unwanted surveillance. The amount of data produced by webcams is also challenging. Similar to the analysis of satellite images, computer-based algorithms are being developed to analyze the data generated from webcams.

Lastly, records of all kinds are increasingly digital. The clearest example of this is the electronic medical record that hold all of an individual's medical information in an online space. Beyond the medical field, city, county, and state's education, crime and safety, social service, and public works records are increasingly kept online (Glaeser et al., 2016). Although much of this data is not publicly available, many cities around the country are developing online data portals where this data can be accessed by community practitioners and researchers (O'Brien, Sampson, & Winship, 2015). In one example of the use of new sources of administrative data, O'Brien and colleagues (2015) used Boston's constituent relationship system's 365,729 geo-referenced service requests to understand neighborhood disorder in the city. The researchers were able to test the reliability of this measure using the eco-metric test outlined by Raudenbush and Sampson (1999) and concluded that, despite some limitation, this provided a viable new source of administrative data that can be used to assess disorder.

CONCLUSION

This chapter has highlighted some of the special methodological decisions that may face a researcher when they undertake community and neighborhood research. The purpose of the chapter is to alert the reader to some of the issues that may present unique challenges when studying neighborhoods and communities. We intentionally touch lightly on these topics because not all of them apply in any particular study. The reader is encouraged to follow up on the works cited to get detailed information about the methods and receive specific guidance about their implementation.

Many of the topics in the chapter, such as reliability and measurement error, come up in most social science research undertakings but may take on different forms when dealing with place-based communities because they have geographic elements or require aggregation of individual measures to capture the concepts. Other themes, exemplified by the discussion of how to define the community or neighborhood as a unit, are fundamental to research in this arena. In all instances, the discussions in the chapter assume a basis of understanding of social science research principles and methods.

REFERENCES

Anselin, L. (1988). Lagrange multiplier test diagnostics for spatial dependence and spatial heterogeneity. *Geographical Analysis, 20*(1), 1–17.

Aramaki, E., Maskawa, S., & Morita, M. (2011). Twitter catches the flu: Detecting influenza epidemics using Twitter. In *Proceedings of the conference on empirical methods in natural language processing* (pp. 1568–1576). Association for Computational Linguistics.

Arceneaux, K., & Nickerson, D. W. (2009). Modeling certainty with clustered data: A comparison of methods. *Political Analysis, 17*(2), 177–190.

Bader, M. D., & Ailshire, J. A. (2014). Creating measures of theoretically relevant neighborhood attributes at multiple spatial scales. *Sociological Methodology, 44*(1), 322–368.

Bagrow, J. P., & Lin, Y. R. (2012). Mesoscopic structure and social aspects of human mobility. *PloS one, 7*(5), e37676.

Banerjee, S., Carlin, B. P., & Gelfand, A. E. (2004). *Hierarchical modeling and analysis for spatial data.* Boca Raton, FL: Chapman & Hall/CRC.

Bingenheimer, J. B., & Raudenbush, S. W. (2004). Statistical and substantive inferences in public health: Issues in the application of multilevel models. *Annual Review of Public Health, 25*, 53–77.

Browning, C. R., & Soller, B. (2014). Moving beyond neighborhood: Activity spaces and ecological networks as contexts for youth development. *Cityscape (Washington, DC), 16*(1), 165.

Carpiano, R. M. (2007). Neighborhood social capital and adult health: An empirical test of a Bourdieu-based model. *Health & Place, 13*(3), 639–655.

Chaix, B., Merlo, J., & Chauvin, P. (2005). Comparison of a spatial approach with the multilevel approach for investigating place effects on health: The example of healthcare utilisation in France. *Journal of Epidemiology & Community Health, 59*(6), 517–526.

Chaix, B., Merlo, J., Evans, D., Leal, C., & Havard, S. (2009). Neighbourhoods in eco-epidemiologic research: Delimiting personal exposure areas. A response to Riva, Gauvin, Apparicio and Brodeur. *Social Science & Medicine, 69*(9), 1306–1310.

Chaix, B., Merlo, J., Subramanian, S. V., Lynch, J., & Chauvin, P. (2005). Comparison of a spatial perspective with the multilevel analytical approach in neighborhood studies: The case of mental and behavioral disorders due to psychoactive substance use in Malmö, Sweden, 2001. *American Journal of Epidemiology, 162*(2), 171–182.

Christopher, S., Watts, V., McCormick, A. K. H. G., & Young, S. (2008). Building and maintaining trust in a community-based participatory research partnership. *American Journal of Public Health, 98*(8), 1398–1406.

Clarke, P., Ailshire, J., Melendez, R., Bader, M., & Morenoff, J. (2010). Using Google Earth to conduct a neighborhood audit: Reliability of a virtual audit instrument. *Health & Place, 16*(6), 1224–1229.

Cockings, S., & Martin, D. (2005). Zone design for environment and health studies using pre-aggregated data. *Social Science & Medicine, 60*(12), 2729–2742.

Coulton, C. (2012). Defining neighborhoods for research and policy. *Cityscape, 14*(2), 231–236.

Coulton, C., Chan, T., & Mikelbank, K. (2011). Finding place in community change initiatives: Using GIS to uncover resident perceptions of their neighborhoods. *Journal of Community Practice, 19*(1), 10–28.

Coulton, C., Jennings, M. Z., & Chan, T. (2013). How big is my neighborhood? Individual and contextual effects on perceptions of neighborhood scale. *American Journal of Community Psychology, 51*(1–2), 140–150.

Cummins, S., Curtis, S., Diez-Roux, A. V., & Macintyre, S. (2007). Understanding and representing "place" in health research: A relational approach. *Social Science & Medicine, 65*(9), 1825–1838.

Dean, R. G., & Fenby, B. L. (1989). Exploring epistemologies: Social work action as a reflection of philosophical assumptions. *Journal of Social Work Education, 25*(1), 46–54.

Dodds, P. S., Harris, K. D., Kloumann, I. M., Bliss, C. A., & Danforth, C. M. (2011). Temporal patterns of happiness and information in a global social network: Hedonometrics and Twitter. *PloS one*, *6*(12), e26752.

Downey, L. (2006). Using geographic information systems to reconceptualize spatial relationships and ecological context. *American Journal of Sociology*, *112*(2), 567–612.

Duncan, G. J., & Raudenbush, S. W. (1999). Assessing the effects of context in studies of child and youth development. *Educational psychologist*, *34*(1), 29–41.

Duran, B., Wallerstein, N., Avila, M.M., Lorenda, B., Minkler, M., & Foley, K. (2013). Developing and marinating partnerships with communities. In B. A. Israel, E. Eng, A. J., Schulz, & E. A. Parker (Eds.), *Methods for community-based participatory research for health* (2nd ed., pp. 43–68). San Francisco, CA: John Wiley & Sons.

Entwisle, B. (2007). Putting people into place. *Demography*, *44*(4), 687–703.

Foster, K. A., & Hipp, J. A. (2011). Defining neighborhood boundaries for social measurement: Advancing social work research. *Social Work Research*, *35*(1), 25–35.

Fotheringham, A. S., & Wong, D. W. (1991). The modifiable areal unit problem in multivariate statistical analysis. *Environment and Planning A*, *23*(7), 1025–1044.

Freire, P. (1987). *Education for critical consciousness*. New York: Continuum.

Fritz, H., Tarraf, W., Saleh, D. J., & Cutchin, M. P. (2017). Using a smartphone-based ecological momentary assessment protocol with community dwelling older African Americans. *The Journals of Gerontology Series B: Psychological Sciences and Social Sciences*, *72*(5), 876–877. doi: 10.1093/geronb/gbw166

Galster, G. (2001). On the nature of neighbourhood. *Urban Studies*, *38*(12), 2111–2124.

Glaeser, E. L., Kominers, S. D., Luca, M., & Naik, N. (2016). Big data and big cities: The promises and limitations of improved measures of urban life. *Economic Inquiry*.

Gonzalez, J., & Trickett, E. J. (2014). Collaborative measurement development as a tool in CBPR: Measurement development and adaptation within the cultures of communities. *American Journal of Community Psychology*, *54*(1–2), 112–124.

Gotham, K. F. (2003). Toward an understanding of the spatiality of urban poverty: The urban poor as spatial actors. *International Journal of Urban and Regional Research*, *27*(3), 723–737.

Gotham, K. F., & Brumley, K. (2002). Using space: Agency and identity in a public–housing development. *City & Community*, *1*(3), 267–289.

Grannis, R. (2005). T-Communities: Pedestrian street networks and residential segregation in Chicago, Los Angeles, and New York. *City & Community*, *4*(3), 295–321.

Green, L. W., George, M. A., Daniel, M., Frankish, C. J., Herbert, C. J., Bowie, W. R., & O'Neill, M. (1995). Study of participatory research in health promotion. University of British Columbia, Vancouver: The Royal Society of Canada.

Greenland, S., & Robins, J. (1994). Invited commentary: Ecologic studies—biases, misconceptions, and counterexamples. *American Journal of Epidemiology*, *139*(8), 747–760.

Guo, J. Y., & Bhat, C. R. (2007). Operationalizing the concept of neighborhood: Application to residential location choice analysis. *Journal of Transport Geography*, *15*, 31–45.

Hausman, A. J., Baker, C. N., Komaroff, E., Thomas, N., Guerra, T., Hohl, B. C., & Leff, S. S. (2013). Developing measures of community-relevant outcomes for violence prevention programs: A community-based participatory research approach to measurement. *American Journal of Community Psychology*, 52(3–4), 249–262.

Haynes, R., Daras, K., Reading, R., & Jones, A. (2007). Modifiable neighbourhood units, zone design and residents' perceptions. *Health & Place*, *13*(4), 812–825.

Heywood, I. (1998). *An introduction to geographical information systems*. New York: Wentley Longman.

Hipp, J. R. (2007). Block, tract, and levels of aggregation: Neighborhood structure and crime and disorder as a case in point. *American Sociological Review*, *72*(5), 659–680.

Jones, M., & Pebley, A. R. (2014). Redefining neighborhoods using common destinations: Social characteristics of activity spaces and home census tracts compared. *Demography, 51*(3), 727–752.

Israel, B. A., Schulz, A. J., Parker, E. A., & Becker, A. B. (1998). Review of community-based research: Assessing partnership approaches to improve public health. *Annual Review of Public Health, 19*(1), 173–202.

Israel, B. A., Schulz, A. J., Parker, E. A., & Becker, A. B. (2001). Community-based participatory research: Policy recommendations for promoting a partnership approach in health research. *Education for Health, 14*(2), 182–197.

Krieger, N., Chen, J. T., Waterman, P. D., Soobader, M. J., Subramanian, S. V., & Carson, R. (2003). Choosing area based socioeconomic measures to monitor social inequalities in low birth weight and childhood lead poisoning: The Public Health Disparities Geocoding Project (US). *Journal of Epidemiology & Community Health, 57*(3), 186–199.

Kwan, M. P. (2012). The uncertain geographic context problem. *Annals of the Association of American Geographers, 102*(5), 958–968.

Lee, C., Moudon, A. V., & Courbois, J. Y. P. (2006). Built environment and behavior: Spatial sampling using parcel data. *Annals of Epidemiology, 16*(5), 387–394.

Lincoln, Y. S. (1994). *Fourth generation evaluation*. Newbury Park, CA: Sage.

Martin, G., Inchley, J., Humphris, G., & Currie, C. (2017). Assessing the psychometric and ecometric properties of neighborhood scales using adolescent survey data from urban and rural Scotland. *Population Health Metrics, 15*(1), 11.

Matthews, S. A. (2011). Spatial polygamy and the heterogeneity of place: Studying people and place via egocentric methods. In L. M. Burton, S. P. Kemp, M. Leung, S. A. Matthews, & D. T. Takeuchi (Eds.), *Communities, neighborhoods, and health: Expanding the boundaries of place* (pp. 35–55). New York: Springer.

Merlo, J., Ohlsson, H., Lynch, K. F., Chaix, B., & Subramanian, S. V. (2009). Individual and collective bodies: Using measures of variance and association in contextual epidemiology. *Journal of Epidemiology & Community Health, 63*(12), 1043–1048.

Moulton, B. R. (1990). An illustration of a pitfall in estimating the effects of aggregate variables on micro units. *The Review of Economics and Statistics, 72*(2), 334–338.

Mujahid, M. S., Diez Roux, A. V., Morenoff, J. D., & Raghunathan, T. (2007). Assessing the measurement properties of neighborhood scales: From psychometrics to ecometrics. *American Journal of Epidemiology, 165*(8), 858–867.

Naik, N., Philipoom, J., Raskar, R., & Hidalgo, C. (2014). Streetscore-predicting the perceived safety of one million streetscapes. In *Proceedings of the IEEE conference on computer vision and pattern recognition workshops* (pp. 779–785).

Nicotera, N. (2007). Measuring neighborhood: A conundrum for human services researchers and practitioners. *American Journal of Community Psychology, 40*(1–2), 26–51.

Nyden, P., & Wiewel, W. (1992). Collaborative research: Harnessing the tensions between researcher and practitioner. *The American Sociologist, 23*(4), 43–55.

O'Brien, D. T., Sampson, R. J., & Winship, C. (2015). Ecometrics in the age of big data: Measuring and assessing "broken windows" using large-scale administrative records. *Sociological Methodology, 45*(1), 101–147.

O'Brien, R. M. (1990). Estimating the reliability of aggregate-level variables based on individual-level characteristics. *Sociological Methods & Research, 18*(4), 473–504.

Openshaw, S. (1984). Ecological fallacies and the analysis of areal census data. *Environment and Planning A, 16*(1), 17–31.

Pearce, N. (2000). The ecological fallacy strikes back. *Journal of Epidemiology and Community Health, 54,* 326–327.

Quercia, D., Capra, L., & Crowcroft, J. (2012). The social world of Twitter: Topics, geography, and emotions. *ICWSM, 12,* 298–305.

Ratti, C., Sobolevsky, S., Calabrese, F., Andris, C., Reades, J., Martino, M., & Strogatz, S. H. (2010). Redrawing the map of Great Britain from a network of human interactions. *PloS one, 5*(12), e14248.

Raudenbush, S. W., & Bryk, A. S. (2002). *Hierarchical linear models: Applications and data analysis methods* (2nd ed.). Thousand Oaks, CA: Sage.

Raudenbush, S. W., & Sampson, R. J. (1999). Ecometrics: Toward a science of assessing ecological settings, with application to the systematic social observation of neighborhoods. *Sociological Methodology, 29*(1), 1–41.

Reades, J., Calabrese, F., & Ratti, C. (2009). Eigenplaces: Analyzing cities using the space–time structure of the mobile phone network. *Environment and Planning B: Planning and Design, 36*(5), 824–836.

Sampson, R. J. (2017). *Urban sustainability in an age of enduring inequalities: Advancing theory and ecometrics for the 21st-century city.* Proceedings of the National Academy of Sciences. (201614433) https://doi.org/10.1073/pnas.1614433114

Sampson, R. J., Raudenbush, S. W., & Earls, F. (1997). Neighborhoods and violent crime: A multilevel study of collective efficacy. *Science, 277*(5328), 918–924.

Savitz, N. V., & Raudenbush, S. W. (2009). Exploiting spatial dependence to improve measurement of neighborhood social processes. *Sociological Methodology, 39*(1), 151–183.

Scherbaum, C. A., & Ferreter, J. M. (2009). Estimating statistical power and required sample sizes for organizational research using multilevel modeling. *Organizational Research Methods, 12*(2), 347–367.

Schootman, M., Nelson, E. J., Werner, K., Shacham, E., Elliott, M., Ratnapradipa, K., . . . & McVay, A. (2016). Emerging technologies to measure neighborhood conditions in public health: Implications for interventions and next steps. *International Journal of Health Geographics, 15*(1), 20.

Schulz, A.J., Israel, B. A., Selig, S.M., Bayer, I. S., & Griffin, C.B. (1998). Development and implementation of principles for community-based research in public health. In R. H Macnair (Ed.), *Research strategies for community practice* (pp. 83–110). New York: Haworth Press.

Schulz, A. J., Parker, E. A., Israel, B. A., Becker, A. B., Maciak, B. J., & Hollis, R. (1998). Conducting a participatory community-based survey for a community health intervention on Detroit's east side. *Journal of Public Health Management and Practice, 4*(2), 10–24.

Schwab, M., & Syme, S. L. (1997). On paradigms, community participation, and the future of public health. *American Journal of Public Health, 87,* 2049–2052.

Sharp, G., Denney J. T., & Kimbro, R. T. (2015). Multiple contexts of exposure: Activity spaces, residential neighborhoods, and self-rated health. *Social Science & Medicine, 146,* 204–213.

Shelton, T., Poorthuis, A., & Zook, M. (2015). Social media and the city: Rethinking urban socio-spatial inequality using user-generated geographic information. *Landscape and Urban Planning, 142,* 198–211.

Sherman, J. E., Spencer, J., Preisser, J. S., Gesler, W. M., & Arcury, T. A. (2005). A suite of methods for representing activity space in a healthcare accessibility study. *International Journal of Health Geographics, 4*(24), 1–24.

Smith, S. E., Willms, D. G., & Johnson, N. A. (1997). *Nurtured by knowledge: Learning to do participatory action research.* IDRC, Ottawa, ON, CA.

Snijders, T. (2005). Power and sample size in multilevel linear models. In B. S. Everitt & D. C. Howell (Eds.), *Encyclopedia of statistics in behavioral science* (Vol. 3., pp. 1570–1573). Hoboken, NJ: Wiley.

Spielman, S. E., & Yoo, E. H. (2009). The spatial dimensions of neighborhood effects. *Social Science & Medicine, 68*(6), 1098–1105.

Stringer, E. T. (1996). *Action research: A handbook for practitioners.* Thousand Oaks, CA: Sage.

Vallée, J., Le Roux, G., Chaix, B., Kestens, Y., & Chauvin, P. (2015). The "constant size neighbourhood trap" in accessibility and health studies. *Urban Studies, 52*(2), 338–357.

Veenhoven, R. (2002). Why social policy needs subjective indicators. *Assessing Quality of Life and Living Conditions to Guide National Policy,* 33–45.

Weden, M. M., Carpiano, R. M., & Robert, S. A. (2008). Subjective and objective neighborhood characteristics and adult health. *Social Science & Medicine, 66*(6), 1256–1270.

4 COMMUNITY READINESS AND CAPACITY FOR CHANGE

Each community, like each person, is different. Community norms, beliefs, traditions, politics, resources, and climates vary widely. This heterogeneity has an impact on how community change processes are conceptualized, catalyzed, implemented, and sustained. Moreover, the burden of different social and health problems also varies across communities.

Differences in risk and contextual factors underpin the concept of community readiness and capacity for change. Two neighborhoods focused on reducing crime rates, for instance, may achieve this goal differently based on existing readiness and capacity. Imagine if one community began a process of change with leadership capacity among residents and police to raise awareness about the social and economic determinants of crime. Imagine that this community also has existing infrastructure within neighborhood associations to effectively mobilize a campaign to promote economic investment within the neighborhood as a strategy to reduce crime trends. Imagine another community with similar rates of crime, yet community leaders are in denial about the problem, and leadership within local civic organizations is in a state of flux, limiting capacity to further neighborhood-level change. These communities require different processes to achieve similar goals related to crime reduction.

The aim of this chapter is to provide measurement tools for assessing community readiness and capacity to better understand the unique assets and needs of each neighborhood. These measures serve as a guide for tailoring change strategies (i.e., interventions) to meet communities where they are. Readiness and capacity measures often illuminate the need for implementation efforts across the ecological spectrum, which was described in Chapter 2, to enhance community readiness and capacity for success and sustainability.

DEFINING COMMUNITY READINESS AND CAPACITY

Foster-Fishman and colleagues (Foster-Fishman, Cantillon, Pierce, & Van Egeren, 2007; Foster-Fishman, Pierce, & Van Egeren, 2009) distinguish between community capacity and community readiness in the context of neighborhood change. Community capacity includes structures and processes that help mobilize residents to take action on neighborhood problems (Foster-Fishman et al., 2007). Community capacity is further defined in the public health field as the "ability (e.g., skills, resources and networks) to identify and act on problems" (Labonte & Laverack, 2001, as cited in Lovell, Gray, & Boucher, 2015). Community capacity is "the interaction of human, organization, and social capital existing within a given community that can be leveraged to solve collective problems and improve or maintain the well-being of that community" (Chaskin, 1999, p. 4). Community resources, relationships, leadership, knowledge, skills, networks, and institutions contribute to community capacity (Foster-Fishman, 2007). Community readiness, on the other hand, "refers to the degree to which communities have accepted that change is needed and feasible and that the program or action that is designed to address a problem will succeed" (Donnermeyer et al., 1997, as cited in Foster-Fishman et al., 2007, p. 94). In short, community readiness is the "overall belief in the possibility of change," and community capacity is "the local ability to implement change" (Foster-Fishman et al., 2007, p. 94). These concepts are interrelated but not necessarily causal.

COMMUNITY READINESS MODEL

The community readiness model developed by Oetting and colleagues (1995) is one of the most commonly used models for assessing community readiness for implementing community-based prevention interventions. This model is guided by three concepts, including individual readiness (Prochaska, DiClemente, & Norcross, 1992), diffusion of innovations (Rogers, 2003), and community development (Beal, 1964). Each of these underlying concepts asserts that change occurs along a continuum. On the one end of the continuum, communities are unaware that a problem exists and therefore lack initiative to change, while those at the other end of the continuum are focused on sustaining changes to solve specific problems.

The community readiness model articulates nine stages of community readiness: (1) community tolerance, (2) denial, (3) vague awareness, (4) preplanning, (5) preparation, (6) initiation, (7) institutionalization, (8) confirmation/expansion, and (9) professionalization (Oetting et al., 1995; Stanley, 2014). The nine stages are summarized in **Table A**. These stages represent the spectrum of community readiness; however, the nine stages are not equally distributed and may not be linearly attained. Movement from the preplanning stage to the preparation stage, for instance, may not require the same level of effort and resources as moving from the preparation stage to the initiation stage. A major event, such as a mass shooting, may shock a community out of the tolerance stage directly into the initiation stage. Likewise, regression may occur, especially if there is a belief that initiation of the change strategy did not result in resolution of the defined problem. In this case, the community may experience a rapid downward spiral from the initiation stage to the denial stage (i.e., denial that change is possible).

TABLE A ■ Nine Stages of Community Readiness for Community Change

Stage of Community Readiness	Description of Stage	Example Sentiment
Stage 1: **No Awareness**	Lack of community knowledge about the issue; no awareness of local efforts to address issue; community members and local leaders believe issue is not a concern; and/or no resources are available to address issue.	We don't have a problem in our community.
Stage 2: **Denial or Resistance**	Limited community knowledge about the issue; limited understanding of current efforts to address issue including misinformation; and/or community members and local leaders do not support use of local resources to address the issue.	It is what it is.

(Continued)

TABLE A ■ (Continued)

Stage 3: Vague Awareness	Community members have vague awareness about the issue; limited awareness of current efforts to address issue; community members and leaders believe the issue may be a concern but are not motivated to act; and/or few community resources are made available to address issue.	We don't know what to do. Maybe someone else in the community is going to do something.
Stage 4: Preplanning	Community members have limited knowledge about the issue; some awareness of current efforts to address issue; community members and leaders agree this is an issue that needs to be addressed, and/or some community resources are made available to address issue.	We need to do something about this community issue, but what?
Stage 5: Preparation	Community members have basic knowledge about the issue and how it can be addressed; most community members have heard of current efforts to address issue; community members and leaders are actively seeking to continue or improve current efforts to address issue; and/or stakeholders are actively seeking new resources to address issue.	We are meeting with a funder tomorrow to move forward on local efforts as soon as possible.
Stage 6: Initiation	Community members have basic knowledge about the issue and aware of its impact locally; most community members have basic knowledge of current efforts to address issue; community members and leaders are taking an active role in executing efforts to address issue; and/or resources are secured to further efforts to address issue.	We are taking action to address this important community issue.
Stage 7: Stabilization	Community members have more than basic knowledge about the issue and its impact locally; most community members have more than basic knowledge about community initiatives to address issue; community members and leadership are focused on long-term sustainability of efforts to address issue; and/or efforts are being made to secure resources to continually address this issue.	This is working in our community. How will we sustain our work over time?
Stage 8: Confirmation and Expansion	Community members have heightened awareness of issue and its impact locally; most community members have extensive awareness of local efforts to address issue, including effectiveness of current work and strong support from community members to sustain work on this issue; community members and leaders are expanding and improving efforts, and/or steady access to resources and new resources are being sought for expansion efforts.	What is needed to scale up and have a bigger impact in our community?
Stage 9: Community Ownership	Community members have substantial knowledge about issue and its impact locally; most community members have detailed knowledge of local efforts to address issue and are highly supportive and actively engaged in efforts to address issue; community members and leaders are reviewing evaluation findings to refine tactics for addressing issue; and/or diversified resources are secured to sustain work.	This work is a part of the culture of our community.

Source: Adapted from content presented in Tri-Ethnic Center for Prevention Research, 2014.

COMMUNITY CAPACITY FOR CHANGE

Community readiness for change is based, in part, on the capacity of people and organizations within communities to initiate action. This type of capacity serves to bridge the gap between evidence-based recommendations for change and corresponding action. The *Interactive Systems Framework*, developed by Wandersman and colleagues (2008), provides a conceptual model for exploring the relationship between community capacity for change and implementation efforts. This model highlights the difference between general capacity and innovation-specific capacity for implementation of prevention interventions, such as teen pregnancy prevention programming and policies (Lesesne et al., 2008), community youth development initiatives (Fagan, Hanson, Hawkins, & Arthur, 2008), and environmental changes to support substance abuse prevention (Florin et al., 2012).

General capacity building is focused on improving the infrastructure, skills, and motivations among people and organizations within communities to support implementation of change initiatives (Wandersman et al., 2008). To promote community readiness for change, general capacity building efforts may focus on enhancing the functioning of organizations within the community to support implementation through staff development, leadership training, organizational structure formation, financial development, and increased cross-sector interaction. These capacities provide the foundation to support a range of community-change efforts.

Innovation-specific capacity building targets the skills and resources needed to support implementation of an intervention that targets a specific topic (e.g., school dropout prevention) or a specific population (e.g., youth). Enhancing innovation-specific capacities may occur through efforts that target individuals, organizations, and/or communities as a whole (Wandersman et al., 2008). At the individual level, innovation-specific capacity may be enhanced through training and peer mentorship to raise awareness about the need for change, promote positive attitudes about alternatives to the status quo, and enhance self-efficacy for implementing new initiatives. Organizations may enhance innovation-specific capacity through the promotion of a learning culture that supports new ideas and risk taking, regularly seeks feedback from outsiders to remain relevant and connected to the latest evidence-based practices, and provides supportive structures such as coaching and networking to facilitate transitions within organizational practices. At the community level, capacity is related to a range of factors, including community readiness (Oetting et al., 1995), community competence (Eng & Parker, 1994), community empowerment (Schultz, Israel, Zimmerman, & Checkoway, 1995), and collective efficacy (Sampson, Raudenbush, & Earls, 1997). In this chapter, measures of community readiness will be explored. See Chapter 6 for more information about measures related to collective efficacy and Chapter 7 for information on community empowerment measures.

MEASURING COMMUNITY READINESS AND CAPACITY

Measures included in Chapter 4 focus on assessing community readiness and community capacity that may be leveraged to promote implementation of evidence-based interventions (e.g., policies, programs, practices) within communities. These measures were developed for use within diverse communities and geographic settings across the world. Thus, the measures have relevance to both domestic and international audiences. The measures of community readiness and capacity address a variety of health and social topics, including substance use, child health and development, crime and safety, chronic disease prevention, and sexual health.

These measures use the term "community" as both a place-based and social concept. Place-based definitions of community are focused on specific geographic areas, such as counties or neighborhoods. Social-based definitions of community are focused on membership within community-based organizations or initiatives, such as coalitions, grassroots organizations, or faith-based groups. The measures take into account the nesting of these community-based organizations within geographic communities.

Measures of Community Readiness

Measures of community readiness build on the community readiness model developed by Oetting and colleagues (1995). The community readiness model asserts communities are at different stages of readiness to implement change. Accordingly, these measures are designed to assist communities in the evaluation of their particular stage along the spectrum of readiness. Community readiness measures may be used by communities to guide practice and/or by researchers to inform evaluation.

The most common measure of community readiness is the **Community Readiness Assessment** developed by the Tri-Ethnic Center for Prevention Research (Plested, Edwards, & Jumper-Thurman, 2006). The Community Readiness Assessment is designed to assess the degree to which a community is prepared to take action on a defined issue (see **Table 4.1**). This 36-item assessment is intended for use by community groups as well as evaluators as a part of a multistep process for creating community change that aligns with readiness of the local context. The five steps include (1) identify issue, (2) define community, (3) conduct key respondent interviews, (4) score to determine readiness level, and (5) develop strategies and conduct work. Data are collected via interviews, including open- and closed-ended questions, with at least four community stakeholders, and interview data are scored by two raters based on five dimensions of readiness. The interviews include questions related to community knowledge about the issue; community efforts to address the issue through programs, activities, policies and community knowledge of these efforts; leadership and community climate; and the availability of resources for prevention, such as money, time, and people. The resulting score for each dimension and an overall community readiness score are presented on a 9-point scale from the lowest level representing no awareness of the need for efforts to address the issue to the highest level representing high level of community ownership of the change process. One indicator of the validity of the tool is its world-wide use over time across diverse communities and topic areas. There are over 30 publications that build on the community readiness assessment tool. Variations of the community readiness assessment have been used by a range of communities to address diverse issues, including obesity (Findholt, 2007), substance use (Ogilvie et al., 2008), and healthy food access (Freedman et al., 2012).

The **Community Readiness Survey** developed by Beebe and colleagues (Beebe, Harrison, Sharma, & Hedger, 2001) is a more focused tool designed to help local prevention planners identify and implement substance use prevention strategies tailored to the needs and perceptions of communities (see **Table 4.2**). The scale was developed based on feedback from residents throughout Minnesota, United States. The 38-item scale has five subscales including: (1) perception of alcohol, tobacco, and other drug problem, (2) support for prevention, (3) permissive attitudes toward teen substance use, (4) perception of adolescent access and (5) perception of community commitment. Reliability measures for each subscale were calculated and are available in Table 4.2.

- Internal validity analysis provided empirical support for some of the theoretical domains originally hypothesized and identified new domains.
- The analyses resulted in removal of more than half of the items that did not result in variability in responses (e.g., majority of the participants responded *strongly agree*) and that were not correlated with empirically derived clusters of items, creating a briefer and easier to administer measure.
- Scale reliability was demonstrated by high levels of internal consistency, and construct validity was demonstrated by the relationships between selected scale scores and community readiness as evaluated by prevention planners.
- There was a statistically significant difference between externally rated measures of community readiness and self-reported perception of community commitment ($p < .001$).
- The four other scales were not significantly associated with externally rated measures of community readiness.
- The final survey included five distinct domains: three domains measure respondents' perceptions of their external community: the level of existing substance use problems, the ease with which teens can obtain tobacco and alcohol, and the sense of community and commitment to change. The other two domains measure respondents' personal beliefs and attitudes: their attitudes toward teen use of tobacco and alcohol and their personal support for prevention activities (Beebe, Harrison, Sharma, & Hedger, 2001).

Feinberg and colleagues (Feinberg, Riggs, & Greenberg, 2005) developed the **Community Readiness for Community-Based Prevention** tool to measure community readiness for prevention programming focused on youth development (see **Table 4.3**). This tool was developed as a part of a broader study focused on members of Communities That Care coalitions in Pennsylvania, United States (Feinberg, Greenberg, Osgood, Anderson, & Babinski, 2002). Communities That Care is a model of community empowerment and community engagement to address risk behaviors among youth, such as substance use, school dropout, and violence (Hawkins & Catalano, 1992). The 15-item scale includes subscales related to community leadership, community readiness, community ties, and community leaders as prevention advocates. Two of the subscales (community leadership, community leaders as prevention advocates) have better reliability than the other four. Validation of the scale was conducted to assess the relationship between community readiness and the social network structure of Communities That Care coalitions.

- Higher levels of community readiness were associated with social ties among coalition members that were noncentralized (i.e., close and direct rather than hierarchical), indicating greater distribution of engagement, and community leadership was associated with greater community readiness.

The **Police Community Readiness for Reducing Youth Access to Tobacco** developed by Kunz and colleagues (Kunz, Jason, Adams, & Pokorny, 2009) represents another targeted measure of community readiness (see **Table 4.4**). This tool was developed based on data from police officers from Illinois, United States. It is designed to measure the readiness of police departments to enforce policies about youth access to tobacco and youth possession of tobacco products. The 74-item tool includes two subscales related to readiness for youth tobacco sales enforcement and readiness for youth tobacco possession enforcement. The tool is administered via a structured interview with yes/no response options for all questions. There was good inter-rater reliability in coding of the response options by interviewers. Each dimension was scored on a 9-point scale of readiness, with higher scores indicating higher levels of police readiness to engage in sales and possession enforcement.

- Higher total readiness rating for tobacco possession law enforcement were related to higher levels of law enforcement activity ($r = .53$, $N = 24$, $p < .01$).
- Significant positive relationships were found between youth reports of knowing someone who received a possession citation and six of the seven possession readiness dimensions.
- Police departments with higher leadership readiness levels for sales law enforcement had significantly fewer numbers of merchants in their community selling tobacco to minors ($r = -.52$, $N = 24$, $p < .05$) (Kunz et al., 2009).

Measures of Community Capacity

Community readiness measures focus more broadly on the range of community resources that may need to be leveraged for change to ignite. In contrast, community capacity measures narrow in on specific skills and abilities of key groups, such as community-based organizations (e.g., grassroots, faith-based, school-based) or community leaders (e.g., elected officials, school leaders) that may facilitate community-wide interventions focused on well-being and equity. Two of the community capacity measures included in this chapter were developed in the United States (Griffin et al., 2005; Lempa, Goodman, Rice, & Becker, 2008), and two were developed outside the United States in New Zealand (Lovell et al., 2015) and India (Thomas et al., 2012). Two of the measures are focused on HIV/AIDS and teen pregnancy prevention (Griffin et al., 2005; Thomas et al., 2012) while the other two are focused on community capacity to address a range of social and health issues, such as HIV/AIDS, nutrition, violence, and environmental hazards.

The **Community and Organizational Capacity for Teen Pregnancy Prevention** developed by Griffin and colleagues (2005) was developed for use by a statewide teen pregnancy prevention initiative in South Carolina, United States (see **Table 4.5**). This is similar to the Community Readiness for Community-Based Prevention (Feinberg et al., 2005) that was developed specifically for evaluating coalitions involved in Community That Care interventions. This 22-item tool includes two subscales related to collaboration community capacity and organizational capacity to support county-level teen pregnancy prevention efforts. The 15-item collaboration community capacity scale uses closed-ended items with Likert scale response options to assess the frequency of engagement in particular activities, such as working with other people in the county to use community input to plan teen pregnancy prevention efforts. The 7-item perceptions of organizational capacity scale includes close-ended items to assess agreement or disagreement with statements such as, Schools in my county effectively communicate their teen pregnancy prevention goals. The organizational capacity scale is designed to assess four specific organizations that may be involved in teen pregnancy prevention (i.e., schools, religious institutions, youth organizations, and local health departments).

- Factor analysis and principal components analysis were conducted to identify the number of factors related to each scale. Both scales retained one factor.
- The reliability of these measures was high, indicating some redundancy among items within the measures.
- Validity assessment revealed the collaboration community capacity subscale scores were significantly correlated with the four organizational capacity scores (i.e., school, religious institutions, etc.).
- There was a significant difference in collaborative community capacity scores and the live birth rate among teens in counties with high live birth rates associated with lower community capacity scores (Griffin et al., 2005).

The **Capacity of Community-Based Health and Social Initiatives** scale developed by Lempa and colleagues (2008) is a 60-item measure designed to assess capacity of leaders and non-leaders of community-based organizations to implement and sustain health and social initiatives (see **Table 4.6**). The scale was developed based on formative research as well as testing with a sample of formal leaders (e.g., elected officials, program staff) and non-leaders (e.g., program participants, residents) from community-based initiatives and grassroots efforts across the United States. Data collection involves three people from each community-based initiative. The overall scale includes two subscales: a 44-item, six-factor scale for leaders and a 38-item, five-factor scale for non-leaders. Twenty-two of these items overlap, resulting in a combined 60-item scale. Internal consistency of the two measures were calculated and are provided in Table 4.6.

- Exploratory factor analysis and principal components analysis were used to identify the factors for the leader and non-leader scales and reduce items.
- This yielded six factors for the **leader scale**: leadership (10 items), resources (5 items), external networking (7 items), visibility and recognition (5 items), ability and commitment to organizing action (10 items), and personnel sustainability (7 items).
- The **non-leader scale** included five factors: leadership (10 items), communication with community members (4 items), resources (4 items), ability and commitment to organize action (10 items), and relationship with influential others (6 items).
- Overall, the leadership factor contributed the greatest amount of variance in both scales (Lempa et al., 2008).

An example leadership indicator that loaded on both the leader and non-leader scales is, Leadership is motivated by helping others.

The **Community Ownership and Preparedness Index (COPI)** developed by Thomas and colleagues (2012) is a 23-item scale designed to assess capacity of community-based groups focused on HIV/AIDS prevention to mobilize for implementation of health and development interventions (see **Table 4.7**). The COPI was developed based on feedback from stakeholders affiliated with 25 community-based groups focused on female sex workers or high-risk men who have sex with men from six states in India and was used to evaluate a large-scale, community-based HIV/AIDS prevention program in this context (Narayanan et al., 2012). COPI is administered via face-to-face interviews to assess close-ended indicators related to four dimensions of community ownership: (1) organizational strength, (2) sustainability, (3) program management, and (4) engagement on issues of rights, entitlements, and stigma reduction. The score for each indicator is weighted to reflect the relative importance of the indicator to community mobilization and transition. The weights were generated by community mobilization experts and community members. The weighted scores for each indicator are summed to create a parameter. These scores are converted to a 7-point scale for evaluating transition readiness. Higher scores reflect (a) transition in leadership of programming from higher-level staff to peer educators and community leaders, (b) transition in the role of community leaders from beneficiary of services to strategic decision maker, and (c) transition of the community's capacity to engage with the state from being invisible to being assertive.

- Across two years of evaluation, the two highest scoring parameters across the 25 CBGs were "Leadership" and "Program Management" while the two lowest scoring areas were "Engagement with Wider Community" and "Decision Making."
- The two-year comparison of the 25 communities using the COPI revealed changes in the parameter scores over time with the greatest gains in the areas of "Engagement with State" and "Governance."
- Community-based groups focused on female sex workers had substantially higher increases in their "Engagement with State" parameter score compared to groups focused on high-risk men who have sex with men. (Narayanan et al, 2012).

The **Community Capacity Scale** developed by Lovell and colleagues (Lovell et al., 2015) is a 26-item scale designed to assess community capacity to come together to address and act on a pressing community issue (see **Table 4.8**). While this scale was tested among residents in New Zealand, we are including it here because it was developed as a geographic-specific measure that has wide applicability in public health and social work. The goal of the study was to develop a generalizable and standard instrument to measure capacity on a community-wide scale. The scale was developed based on feedback from community residents from small towns in southern New Zealand. Similar to other researchers, Lovell and colleagues (2015) view community capacity as a multidimensional construct, including the following domains that were supported by their review of the literature: (a) participation, (b) leadership, (c) connections, (d) sense of place, (e) community attitudes, and (f) problem assessment. The scale is scored on a 7-point Likert scale to reflect agreement with each statement. Reliability and validity analyses were used to examine the instrument, which was initially a total of 41 items. The reliability analysis was used to reduce the items to minimize respondent burden and enhance validity; therefore, items were removed to improve internal consistency (Lovell et al., 2015). The weakest subscale was also removed. All of the remaining items were reviewed for validity by interviewing key community informants. The internal consistency of the full scale is good, and two of the six subscales (i.e., leadership, community attitudes) have acceptable internal consistency. Validity assessment revealed the six subscales are significantly correlated, with the highest correlation between the problem assessment subscale and all of the other subscales (Pearson correlation between 0.50–0.54).

- The scale was validated in terms of associations with anticipated predictors of community capacity (time spent living in location, local voting behavior, and volunteering) in unadjusted and adjusted linear regression models (Lovell et al., 2015).

Residents who lived in the community longer, voted in the last local election, and volunteered in the community had significantly higher community capacity scores.

- The study found differences in community capacity between places that cannot be explained by the composition of the population, which suggests that a collective approach (rather than individually focused) may be an effective means of boosting community capacity.
- The residual differences in community capacity between the towns suggest that contextual influences—that is, their material and collective features—effect community capacity to a much greater degree than might be expected given the composition of the communities, thus, supporting the presence of "place effects" (Lovell et al., 2015).

This study resulted in a community capacity instrument that has adequate face, content, and construct validity, and the instrument also was associated with expected sociodemographic and behavioral predictors (Lovell et al., 2015).

Combined Measures of Community Readiness and Capacity

While concepts of community readiness and capacity are interrelated, the prior measures treated them more distinctly. In contrast, Foster-Fishman and colleagues (2007; 2009) developed and tested measures that combine community capacity and readiness in their study of a comprehensive community building initiative in Michigan called Yes we can! (YWC!). Community participation measures that were developed in these studies are discussed in Chapter 5. The goal of the YWC! was to "bring about a more just and sustainable community by reducing gaps in economic and educational outcomes" by engaging residents and neighborhood leaders as change agents through their "informed and full participation in public life" (Foster-Fishman et al., 2009, p. 556). The project took place in seven distressed neighborhoods within the city of Battle Creek, Michigan, United States. **Table 4.9** describes the initial study and measures, and **Table 4.10** describes the follow-up study and measures.

The first study was a community-wide survey to a random sample of residents in the seven neighborhoods targeted for the intervention while the second study focused on a purposive sample of residents from the targeted neighborhoods who were engaged in the initiative or in neighborhood organizations. Thus slightly different measures were used in both studies, so they are reported separately. The measure of community readiness in the first study (Foster-Fishman et al., 2007) consisted of two elements that were considered important for facilitating community mobilization and resident engagement and participation: social ties/networks and neighborhood leadership (see Table 4.9). Measures of community capacity focused on collective efficacy and a sense of hope for change. It is important to note that this study did not use Sampson and colleagues' (1997) measure of collective efficacy (which is included in Chapter 6); the researchers developed their own measure of collective efficacy for their program. The researchers also include measures of neighborhood problems that could impact the desire and willingness of residents to become involved in improving their communities, including neighborhood disorder and crime (Note: these types of measures are described in Chapter 11). The main goal of this study was to examine how community readiness and capacity as well as neighborhood problems have an impact on levels of citizen engagement.

- Results from Study 1 found residents who reported higher social ties had statistically significantly higher rates of engagement in individual activism when demographics and neighborhood problems were included in the model as well as the measure of community readiness.
- The researchers found all four of the measures of community readiness and community capacity were significantly associated with increased odds of engaging in collective action.
- Validity assessments including predictive validity using proportional chance criterion and Cohen's kappa both found that the models that include the community readiness and community capacity measures for predicting individual activism and collective activism are better than chance.
- Neighborhood leadership was significantly associated with both individual and collective action among those who took part, revealing participants who reported higher levels of neighborhood leadership were more likely to be in the high involvement group regardless of the type of activism.
- The measure of hope was the only readiness and capacity factor associated with individual activism among the high-involved group. Both of these models were found to be better at predicting involvement in individual and collective action compared to chance (Foster-Fishman et al., 2007).

In the second study (see **Table 4.10**), the researchers refined their definition of community capacity to focus on a single factor (i.e., sense of community) while community readiness was similarly defined to include two concepts (i.e., collective efficacy, sense of hope for change), yet measurement of these concepts changed from Study 1 to Study 2 (Foster-Fishman et al., 2009). The collective efficacy measure was somewhat different than the one used in the first study, and the format was based on Sampson and colleagues' measure (1997). The sense of community measure was based on two prior measures: one by Chavis and colleagues (Chavis, Hogge, McMillan, & Wandersman,1986) described in Chapter 4 and one by Coulton and colleagues (Coulton, Korbin, & Su, 1996). The hope scale is slightly different than the first study.

- In Study 2, the researchers used structural equation models to examine the hypotheses. Greater neighborhood capacity and readiness for change were associated with an individual's perception that their neighbors would be engaged citizens; when they thought their neighbors would be engaged, individuals were more likely to be active in their neighborhoods.
- Norms for activism were significant direct predictors of citizen participation and were predicted by both collective efficacy and sense of community.
- Hope was a significant predictor of collective efficacy, which had a significant direct effect on norms. The indirect effect from hope on norms for activism was small.
- Organizing skills was a significant direct predictor of norms for activism.
- Neighborhood norms for activism had a strong mediational role for followers but not for leaders.

- Organizing skills was a positive predictor of citizen participation. It was stronger for leaders than followers (Foster-Fishman et al., 2009).

Results of this study revealed residents who feel connected to their neighbors and believe that by working together change is possible; they are more likely to be active, engaged citizens.

These two studies by Foster-Fishman and colleagues provide multidimensional measures for community readiness and capacity. While the intent of these studies was not to create and test these measures, the research from both studies demonstrates mostly strong reliabilities as well as expected relationships among most of the hypothesized variables. The researchers emphasize that it is important to clarify measures of community capacity and readiness based on the targeted outcome of an intervention or relevant community needs (Foster-Fishman et al., 2007; Foster-Fishman et al., 2009).

CONCLUSION

For over two decades, researchers and community practitioners worked to develop tools to assess community factors that have an impact on implementation of social and health development programs, policies, and practices. Underpinning each of the measures included within this chapter is an emphasis on the heterogeneity of communities. Neighborhoods and community-based organizations each possess unique strengths and limitations that contribute to their ability to acknowledge the existence of a community need and move forward to implement and sustain interventions to shift the status quo. These measures challenge the notion that "one size fits all" when it comes to community-wide change.

A key feature to the measures of community readiness and community capacity is the inclusion of multiple stakeholders in data collection. Whether its "leaders" and "non-leaders" of community-based initiatives (Lempa et al., 2008) or a minimum of four community stakeholders representing diverse interests (Plested et al., 2006), it is critical to capture different perspectives during assessment. This may create challenges in terms of scoring the community readiness and capacity measures, especially since several are qualitative in nature. Reliability assessments of the measures included in this chapter reveal raters achieved high levels of agreement through the scoring process among trained data collectors.

There were commonalities in the subscales included in the eight measures described in this chapter. Seven of the measures included assessment of leadership for change (Feinberg et al., 2002; Foster-Fishman et al., 2007; Kunz et al., 2009; Lempa et al., 2008; Lovell et al., 2015; Plested et al., 2006; Thomas et al., 2012), highlighting the salience of this construct to community readiness and community capacity. Other salient constructs across the eight measures included knowledge and attitudes about the issue (Beebe et al., 2001; Kunz et al., 2009; Lovell et al., 2015; Plested et al., 2006), social ties and networks for leveraging change (Feinberg et al., 2002; Foster-Fishman et al., 2007; Lempa et al., 2008; Lovell et al., 2015; Thomas et al., 2012), and availability of resources to support action (Kunz et al., 2009; Lempa et al., 2008; Plested et al., 2006; Thomas et al., 2012). The COPI was unique in its inclusion of a subscale that explicitly assessed the political aspects of community readiness and capacity (Narayanan et al., 2012; Thomas et al., 2012). This subscale measured community leadership to "create and build new spaces of engagement with state bodies to realise the rights and welfare entitlements of the community members" (Thomas et al., 2012, p. ii30).

All but one of the measures ranked each dimension of community readiness and capacity as being equally important. In other words, if a community lacked leadership and social ties and networks to support change, these limitations would be equally scored to bring down the overall readiness or capacity score. In contrast, the COPI weighted the relative significance to success for each subscale based on community feedback, resulting in a total score that placed more emphasis on subscales considered to be more important compared to others. Moreover, most of the measure assessed community readiness and community capacity separately. The two studies by Foster-Fishman and colleagues provide examples of how these constructs may be assessed together (Foster-Fishman et al., 2007; Foster-Fishman et al., 2009). Future research on community readiness and capacity is beginning to weight different dimensions to guide strategic action (Lee et al., 2017).

These measurement tools raise questions about their relevance to diverse communities and topics. In general, the authors of the readiness and capacity measures recommend tailoring to ensure the tools measure concepts that are uniquely important for a specific topic or community. Tailoring will likely involve a process of gaining feedback from the community about factors perceived to influence successful intervention implementation.

Finally, use of these measures provides an opportunity to assess readiness and capacity to support change within communities. Feedback resulting from these assessments may further ignite action if scores are returned to communities with corresponding action steps that are staged based on the community's score. This type of feedback loop between assessment and resource sharing may catalyze community-wide intervention implementation and sustainability.

LIST OF MEASURES AND TABLE NUMBERS

TABLE 4.1 ■	Community Readiness Assessment
Primary Reference	Plested, B. A., Edwards, R. W., & Jumper-Thurman, P. (2006). *Community readiness: A handbook for successful change*. Fort Collins, CO: Tri-Ethnic Center for Prevention Research.
Purpose	Assesses the degree to which a community is prepared to take action on an issue
Description	This 36-item assessment is intended for use by community groups as well as evaluators as a part of a multistep process for creating community change that aligns with readiness of the local context. • The steps include: identify issue, define "community," conduct key respondent interviews, score to determine readiness level, develop strategies, and conduct work. • The community readiness assessment has been used with a range of communities to address diverse issues, including obesity, substance use, intimate partner violence, child abuse, head injury, and suicide. For a description of all of the items included in the assessment, please see the primary reference. The community readiness assessment is completed via interview format and includes open- and closed-ended questions related to the following dimensions: • Community efforts to address the issue • Community knowledge of efforts • Leadership • Community climate • Knowledge about the issue • Resources for prevention (e.g., money, time, people) At least two interviewers code the data based on a 9-point anchored rating scale that corresponds to the nine levels of community readiness in Table A in this chapter (level 1 = *no awareness* to level 9 = *high level of community ownership*).
Sample	• The community readiness assessment should be administered to a minimum of four to six key stakeholders who represent different perspectives about the issue. • Stakeholders may include people from education, government, law enforcement, social services, mental health, faith-based groups, community at large, and youth. • Interviews take between 30–60 minutes to complete.
Scoring	An average score for each interview is generated based on agreement by the interviewers, and then scores from all interviews are averaged to generate an overall community score and score for each dimension.
Assessment	• Inter-rater reliability scores for two scorers working independently to code the interview data using the 9-point anchor ratings for each dimension was high. • In 92% of the cases, the same rating was given by the two scorers.
Related References	Stanley, L. R. (2014). *Tri-Ethnic Center for Community Readiness handbook* (2nd ed.). Fort Collins, CO: Tri-Ethnic Center for Prevention Research.
Language	English
Contact	Tri-Ethnic Center for Prevention Research Colorado State University Fort Collins, CO 80523 Email: tecweb@lamar.colostate.edu
Website	Publication available at http://tinyurl.com/h7zvqvh Study website: http://triethniccenter.colostate.edu/communityreadiness_home.htm
Other Comments	Original community readiness assessment tool

TABLE 4.2 ■ Community Readiness Survey	
Primary Reference	Beebe, T. J., Harrison, P. A., Sharma, A., & Hedger, S. (2001). The community readiness survey: Development and initial validation. *Evaluation Review*, 25(1), 55–71.
Purpose	Designed to help local prevention planners identify and implement substance use prevention strategies tailored to the needs and perceptions of communities.
Description	Tool for measuring population attitudes toward substance use and the potential receptivity of communities to different prevention efforts. The initial 89-item survey included questions related to eight dimensions of readiness. Each item was hypothesized to be associated with only one dimension. Ultimately, the survey was reduced to 38 items related to five distinct domains. Questions were assessed using a Likert scale from *strongly disagree* to *strongly agree*. Several methods were employed to guide scale development, including assessment of item-response variability and factor analysis. **Perception of alcohol, tobacco, or other drug problem (12 items):** Assessed levels of agreement about use of different substances, such as alcohol, marijuana, and tobacco, by adults and youth in the community and the extent to which substance use contributes to crime. • Marijuana use by teenagers • Alcohol use by adults • Other drug use by teenagers • Extent use contributes to crashes • Often see teens smoking in public • Often see someone drunk in public **Support for prevention (9 items):** Assessed community support for prevention efforts, such as • Willingness to pay increase in tobacco tax • Tobacco advertising should be banned • Alcohol/drug prevention are programs good • Community set up prevention programs **Permissive attitudes toward teen substance use (7 items):** Assessed beliefs, such as: • It is OK for teens to drink at a party. • Parents tell kids to drink with them. • Tell teens to use alcohol carefully. **Perception of adolescent access (8 items):** Assessed barriers to accessing illegal substances among youth through items such as: • Difficult to sneak alcohol from home. • Difficult to purchase tobacco in a store. • Difficult to get adult to buy alcohol. • Difficult to order a drink in a bar. **Perception of community commitment (2 items):** • My community is not interested in changing. • There is no sense of commitment in my community.

Sample	A random sample of 7,151 adults (52% response rate) from 30 communities located in different regions of Minnesota
Scoring	Mean scores were calculated.
Assessment	Chronbach's alpha ranged from .90 to .77 for the following scales: • Perception of alcohol, tobacco, or other drug problem (α = .90) • Support for prevention (α = .79) • Permissive attitudes toward teen substance use (α = .78) • Perception of adolescent access (α = .77) • Perception of community commitment (α = .80)
Related References	Sharma, A., Botzet, A., Sechrist, R. A. J., Arthur, N., & Winters, K. C. (2006). Community readiness survey: Norm development using a Q-sort process. *Journal of Child and Adolescent Substance Abuse, 16*(1), 25–38.
Language	English
Contact	Timothy Beebe Minnesota Department of Human Services Health Care Research Division 444 Lafayette Road St. Paul, MN 55155-3865 Email: t m.beebe@state.mn.us
Other Comments	Builds on community readiness model

TABLE 4.3 ■ Community Readiness for Community-Based Prevention	
Primary Reference	Feinberg, M. E., Riggs, N. R., & Greenberg, M. T. (2005). Social networks and community prevention coalitions. *Journal of Primary Prevention, 26*(4), 279–298.
Purpose	Measure community readiness for community-based prevention programming focused on youth development
Description	This measure includes four scales related to different aspects of community readiness. The four subscales and sample questions are provided below. Response options were on a Likert scale from 1 = *strongly disagree* to 4 = *strongly agree*. See the primary reference for a description of all of the items. **Community leadership (4 items):** Evaluates the degree to which leaders include all sectors of the community, build consensus, and involve the community in decisions through items such as the following: ○ Willing and able to involve community members in decision-making • **Community readiness (5 items):** Assessed prior community initiative success and sense of efficacy, residents' engagement in decision-making processes, and conflict management through items such as the following: ○ The community never seems to be able to accomplish much at all. ○ In the past the community has been successful at addressing social problems. **Community ties (3 items):** Evaluates the extent to which residents are interested in and committed to the community through items such as the following: • Most people in your area are committed to addressing community issues. **Community leaders as prevention advocates (3 items):** Assesses knowledge of and commitment to prevention programming among local leaders through items such as the following: • Able to obtain necessary resources for community initiatives
Sample	Participants included 219 members who were actively involved in Communities That Care (CTC) programs and coalitions in 23 rural and semirural communities in Pennsylvania.
Scoring	The 15-item survey included questions related to four dimensions of readiness that were measured at individual and community levels. Individual-level scores for all scales were calculated by standardizing items prior to generating the mean. A community-level score was computed by calculating the mean scale score for all individual respondents from a specific community.
Assessment	Chronbach's alpha for the four scales ranged from .63 to .84: • Community leadership (α = .83) • Community readiness (α = .64) • Community ties (α = .63) • Community leaders as prevention advocates (α = .74)
Related References	Feinberg, M. E., Greenberg, M. T., Osgood, D. W., Anderson, A., & Babinski, L. (2002). The effects of training community leaders in prevention science: Communities That Care in Pennsylvania. *Evaluation and Program Planning, 25*, 245–259.
Language	English

Contact	Mark Feinberg Prevention Research Center Henderson Building South Room 109 The Pennsylvania State University University Park, PA 16802 Email: mef11@psu.edu
Other Comments	Builds on community readiness model

TABLE 4.4 ■ Police Community Readiness for Reducing Youth Access to Tobacco

Primary Reference	Kunz, C. B., Jason, L. A., Adams, M., & Pokorny, S. B. (2009). Assessing police community readiness to work on youth access and passion of tobacco. *Journal of Drug Education, 39*(3), 321–337.
Purpose	Tool for measuring the readiness of police departments to address policies about youth access to tobacco and youth possession of tobacco products
Description	Community readiness 74-item assessment for use by police departments that includes two separate scales related to readiness for youth tobacco sales enforcement and readiness for youth tobacco possession enforcement. The community readiness assessment included seven dimensions related to the following areas. All questions had yes/no responses. Sample items for each dimension are listed below. **Knowledge regarding problem of tobacco sales to minors (18 items):** • Do police officers in your department believe that youth tobacco use is a national/U.S. problem? **Resources available for tobacco control law enforcement (9 items):** • Do officers in your department know of any internal/external resources available for tobacco possession law enforcement? **Efforts by police for tobacco control law enforcement (11 items):** • Do officers in your department believe that they can reduce illegal sales of tobacco to youth by enforcing a tobacco sales law? **Knowledge of tobacco control law enforcement efforts (9 items):** • Would you characterize officers as being informed of the department's sales enforcement efforts? **Police climate toward tobacco control law enforcement (9 items):** • Have officers expressed support for the initiation of possession enforcement by the department? **Town climate toward police enforcement of tobacco control laws (9 items):** • Do schools and community leaders in your town support plans for the police department to conduct compliance checks with tobacco merchants? **Attitudes, knowledge, and behaviors of leaders for tobacco control enforcement (9 items):** • Have officers been identified to lead in the development and organization of the department's possession enforcement efforts?
Sample	• Key informant interviews were conducted with 24 police officers from 24 communities in northern and central Illinois. Key informants were chosen by asking the chief of police in each police department to identify the officer with the most knowledge of tobacco sales and possession enforcement efforts in the department. • The readiness for youth tobacco sales enforcement and readiness for youth tobacco possession enforcement scale scores were determined by averaging the stage ratings from the seven dimensions that make up the scales.
Scoring	The 74-item structured interview included yes/no questions related to seven dimensions of readiness. Each dimension was rated on a 9-point scale, with higher scores indicating higher levels of readiness to engage in sales and possession enforcement.
Assessment	Cohen's kappa measuring inter-rater reliability for each dimension on the sales and possession scales were high, with Kappa's between 0.65 and 1.0.

Language	English
Contact	Leonard Jason DePaul University Center for Community Research 990 Fullerton Avenue, Suite 3100 Chicago, IL 60614 Email:5.jason@depaul.edu
Other Comments	Builds cn community readiness model

TABLE 4.5 ■	Community and Organizational Capacity for Teen Pregnancy Prevention
Primary Reference	Griffin, S. F., Reininger, B. M., Parra-Medina, D., Evans, A. E., Sanderson, M., & Vincent, M. L. (2005). Development of multidimensional scales to measure key leaders' perceptions of community capacity and organizational capacity for teen pregnancy prevention. *Family and Community Health, 28*(4), 307–319.
Purpose	Assess involvement in community capacity building and organizational capacity to support teen pregnancy prevention efforts in counties
Description	This 22-item tool includes two subscales related to collaboration community capacity and organizational capacity to support county-level teen pregnancy prevention efforts. The tool was developed as a part of the South Carolina Adolescent Pregnancy Prevention Initiative Evaluation. Scale development was informed by prior literature, best practices in teen pregnancy prevention, the community readiness model, the stages of change theory, and pilot testing. For a description of all of the items, please see the primary reference. **Collaboration community capacity (15 items):** Likert scale response options ranging from 1 = *never done activity* to 5 = *regularly done activity* for several years. Respondents were asked: "How often have you worked with other people in your county to . . ." Sample items included • Use community input to plan teen pregnancy prevention efforts? • Use local statistics and survey information to guide planning of teen pregnancy efforts? • Involve the community in the planning of teen pregnancy prevention programs? • Clearly communicate measurable goals for teen pregnancy prevention? • Ensure all people, regardless of color or beliefs, receive teen pregnancy prevention programs? • Actively help people become leaders in teen pregnancy prevention? • Involve youth in meaningful leadership roles regarding teen pregnancy? **Perceptions of organizational capacity (7 items):** Likert scale response options ranging from 1 = *strongly disagree* to 5 = *strongly agree*. The organizations assessed via this scale included schools, religious institutions, youth organizations, and local health departments. Respondents were asked: "(X Organization) in my county . . . " Sample items include • Effectively communicate their teen pregnancy prevention goals • Are actively working to change or enhance their policies to prevent teen pregnancy • Are good at identifying resources to use in teen pregnancy prevention • Use community input to plan their teen pregnancy prevention efforts
Sample	• Participants included 1,516 formal leaders (e.g., elected officials, superintendent) and informal leaders (e.g., community residents, parent) from counties across South Carolina who were nominated by program staff working on the South Carolina Adolescent Pregnancy Prevention Initiative Evaluation. • The goal was to recruit at least five leaders across eight sectors (e.g., government, community organizations, youth organizations, schools) per county, including rural and urban counties.
Scoring	Scale scores are calculated by generating the mean for each scale. The mean collaborative community capacity score was 2.41 (range: 1–4). Local health departments had the highest mean organizational capacity score, 3.76 (range: 1–5), whereas religious institutions had the lowest organizational capacity score, 3.24 (range: 1–5).

Assessment	Chronbach's alpha for the collaboration community capacity scale was very high at $\alpha = .97$, indicating item reduction may be possible. The four organizational capacity scales (e.g., schools, religious institutions) also had a high internal consistency with Chronbach's alpha ranging from .93 to .97, indicating there may be redundancy in some of the indicators that could be streamlined for a more parsimonious scale.
Language	English
Contacts	S. F. Griffin, PhD Department of Health Promotion Education and Behavior Prevention Research Center Norman J. Arnold School of Public Health University of South Carolina, Columbia, SC 29208 Email: sgriffin@sc.edu Deborah Parra-Medina, PhD University of Texas, Austin Latino Research Initiative 210 W. 24th St., Mailcode F9200 Austin, TX 78712 Email: parramedina@austin.utexas.edu
Other Comments	Measure of community capacity for change

TABLE 4.6 ■ Capacity of Community-Based Health and Social Initiatives	
Primary Reference	Lempa, M., Goodman, R. M., Rice, J., & Becker, A. B. (2008). Development of scales measuring the capacity of community-based initiatives. *Health Education & Behavior, 35*(3), 298–315.
Purpose	Assess capacity of leaders and non-leaders of community-based organizations to implement and sustain health and social initiatives
Description	Measure development was informed by qualitative research with core members of eight community initiatives representing diverse topics, including HIV/AIDS, housing quality, violence, and neighborhood improvement. Findings informed the development of initial thematic areas and resulting indicators, which were reviewed for content validity by an expert panel. The resulting 160-item scale was tested among a sample of leaders and non-leaders from community-based initiatives across the USA. Two scales emerged representing capacity of leaders and capacity of non-leaders for implementing community-based health and social initiatives. The final combined scale includes 60 items and response options were on a 10-point Likert scale from 1 = *not at all* to 10 = *completely.* Sample items for each scale are listed below. For a description of all of the items, please see the primary reference. **Capacity of Leaders (44 items):** assessed capacity among formal leaders within communities for implementing community-based health and social initiatives. This scale has 6 subscales: • **Leadership (10 items):** ○ The leadership is motivated by helping others. ○ The leadership shows compassion for people. ○ The people involved with the project support the principles or values of the leadership. ○ People involved with the project agree with the leadership's vision. ○ The leadership tries to develop agreement in group decision-making. • **Resources (5 items):** ○ The project has adequate space or has access to adequate space to conduct its business. ○ The project has adequate space or access to adequate space for meetings. • **External networking (7 items):** ○ The project knows where to go to find funding. ○ The project can gain support from political figures when needed. ○ The project has access to powerful people. • **Visibility and recognition (5 items):** ○ People outside the community know who the project's leaders are. ○ People outside the community know the name of the project. • **Ability and commitment to organizing action (10 items):** ○ The project can obtain information necessary for its work. ○ People involved with the project have or can obtain information the project needs to succeed. ○ The community has access to people involved with the project. ○ People involved with the project do not give up when the project faces challenges. ○ The project has a core group that organizes its efforts.

	• **Personnel sustainability (7 items):** ○ The leadership develops new leaders for the project. ○ Staff and/or volunteers are adequately trained. **Capacity of non-leaders (38 items):** assessed capacity among community residents (i.e., non-leaders) for implementing community-based health and social initiatives. This scale has 5 subscales: • **Leadership (10 items):** ○ People involved with the project trust the leadership. ○ The leadership listens to the ideas and opinions of project members. ○ The leadership shows compassion for people. ○ The leadership is consistent in its principles and values. ○ Project members support the leadership's principles or values. • **Communication with community members (4 items):** ○ People in the community know the name of the project. ○ People in the community are knowledgeable about what the project does. • **Resources (4 items):** ○ The project has the supplies it needs (e.g., paper, postage). ○ The project has adequate space or has access to adequate space to conduct its business. • **Ability and commitment to organize action (10 items):** ○ Project members treat people outside the community with respect. ○ Project members treat community members with respect. ○ Project members can work with diverse groups with different interests. ○ Project members do not give up when the project faces challenges. ○ Project members put in extra time when necessary. • **Relationships with influential others (6 items):** ○ The leadership has relationships with public officials who can help the project. ○ The project can gain support from political figures when needed. ○ The project has access to powerful people. ○ Public officials listen to the ideas and opinions of the leadership. ○ The leadership has relationships with diverse groups that can help the project.
Sample	• Data were collected in 2002–2003 from 702 respondents representing 291 community-based initiatives across the USA. Three people from each community-based initiative were included: a person central to the initiative's leadership, a participant in the initiative but not a leader, and an individual more sporadically involved with the initiative. • Participants represented local community-based initiatives operating out of community-based organizations or grassroots citizen ventures that focused on a range of health and social topics, including HIV/AIDS, nutrition, violence, environmental hazards.
Scoring	Data from the three types of respondents were aggregated into two groups: leaders and non-leaders, with the non-leader group including the two participant categories. This resulted in two scales: a 44-item six factor scale for leaders accounting for 64.9% of the variance and a 38-item, five factor scale for non-leaders accounting for 67.8% of the variance. Twenty-two of these items overlapped, resulting in a combined scale of 60 items. An overall scale score is generated.

(Continued)

TABLE 4.6 ■ (Continued)	
Assessment	• Chronbach's alpha coefficients for the factors related to the leader and non-leader scales were high, ranging from .82 to .96. • The authors indicated further reduction of items may be possible while still retaining high internal consistency; however, these analyses were conducted with the test sample.
Related References	Anderson-Lewis, C., Cuy-Castellanos, D., Byrd, A., Zynda, K., Sample, A., Blakely Reed, V., Beard, M., Minor, L., & Yadrick, K. (2012). Using mixed methods to measure the perception of community capacity in an academic–community partnership for a walking intervention. *Health Promotion Practice, 13*(6), 788–796.
Language	English
Contact	Robert Goodman, PhD School of Public Health Indiana University at Bloomington 1025 E. 7th Street, Suite 111 Bloomington, IN 47405 Email: rmg@indiana.edu
Other Comments	Measure of community capacity for change

TABLE 4.7 ■	Community Ownership and Preparedness Index (COPI)
Primary References	Thomas, T., Narayanan, P., Wheeler, T., Kiran, U., Joseph, M. J., & Ramanathan, T. V. (2012). Design of a community ownership and preparedness: Using data to inform the capacity development of community-based groups. *Journal of Epidemiology and Community Health, 66*, ii26–ii33. Narayanan, P., Moulasha, K., Wheeler, T., Baer, J., Bharadwaj, S., Ramanathan, T. V., & Thomas, T. (2012). Monitoring community mobilisation and organizational capacity among high-risk groups in a large-scale HIV prevention programme in India: Selected findings using a community ownership and preparedness index. *Journal of Epidemiology and Community Health, 66*, ii34–ii41.
Purpose	Assess mobilization capacity of community-based groups to support implementation of health and development interventions
Description	The COPI questionnaire includes 23 items that are prioritized to generate an aggregated score based on feedback from diverse stakeholders affiliated with community-based groups focused on HIV prevention among high-risk groups. COPI is designed to be a participatory method for evaluating mobilization efforts to inform future practice. The scale is completed via face-to-face interviews to assess four dimensions of community ownership: organizational strength; sustainability; program management; and engagement on issues of rights, entitlements, and stigma reduction. These four dimensions are operationalized into eight parameters that include 2–5 indicators per parameter. The eight parameters and sample indicators are listed below. For a description of all of the items, please see Thomas et al. (2012). Items were scaled on a 7-point Likert scale as described in the Measurement and Scoring section of this table. **Dimension 1: Capacity in terms of strong leadership, governance mechanisms, and decision-making systems** **Leadership (5 main indicators):** can address immediate and strategic needs of community members and has emerged out of the shadow of the implementing partner • Leadership team has demonstrated capacity to show solidarity during crises faced by community members. • LT has demonstrated strength in mobilizing community members to assert their identity and to engage issues through collective action. **Governance (3 main indicators):** system that is inclusive and participatory, with a democratic selection process and robust accountability arrangements • Inclusion of all groups on the leadership team **Decision-making system (3 main indicators):** respects participation as well as the need for delegation and time-bound decision-making • Define system for decision-making with community-based group becoming the decision maker **Dimension 2: Capacity to sustain itself through resource mobilization and networking** **Resource mobilization (2 main indicators):** The group is self-sustaining and has the capability to raise and manage resources, and individual community members are economically empowered. • Strong, diversified resource base **Community collective networks (3 main indicators):** has the networking strength to assert its identity and to legitimize as well as realize its demands beyond its own members • Regular increase in outreach

(Continued)

TABLE 4.7 ■ (Continued)

	Dimension 3: Capacity to lead and manage the targeted intervention program **Project and risk management (2 main indicators):** • Leadership is competent and confident in contributing toward project processes. **Dimension 4: Capacity to engage with state bodies and broader society to realize rights and address issues of stigma** **Engagement with the state (3 main indicators):** to secure civil and political rights and welfare entitlements • Leadership team has demonstrated capacity to deal with issues of violation of freedom. **Engagement with other key influencers (2 main indicators):** can assert itself with respect to many other influential groups and individuals • Leadership team has demonstrated collective actions in engaging with gatekeepers to assert the identity of community members.
Sample	• Data were collected in 2009 and 2010 from stakeholders affiliated with 25 community-based groups focused on female sex workers or high-risk men who have sex with men from six states in India. • Participants included four groups of stakeholders: the leadership team of the community-based group, committee members, staff of the implementing nongovernmental organization, and members of the high-risk community.
Scoring	Each indicator was scored to assess if the activity took place and the level of involvement of the community-based group in planning and executing the activity. The score for each indicator was weighted to reflect the relative importance of the indicator to community mobilization and transition. The weights were generated by community mobilization experts and community members. The weighted scores for each indicator are summed to create a parameter score (expressed as a percentage of the maximum score possible). These scores are converted to a 7-point scale for evaluating transition readiness: 1 = Basic (0–14.3% of maximum score for parameter) 2 = Foundation (14.4–28.6%) 3 = Promising 1 (28.7–42.9%) 4 = Promising 2 (43.0–57.1%) 5 = Promising 3 (57.2–71.4%) 6 = Vibrant 1 [transition ready] (71.5–85.7%) 7 = Vibrant 2 [transition ready] (85.8–100%) Higher scores reflected (1) transition in leadership of programming from higher level staff to peer educators and community leaders, (2) transition in the role of community leaders from beneficiary of services to strategic decision maker, and (3) transition of the community's capacity to engage with the state from being invisible to being assertive.
Assessment	Reliability assessment was not conducted.

Related Reference	Sadhu, S., Manukonda, A. R., Yeruval, A. R., Patel, S. K., Saggurti, N. (2014). Role of a community-to-community learning strategy in the institutionalization of community mobilization among female sex workers in India. *PLOS One, 9*(3), e90592. doi:10.1371/journal.pone.0090592
Language	English
Contact	Pradeep Narayanan Research and Consultancies, Praxis Institute for Participatory Practice C-75, South Extension Part II New Delhi-110049, India Email: pradeepn@praxisindia.org
Other Comments	Measure of community capacity for change

TABLE 4.8 ■ Community Capacity Scale

Primary Reference	Lovell, S. A., Gray, A. R., & Boucher, S. E. (2015). Developing and validating a measure of community capacity: Why volunteers make the best neighbours. *Social Science & Medicine, 133,* 261–268.
Purpose	Assess community capacity among residents to come together to address and act on a pressing issue.
Description	The 26-item scale was developed based on a review of the literature and feedback from community residents from small towns in southern New Zealand. The community capacity scale includes six subscales with 3–6 items per subscale. The subscales are related to the following aspects of community capacity with sample items listed below. All response options are scored on a using a 7-point Likert scale to reflect agreement or disagreement with each statement. For a description of all of the items, please see Appendix A in the primary reference. **Participation (4 items):** • I attend local events whenever I can. • Participating in local clubs and events is good for the community. **Leadership (4 items):** • If I share my ideas and opinions with local leaders, they will listen. • My town/neighborhood has strong leaders who are moving it forward. **Connections (5 items):** • I have little in common with most people who live here (reverse scored). • Residents are friendly and inclusive of newcomers. • I don't feel welcome to join local groups and activities (reverse scored). **Sense of place (3 items):** • I see how economic changes have affected [place name]. **Community attitudes (4 items):** • What is good for the neighborhood is good for me. • [Place name]'s youth often go on to achieve great things. **Problem assessment (6 items):** • [Place name]'s residents bounce back in hard times. • I frequently discuss community issues with my friends and neighbors. • I am quick to work with others when I see a need within the community.
Sample	• Data were collected in 2011. The study sample included 306 residents of four small (populations 1500–2000), high-deprivation towns in southern New Zealand. • These residents were matched demographically (using age groups, sex, and New Zealand Deprivation Index quintiles) with the Mataura study sample. • The survey response rate of the control group was 58% while that of the comparison group was 54%. • Most respondents (75%) were educated to a primary or secondary school level; 58% had a household income of $50,000 a year or less (which was lower than the New Zealand medium household income of $62,853).
Scoring	Total and mean subscale scores were calculated. Missing data were imputed based on the mean scores for the subscales based on answered items if at least 80% of the relevant items had responses.

Assessment	• Chronbach's alpha for the overall community capacity scale was high with $\alpha = .88$. • Internal consistency of two of the six subscales (leadership, community attitudes) was above $\alpha = .70$. • The remaining four subscales had questionable internal consistency with α ranging between .62 and .66.
Language	English
Contact	Sarah Lovell School of Health Sciences University of Canterbury Private Bag 4800 Christchurch 8140, New Zealand Sarah.lovell@canterbury.ac.nz
Other Comments	Measure of community capacity for change

TABLE 4.9 ■	Community Readiness, Community Capacity, and Citizen Participation (Study 1)
Primary Reference	Foster-Fishman, P. G., Cantillon, D., Pierce, S. J., & Van Egeren, L. A. (2007). Building an active citizenry: The role of neighborhood problems, readiness, and capacity for change. *American Journal of Community Psychology, 39*, 91–106.
Purpose	The purpose of this study was to investigate the conditions related to resident involvement in neighborhood-based activities within the context of one comprehensive community-building effort. The study was designed to give funders, programming staff, and residents insight into those conditions that could be leveraged to foster resident involvement within the initiative.

Description	This scale includes measures of both community readiness and community capacity. Community readiness includes two subscales (collective efficacy, hope) and community capacity includes two subscales (neighborhood leadership, social ties). Information about each of the subscales is provided below.
	
	Collective efficacy (7 items): Developed for this study, this measure asked residents to rate their neighborhood's ability to collectively address neighborhood problems on a 3-point Likert scale (1 = *no control*, 2 = *some control*, and 3 = *a lot of control*). Two subscales:
	• Collective efficacy around housing and social problems
	    ○ Improving the physical conditions of your neighborhood
	• Collective efficacy around crime
	    ○ Reducing drug dealing
	
	Hope (1 item): Residents were asked to respond to one item, "In the next year, I think that conditions on my block will improve," on a 5-point Likert scale (from 1 = *strongly disagree* to 5 = *strongly agree*).
	
	Neighborhood leadership (3 items): measured neighborhood leadership by asking residents about perceptions of the quality of neighborhood leadership, neighborhood organizations, and faith-based leadership. Residents were asked to rate how much they agreed that each statement portrayed current conditions in their neighborhood on a 5-point Likert scale (1 = *strongly agree* to 5 = *strongly disagree*).
	• There is strong neighborhood leadership in my neighborhood.
	
	Social ties (7 items): described common interactions with neighbors (e.g., socializing, visiting, exchanging favors, asking advice). Residents responded by how much they agreed that each statement portrayed the current conditions on their block on a 5-point Likert scale (1 = *strongly agree* to 5 = *strongly disagree*).
	• People on my block socialize with each other.
	
	Note: The Individual Activism and Collective Action Measures in this study are explained in Chapter 7.

Sample	Seven distressed neighborhoods were defined and included in this study. Criss-cross directory was used to randomly select from the 3,301 households with phone numbers in the seven neighborhoods, 509 of the households participated (30%). Median length of residency was 10 years; 85% owned their own homes; 68% were females; 16% were African American; 79% were White; 42% had children under age 18 living in their homes.
Scoring	*Z*-scores for the two collective efficacy subscales were averaged to create one collective efficacy score. A *z*-score was created for the hope subscale. For the two subscales of community capacity (leadership, social ties), mean scores were calculated.

Reliability	Chronbach's alpha ranged from .67 to .90 for the following scales: • Collective efficacy around neighborhood housing and social problems (α = .74) • Collective efficacy around crime (α = .90) • Neighborhood leadership (α = .67) • Social ties (α = .76)
Related Reference	Foster-Fishman, P. G., Pierce, S. J., & Van Egeren, L. A. (2009). Who participates and why: Building a process model of citizen participation. *Health Education & Behavior, 36*(3), 550–569.
Language	English
Contact	Pennie G. Foster-Fishman, PhD Department of Psychology Michigan State University 125D Psychology Building East Lansing, MI 48824, USA fosterfi@msu.edu

TABLE 4.10 ■ Community Readiness, Capacity, and Citizen Participation (Study 2)	
Primary Reference	Foster-Fishman, P. G., Pierce, S. J., & Van Egeren, L. A. (2009). Who participates and why: Building a process model of citizen participation. *Health Education & Behavior, 36*(3), 550–569.
Purpose	The purpose of this study is to expand understanding of the factors that are associated with citizen participation by investigating who gets involved and under what circumstances. This will help practitioners and funders design interventions that are more capable of leveraging the levels of participation desired.
Description	This scale builds on the measures of community readiness and community capacity developed in Foster-Fishman et al., 2007, presented in Table 4.10. Community readiness incudes two subscales (collective efficacy, hope), and community capacity includes one subscale (sense of community). Information about each of the subscales is provided below. **Collective efficacy (6 items):** examined degree to which residents believe that they can make change happen by working together on a 6-point Likert scale. Format was based on Sampson, Raudenbush, and Earls (1997). Respondents were asked to rate from 1 (*not at all*) to 6 (*completely*) the extent to which, working together with their neighbors, they could achieve neighborhood change such as improving • Neighborhood physical conditions • The schools **Hope (3 items):** assessed whether residents see the possibility of positive change and a better future by rating items on 6-point Likert scale (1 = *strongly disagree* to 6 = *strongly agree*). • Residents believe that change is possible in this neighborhood. • Parents in this neighborhood are hopeful about their child's future. **Sense of community (10 items):** measured the degree of social bonding that residents perceive in their neighborhood on a 6-point Likert Scale (1 = *strongly disagree* to 6 = *strongly agree*). Scale was adapted from previous studies by Chavis, Hogge, McMillan, and Wandersman (1986) and Coulton, Korbin, and Su (1996). • In my neighborhood, people socialize with each other. • In my neighborhood, most people agree about what is best for the neighborhood. Note: This study also includes measures of Citizen Participation, Norms for Neighborhood Activism and Organizing Skills, which are explained in Chapter 7.
Sample	• The study was part of a broader evaluation of a comprehensive community-building effort in Battle Creek, Michigan. Data were collected in 2003, one year after the program was launched. • Purposive sampling was used to target 333 residents living in the seven distressed neighborhoods involved with the program in two ways: ○ All residents who had demonstrated some commitment to the program's goals (e.g., served on a steering committee) ○ All known residents who held formal and informal leadership positions in neighborhood-based groups (e.g., PTA, neighborhood associations, and planning councils) • Residents were sent a mail survey to complete, resulting in a sample of 201 participants (62% response rate). • The majority of participants were female (77%); mean age was 48.9; 56% White, 35% African American, 4.5% Hispanic; and mostly low-income (75% at $45,000 or less a year).

Assessment	Chronbach's alpha ranged from .84 to .91 for the following scales: • Collective efficacy (α = .91) • Hope (α = .84) • Sense of community (α = .90)
Related Reference	Foster-Fishman, P. G., Cantillon, D., Pierce, S. J., & Van Egeren, L. A. (2007). Building an active citizenry: The role of neighborhood problems, readiness, and capacity for change. *American Journal of Community Psychology, 39*, 91–106.
Language	English
Contact	Pennie G. Foster-Fishman, PhD Department of Psychology Michigan State University 125D Psychology Building East Lansing, MI 48824, USA fosterfi@msu.edu

REFERENCES

Beal, G. M. (1964). Social action: Instigated social change in large social systems. In J. H. Copp (Ed.), *Our changing rural society: Perspectives and trends.* Ames, IA: Iowa State University Press.

Beebe, T. J., Harrison, P. A., Sharma, A., & Hedger, S. (2001). The Community Readiness Survey. Development and initial validation. *Evaluation Review, 25*(1), 55–71.

Chaskin, R. J. (1999). *Defining community capacity: A framework and implications from a comprehensive community initiative.* Paper prepared for Urban Affairs Association Annual Meeting, Fort Worth, TX. Retrieved from http://www.chapinhall.org/sites/default/files/old_reports/41.pdf

Chavis, D. M., Hogge, J. H., McMillan, D. W., & Wandersman, A. (1986). Sense of community through Brunswik's lens: A first look. *Journal of Community Psychology, 14*(1), 24–40.

Coulton, C. J., Korbin, J. E., & Su, M. (1996). Measuring neighborhood context for young children in an urban area. *American Journal of Community Psychology, 24*(1), 5. doi:10.1007/bf02511881

Eng, E., & Parker, E. (1994). Measuring community competence in the Mississippi Delta: The interface between program evaluation and empowerment. *Health Education Quarterly, 21*(2), 199–220.

Fagan, A. A., Hanson, K., Hawkins, J. D., & Arthur, M. W. (2008). Bridging science to practice: Achieving prevention program implementation fidelity in the Community Youth Development Study. *American Journal of Community Psychology, 41*(3–4), 235–249. doi:10.1007/s10464-008-9176-x

Feinberg, M. E., Greenberg, M. T., Osgood, D. W., Anderson, A., & Babinski, L. (2002). The effects of training community leaders in prevention science: Communities That Care in Pennsylvania. *Evaluation and Program Planning, 25*(3), 245–259. doi: http://dx.doi.org/10.1016/S0149-7189(02)00019-8

Feinberg, M. E., Riggs, N. R., & Greenberg, M. T. (2005). Social networks and community prevention coalitions. *J Prim Prev, 26*(4), 279–298.

Findholt, N. (2007). Application of the community readiness model for childhood obesity prevention. *Public Health Nursing, 24*(6), 565–570.

Florin, P., Friend, K. B., Buka, S., Egan, C., Barovier, L., & Amodei, B. (2012). The interactive systems framework applied to the strategic prevention framework: The Rhode Island experience. *American Journal of Community Psychology, 50*(3), 402–414. doi:10.1007/s10464-012-9527-5

Foster-Fishman, P. G., Cantillon, D., Pierce, S. J., & Van Egeren, L. A. (2007). Building an active citizenry: The role of neighborhood problems, readiness, and capacity for change. *American Journal of Community Psychology, 39*(1–2), 91–106.

Foster-Fishman, P. G., Pierce, S. J., & Van Egeren, L. A. (2009). Who participates and why: Building a process model of citizen participation. *Health Education and Behavior, 36*(3), 550–569.

Freedman, D. A., Whiteside, Y. O., Brandt, H. M., Young, V., Friedman, D. B., & Hebert, J. R. (2012). Assessing readiness for establishing a farmers' market at a community health center. *Journal of Community Health, 37*(1), 80–88.

Griffin, S. F., Reininger, B. M., Parra-Medina, D., Evans, A. E., Sanderson, M., & Vincent, M. L. (2005). Development of multidimensional scales to measure key leaders' perceptions of community capacity and organizational capacity for teen pregnancy prevention. *Family & Community Health: The Journal of Health Promotion & Maintenance, 28*(4), 307–319.

Hawkins, J. D., & Catalano, R. F. (1992). *Communities that care: Action for drug abuse prevention.* San Francisco: Jossey-Bass.

Kunz, C. B., Jason, L. A., Adams, M., & Pokorny, S. B. (2009). Assessing police community readiness to work on youth access and possession of tobacco. *Journal of Drug Education, 39*(3), 321–337.

Lee, E., Dalton, J., Ngendahimana, D., Bebo, P., Davis, A., Remley, D., Smathers, C., & Freedman, D.A. (2017). Consensus modeling to develop the farmers' market readiness assessment and decision instrument. *Translational Behavioral Medicine, 7*(3), 506–516.

Lempa, M., Goodman, R. M., Rice, J., & Becker, A. B. (2008). Development of scales measuring the capacity of community-based initiatives. *Health Education and Behavior, 35*(3), 298–315.

Lesesne, C., Lewis, K., White, C., Green, D., Duffy, J., & Wandersman, A. (2008). Promoting science-based approaches to teen pregnancy prevention: Proactively engaging the three systems of the interactive systems framework. *American Journal of Community Psychology, 41*(3–4), 379–392.

Lovell, S. A., Gray, A. R., & Boucher, S. E. (2015). Developing and validating a measure of community capacity: Why volunteers make the best neighbours. *Social Science and Medicine, 133*, 261–268.

Narayanan, P., Moulasha, K., Wheeler, T., Baer, J., Bharadwaj, S., Ramanathan, T. V., & Thomas, T. (2012). Monitoring community mobilisation and organisational capacity among high-risk groups in a large-scale HIV prevention programme in India: Selected findings using a Community Ownership and Preparedness Index. *Journal of Epidemiology and Community Health, 66 Suppl 2*, ii34–41.

Oetting, E. R., Donnermeyer, J. F., Plested, B. A., Edwards, R. W., Kelly, K., & Beauvais, F. (1995). Assessing community readiness for prevention. *International Journal of the Addictions, 30*(6), 659–683.

Ogilvie, K. A., Moore, R. S., Ogilvie, D. C., Johnson, K. W., Collins, D. A., & Shamblen, S. R. (2008). Changing community readiness to prevent the abuse of inhalants and other harmful legal products in Alaska. *Journal of Community Health, 33*, 248–258.

Plested, B. A., Edwards, R. W., & Jumper-Thurman, P. (2006). *Community readiness: A handbook for successful change* Retrieved from http://www.ndhealth.gov/injury/ND_Prevention_Tool_Kit/docs/Community_Readiness_Handbook.pdf

Prochaska, J. O., DiClemente, C. C., & Norcross, J. C. (1992). In search of how people change: Applications to addictive behaviors. *American Psychologist, 47*(9), 1102–1114.

Rogers, E. M. (2003). *Diffusion of innovations* (5th ed.). New York: Free Press.

Sampson, R. J., Raudenbush, S. W., & Earls, F. (1997). Neighborhoods and violent crime: A multilevel study of collective efficacy. *Science, 277*(15), 918–924.

Schultz, A. J., Israel, B. A., Zimmerman, M. A., & Checkoway, B. N. (1995). Empowerment as a multilevel construct: Perceived control at the individual, organizational and community levels. *Health Education Research, 10*(3), 309–327.

Stanley, L. R. (2014). *Tri-Ethnic Center for Community Readiness handbook* (2nd ed.). Fort Collins, CO: Tri-Ethnic Center for Prevention Research.

Thomas, T., Narayanan, P., Wheeler, T., Kiran, U., Joseph, M. J., & Ramanathan, T. V. (2012). Design of a Community Ownership and Preparedness Index: Using data to inform the capacity development of community-based groups. *Journal of Epidemiology and Community Health, 66*(Suppl 2), ii26–ii33.

Tri-Ethnic Center for Prevention Research. (2014). *Community readiness for community change.* Retrieved from http://triethniccenter.colostate.edu/docs/CR_Handbook_8-3-15.pdf

Wandersman, A., Duffy, J., Flaspohler, P., Noonan, R., Lubell, K., Stillman, L., . . . Saul, J. (2008). Bridging the gap between prevention research and practice: The interactive systems framework for dissemination and implementation. *American Journal of Community Psychology, 41*, 171–181.

5 STRATEGIC COLLECTIVE ACTION IN COMMUNITIES

Research focusing on communities and neighborhoods generally includes an intersection of theories, practice approaches, and research methods aimed at individuals, groups, organizations, and communities at large within a geographical area or target boundary. This is particularly true when conducting research on social change that involves community practice approaches, such as local organizing, coalition building, and other forms of communal collaboration. In this context, one is theorizing and measuring the work of individuals and/or collective actors within the larger group. For example, when using a frame of individual social action, the focus is largely based on theories at an individual (micro) level—measuring psychological constructs of motivation, cognition, or skill of the individual. However, this focus ignores the theory that groups collectively also seek advantage or change. Aggregate social actors like organizations, coalitions, government agencies, and communities engage in social action that also uses resources, power, and agency. They coalesce and strengthen ties between individuals and other organizations that can be leveraged for mutual advantage. In such cases, a meso-level theoretical approach may more appropriately illuminate the complex web of interactions, structures, relationships, and outcomes to highlight the intersection between the individual and social change (Fligstein & McAdam, 2011).

For research studies that involve various forms of community collaboration (e.g., coalition building, organizational alliances) and social action (community organizing), Fligstein and McAdam's theory of strategic action fields (2011) is useful in framing the concepts and measures of strategic collective action. This middle range theory captures the "efforts of collective actors who vie for strategic advantage in and through interaction with other groups in what can be seen as meso-level social orders" (Fligstein & McAdam, 2011, p. 2). Strategic collective action is an "action taken by a group (either directly or on its behalf through an organization) in pursuit of members' perceived shared interests" (Marshall, 1988).

This chapter will make a case for why it is important to document, assess, and evaluate strategic collective action. It will summarize the methods used to measure collective action tactics, such as community organizing and community collaboration, and it will outline the difficulties in assessing collective action as a practice, process, or outcome. The measures included in this chapter represent the effort of researchers, organizers, and administrators who recognize the critical importance of understanding and measuring how collective action works in neighborhoods and communities.

THE IMPORTANCE OF MEASURING STRATEGIC COLLECTIVE ACTION

Measuring collective action has received limited attention. In part, the difficulty stems from the wide range of strategies involved in collective action. For example, legal actions such as class action lawsuits may be used by actors to fight an issue through the court system on behalf of disenfranchised groups. A specific issue or event may mobilize people or a local community to meet or demand change, a short-term tactic that often prompts collective action. For example, school closures generally prompt parents to mobilize quickly to attend meetings and voice their opinions about issues such as poor school performance or the lack of available resources to support learning. Political campaigning is used by candidates to convince voters to elect them on the basis of issues that are important to voters. Voters come together to assert their collective power before and after campaigns. Community-organizing activities are distinguished by an "emphasis on grassroots process, the exercise of social power, and by their pursuit of social transformation" (Christens & Speer, 2011, p. 254). Similarly, advocacy groups emerge to fight for the rights of others, offering resources and protection for those who are without the capacity to organize on their own. Community development in all its forms, including service delivery, leadership development, organizational capacity building, and coalition building, seeks to develop the assets of communities through collaboration and consensus (Ohmer & DeMasi, 2009). Finally, social movements emerge when multiple groups and institutions coalesce around a problem or issue and when conditions allow opportunities for groups to use different tactics and develop resources necessary to sustain the movement over time. Although these various forms of collective action present challenges for researchers, they also offer a rich backdrop for the measurement and evaluation of the key principles, values, and practices that underlie social change.

Another reason for measuring strategic collective action is that it allows a community or group to measure their progress as well as evaluate the strategies they used to achieve their goals. Documenting specific tactics or tasks, such as door knocking, alerting social media, letter writing, and demonstrations, records the different types of effort required to bring about community change. As short-term tactics, these activities have multiple goals, beginning with community engagement and continuing to action planning and eventual implementation of a social action agenda. By specifically listing or tracking community-organizing tactics, for example, we can also learn if there is a chronological sequence to the activities. Early advocates like Alinsky (1971) recommend using different tactics and actions based on the specific purpose. Organizing traditionally began building awareness through door knocking (Rubin & Rubin, 1986). Today, organizers also use social media and other forms of informal and formal communication to alert neighborhood residents about problems in their community. Organizers can also move directly to engaging community members in protests or actions that apply political pressure on office holders or others with political and authoritative control. Through a comparative lens, we can identify which collective action strategies are commonly used across communities and separate those that are unique to the context and problem.

Measuring organizing tactics can also document the impact of the processes on the community organizations involved (Hardina, 2002). Did the action increase membership? Did it stimulate new leaders or enhance the reputation of the organization? Did the strategies result in generating additional financial donations to support the organization? Measuring organizing tactics can also document the resources needed in the effort to unify residents against a community problem. Pyles (2009) adds that by measuring participation (e.g., member characteristics) and frequency of collective action, we can determine who is missing from the collective and identify the next target for creating a larger coalition of interests.

Documenting activities that organize and mobilize collective groups for change can also help to standardize what community practitioners "do" in a community. Kettner, Moroney, and Martin (2013) argue that knowing the tasks that are being completed by staff or volunteers brings focus to the question of who does what with residents, for what purpose, and under what conditions.

Lastly, when actual efforts and outcomes are compared against the original plan (whether it is for coalition development or neighborhood mobilization), we compare actions with assumptions about the model of practice being used by the organizers. Research on building coalitions, for example, shows that coalitions may not follow a linear line of development as called for in the practice model (Hays, Hays, DeVille, & Mulhall, 2000). Comparisons also provide another benefit by documenting the effectiveness of a strategy. We can improve the practice of unifying residents against a community problem by measuring the process and outcomes of strategic collective effort.

Moreover, documenting organizing and collective action efforts can also contribute to the evidence base for community and neighborhood research, particularly community organizing and community-level interventions (Ohmer & Korr, 2006; Ohmer, 2008). With limited resources and funding, it has become increasingly important for researchers and practitioners to document that their process and outcomes are working and have tangible results (Ohmer, 2008). It is also important to have clear and reliable measures that show residents and community stakeholders that the time and energy they invest in collective action efforts is not wasted. Ohmer and DeMasi (2009) argue that engaging residents and community stakeholders over the long haul is one of the most difficult things to do when organizing in vulnerable communities. Therefore, having clear and reliable measures can help organizers document and celebrate their successes along the way and continue to work on challenging issues, even when things are difficult. Strong evaluation, research, and measurement can also help organizers catch potential problems earlier in the process, which can improve organizing strategies, outcomes, and long-term community engagement.

METHODS FOR MEASURING STRATEGIC COLLECTIVE ACTION

Researchers who study strategic collective action focus on relations, networks, communities, or organizations. However, tracing collective action behaviors and understanding the identities, ties, and motivation of both individual actors and the structure of their actions present a challenge. This is a problem of location—that is, trying to identify or locate the drivers or predictors and what is the "collective action" group. For example, Glickman and Scaly (2008) direct our attention to the strengths of education organizing and the impact of such efforts in enhancing school and community outcomes and on the relationships of those involved in such initiatives. A policy coalition evaluation tool was used to study the contributions for policy development, which allows researchers to record measurable activities that can move a coalition toward policy change (Hardy, Wertheim, Bohan, Quezada, & Henley, 2013). Butterfoss, Goodman, and Wandersman (1996) examine the influence and decision-making of community coalition members. Wolff (2001) suggests that we should take a relational approach between actors in a coalition and elected officials, institutional leaders, and other power players. Each of these examples uses a different focus and approach to change.

In research on collective action, "the group" is the unit of analysis (Poteete & Ostrom, 2004). The relevant set of people can be those who share some interests or those who fail to act collectively. Groups may form together as an association or a coalition with rules for collective decision-making and action. For most definitions, boundaries are usually drawn to differentiate between those who are contributors versus those who are not. However, there are many instances when community members come together to organize but may not know who is involved. This means that there are groups of individuals involved in collective action associated with organized and bounded collective action entities but there is also social action connected with loose social networks (Weick, 1976).

Identifying the unit of analysis is critical because it identifies the purpose and focus of the "collective action," be it process, outcome, or impact. For example, is the purpose to identify determinants (e.g., relationships or ties between social actors or organizations) of a specific collective action effort? Is it to assess the processes or tactics (e.g., community organizing, neighborhood canvassing) used for collective action? Is the intent to assess outcomes and impact (e.g., resources obtained, policies changed)? Is the goal to compare collective action used in one group versus another group formed to address similar neighborhood problems? Depending on the purpose and type of study, the research methods and measures will vary.

Research on social action strategies, such as community organizing, has been documented through case studies and self-reports or organizational records of participation. Semistructured interviews and web-based surveys are commonly used to capture the efforts and outcomes realized by those who form a coalition. Many organization efforts also use community dashboards and other forms of summary analytics to track progress and impact of their collective action. For example, network analysis, which maps formal and informal links between collaborators, offers a methodology that traces the quality and frequency of interactions of residents engaging in a change process.

To measure collective action, we have to translate a complex set of interactions and events into clear and applicable sets of observable steps or actions from community practitioners as they implement these strategies in their practice. As mentioned above, there are several approaches and tactics that can be the target of measurement, but operationalizing and quantifying the various dimensions of collective action is a challenge. Christens and Speer (2015) point out that there are many types of organizing, for example, and it's difficult to come up with one tool that can be used in one context or one issue area or with a heterogeneous group of citizens or populations.

Challenges in measuring collaborations are well documented (Roussos & Fawcett, 2000). When a community or neighborhood is the unit of analysis, a lack of an appropriate comparison group and random assignment are common threats to inferences of causality attributed to collaborative partnerships or coalitions. Another challenge in measuring collective action, such as organizing, is the inherent difficulty of separating the impact of organizing in one neighborhood and city and their specific conditions from other efforts (Rothstein, 2004). Brown and colleagues (Brown, Feinberg, & Greenberg, 2012) suggest that measuring coalition functioning requires identifying constructs that are empirically distinct from one another. With distinct constructs, we can be more precise in identifying which specific factors of coalition functioning lead to different indicators of success.

MEASURES OF STRATEGIC COLLECTIVE ACTION

Concepts that are measured in strategic collective action include ideas of participation, representation, activities, power, collaboration, and coalitions. In some cases, the focus reflects the input or intent behind various common practices or tactics of collective strategic action. For example, the number of individuals or organizations involved may be a significant factor in collective action efforts. However, the optimal group size is unknown. Are 100 people sufficient or 1000? In small towns, 100 people attending a rally may be sufficient to focus attention on a problem, but in a city of two million, it may not be enough to change a political opinion or result in action. Some studies examine who is involved or the heterogeneity of the groups

(Kegler & Swan, 2011). Group diversity may be important in some contexts, while in others, homogeneity of values may be central. Chaskin and colleagues (Chaskin, Brown, Venkatesh, & Vidal, 2001) point out that selecting the "right" actors to participate in collective action can be critical in shaping dynamics and ultimate success.

Other targets of measurement for collective action focus on the purpose, the processes used, and outcomes achieved. Defining specific activities of community organizing (Pyles, 2009) and identifying specific goals (Glickman & Scaly, 2008) bring clarity and can demonstrate both the difficulty and success of acting collectively. Outcomes of collective action range from the personal to communal and organizational, including such measurable results as specific efforts that result in park improvements, increased street lighting, or community policing (Wood & Warren, 2002). Some organizing has reached levels affecting social policy where mass-based community organizations of low- and moderate-income individuals have been effective at changing policy. For example, People Improving Communities through Organizing and the Association of Community Organizations for Reform Now have changed state policies affecting health care and minimum wage (Swarts, 2008).

Power is another construct that represents an important aspect of collective action. If groups have power, whether formal or informal, it can influence resources and the likelihood of change occurring in communities. Increasing power by building relationships, either through community organizing or forming coalitions and collaboration across organizations, can be effective in addressing a variety of issues, such as substance abuse, youth violence, education issues, workforce development, and homelessness (Speer, Tesdahl, & Ayers, 2014).

A number of researchers study various forms of collaboration and coalition building as a form of collective action (Brown et al., 2012; Greenbaum & Dedrick, 2007; Shapiro, Oesterle, Abbott, Arthur, & Hawkins, 2013). Many advantages accrue when groups or organizations deliberate about problems, strategically align their combined resources, and take collective action.

Participation, Representation, and Activities

Research on collective action begins with attendance counts and frequencies but also includes collecting demographics on the participants, such as gender, age, race, and social class. Knowing who is participating is also important because it collects information related to representation (Speer et al., 2014). Knowing if participants are there as residents or if they represent a group or organization helps to determine the extent of coalition involvement or other community group participation in collective action efforts. While participation is a basic measure of collective action and community building (see Chapter 6), assessing the number or type of activities can also be helpful in creating operational direction for a variety of settings. Tracking the implementation of collective action activities can establish if the activity is effective and should be continued and if it is translatable across different community settings and efforts. Activities may include face-to-face meetings in communities or with organizations, participation in political discussions, involvement in public action, participation in demonstrations, demonstrating collective efficacy (see Chapter 6), community-based research and learning, involvement with other organizations, and helping others in need through volunteering. Measures are included in this section that can be used to document and describe participation, representation, and activities of collective action.

Christens and Speer (2011) conducted a longitudinal study of congregation-based community organizing over five years. The researchers sought to understand how the influence of contextual variables, such as neighborhoods, networks, and settings, can explain the differences in outcomes in attrition or sustained participation in organizing. Unique to this study is the use of longitudinal data from sign-in sheets at group meetings. Individual participation, neighborhood characteristics, and affiliation network engagement was assessed over five years (see **Table 5.1 Contexts Affecting Community Organizing**) on measures of contextual variables influencing community organizing. A nested three-level model of analysis was used where participation in group meetings was used each successive year as the control. The results showed that characteristics of organizational settings (types of meetings attended and frequency of face-to-face contact) predicted future participation in group meetings. Individual and neighborhood demographics characteristics were generally not predictive of future participation in community organizing activities. The results on the group meeting types (or setting phenotypes) underscores the importance of defining and measuring different community organizing meetings, particularly those that build interpersonal relationships. Measuring the size of the group meetings also helped the researchers learn that large action meetings were found to be negatively predictive of future participation in community organizing. Hosting smaller, goal-focused meetings may increase and sustain resident participation over time.

In a more comprehensive study, Kegler and Swan (2011) analyzed data from an evaluation of twenty California Healthy Cities and Community Coalitions to test relationships between coalition factors and outcomes. Multiple sources of data based on coalition member surveys, interviews, and semiannual progress reports were analyzed to test relationships in both the formative and maintenance stages of coalition development as predicted by the Community Coalition Action Theory. This theory asserts that coalitions form because of a threat, opportunity, or mandate, with coalition leadership facilitating member engagement to ensure that benefits of participation outweigh the costs (Butterfoss & Kegler, 2009). The researchers identified and defined four factors related to coalition development, including membership/representation, coalition processes (communication, decision-making, task focus, cohesion), leadership and staffing, and structure. In addition, they used measures of member engagement (role, participation, satisfaction) and indicators of community capacity (new skills and new partnerships) as expected outcomes. All measures had reliable coefficients ranging from .73 through .93 (see **Table 5.2 Coalition Representation, Participation, and Engagement**). Membership was examined in relation to its influences on coalition processes, leadership and staffing, and structures in the early stage of coalition development. Findings indicate that broad representation was significantly correlated with coalition size and negatively correlated with cohesion. Having broad representation in the maintenance stage was correlated with the number of leadership opportunities created and number of new partners engaged. Shared decision-making and leadership were also correlated with participation.

- Finally, the researchers also found that staff competence, task focus, and cohesion were correlated with member satisfaction.
- Longitudinally, member satisfaction in the formation stage was associated with new skills in the maintenance stage (Kegler & Swan, 2011).

These results demonstrate how researchers can use data to test theoretical assumptions about the links between constructs of participation and membership and their impact on outcomes as well as help to expand the knowledge base about stages of coalition development.

Mannarini and Talo (2013) take a broader view of participation and report that it can range from passive forms (where people are told what to do and have no control over processes) and outcomes to very active and interactive forms where community members have control over the processes and outcomes. In this range, there are a number of activities that enable community residents to be active participants in public deliberations about policy options, which in turn lead to citizen empowerment. While research described in Chapter 7 presents measures of empowerment, including participation in community activities, Mannarini and Talo (2013) offer measures of process and outcomes of public participation that may affect whether community members continue to participate or withdraw their willingness to be actively engaged in social change (see **Table 5.3 Deliberative Process Perceptions of Quality Scale and Outcome Rating Scale**). They measured the quality of the deliberative processes used and the outcomes reporting reasonable Cronbach's alpha ranging from .76 through .89.

- Researchers found that the likelihood of participating was correlated with all variables but time, and more strongly associated with processes (dialogue and knowledge/understanding).
- Regression analysis found that participant likelihood of engaging in future public forms depends on the dialogical exchange of ideas, the perceived results of the interaction, perceived benefits of participation that outweigh the costs, and perception that information received on the topic was adequate.
- Their research also found that participants who reported a "good quality" experience (e.g., open, respectful, and collaborative communication) did not perceive serious costs, felt informed about the issue, and were more likely to participate in future events (Mannarini & Talo, 2013).

Power

Strategic collective action contains many references to power. However, the concept is not easily defined and is difficult to disentangle from empowerment (Chapter 7). Empowerment is about the feelings of power (e.g., self-efficacy) and the process of control (power to) while ignoring actual control over resources (power over). Critics have pointed out that empowerment does not confer actual power over resources (Angelique, Rodriguez, Culley, Brown, & Binette, 2013). Power over resources stems from possession of resources and the ability to make decisions about the distribution of resources (through positions, privilege). Neal and Neal's (2011) review of the literature on power offers three overlapping conceptions of power—social power, psychopolitical power, and relational power. Each will be used to frame power measures (where available) that are important for strategic collective action research.

Social power is multidimensional and describes the relationship between power and empowerment. There are three instruments of social power: The first is power over resources, which allows for domination and control of others. The second instrument of power is the ability to set agendas or control issues up for public discussion. The third instrument of power is the influence of shared consciousness, the ability to distribute materials, information, and ideology that influences the perceptions of others. Oetzel and colleagues (2015) used three types of measures that relate to the instruments of social power in a larger study that sought to establish psychometric properties of twenty-two measures from a community-based participatory research (CPBR) model (see **Table 5.4 Measures of Community-Based Participatory Research Projects**). A measure of influence and power dynamics assessed the extent of equal voice and influence over decisions made in the partnership. As a three-item measure, the reliability was low (.58). A participatory decision-making measure that relates to the influence and being a part of decisions made by the group had a Cronbach's alpha of .83. Finally, the study measured power as an outcome and assessed the degree to which power and capacity have been developed in the community (Cronbach's alpha = .81). In this last application, the measure of power as an outcome seeks to understand how structural relations between researchers and community members were impacted through their partnership.

- Using a rigorous three-stage random sampling of CBPR research projects, the study found evidence that 15 of the 22 multi-item measures achieved good fit, while the other measures had to be modified.
- The study also demonstrated the proximal, intermediate, and distal outcomes to test relationships among context, process, and outcome (Oetzel et al., 2015).

While many of the constructs measured in this study were important for theorizing and modeling the science of community-based participatory research (CBPR), there are several other measures (e.g., partnership capacity, leadership, synergy, agency capacity) that may be useful in research examining collective action of individuals and groups involved in CBPR or community-engaged research projects.

The second conception of power is psychopolitical power (Prilleltensky, 2008). In this view, psychology and politics are combined as the "capacity and opportunity to fulfill or obstruct personal, relational or collective needs" (p. 119). Power is exercised by manipulating resources and excluding people but also influenced by external forces (military, economic). For example, elected officials and bureaucrats use psychopolitical power when they make decisions about where to locate recreation services in a community or which properties in a neighborhood become a candidate for demolition or rehabilitation. The psychological component is the ability to shape others' viewpoints by manipulating various affective, behavioral, cognitive, and cultural mechanisms, which can operate at the individual or collective level. At an aggregate level, policy decisions, for example, can be mapped onto local communities demonstrating the use of resources and the power to include or exclude certain groups or communities from benefiting over others.

Relational power is a struggle or conflict between advantaged and disadvantaged parties; power is a social relationship. Neal and Neal (2011) describe a structural measure of power "that emphasizes the privileged position of the agent (i.e., individual or group) within a pattern of relationships through which resources are exchanged" (p. 9). In social change, if the goal is to change social structures, then an analysis of structural power imbalances helps to determine targets for social change strategies. This is the focus of transformation in communities. Structural analyses of power can be useful in examining marginalization of oppressed political status (race, ethnicity, class/poverty, gender, or mental illness) and to pinpoint where powerful relationships exist between individuals, agencies, or community groups. Neal and Neal's (2011) measure of power is a calculation of the amount of power A has over B by answering (a) Does A have a resource desired by B? and (2) How many sources does B have for this resource? The equation is

$$\text{Power of A over B} = \frac{R_{AB}}{R_B}$$

This quantitative measure specifies the relationship between resources, exchange opportunities, and power in a way that can be applied to a range of groups or organizations. Patterns can be examined to assess various resource dependencies between groups and how they may evolve over time. By analyzing the power of various groups, community practitioners can target capacity-building strategies that can help under resourced groups be more successful in achieving their goals.

In one of the few research studies that measured partnership power, Jones and Barry (2011) explored key factors that influence health promotion partnership synergy. Although understudied, the authors hypothesized that power among other factors was an important predictor in partnership synergy, assuming that it facilitated cooperation and may be viewed as an equivalent to trust (Bachmann, 2006). Power was a nine-item scale with pattern coefficients that ranged from .512 to .918. Synergy was conceptualized as the product or capability of partnership (Weiss, Miller Anderson, & Lasker, 2002)—that is, it can be measured as both a process and product. These researchers also measured trust, organizational culture, leadership, administrative and management activities, efficiency, and partnership outcomes (see **Table 5.5 Power, Trust, and Partnership Synergy**). Positive trust, leadership, and efficiency were found to be key predictors of partnership synergy. Power was not a significant predictor of synergy. However, the authors note that trusting relationships among partners can exist only when power is shared.

These measures can help one understand who has power, who controls resources, and who is involved in decision-making that impacts resource distribution and the shared consciousness of the group. Other techniques are also available, such as social network analysis (described later in the chapter). This type of measurement and analysis can identify how groups act collectively through collaboration or coalitions to increase their power by forming resource exchange opportunities (e.g., transportation, service referrals), which can strengthen the group's ability to secure resources for social change.

Collaboration

Collaborating in communities is a strategy used by community activists, nonprofit leaders, and government officials to bring stakeholders in a community together with citizens to address common concerns. Collaboration is generally used by nonprofits to enhance their programs, generate support for their organization, and to enhance relations with other entities in a community. Gray (1985) defines collaboration as "the pooling of appreciations and/or tangible resources, e.g., information, money, labor, by two or more stakeholders, to solve a set of problems which neither can solve individually" (p. 912). Collaboration has been used successfully to tackle complex and controversial issues facing communities, including housing, education, employment, public health, and child and family well-being (Berkowitz & Cashman, 2000; Butterfoss, Goodman, & Wandersman, 1996; Harper, Kuperminc, Weaver, Emshoff, & Erickson, 2014).

Collaboration is measured in many ways, including tracking service coordination, collaborative activities (planning, program development), processes, practices, administration and management, network linkages, and outcomes. Because the literature on collaboration is vast and crosses over into the areas of coalitions, partnerships, and coordinating councils, this section focuses on interagency collaboration where shared power, responsibility, and interdependences exist. Interagency collaboration theoretically offers opportunities for researchers to explore how combining diverse perspectives at the individual and organizational level can develop comprehensive community interventions targeted at multiple levels of the community and how to build their numbers to leverage resources and exert influence on policy makers.

Dedrick and Greenbaum (2011) developed a measure specific to organizational collaborative practices and activities in three areas: financial and physical resources, program development and evaluation, and collaborative policies (see **Table 5.6 Interagency Collaboration Activities Scale**). Unlike previous studies on collaboration that use factor analysis to measure interagency collaboration at the individual level, this study shifts the items from the *individual's* level of collaboration to the *agency's* level of collaboration and uses a multilevel analysis approach. Thus, rather than asking the participant to report his or her own level of collaboration, the participant was asked about the extent his or her agency collaborated with other agencies. The analysis used to test the equivalence of a three-factor structure across individual and agency levels found that the reliability of the scores of the financial and physical resources, program development and evaluation, and collaborative policy activities factors were different. Reliability estimates at the organizational level were .81, .60, and .72, respectively, compared to the reliability estimates obtained when ignoring the nesting of individual informants within agencies (.79, .82, and .85, respectively).

- Employee's age, job role, gender, educational level, and number of months employed were not significantly related to interagency collaboration (Dedrick & Greenbaum, 2011).

As the authors suggest, using an individual-level model to represent agency-level factors may produce distorted relationships with other variables, such as collaboration outcomes.

It should be noted that the Wilder Collaboration Factors Inventory is a good example of a tool that is widely used to assess the elements of effective collaboration. The inventory identifies 20 factors organized around six domains: purpose, membership characteristics, process and structure, communication, environment, and resources. Although the inventory is used mostly as a diagnostic tool, the RAND Corporation published a report on the Evaluation of Community Voices Project in Miami, which describes a five-year initiative aimed at enhancing health care access and quality for the underserved (Derose, Beatty, & Jackson, 2004). The report provides reliability coefficients for each factor; however, readers are encouraged to review the Amherst H. Wilder Foundation website (www.wilder.org) and the following citation on the development and use of the collaboration inventory (Mattessich, Murray-Close, & Monsey, 2001).

Coalitions

Solutions to address the range of social, human, and environmental issues affecting communities and neighborhoods require the support and partnerships of multiple stakeholders and groups. They can work together to coordinate messages, relationships, and identify priorities for action. When problems are too large or complex, a coalition of interest groups and individuals come together to develop a coordinated response. Chavis (1995) defines a coalition as a loosely structured intra- and inter-organizational alliance of individuals representing diverse organizations, factions, or constituencies who agree to work together to achieve a common goal. Coalitions have the potential to influence many outcomes, such as a community benefits policy for economic development or improved access to health services. However, coalitions can also shape the capacity of its members as well as the individual organizations.

Granner and Sharpe (2004) published an inventory of measurement tools for evaluating community coalition characteristics and partnership functioning. Their review of the literature at the time found 146 measurement scales/indexes reporting on numerous constructs and conceptual definitions. The authors organized the tools into five groups: (1) member characteristics and perceptions (e.g., representation, skills and experience, participation, role clarity, sense of ownership, perceived effectiveness, satisfaction, commitment, participation, benefits and costs); (2) organizational or group characteristics (e.g., leadership, staff performance, formal organizational structure, task focus); (3) organizational or group processes and climate (e.g., stages of development, community capacity and organizational climate, group relationships, conflict, decision-making, recruitment, quality implementation, resources); (4) general coalition function or scales bridging multiple constructs (e.g., member characteristics, collaboration, group functioning); and (5) impacts and outcomes (e.g., community linkages, impacts, institutionalization, capacity). Although some of the measures have little or no data available supporting reliability and validity, the ones with reported reliabilities > .80 have been selected to complement the other coalition measures covered below.

Building on previous research conducted during the 1990s on community coalitions for the prevention of substance abuse, Hays et al. (2000) studied the impact of twenty-eight Illinois coalitions (see **Table 5.7 Coalition Characteristics and Impacts**). In particular (and not included in other more current scales below), the researchers examined several independent variables on leadership effectiveness, member diversity and participation, and collaboration and their impact on perceived changes in their community's prevention system, planning, and policy changes. The scales that were reported had good reliabilities and reflected concepts important to coalition functioning and outcomes. For example, coalition member resources and organizational and structural characteristics such as leadership, decision-making processes, and member participation were measured as critical determinants of coalition action and achievements. Measures for specific impacts included increased awareness of the problem, the extent of logical connections between programs and outcomes, and the extent of stronger policies and regulations in the community.

- The findings showed that different structural characteristics of coalitions were related to three different community impacts.
- A larger number of sectors represented in a coalition and having more complex collaborative interactions was associated with an increased likelihood of developing prevention plans and changes in public policy.
- Collaboration, however, was negatively related to changes in public policy and system changes (Hays et al., 2000).

The authors suggested that the age range of coalitions used in the analysis may mean that coalition impacts depend on their stage of development. Older coalitions may lose their momentum and focus and may benefit from technical assistance aimed at facilitating capacity building in new ways, depending on structural and organizational features of a coalition.

Brown and colleagues (2012) developed an instrument to measure coalition functioning based on Communities That Care (CTC) coalitions funded by the Pennsylvania Commission on Crime and Delinquency. They examined and organized coalition functioning into six domains: leadership, task focus, interpersonal relationships, participation benefits and costs, sustainability planning, and community support (see **Table 5.8 Coalition Functioning**). An exploratory factor analysis of all items led to removing items based on low factor loadings or low cross-loadings resulting in empirically distinct scales reflecting the domains of coalition functioning. Empirically distinct scales included coalition leadership style, mobilizer skill, coalition efficiency, community support, participation benefits, participation difficulties, and sustainability planning, and were all found to be psychometrically sound multidimensional measures of coalition functioning.

- In addition, the researchers examined the relationships between the distinct scales and five criterion variables for construct validity. For example, coalitions with members who had greater mobilizing skills were more likely to have stronger fidelity to the CTC model. Those with the higher community support were also less likely to need technical assistance.
- Compared to previous research, however, the new scales on participation benefits and difficulties found little association with the criterion variables, suggesting that further work is needed to examine how participation difficulties predict coalition involvement and attrition (Brown et al., 2012).

Shapiro and colleagues (2013), in their work evaluating Communities That Care, developed a measure of coalition functioning to assess relationships to successful practice outcomes. Based on economic theory, population ecology, human ecology, and network theory, researchers focused on four dimensions: efficiency, goal directedness, opportunities for participation, and cohesion (see **Table 5.9 Community Board Interview**).

- A 2-index strategy (the comparative fit index and the root mean square error of approximation) was used to determine the adequacy of the factor structure at the early, mid-, and late points of the intervention.
- The four-factor model was found to be a better fit over time rather than a single factor model.
- As a test of validity, the constructs used to measure the four distinct dimensions of coalition functioning had significant commonality between member observations and external observers (Shapiro et al., 2013).

Although these dimensions had a consistent factor structure over time and good construct validity, the reliability coefficients of the measures were lower than expected. As the authors suggest, further research with larger and more varied samples could help to build on these measures for coalition-based community-practice models.

A more recent method used to understand partnerships or coalitions of organizations in communities is network analysis. Network analysis is used to examine the connections and relationships among organizations using data from multiple individuals or organizations that may be interacting with each other (Provan, Veazie, Staten, & Teufel-Shone, 2005). The unit of analysis is the relationship and not the organization itself. By reflecting on the structure, strong or weak ties, we can learn how to build stronger networks. Organizations can also see the role they play in partnerships. Provan and colleagues developed a network data collection instrument that was administered to organizations who were providing health and support services for persons with chronic diseases (see **Table 5.10 Partnership Networks and Processes**). They also offer eight questions that researchers and others can use to provide information for those involved in collaborative, multiorganizational partnerships to understand what the partnership looks like, how it has evolved, and what can be done to enhance and sustain collective action.

Network analysis can also help us understand what is significant about relationships and thus can index resources, trust, and information. In an analysis of ninety-nine organizations, Bess (2015) examined patterns of structural change with youth violence prevention organizations involved in the development of a community coalition. In this study, the coalition represents the network or system of interest theorized to include individuals and organizations working together to solve a problem through the citywide intervention system. The conceptualization of a coalition is viewed as a systems event that can influence relational dynamics within the intervention network that are both serendipitous and goal directed. Serendipitous networks lack structure, with no single leaders or plan that directs their activity. The structure of these organizations merges from dynamic and shifting patterns. Goal-directed networks represent a structural response to a need to organize and coalesce together. Pooling resources with centralized leadership are common. Bess (2015) measured perceived collaboration, coalition attendance, and organizational type (see **Table 5.11 Youth Prevention Coalition Measure of Network Capacity**). Patterns of density and centralization were analyzed across five years of data. The findings show that the coalition extended its reach beyond its own boundaries and influenced the structure of the youth violence prevention system overall by generating new opportunities for collaboration and through an increased hierarchy.

CONCLUSION

The concept and application of collective action and the family of community-based cooperative activities continue to grow and be used across communities and neighborhoods. There are literally thousands of partnerships, coalitions, and consortiums of groups across the United States, with common and unique activities, processes, and outcomes. Individual-level measures dominate and are fruitful in testing conceptual linkages between individual action and social change. However, the pace of methodological development has not kept up with the practice. Collective action is a complex and often context-dependent process, which challenges the development of valid and reliable measures that can be used consistently to test hypotheses and theories. In a recent scoping review, Stolp and colleagues (2017) called for the use of reliable and validated tools for assessing effective collaboration. As we continue to expand the definition of where we engage, measure, and practice our work to address some of the most intractable problems in communities and neighborhoods, we will need a variety of measures.

Numerous applications of collective action practice and various operational definitions of concepts indicate that we do not fully understand the processes. Christens and Speer (2015) argue that while research on collective action strategies, like community organizing, has been shown to be beneficial for individual participants, more research is needed to help specify the mechanisms of influence or the ways they are mediated by contextual or personal characteristics. In addition, more emphasis is needed on using multilevel approaches that link individual changes in participants with the development of community capacity and outcomes at the community or neighborhood level. By using more reliable measures, nested designs, and hierarchical analysis, we hope to understand collective action, a concept that begs for more methodological innovation.

LIST OF MEASURES AND TABLE NUMBERS

TABLE 5.1 ■ Contexts Affecting Community Organizing

Primary Reference	Christens, B. D., & Speer, P. W. (2011). Contextual influences on participation in community organizing: A multilevel longitudinal study. *American Journal of Community Psychology*, *47*, 253–263.
Purpose	The purpose of the study was to assess differences in participatory contexts like neighborhoods and if they can account for divergent outcomes in attrition or sustained participation in organizing.
Description	This measure consists of a total of eight items with five subscales (ranging from 1–3 items). **Individual participation** was measured as a count variable for each year over five years. **Neighborhood characteristics** measured the effects of median income, economic heterogeneity (index of qualitative variation based on likelihood that any two households within the geographical area will fall into different income categories, as opposed to the same category), and residential stability using census data. **Affiliation network engagement** assessed the level of involvement of the other attendees at meetings that an individual attends during the year in which the attendance occurs (i.e., organizing engagement of an individual's network of affiliation). **Group meeting types** measured the frequency of and attendance at different group meeting types, including • Action meetings • Research action meetings • Planning meetings **One-to-one meetings** were defined as the number of face-to-face meetings between participants that last approximately 30 minutes.

Sample	• Data were collected over five years among people involved in congregation-based community organizing.
	• 11,583 individuals from 115 congregations were involved in one of five local organizing initiatives in different cities.
	• Demographic information collected for a subset of participants ($N = 461$):
	  ○ Mean level of income: $35,000 to $45,000
	  ○ Mean education: between some college and a college degree

Scoring	• Individual participation was transposed into a binary indicator of participation/nonparticipation in group meetings. • Census data was used as measures of neighborhood characteristics and converted to discrete scores. • Affiliated network engagement was measured as an average level of outside attendance of co-attendees. • Group meeting type was assessed as the frequency of group meeting types, and average attendance levels across all organizing initiatives. • One-to-one meetings was summed for an annual count.
Assessment	Measures of reliability do not apply to this scale.
Language	English
Contact	B. D. Christens Department of Interdisciplinary Studies, School of Human Ecology University of Wisconsin-Madison 2406 Sterling Hall, 475 N. Charter Street, Madison, WI Email: bchristens@wisc.edu

TABLE 5.2 ■ Coalition Representation, Participation, and Engagement	
Primary Reference	Kegler, M. C., & Swan, D. W. (2011). An initial attempt at operationalizing and testing the community coalition action theory. *Health Education & Behavior, 38*(3), 261–270.
Purpose	To test relationships between coalition factors and outcomes as predicted by community coalition action theory implemented in two stages of development.
Description	Relevant constructs in this measure include **Coalition membership** • **Representation:** Number of community sectors represented on a coalition out of 15; sectors were summed for coalition-level measure. The sectors included ○ Social services ○ Health care ○ Education ○ Business **Coalition processes** • **Communication (2 items)** was assessed as the frequency and productivity of communication among members and between members and staff on a 5-point semantic differential scale • **Decision-making** was assessed as the perception of members influence over four types of decisions on a scale of 1 = *a lot of influence*, 4 = *no influence* ○ Setting goals and objectives for the program • **Task focus** was assessed by averaging 4 items, such as ○ This is a down-to-earth, practical coalition • **Cohesion** was assessed by averaging 4 items, such as ○ Group spirit among members **Leadership and staffing** • **Leadership** assessed skills of the coalition leaders in guiding the coalition with eight items (e.g., asks you to assist with specific tasks). • **Staffing** referred to the staff skills in supporting the coalition with 8 items (e.g., usually available for assistance). **Member engagement** • **Member participant role** was assessed by asking participants which of seven roles they played during the planning phase in the coalition (e.g., helped with needs and/or assets of the community) and which roles they played in the implementation phase. Number of roles was summed for members then averaged to form a coalition-level variable. • **Participation** was assessed by summing the hours members spent in coalition meetings and coalition activities outside of monthly meeting. • **Satisfaction** was assessed by asking how satisfied members were with seven areas of the coalition in the planning stage (e.g., programs and/or activities of the coalition) and 11 items in the implementation phase. **Indicators of community capacity** • **New skills** was measured by asking members the extent to which 13 skills (e.g., communicating effectively in groups) had improved because of their participation in the initiative. • **New partnerships** was assessed by asking members if the number of organizations they related to had changed for a range of typical inter-organizational activities.

	Coalition structure • **Size** was the number of active coalition members. • **Complexity** was scored by counting the number of committees per coalition: 1 = one coalition with no committees to 5 = 5 or more committees or groups. **Indicators of community change** • **Level of policy achievement** measures the self-report of polices that the coalition was able to influence and categorized as substantive, moderate, or limited. • **Level of program expansion** was assessed through qualitative categories of three levels of change (number of new or expanded programs, new program developed in addition to those in action plan, and evidence of proved infrastructure for program development).
Sample	• Secondary data analysis of quantitative and qualitative data collected from 20 sites implementing the California Healthy Cities and Communities program. • Multiple methods of data collection including interviews with coordinators, community leaders, focus groups, and review of documents. • A majority of data were gathered from a survey of coalition members in each community at the end of the first year and at the end of the three years during the implementation phase.
Scoring	Responses from individual coalition members were averaged to create coalition-level measures.
Assessment	• Communication (α = .85) • Decision-making (α =.86) • Task focus (α = .73) • Cohesion (α = .78) • Leadership (α =.88) • Staffing (α =.92) • Member participation role (α = .78) • Participation is the sum of hours members spent • Satisfaction (α = .92) • New skills (α = .93) • New partnerships (α = .70)
Language	English
Contact	Michelle C. Kegler 1518 Clifton Road NE 5th floor Atlanta, GA 40444 Email: mkegler@sph.emory.edu

TABLE 5.3 ■	Deliberative Process Perceived Quality Scale (DPPQS) and Outcome Rating Scale (ORS)
Primary Reference	Mannarini, T., & Talo, C. (2012). Evaluating public participation: Instruments and implications for citizen involvement. *Community Development*, *44*(2), 239–256.
Purpose	The purpose of this study was to validate two instruments for measuring process and outcomes of a participatory procedure and explored if participants' evaluation predicted future involvement in the same type of practice.
Description	Two scales were tested for evaluating public participation: DPPQS and ORS. The original DPPQS contained 18 items with six subscales while the original ORS contained 15 items with five subscales. All items were measured on a seven-point scale (1 = *strongly disagree* to 7 = *strongly agree*). Sample items for the DPPQS-11 include **Dialogue (6 items)** • None of the ideas proposed was considered wrong or useless. • When I spoke, others paid attention to what I was saying. • Everyone had the opportunity to speak and to make him/herself heard. **Knowledge/Understanding (5 items)** • I think that the discussion made me consider new perspectives on the issue at stake. • Through the discussion, I increased my knowledge of the problem. • Participants sought clarification and explanation of the views expressed. **Outcome rating scale (4 items)** measures outcomes achieved through participatory discussion techniques like open space technology. • The [participatory setting] generated new knowledge on the issue under discussion. • Through the [participatory setting], new relational networks were established.
Sample	• Residents of the Apulia region in Italy participated in one of five open space technology processes designed to encourage discursive interaction through group discussion in low-structured settings. • A total of 283 individuals participated in assessing the measures while another 188 completed the revised versions of the scales.
Scoring	Information on how the items were scored was not provided.
Assessment	A confirmatory factor analysis indicated two factors that should be considered as two distinct subscales: dialogue and knowledge/understanding. The reliability scores were • Dialogue: $\alpha = .86$ • Knowledge/understanding: $\alpha = .76$ • DPPQS-11: = $\alpha = .89$ • Outcome rating: $\alpha = .78$
Language	English and Italian
Contact	Terri Mannarini Department of History, Society and Human Studies University of Salento, via Stampacchia 45 Lecce 73100, Italy Email: terrimannarini@hotmail.com

TABLE 5.4 ■ Measures of Community-Based Participatory Research Projects

Primary Reference	Oetzel, J. G., Zhou, C., Duran, B., Pearson, C., Magarati, M., Lucero, J., Wallerstein, N., & Villegas, M. (2015). Establishing the psychometric properties of constructs in a community-based participatory research conceptual model. *American Journal of Health Promotion, 29*(5), 188–202.
Purpose	To establish psychometric properties of 22 measures from a community-engaged research project
Description	The measures of community-based participatory research included five conceptual domains with 24 subscale constructs. **Partnership capacity (6 items):** using 5-point scale: 1 = *not at all*, 5 = *a great extent* • Diverse membership • Ability to bring people together for meetings and activities • Connections to political decision makers, government agencies, other organizations/ groups **Influence and power dynamics (3 items):** using 5-point scale: 1 = *not at all*, 5 = *a great extent* • All partners had equal voice in deciding which funding opportunities were sought for this project. • Overall, I am satisfied with the amount of influence that each partner has over decisions that this partnership makes. **Participatory decision-making (4 items):** using 5-point scale: 1 = *not at all*, 5 = *a great extent* • Feel comfortable with the way decisions are made in the project • Support the decisions made by the project team members **Leadership (10 items):** using a 5-item scale: 1 = *very ineffective*, to 5 = *very effective* • Taking responsibility for moving project forward • Inspiring or motivating people involved in the project • Fostering respect between partners • Developing trust between partners • Creating an environment where differences of opinion can be voiced • Resolving conflict among partners **Partnership synergy (5 items):** using 5-point scale: 1 = *not at all*, 5 = *a great extent* By working together, how well are/were you and your partner able to • Develop goals that are widely understood and supported in the partnership • Recognize challenges and come up with good solutions • Respond to needs and problems of your stakeholders or community as a whole **Partner capacity building (3 items):** using 5-point scale: 1 = *not at all*, 5 = *a great extent* • Enhanced my own reputation • Increased utilization of my expertise or services **Agency capacity building (3 items):** using 5-point scale: 1 = *not at all*, 5 = *a great extent* • Enhanced the agencies' reputation • Enhanced the agencies' ability to affect public policy

(Continued)

TABLE 5.4 ■ (Continued)	
	Changes in power relations (5 items): using 5-point scale: 1 = *not at all*, 5 = *a great extent* • Community team members have increased participation in the research process. • Community team members can talk about the project in other settings, such as a community or political meeting. • Community team members can apply the findings of the research. **Health outcomes: Community transformation (4 items):** using 5-point scale: 1 = *not at all*, 5 = *a great extent* • Resulted in policy changes • Improved the overall health status of individuals in the community Other measures also included structural/individual dynamics, research tasks and communication, dialogue and learning, sustainability of partnership/project, resource management.
Sample	294 CBPR projects in United States with federal funding; 312 (77.2% response) academic and community partners and 138 principal investigators (69%)
Scoring	Confirmatory factor analysis was used to establish factorial validity and Pearson correlations to establish convergent and divergent validity.
Assessment	• Partnership capacity, α = .78 • Influence and power dynamics, α = .58 • Participatory decision-making, α = .83 • Leadership, α = .94 • Partnership synergy, α = .90 • Partner capacity building, α = .80 • Agency capacity building, α = .87 • Changes in power relations, α = .81 • Health outcomes: Community transformation, α = .79
Language	English
Contact	John G. Oetzel Department of Management Communication, University of Waikato Private Bag 3105, Hamilton, New Zealand 3240 Email: joetzel@waikato.ac.nz

TABLE 5.5 ■ Power, Trust, and Partnership Synergy	
Primary Reference	Jones, J., & Barry, M. M. (2011). Exploring the relationship between synergy and partnership functioning factors in health promotion partnerships. *Health Promotion International*, *26*(4), 408–420.
Purpose	The purpose of this study was to identify factors that influence health promotion partnership synergy, including the testing of new multidimensional scales of power, trust, mistrust, and synergy.
Description	This measure consists of the following four scales: **Power** was assessed with a 9-item scale asking the frequency of partnership experiences with a 5-point response option where 1 = *always* and 5 = *never*. Sample items include • Credit is shared among all the partners • Partners withhold their expertise or apply it arrogantly • Power is shared equally between partners **Trust** was measured with two subscales comprised of 14-items using a 5-point response option where 1 = *never* and 5 = *always*. Sample items include Positive trust • Partners eagerly volunteer to take on tasks associated with the partnership. • Partners' roles are clearly understood and they fulfill these roles. • Partners keep promises they make to the partnership. Mistrust • Partners have hidden agendas and bring these into the partnership. • Partners withhold information of relevance to the partnership. • Partnership time and energy is wasted because of mistrust. **Partnership synergy** was a 9-item scale asking the frequency of partnership experiences with a 5-point response option where 1 = *always* and 5 = *never*. Sample items include • Feelings of energy, excitement, and passions • The skills and unique perspective of the partnership complement each other • The work of the partnership is broken down or shared by all partners Other concepts in the study included the following: **Organizational culture** was a 9-item scale asking about the frequency of partnership experiences using a 5-point response option where 1 = *always* and 5 = *never*. Sample items include • The partnership has a common language to talk about health. • Professionals on the partnership have a tendency to assume they know the answers before the questions have even been asked. **Leadership effectiveness** was an 11-item scale that rates total effectiveness of the partnership's leadership (both informal and formal) using a 5-point option where 1 = *poor* and 5 = *excellent*. Sample items include • Communicating the vision of the partnership • Creating an environment where differences of opinion can be voiced • Recruiting diverse people and organizations into the partnership **Administration and management effectiveness** was measured with 10 items with a 5-item response option where 1 = *poor* to 5 = *excellent*. Sample items include • Coordinating communication with people and organizations outside of the partnership

(Continued)

TABLE 5.5 ■ (Continued)

	• Applying for and managing grants and funds • Evaluating the progress and impact of the partnership **Partnership efficiency** was assessed using 3 items that asked how efficient the partnership was in using resources with a 5-item response option where 1 = *very inefficiently* to 5 = *very efficiently*. Sample items include • Financial resources • In-kind resources (partners skills, experience, and knowledge) **Partnership outcomes** was an 8-item measure that asked partnership achievements using a 3-item response option where 1 = *yes*, *no* = 2, and 3 = *did not measure*. Sample items include • Change in the capacity of community members • Policy changes that affected people in a positive way • Service changes that affected people in a positive way
Sample	• Study based on surveys conducted with chair/lead members representing 40 health promotion partnerships • 337 surveys completed (72% response rate) • More than half engaged in 5–6 activities (i.e., training, research, education). • Almost half (47.5%) of partnerships were 3–5 years old and 30% were more than 5 years old.
Scoring	• Two units of analysis were considered: (1) partner level and (2) partnership level. Scores were obtained for each respondent and then calculated for an aggregate score for respondents in each partnership. • Reliability and validity tests were carried out on individual partner-level data, and Pearson's correlations and regression analysis were conducted on partner-level data. Convergent and discriminate validity were established for power, positive trust, mistrust, synergy, and leadership.
Assessment	Power: $\alpha = .87$ Positive trust: $\alpha = .91$ Mistrust: $\alpha = .82$ Synergy: $\alpha = .91$ Organizational culture: $\alpha = .90$ Leadership: $\alpha = .96$ Efficiency: $\alpha = .84$
Related Reference	Weiss, E. S., Miller Anderson, R., & Lasker, R. D. (2002). Making the most of collaboration: Exploring the relationship between partnership synergy and partnership functioning. *Health Education and Behaviour, 29*, 683–698.
Language	English
Contact	Jacky Jones Health Promotion Services, Health Service Executive West West City Centre, Seamus Quirke Road Galway, Republic of Ireland Email: drjackyjones@gmail.com

TABLE 5.6 ■ Interagency Collaboration Activities Scale (ICAS)

Primary Reference	Dedrick, R. F., & Greenbaum, P. E. (2011). Multilevel confirmatory factor analysis of a scale measuring interagency collaboration of children's mental health agencies. *Journal of Emotional and Behavioral Disorders, 19*(1), 27–40. http://doi.org/10.1177/1063426610365879
Purpose	To evaluate the factor structure underlying the 12-item IACS at the informant and at the agency levels
Description	The ICAS scale consists of 12 items covering four areas of collaborative activities, reflecting aspects of an organization's culture. "To what extent does your organization share with other like serving organizations . . ." using a response scale that ranged from 1 = *not at all* to 5 = *very much.* • **Financial and physical resources (4 items):** funding, purchasing • **Program development and evaluation activities (4 items):** developing programs or services, program evaluation • **Collaborative policy activities (4 items):** formal written agreements, voluntary contractual relationships, case reviews, informal agreements
Sample	• Professionals from 32 children's mental health agencies were recruited at a national conference; 23 agencies were from California, six from Michigan, and three from Ohio. • Once agencies were selected, mental health professionals within each agency were recruited for the study. • A total of 378 professionals responded representing 104 administrators, 201 service providers, and 73 case managers. Most were female (74%), White (60%), with a mean age of 41.2 years. • The mean number of participants representing the 32 agencies equaled 11.81.
Scoring	• Multilevel confirmatory factor analysis was conducted to test the equivalence of a three-factor structure across levels (individual and agency-level).
Assessment	• Financial and physical resources: $\alpha = .79$ • Program development and evaluation activities: $\alpha = .82$ • Collaborative policy activities: $\alpha = .85$
Related Reference	Greenbaum, P. E., & Dedrick, R. F. (2007). Multilevel analysis of interagency collaboration of children's mental health services. In C. Newman, C. Liberton, K. Kutash, & R. M. Friedman (Eds.), *The 19th annual research conference Proceedings, A system of care for children's mental health: Expanding the research base.* Tampa, FL: University of South Florida, The Louis de la Parte Florida Mental Health Institute, Research and Training Center for Children's Mental Health.
Language	English
Contact	Robert Dedrick University of South Florida, Department of Measurement and Research, EDU 105 Tampa, FL 33620 Email: dedrick@usf.edu

TABLE 5.7 ■	Coalition Characteristics and Impacts
Primary Reference	Hays, C. E., Hays, S. P., DeVille, J. O., & Mulhall, P. F. (2000). Capacity for effectiveness: The relationship between coalition structure and community impact. *Evaluation and Program Planning*, *23*, 373–379.
Purpose	The study evaluated the structural characteristics of community coalitions and their impacts on the community.
Description	The independent variables assessed representation, membership diversity, leadership effectiveness, member's participation, and collaboration. Sample items include **Leadership effectiveness (6 items)** using 5-point Likert-type scale • The leader encourages and explores all points of view. • The leader effectively manages conflict and channels it toward coalition goals. **Member Participation (10 items)** with a response option 1 = *strongly agree* to 5 = *strongly agree* • Coalition members share a common vision for our community. • My abilities are effectively used by the coalition. • I feel strongly committed to this coalition. **Collaboration (6 items)** using a frequency scale of 1 = *infrequent* to 5 = *more frequent* • How often do members engage in six increasingly complex activities with other members of their coalition? These activities ranged from "exchanged information about meetings, conferences and training opportunities" to "jointly planned and implemented programs with one or more coalition partners." The dependent variables included perceived impact on community's prevention system, planning prevention, and public policy change. Sample items include **Impact on prevention system (7 items)** using a scale ranging from 0 = *not at all* to 4 = *a great extent* • To what extent has your coalition increased community-wide awareness of community ATOD problems . . . helped organizations working for ATOD prevention to increase their share of community resources . . . improved communication with broader community sectors about research related ATOD prevention strategies? **Planning prevention (8-item rating index assessing designed logic models)** • Extent of logical connections between programs and outcomes, the comprehensiveness of effect, and sufficiency of reach to achieve community change **Public policy change (1 item)** using response option of a 4-point scale • To what extent has your coalition strengthened ATOD-related policies and regulations in the community?
Sample	• 28 community-based substance abuse prevention coalitions in Illinois; 2–12 years in existence
Scoring	• Regression analysis was used to examine 28 coalition-member resources and organizations with structural characteristics as determinants of coalition activities and accomplishments.
Assessment	• Leadership effectiveness: $\alpha = .92$; responses were scored by calculating the mean of each member's rating on the 6-item scale and averaging members' rating for each coalition. • Member participation: $\alpha = .87$; responses were scored by calculating the mean of each member's rating on the 10-item scale and then averaging members' rating for each coalition.

	• Collaboration: $\alpha = .87$; complex interactions were weighted more heavily, with a variables created by summing weighted frequencies for each member and averaging member response by coalition. • Prevention impact: $\alpha = .91$ • Planning prevention: $\alpha = .70$
Language	English
Contact	C.E. Hayes Center for Prevention Research and Development Institute of Government and Public Affairs 510 Devonshire Drive Champaign, IL 61820 University of Illinois at Urbana-Champaign Email: cehays@uiuc.edu

TABLE 5.8 ■ Coalition Functioning	
Primary Reference	Brown, L. D., Feinberg, M., & Greenberg, M. (2012). Measuring coalition functioning: Refining constructs through factors analysis. *Health Education and Behavior, 39*(4), 486–497.
Purpose	The purpose was to examine and refine measures of unique coalition functioning constructs. The measures were created from Communities That Care coalitions funded by Pennsylvania Commission on Crime and Delinquency.
Description	This measure consists of seven empirically distinct scales: **Leadership**: response options range from 1 = *strongly disagree* to 7 = *strongly agree* Coalition leadership style **(3 items)** • Leadership asks you to assist with specific tasks. • Leadership creates an environment where differences of opinion can be voiced. Mobilizer skill (4 items) • Interpersonal and communication skills • Enthusiasm and passion for the mission **Task focus:** response options range from 1 = *strongly disagree* to 7 = *strongly agree* Coalition efficiency **(3 items)** • Team members work very hard • People pay a lot of attention to getting work done **Community support: (4 items)** response options range from 1 = *no* to 7 = *a great deal* • Do influential community leaders understand CTC and why it is important? • Does the administrative leadership in the school system champion CTC? **Participation benefits and costs**: response options range from 1 = *not at all* to 7 = *a great deal* Participation benefits **(3 items)** • Learning new skills • Developing valuable relationships Participation difficulties **(3 items)** • Interfered with your work schedule and responsibilities • Interfered with your family life **Sustainability planning: (3 items)**, response options range from 1 = *not at all* to 7 = *yes*; 1 = *highly unlikely* to 7 = *highly likely* • How likely do you think it is that the CTC process will continue beyond the funding period? • CTC has developed a realistic, concrete plan for how to continue offering prevention programs when funded ceases.
Sample	• Data were collected over five years in an annual survey of coalition members. • The number of respondents ranged from 732 in 2010 to 988 in 2007 representing 53 coalitions in 2010 and 75 coalitions in 2010. • Respondents from 2010 were 70% female, 89% White, 7% Black, 1% Hispanic, and 2% of another ethnicity.

Scoring	Scoring of the scales was not provided—however, overall coalition functioning scale was created using the mean scores of the seven subscales.
Assessment	• Coalition leadership style: $\alpha = .85$ • Mobilizer skill: $\alpha = .92$ • Coalition efficiency: $\alpha = .94$ • Community support: $\alpha = .88$ • Participation benefits: $\alpha = .87$ • Participation difficulties: $\alpha = .84$ • Sustainability planning: $\alpha = .85$
Language	English
Contact	Louis D. Brown The University of Texas Health Science Center at Houston (UTHealth) School of Public Health in El Paso 1101 North Campbell Street, Room 409 El Paso, Texas 79902 Email: louis.d.brown@uth.tmc.edu

TABLE 5.9 ■ Community Board Interview (Coalition Functioning)

Primary Reference	Shapiro, V. B., Oesterle, S., Abbott, R. D., Arthur, M. W., & Hawkins, J. D. (2013). Measuring dimensions of coalition functioning for effective and participatory community practice. *Social Work Research, 37*(4), 349–59.
Purpose	Designed to measure coalition functioning, which is defined as "the way in which coalitions operate to marshal resources and exercise power to influence their objectives" (Shapiro et al., 2013, p. 350). This particular measure was created specifically for use by Communities That Care (CTC), a coalition-based model of community practice that works to transform communities and change rates of problem behavior among youth.
Description	The 17-item scale was divided into four subscales. Participants rated each item on a 4-point scale, with 1 meaning *strongly disagree* and 4 meaning *strongly agree*. Sample items are listed below. **Goal-directedness (5 items)** • The CTC leadership adheres to the decision-making procedures. • The CTC leadership has control of meetings. • Team has agreed how to govern itself and make decisions. **Efficiency (6 items)** • Board members work very hard. • This is a highly efficient, work-oriented board. • This board rarely has anything concrete to show for its efforts. **Opportunities for participation (4 items)** • The CTC leadership asks you to assist with specific tasks. • The CTC leadership intentionally seeks out your views. • Everyone is involved in the discussion, not just a few. **Cohesion (3 items)** • There is not much group spirit among this board. • There is a sense of unity and cohesion in our board.
Sample	• The 432 respondents were randomly selected from the rosters of active coalition members (provided by community coordinators in CTC communities). • The interviews took place annually for five years, and over 40% of the coalition members participated in more than one annual interview.
Scoring	• Higher scores indicate higher levels of coalition functioning. • The interview was based on the Coalition Web-Based Self-Report Questionnaire but was revised to better assess how coalitions were functioning. • CTC implementation specialists provided additional ratings of coalition functioning (the specialists had no knowledge of what was said during the coalition member interviews). Details of how each measure was scored was not included.
Assessment	• Reliability coefficients were reported to be lower than what was found on a previous study; authors suggested these may be due to instrument modifications or sample differences.
Language	English
Contact	Valerie B. Shapiro School of Social Welfare University of California, Berkeley 120 Haviland Hall Berkley, CA 94720-7400 Email: vshapiro@berkeley.edu

TABLE 5.10 ■ Partnership Networks and Processes

Primary Reference	Provan, K.G., Veazie, M.A., Staten, L.K., & Teufel-Shone, N.I. (2005). The use of network analysis to strengthen community partnerships. *Public Administration Review, 65*(5), 603–613.
Purpose	To demonstrate how the information from network analysis can be used by communities and leaders to build community capacity through the development of a network of collaborating organizations
Description	This measure consists of the follow items: **Types of links** For each organization in the community, the respondent organization is asked to indicate with a check the extent of their involvement across four types of relationships. Examples include • Through shared resources (e.g., joint funding, shared equipment, or personnel, shared facilities) • Through patient client referrals (either sent or received or both) between your organization and the agency listed The overall **quality of the working relationship** with each agency is also indicated using a 4-point scale: 1 = *poor relationship* (little trust), 2 = *fair relationship* (some trust), 3 = *good relationship* (trust), 4 = *excellent relationship* (high trust). **Trust scores** are compiled for each organization in the network or partnership based on an average of all trust scores assigned to that particular organization by its network partners; averaging all scores produces an overall trust score for the network. **Benefits and drawbacks** from cooperating and collaborating with other agencies are assessed using 14 items. Participants responded when it (1) already occurred, (2) expect to occur, or (3) do not expect it to occur. **Benefits (9 items)** • Ability to serve my clients better • Acquisition of new knowledge or skills • Better use of my organization's services • Heightened profile of my organization • Increased ability to reallocate resources **Drawbacks (5 items)** • Takes too much time and resources • Loss of control/autonomy over decisions • Strained relations within my organization
Sample	• The development of the questions was based on the work of the University of Arizona's Southwest Center for Community Health Promotion, which conducted network analysis at two sites along the U.S.–Mexico border and collaborations among a range of public and nonprofit agencies.
Scoring	• Organizations with the greatest number of links (interactions) to others are central in the network; those with the fewest links are least central.
Assessment	• Unit of analysis is the relationship among organizations comparing relationships between two organizations, clusters of organizations, and among all of the organizations comprised in the network.
Language	English
Contact	Keith G. Provan Public Administration and Policy at the University of Arizona Email: kprovan@eller.arizona.edu

TABLE 5.11 ■	Youth Prevention Coalition Measure of Network Capacity
Primary Reference	Bess, K. (2015). Reframing coalitions as systems interventions: A network study exploring the contribution of a youth violence prevention coalition to broader system capacity. *American Journal of Psychology, 55*, 381–395.
Purpose	To assess the contributions coalitions make, through their collaborative activities of their members, to the broader intervention systems in which they are embedded.
Description	**Perceived Collaboration** was measured as a tie when Organization A collaborates with Organization B in at least one category regardless of reciprocity. • Based on the responses, a matrix was created for each question or network relation based on collaboration time (e.g., program/service delivery) or leadership for each of five years. **Coalition Participation** was assessed through attendance sheets at official coalition events and meetings. **Organizational type** was measured as • Community based • Human service • Youth development • K–12 school • Education • Faith • Government • Immigrant • Health
Sample	• Sample consisted of 99 public and private nonprofit organizations involved in youth violence prevention in a midsized southeastern city. • Social network analysis assessed collaborations over the past 12 months using a roster of organizations they had collaborated with for the purpose of policy/advocacy work, information sharing, involvement with a community coalition or event service delivery, resource sharing or training, and education.
Scoring	Perceived collaboration: One is assigned in the matrix to denote if Organization A identifies Organization B as a collaborator, and 0 is assigned if no relationship. Organizational type was measured as "1" if organizations were the same or "0" if they were of different types.
Assessment	Measures of reliability do not apply to this measure.
Language	English
Contact	Kimberly Bess Department of Human and Organizational Development Vanderbilt University Peabody 90, Nashville, TN 37203 Email: Kimberly.d.bess@vanderbilt.edu

REFERENCES

Alinsky, S. D. (1971). *Rules for radicals: A primer for realistic radicals.* New York: Random House.

Angelique, H. L., Rodriguez, R., Culley, M. R., Brown, R., & Binette, A. J. (2013). Empowering community psychology through an examination of social power. *Community Psychology, 41,* 725–742. doi:10.1002/jcop.21567.

Bachmann, R. (2006). Trust and/or power: Towards a sociological theory of organizational relationships. In R. Bachmann & Z. Zaheer (Eds.), *Handbook of trust research.* Cheltenham, UK: Edward Elgar Publishing.

Berkowitz, B., & Cashman, S. (2000). Building healthy communities: Lessons and challenges. *Community, 3*(2), 1–7.

Bess, K. (2015). Reframing coalitions as systems interventions: A network study exploring the contribution of a youth violence prevention coalition to broader system capacity. *American Journal of Psychology, 55,* 381–395.

Brown, L. D., Feinberg, M., & Greenberg, M. (2012). Measuring coalition functioning: Refining constructs through factor analysis. *Health Education and Behavior, 39*(4), 486–497.

Butterfoss, F. D., Goodman, R. M., & Wandersman, A. (1996). Community coalitions for prevention and health promotion: Factors predicting satisfaction, participation, and planning. *Health Education Quarterly, 23*(1), 65–79.

Butterfoss, F., & Kegler, M. (2009). The community coalition action theory. In R. J. Clemente, R. A. Crosby, & M. C. Kegler (Eds.), *Emerging theories in health promotion practice and research: Strategies for improving public health* (2nd ed., pp. 157–193). San Francisco, CA: Jossey-Bass.

Chaskin, R. J., Brown, P., Venkatesh, S., & Vidal, A. (2001). *Building community capacity.* New York: Aline De Gruyter.

Chavis, D. M. (1995). Building community capacity to prevent violence through coalitions and partnerships. *Journal of Health Care for the Poor and Underserved, 6*(2), 234–245.

Christens, B. D., & Speer, P. W. (2011). Contextual influences on participation in community organizing: A multilevel longitudinal study. *American Journal of Community Psychology, 47,* 253–263.

Christens, B. D., & Speer, P. W. (2015). Community organizing: Practice, research, and policy implications. *Social Issues and Policy Review, 9,* 193–222.

Dedrick, R. F., & Greenbaum, P. E. (2011). Multilevel confirmatory factor analysis of a scale measuring interagency collaboration of children's mental health agencies. *Journal of Emotional and Behavioral Disorders, 19*(1), 27–40. http://doi.org/10.1177/1063426610365879

Derose, K. P., Beatty, A., & Jackson C. A. (2004). *Evaluation of community voices Miami: Affecting health policy for the uninsured.* Santa Monica, CA: RAND Corporation. https//www.rand.org/pubs/technical_reports/TR177.html

Fligstein, N., & McAdam, D. (2011). Toward a general theory of strategic action fields. *Sociological Theory, 29,* 1–26.

Glickman, N. J., & Scaly, C. P. (2008). Can community and education organizing improve inner-city schools? *Journal of Urban Affairs, 30,* 5, 557–577.

Granner, M. L., & Sharpe, P. A. (2004). An inventory of measurement tools for evaluating community coalition characteristics and functioning. Last updated April 2003. Retrieved from http://prevention.Sph.sc.edu/tools/CoalitionEvalInent.pdf

Gray, B. (1985). Conditions facilitating interorganizational collaboration. *Human Relations, 38*(10), 911–936.

Greenbaum, P. E., & Dedrick, R. F., (2007). *Multilevel analysis of interagency collaboration of children's mental health agencies.* In C. Newman, C. Liberton, K. Kutash, R. M. Friedman (Eds.), The 19th Annual Research Conference Proceedings, A System of Care for Children's Mental Health: Expanding the Research Base. University of South Florida, The Louis de la Parte Florida

Mental Health Institute, Research and Training Center for Children's Mental Health, Tampa, FL.

Hardina, D. (2002). *Analytical skills for community organization practice.* New York: Columbia University Press.

Hardy, L. J, Wertheim, P., Bohan, K., Quezada, J. C., & Henley, E. (2013). A model for evaluating the activities of a coalition-based policy action group: The case of Hermosa Vida. *Health Promotion Practice, 14*(4), 514–523.

Harper, C. R., Kuperminc, G. P., Weaver, S. R., Emshoff, J., & Erickson, S. (2014). Leveraged resources and systems changes in community collaboration. *American Journal of Community Psychology, 54*, 348–357.

Hays, C. E., Hays, S. P., DeVille, J. O., & Mulhall, P.F. (2000). Capacity for effectiveness: The relationship between coalition structure and community impact. *Evaluation and Program Planning, 23*, 373–379.

Jones, J., & Barry, M. M. (2011). Exploring the relationship between synergy and partnership function factors in health promotion partnerships. *Health Promotion International, 26*(4), 408–420.

Kegler, M. C., & Swan, D. W. (2011). An initial attempt at operationalizing and testing the community coalition action theory. *Health Education & Behavior, 38*(3), 261–270.

Kettner, P. M., Moroney, R. M., & Martin, L. L. (2013). *Designing and managing programs: An effectiveness-based approach.* Thousand Oaks, CA: Sage.

Mannarini, T., & Talo, C. (2012). Evaluating public participation: Instruments and implications for citizen involvement. *Community Development, 44*(2), 239–256.

Marshall, G. (1988). *A dictionary of sociology.* New York: Oxford University Press.

Mattessich, P., Murray-Close, M., & Monsey, B. (2001). *Collaboration: What makes it work* (2nd ed.). St. Paul, MN: Amherst H. Wilder Foundation.

Neal, J. W., & Neal, Z. P. (2011). Power as a structural phenomenon. *American Journal of Community Psychology, 48*(3–4), 157–67.

Oetzel, J. G., Zhou, C., Duran, B., Pearson, C., Magarati, M., Lucero, J., Wallerstein, N., & Villegas, M. (2015). Establishing the psychometric properties of constructs in a community-based participatory research conceptual model. *American Journal of Health Promotion, 29*(5), 188–202.

Ohmer, M., & DeMasi, K. (2009). *Consensus organizing: A community development workbook: A comprehensive guide to designing, implementing, and evaluating community change initiatives.* Thousand Oaks, CA: Sage.

Ohmer, M. L. (2008). Assessing and developing the evidence base of macro practice interventions with a community and neighborhood focus. In M. Roberts-DeGennaro (Ed.), Paradigm of evidence-based macro practice [Special issue]. *Journal of Evidence-Based Social Work, 5*(3/4), 519–547.

Ohmer, M. L., & Korr, W. S. (2006). The effectiveness of community practice interventions: A review of the literature. *Research on Social Work Practice, 16*(2), 132–145.

Orsi, R. (2014). A method for articulating grassroots community organizing. *Journal of Community Psychology*, 42(4), 398–413.

Poteete, A. R., & Ostrom, E. (2004). In pursuit of comparable concepts and data about collective action. *Agricultural Systems, 82*(3), 215–232.

Prilleltensky, I. (2008). The role of power in wellness, oppression, and liberation: The promise of psychopolitical validity. *Journal of Community Psychology, 36*, 116–136.

Provan, K. G., Veazie, M. A., Staten, L. K., & Teufel-Shone, N. I. (2005). The use of network analysis to strengthen community partnerships. *Public Administration Review, 65*(5), 603–613.

Pyles, L. (2009). *Progressive community organizing: A critical approach for a globalizing world.* New York: Routledge.

Rothstein, R. (2004). *Class and schools: Using social, economic, and educational reform to close the black-white achievement gap.* New York: Teachers College, Columbia University.

Roussos, S. T., & Fawcett, S. B. (2000). A review of collaborative partnerships as a strategy for improving community health. *Annual Review of Public Health, 21*, 369–402.

Rubin, H. J., & Rubin, I. (1986). *Community organizing and development.* Columbus, OH: Merrill.

Shapiro, V. B., Oesterle, S., Abbott, R. D., Arthur, M. W., & Hawkins, J. D. (2013). Measuring dimensions of coalition functioning for effective and participatory community practice. *Social Work Research, 37*(4), 349–59.

Shlay, A., & Whitman, G. (2006). Research for democracy: Linking community organizing and research to leverage blight policy. *City & Community, 5*(2), 153–171.

Speer, P. W., Tesdahl, E. A., & Ayers, J. F. (2014). Community organizing practices in a globalizing era: Building power for health equity at the community level. *Journal of Health Psychology,* 19(1), 159–169.

Stolp, S., Bottorff, J. L., Seaton, C. L., Jones-Bruker, M., Oliffe, J. L., Johnson, S. T., . . . Lamont S. (2017). Measurement and evaluation practices of factors that can contribute to effective health promotion collaboration functioning: A scoping review. *Evaluation and Program Planning, 61,* 38–44.

Swarts, H. J. (2008). *Organizing urban America: Secular and faith-based progressive movements.* Minneapolis, MN: University of Minnesota Press.

Weick, K. E. (1976). Educational organizations as loosely coupled systems. *Administrative Science Quarterly, 21*(1), 1–19.

Weiss, E. S., Miller Anderson, R., & Lasker, R. D. (2002). Making the most of collaboration: Exploring the relationship between partnership synergy and partnership functioning. *Health Education and Behaviour, 29,* 683–698.

Wolff, T. (2001). Community coalition building-contemporary practice and research: An introduction. *American Journal of Community Psychology, 29*(2), 165–191.

Wood, R. L., & Warren, M. R. (2002). A different face of faith-based politics: Social capital and community organizing in the public arena. *International Journal of Sociology and Social Policy, 22,* 6–54.

6 SOCIAL CONNECTIONS AND PROCESSES IN COMMUNITIES

This chapter provides an overview of measurement instruments that assess connections among residents and/or their connections to a neighborhood or place. Social connections in communities are the relationships and ties that demonstrate how residents are associated to their geographic place of residence (e.g., neighborhood, town, city) but also to the people, institutions, and social structures in that place. This chapter focuses on the relational aspects of community, including the quality and character of human relationships and associations that exist because of one's connection to and membership in a community. The chapter includes measures of social connections and processes among members of place-based communities, including sense of community, collective efficacy, and social capital.

WHY IS IT IMPORTANT TO MEASURE SOCIAL CONNECTIONS AND PROCESSES IN COMMUNITIES?

Strong social connections and sense of community among residents can lead to a range of positive outcomes, including increased civic and political participation, community engagement, trust in local government, as well as improved neighborhood and life satisfaction, well-being, psychological empowerment, social support and mental health (Hughey, Speer, & Peterson, 1999; McCarthy, Pretty, & Catano, 1990; Perkins, Florin, Rich, Wandersman, & Chavis, 1990; Peterson, Speer, & Hughey, 2006; Pretty, 1990). Neighborhood social processes, including collective efficacy and social capital, are tied to lower levels of community violence (Sampson, Raudenbush, & Earls, 1997) and decreased levels of major depression (Ahern & Galea, 2011). Collective efficacy and social capital are also protective against a range of physical health problems, including asthma, obesity and overweight, cardiovascular disease, cancer, and premature mortality as well as improved self-reported health and lower neighborhood death rates (Browning & Cagney, 2002; Cohen, Finch, Bower, & Sastry, 2006; Cohen, Inagami, & Finch, 2008; Lochner, Kawachi, Brennan, & Buka, 2003; Kawachi, Kennedy, Lochner, & Prothrow-Stith, 1997; Kim, Subramanian, & Kawachi, 2006; Schultz, O'Brien, & Tadesse, 2008; Subramanian, Kim, & Kawachi, 2002). Social capital has also been linked to economic development and the stable functioning of democracies (Putnam, 2000).

The social processes that occur when residents have higher levels of social cohesion, trust, and stronger connections are considered necessary for engaging in positive behaviors that promote health, collective action, civic participation, reciprocity, and a greater willingness to take action or intervene to address neighborhood problems (Kawachi & Berkman, 2000). Social capital and sense of community may also act as resources that people have with one another and that residents in a neighborhood can draw upon to accomplish goals and engage in actions to improve their own lives as well as their communities (Coleman, 1990; Kawachi & Berkman, 2000; Putnam, 1993; Veenstra, 2001). Community researchers and practitioners are increasingly engaged in analyzing the impact of social processes and connections on a range of individual and community outcomes, and some are also developing interventions to facilitate neighborhood social processes as a strategy for improving a range of outcomes. Valid and reliable measures in this field, therefore, are critical to analyze these connections as well as the impact of potential strategies to facilitate social processes among neighborhood residents. The following sections synthesize prior research on some of the most widely used and tested measures of neighborhood social connections.

SENSE OF COMMUNITY (SOC) MEASURES

Community psychologists have conducted extensive research on sense of community in order to establish a theoretical foundation for the field's values, principles, and areas of inquiry (Chavis & Pretty, 1999). Measuring and evaluating how community interventions impact sense of community has become increasingly important for practitioners in the field, particularly understanding how sense of community can sustain the health of neighborhoods (Chavis & Pretty, 1999). Sense of community is an important concept and measure that both researchers and practitioners can use to understand and improve the social connections among residents in neighborhoods.

One of the earliest definitions of sense of community was developed by Sarason (1974), who conceptualized psychological sense of community (PSC) as an individual "perception of similarity to others, an acknowledged interdependence with others, a willingness to maintain this interdependence by giving to or doing for others what one expects from them, and the feeling that one is part of a larger dependable and stable structure" (p. 157). Glynn (1981) argued that PSC was a "desirable feeling, difficult to describe in an operational manner, but associated with the presence or development of a common bond with other people" (p. 790). Sarason and Glynn both felt that the conditions that supported PSC were declining in society and that ways should be explored for increasing or at least maintaining it. Glynn conducted an extensive research project in the United States and Israel to operationalize and measure PSC, which resulted in a measure that contained 60 items related to perceptions of the respondents' own community, while another 60 items related to an ideal sense of community (note: see Glynn [1981] for a copy of the community questionnaire and the items on the PSC scale).

After Glynn's 1981 study, further theoretical and empirical research was conducted to develop and measure sense of community. Chavis and colleagues (Chavis, Hogge, & McMillan, 1986) created a Sense of Community Profile, which consisted of a broad 46-item scale developed as part of the New York City Block Booster Action Research Project. McMillan and Chavis' (1986) theory and definition of sense of community theory has been used to develop subsequent measures of sense of community. They define sense of community as "a feeling that members have of belonging, a feeling that members matter to one another and to the group, and a shared faith that members' needs will be met through their commitment to be together" (McMillan & Chavis, p. 9). Their SOC theoretical model had four dimensions: (a) *membership*—a sense of belonging or identification with a larger collective, interpersonal relatedness; (b) *influence*—reciprocal relationships between the individual and the community in terms of the ability to make a difference or affect change in each other and in the community; (c) *fulfillment of needs*—individuals' needs can be met through cooperative behavior within the community, reinforcing appropriate community behaviors;

and (d) *shared emotional connection*—emotional support members share from struggles and successes living in the community, including history, place, and experiences (McMillan & Chavis, 1986). Several researchers have used the theory and conceptualization of sense of community developed by McMillan and Chavis (1986) to refine its measurement. This research is explained in what follows.

A theoretically based sense of community scale was developed from the responses of 1,200 adults to a Neighborhood Participation Project Questionnaire (Chavis et al., 1986). Chavis and colleagues (1986) 23-item Sense of Community Index (SCI) index was an individual construct that was conceptualized to include four subscales based on the original four dimensions of SOC developed by McMillan and Chavis (1986). This 23-item sense of community scale was then developed into a short 12-item version called the Sense of Community Index (SCI), which included a True/False response scale. The 12-item version of the SCI, which was initially used in the New York City Block Booster action research project, is described in **Table 6.1** (Perkins et al., 1990). The construct validity of the SCI measure in this study was demonstrated by the following results:

- The SCI predicted several outcome variables: Higher SCI scores were significantly associated with length or residence, higher ratings of block satisfaction, neighboring, informal social control, communitarianism, and lower ratings of fear of crime (Peterson et al., 1990, p. 110).

The 12-item SCI has been widely debated and critiqued (Peterson, Speer, & Hughey, 2006). Peterson and colleagues review and discuss some of the main criticisms of the SCI, including the lack of specificity, inconsistent level of analysis, measurement referent, conceptualization of community as a collective as well an individual experience, and issues with the psychometric properties, including factor structure and reliability. Attempts to address the criticisms of the SCI and refine its measurement properties are described next.

Chipuer and Pretty (1999) conducted a review of the SCI examining its use, factor structure, and reliability among adults and youth in neighborhoods and adults in the workplace. Their results demonstrated reliabilities ranging from .64 to .69 for the total SCI scale, but reliabilities were mostly below acceptable levels for the subscales (.16 to .72). Moreover, results from their exploratory factor analysis did not support the four dimensions of the SCI, with items loading on multiple scales, items loading on different subscales among the different samples, and item loadings deviating from the dimensions proposed by McMillan and Chavis (Peterson et al., 2006). Chipuer and Pretty suggested that the SCI be used as a unidimensional measure "until the items making up the SCI are reformulated to reflect the four underlying dimensions as conceptualized" (p. 654).

Long and Perkins (2003) conducted further research on the SCI, which resulted in the creation of a brief Sense of Community (SOC) Index. Long and Perkins reviewed prior attempts to measure sense of community, including Buckner's (1988) neighborhood cohesion index. The authors argue that Buckner's (1988) research did not support his proposed three-dimensional model of sense of community cohesion but resulted in a nonfactorial 18-item scale containing nine items originally designed to tap SOC, including five for neighboring and three for attraction to a neighborhood (Long & Perkins, 2003, p. 281). Long and Perkins (2003) further argue that Chavis et al.'s (1986) scale poses similar issues, in that "neighboring is a behavior rather than a cognitive-perceptual construction; attraction to neighborhood is more similar to place attachment and/or community satisfaction than SOC; and some of the SOC items even appear to tap constructs other than SOC" (p. 281).

Therefore, Long and Perkins (2003) attempted to empirically verify the four dimensions of the SCI proposed by Chavis and colleagues (Chavis, Hogge, McMillan, & Wandersman, 1986) by conducting a confirmatory factor analyses (CFA), which was used to test how well the variables in the measure represented the constructs proposed by the theory. Long and Perkins (2003) argued that "when theoretical or empirical evidence exists for a multidimensional construct, CFA is the appropriate analysis for (dis)confirming the fit of the theoretical construct to the empirical data" (p. 282). Their results yielded a poor model fit for the original theoretical formulation of the four dimensions as well as for a single-factor index. Therefore, they created a brief eight-item SOC index, which showed a good model fit for CFA. Moreover, they found that the new measure differentiated street level block reliability based on intragroup agreement, while maintaining the profile of a cognitive-perceptual construct. They also recommend using a 5-point Likert response agreement scale in order to increase reliability versus the "yes/no" or "true/false" response formats previously used in earlier studies. Long and Perkins (2003) **brief SOC** is summarized in **Table 6.2**. The following summarizes the results from this study:

- Results suggest the new Brief Sense of Community Index is a valid measure of the cognitive-perceptual construct popular in the field.
- There was no relationship between the items and other constructs separate but related to sense of community, including behavioral (e.g., participation, neighboring) or other cognitive-affective-perceptual constructs (e.g., community satisfaction, place attachment, collective efficacy).
- The BSCI's three-factor structure was found to have generally good fit according to rigorous confirmatory factor analysis standards, despite having marginal internal reliability (apparently due to weak response set sensitivity) (Long & Perkins, 2003, p.292).

Further research was later conducted by Peterson and colleagues (Peterson, Speer, & Hughey, 2006) examining the factor structure of the SCI using confirmatory factor analysis with two data sets. The researchers argued that a possible explanation for the psychometric problems of the SCI was the systematic error that occurred from the use of negatively worded items. The researchers demonstrated that the SCI was "best described by four factors in combination with two method factors (i.e., one factor including only positively worded items and another including only negatively worded items) . . . and that the SCI should be revised to exclude negatively worded items and new positively worded items should be developed and tested" (Peterson et al., 2006, p. 453).

Additional methods for measuring sense of community have emerged more recently in the literature. In 2008, a newly created brief SOC Index was developed by Peterson, Speer, and McMillan (2008), and a newly developed longer version of the SOC was created by Chavis and colleagues (2008). The newly created brief SOC Index or BSCS was developed because Peterson and colleagues (2008) argued that "little theoretical justification was provided by Long and Perkins (2003) for their new dimensional structure" for the brief SOC (p. 63). Peterson and colleagues' (2008) new measure was based on the original four theoretical SOC dimensions created by McMillan and Chavis (1986). Both the first and second-order factor structure of the SOC measure was evaluated using confirmatory factor analysis (CFA). The validity of the BSCS was assessed by examining its relationship to a set of variables that might be differentially associated with the dimensions of SOC (i.e., community participation, empowerment, mental health, and depression). Information on the **2008 brief SOC**

(BSCS) measure is discussed in **Table 6.3**. Below is a summary of the results from this study:

- Confirmatory factor analysis: Supported both the scale's hypothesized first-order and second-order factor structure.
- Results showed that the BSCS was correlated with community participation, psychological empowerment, mental health, and depression.
- Findings "provide empirical support for the BSCS and its underlying multidimensional theory of SOC" (Peterson et al., 2008, p. 61).

Chavis, who was involved in the creation of the original SCI 12-item scale (McMillan & Chavis, 1986), went back to the drawing board in 2008 to create a newly revised sense of community measure incorporating several of the recommendations from the prior research discussed above. The SOC Index 2 (SCI-2) was presented by Chavis, Lee, and Acosta (2008) at the International Community Psychology Conference. The authors piloted their revised measure with 36 culturally distinct respondents in seven U.S. settings and then further tested the scale with a large sample of 1,800 respondents, resulting in a reliable measure overall (coefficient alpha = .94) and reliable subscales ranging from .79 to .86. Because this scale attempts to address prior issues, we include the measure of the **SCI-2** in **Table 6.4**. The two most recent scales measuring sense of community (Chavis et al., 2008; Peterson et al., 2006) use only positively worded items and a Likert scale to address issues uncovered in prior research. However, the major weakness of the new scale by Chavis and colleagues (2008) is the lack of analyses examining the scale's factor structure and research demonstrating its validity.

Finally, Prezza and colleagues (Prezza, Pacilli, Barbaranelli, & Zampatti, 2009) developed a multidimensional territorial measure for sense of community (MTSOCS) to examine different geographical communities in Italy (small towns, cities, and metropolis neighborhoods). It is included here because it focuses specifically on geographical communities and attempts to address several prior measurement issues. In order to address prior concerns, Prezza and colleagues use Chipuer and Pretty's (1990) advice to operationalize McMillan and Chavis' (1986) theory of SOC as well as Long and Perkins' (2003) advice to conduct a confirmatory factor analysis. Their research resulted in a 19-item scale with five subscales that were similar across different-sized territorial communities and demonstrated good construct validity. Please see **Table 6.5** for more information on Prezza and colleagues **MTSOCS**. The following summarizes the results from this study:

- A confirmatory factor analysis resulted in the elimination of seven items.
- Tests of factorial invariance showed that the five-factor model was basically the same across different-sized territorial communities.
- A significant relationship was found between the total scale and participation in groups/organizations, cohabitation, community identity, life satisfaction, perceived social support, interpersonal trust, and trust in local government.
- There was a higher sense of community among those cohabiting and those who participated in community groups and a lower sense of community for those who lived in small towns (Prezza et al., 2009, pp. 321–322).

Construct Validity of the SOC

While the construct validity the SOC measures is discussed where available above, we provide an overall assessment here as well. Construct validity involves relating a measurement instrument to an overall theoretical framework to determine whether the measure is correlated with all the concepts and propositions that comprise the theory (Monette, Sullivan, & DeJong, 2005). Measures are typically assessed in terms of how they relate to some criteria derived from theory. Peterson and colleagues (2006) argued that the construct validity and utility of the McMillan and Chavis (1986) SOC model is supported by prior research. Peterson and colleagues (2006) cite other studies demonstrating that SOC is positively associated with a number of outcomes including "length of residency, neighboring, satisfaction, informal social control, political participation, community involvement, perceptions of social climate and well-being" (Perkins et al., 1990; Hughey, et al., 1999; McCarthy et al., 1990; and Pretty, 1990 as cited in Peterson, et al., 2006, p. 454). The newer versions of sense of community also demonstrate construct validity. Peterson, Speer, and McMillan (2008) found that the "overall brief BSCS scale and its subscales were found to be correlated as expected with community participation, psychological empowerment, mental health, and depression" (p. 61). Prezza and colleagues (2009) found a significant relationship between the total MTSOCS scale and participation in groups/organizations, cohabitation, community identity, life satisfaction, perceived social support, interpersonal trust, and trust in local government.

SOC as an Individual- and Community-Level Construct

Buckner (1988), Perkins et al. (1990), and Long and Perkins (2003) examined SOC at both the individual and collective levels (Long & Perkins, 2003). The SOC measures can be used to assess individual residents' sense of community as well as collective or neighborhood level sense of community. Long and Perkins (2003) argued that their examination of the social climate properties of SOC showed "significant agreement among individuals within a community about the level of social cohesion, that communities vary in their degree of cohesion, and that those variables significantly relate to other variables of interest (e.g., civic participation) at the community level" (Long & Perkins, 2003, p. 281). While the majority of the measures for sense of community are used at the individual level of analysis (one's own sense of connection to their community), scholars have also measured SOC at the community level (the neighborhood's overall sense of community).

MEASURES OF NEIGHBORHOOD SOCIAL PROCESSES

The measures of neighborhood social processes that are discussed in this section of the chapter reflect community- or neighborhood-level perspectives. The majority of neighborhood social process measures have emerged from the work of researchers involved in the Project on Human Development in Chicago Neighborhoods, which was a large-scale, interdisciplinary study of the impact of families, schools, and neighborhoods on child and adolescent development (PHDCN, n.d.). The project had two major components, including a study of the social, economic, organizational, political, and cultural structures and changes in Chicago's neighborhoods over time, and a series of longitudinal studies following 6,000 randomly selected children, adolescents, and young adults to examine circumstances and personal characteristics that could impact antisocial behaviors (PCDCN, n.d.). The measures in this major research study that assess neighborhood social processes include collective efficacy—including informal social control and social cohesion—social norms, and social connections as well as social capital (which is explained in the next section of this chapter).

Neighborhoods matter because their characteristics have a strong influence on individual outcomes, particularly among youth, including reducing youth violence and increasing academic achievement (Henry, Gorman-Smith, Schoeny, & Tolan, 2014). Measures of neighborhood characteristics (e.g., poverty, inequality, etc.) are important because they can inform and help to assess the outcomes of interventions that address neighborhood problems, such as crime and youth violence. This section discusses research and measures that have been used to examine how social relationships within neighborhoods explain differences in the rate or level of community problems (Henry et al., 2014). These measures are explained next.

Collective Efficacy

Collective efficacy describes residents' perceptions regarding their ability to work with their neighbors to intervene in neighborhood issues to maintain social control and solve problems (Wandersman & Florin, 2000). Neighborhood collective efficacy is the combination of mutual trust/social connections and informal social control (Sampson et al., 1997). Mutual trust and social connections or ties among neighbors include the relationships that neighbors have with each other, including friendship networks, civic participation, or faith-based ties. When neighbors know each other and share social ties and norms, they are more likely to intervene in problems and thereby support prosocial behaviors and informal social control (Sampson et al., 1997). Informal social control refers to neighbors' willingness to intervene to address neighborhood problems. Informal social control can include indirect intervention or surveillance of the area—such as keeping an eye on a neighbor's property and actions during the course of day-to-day activities—or direct intervention, such as residents interceding to confront antisocial behaviors (Greenberg, Rohe, & Williams, 1982). It can also include direct intervention, which involves residents "questioning both strangers and residents of the neighborhood about suspicious activities. It may also include chastening people for certain behavior and admonishing children" (Greenberg et al., 1982, p.10). Research conducted as part of the Project on Human Development in Chicago Neighborhoods demonstrated the important connection between relationships among neighbors and their willingness to intervene. Findings from the project revealed that where collective efficacy was strong, crime and violence were low regardless of sociodemographic characteristics and the level of disorder in the neighborhood (Sampson et al., 1997).

Sampson and colleagues developed a widely used 10-item measure for **neighborhood collective efficacy** that consists of two subscales that reflect the theoretical and conceptual definition described above. The first subscale consists of five items measuring informal social control, examining residents' perceptions of the likelihood that their neighbors can be counted on to intervene in neighborhood problems. The second subscale measures social cohesion and trust by asking residents questions about their social ties to and within their community. Sampson, Raudenbush, and Earls (1997) used a spatial definition of neighborhood, defined as a collection of people and institutions occupying a subsection of a larger community. They combined 847 census tracts in the city of Chicago to create 343 ecologically meaningful "neighborhood clusters" (NCs) of about 8,000 people, using geographically contiguous census tracts that were internally homogeneous on key census indicators. The researchers examined the reliability of their collective efficacy measure using a hierarchical statistical model representing item variation within persons, person variation within neighborhoods, and variation between neighborhoods (Sampson et al., 1997, p. 920). Their results demonstrated that their measure of collective efficacy was reliable at a neighborhood level. Moreover, the results demonstrated that neighborhood collective efficacy was associated with theoretically proposed neighborhood-level outcomes, including reduced neighborhood-level crime and violence (Sampson et al., 1997). More information on this measure is described in **Table 6.6**. In summary, the study results showed:

- Together, three dimensions of neighborhood stratification, concentrated disadvantage, immigration concentration, and residential stability, explained 70% of the neighborhood variation in collective efficacy.
- Collective efficacy mediated a substantial portion of the association of residential stability and disadvantage with multiple measures of violence, which is consistent with a major theme in neighborhood theories of social organization.
- After adjustment for measurement error, individual differences in neighborhood composition, prior violence, and other potentially confounding social processes, the combined measure of informal social control and cohesion and trust remained a robust predictor of lower rates of violence (Sampson et al., 1997, p. 923).

Neighborhood Matters Measure

Henry and colleagues (2014) used a developmental-ecological perspective on risk, protection, and prevention to inform their approach to measuring neighborhood social processes that impact youth development (p. 188). Their approach is informed by Bronfenbrenner's (1979) ecological development model, which takes into consideration one's social setting in determining one's development. Henry and colleagues also consider the impact of the microsystem of the family on development and the impact of neighborhood social connections on parenting and control exercised by the family. The authors developed a measure they called "neighborhood matters," which consists of three broad measurement areas that can influence child development, including (a) neighborhood social norms (b) informal social control (which is also part of collective efficacy); and (c) social support and connection (p. 189). Henry and colleagues (2014) define social norms as "shared beliefs about expected or acceptable behavior and attitudes" (p. 189). The social norms measure includes (a) "items tapping beliefs about various aspects of neighborhood life that impact child and adolescent development"; and (b) "perceived neighborhood support for such beliefs" (Henry et al., p. 190). The authors use Sampson and colleagues' (1997) definition of informal social control, particularly focusing on "neighborhood residents taking responsibility for and authority to help regulate each other's behavior collectively and informally" (Henry et al., 2014, p. 190). Norms and informal social control "refer to ways neighborhoods might regulate resident behavior, while social connection and support express the extent of neighborliness experienced in a neighborhood" (Henry et al., p. 191).

Henry and colleagues' (2014) study was conducted in poor urban communities in Chicago. Their purpose was to develop and validate an inventory of measures for neighborhood social organization as well as measures that assess likely correlates of social processes, such as neighborhood change, problems, and resources. Key areas addressed in their research include "how many dimensions are needed to characterize neighborhood measures, the internal consistency at the individual level, and the shared variance at the neighborhood level of analysis" (Raudenbush & Sampson, 1999, as cited in Henry et al., 2014, p. 191). They also assess the "criterion-related validity of their measures by predicting neighborhood crime contemporaneous with collection of the neighborhood social processes scales" (Henry et al., 2014, p. 191). Henry and colleagues' (2014) research resulted in valid and reliable measures of neighborhood social processes. Their results support the internal consistency of most of their measures at the individual level and reliability as indicators of neighborhood-level phenomena as well (Henry et al., 2014). The **neighborhood matters** measures are described in **Table 6.7**. In summary, the study results showed:

- Controlling for population and poverty, neighborhood social norms about adolescent behavior correlated significantly with police reports about property crime and marginally with police reports about neighborhood violent crime.
- All of the subscales and the general informal social control scales were significantly associated with crime levels, except the subscales for the citizen responsibility and neighborhood organization, indicating the higher informal social control, the lower neighborhood violent crime.
- Neighborhood social cohesion was significantly associated with violent and drug-related crime, indicating that higher social cohesion was associated with lower levels of crime. However, cohesion was marginally positively related to violent crime, indicating that higher crime neighborhoods tended to have more resources (Henry et al., 2014, pp. 196–198).

SOCIAL CAPITAL MEASURES

Social capital, whose meaning has evolved over time, is one of the more difficult neighborhood- or community-level concepts to measure. Coleman (1988) originally conceptualized social capital by its function or form in terms of obligations and expectations, information channels, and social norms. Social capital depends on the trustworthiness of the social environment, which means that "obligations will be repaid [and the] actual extent of obligations held" (Coleman, 1988, p. S102). Another important form of social capital is the information that is part of one's social relationships and the basis for action, including social norms as well as effective sanctions for not upholding social norms. For example, an important form of social capital are norms that "one should forgo self-interest and act in the interests of the collectivity" (Coleman, 1988, p. S104). Moreover, social relations and social structures facilitate some forms of social capital: "actors establish relations purposefully and continue them when they continue to provide benefits" (Coleman, 1988, p. S105).

Putnam (1993) later argued that social capital was defined in terms of social organization, including trust, norms, and networks that can improve the efficiency of society by facilitating coordinated actions. Putnam (2000) also differentiates between bonding social capital, which is based on relationships of mutual trust found between neighbors, and bridging social capital, which is based on connections between residents and individuals and organizations external to the neighborhood. Social capital is also considered a condition for collective efficacy, but residents must take action for collective efficacy to be realized (Sampson et al., 1997). Several measures of social capital have evolved out of Putnam's work but also in connection with the Project on Human Development in Chicago Neighborhoods described above. In addition, a more recent measure of social capital based on both international and national research is discussed below.

Saguaro Seminar on Civic Engagement

The Saguaro Seminar on Civic Engagement (John F. Kennedy School of Government, Harvard University) built on Putnam's work and developed a comprehensive measure of social capital known as the **Social Capital Benchmark Survey** (see **Table 6.8** for a description of the content areas included in the survey). The effort engaged over three-dozen local community foundations in assessing social capital in their communities, with the goal of understanding community strengths and areas for improvement in community civic behavior and creating a baseline against which future progress could be measured (Kennedy School of Government, 2000). The national survey sample included approximately 3,000 national respondents as well as 26,200 respondents from representative samples in 40 communities across 29 states. While there has been considerable reporting about the results of this survey, there has been little empirical research analyzing the validity and reliability of the social capital measures used in the study. In addition to revealing the character of civic engagement in each community, the results suggest two very large challenges and opportunities across all the communities sampled:

- The opportunity and challenge of faith-based civic engagement. From a civic perspective, the special challenge associated with faith-based civic engagement is to encourage greater tolerance for minority viewpoints and greater sensitivity to imperatives of social reform. However, the survey shows that faith-based communities have some matchless strengths as sources of civic engagement.

- The opportunity and challenge of diversity. The opportunities for social capital building in America's increasingly diverse communities are substantial, but the challenges are great, as well. The evidence suggests that community activists in settings of unusual diversity need to redouble their efforts to build trust (and not just across racial lines), to reduce social isolation, to expand political participation, and to bridge class barriers (JFK School of Government, 2000, pp. 2–4).

We included in this chapter a few studies that examined data from the survey to assess the association between social capital and self-rated health. Two of those studies used the national data from the Social Capital Benchmark Survey, while the third used data from a specific geographic community that participated in the Benchmark Survey. The social capital measures that were examined in these studies are explained below.

The first two studies used national data from the Social Capital Benchmark Survey. Subramanian, Kim, and Kawachi's (2002) measure of **social capital** (see **Table 6.9**) included individual trust, defined as general interpersonal trust and degrees of trustworthiness of neighbors, and coworkers; and community-level social trust, which was aggregated from individual responses to questions on the interpersonal trust scale. Community-level measures were developed using these variables and then a contextual social trust variable was aggregated from individual responses to questions on interpersonal trust. Below is a summary of this study's results:

- Higher levels of community social trust were associated with a lower probability of reporting poor health.

- Individual demographic and socioeconomic predictors did not explain the association of community social trust with self-rated health.

- Controlling for individual trust perception, however, rendered the main effect of community social trust statistically insignificant.

- A complex interaction effect was observed, such that the health-promoting effect of community social trust was significantly greater for high-trust individuals. For low-trust individuals, the effect of community social trust on self-rated health was the opposite (Subramanian et al., 2002, pp. S31–S32).

Kim, Subramanian, and Kawachi's (2006) measure of **social capital** (see **Table 6.10**) examined bonding versus bridging social capital, including formal group/associational involvement, diversity of friendships, and level of trust in one's race/ethnicity. Community-level measures of bonding and bridging social capital were created by aggregating individual responses to these subscales. It is important to note that the results from both studies demonstrated that community-level social capital was associated with a lower probability of reporting poor health. The second study showed that:

- Adjusting for individual-level factors (except for social capital) and community level covariables, community bonding social capital and community bridging social capital were associated with 14% and 5% lower odds of self-reported fair/poor health, respectively.
- The two forms of community social capital did not interact with one another or with community level SES, and the main effects did not differ significantly by individual sex or income.
- The validity of the study's results was strengthened by controlling for a number of compositional characteristics, community-level SES and age.
- The survey sampling from multiple, diverse U.S. communities favors the generalizability of the findings to other U.S. communities (Kim et al., 2006, pp. 119–120).

Schultz, O'Brien, and Tadesse (2008) (see **Table 6.11**) used data from the SCBS in Duluth, Minnesota, and Superior, Wisconsin, and examined **bonding social capital** (informal socializing/interactions), **bridging social capital** (formal group/associational involvement and organizational group interaction), as well as the related social capital constructs of social trust, social support, and volunteer activity. The researchers address the endogenous nature of social capital by estimating it as a function of both individual and household characteristics and then estimating self-reported health as a function of the individual and social capital as well as individual and household characteristics (Schultz et al., 2008, p. 610). The researchers also included explanatory measures that acted as proxies for the ability of individuals to produce social capital, including length of residency and religiosity. The results of this study demonstrated that:

- Individuals with higher social trust, greater associational involvement and participation in organized interactions, and more informal socializing or volunteering reported stronger health than those with lower levels of these social capital indices.
- The production and demand for social capital, through social engagement, are related to individual characteristics, including income and education
- While religiosity had a positive impact on social capital, it did not predict self-reported health status.
- The research suggests that individuals with higher levels of social trust, associational involvement, more participation in organized interactions and informal socializing, and those who volunteer perceive themselves to be healthier compared to those with lower levels of these individual social capital measures.
- Summing all social capital measures results in approximately a 10% increase in the probability of being healthy when each index increases by 1% (Schultz et al., 2008, pp. 613–616).

The major weakness of above studies examining social capital and self-reported health is that none of them assessed the reliability of the social capital measures they used, nor did they conduct any type of factor analysis to examine the dimensions of their measures. These studies, however, demonstrate empirical validity through the association of social capital with other potentially related constructs, such as self-rated health.

Social Capital Measure From the Project on Human Development in Chicago Neighborhoods

This section discusses two studies that empirically examined measures of social capital from the PHDCN. The first study by Chaskin, Goerge, Skyles, and Guiltinan (2006) used a convenience sample in two Chicago communities and includes the following **social capital** constructs: voluntary association/organizational involvement, collective efficacy, and neighborhood activism (see **Table 6.12**). The researchers argue that these three concepts were selected because they reflect different dimensions of civic engagement, including informal and formal, theory supporting their interaction with community well-being, and their relationship to personal efficacy and Putnam's notion of democratic activism (Chaskin et al., 2006, p. 492). The researchers tested practical options for community-based organizations to measure social capital. They found that the community partners in their study had a basic understanding of and interest in social capital in their communities, including the interactions between residents and community stakeholders and how neighborhood organizations and the environment impacted those interactions, the social fabric, and quality of life. The strength of their study was that they examined the reliability of their social capital constructs and tested empirical validity by examining differences between the results from their sample and the PHDCN sample. Below is a summary of the study results:

- A regression model of social capital examined whether it was possible to measure aspects of social capital in partnership with CBOs.
- Some social capital measures translated better than others to methods more generally accessible to CBOs.
- There was no statistically significant difference between how individuals in the current study's sample responded to items measuring collective efficacy as compared to those in the PHDCN study.
- Measures of neighborhood activism and voluntary association were overestimated in the CBO community survey, possibly due to a systematic sampling bias in favor of more active and engaged residents.
- Some public venues like supermarkets were more promising for strategic convenience sampling because they offered a cross-section of the local population and an efficient mechanism for collecting relatively high numbers of completed surveys (Chaskin et al., 2006, pp. 510–511).

The second study by Sampson and Graif (2009) examined the following **neighborhood social capital** and related constructs: neighborhood collective efficacy, neighborhood activism, conduct norms; moral legal cynicism, intergenerational closure, reciprocal exchange, density of local friend/kinship ties, organizational involvement, tolerance of deviance, and police efficacy (see **Table 6.13**). Sampson and Graif (2009) examine the structural dimensions and predictors of social capital and thus significantly contribute to the literature on measuring social capital at the neighborhood level. Sampson and Graif (2009) examine the reliability of their constructs and their dimensionality, and they assess empirical validity by examining potential predictors of social capital. The results demonstrated a reliable measure of social capital at the residential level that consisted of four major factors that were extracted using a principal components factor analysis: collective efficacy, local networks, organizational involvement, and conduct norms. A measure of leadership-based social capital was also developed using a survey of positional leaders in Chicago (see Sampson & Graif, 2009, for more details on this measure). The authors used the results to develop a conceptual typology of communities that can inform future studies of social capital. Sampson and Graif (2009) "caution future research against the notion that there is one or even a small number of indices of neighborhood-level social capital that can coherently reflect all of its relevant and yet simultaneously distinct facets" (p. 1601). Below is a summary of the study results:

- Principal component factor analyses were conducted with a varimax rotation.
- Based on the main conceptual commonalities of the indices bearing the highest loadings on each, the community survey yielded four major factors:
    - Collective efficacy (Eigenvalue = 7.821): social cohesion, social control, moral/legal cynicism, neighborhood dissatisfaction, and police efficacy
    - Local networks (Eigenvalue = 2.210): friends and kin density, reciprocal exchange, intergenerational closure, anonymity, unlikely to move out
    - Organizational involvement (Eigenvalue = 1.554): organizational participation, neighborhood activism, involvement in neighborhood organization
    - Conduct norms (Eigenvalue = .923): conduct norms for both 13-year-olds and 19-year-olds
- The above dimensions "cluster differently across Chicago communities and are differently influenced by structural disadvantage, residential instability, and diversity of population."
- Communities with high scores on collective efficacy had low scores on residents' networks in the neighborhood, conduct norms, and leadership involvement in traditional religious or school organizations.
- For local networks and conduct norms, disadvantage was not a significant predictor net of other structural indices (Sampson & Graif, pp. 1600–1601).

More Recent Social Capital Measures

Two other unrelated studies on social capital also may be worth exploring, including Whitman (2012), who developed and examined the following social capital constructs to asses community success: civic network density—interorganizational connectedness via residents' overlapping organizational affiliations (note: this is similar to associational/organizational involvement in other studies)—and gathering place density—extent to which residents socialize/co-frequent local gathering places (this is similar to informal social interactions in other studies).

Alaimo, Reischl, and Allen (2010) examined the relationship between community gardening and social capital. Their social capital measures included (a) bonding social capital—trust/reciprocity, know neighbors, get along, intergenerational relationships, (b) social support, linking social capital—connections, get to know police, neighborhood organizations, and (c) norms/values—feel responsible, involvement, informal social control, collective efficacy, neighborhood influence, and satisfaction. Moreover, there are numerous international measures of social capital that can be explored when conducting global research, such as those developed by international agencies (e.g., the World Bank), including the integrated questionnaire for the measurement of social capital, the social capital inventory, and the social capital assessment tool (Grootaert, Narayan, Nyhan-Jones, & Woodcock, 2004; Grootaert & Van Bastelaer, 2001; Narayan & Cassidy, 2001). However, an analysis of these extensive international measures is beyond the primary scope of this book.

The final measure of social capital in this chapter draws on lessons learned about social capital measurement at the international and domestic levels discussed in a recent article by Enfield and Nathaniel (2013) on social capital constructs and survey development. The authors argue that, while measuring social capital can be difficult, researchers from around the globe and in the United States have demonstrated the beneficial presence, utility, and impact of social capital in communities. Enfield and Nathaniel (2013) provide a thorough review of the national and international literature on social capital measurement and introduce a measure that was developed by researchers at the University of Minnesota (Chazdon, Allen, Horntvedt, & Scheffert, 2013).

Chazdon, Allen, Horntvedt, and Scheffert's (2013) measure of **social capital** was developed and tested using a participatory and community-engaged approach (**Table 6.14**). The measure includes behavioral and cognitive traits associated with three kinds of social capital, bonding (strong internal ties among individuals with similar backgrounds), bridging (weak ties with external resources and support), and linking (vertical networks) (Chazdon et al., 2013). Similar to bridging social capital, linking social capital includes networks with external players or institutions, but these networks are not among individuals who are alike or share power or status (Chazdon et al., 2013, p. 2). The researchers created a conceptual model of overall social capital that contains six related subconstructs, including bonding engagement, bonding trust, bridging engagement, bridging trust, linking engagement, and linking trust. They also add a seventh dimension called efficacy, which is an individual measure that lacks the shared definition of collective efficacy. Their conceptualization of efficacy aggregates individual-level data from their survey to measure the "ability to make a difference in social contexts" (Chazdon et al., 2013, p. 4).

Chazdon and colleagues (2013) tested their measure of social capital in three rural communities (because of their long standing work there) as well as one community located close to a major metropolitan area. Their conceptual model of social capital (illustrated in Chazdon et al., 2013) was derived by conducting both exploratory and confirmatory factor analyses of the seven dimensions discussed above. The results demonstrated that their measure of social capital was valid and reliable and the "overall model held together as a conceptual framework for measuring social capital," with "efficacy at the center of the model, reflecting its importance as the energy needed to animate community social capital" (Chazdon et al., 2013, p. 10). Their findings are similar to prior research discussed earlier in this chapter demonstrating that efficacy is needed to activate social networks, ties, and cohesion:

- A model generating CFA was used to test the conceptual model of social capital by identifying the model based on theory and statistical analyses in order to derive the best fit and most efficient model.
- The results showed that the seven conceptual domains were valid and reliable as measurement scales. The overall conceptual model held together as framework for measuring social capital (Chazdon et al., 2013, p. 10).

Chazdon and colleagues (2013) note that their measure needs further testing among low-income people, youth, less-educated residents, and residents of inner-city and urban areas. Enfield and Nathaniel (2013) are piloting a revised version of the Chazdon et al. survey among youth in the 4-H program, with the goal of making the survey youth friendly and meaningful to youth from various geographical and cultural backgrounds.

CONCLUSION

The social fabric of communities, including the social connections and networks residents share, has been recognized as a powerful and important characteristic of communities for generations (Ahlbrandt, 1984; Glynn, 1981; McMillan & Chavis, 1986). As early as 1979, social fabric was described as "the fragile, sacred, essential, and complex ingredient that holds neighborhoods together" (Baroni, 1979, p. vii). Measurement in this area has advanced over the last 50 years, resulting in measures with increased validity and reliability. While there is still work to be done, the measures in this chapter provide researchers and practitioners with tangible methods to quantify and examine the complex social processes that make up a neighborhood's social fabric and that impact a range of individual and community-level outcomes.

LIST OF MEASURES AND TABLE NUMBERS

TABLE 6.1 ■ Sense of Community Index

Primary Reference	Perkins, D. D., Florin, P., Rich, R. C., Wandersman, A., & Chavis, D. M. (1990). Participation and the social and physical environment of residential blocks: Crime and community context. *American Journal of Community Psychology, 18*(1), 83–115.
Purpose	• Measures sense of community, defined as a feeling that members have of belonging and being important to each other and a shared faith that members' needs will be met by their commitment to be together. (McMillian & Chavis, 1986) • The short SCI was part of a larger survey designed to understand the relationship between participation in block associations and a wide range of block-level variables (demographics, the built environment, crime, and the transient social and physical environment).
Description	The Sense of Community Index (SCI) is a 12-item self-report scale with four subscales based on the original four dimensions developed by McMillan and Chavis (1986). Responses are True or False. Please see the article for all of the items. **Reinforcement of needs (3 items)** • I think my [block] is a good place for me to live. • People on this [block] do not share the same values. **Membership (3 items)** • I can recognize most of the people who live on my [block]. • Very few of my [neighbors] know me. **Influence (3 items)** • I care about what my [neighbors] think of my actions. • If there is a problem on this [block] people who live here can get it solved. **Shared emotional connection (3 items)** • It is very important to me to live on this particular [block]. • People on this [block] generally don't get along with each other.
Sample	• Forty-eight blocks in three New York City neighborhoods were selected to participate in the study. • A telephone survey was conducted over five weeks in the spring of 1985 with randomly selected block residents from 48 New York City blocks using the criss-cross directory. Selected sample characteristics • 58% response rate • Mean age: 42 years old • Median estimated annual family income: $19,000 • Median length of residence: 9 1/2 years (Perkins et al., 1990, pp. 95–96)
Scoring	To get a total score for the SCI, Q2, Q6, Q8, & Q11 need to be reversed before scoring. Then you add scores to get the total score for all 12 questions.
Assessment	The total scale was shown to have an internal reliability coefficient of .80 (Perkins et al., 1990, p. 110). However, there is no report of internal reliabilities of subscales in this study.
Related Reference	The SCI was also used in several other place-based studies; however, only a few use the 12-item T/F SCI discussed here. One example is Kingston, S., Mitchell, R., Florin, P., & Stevenson, J. (1999). Sense of community in neighborhoods: A multilevel construct. *Journal of Community Psychology, 27*(6), 681–694.

(Continued)

TABLE 6.1 ■ (Continued)	
Language	English
Contact	Douglas D. Perkins Department of Human and Organizational Development, Box 90 Peabody College, Vanderbilt University Nashville, TN 37203 Email: douglas.d.perkins@vanderbilt.edu
Other Comments	Further development and assessment of this instrument is discussed in this chapter.

TABLE 6.2 ■ Brief Sense of Community Index (2003)	
Primary Reference	Long, D. A., & Perkins, D. D. (2003). Confirmatory factor analysis of the sense of community index and development of a brief SCI. *Journal of Community Psychology, 31*(3), 279–296.
Purpose	• Confirmatory factor analysis of the 12-item SCI Index developed by McMillan and Chavis (1986) and used in Perkins et al. (1990). • Study used findings to create the brief SCI.
Description	This scale consists of eight items divided into three subscales. The items from the SCI that were retained in the brief SCI (McMillan & Chavis, 1986) are indicated in parentheses. This scale also uses a True or False response format, except for the open-ended questions listed below. Please see the article for all of the items. **Social connections (membership subscale in the SCI): (3 items) All three items from the original SCI were retained in this subscale, including** • I can recognize most of the people who live on my block. • I have almost no influence over what this block is like. **Mutual concerns (reinforcement of needs and influence subscales in the SCI): (2 of the 3 items were retained and a 3rd added):** • My neighbors and I want the same things from the block (from original SCI). • If there is a problem on this block, people who live here can get it solved (from original SCI). • In general, would you say that people on your block help out when they can, or do they pretty much go their own way? **Community values (new items):** • Would you say that it is very important, somewhat important, or not important to you to feel a sense of community with the people on your block? • Would you say that you feel a strong sense of community with others on your block, very little sense of community, or something in between?
Sample	• The original SCI and other resident survey data from the 1985–1986 Block Booster Project are used to develop this measure (Perkins et al., 1990). • Clustered, resident survey data from 47 street blocks in five neighborhoods in Brooklyn and Queens, New York, were collected at two points in time and through a household panel: ○ T1 $N = 1{,}081$ ○ T2 $N = 638$ • This study uses both waves of data, not just the first wave; however, respondent panel verification was limited. • Thus, the analyses are of two semi-independent, cross-sectional data sets.
Scoring	Similar to the SCI, the negatively phrased items (Questions 2 and 3) need to be reversed scored. Then the scores from all of the items are added together to create a total Brief SCI score.

(Continued)

TABLE 6.2 ■ (Continued)	
Assessment	• Brief Sense of Community overall reliability $\alpha = .65$ (Time 1; $N = 713$), $\alpha = .73$ (Time 2; $N = 422$). Subscale Reliabilities • Mutual concerns: $\alpha = .50$ (Time 1; $N = 820$), $\alpha =. 64$ (Time 2; $N = 485$) • Social connections: $\alpha = .55$ (Time 1; $N = 917$), $\alpha = .50$ (Time 2; $N = 544$) • Community values: $\alpha = .51$ (Time 1; $N = 1040$), $\alpha = .61$ (Time 2; $N = 621$)
Language	English
Contact	Douglas D. Perkins Department of Human and Organizational Development Box 90 Peabody College, Vanderbilt University Nashville, TN 37203 Email: douglas.d.perkins@vanderbilt.edu

TABLE 6.3 ■ Brief Sense of Community Scale (BSCS)

Primary Reference	Peterson, N. A., Speer, P. W., & McMillan, D. W. (2008). Validation of a brief sense of community scale: Confirmation of the principal theory of sense of community. *Journal of Community Psychology, 36*(1), 61–73.
Purpose	This study examined a brief measure for SOC that included completely new items designed to be consistent with the McMillan and Chavis (1986) model of the four SOC dimensions.
Description	The BSCS followed recommendations in the SOC literature (Peterson, Speer, & Hughey, 2006), including using only positively worded items. In addition, all BSCS items were designed to reference the respondents' neighborhood and used a 5-point, Likert-type response option format ranging from strongly agree to strongly disagree. Sample items are provided below. Please see the article for a complete list of the items. **Needs Fulfillment: (2 items)** • I can get what I need in this neighborhood. **Membership: (2 items)** • I feel like a member of this neighborhood. **Influence: (2 items)** • People in this neighborhood are good at influencing each another. **Emotional Connection: (2 items)** • I have a good bond with others in this neighborhood.
Sample	• Part of a larger study evaluating a community health promotion initiative in the mid-western United States. Sample: • 308 randomly selected residents participated in the study. • 293 who completed all BSCS items and were included in the present study. • The majority were non-Hispanic White females.
Scoring	A total score is created by adding the responses to all of the items.
Assessment	Cronbach's alpha for the overall BSCS was .92 Subscale reliabilities • α = .86 for needs fulfillment • α = .94 for group membership • α = .77 for influence • α = .87 for emotional connection
Language	English
Contact	N. Andrew Peterson School of Social Work Rutgers University 536 George Street, 303A New Brunswick, NJ 08901. Email: andrew.peterson@ssw.rutgers.edu

TABLE 6.4 ■ Sense of Community Index-2

Primary Reference	Chavis, D. M., Lee, K. S., & Acosta, J. (2008). *The sense of community (SCI) revised: The reliability and validity of the SCI-2.* Paper presented at the 2nd International Community Psychology Conference, Lisboa, Portugal.
Purpose	Designed to expand and improve the original Sense of Community Index (SCI) based on McMillian and Chavis (1986) theory of sense of community.
Description	The Sense of Community Index-2 is a 24-item scale divided into four subscales. Respondents rate each item, which measures how they feel on a 4-point Likert-like scale (*not at all* = 0, *somewhat* = 1, *mostly* = 2, and *completely* = 3). The full report on this article is publicly available at the website listed below. **Reinforcement of needs** • I get important needs of mine met because I am part of this community. • Community members and I value the same things. • This community has been successful in getting the needs of its members met. • Being a member of this community makes me feel good. • When I have a problem, I can talk about it with members of this community. • People in this community have similar needs, priorities, and goals. **Membership** • I can trust people in this community. • I can recognize most of the members of this community. • Most community members know me. • This community has symbols and expressions of membership, such as clothes, signs, art, architecture, logos, landmarks, and flags that people can recognize. • I put a lot of time and effort into being part of this community. • Being a member of this community is a part of my identity. **Influence** • Fitting into this community is important to me. • This community can influence other communities. • I care about what other community members think of me. • I have influence over what this community is like. • If there is a problem in this community, members can get it solved. • This community has good leaders. **Shared emotional connection** • It is very important to me to be a part of this community. • I am with other community members a lot and enjoy being with them. • I expect to be a part of this community for a long time. • Members of this community have shared important events together, such as holidays, celebrations, or disasters. • I feel hopeful about the future of this community. • Members of this community care about each other.

Sample	• The original draft was piloted with 36 culturally diverse persons in seven different settings from Maryland to Hawaii. • Strong reliability was found, but there were several suggestions for improvement that were incorporated (i.e., rewording of the statement to increase clarity). • The SCI-2 was revised and tested with a larger survey of 1,800 people.
Scoring	A total score is created by adding the responses to all of the items.
Assessment	The analysis of the SCI-2 showed that it is a very reliable measure (coefficient alpha = .94). The subscales also proved to be reliable with coefficient alpha scores of .79 to .86.
Language	English
Contact	David Chavis, PhD Community Science 438 N. Frederick Ave, Suite 315 Gaithersburg, MD 20877 301-519-0722 (office) or 301-519-0724 (fax) Email: dchavis@communityscience.com
Website	This article is available at http://www.communityscience.com/pdfs/Sense%20of%20Community%20Index-2%28SCI-2%29.pdf

TABLE 6.5	**Multidimensional Territorial Sense of Community Scale (MTSOCS)**
Primary Reference	Prezza, M., Pacilli, M. G., Barbaranelli, C., & Zampatti, E. (2009). The MTSOCS: A multidimensional sense of community scale for local communities. *Journal of Community Psychology, 37*(3), 305–326.
Purpose	Designed to measure the sense of community across different geographical communities (small towns, cities, and metropolis neighborhoods). Sense of community is based on McMillan and Chavis' (1986) definition of sense of community.
Description	This measure consists of 19 items divided into five subscales. Respondents rate each item on a 4-point scale, with 4 meaning *strongly agree* and 1 meaning *strongly disagree*. Sample items are provided for each subscale. For a list of all of the items, see Prezza and colleagues (2009). **Membership (4 items)** • I feel like I belong here. • This town is a part of me. **Shared influence (3 items)** • If the people here get organized, they can achieve their goals. • If there is a serious problem in this town, the people who live here can get it solved. **Help in case of need (4 items)** • Many people in this town are available to give help if somebody needs it. • If I had a problem, few people in this town would try to help me. **Social climate and bonds (4 items)** • I have good friends in this town. • I feel at ease with the people in my town. **Needs fulfillment (4 items)** • This town provides opportunities for me to do a lot of different things. • In this town I have few opportunities to satisfy my needs.
Scoring	The scores are added for all items to create a total score.

Sample	• 781 participants were divided into three groups:
	  ○ 316 participants from four small Italian towns
	  ○ 227 participants from two Italian cities
	  ○ 238 participants from neighborhoods in Rome

Assessment	• Overall reliability of the 19 item MTSCOS scale: $\alpha = .88$ Reliability for the subscales • Membership: $\alpha = .80$ • Shared influence: $\alpha = .61$ • Help in case of need: $\alpha = .69$ • Social climate and bonds: $\alpha = .75$ • Needs fulfillment: $\alpha = .71$
Languages	English and Italian
Contact	Miretta Prezza Department of Psychology "Sapienza" University of Rome Via dei Marsi 78 00185 Rome, Italy Email: miretta.prezza@uniroma1.it

TABLE 6.6 ■ Neighborhood Collective Efficacy

Primary Reference	Sampson, R. J., Raudenbush, S. W., & Earls, F. (1997). Neighborhoods and violent crime: A study of collective efficacy. *Science, 277*, 918–924.
Purpose	Designed to measure neighborhood collective efficacy, which is the combination of informal social control and social cohesion/trust. It is designed to measure a neighborhood- or community-level construct.
Description	Neighborhood collective efficacy is a 10-item self-report scale, consisting of two subscales: informal social control and social cohesion/trust (Sampson et al., 1997). This measure and the complete community survey are available on the PHDCN (Project on Human Development in Chicago Neighborhoods) website (see below). The **social cohesion/trust** subscale contained five conceptually related items that asks residents how strongly they agree (1 = *strongly disagree*, 2 = *disagree*, 3 = *neither agree nor disagree*, 4 = *agree*, and 5 = *strongly agree*) with several statements including the following: • People around here are willing to help their neighbors. • This is a close-knit neighborhood. • People in this neighborhood can be trusted. The 5-item **informal social control** subscale asks residents about the likelihood (1 = *very unlikely*, 2 = *likely*, 3 = *neither likely nor unlikely*, 4 = *likely*, and 5 = *very likely*) that their neighbors can be counted on to intervene in various ways if, including the following: • Children were skipping school and hanging out on a street corner. • A fight broke out in front of their house. • The fire station closest to their home was threatened with budget cuts.
Sample	• The sample consisted of 8,782 Chicago residents representing 343 neighborhood clusters (NC), who were interviewed in their homes as part of the community survey (CS). • The CS was designed to yield a representative sample of households within each NC, with sample sizes large enough to create reliable NC measures (Sampson et al., 1997, p. 919). • The sample neighborhoods were categorized into low, medium, and high socioeconomic status (SES). There were no low-SES White neighborhoods and no high-SES Latino neighborhoods. There were Black neighborhoods in all three categories of SES and many heterogeneous neighborhoods that varied in SES (Sampson et al., 1997, p. 919).
Scoring	• A mean score is calculated after the last two items in the social cohesion scale are reverse coded. • Responses were aggregated to the neighborhood level as initial measures. Social cohesion and informal social control were closely associated across neighborhoods ($r = 0.80$, $p < 0.001$), which suggested that the two measures were tapping aspects of the same latent construct. • The two scales were combined into a summary measure labeled collective efficacy (Sampson et al., 1997, p. 920).
Assessment	The reliability with which neighborhoods could be distinguished on collective efficacy ranged between 0.80 for neighborhoods with a sample size of 20 raters to 0.91 for neighborhoods with a sample size of 50 raters.

(*Continued*)

TABLE 6.6 ■ (Continued)

Related Reference	Sampson, R. J., & Raudenbush, S. W. (1999). Systematic social observation of public spaces: A new look at disorder in urban neighborhoods. *American Journal of Sociology, 105*(3), 603–651.
Language	English
Contact	Robert J. Sampson, PhD Professor and Chair, Department of Sociology Harvard University William James Hall 33 Kirkland St. Cambridge, MA 02138 Email: rsampson@wjh.harvard.edu
Website	For more information on neighborhood collective efficacy, related measures, and this research, see the study website: Project on Human Development in Chicago Neighborhoods: http://www.icpsr.umich.edu/icpsrweb/PHDCN/instruments.jsp.

TABLE 6.7 ■	Neighborhood Matters Measure of Neighborhood Social Processes
Primary Reference	Henry, D. Gorman-Smith, D., Schoeny, M., & Tolan, P. (2014). "Neighborhood matters": Assessment of neighborhood social processes. *American Journal of Community Psychology, 54,* 187–204.
Purpose	Designed to measure neighborhood social processes that impact youth development and outcomes and evaluate their reliability at the individual level, their shared variance at the neighborhood level, and criterion-related validity.
Description	The following measures for three neighborhood social processes were developed and assessed in this study. **Neighborhood social norms** The original scale had 45 items; 12 items were eliminated based on the confirmatory factor analysis. Each item contained the stem: "People in this neighborhood believe that . . . " followed by the specific item content. Responses were on a 5-point Likert scale from 1 = *strongly disagree* to 5 = *strongly agree*. The subscales are described below, along with sample items: • **Child welfare (6 items):** "Adults should know who the neighborhood children and teenagers are." "Adults should do something if they see a child in danger or hurt or being mistreated." • **Child management (10 items):** "Children and teenagers should be expected to respect adults." "If adults see a child doing something wrong, they should tell that child's parent(s)." • **Adolescent behavior (4 items):** "It is always wrong for teenagers to drink alcohol." "It is always wrong for teenagers to smoke cigarettes." • **Crime (5 items):** "People should call the police if they see a crime being committed." "People should do something if a neighbor's house is being vandalized." • **Neighborhood management (4 items):** "People should be considerate of their neighbors." "People should keep their neighborhood looking nice." **Informal social control** The original scale had 62 items; 15 items were eliminated based on the confirmatory factor analysis. For each item, respondents were asked: "What would people in your neighborhood do if . . . " followed by the specific content for each item. Responses were on a 4-point Likert scale, from 1 = *do nothing*, 2 = *complain to or discuss with other neighbors*, 3 = *talk to someone who can do something about it* (e.g., police, etc.), or 4 = *do something directly* (e.g., stepping in and talking directly to the persons involved). The subscales are described below, along with sample items: • **Child welfare (8 items):** "A child falls or hurts him/herself is crying?" "A child is left at home alone during the evening?" • **Child management (11 items):** "Some children are spray-painting graffiti (tagging)?" "A child (or children) is/are bullying or hassling another child?" • **Adolescent behavior (6 items):** "A teenager is recruiting for a gang?" "Someone is trying to sell drugs to a teenager in plain sight?" • **Crime (10 items):** "They hear about planned gang retaliation?" "A neighbor is physically abusing (beating) their partner?" • **Neighborhood management (5 items):** "Someone who lives in the neighborhood rarely or never shovels snow?" "A neighbor is blasting music out of their home or apartment?" • **Neighborhood organization (7 items):** "They want more resources or recreation programs for youth?" "There is violence or shootings?"

(Continued)

TABLE 6.7 ■ (Continued)	
	Social support and connection The original scale had 45 items, 32 of which tapped social cohesion (e.g., none were eliminated) and the remaining assessing existence and use of neighborhood resources that might promote social connection (one was eliminated). • **Neighborhood social cohesion (32 items):** Responses were on a 5-point Likert scale from 1 = *strongly disagree* to 5 = *strongly agree*. Twenty-five items included the stem: "In general, people in this neighborhood . . . ," for example, "look out for one another," "introduce themselves when someone new moves into the neighborhood." Seven items had no stem—for example, "This neighborhood is a good neighborhood for families." • **Neighborhood social resources (5 items):** Responses were "yes" or "no" followed by a 3-point Likert scale indicating whether none, some, or most community residents made use of a resource if the answer was "yes." Sample items include the following: "Does this neighborhood have a neighborhood newsletter?" "Does this neighborhood have organized activities for children?"
Sample	• Neighborhoods were selected through a stratified random sample from pools of eligible census tracks in Chicago, including minority population, size, poverty, and crime level. • To form the sample of neighborhood informants, 20 participants within each of the 30 census tracks were recruited. A stratified sample was used to ensure an even number of male/female, youth/adults. • Data were collected via an in-person interview; 86.2% of households with an eligible resident participated.
Scoring	Mean scores are calculated to determine the scores for each subscale and for the overall scale.
Assessment	**Neighborhood social norms** • Internal consistency reliabilities were all above .70. • At the neighborhood level, three of the five subscales had significant shared variance at the neighborhood level: child management, crime, and neighborhood management. **Informal social control** • Internal consistency reliabilities were above .80 with one exception, neighborhood organization, which was at .74. • Shared variance at the neighborhood level was significant for all subscales except for citizen responsibility and the general informal social control factor. **Social cohesion** • Internal consistency reliability was .92. • At the neighborhood level, the shared variance was significant.
Language	English
Contact	David Henry, PhD Institute for Health Research and Policy University of Illinois at Chicago (MC 275) 512 Westside Research Office Bldg. 1747 West Roosevelt Road Chicago, IL 60608 Email: dhenry@uic.edu
Website	The online version of the article contains supplementary material, including the complete survey with the final items, available to authorized users.

TABLE 6.8 ■ Social Capital Benchmark Survey

Primary Reference	J. F. Kennedy School of Government: Harvard University. (2000). *Social Capital Community Benchmark Survey: Executive summary.* The Saguaro Seminar: Civic Engagement in America Project. Retrieved from http://www.hks.harvard.edu/saguaro/communitysurvey/results.html
Purpose	Designed to measure social capital in communities
Description	The instrument is a 25-minute phone survey with 66 questions that measure social capital in 11 dimensions • **Social trust** measures whether or not people trust each other. • **Inter-racial trust** measures the extent to which different racial groups trust one another and is a proxy for health of inter-racial relations in the community. • **Conventional politics participation** measures how many people in the community are involved politically because political involvement is a key measure of community engagement. • **Protest politics participation** measures participation in political protest forms like marches, demonstrations, boycotts, and so forth. The data in the benchmark survey indicates communities with low conventional political participation exhibit high levels of protest politics participation. • **Civic leadership** measures how frequently respondents were engaged in community and civic groups and whether respondents took a leadership role in these groups. • **Associational involvement** measures associational involvement across 18 categories of groups including senior groups, ethnic groups, musical, service and fraternal, and so forth. • **Informal socializing**: While civil leadership and associational involvement measure "formal" social ties, this measure looks at informal socializing, like socializing with neighbors, coworkers, and "hanging out" in public spaces. • **Diversity of friendships** measures how diverse a person's social network is (and by extension diversity in the community's network). This measure of diversity is important in producing community solidarity and forming larger consensus of how communities should work together. • **Giving and volunteering** measures how often community residents volunteer and how generous their giving is. • **Faith-based engagement** measures attendance, participation, and affiliation with religion and religious activities because religion is a big part of social capital. • **Equality of civic engagement across the community** measures how skewed civic participation is across socioeconomic status within a community. Communities with more egalitarian civic participation score higher.
Sample	• Sample: 30,000 Americans, with 27,000 respondents surveyed across 40 communities and 3,000 nationally representative respondents using random digit dialing. • Average response rates: 28.9% for the community samples and 28.7% for the national sample.

(Continued)

TABLE 6.8 ■ (Continued)

Scoring	• The Roper Center at the University of Connecticut offers a codebook to assist with the actual scoring of the survey. The Social Capital Benchmark survey used "community quotients" as a measure to compare results across the communities surveyed since they were so varied. • Along every dimension of social capital, a community quotient (CQ) score shows a community's performance on this dimension relative to what was predicted given its urbanicity, ethnicity, levels of education, and age distribution. • A score *above* 100 indicates that a community shows more of this community connectedness than its demographics would predict; conversely, a score below 100 indicates that a community shows *less* of this type of social capital than its demographics would suggest.
Assessment	No information on reliability is provided.
Related References	The Social Capital Benchmark Survey Website has a listing of papers published using the survey: http://www.hks.harvard.edu/saguaro/pdfs/SCCBSpapers0108.pdf. Three research studies using the survey are also reported on in this chapter.
Language	English
Contact	The Roper Center for Public Opinion Research University of Connecticut Homer Babbidge Library 369 Fairfield Way, Unit 1164 Storrs, CT 06269-1164 Telephone: 860.486.4440 Fax: 860.486.6308
Website	Social Capital Benchmark Survey Website http://www.hks.harvard.edu/saguaro/communitysurvey/index.html Roper Center at University of Connecticut (*Survey Codebook*, methodology) http://www.ropercenter.uconn.edu/misc/USMISC2006-SOCCAP/usmisc2006-soccap.pdf For a copy of the executive summary of the results, please see http://www.ksg.harvard.edu/saguaro/communitysurvey/docs/exec_summ.pdf Study Results: http://www.hks.harvard.edu/saguaro/communitysurvey/results5.html

TABLE 6.9 ■ Social Capital Benchmark Survey: Social Trust and Self-Rated Health

Primary Reference	Subramanian, S. V., Kim, D. J., & Kawachi, I. (2002). Social trust and self-rated health in U.S. communities: A multilevel analysis. *Journal of Urban Health: Bulletin of the New York Academy of Medicine, 79*(4), S21–S34.
Purpose	This study examined social trust and self-rated health using data from the Social Capital Benchmark Survey (SCBS) from all 40 communities participating in the survey. A multilevel analysis was conducted with 21,456 individuals nested within the 40 communities.

Description	The instrument was a 25-minute phone survey with 66 questions that measure social capital in 11 dimensions. This study used the following variables from the SCBS:
	• **Perceptions of individual trust:** derived by summing individual responses to questions on
	  ○ General interpersonal trust (whether most people can be trusted) with potential responses being "people can be trusted," "you can't be too careful," and "depends"
	  ○ Degree of trustworthiness (how much you can trust people) of neighbors, coworkers, fellow congregants, store employees where the individual shops, and local police, with potential responses being "trust them a lot," "trust them some," and "trust them not at all." Individual scores on this scale were dichotomized as low and high, using the average as the cut point.
	• **Self-rated health** was also measured to determine the association between social capital and health. Respondents were asked: "How would you describe your overall health these days? Would you say it is excellent, very good, good, fair or poor?" The five responses were collapsed into dichotomous variables: 0 for excellent, very good and good, and 1 for fair or poor.

Sample	Social Capital Benchmark Survey Sample (see Table 6.8)
Scoring	**Community-level measures** were then developed using the above measures. • A contextual social trust variable was aggregated from individual response to questions on interpersonal trust. • Values were calculated as the average of the standardized responses to the questions using the U.S. average of the response to each question for standardization. • Aggregate community-level measures of social trust were calculated by taking the arithmetic average of the weighted individual level measures.
Assessment	No information on reliability is provided.
Related Reference	Kim, D., Subramanian, S. V., & Kawachi, I. (2006). Bonding versus bridging social capital and their association with self-rated health: A multilevel analysis of 40 U.S. communities. *Journal of Epidemiology & Community Health, 60*(2), 116–122. (see Table 6.10)
Language	English
Contact	Dr. S. V. Subramanian Department of Health and Social Behavior Harvard School of Public Health 677 Huntington Avenue, 7th Floor Boston, MA 02115 svsubram@hsph.harvard.edu

TABLE 6.10 ■	Social Capital Benchmark Survey: Bonding/Bridging Social Capital and Self-Rated Health
Primary Reference	Kim, D., Subramanian, S. V., & Kawachi, I. (2006). Bonding versus bridging social capital and their association with self-rated health: A multilevel analysis of 40 U.S. communities. *Journal of Epidemiology & Community Health, 60*(2), 116–122.
Purpose	This study examined bonding versus bridging social capital and self-rated health using data from the Social Capital Benchmark Survey (SCBS) from all 40 communities participating in the survey. A multilevel analysis was conducted with 21,456 individuals nested within the 40 communities.
Description	The instrument is a 25-minute phone survey with 66 questions that measure social capital in 11 dimensions. This is the same measure used above, but this study used the following variables from the SCBS for their measure of social capital. • **Formal group involvement (called associational involvement in SCBS):** This includes participation in 19 different types of formal groups, including neighborhood associations, senior groups, labor unions, and religious organizations. They also measured the respondent's stated most important formal group and how its composition was characterized in terms of race/ethnicity, sex, and education. • **Diversity of friendships (same name as SCBS)**: This was a count of the number of different kinds of personal friends, including having a friend who owns their own business, has been on welfare, is White, Hispanic, Asian, or African American, or has a different religion. • Level of trust in one's race/ethnicity (part of the measure of **social trust**) • The number of times one had invited or been invited to the home of a person of a different race/ethnicity over the previous year The same self-rated health measure was used as in the study in Table 6.9.
Sample	Social Capital Benchmark Survey Sample (same as Table 6.8)
Scoring	**Community level measures** were then developed using the preceding **measures**: • **Community bonding social capital:** calculated as the mean of the (1) standardized proportion of individuals in the community sample that was both at or above the national median on the number of formal group involvements and for whom most of the respondents stated most important formal group was similar to the respondent on race/ethnicity, sex, and education; and (2) the standardized mean level of trust in members of one's racial/ethnic group. • **Community bridging social capital**: calculated as the mean of (1) standardized proportion of individuals in the community sample that was both at or above the national median on the number of formal group involvements and for whom most of the respondents stated most important formal group was dissimilar to the respondent on race/ethnicity, sex, and education; and (2) the standardized mean of the number of times one had invited or been invited to the home of a person of a different race/ethnicity; and (3) the standardized community-level mean for diversity of friendships. • To generate community level proportions, individual level measures were weighted according to previously assigned survey weights.
Assessment	No information on reliability is provided.
Related Reference	See study by Subramanian et al., in Table 6.9.
Language	English

Contact	D. Kim Department of Society, Human Development, and Health Harvard School of Public Health 677 Huntington Avenue Boston, MA 02446 dkim@hsph.harvard.edu

TABLE 6.11 ■ Social Capital Benchmark Survey: Social Capital and Self-Rated Health	
Primary Reference	Schultz, J., O'Brien, M. A., & Tadesse, B. (2008). Social capital and self-rated health: Results from the US 2006 social capital survey of one community. *Social Science and Medicine, 67*(4), 606–617.
Purpose	This study examined individual social capital and self-rated health, after controlling for individual and economic characteristics, using data from the Social Capital Benchmark Survey (SCBS) in Duluth, Minnesota, and Superior, Wisconsin. The researchers address issues of social capital as an endogenous determinant of self-reported health using instrumental variables probit estimation.
Description	The instrument was a 25-minute phone survey with 66 questions that measure social capital in 11 dimensions. This study used the following variables from the SCBS: • **Social trust** (same scale used in Subramanian et al., 2002): Five questions were used to construct the social trust index, one question on general trust and four others on degrees of trustworthiness with specific types of people (see Table 6.9 for details). • **Associational involvement:** counts the number of groups the respondent has been involved with in the past 12 months prior to the interview. The index consists of 17 questions that cover the following types of groups: religious, sports, neighborhood association, ethnic group, political groups, hobby, garden, singing group, and so forth. • **Organized group interaction:** constructed from three questions: the number of times in the past 12 months the respondent (1) attended any public meeting in which town or school affairs were discussed, (2) attended a club meeting, and (3) attended a celebration, parade, or local sports or art event. • **Information social interaction:** based on the answers to five questions about socializing over the past 12 months. Respondents were asked how many times they had done things such as "had friends over to their home," "socialized with coworkers outside of work," and "hung out with friends at park, shopping mall or public place." • **Social support:** based on answers to four questions, including how often they communicate with immediate neighbors, how many close friends they have, and number of times they have been in the home of a neighbor. • **Volunteer activity**: continuous variable, asked respondents how many times they volunteered in the past 12 months prior to the survey. This study used the same self-rated health measure as the studies in Tables 6.9 and 6.10.
Sample	• Data were analyzed from the 2006 Social Capital Community Survey of Duluth, Minnesota, and Superior, Wisconsin. • A random telephone survey was conducted with 500 households in mid-April 2006. The response rate was 24.5%, which was higher than the national rate of the SCCS.
Scoring	See description of measures above for scoring (where applicable and available).
Assessment	No information was provided on reliability.
Language	English
Contact	Jennifer Schultz Department of Economics University of Minnesota 165 SBE, 412 Library Drive Duluth, MN 55812 (218) 726-6695 Email: jschultz@d.umn.edu

TABLE 6.12 ■ Social Capital Measure From the PHDCN

Primary Reference	Chaskin, R. J., Goerge, R. M., Skyles, A., & Guiltinan, S. (2006). Measuring social capital: An exploration in community–research partnership. *Journal of Community Psychology, 34*(4), 489–514. doi:10.1002/jcop.20111
Purpose	The study tests practical options for community-based organizations to measure aspects of social capital at the neighborhood level. The study used findings from PHDCN to provide comparison measures to test strategic nonrandom approaches to neighborhood survey administration.
Description	• The community survey was developed in consultation with community partners, building from items contained in the PHDCN community survey. • The survey combined the following three scales of social capital from the PHDCN, available on the PHDCN website (see below): **Collective efficacy:** This measure includes two subscales: **social cohesion and trust** and **informal social control,** described in **Table 6.6** in this chapter. (Sampson et al., 1997) **Neighborhood activism (5 items):** Respondents were asked the following: "Sometimes people in a neighborhood do things to take care of a local problem or to make the neighborhood a better place to live. Please tell me if you have been involved in the following activities in your neighborhood in the past year. Have you (or any member of your household) . . . " (Sample items include:) • Talked to a person or group causing a problem in the neighborhood • Attended a meeting of a neighborhood group about a problem • Gotten together with neighbors to do something about a problem in the neighborhood **Voluntary association (6 items):** asking the respondent whether he or she or a member of his or her household belongs to local organizations, such as • A church or other religious organization • A neighborhood watch program • A business or civic group • A local political organization
Sample	• Strategic convenience sampling of two communities, North Lawndale and Southwest Side in Chicago, was used to deliberately select sites based on local knowledge of community characteristics and dynamics. • Sample size: 355 people in North Lawndale and 248 in Southwest Side. • The researchers used the PNDCN definition of Chicago neighborhoods and information on neighborhood definitions from the community organizations they worked with on the study. • Researchers compared characteristics of respondents with data from the U.S Census and also the findings of the PHDCN Survey.
Scoring	No information is provided on scoring
Assessment	• Collective efficacy ○ Social cohesion: $\alpha = .72$ ○ Informal social control: $\alpha = .80$ • Neighborhood activism: $\alpha = .77$ • Voluntary association: $\alpha = .43$

(Continued)

TABLE 6.12 ■ (Continued)

Language	English
Contact	Robert J. Chaskin University of Chicago 1313 East Sixtieth Street Chicago, IL 60637 Email: rjc3@uchicago.org
Website	For more information see: Project on Human Development in Chicago Neighborhoods: http://www.icpsr.umich.edu/icpsrweb/PHDCN/instruments.jsp.

TABLE 6.13 ■	Extended Social Capital Measure From the PHDCN
Primary Reference	Sampson, R., & Graif, C. (2009). Neighborhood social capital as differential social organization: Resident and leadership dimensions. *American Behavioral Scientist, 52,* 1579–1605.
Purpose	The study treats social capital as a multidimensional phenomenon along which neighborhoods are differentially organized. The authors use data from the PHDCN to examine the dimensionality and structural predictors of neighborhood social organization.
Description	This measure includes the following dimensions using data from the PHDCN, which is available online (see website below): • **Neighborhood collective efficacy** (same as Table 6.6 in this chapter) • **Neighborhood activism** (same as Table 6.12) • **Moral/legal cynicism (5 items):** based on responses to five statements, on a scale from 1 to 4, with a high value signifying greater cynicism: ○ Laws were made to be broken. ○ Fighting between friends or within families is nobody else's business. • **Intergenerational closure (5 items):** Respondents were asked about their level of agreement (on a scale from 1, *disagree strongly*, to 4, *agree strongly*) to five statements such as the following: ○ There are adults in this neighborhood that children can look up to. ○ Parents in this neighborhood know their children's friends. • **Reciprocal exchange (5 items):** based on responses to five statements (on a scale from 1, *never*, to 4, *often*), such as ○ When a neighbor is not at home or on vacation, how often do you and other neighbors watch over their property? ○ How often do you and other people in this neighborhood visit in each other's homes or on the street? • **Density of local friend/kinship ties:** based on responses to two questions (on a scale from 1, *none*, to 5, *ten or more*): ○ Not counting those who live with you, how many of your relatives or in-laws live in your neighborhood? ○ How many friends do you have who live in your neighborhood? • **Organizational participation:** (same as voluntary association in Table 6.12) • **Tolerance of deviance (4 items):** asks respondents four questions on a scale from *not at all wrong* to *very wrong*, including ○ How wrong is it for teenagers around 13 years of age to smoke cigarettes? ○ How about getting into fistfights? (The same four questions are repeated for "teenagers around 19 years of age.") • **Police efficacy (5 items):** asks respondents about their level of agreement to five statements, such as ○ The police in this neighborhood are responsive to local issues. ○ The police are not doing a good job in preventing crime in this neighborhood.

(Continued)

TABLE 6.13 ■ (Continued)

	◦ Three single item measures were also included the following: Anonymity: how easy is it to spot strangers in the neighborhood; Attachment to neighborhood: how much respondents like living in the neighborhood: Intentions to move: how likely respondents will move in the next five years. Please see the article and the PHDCN website for all of the items for each of the above measures.
Sample	• The study uses data from the PHDCN. In 1995 the community survey was conducted; 8,782 Chicago residents representing all Chicago community areas were interviewed in their homes. • The survey consisted of three stages. At Stage 1, city blocks were sampled within each neighborhood cluster; Stage 2, dwelling units were sampled within blocks; Stage 3, one adult resident (18 or older) was sampled within each selected dwelling unit. • The final response rate was 75%. • A key informant (KI) survey was also conducted.
Scoring	Information on scoring is provided in the preceding section where available.
Assessment	• Collective efficacy: $\alpha = .85$ and intraclass correlation of .20 ◦ Social cohesion: community-area reliability of .92 ◦ Social control: community-area reliability of .87 • Neighborhood activism: aggregate reliability was .66 • Moral/legal cynicism: community-level reliability was .73 • Intergenerational closure: community-level reliability was .87 • Reciprocal exchange: community-level reliability was .82 • Density of local friend/kinship ties: $\alpha = .79$ • Tolerance of deviance: between community level reliabilities were .67 for questions asked about 13-year-olds and .78 for questions about 19-year-olds • Police efficacy: $\alpha = .92$.
Language	English
Contact	Robert J. Sampson, PhD Professor and Chair, Department of Sociology Harvard University William James Hall 33 Kirkland St. Cambridge, MA 02138 Email: rsampson@wjh.harvard.edu
Website	For more information see the study website: Project on Human Development in Chicago Neighborhoods. http://www.icpsr.umich.edu/icpsrweb/PHDCN/instruments.jsp.

TABLE 6.14 ■ Measure of Social Capital in Rural Communities

Primary Reference	Chazdon, S., Allen, R. P., Horntvedt, J., & Scheffert, D. R. (2013). *Developing and validating University of Minnesota extension's social capital model and survey.* Regents of the University of Minnesota: University of Minnesota Extension.
Purpose	The goal of this study was to develop and validate a conceptual framework for measuring social capital by pilot testing the measure using a participatory approach in rural communities.
Description	The scale includes 34 items, broken down into seven subscales measuring the conceptualized dimensions of social capital. Sample items are provided below (please see primary and secondary sources for all items and additional information). **Bonding trust (4 items)** • I trust my family members who live nearby. • I trust the people on my block who live nearby. **Bonding engagement (4 items)** • When my family or I need extra help with daily tasks (like shopping, childcare, meals, rides to school or appointments), there are people who live nearby whom we can count on for support. • In the area where I live, I help people out with daily tasks (like helping with chores or homework, giving rides, or other small acts of kindness), and I can count on them to help me. **Bridging trust (4 items)** • I trust people new to the area. • I trust people who don't share my cultural, racial, or ethnic background. **Bridging engagement (6 items)** • In the past month, how often have you spent at least fifteen minutes interacting directly with people of a different racial or ethnic background from you? • In the past month, how often have you spent at least fifteen minutes interacting directly with people whose first language is different from yours? **Linking trust (5 items)** • I trust the people who own and work at the places where I shop. • I trust people in local law enforcement. • I trust the hospitals and health clinics in my community. **Linking Engagement (7 items).** Asks respondents the number times they: • Attended any public meeting in which there was discussion of school or other local affairs? • Hosted or visited the home of a nonfamily member you consider to be a community leader? • Tried to get your local government to pay attention to something that concerned you? **Efficacy (4 items):** • I believe I can make a difference by helping out my circle of closest friends. • I believe I can make a difference helping newcomers get involved in groups or organizations.

(Continued)

TABLE 6.14 ■ (Continued)

Sample	• The survey was administered in four communities, three of which were rural and one that was located close to a major urban area. A project team of volunteers was organized to conduct the survey in each community. • The sample was a nonrandom convenience sample in order to capture a representative cross section of the community, including civic and community organizations, private businesses, schools, food shelves, churches, community service agencies, libraries, and coffee shops. • Total sample: 1,293 adults; ranging from 168 to 465 in each community. • Sample characteristics: Compared to the populations in each community, the samples were disproportionately female, well educated, and wealthy.
Scoring	See primary and secondary references
Assessment	Subscale reliabilities • Bonding trust: $\alpha = 0.669$ • Bonding engagement: $\alpha = 0.764$ • Bridging trust: $\alpha = 0.808$ • Bridging engagement: $\alpha = 0.800$ • Linking trust: $\alpha = 0.786$ • Linking engagement: $\alpha = 0.788$ • Efficacy: $\alpha = 0.835$
Related References	• Chazdon, S., Allen, R. P., Horntvedt, J., & Scheffert, D. R. (2013). *Methodological appendix: Steps before confirmatory factor analysis.* Regents of the University of Minnesota: University of Minnesota Extension. • Enfield, R. P., & Nathaniel, K. C. (2013). Social capital: Its constructs and survey development. *New Directions for Youth Development, 138,* 15–30.
Language	English
Contact	Scott Chazdon, Evaluation & Research Specialist, Community Vitality University of Minnesota Extension 454 Coffey Hall, 1420 Eckles Avenue Saint Paul, MN 55108 Email: schazdon@umn.edu Phone: 612-624-0982 Cell Phone: 612-251-2178 Fax: 612-625-1955
Website	For the full report on this measure please see http://www.extension.umn.edu/community/research/reports/docs/Validating-Social-Capital-Report.pdf For the methodological appendix listed above, please see http://www.extension.umn.edu/community/research/reports/docs/Validating-Social-Capital-Appendix.pdf

REFERENCES

Ahern, J., & Galea, S. (2011). Collective efficacy and major depression in urban neighborhoods. *American Journal of Epidemiology, 173*(12), 1453–1462.

Ahlbrandt, R. S. (1984). *Neighborhoods, people and communities.* New York: Plenum.

Alaimo, K., Reischl, T.M., & Allen, J. O. (2010). Community gardening, neighborhood meetings, and social capital. *Journal of Community Psychology, 38*(4), 497–514.

Baroni, G. (1979). Forward. In R. S. Ahlbrandt & J. V. Cunningham, *A new public policy for neighborhood preservation* (pp. vii–ix). New York: Praeger.

Bronfenbrenner, U. (1979). *The ecology of human development: Experiments in nature and design.* Cambridge, MA: Harvard University Press.

Browning, C. R., & Cagney, K. A. (2002). Neighborhood structural disadvantage, collective efficacy, and self-rated physical health in an urban setting. *Journal of Health and Social Behavior, 43*(4), 383–399.

Buckner, J. C. (1988). The development of an instrument to measure neighborhood cohesion. *American Journal of Community Psychology, 16*, 771–791.

Chaskin, R. J., Goerge, R. M., Skyles, A., & Guiltinan, S. (2006). Measuring social capital: An exploration in community–research partnership. *Journal of Community Psychology, 34*(4), 489–514.

Chavis, D. M., Hogge, J. H., McMillan, D. W., & Wandersman, A. (1986). Sense of community through Brunswick's lens: A first look. *Journal of Community Psychology, 14*(1), 24–40.

Chavis, D. M., Lee, K. S., & Acosta, J. (2008). *The sense of community (SCI) revised: The reliability and validity of the SCI-2.* Paper presented at the 2nd International Community Psychology Conference, Lisboa, Portugal.

Chavis, D. M., & Pretty, G. M. H. (1999). Sense of community: Advances in measurement and application. *Journal of Community Psychology, 27*, 635–642.

Chazdon, S., Allen, R. P., Horntvedt, J., & Scheffert, D. R. (2013). *Developing and validating University of Minnesota Extension's Social Capital Model and Survey*: Regents of the University of Minnesota: University of Minnesota Extension. Retrieved from http://www.extension.umn.edu/community/research/reports/docs/Validating-Social-Capital-Report.pdf

Chipuer, H. M., & Pretty, G. M. H. (1999). A Review of the Sense of Community Index: Current uses, factor structure, reliability, and further development. *Journal of Community Psychology, 27*(6), 643–658.

Cohen, D. A., Finch, B. K., Bower, A., & Sastry, N. (2006). Collective efficacy and obesity: The potential influence of social factors on health. *Social Science & Medicine, 62*(3), 769–778.

Cohen, D. A., Inagami, S., & Finch, B. (2008). The built environment and collective efficacy. *Health and Place, 14*(2), 198–208.

Coleman, J. S. (1988). Social capital in the creation of human capital. *American Journal of Sociology, 94*, S95–S120.

Coleman, J. S. (1990). *Foundations of social theory.* Cambridge, MA: Harvard University Press.

Enfield, R. P., & Nathaniel, K. C. (2013). Social capital: Its constructs and survey development. *New Directions for Youth Development, 138*, 15–30.

Glynn, T. J. (1981). Psychological sense of community: Measurement and application. *Human Relations, 34*, 780–818.

Greenberg, S. W., Rohe, W. M., & Williams, J. R. (1982). *Safe and secure neighborhoods: Physical characteristics and informal territorial control in high and low crime neighborhoods.* Washington, DC: Community Crime Prevention Division, National Institute of Justice, U.S. Department of Justice.

Grootaert, C., & Van Bastelaer, T. (2001). *Understanding and measuring social capital: A synthesis of findings from the social capital initiative.* Social capital initiative working paper

Number 24. Washington, DC: Social Development Department, World Bank.

Grootaert, C, Narayan, D, Nyhan-Jones, V., & Woodcock, M. (2004). *Measuring social capital: An integrated questionnaire* (No. 18). Washington, DC: World Bank. Retrieved from https://openknowledge.worldbank.org/bitstream/handle/10986/15033/281100PAPER0Measuring0social0capital.pdf? sequence=1

Henry, D., Gorman-Smith, D., Schoeny, M., & Tolan, P. (2014). "Neighborhood Matters": Assessment of neighborhood social processes. *American Journal of Community Psychology, 54,* 187–204.

Hughey, J., Speer, P. W., & Peterson, N. A. (1999). Sense of community in community organizations: Structure and evidence of validity. *Journal of Community Psychology, 27,* 97–113.

John F. Kennedy School of Government: Harvard University. (2000). *Social Capital Community Benchmark Survey: Executive summary.* The Saguaro Seminar: Civic Engagement in America Project. Retrieved from http://www.hks.harvard.edu/saguaro/communitysurvey/results.html

Kawachi, I., & Berkman, L. (2000). Social cohesion, social capital, and health. In L. F. Berkman & I. Kawachi (Eds.), *Social epidemiology.* New York: Oxford University Press.

Kawachi, I., Kennedy, B. P., Lochner, K., & Prothrow-Stith, D. (1997). Social capital, income inequality and mortality. *American Journal of Public Health, 87,* 1491–1498.

Kim, D., Subramanian, S. V., & Kawachi, I. (2006). Bonding versus bridging social capital and their association with self-rated health: A multilevel analysis of 40 U.S. communities. *Journal of Epidemiology & Community Health, 60*(2), 116–122.

Lochner, K. A., Kawachi, I., Brennan, R. T., & Buka, S. L. (2003). Social capital and neighborhood mortality rates in Chicago. *Social Science & Medicine, 56,* 1797–1805.

Long, D. A., & Perkins, D. D. (2003). Confirmatory factor analysis of the Sense of Community Index and development of a Brief SCI. *Journal of Community Psychology, 31,* 279–296.

McCarthy, M. E., Pretty, G. M., & Catano, V. (1990). Psychological sense of community and student burnout. *Journal of College Student Development, 31*(3), 211–216.

McMillan, D., & Chavis, D. (1986). Sense of community: A definition and theory. *American Journal of Community Psychology, 14,* 6–23.

Monette, D. R., Sullivan, R. J., DeJong, C. R. (2005). *Applied social research: A tool for the human services* (6th ed.). Belmont, CA: Brooks/Cole.

Narayan, D., & Cassidy, M.F. (2001). A dimensional approach to measuring social capital: Development and validation of a social capital inventory. *Current Sociology, 49*(2), 59–102.

Perkins, D. D., Florin, P., Rich, R. C., Wandersman, A., & Chavis, D. M. (1990). Participation and the social and physical environment of residential blocks: Crime and community context. *American Journal of Community Psychology, 18*(1), 83–115.

Peterson, N. A., Speer, P. W., & Hughey, J. (2006). Measuring sense of community: A methodological interpretation of the factor structure debate. *Journal of Community Psychology, 34*(4), 453–469.

Peterson, N. A., Speer, P. W., & McMillan, D. W. (2008). Validation of A brief sense of community scale: Confirmation of the principal theory of sense of community. *Journal of Community Psychology, 36*(1), 61–73.

Pretty, G. M. (1990). Relating psychological sense of community to social climate characteristics. *Journal of Community Psychology, 18*(1), 60–65.

Prezza, M., Pacilli, M. G., Barbaranelli, C., & Zampatti, E. (2009). The MTSOCS: A multidimensional sense of community scale for local communities. *Journal of Community Psychology, 37*(3), 305–326.

Project on Human Development in Chicago Neighborhoods (n.d.). *About.* Retrieved from http://www.icpsr.umich.edu/icpsrweb/PHDCN/about.jsp

Putnam, R. D. (1993). What makes democracy work? *National Civic Review, 82*(2), 101–107.

Putnam, R. D. (2000). *Bowling alone: The collapse and revival of American community.* New York: Simon & Schuster.

Sampson, R. J., & Graif, C. (2009). Neighborhood social capital as differential social organization: Resident and leadership dimensions. *American Behavioral Scientist, 52*(11), 1579–1605.

Sampson, R. J., & Raudenbush, S.W. (1999). Systematic social observation of public spaces: A new look at disorder in urban neighborhoods. *American Journal of Sociology, 105*(3), 603–651.

Sampson, R. J., Raudenbush, S. W., & Earls, F. (1997). Neighborhoods and violent crime: A multilevel study of collective efficacy. *Science, 277,* 918–924.

Sarason, S. B. (1974). *The psychological sense of community: Prospects for a community psychology.* San Francisco: Jossey-Bass.

Schultz, J., O'Brien, M. A., & Tadesse, B. (2008). Social capital and self-rated health: Results from the US 2006 social capital survey of one community. *Social Science and Medicine, 67*(4), 606–617.

Subramanian, S. V., Kim, D. J., & Kawachi, I. (2002). Social trust and self-rated health in US communities: A multilevel analysis. *Journal of Urban Health: Bulletin of the New York Academy of Medicine, 79*(4), S21–S34).

Veenstra, G. (2001). Social capital and health. *ISUMA: Canadian Journal of Policy Research, 2,* 72–81.

Wandersman, A., & Florin, P. (2000). Citizen participation and community organizations. In J. Rappaport & E. Seidman (Eds.), *Handbook of community psychology.* New York: Kluwer Academic/Plenum Publishers.

Whitman, M. M. (2012). Community connections: Social capital and community success. *Sociological Forum, 27*(2), 441–457.

7 COMMUNITY EMPOWERMENT AND ENGAGEMENT

This chapter provides an overview of measurement instruments that assess community empowerment and engagement, including measures of psychological empowerment in a community setting, sociopolitical control, community participation, neighborhood activism, and civic engagement. There is a bidirectional and important relationship between community empowerment and engagement: As a community becomes more empowered, they have the motivation to become more engaged in community change efforts, and as residents become more active, they become more personally empowered and the overall community becomes more empowered as well.

Community in this chapter, as in other chapters, is defined by a specific territory or geographical location (e.g., a neighborhood, town, or city). Israel, Checkoway, Schulz, and Zimmerman (1994) identified the following elements as important to community empowerment and engagement:

- **Membership:** a sense of identify and belonging; common symbol systems, including similar language, rituals, and ceremonies
- **Shared values and norms**
- **Mutual influence:** community members have influence and are influenced by one another
- **Shared needs and commitment to meeting them**
- **Shared emotional connection:** members share common history, experiences and mutual support (p. 151)

WHY IS IT IMPORTANT TO MEASURE COMMUNITY EMPOWERMENT AND ENGAGEMENT?

Community empowerment and engagement are central elements in community research and practice. Community engagement includes the various ways residents and citizens become actively involved in their communities and neighborhoods, while community empowerment can be the result of such engagement, as well as community capacity building strategies. Zimmerman and Rappaport (1988) argue that citizen participation and engagement are important mechanisms for the development of personal and community empowerment because it is through their engagement that residents gain experience in organizing people, identifying resources, and developing strategies to achieve the community's goals (p. 727). As mentioned previously, these concepts are bidirectional; increased responsibility, engagement, and action in the community increase residents' feelings of competence and control and decreases isolation, which increases one's feeling of empowerment. Increased feelings of empowerment can also motivate residents to engage more in their communities and take on more challenging tasks (Peterson, Lowe, Hughey, Reid, Zimmerman, & Speer, 2006; Zimmerman & Rappaport, 1988).

The concept of empowerment has become a central feature in community interventions and prevention science among multiple disciplines, including public health, community psychology, social work, and community practice (Peterson et al., 2006). Israel and colleagues (1994) argue that public health problems, such as exposure to toxic chemicals, racial disparities, poor sanitation, inadequate housing, and lack of access to healthy foods, are beyond the ability of any one individual to address, control, or change. Community empowerment approaches are needed to take the blame off of the victim and focus on eliminating the root causes of the problem. Empowerment approaches focus on positive and proactive strategies for change versus reactive approaches based on clinical treatment or illness models of intervention (Israel et al., 1994).

The development and use of reliable and valid measures is particularly important for improving community empowerment and engagement interventions and assessing their outcomes. Peterson and colleagues (2006) argue that efforts are needed to improve the psychometric properties of measures commonly used in empowerment research so that researchers and practitioners can influence policy debates about vulnerable populations, social determinants of health and well-being, as well improve interventions that increase empowerment and address inequities. Citizen engagement and participation are critical to building healthy communities and "creating empowered constituencies who can leverage greater and more equal access to available resources" (Foster-Fishman, Pierce, & Van Egeren, 2009, p. 550). Citizen engagement is associated with positive individual outcomes, such as educational attainment, and social competence as well as social outcomes, including improved democratic participation (Bobek, Zaff, Li, & Lerner, 2009). Citizen participation in neighborhood organizations is positively linked to increased leadership, policy control, neighborhood policy control, organizational collective efficacy, and sense of community (Ohmer, 2007).

It has also become increasingly important to engage youth, particularly youth of color, in community interventions that focus on participatory research, youth organizing, and community and school improvement projects (Bobek et al., 2009; Ozer & Schotland, 2011; Zaff, Boyd, Li, Lerner, & Lerner, 2010). Many initiatives focus on giving youth a voice in their communities by providing opportunities for them to improve their schools and neighborhoods. Research demonstrates that there are important differences in how youth and adults engage and become empowered in communities (e.g., engagement through peer relationships among youth versus relationships between youth and adults) (Peterson et al., 2006). Zaff and colleagues (2010) argue that "when young people are engaged in improving the well-being of their communities and their country, their own development is enhanced and civil society benefits" (p. 736). Community engagement and empowerment measures targeted for youth may help researchers better understand youth behavioral and developmental outcomes, including identity development, violence, substance abuse, and educational attainment (Peterson et al., 2006). Therefore, this chapter also describes measures of community empowerment and engagement that have been used in studies and interventions targeting youth.

EMPOWERMENT IN COMMUNITIES

The concept of empowerment has been examined among multiple disciplines and professions, including social work, community psychology, and public health; however, there has been a lack of clarity regarding how it is conceptualized, operationalized, and measured (Israel et al., 1994). To better understand community empowerment, it is important to trace how the concept of "empowerment" has been historically defined in the literature. Zimmerman and Rappaport (1988) provide one of the earliest definitions, stating that empowerment "links individual strengths and competencies, natural helping systems, and proactive behaviors to matters of social policy and social change" (p. 726). Other scholars have defined empowerment as

- "A process by which individuals gain mastery or control over their own lives and democratic participation in the life of their community" (Zimmerman & Rappaport, 1988, p. 726).
- "A process of increasing personal, interpersonal, or political power so that individuals can take action to improve their life situations" (Gutierrez, 1990, p. 149).
- "The ability of people to gain understanding and control over personal, social, economic, and political forces in order to take action to improve their life situations" (Israel et al., 1994, p. 152).

These definitions refer to individual power as a key component of community empowerment as well as control over the environment, including the ability to take action on issues, change policies impacting communities, and mobilize for social change.

The concept of community empowerment is often conceptualized as a multidimensional construct, including individual, organizational, and community levels of analysis (Israel et al., 1994; Zimmerman, 1995). At the individual level, scholars refer to the concept of psychological empowerment, which incorporates cognitive, emotional, and behavioral domains (Speer & Peterson, 2000):

- Cognitive domains of empowerment include self-efficacy (Bandura, 1982), personal efficacy, and competence (Israel et al., 1994).
- Emotional or personality domains include locus of control or feelings about one's competency or ability to affect change in the community (Speer & Peterson, 2000; Zimmerman & Rappaport, 1995).
- Behavioral domains focus on both the motivation to control one's environment as well as participatory activities to engage in social change or social action to influence decisions and community institutions (Israel et al., 1994; Speer & Peterson, 2000; Zimmerman & Rappaport, 1995).

Empowerment theory has also been used to characterize empowering organizations, which are "democratically managed" and include structures through which members share information and power, engage in cooperative decision-making, and design, implement, and control efforts toward mutually defined goals (Israel et al., 1994, p. 152). An empowering organization also allows people to gain control over their lives as well as the quality of life in their communities through shared responsibility and leadership opportunities (Zimmerman, 2000). Opportunities are provided for members to increase their control over policies and decisions that are made in the larger systems or communities in which they operate (Israel et al., 1994). Moreover, empowering organizations have a healthy social climate, fostering positive relationships between members, support and control among leaders, and functioning structures (Wandersman & Florin, 2000). Measures of community coalitions and partnerships that exemplify organizational empowerment are included in Chapter 5.

At the community level of analysis, "individuals and organizations apply their skills and resources in collective efforts to meet their respective needs, . . . provide enhanced support for each other, address conflicts within the community, and gain increased influence and control over the quality of life in their communities" (Israel et al., 1994, p. 153). While community empowerment has frequently been defined or viewed as an outcome, it is more often viewed as a process that involves empowerment at a personal, group (e.g., small mutual groups, community organizations, and partnerships), or social/political level (Laverack & Wallerstein, 2001, p. 182). Achieving community empowerment as an outcome is a long-term process that is contingent on many internal and external factors. Measuring community empowerment as a process allows researchers and practitioners to "monitor the interaction between capacities, skills and resources at the individual and organizational levels during the time frame of a programme, as well as community-level changes in healthy conditions, policies and interpersonal structures" (Laverack & Wallerstein, 2001, p. 182).

Three measures of personal empowerment used in community settings are discussed below, including psychological empowerment related to citizen participation (Zimmerman & Rappaport, 1988); personal empowerment in a community organizing context (Speer & Peterson, 2000); and psychological empowerment among urban youth (Ozer & Schotland, 2011). These measures are followed by a discussion of an overall measure of community empowerment (Israel et al., 1994).

Psychological Empowerment Measures

One of the earliest attempts at developing and measuring psychological empowerment was by Zimmerman and Rappaport (1988). Their research integrated the literature on citizen participation and perceived control to combine 11 indices of empowerment representing personality, cognitive, and emotional domains. Three studies were conducted to examine the relationship between psychological empowerment and participation among college students and community residents. A second goal of the research was to identify common themes to describe an empowered individual (Zimmerman & Rappaport, 1988, p. 728). Moreover, "a single dimension comprised of personality, cognitive and motivational measures was expected to provide convergent and discriminant validity for the construct" (Zimmerman & Rappaport, 1988, p. 728). **Table 7.1** provides information about the measure of **psychological empowerment** developed by Zimmerman and Rappaport (1988). The results of their study showed moderate correlations among the 11 indices for psychological empowerment, indicating that "each measure assesses both an overlapping and a unique aspect of empowerment" (Zimmerman & Rappaport, 1988, p. 746). Moreover, "only one discriminant function significantly distinguished groups," suggesting that each domain contributed to a single function representing the construct better than the individual measures alone (Zimmerman & Rappaport, 1988, p. 746). This study also developed two measures of **citizen participation**: participation in community activities and level of involvement in community organizations. These measures are described in Table 7.1. The researchers argue that the validity of their psychological empowerment measure was demonstrated because the results were replicated among student and community samples. Moreover, their results demonstrated convergent validity (psychological empowerment was associated with leadership) as well as divergent validity (psychological empowerment was associated in the expected direction with alienation) (Zimmerman & Rappaport, 1988).

- The results of the three studies supported the hypothesis that greater participation in community activities and organizations is associated with psychological empowerment.

- In each study, personality, cognitive, and motivational measures significantly contributed to distinguishing high and low participation groups.
- Students and residents involved in community organizations had a greater sense of empowerment than their less-involved counterparts.
- Student and residents reported a greater sense of political efficacy, competence and mastery, desire for control, more civic duty, and a belief that their success is a result of internal rather than external factors (Zimmerman & Rappaport, 1988, p. 746).

However, this study did not examine the reliability or the underlying factor structure of the construct of psychological empowerment, which may have produced a multidimensional measure. While this is an older study, it is important to understand how researchers initially defined, operationalized, and measured empowerment, particularly among residents participating in community organizations.

Speer and Peterson (2000) later developed a measure of **psychological empowerment** that was used in a **community organizing context** (see **Table 7.2**). Their research examined the psychometric properties of a 27-item empowerment scale from a sample of 974 randomly selected residents in six municipalities in the northeastern United States that were part of community-wide partnerships to prevent substance abuse. The factor analysis results did not support a one-dimensional measure of psychological empowerment; however, positive associations were found between empowerment and measures of citizen engagement and residents' perceptions of their community.

- A principal components factor analysis was used to assess content validity, including the dimensions of empowerment (Speer & Peterson, 2000).
    - While seven factors were hypothesized, six were extracted. The factor analysis yielded three subscales for cognitive empowerment, two subscales for emotional empowerment, and one subscale for behavioral empowerment. The defining debate scale items (the seventh dimension) were split evenly between the political functioning and shaping ideology factors included in the cognitive dimension.
- Construct validity was examined using bivariate correlational analysis, which showed that the relationships among the factors of the empowerment scale had greater associations within the cognitive and behavioral domains but were weak across domains.
    - Specifically, the cognitive domain was not associated with the emotional or behavioral domains, and the behavioral and emotional domains were only moderately correlated.
    - The results of the bivariate analysis showed that empowerment was related to community involvement and perceptions of the community (e.g., sense of community, institutional involvement), but these associations were weak.
    - The multivariate analyses demonstrated that greater behavioral empowerment, stronger beliefs that power was developed through relationships, and lower-political efficacy were associated with greater sense of community, membership in community organizations, and perception of greater involvement by institutions in the local community (Speer & Peterson, 2000, p. 112–116).

Furthermore, the cognitive and behavioral subscales demonstrated higher levels of reliability than the emotional empowerment subscale (see Table 7.2). The findings suggest empowerment is a complex, multivariate phenomenon (Speer & Peterson, 2000).

Finally, two more recent measures of **psychological empowerment among urban youth** are examined in this chapter. The first measure was developed by Ozer and Schotland (2011) to assess youth-led organizing and participatory research approaches for addressing social and community problems (see **Table 7.3**). The goal of the study was to develop a measure of youth empowerment that could be used for evaluating youth-driven approaches to adolescent development in schools and communities. In youth-led initiatives, "young people themselves identify the focus of their project and which issues they want to research and change" (Ozer & Schotland, 2011, p. 349). The researchers argued that youth-led initiatives require a measure of empowerment that is not issue specific but one that can assess empowerment domains associated with adolescent psychosocial outcomes. Their measure of adolescent psychological empowerment included four domains: sociopolitical skills, motivation to influence their schools or communities, participatory behavior, and perceived control (Ozer & Schotland, 2011, p. 349). Criterion validity was examined by comparing their measure of empowerment with distinct but related measures of adolescent functioning. The authors "hypothesized that higher levels of psychological empowerment might also demonstrate good functioning in other domains" but differ from global measures of self-esteem and relationships (Ozer & Schotland, 2011, p. 349). The researchers also developed a measure of adolescent skills and efficacy in communication, advocacy, and research related to psychological empowerment (see Table 7.3).

Ozer and Schotland's (2011) measure of youth psychological empowerment was informed by Zimmerman and Zahniser's (1991) sociopolitical control scale (which is discussed in the next section) as well as the perceived autonomy in school scale (Developmental Studies Center, 2000). Formative research methods were used to develop the measure, including group interviews with youth and community-based organization staff members as well as pilot tests.

- After the initial review of psychometric properties of each item, 16 items were removed (e.g., because of low response rate or variability).
- The remaining 45 items were tested for reliability; 17 items that were not theoretically central and did not correlate highly with other subscale items were removed.
- Confirmatory factor analysis was used to examine the factor structure, and correlational analyses were conducted to assess associations with other measures of adolescent functioning (Ozer & Schotland, 2011). The factor analysis resulted in a four-factor model of adolescent psychological empowerment that included 19 items.
    - After, the four-factor model was tested using confirmatory factor analyses. The final four factors demonstrated good internal consistency, and the four-factor model showed adequate goodness of fit based on four fit indices. Six items were removed based on these analyses, resulting in a four-factor model that showed improved fit.
- All four subscales were correlated with each other and moderately and positively associated with traditional indicators of adolescent psychosocial

> functioning, including self-esteem, caring relationships with adults at school, and greater perceived social support from peers at school. However, for the external criterion of GPA, correlation effects sizes were low (Ozer et al., 2011, pp. 352–354).

This was the first study to operationalize a measure of psychological empowerment among young people of diverse ethnic backgrounds living in urban neighborhoods (Ozer & Schotland, 2011). The researchers argue that the measure can be used to examine outcomes in youth-led programs in a variety of school and community contexts.

Eisman and colleagues (2016) also developed a measure of **psychological empowerment among urban youth (Table 7.4)** that was guided by Zimmerman and Rappaport's (1988) conceptual framework, which includes intrapersonal, interactional, and behavioral components. They also examined the relationship between psychological empowerment and positive and negative outcomes among urban youth, including aggressive behavior and prosocial engagement. The researchers used confirmatory factor analysis and structural equation modeling (SEM) to examine their hypotheses. The results demonstrated that each of the "latent factors for the three PE components demonstrated a good fit with the data"; and "three components loaded onto a higher-order PE factor" (Eisman et al., 2016, p. 410). The reliability of each of the component measures was also examined and is presented in Table 7.4. Eisman and colleagues (2016) also found that a second order PE factor was negatively associated with aggressive behavior and positively associated with prosocial engagement (p. 410). However, the higher order PE factor was associated with prosocial behavior but not with aggressive behavior.

Community Empowerment Measure

Israel and colleagues (1994) developed a measure of community empowerment for use in a health education initiative to assess the extent and development of community empowerment over time. The measure was developed as part of the Detroit Area Study, which is a random sample survey conducted yearly at the University of Michigan. The survey examines social, economic, and political issues, residents' views of issues facing their communities, and public involvement in community problem solving. Israel and colleagues' (1994) measure of **community empowerment** examined individual perceptions of control or influence at three levels: individual, organizational, and community (see **Table 7.5**). The researchers conducted a factor analysis, which resulted in three subscales. Reliability analyses were also conducted for each subscale as well as the overall scale, demonstrating moderate to good reliability (see Table 7.5). The researchers reported that the correlations among the three subscales were rather weak, indicating that the combined items may not fully represent an overall measure of community empowerment (Israel et al., 1994). Validity was not discussed in detail in this study; however, the researchers stated that perceived control at the organizational and community levels were predicted by public policy influence, active leadership in voluntary organizations, and the belief that taking action is effective in influencing community decisions (Israel et al., 1994, p. 161). The researchers suggest that the instrument can be used by health and community educators to assess the outcomes of community empowerment interventions. However, Israel and colleagues (1994) state that their instrument is limited by the weak associations among the subscales, validity issues, and the use of closed-ended questions that don't capture the complexity of community empowerment. Moreover, there are no known recent attempts to develop and test a multilevel measure of community empowerment, representing a significant gap in this area of community measurement.

SOCIOPOLITICAL CONTROL MEASURES

Sociopolitical control is a measure of personal empowerment and efficacy in community settings. Zimmerman and Zahniser (1991) define sociopolitical control as "beliefs about one's capabilities and efficacy in social and political systems," including "beliefs that one can influence policy decisions, lead a group of people, or organize one's neighbors" (p. 189). The sociopolitical control scale (SPCS) is a "sphere-specific measure of perceived control that integrates personality, cognitive and motivational domains" (Zimmerman & Zahniser, 1991, p. 191). Several components of sociopolitical control are often integrated into the psychological empowerment measures discussed above. However, sociopolitical control is distinct because it focuses on perceived control in public and sociopolitical contexts, including involvement in community organizations and activities. Since its development, sociopolitical control has been examined in multiple studies, including a community-based training program to improve adaptive behaviors among low-income women immigrants in Israel (Itzhaky, 2003, as cited in Peterson et al., 2006) and a school-based effort to promote adolescent engagement in health advocacy programs (Altman et al., 1998, as cited in Peterson et al., 2006). Ohmer (2007) found that citizen participation among members of neighborhood organizations in poor urban communities was positively related to sociopolitical control. Moreover, the U.S. "Center for Substance Abuse and Prevention (CSAP) recognized the SPCS as a useful tool for assessing empowerment-related outcomes of substance abuse prevention interventions" (Kumpfer et al., 1993, as cited in Peterson et al., 2006, p. 288).

The conceptual foundation for the sociopolitical control scale was provided by several early studies on sociopolitical control and psychological empowerment (e.g., all of the following are cited in Zimmerman and Zahniser, 1991: Zimmerman, 1989; 1990; Gerschick, Israel, & Checkoway, 1990; Rappaport, 1981, 1987; Swift & Levin, 1987, as cited in Zimmerman & Zahniser, 1991, p. 288). Zimmerman and Zahniser (1991) clarified and linked prior literature and research in three studies to develop an integrated measure of sociopolitical control. The first two studies (one with college students and the other with community residents) were also used by Zimmerman and Rappaport (1988) to develop their measure of psychological empowerment. An additional study with members of four Free Methodist churches located in different geographical regions of the United States was also used to develop the sociopolitical control scale (Zimmerman & Zahniser, 1991). In the first study, the researchers selected items from 10 instruments that represented personality, cognitive, and motivational domains of sociopolitical control, including political efficacy (Craig & Maggiotto, 1982, as cited in Peterson et al., 2006), perceived competence (Florin & Wandersman, 1984, as cited in Peterson et al., 2006), locus of control (Levenson, 1974, as cited in Peterson et al., 2006), and sense of mastery (Perlin, Menaghan, Lieberman, & Mullen, 1981, as cited in Peterson et al., 2006).

The following validity criteria were used to select the items for the sociopolitical control scale: (a) items were retained that significantly correlated in the hypothesized direction across two types of community involvement (e.g., level of participation in voluntary organizations and extent of involvement of in community activities), and (b) the item content had to be theoretically relevant to sociopolitical control and psychological empowerment (Zimmerman & Zahniser, 1991; Peterson et al., 2006). Their analysis resulted in a final pool of 17 items that represented the cognitive and motivational domains of perceived control (see **Table 7.6**) from five of the 10 scales they examined: political efficacy (Craig & Maggiotto, 1982, as cited in Peterson et al., 2006), self-efficacy (Tipton & Worthington, 1984, as cited in Peterson et al., 2006), desirability of control (Burger & Cooper, 1979, as cited in Peterson et al., 2006), perceived competence (Florin & Wandersman, 1984, as cited in Peterson et al., 2006), and civic duty scales (Campell, Gurin, & Miller, 1954, as cited in Zimmerman & Zahniser, 1991).

- Study 1
  - A factor analysis was conducted on the 17 items.
  - Convergent validity was also examined using an alienation scale (consisting of three subscales) and leadership.
  - Two factors were retained in the analysis, with eight items loading on leadership skills and nine on policy control.
  - Both subscales correlated negatively with alienation and positively with leadership (Zimmerman and Zahniser, 1991, pp. 192–195).

- Study 2 and Study 3
  - A two-factor solution was produced that was similar to Study 1.
  - Independent variables related to participation were also used to validate the factor structure with community residents and with congregation members in Study 3.
  - Results demonstrated that all correlations were significant and in the expected direction.
  - Multivariate analysis of variance was also conducted (Zimmerman & Zanhiser, 1991, pp. 195–200).

- Overall results
  - The psychometric properties of the two subscales were acceptable and were replicated across the three study samples that differed in age, life stage, and geographical location but were similar in socioeconomic status.
  - Replication of the factor structure and item consistency within the subscales supported internal reliability.
  - Construct validity was supported by the significant correlations with the alienation and leadership measures in all three samples. The multivariate analysis demonstrated that individuals more involved in voluntary organizations and community activities had greater sociopolitical control than those less involved, even when age and education were statistically controlled for in Study 3 (Zimmerman & Zanhiser, 1991, pp. 200–201).

A major limitation of this research is the lack of validation on minority samples and the exclusion of behavioral measures for additional validation. The SPCS was developed using White, middle-class samples and may not be appropriate for other groups (Zimmerman & Zahniser, 1991). The two factors in the SPCS enrich the understanding of sociopolitical control because they distinguish specific skills (leadership competence) from participatory expectations (policy control) and they are not limited to social change activities. The subscales also represent significant aspects of psychological empowerment (competence and efficacy) (Zimmerman & Zahniser, 1991).

A more recent study (Peterson et al., 2006) extended research on the sociopolitical control scale to test the hypothesized factor structure and a revised version of the scale that used positively versus negatively worded items. Confirmatory factor analyses were conducted with two samples to test the structure, potential effects of method bias on the psychometric properties, and whether the revised version of the scale yielded improved model fit (Peterson et al., 2006). While the original SPCS scale had several strengths in terms of reliability and validity, there were two negatively worded items that did not load on the expected factor (Zimmerman & Zahniser, 1991; Peterson et al., 2006). Smith and Propst (2001) also examined the factor structure of the SPCS and had similar results: The hypothesized factors emerged but "several negatively worded items failed to produce significant loadings." The researchers also argued that "method bias from the use of negatively worded items may have a detrimental effect on the SPCS's psychometric properties" (Peterson et al., 2006, p. 288).

It is important to note that researchers have traditionally advised using both positively and negatively worded items to reduce response bias; however, problems with factor structure and internal consistency can occur with this practice (Anastasi, 1982, as cited in Peterson et al., 2006; Barnette, 2000, as cited in Peterson et al., 2006). Positively and negatively worded items may be too complex, causing respondents to "misunderstand an item or answer differently than they would to a positively worded statement" (Peterson et al., 2006, p. 288). Negatively worded items may also more accurately represent different constructs of interest than what they are intended to measure (Roberts, Laughlin, & Wedell, 1999, as cited in Peterson et al., 2006, p. 289).

Table 7.7 describes the revised version of the **sociopolitical control scale (SPCS-R)**, indicating which items were revised and how they were changed from negatively to positively worded statements. The findings from Peterson and colleagues (2006) demonstrate improvements to the validity, reliability, and factor structure of the revised SPCS scale.

- The two-factor solution for the original SPCS provided the poorest fit to the data from both samples.
- Rephrasing negative items into positively worded statements produced results that confirmed the hypothesized two-factor model of leadership competence and policy control.
- The revised subscale that rephrased items was found to be reliable and related to measures of community involvement, which improved the validity of the SPCS (Peterson et al., 2006, p. 288).

Moreover, Peterson and colleagues (2006) extended research on the SPCS by including a more diverse sample in their second study, which included predominantly African American and Hispanic respondents. The authors recommend using the revised measure to strengthen the validity of future studies, "particularly those that evaluate interventions for improving community involvement, citizenship and intrapersonal PE" (psychological empowerment) (Peterson et al., 2006, p. 294).

Peterson, Peterson, Agre, Christens, and Morton (2011) developed a measure of **sociopolitical control for youth** engaged in empowerment efforts in urban areas (see **Table 7.8** for a description of the **SPCS-Y**). Their study extended research by Holden and colleagues (Holden, Crankshaw, Nimsch, Hinnant, & Hund, 2004; Holden, Evans, Hinnant, & Messeri, 2005) that tested a unidimensional measure of sociopolitical control among youth participating in a program to prevent tobacco use. Peterson and colleagues (2011) examined the factor structure, reliability, and validity of the two dimensional measure of youth sociopolitical control, testing both the one- and two-factor models. The survey was conducted as part of a comprehensive needs assessment to prevent substance abuse and sexual risk taking behaviors among racial and ethnic minority youth in urban communities (Peterson et al., 2011). This sample extended prior research on the SPCS by including minority youth from some of the poorest school districts in the United States with the highest rates for substance abuse. The following measures were included to examine their relationships with sociopolitical control: community and school participation, neighborhood attachment, perceived school importance, and alcohol and drug use. Participants were divided into four profile groups based on scores from the two subscales to determine if they differed on the four additional measures (Peterson et al., 2011).

- The results of the confirmatory factor analysis supported the two-factor model, consisting of leadership competence and policy control subscales.
  - The two-factor solution provided an adequate fit to the data, which was significantly better than the one-factor model. The results also support the validity of the Sociopolitical Control Scale for Youth (Peterson et al., 2011, p. 600).
- Moreover, validity was confirmed by statistically significant associations between the SPCS-Y and variables related to neighborhood and community engagement, attachment, and use of alcohol and drugs (Peterson et al., 2011).
  - Statistically significant differences were found between the four profile groups for all of the conceptually relevant variables.
  - Participants in Group 1 (those with higher scores on both subscales) had higher scores on community and school participation than the other three groups.
  - Participants in Groups 1 and 3 (those with higher scores on policy control and lower scores on leadership competence) had significantly higher scores on neighborhood attachment and significantly lower scores on alcohol and drug use than Groups 2 and 4 (those with lower scores on both subscales).
  - Participants in Groups 1 and 3 had higher scores on perceived school importance than individuals in Group 4 (Peterson et al., 2011, pp. 599–600).

These findings confirm prior research by Zimmerman and Zahniser (1991) supporting a two-factor model as well as Peterson and colleagues' use of positively worded items to measure sociopolitical control. Peterson and colleagues (2011) advocate the use of the sociopolitical control scale to assess social change efforts, citizen participation in community organizations, and outcomes of youth and community empowerment initiatives. However, the researchers argue that the items in the scale for youth SPCS may need to be tailored for use with other youth populations and in different contexts and settings (Peterson et al., 2011, p. 602).

COMMUNITY AND CITIZEN PARTICIPATION

This section describes measures of community engagement and citizen participation. These measures are often used in studies about sense of community, social capital, and community empowerment, including research discussed in this chapter and in

Chapters 4 and 6. Several studies combine measures of community participation and capacity; this chapter includes measures of community participation while measures of community capacity and readiness are included in Chapter 4.

Defining Community and Citizen Participation

Gamble and Weil (1995) define citizen participation as "the active, voluntary involvement of individuals and groups in changing problematic conditions in communities and influencing the policies and programs that affect the quality of their lives and the lives of other residents" (as cited in Ohmer, 2007, p. 109). Zimmerman and Rappaport (1988) define citizen participation broadly as "involvement in any organizing activity in which the individual participates without pay in order to achieve a common goal" (p. 726). More recently, community-based and comprehensive community initiatives have emphasized engaged and active residents in their initiatives as key strategies for improving and creating healthy communities (Foster-Fishman, Cantillon, Pierce, & Van Egeren, 2007; Smallwood et al., 2015). An active citizenry can leverage resources and shape programs and policies to better serve their needs (Foster-Fishman et al., 2009). By engaging in their communities, "residents can influence external social systems and work with neighbors and community organizations to improve their neighborhoods" (Ohmer, 2007, p. 110).

Residents become engaged in their communities in several ways, including involvement in decision-making roles, such as planning and designing, or on decision-making bodies; participating in community and organizational activities or projects to improve their neighborhoods; or advocacy, collective action, or mobilization efforts (Foster-Fishman et al., 2007; Foster-Fishman et al., 2009). Residents may also become involved in their communities through private and/or public organizations, such as neighborhood or civic organizations, community development corporations, advisory boards, planning groups, social service and public health agencies, and environmental or advocacy organizations. Another term often used to describe community participation is neighborhood activism, which focuses on the collective action of residents in their communities (Foster-Fishman et al., 2007, 2009; Sampson & Graif, 2009). Finally, community mobilization is another term used to signify resident engagement around common neighborhood goals (Lippman et al., 2016).

Measures of Community and Citizen Participation

An early measure of **citizen participation** was developed by Perkins and colleagues (1990) for a study on the relationship between participation in block associations and the social and physical environment (see **Table 7.9**). Their study examined crime-related physical and social conditions as the context for community participation and empowerment. Twenty-one potential sample neighborhoods were selected to be in the study based on having a sufficient number of active block associations (e.g., according to the civic organization's mailing list) and having increased robbery and burglary rates (e.g., based on police reports). Letters were sent the block association leaders asking about their interest and willingness to participate in the study; a total of 48 blocks in three neighborhoods were selected for the study based on the response (10% return rate) (Perkins et al., 1990). Blocks that were selected had to be predominantly residential areas, and block associations had to be at least one year old and minimally active with regular meetings. The authors used a continuous, multidimensional scale from two different data sources to develop a more valid and reliable measure of block association participation than a simple dichotomy of organized/unorganized blocks. Their measures examined the proportion of residents participating at different levels of responsibility and the amount of time they participated as well as a wide cross section of information through the inclusion of nonmembers' perceptions of block association activities (Perkins et al., 1990).

- The researchers found that participation in block associations was impacted by a combination of catalysts in the physical environment (e.g., such as poorly maintained properties) and social environment (e.g., such as block satisfaction and neighboring).
    - The results showed that the built environment, the social climate, and the transient physical environment are significantly and independently related to collective participation in block associations (Perkins et al., 1990).
- However, they did not find a connection between participation and crime nor reactions to crime.
    - Length of residence, home ownership, and income were all positively related to individual-level but not block-level participation. The researchers suggest that poor and residentially unstable neighborhoods are able to develop a level of participation equal to other communities. However, those individuals with more resources and a greater vested interest in property are still more likely to participate within these communities.
    - The results also suggest that the social and physical environment is more important for block-level participation than demographic characteristics or crime-related problems, perceptions, and fears (Perkins et al., 1990, pp. 106–107).

While the authors in this study did not examine the reliability or factor structure of their citizen participation measure, this measures of citizen participation is included here as an early attempt to conceptualize participation that demonstrated validity because of its relationship with other theoretically conceptualized measures. It is important to note that a later study by Perkins and Long (2002) examined the reliability of this measure and found that it was reliable at multiple time periods.

Foster-Fishman and colleagues (2007, 2009) developed and tested measures of citizen participation and community capacity in their study of a comprehensive community building initiative in Michigan called Yes we can! (YWC!), which was funded by the W. K. Kellogg Foundation. The citizen participation measures are included in this chapter and the community capacity and readiness measures are described in Chapter 4. Comprehensive community building initiatives (CCIs or CBIs) are designed to address social issues at multiple levels by "fostering partnerships between and among neighborhood residents and local organizations and institutions, engaging local residents in the work, and building local capacity to resolve issues" (Foster-Fishman et al., 2007, p. 91). The goal of the YWC! was to "bring about a more just and sustainable community by reducing gaps in economic and educational outcomes" by engaging residents and neighborhood leaders as change agents through their "informed and full participation in public life" (Foster-Fishman et al., 2009, p. 556). CBIs "emphasize broad-based resident or grassroots involvement in most, if not all, phases of the programming efforts" (Chaskin & Peters, 2000, as cited in Foster-Fishman et al., 2007; Smock, 1997, as cited in Foster-Fishman et al., 2007, p. 92).

Foster-Fishman and colleagues (2007, 2009) developed measures of **citizen participation** as part of their evaluation of YWC! The CBI took place in seven distressed neighborhoods within the city of Battle Creek, Michigan. **Table 7.10** describes the initial study and measures, and **Table 7.11** describes the follow-up study and measures. The first study included a community-wide survey to a random sample of residents in the seven neighborhoods targeted for the intervention, while the second study focused on a purposive sample of residents from the targeted neighborhoods who were engaged in the initiative or in neighborhood organizations. Thus slightly different measures were used in both studies, so they are reported separately. The researchers included the following citizen participation measures: **individual activism,** which "refers to the actions of individual residents intended to express their concerns about specific problems within a neighborhood to groups or key decision makers such as local politicians or neighborhood leadership," and **collective action**, which "refers to an individual's participation in collaborative resident efforts to address issues or influence decision-making, such as engagement in neighborhood block groups, citizen's committees, or neighborhood organizing efforts" (Foster-Fishman et al., 2007, p. 95). Measures of strategic collective action in communities are discussed in Chapter 5. Foster-Fishman and colleagues (2007) also include measures of neighborhood problems that could impact the desire and willingness of residents to become involved in improving their communities, including neighborhood disorder and crime (note: these types of measures are described in Chapter 11). The main goal of this study was to examine how community readiness and capacity as well as neighborhood problems impact the level of citizen engagement.

The above two studies provide multidimensional measures for citizen participation in neighborhoods. While the intent of these studies was not to create and test these measures, the researchers examined their reliability and validity, including testing the expected relationships among the hypothesized variables (see Tables 7.10 and 7.11 for these results). The researchers emphasize that it is important to clarify measures based on the targeted outcome of an intervention or relevant community needs (Foster-Fishman et al., 2007, 2009). Thus the items may change, as illustrated in differences among these measures in study one, which focused on residents living in the targeted communities versus study two, which purposively targeted residents who were engaged in the community building initiative and/or their neighborhoods. The overall findings from the first study demonstrated that neighborhood conditions were significantly related to whether and how much an individual engaged in individual or collective action. Moreover, different elements of neighborhood conditions seem to be important for different types and levels of resident involvement (Foster-Fishman et al., 2007, 2009).

- The overall findings from this research show that neighborhood conditions matter and are significantly related to whether and how much an individual engaged in individual or collective action. Logistic regressions were conducted to examine the following questions (Foster-Fishman et al., 2007, pp. 99–102):
- How are neighborhood capacity, readiness and problems related to whether individuals participate in individual activism or collective action?
    - Demographic variables were largely unimportant. Parenthood was marginally statistically significant to neighborhood activism but not collective action.
    - Residents who had children were 1.54X more likely to be involved in individual activism than those without children.
    - Neighborhood problems were the strongest predictor of individual activism and collective action.

- What neighborhood conditions (readiness, capacity, or problems) are related to how much residents participate in individual activism and collective action?
    - Results of the study indicated that neighborhood problems were significantly associated with individual activism but not with collective action.
    - Neighborhood leadership was statistically significant with both individual activism and collective action.
    - Hope was statistically associated with individual activism but not with collective action.
- Demographic variables predicted individual activism, but race was statistically associated with collective action.

The second study used structural equation models with observed variables to examine the hypotheses. The results showed that, when residents felt connected to their neighbors and believed that working together helped to create change, they were more likely to be active, engaged citizens. Greater neighborhood capacity and readiness for change was associated with individuals' perception that their neighbors would be engaged citizens and when they thought their neighbors would be engaged, residents were more likely to be active in their neighborhoods (Foster-Fishman et al., 2009).

- Norms for activism were significant direct predictors of citizen participation and were predicted by both collective efficacy and sense of community
- Hope was a significant predictor of collective efficacy that had a significant direct effect on norms. The indirect effect from hope on norms for activism was small.
- Neighborhood problems did not have a significant effect on citizen participation.
- Organizing skills was a significant direct predictor of norms for activism.
- Strong support that leadership status moderates the relationships between neighborhood conditions, skills, and citizen participation.
- Neighborhood norms for activism had a strong mediational role for followers but not leaders.
- Organizing skills was a positive predictor of citizen participation. It was stronger for leaders than followers.
- Sense of community and neighborhood problems were positive predictors of collective efficacy among followers but not leaders (Foster-Fishman et al., 2009, pp. 565–566).

Sampson and Graif (2009) developed a measure of **neighborhood activism** as part of the Project on Human Development in Chicago Neighborhoods (**Table 7.12**). Neighborhood activism is part of a measure of neighborhood social capital that is discussed in Chapter 6. Sampson and Graif's (2009) measure balances neighborhood activism to address a problem and to improve the neighborhood, including multiple vehicles for collective participation (e.g., political and religious), as well as participation in local organizations. The results demonstrated that the reliability, which was examined at the neighborhood level, was moderate to good (see Table 7.12).

- The results from this study suggest that the social capital of communities in Chicago encapsulates distinct and even divergent dimensions of social organization at the resident level and at the leadership level, including distinct dimensions of neighborhood social activism.
- Four dimensions of social capital emerge at the residential level, including collective efficacy, local networks, organizational involvement (which includes neighborhood activism), and conduct norms (Sampson & Graif, 2009, p. 1599–1600).

More information about the Project on Human Development in Chicago Neighborhoods is included in Chapter 6.

More recently, a multidimensional measure of **community mobilization (Table 7.13)** was developed by Lippman and colleagues (2016) that was designed to examine change at the community level as part of an HIV/AIDs prevention program in South Africa. The measure included six domains that synthesized prior community mobilization literature on social movements, community empowerment, development, and capacity, including: (a) **shared concerns** or community issues that may address power imbalances, improve access to resources and services, or promote social inclusion (the following as cited by Lippman et al., 2016: Tilly, 2004; Minkler and Wallerstein, 2002; Buechler, 1995; Edelman, 2001); (b) **critical consciousness**, collective sensitization processes and learning cultures (Freire, 1970, as cited by Lippman et al., 2016), which are at the heart of the community empowerment literature (the following as cited by Lippman et al., 2016: Minkler & Wallerstein, 2002; Laverack & Wallerstein, 2001; Norton et al., 2002); (c) **organizational structures, networks** or vehicles "through which people mobilize and engage in collective action" (McAdam, 1999, as cited by Lippman et al., 2016); (d) **leadership** at the individual, institutional, or coalition level (Laverack & Wallerstein, 2001; Norton et al., 2002); (e) **collective actions** (the "social movement repertoire") (Tilly, 2004, as cited in Lippman et al., 2016) and public participation in mobilization (Fawcett et al., 1995, as cited by Lippman et al., 2016); and (f) **social cohesion**, which is the "glue" that holds people together (Diani & Bison, 2004, as cited by Lippman et al., 2016), shared trust (Sampson, 2003, as cited by Lippman et al., 2016; Sampson et al., 1997), and sense of community (Norton et al., 2002; McMillan & Chavis, 1986, as cited in Lippman et al., 2016, p. 128).

Lippman and colleagues (2016) used "construct mapping" to develop and assess the items in their measure using a deductive approach, including qualitative research and multiple iterative steps (p. 128). The items for each of the six domains are included in Table 7.13. The researchers used item response modeling (IRM), exploratory factor analyses (EFA in the pilot), and confirmatory factor analysis (CFA in the main study) to examine each of the community mobilization instrument's domains. The CMM demonstrated robust reliability, while the factor analyses demonstrated a seven-dimensional model that fit the data the best, with linked domains but no higher order construct (Lippman et al., 2016, p. 128).

- The measure demonstrated robust reliability; the internal consistency reliability of the factors was strong, with r values ranging from 0.81 to 0.93.

- Results indicate the seven-dimensional model, with linked domains but no higher order construct, fit the data best.
- Construct validity was demonstrated at the individual level, based on model performance and synergies between the theory guiding the measure, qualitative data, and measurement results.
- Initial community-level analysis suggests evidence of construct validity, although evidence from larger, more heterogeneous samples is required to fully determine higher-level validity and reliability.
- At the village level, CMM subscales were correlated with other metrics of village social capital and integrity, providing initial evidence of higher-level validity; however, additional evaluation of the measure at the community-level is needed (Lippman et al., 2016, pp. 132–135).

CIVIC ENGAGEMENT

Defining Civic Engagement

Broadly defined, civic engagement "refers to the ways in which citizens participate in the life of a community in order to improve conditions for others or to help shape the community's future" (Adler & Goggin, 2005, p. 236). Civic engagement is conceptualized as a construct that "includes attitudes, behaviors, knowledge and skills that benefit society and derive from the interest in improving the common good" (Lenzi et al., 2012). Engaged citizens feel responsibility toward the communities in which they are embedded as well as toward the well-being of society as a whole. Engaged citizens exhibit civic behaviors and actions to "resolve community issues and improve the welfare of society, such as volunteer work and supporting charities," but they may also be a member of and/or participate in local organizations and institutions (Lenzi et al., 2012, p. 2). Zaff and colleagues (2010) define an active and engaged citizen as "someone who has a sense of civic duty, feeling of social connection to their community, confidence in their abilities to effect change, as well as someone who engages in civic behaviors" (p. 737).

The term *civic engagement* was traditionally applied to young people, so multiple methods have emerged to measure youth civic engagement. However, in the late 1990s, the term was used to promote greater civic engagement among adults (Adler & Goggin, 2005). *Civic Engagement* has been used to refer to political engagement, community service, and involvement in collective action or social change. It can also include individual levels of volunteerism, organizational participation, and involvement in the electoral process (Adler & Goggin, 2005). This section describes measures of civic engagement among young people as well as adults in the United States.

Civic Engagement Measures

Measuring civic engagement has taken multiple forms. For example, in a national survey research project sponsored by the Pew Charitable Trusts called *The Civic and Political Health of the Nation* (Keeter, Zukin, Andolina, & Jenkins, 2002), researchers examined civic engagement among Americans aged 15 to 55+. Keeter and colleagues (2002) created 19 indicators consisting of three main categories: (a) indicators of community-focused activities ("civic indicators"), including volunteering and raising funds for charitable causes; (b) indicators of participation in the electoral process, including voting and working for a candidate or a political party; and (c) indicators of political activity, including advocacy around particular issues or policies (Adler & Goggin, 2005, p. 242). Keeter and colleagues' (2002) **Civic Indicators Measure** is described in **Table 7.14.** Their study focused on developing a set of reliable indicators to measures political and civic engagement that could be used to identify community problems, compare communities across the country, and measure the impact of civic engagement programs before and after implementation (Keeter et al., 2002). The researchers examined civic engagement over the following four generations: (a) *DotNet generation* (born between 1977 and 1987); (b) *Generation X* (born between 1965 and 1976); (c) *Baby Boomers* (born between 1946 and 1964); and (d) the *Matures* (born in 1945 and before) (Keeter et al., 2002, p. 44). The study results showed that overall older adults or *Matures* are more civically engaged than other age groups, particularly in electoral activities. However, *Baby Boomers* and *GenXers* are more involved in community or civic engagement activities. Young people, particularly those in high school, volunteer the most, typically through service learning projects (Adler & Goggin, 2005). In fact, most young people are now expected to volunteer or participate in community service, because these factors are often examined on applications for higher education along with test scores and grades (Adler & Goggin, 2005). In addition, this study had the following specific results:

- Younger groups paid less attention to public affairs and electoral participation but were engaged in community-related and volunteer activities and in activities where they could voice to their concerns.
- Consumer activism was practiced by many individuals, with over 50% boycotting a company or product at some time in their lives, and almost as many bought something to reward a company for its practices.
- The results showed two distinct modes of engagement: the civic and political. Many choose one or the other forms of engagement: one in five (20%) specialize in the electoral realm (by voting, working for a candidate or party, for example); another 16% confined their efforts to the civic realm (working on problems in their community, raising money for charities or volunteering). Those who are active in *both* the civic and electoral arenas (16% overall) do not differ by race, gender, or political affiliation, but they are unique in their means of political expression, speaking more loudly and through a broader variety of channels than other citizens.
- Over half of those ages 15 to 25 are disengaged; 15% are involved in electoral politics only (compared to 20% overall); 17% limit their activities to the civic world. Just one in ten (11%) qualify as dual activists (Keeter et al., 2002, p. 1–2).

Doolittle and Faul (2013) report on the development and validation of the **Civic Engagement Scale (CES)** (see **Table 7.15**), which was developed for young adult social work and education college majors at three universities. The scale assesses the attitudes and behaviors affected by service-learning experiences. The researchers used Thomas Ehrlich's (1997) definition of civic engagement: "the process of believing that one *can* and *should* make a difference in enhancing his or her community" (Doolittle & Faul, 2013, p. 2). The CES measures two specific aspects of engagement: (a) *attitudes,* which are "the personal beliefs and feelings that individuals have about their own involvement in their community and their perceived ability to make a difference in that community," and (b) *behaviors,* which are "the actions that people take to actively attempt to engage and make a difference in their community" (Doolittle & Faul, 2013, p. 2). A pilot version of the scale was developed based on prior literature and then feedback was provided by a group of bachelor's students as well as faculty members who assessed the content, comprehensiveness, and language (Doolittle & Faul, 2013, p. 2). The purpose of this study was to examine the psychometric characteristics of the scale, including the reliability and validity. Reliability of the final scale was good, and the principal components factor analysis resulted in a two-dimensional scale with high loadings on both factors.

- For factorial validity, principal component analysis (PCA) with a varimax rotation was used to examine the factorial structure of the scale.
- PCA indicated a two-dimensional scale with a high loading on both factors (mean factor loading for the attitude factor = .79, and mean factor loading for the behavior factor = .77). These results indicate evidence of acceptable factorial validity.
- Content validity was also assessed: An item analysis was conducted for the CES to determine whether its items significantly contributed to the total score. Each item on the CES was correlated with its own total score and with the subscale. The removal of item self-correlations resulted in a content validity coefficient of .71 for the attitudes scale and .65 for the behaviors scale.
- The attitude scale was reduced from 11 to 8 items, and the behavior scale was reduced from 11 to 6 items (Dolittle & Faul, 2013, pp. 3–5).
- Discriminant validity was demonstrated by the CES not correlating demographic variables such as gender, number of children, and age.
- Convergent validity, on the scale level, was demonstrated by the CES correlating moderately with another measure called the CSAS (e.g., which consists of eight factors: normative helping, connectedness, costs, awareness, benefits, seriousness, career benefits, and intentions).

The authors state that the limitation of this scale was its development among White, college-educated women, so additional research is needed to generalize this measure for use in other populations (Doolittle & Faul, 2013).

Several civic engagement measures for young people have been developed by researchers examining data from students involved in the 4-H positive youth development study (Bobek et al., 2009; Zaff et al., 2010). The 4-H national longitudinal research study examined the connections between "youth development and individual and ecological resources for positive, healthy development present in the homes, schools and communities of youth" (Bobek et al., 2009, p. 616). Bobek and colleagues (2009) developed an integrated measure of civic engagement (see **Table 7.16**) to include civic behaviors, civic skills, civic connections, and civic commitment of youth, which they call **Civic Identity/Civic Engagement (CICE).** The CICE is rooted in several theories. The first theory is "Erikson's ego identity theory," which involves "a search for a sense of self that reflects a role meeting individual and societal needs" (Erikson, 1963, as cited in Bobek et al., 2009; Marcia, 1980, as cited in Bobek et al., 2009, p. 615). The measure is also informed by German action theories suggesting that "adaptive development involves mutually beneficial relations between the actions of the individual on the context (e.g., engagement with or contributes to the institutions of civil society) and the actions of the context on the individual (e.g., constraining or promoting individual behavior)" (Baltes, 1987, as cited in Bobek et al., 2009; Baltes, Lindenberger, & Staudinger, 2006, as cited in Bobek et al., 2009; Freund & Baltes, 2002, as cited in Bobek et al., 2009, p. 615). The CICE includes the following emotional, cognitive, and behavioral components of civic engagement among youth: social cohesion, civic skills, civic commitment or duty, and civic action. The researchers used a three-step expert rater validation process to identify the set of items within the 4-H study data set that could be used to operationalize the CICE constructs, including engaging current or past graduate-level researchers involved in the 4-H study and getting feedback on the final list of items from 21 "expert" raters in the field of civic engagement and identity development (Bobek et al., 2009). Once a final set of items was agreed upon, Bobek and colleagues (2009) used confirmatory and exploratory factor analyses to develop the CICE and also examined differences in CICE between participation in the 4-H program and other youth development activities. Their research resulted in a six-factor structure for the CICE with 42 items. Reliability of the overall measure and subscales was also assessed and is reported in Table 7.16. Moreover, participation in 4-H predicted five of the six CICE factors, and three factors were significantly related to 4-H participation versus other youth development programs.

- Confirmatory and exploratory factor analyses were conducted to examine whether the 48 indicators identified by the expert raters corresponded to the hypothesized four factors (positive civic attitudes; civic engagement; social capital and social trust; and civic knowledge and skills).
- A four-component model of the CICE was not supported. Eight factors were identified and then reduced to six factors based on theory. The six factors included civic duty, civic skills, neighborhood social connection, peer social connection, adult social connection, and civic participation. Of the 48 original items, 42 were found theoretically meaningful and comprised these six factors that integrated cognitive (skills), emotional (connection and duty), and behavioral (participation) aspects of civic engagement.
- Presence of discriminant validity was supported by the finding that none of the 15 distractor items rated was substantively relevant by the 80% criterion.
- The Cronbach alphas were sufficiently high, and the mean score of CICE suggests that the measure may be tapping a development process for young people.
- A regression analysis demonstrated that 4-H participation predicted five of the six CICE factors and overall CICE, even when holding for race, gender, socioeconomic status. 4-H participation significantly predicted three of the factors (civic duty, civic voice, and peer social connection) while participation in other youth development organizations did not (Bobeck et al., 2009, pp. 624–626).

Zaff and colleagues (2010) examined a measure of civic engagement for youth that built on the work of Bobek and colleagues (2009) (see **Table 7.17** for a description of the **Active and Engaged Citizenship** measure). The goal of the study was to "refine the initial measurement model and test the factor structure and validity of the refined model across three years of adolescence and for boys and girls," using data from the 4-H Study of Positive Youth Development (Zaff et al., 2010, p. 737). The sample for Zaff and colleagues' study included data from 909 adolescents who took part in assessments for Grades 8 through 10 in the longitudinal study. In addition, they assessed whether social connections to peers and adults in one's neighborhood were necessary components or rather predictors of civic engagement. They hypothesized that a valid measurement model for boys and girls could be identified and that there would be measurement invariance for boys and girls as well as longitudinally (Zaff et al., 2010, p. 738). The researchers conducted a series of second order confirmatory factor analyses to assess their hypotheses. Four first order factors of civic engagement were produced, and reliability analyses were also conducted (as described in Table 7.17). Their research resulted in a more parsimonious and theoretically refined measurement model of civic engagement than the one developed by Bobek and colleagues (2009) by eliminating the items examining social connections to adults and peers (Zaff et al., 2010). The results also demonstrated that the factor structure held across time, "thus enabling researchers to examine change, such as growth or trajectories of engagement" (Zaff et al., 2010, p. 747). Finally, the researchers found that the structure of their measure of civic engagement held across sex, which allowed a comparison across the groups (Zaff et al., 2010).

- Confirmatory factor analysis was used to identify four first-order factors of civic engagement (civic participation, civic duty, civic skills, and neighborhood social connection) that comprised a second-order factor of AEC.
- The authors believe that the current model provides a more theoretically refined measurement model of AEC than the 6-factor model identified in Bobek et al., 2009.
- By focusing on the community, the authors believe that this study is more theoretically sound because feeling a connection to community appears to be essential for engaging in community affairs. This differs from the previous model that included social connection to adults and peers.
- Connections to adults and peers were a predictor of future engagement but not an essential component of current engagement. The study found that the factor structure held across time, enabling researchers to examine change (Zaff et al., 2010, pp. 746–748).

Limitations to this research (Bobek et al., 2009; Zaff et al., 2010) include not testing for cultural relevance or sensitivity to accurately portray civic engagement among diverse ethnic/racial, income, or geographic groups. Moreover, these measures of civic engagement are focused primarily on community service versus other forms of engagement, such as advocacy or working within the political system (Zaff et al., 2010).

CONCLUSION

The earliest measures of community engagement and empowerment were developed by community psychologists in the late 1980s to assess the connection between community participation and cognitive, behavioral, personality, and emotional empowerment among residents and college students. Empowerment measures were developed to assess an individual's efficacy, confidence, leadership ability, and general and political perceptions of control as they related to their engagement in communities. Measures for psychological empowerment and sociopolitical control were developed for both adults and youth, which allow for a more targeted assessment of the ways in which these two groups are empowered. The measure of community empowerment assesses three areas of perceived control at the individual, organizational, and community levels. While a substantive amount of research has been conducted to develop individual measures of empowerment in community settings, additional research is needed to examine overall community empowerment measures.

The majority of community participation and neighborhood activism measures focus on involvement in community organizations and engaging behaviors, including actions taken to address community issues. One study also examined neighborhood norms for activism as well as organizing skills, which are also important for the efficacious and mutual engagement of residents in addressing neighborhood problems (Foster-Fishman et al., 2009). Community participation and neighborhood activism measures focus on smaller geographic areas and a more narrow focus on involvement in local organizations, while civic engagement measures are broader, focusing on civic skills and duty as well as social connections that advance, motivate, and/or encourage engagement. Measures of civic engagement have also been developed specifically for youth; however, additional research is needed to develop community participation and neighborhood activism measures for youth, particularly given the growth of youth organizing and community engagement initiatives.

Community empowerment and engagement have become central features in community-based prevention and intervention research among multiple disciplines. Communities today face complicated issues that are beyond the ability of any one organization and/or individual to address. Engaging and empowering residents is needed to focus on proactive solutions developed by the people who are the most impacted by neighborhood problems. Reliable and valid measures are needed to accurately capture how residents become engaged and empowered as they address the multiple issues in their communities and advocate for changes in policies and programs.

LIST OF MEASURES AND TABLE NUMBERS

TABLE 7.1 ■ Psychological Empowerment and Citizen Participation	
Primary Reference	Zimmerman, M. A., & Rappaport, J. (1988). Citizen participation, perceived control and psychological empowerment. *American Journal of Community Psychology, 16*(5), 725–750.
Purpose	The authors used a series of three studies to examine the relationship between psychological empowerment and participation among college students and community residents. A goal of the study was to identify a common theme that describes an empowered individual.

Description	**Psychological empowerment** was measured using 11 dependent variables that were selected to represent personality, cognitive, and motivational aspects of empowerment.
	• **Personality Measures**: locus of control, chance control, believe in powerful others, and control ideology. Taken from:
	  ○ Levenson (1974)
	  ○ Gurin, Gurin, Lao, and Beattie (1969)
	• **Cognitive Measures**: self and political efficacy expectations: the belief that one has the skills and ability to achieve goals.
	  ○ General Self-Efficacy: Tipton and Worthington (1984), 10-item scale
	  ○ Sense of Mastery: Pearlin, Menaghan, Lieberman, and Mullan (1981)
	  ○ Perceived confidence: 4-item scale developed by Florin and Wandersman (1984)
	• **Political Efficacy**: belief that it is possible to influence the political process and community decision-making. Developed by Craig and Magiotto (1982)
	• **Motivational measures**:
	  ○ Desire for Control Scale (Burger & Cooper, 1979)
	  ○ Civic Duty (Florin & Wandersman, 1984)
	Measures to assess convergent and discriminant validity
	• **Leadership**: Respondents asked to indicate on 4-point Likert scale whether or not they would be willing to volunteer to be a group leader
	• **Alienation** (Dean, 1961): 3 subscales (powerlessness, normlessness, and social isolation)
	Covariates: to control for possible confounds introduced by response bias and one's need for affiliation:
	• Social desirability scale (Jackson's Personality Research Form ([PRF], 1967)
	• Desire to affiliate with others (Buss & Plomin, 1975)
	Citizen Participation Measures:
	• **Participation in Community Activities**: measured by a checklist of 26 activities. Participants were asked to check all activities that they had participated in during the past year, such as
	  ○ Voting
	  ○ Signing a petition
	  ○ Organizing people
	  ○ Attending meetings
	  ○ Contributing money to organizations
	  ○ Writing letters to government officials
	  ○ Working on political campaigns
	• **Level of involvement in community organizations:** was operationalized as the amount of effort participants expended in organizations that they are involved in. For each organization, participants were asked to report things such as

	○ Number of hours spent volunteering ○ Length of time involved in the organization ○ How regularly they attended meetings ○ Number of leadership positions held (e.g., political groups, self-help groups, service organizations, church groups) A composite measure was computed, resulting in high, moderate, and low involvement. A fourth group of not involved in any organizations was used as a comparison.
Sample	**Study 1**: Three hundred ninety-two students randomly selected from students enrolled in an introductory psychology course. Ten groups of 40 students were given a questionnaire to complete in a one-hour session: mean age (18.95), White (88%), and middle class. Hypothetical scenarios were used. **Study 2**: Respondents were the same, but naturalistic behaviors were used; groups were classified into involvement in community activities and membership in voluntary organizations. **Study 3**: There were 176 community residents. Nine organizational leaders were asked to invite their membership to participate in the research. Organizations were selected to represent several political viewpoints and goals. Questionnaires were distributed to members at an organizational meeting • Return rate was 85% (176 out of 205). • The sample was mostly White (92%), married (66%), men (45%), women (55%), mean age (41.94), mostly middle class. • Comparison group participants were recruited by random telephone numbers. After screening, those who agreed to participate were mailed a questionnaire: 22 individuals completed questionnaires (64% response rate).
Assessment	• Reliability was not provided in the article. • The authors conducted a discriminant function analysis to examine the dimensions of psychological empowerment in each study sample. They found one significant dimension that they identified as psychological empowerment that was positively correlated with leadership and negatively correlated with alienation.
Results	• The results of the three studies supported the hypothesis that greater participation in community activities and organizations is associated with psychological empowerment. • In each study, personality, cognitive, and motivational measures significantly contributed to distinguishing high and low participation groups. • Students and residents involved in community organizations had a greater sense of empowerment than their less-involved counterparts. • Student and residents reported a greater sense of political efficacy, competence and mastery, desire for control, more civic duty, and a belief that their success is a result of internal rather than external factors (Zimmerman & Rappaport, 1988, p. 746).
Language	English
Contact	Marc A. Zimmerman, PhD Department of Health Behavior and Health Education School of Public Health, University of Michigan 3702 SPH 1 1415 Washington Heights Ann Arbor, Michigan 48109 Email: marcz@umich.edu

TABLE 7.2 ■ Empowerment Scale for Citizen Participation in Community Organizing Contexts

Primary Reference	Speer, P. W., & Peterson, N. A. (2000). Psychometric properties of an empowerment scale: Testing cognitive, emotional, and behavioral domains. *Social Work Research, 24*(2), 109–117.
Purpose	Designed to measure empowerment at an individual level of analysis that captured cognitive, emotional, and behavioral dimensions in community organizing contexts.
Description	The empowerment scale is a 27-item instrument with three scales (please see the primary source for information on all of the items) **Cognitive empowerment** is measured with 16 items in three subscales: • **Power developed through relationships (5 items):** sample items include: ○ I can have power in my community only by working in an organized way with other people ○ Power is collective, not individual ○ Power lies in the relationships among people • **Political functioning (5 items):** sample items include ○ Public officials make decisions to please those with power ○ Things happen in my community because those with power reward their friends ○ The powerful control what information gets to the public • **Shaping ideology (4 items):** sample items include ○ What a community talks about depends on what residents are interested in ○ Community perceptions depend on the quality of individuals in that community **Emotional Empowerment** was measured with an abbreviated 6-item Social Political Control Scale (SPCS), which consisted of two subscales: • **Perceived Leadership Competence (3 items):** sample items include ○ I am often a leader in groups • **Political Efficacy (3 items):** sample items include ○ I feel like I have a pretty good understanding of the important political issues that confront our society **Behavioral Empowerment:** This scale is a measure of **Citizen Participation:** the measure included an 8-item self-report of **community action behavior** over a three month period. Sample items include • Signed a petition • Attended an event promoting information about community services • Attended a meeting to gather information about a neighborhood issue Other variables measured in this study included • Sense of community (McMillan & Chavis, 1986; included in Chapter 6) • Organizational membership: asked whether respondents were members of community groups such as faith organizations, school or parent groups, and civic or community organizations (these types of measures are in Chapter 5) • Perceived involvement of institutions in the local community: asked participants to rate the level of involvement of institutions such as the police and government in working with residents to improve their neighborhood

Sample	• A sample of 974 randomly selected residents of six municipalities in North Eastern United States; the response rate was 56%. • The survey was administered by eight trained interviews via phone. The survey lasted 20–30 minutes. • The sample was 60% female, 85% White, and 60% were between the ages of 18 and 45 years old; 65% were homeowners.
Scoring	No information is provided on measurement or scoring.
Assessment	The following alphas were reported for the psychological empowerment subscales: Cognitive empowerment • Power developed through relationships: 0.72 • Political functioning: 0.78 • Shaping ideology: 0.77 Emotional empowerment • Perceived leadership competence: 0.47 • Political efficacy: 0.56 Behavioral empowerment: 0.78
Language	English
Contact	Paul W Speer, PhD Department of Human & Organizational Development Vanderbilt University Box 90 GPC, Nashville, Tennessee 37203 Email: paul.w.speer@vanderbilt.edu

TABLE 7.3 ■ Psychological Empowerment Among Urban Youth

Primary Reference	Ozer, E. J., & Schotland, M. (2011). Psychological empowerment among urban youths. Measure development and relationship to psychological functioning. *Health Education & Behavior, 38*(4), 348–356.
Purpose	The purpose of this study was to develop a self-report survey measure of psychological empowerment that is not linked to an intervention but can be used to operationalize and investigate this construct for the study of child and adolescent development.
Description	This measure initially consisted of 61 items covering four conceptual areas. Following analysis, the final measure included 26 items. Response scales were on a 4-point Likert scale (*strongly disagree* to *strongly agree*). Community researchers can adapt the items to focus more on community versus school youth-led programs. The four domains are described below (please see primary source for information on all items): **Sociopolitical skills (8 items):** Sample items include • I feel like I have a pretty good understanding of the important political issues that confront our society. • I am often a leader in groups. • I can usually figure out how much to get an adult to see my point of view, even if they don't agree with me. • If I want to improve a problem in my city, I know how to gather useful data about the issue. **Motivation to influence (4 items):** Sample items include • It is important for youth to try to improve our city even if we can't always make the changes we want. • I want to have as much say as possible in making decisions in my city. **Participatory behavior (8 items):** Sample items include • I have led a group of young people working on an issue we care about. • I have interviewed an adult to learn their perspectives about an issue. • If issues come up that affect youth in my city, we do something about it. • I have spoken with other youth about issues that I want to improve in the city. **Perceived control (6 items):** Sample items include • Students at this school get to help plan special activities and events. • There are plenty of ways for young people like me to have a say in what our city government does. • Youth have a say in what happens in this city.
Scoring	Mean scores are calculated.
Sample	• A sample of 439 high school students from four schools and several summer programs in a West Coast urban community were used in this study. • Sample recruitment was intended to maximize diversity of the adolescents. • The average age was 16 years old, 61% were female, 29% were Chinese, 28% were Latino, 8% were African American, 7% European American, 5% Filipino, 23% Other. The ethnic diversity of the sample paralleled the overall school district. • Graduate-level members of the research team administered the 45-minute survey and assisted with questions.

Assessment	• Sociopolitical skills: $\alpha = 0.81$ • Motivation to influence: $\alpha = 0.80$ • Participatory behavior: $\alpha = 0.83$ • Perceived control: $\alpha = 0.80$
Related Reference	Zimmerman, M. A., & Zahniser, J. H. (1991). Refinements of sphere-specific measures of perceived control: Development of a sociopolitical control scale. *Journal of Community Psychology, 19*(2), 189–204.
Language	English
Contact	Emily J. Ozer 50 University Hall Berkeley, CA 94720-7360 Email: eozer@berkeley.edu

TABLE 7.4 ■	Psychological Empowerment Among Urban Youth
Primary Reference	Eisman, A. B., Zimmerman, M. A., Kruger, D., Reischl, T. M., Miller, A. L., Franzen, S. P., & Morrell-Samuels, S. (2016). Psychological empowerment among urban youth: Measurement model and associations with youth outcomes. *American Journal of Community Psychology, 58,* 410–421.
Purpose	The purpose of this study was to develop a survey measure of psychological empowerment that consisted of three domains: intrapersonal, interactional, and behavioral.
Description	The measure examined the following three components (please see the primary source for information on all of the items): **1. Intrapersonal component:** Respondents were asked about their level of agreement regarding the following areas, on a scale from 1 = *strongly disagree* to 5 = *strongly agree:* **Leadership efficacy (3 items):** (adapted from Zimmerman & Zahniser, 1991; see Table 7.5 below) • I am often a leader in groups. • I can usually organize people to get things done. **Civic efficacy (3 items):** Asked participants if they felt they could • Be involved in community change • Make their community better by helping others **Self esteem (5 items):** (Rosenberg, 1965) • On the whole, I am satisfied with myself. • I am able to do things as well as most other people. • I feel I do not have much to be proud of (reverse coded). **2. Interactional component** **Adult mentorship (5 items):** Participants indicated how often a mentor engaged in the following behaviors, on a scale from 1 = *once a year* or less to 5 = *every day*: • Encouragement • Providing useful information and advice • Listens when you need to talk **Adult resources (3 items):** asked participants how many adults young people knew who could provide cognitive and/or instrumental support in the following areas, on a scale from 1 = *none* to 5 = *four or more*: • Solve a neighborhood problem • Solve the city/town problems **Resource mobilization (4 items):** asked respondents their level of agreement with the following statements, on a scale from 1 = *strongly disagree* to 5 = *strongly agree*: • Working with others on a community project makes the project better • Adults can help me do a community project

	3. Behavioral component **Leadership behavior (3 items):** (adapted from Zimmerman & Zahniser, 1991) asked participants how often they engaged in the following behaviors, on a scale from 1 = *never* to 5 = *always*: • Being a leader in groups • Organizing people to get things done **Community and school engagement (4 items):** (adapted from the Dept. of Education's community engagement scale, U.S DOE, 2004) asked participants about their level of agreement regarding participating in the following activities, on a scale from 1 = *strongly disagree* to 5 = *strongly agree*: • Participate in neighborhood/school activities • Encourage others to do things to help improve their school/neighborhood
Scoring	Mean scores are calculated.
Sample	• Participants were involved in a longitudinal study evaluating the developmental outcomes of the Youth Empowerment Solutions (YES) afterschool program. • They were randomly assigned to the YES program after completing a pre-test or the usual afterschool program. • The participants were middle school students from Michigan. • The sample included 367 youth aged 11–16 (M=12.71), 60% were female; 32% White, 46% African American; 22% mixed race; 14% were from Flint City schools with the rest from adjacent school districts (none from rural areas); 61–75% of the students participated in the free/reduced lunch program.
Assessment	• Leadership efficacy: $\alpha = 0.67$ • Civic efficacy: $\alpha = 0.81$ • Self-esteem: $\alpha = 0.68$ • Adult mentorship: $\alpha = 0.87$ • Adult resources: $\alpha = 0.66$ • Resource mobilization: $\alpha = 0.78$ • Leadership behaviors: $\alpha = 0.76$ • School and community engagement: $\alpha = 0.85$
Related Reference	Zimmerman, M. A., & Zahniser, J. H. (1991). Refinements of sphere-specific measures of perceived control: Development of a sociopolitical control scale. *Journal of Community Psychology, 19*(2), 189–204.
Language	English
Contact	Andria B. Eisman Department of Health Behavior and Health Education University of Michigan School of Public Health Ann Arbor, MI USA aeisman@umich.edu

TABLE 7.5 ■	Community Empowerment
Primary Reference	Israel, B. A., Checkoway, B., Shultz, A., & Zimmerman, M. A. (1994). Health education and community empowerment: Conceptualizing and measuring perceptions of individual, organizational and community control. *Health Education Quarterly, 21,* 149–170.
Purpose	Designed to measure community empowerment at three levels of analysis, individual, organizational, and community. The indices measure the perceptions of control at the three levels.
Description	This is a **12-item measure** with three subscales. Respondents rated each item on a four-point scale with 1 = *disagree strongly* to 4 = *agree strongly*. Please see the primary source for information on all of the items. **Perceived control at organizational level: (5 items)** • I can influence the decisions that this organization makes. • This organization is effective in achieving its goals. • This organization can influence decisions that affect the community. **Perceived control at the individual level: (2 items)** • I have control over the decisions that affect my life. • I am satisfied with the amount of control I have over decisions that affect my life. **Perceived control at the community level: (5 items)** • My community has influence over decisions that affect my life. • I can influence decisions that affect my community. • By working together, people in my community can influence decisions that affect the community.
Sample	916 randomly selected adults from 47 communities in the Greater Detroit Area. (This study was conducted through the Detroit Area Study, a large random survey conducted yearly with different yearly objectives.)
Scoring	Scoring constitutes the sum of items in the subscale. The sum of all 12 items is perceived control at multiple levels.
Assessment	Overall scale: $\alpha = 0.71$ Perceived control at organizational level: $\alpha = 0.61$ Perceived control at the individual level: $\alpha = 0.66$ Perceived control at the community level: $\alpha = 0.63$
Language	English
Contact	Barbara A. Israel, PhD Department of Health Behavior and Health Education School of Public Health The University of Michigan 1420 Washington Heights Ann Arbor, MI 48109-2029

TABLE 7.6 ■ Sociopolitical Control Scale (SPCS)

Primary Reference	Zimmerman, M. A., & Zahniser, J. H. (1991). Refinements of sphere-specific measures of perceived control: Development of a sociopolitical control scale. *Journal of Community Psychology, 19*(2), 189–204.
Purpose	Designed to measure sociopolitical control. Sociopolitical control refers to beliefs about one's capabilities and efficacy in social and political systems.
Description	The Sociopolitical Control Scale is a self-report, 17-item instrument with two subscales. Participants are asked to respond by using a five-point Likert-scale ranging from *strongly disagree* to *strongly agree*. Please see the primary source for a description of all of the items. **Leadership competence: (8 items)** (one's confidence in leadership skills) • I am often a leader in groups. • I would prefer to be a leader rather than a follower. • I can usually organize people to get things done. • Other people usually follow my ideas. **Policy control: (9 items)** (the belief that one can influence policy decisions) • I enjoy political participation because I want to have as much say in running government as possible. • I feel like I have a pretty good understanding of the important political issues which confront our society. • People like me are generally well qualified to participate in political activity and decision-making in our country. • There are plenty of ways for people like me to have a say in what our government does. • Most public officials wouldn't listen to me no matter what I did.
Sample	Three studies and samples were used: **Study 1**: 392 students randomly selected from students enrolled in an introductory psychology course. Ten groups of 40 students were given a questionnaire to complete in a one-hour session. Mean age (18.95), White (88%), and middle class. **Study 2**: 205 community residents. They were recruited at voluntary organization meetings (*N* = 183; 85% return rate) and by random digit dialing (*N* = 22; 64% return rate). The sample was mostly White (92%); men (45%), and women (55%); mean age (41.94); mostly middle class. Comparison group participants were recruited by random telephone numbers. **Study 3:** 143 members (55% return rate) of four Free Methodist churches located in geographic regions different from the first two studies; 52% were women; predominantly White (96%); average age was 38.
Scoring	Mean scores were calculated.
Assessment	Internal consistency of scales was similar in all three studies: • Study 1: Cronbach alpha for leadership competence = .78 Policy control = .75 • Study 2: Cronbach alpha for both subscales = 0.76 • Study 3: Cronbach alpha for leadership competence = .76 Policy control = .75

(*Continued*)

TABLE 7.6 ■ (Continued)	
Related References	Peterson, N. S., Lowe, J. B., Hughey, J., Reid, R. J., Zimmerman, M. A., & Speer, P. W. (2006). Measuring the intrapersonal component of psychological empowerment: Confirmatory factor analysis of the sociopolitical control scale. *American Journal of Community Psychology, 38,* 287–297. Peterson, N. A, Peterson, C. H., Agre, L, Christens, B. D., & Morton, C. M. (2011). Measuring youth empowerment: Validation of a sociopolitical control scale for youth in an urban context. *Journal of Community Psychology, 39*(5), 592–605. Christens, B. D., Peterson, N. A., & Speer, P. W. (2011). Community participation and psychological empowerment: Testing reciprocal causality using a cross-lagged panel design and latent constructs. *Health Education & Behavior, 38*(4), 339–347.
Language	English
Contact	M. A. Zimmerman Department of Health Behavior & Health Education School of Public Health University of Michigan Ann Arbor, MI, USA

TABLE 7.7 ■ Sociopolitical Control Scale-Revised (SPCS-R)	
Primary Reference	Peterson, N. S., Lowe, J. B., Hughey, J., Reid, R. J., Zimmerman, M. A., & Speer, P.W. (2006). Measuring the intrapersonal component of psychological empowerment: Confirmatory factor analysis of the sociopolitical control scale. *American Journal of Community Psychology, 38,* 287–297.
Purpose	The purpose of this study was to use confirmatory factor analysis to test the hypothesized structure of the SPCS, potential effects of method bias on the psychometric properties, and whether a revised version of the scale (negatively items rephrased to positive) resulted in an improved fit.
Description	This study revised items from the original 17-item SPCS developed and tested by Zimmerman and Zahniser (1991). All items were answered using a 5-point Likert scale (*strongly disagree* to *strongly agree*). A subsample received the alternate version, where all items were rephrased positively. The following shows the items that were revised from the original SPSC scale and how they were revised in the current study. **Leadership competence: (4 out of 8 items were revised)** • Original item: I would rather someone else took over the leadership role when I'm involved in a group project. ○ Revised: I would rather have a leadership role when I'm involved in a group project. • Original item: I find it very hard to talk in front of a group. ○ Revised: I find it very easy to talk in front of a group. • Original item: I like to wait and see if someone else is going to solve a problem so that I don't have to be bothered by it. ○ Revised: I like to work on solving a problem myself rather than wait and see if someone else will deal with it. • Original item: I would rather not try something I'm not good at. ○ Revised: I like trying new things that are challenging to me. **Policy control: (5 out of 9 items were revised)** • Original item: Sometimes politics and government seem so complicated that a person like me can't really understand what's going on. ○ Revised: A person like me can really understand what's going on with government and politics. • Original item: It hardly makes any difference who I vote for because whoever gets elected does whatever he wants to do anyway. ○ Revised: It makes a difference who I vote for because whoever gets elected will represent my interests. • Original item: So many other people are active in local issues and organizations that it doesn't matter much to me whether I participate or not. ○ Revised: It is important to me that I actively participate in local issues. • Original item: Most public officials wouldn't listen to me no matter what I did. ○ Revised: Most public officials would listen to me. • Original item: A good many local elections aren't important enough to bother with. ○ Revised: A good many local elections are important to vote in.

(*Continued*)

TABLE 7.7 ■ (Continued)	
Sample	Two samples were used in this study. • The first sample included 316 participants who were from a rural Midwestern community. Participants were selected using random sampling from a telephone directory. Participants were interviewed face-to-face; the interviews lasted approximately 60–90 minutes. Most participants were female (58%) and non-Hispanic White (98.4%). • The second sample included 750 participants from a large Northeastern U.S. city. Probability proportionate to size sampling procedures was used to select the sample. Measures were administered via phone interviews that lasted approximately 25–45 minutes. Most participants were female (58%); 46% were African American, 29% were Hispanic, and 20% were non-Hispanic White.
Scoring	Mean scores were calculated.
Assessment	Alpha values are for subscale where items that were rephrased positively. • Leadership competence: $\alpha = 0.78$ • Policy control: $\alpha = 0.81$
Related Reference	Smith, P. D., & Propst, D. B. (2001). Are topic-specific measures of socio-political control justified? Exploring the realm of citizen participation in natural resource decision making. *Journal of Community Psychology, 29*, 179–187.
Language	English
Contact	N. Andrew Peterson Rutgers University, School of Social Work 536 George Street New Brunswick, NY 08901 Email: Andrew.peterson@ssw.rutgers.edu

TABLE 7.8 ■ Sociopolitical Control Scale for Youth (SPCS-Y)

Primary Reference	Peterson N. A, Peterson, C. H., Agre, L., Christens, B. D., & Morton, C. M. (2011). Measuring youth empowerment: Validation of a sociopolitical control scale for youth in an urban context. *Journal of Community Psychology, 39*(5), 592–605.
Purpose	Designed to measure youths' sense of sociopolitical control, through the two dimensions of leadership competence and policy control

Description	The 17-item scale consists of two subscales: leadership competence **(eight items)** and policy control **(nine items)**. All items are positively worded to be consistent with Peterson and colleagues (2006) and rated on a 5-point scale ranging from *strongly disagree* to *strongly agree*.
	
	The **leadership competency** scale remained the same as SPCS-R (please see **Table 7.7** for this scale, Peterson et al., 2006). Below are the items from the SPCS-R that were changed to specifically assess youth sociopolitical control. The policy control items were revised to reference "community or school" to be consistent with a study by Holden and colleagues (2004).
	
	Policy Control (all items were revised). Some of the revised items include
	• A person like me can really understand what's going on with government and politics.
	  ○ Revised: Youth like me can really understand what's going on with my community or school.
	• I feel like I have a pretty good understanding of the important political issues which confront our society.
	  ○ Revised: I feel like I have a pretty good understanding of the important issues which confront my community or school.
	• People like me are generally well qualified to participate in political activity and decision making in our country.
	  ○ Revised: Youth like me have the ability to participate effectively in community or school activities and decision-making.
	• There are plenty of ways for people like me to have a say in what our government does.
	  ○ Revised: There are plenty of ways for youth like me to have a say in what our community or school does.
	• It is important to me that I actively participate in local issues.
	  ○ Revised: It is important to me that I actively participate in local teen issues.
	• A good many local elections are important to vote in.
	  ○ Revised: Many local activities are important to participate in.

Sample	The sample consisted of 865 urban high school students from the northeastern United States; 60% were female and 40% male; 55% Hispanic, 37% African American, 4% Asian and 4% White, non-Hispanic; 16% of the students were in 9th grade, 23% were in 10th grade, 29% were in 11th grade, and 33% were in 12th grade.
Scoring	Mean scores were calculated. Higher scores indicate higher levels of sociopolitical control.
Assessment	Cronbach's alpha for the overall scale = .81.

(Continued)

TABLE 7.8 ■ (Continued)	
Related References	Holden, D. J., Crankshaw, E., Nimsch, C., Hinnant, L. W., & Hund, L. (2004). Quantifying the impact of participation in local tobacco control groups on the psychological empowerment of involved youth. *Health Education & Behavior, 31*, 615–628. Holden, D. J., Evans, W. D., Hinnant, L. W., & Messeri, P. (2005). Modeling psychological empowerment among youth involved in local tobacco control efforts. *Health Education & Behavior, 32*, 264–278.
Language	English
Contact	N. Andrew Peterson Rutgers University, School of Social Work 536 George Street New Brunswick, NY 08901 Email: Andrew.peterson@ssw.rutgers.edu

TABLE 7.9 ■	Citizen Participation in Block Associations
Primary Reference	Perkins, D., Florin, P., Rich, R., Wandersman, A., & Chavis, D. (1990). Participation and the social and physical environment of residential blocks: Crime and community context. *American Journal of Community Psychology, 18*, 83–115.
Purpose	The purpose of this study was to examine the characteristics of community environments related to resident participation in block associations, focusing on contextual factors as predictors of participation.

Description	The participation scale consists of four equally weighted dimensions each aggregated by block: from the resident survey, (a) how active the association is perceived to be, (b) the mean time (hours per month) working for the association outside of meetings, (c) the mean level of different forms of organizational responsibility among residents in the preceding year, and (d) the mean of ten, more detailed, level of responsibility items from the block association member survey. Please see the primary source article and its appendix for a detailed description of all of the measures and items in the study.
	
	Participation in block association activities. This scale asked several questions about residents' participation in their block association, including
	• Would you say that this block association is very active, moderately active, or largely inactive?
	• Have you ever taken part in an activity sponsored by the block association?
	• How many hours would you say you give to the block association each month outside of meetings, if any?
	• In the past year, have you **(5 items)**
	  ○ Served as an officer or as a committee chair?
	  ○ Spoken up during a meeting?
	  ○ Done work for the organization outside of meetings?
	
	Block Association Member Survey: includes the last four measures above and six additional measures, where members were asked: In the past 12 months, have you . . .
	• Helped organize activities (other than meetings) for the association?
	• Participated in activities other than meetings (block party, cleanup)?
	• Tried to recruit new members?
	• Served as a representative of the association to other community groups?
	
	Several other measures were included in this study and explained in the article, including communitarianism, sense of community, perceived block association efficacy, block satisfaction, perceived incivilities, perceived crime problems. A measure was also developed for the purpose of assessing both the built and transient, crime and fear-related physical environment of urban residential areas. Rates of reported crime data at the block level were also collected from the New York City Police Department. (Note: because several of these types of measures are discussed in other chapters of this book, we do not include a detailed description here.)

Sample	• Data were obtained from 48 New York City blocks using (a) a telephone survey of residents (n = 1,081), (b) the Block Environmental Inventory (BEI), (c) police records of reported crime, and (d) a survey of block association members (n = 469). • The telephone survey (response rate 58.7%) sample characteristics included 30.7% active members; 39.7% non- or inactive members; 25% lived on 13 blocks without organizations; 67% lived on three blocks with either dormant or incipient block associations. Survey responses confirmed that the residents of organized and unorganized blocks did not differ significantly in age, race, or socioeconomic status.

(Continued)

TABLE 7.9 ■ (Continued)

	• The number of respondents per block ranged from 10 to 41 with a mean of 24. 65% were female; 47% were Black, 47% were White; 62% owned their home. Of the renters, approximately 60.7% lived in apartment buildings and the rest lived in private homes; 29% were college graduates and 42% had a high school education or less; mean age was approximately 42 years old; the median estimated annual family income was approximately $19,000; the median length of residence was approximately nine and a half years.
Scoring	Mean scores were calculated to create continuous variables.
Assessment	No information is provided on reliability in this study. However, a follow-up study by Perkins and Long (2002; see citation below) found the scale to be reliable at multiple time periods (α (T1) = .78, α (T2) = .80).
Related Reference	Perkins, D. D., & Long, D. A. (2002). Neighborhood sense of community and social capital: A multi-level analysis. In A. Fisher, C. Sonn, & B. Bishop (Eds.), *Psychological Sense of Community: Research, Applications, and Implications* (pp. 291–318). New York: Plenum.
Language	English
Contact	Douglas A. Perkins Department of Human and Organizational Development Box 90 Peabody College, Vanderbilt University Nashville, TN 37203 Email: douglas.perkins@vanderbilt.edu

TABLE 7.10 ■ Citizen Participation Measures: Study 1	
Primary Reference	Foster-Fishman, P. G., Cantillon, D., Pierce, S. J., & Van Egeren, L. A. (2007). Building an active citizenry: The role of neighborhood problems, readiness, and capacity for change. *American Journal of Community Psychology, 39*, 91–106.
Purpose	The purpose of this study was to investigate the conditions related to resident involvement in neighborhood-based activities within the context of one comprehensive community-building effort. The study was designed to give funders, programming staff, and residents with insight into those conditions that could be leveraged to foster resident involvement within the initiative.
Description	**Citizen participation measures:** consisted of the following two subscales (please see primary source for a description of all of the items) • **Individual activism (3 items):** asked respondents to indicate whether they or anyone in their family had in the last year (yes/no) ○ Spoken to a local politician about a neighborhood problem ○ Talked to a local religious leader or minister to help with a neighborhood problems or with neighborhood improvement • **Collective action (4 items):** asked respondents to indicate whether they or anyone in their family in the past two months had (yes/no) ○ Attended a meeting of a block or neighborhood group, such as a neighborhood partnerships, neighborhood planning councils, and so forth ○ Gotten together with neighbors to do something about a neighborhood problem or to organize neighborhood improvement
Sample	• Seven distressed neighborhoods were defined and included in this study. Criss-cross directory was used to randomly select from the 3,301 households with phone numbers in the seven neighborhoods. • Sample: 509 of the households participated (30%); median length of residency was 10 years; 85% owned their own homes; 68% were females; 16% were African American; 79% were White; 42% had children under age 18 living in their homes
Scoring	The number of activities were tallied and categorized according to the above guidelines.
Assessment	No information is provided on reliability.
Related Reference	Foster-Fishman, P. G., Pierce, S. J., & Van Egeren, L. A. (2009). Who participates and why: Building a process model of citizen participation. *Health Education & Behavior, 36*(3), 550–569.
Language	English
Contact	Pennie G. Foster-Fishman, PhD Department of Psychology Michigan State University 125D Psychology Building East Lansing, MI 48824, USA Email: fosterfi@msu.edu

TABLE 7.11 ■ Citizen Participation Measures: Study 2	
Primary Reference	Foster-Fishman, P. G., Pierce, S. J., & Van Egeren, L. A. (2009). Who participates and why: Building a process model of citizen participation. *Health Education & Behavior, 36*(3), 550–569.
Purpose	The purpose of this study was to expand understanding of the factors that are associated with citizen participation by investigating who gets involved and under what circumstances. This study intends to help practitioners and funders design interventions that are more capable of leveraging the levels of participation desired.
Description	**Citizen participation measure:** 11 items measuring the extent to which the respondent had been involved with neighborhood and community-level change activities on a 6-point scale (1 = *never* to 6 = *more than seven times*). The scale was adapted from Speer and Peterson's (2000) Behavioral Empowerment Scale and the Interaction Scale developed by Chavis, Hogge, McMillan, and Wandersman (1986). • **Organizational participation (6 items):** asked respondents: "How many times in the past 12 months have you attended a meeting of any of the following associations or organizations?" followed by the items such as ○ Your local neighborhood planning council ○ P.T.A. ○ City commission • **Neighborhood change activities (5 items):** asked respondents, "How many times in the past 12 months have you . . ." followed by items such as ○ Organized your neighbors to take action on some issue ○ Worked on a neighborhood improvement project Other measures related to participation **Organizing skills (10 items):** measured residents' self-reported abilities on skills needed to be effective at promoting neighborhood change, on 6-point Likert scale (1 = *not at all* to 6 = *excellent*). Asked respondents, "How good are you at . . . " followed by items such as • Running effective meetings • Organizing a neighborhood group • Getting city leaders to listen to you **Neighborhood norms for activism (8 items):** measured residents' perception that people in the neighborhood could be counted on to engage in social change activities that they might have either seen their neighbors engage in or that neighbors may have mentioned in a conversation, on a 6-point Likert scale (1 = *not at all* to 6 = *always*). Asked respondents, "How much are residents in your neighborhood likely to . . . " followed by items such as • Work with other residents on projects to improve the neighborhood • Participate in a letter writing campaign **Collective efficacy (6 items)** (format based on Sampson et al., 1997, scale in Chapter 6): assessed the degree to which residents believe that they can make change happen by working together. Respondents were asked to rate from (1 = *not at all* to 6 = *completely*) the extent to which, working together with their neighbors, they could achieve neighborhood change such as • Improving neighborhood physical conditions • Improving the schools **Hope (3 items)** assessed residents' belief that, in their neighborhood, residents see the possibility of positive change and a better future for themselves and their children. Items were rated using a 6-point Likert-type scale (1 = *strongly disagree*, 6 = *strongly agree*) and included

	• Residents believe that change is possible in this neighborhood • Parents in this neighborhood are hopeful about their child's future **Neighborhood problems (3 items)** (adapted from Coulton and colleagues, 1996 Social Disorder scale): residents' perceptions of problems in their neighborhood. Residents were asked to rate the extent to which they agreed with a set of statements about physical and social disorder using a 6-point Likert-type scale (1 = *strongly disagree*, 6 = *strongly agree*). Sample items include • Crime is a problem • Abandoned, vacant, or neglected buildings are a problem **Sense of community (10 items)** (adapted from Chavis et al., (1986) and Coulton et al., (1996)): measured the degree of social bonding that residents perceived in their neighborhood using a 6-point Likert-type scale (1 = *strongly disagree*, 6 = *strongly agree*). Sample items included • In my neighborhood, people socialize with each other • In my neighborhood, most people agree about what is best for the neighborhood
Sample	• The study was part of a broader evaluation of a comprehensive community-building effort in Battle Creek, Michigan. • Data were collected in 2003, 1 year after the program was launched. • Purposive sampling was used to target 333 residents living in the seven distressed neighborhoods involved with program in two ways: all residents who had demonstrated some commitment to the program's goals (e.g., served on a steering committee) and all known residents who held formal and informal leadership positions in neighborhood-based groups (e.g., PTA, neighborhood associations, and planning councils). • Residents were sent a mail survey to complete, resulting in a sample of 201 participants (62% response rate). • The majority of participants were female (77%); mean age was 48.9; 56% White, 35% African American, 4.5% Hispanic; mostly low-income (75% at $45,000 or less a year).
Assessment	Citizen participation: $\alpha = 0.80$ Other related participation measures • Neighborhood norms for activism: $\alpha = 0.91$ • Organizing skills: $\alpha = 0.95$ • Collective efficacy: $\alpha = 0.91$ • Hope: $\alpha = 0.84$ • Neighborhood problems: $\alpha = 0.86$ • Sense of community: $\alpha = 0.90$
Related Reference	Foster-Fishman, P. G., Cantillon, D., Pierce, S. J., & Van Egeren, L. A. (2007). Building an active citizenry: The role of neighborhood problems, readiness, and capacity for change. *American Journal of Community Psychology, 39*, 91–106.
Language	English
Contact	Pennie G. Foster-Fishman, PhD Department of Psychology Michigan State University 125D Psychology Building East Lansing, MI 48824, USA Email: fosterfi@msu.edu

TABLE 7.12 ■ Neighborhood Activism Measure

Primary Reference	Sampson, R. J., & Graif, C. (2009). Neighborhood social capital as differential social organization resident and leadership dimensions. *American Behavioral Scientist, 52*(11), 1579–1605.
Purpose	This measure was developed as part of a larger study on collective efficacy and social capital (PHDCN: Project on Human Development in Chicago Neighborhoods).
Description	**Neighborhood activism**: summarizes responses to five questions. Respondents were asked, "Sometimes people in a neighborhood do things to take care of a local problem or to make the neighborhood a better place to live. Please tell me if you have/if any member of your household has been involved in the following activities since you lived in this neighborhood. Have you (or any member of your household) . . ." Sample items include • Talked to a person or group causing a problem in the neighborhood? • Attended a meeting of a block or neighborhood group about a neighborhood problem or neighborhood improvement? • Gotten together with neighbors to do something about a neighborhood problem or to organize neighborhood improvement? Community participation is also examined through a measure of **organizational participation** that taps involvement by residents in five organizations including • Local religious organizations • Neighborhood watch programs • Business or civic groups
Sample	• Spatial definition of neighborhood: a collection of people and institutions occupying a subsection of a larger community. Combined 847 census tracts in Chicago to create 343 ecologically meaningful "neighborhood clusters" (NCs) with about 8,000 people in geographically contiguous census tracts, which were internally homogeneous on key census indicators. • Sample: 8,782 Chicago residents representing 343 NCs were interviewed in their homes as part of the community survey (CS). Representative sample of households within each NC, with sample sizes large enough to create reliable measures. • Neighborhoods were categorized into low, medium, and high socioeconomic status (SES). There were no low-SES White neighborhoods and no high-SES Latino neighborhoods. There were Black neighborhoods in all three categories of SES and many heterogeneous neighborhoods with varying SES.
Scoring	No information is provided on scoring.
Assessment	• The aggregate reliability of the neighborhood activism scale is $\alpha = .66$. • The reliability of organizational participation density at the community level is $\alpha = .85$.
Language	English
Contact	Robert J. Sampson, PhD Professor and Chair, Department of Sociology Harvard University William James Hall 33 Kirkland St. Cambridge, MA 02138 Email: rsampson@wjh.harvard.edu
Website	For more information on neighborhood collective efficacy and this research, see the study website: Project on Human Development in Chicago Neighborhoods: http://www.icpsr.umich.edu/icpsrweb/PHDCN/instruments.jsp.

TABLE 7.13 ■ Community Mobilization	
Primary Reference	Lippman, S. A., Neilands, T. B., Leslie, H. H., Maman, S., MacPhail, C., Twine, R., . . . Pettifor, A. (2016). Development, validation, and performance of a scale to measure community mobilization. *Social Science & Medicine, 157*, 127–137.
Purpose	The goal of this study was to develop a Community Mobilization Measure (CMM) composed of a set of scales to measure mobilization domains hypothesized to operate at the community level. The six domains include shared concerns, critical consciousness, leadership, collective action, social cohesion, and organizations and networks. The domain of social control was included to explore synergies with the related construct of collective efficacy.
Description	The Community Mobilization Measure is multidimensional and includes the following domains (see Lippman et al., pp. 129 and 133): **Social control (8 items):** (adapted from Sampson, Raudenbush, & Earls, 1997, see Chapter 6) asked respondents on a scale from 1 = *very likely* to 3 = *somewhat unlikely* that • Your neighbors would intervene if children were breaking windows on a local building/ destroying public property? • Your neighbors would intervene if children were showing disrespect to an adult? • Your neighbors would intervene if a family didn't have enough food? • Your neighbors would intervene if an elderly person was robbed? **Social cohesion (6 items):** (adapted from Sampson, Raudenbush, & Earls, 1997, see Chapter 6) Asked respondents their level of agreement regarding the following statements, on a scale from 1 to 3: 1 = *agree*, 2 = *somewhat agree*, and 3 = *disagree*: • People in this village are willing to help their neighbors. • People in this village generally get along well with each other. • People in this village share the same values. **Shared concerns (10 items):** asked respondents about their shared concerns regarding HIV on a scale from 1 to 3: 1 = *agree*, 2 = *somewhat agree*, and 3 = *disagree*: • People in your village are concerned about HIV. • People in your village believe that HIV impacts the community. • People in your village talk about HIV/AIDS at community meetings. • People in your village work together to reduce the effects of HIV. • People in your village take HIV/AIDS seriously. **Critical consciousness (11 items):** asked respondents about the following statements, on a scale from 1 to 3: 1 = *agree*, 2 = *somewhat agree*, and 3 = *disagree*: • People work together to solve problems in the village. • People in your village talk to each other about how to solve village problems. • People in your village enjoy discussing different ways to solve village problems. • People in your village volunteer to help solve village problems. • People in your village think about why there are problems so they can address the cause of problems. • People in this village not only talk about problems but they also try to solve them.

(Continued)

TABLE 7.13 ■ (Continued)

	Leadership (14 items): asked respondents about the following statements, on a scale from 1 to 3: 1 = *agree*, 2 = *somewhat agree*, and 3 = *disagree*: • The leaders in your community work effectively together. • The leaders in your village get a lot done for the community. • The leaders in your village represent all the different kinds of people who live in your community. • The power to make community decisions is shared among leaders and the people in this village. • The leaders in this village are trustworthy. • The leaders in this village act responsibly with the power they have. • The leaders in this village are honest; there is little corruption here. **Organizations and networks (10 items in two sets of questions):** asked respondents to reply yes or no to the following two questions: • Are there any organizations or groups that help to make your community better in your village? • Are there groups with which you can volunteer to help people in your community? Asked respondents how important eight things were on a scale from 1 to 3 (1 = *very important*, 2 = *a little important*, and 3 = *not important/no such organizations*). Sample items include: • How important are police/safety organizations in this community? • How important are youth organizations in this community? • How important are religious/church organizations in this community? • How important are cultural organizations in this community? **Collective action: (6 items)** • How many community members participate in community meetings on average in the last three months? • How many times has the community worked together to fix a problem in the past three months? • How many times have you worked to fix a community problem?
Sample	• The study took place in South Africa. A pilot test was initially completed with a random sample of 101 participants, between 18 and 35 years of age, from five villages in the sampling frame (20 people per village); 50.5% were male, 49.5% female; most completed some secondary school (66.3%) while 27.7% completed secondary school; 77.2% were never married. • Villages were selected purposefully to garner responses from inhabitants of communities that varied in size, socio-demographic attributes, and community resources. • Data for the main survey were from a random sample of 1181 young adults aged 18 and 35 years, approximately 55 people in each of 22 villages participating in an HIV prevention trial (Pettifor et al., 2015); 49.2% were male, 50.8% female; 56.1% completed some secondary school and 33.3% completed secondary school; 73.1% were never married. • Surveys were administered to one eligible respondent per household in English or Shangaan via computer-assisted personal interviews (CAPI) at the respondent's home (pp. 130–131).

Scoring	Mean scores were calculated for most of the subscales. For the collective action scale, the responses were quantified and coded.
Assessment	• Social control: $\alpha = 0.89$ • Social cohesion: $\alpha = 0.81$ • Shared concerns: $\alpha = 0.85$ • Critical consciousness: $\alpha = 0.93$ • Leadership: $\alpha = 0.92$ • Organizations and networks: $\alpha = 0.81$ • Collective action: $\alpha = 0.84$
Languages	English and Shangaan
Contact	Dr. Sheri Lippman University of California, San Francisco Center for AIDS Prevention Studies Department of Medicine 550 16th Street, 3rd Floor San Francisco CA, 94158-2549, USA Email address: sheri.lippman@ucsf.edu

TABLE 7.14 ■ Civic Engagement Indicators

Primary Reference	Keeter, S., Zukin, C., Andolina, M., & Jenkins, M. (2002). *The civic and political health of the nation: A generational portrait*. College Park, MD: Center for Information and Research on Civic Learning and Engagement (CIRCLE), School of Public Policy, University of Maryland.
Purpose	The purpose of the study was to understand and document the ways in which citizens participate in civic and political life.
Description	The 19 civic indicators are included in three main domains. Please see the primary reference for a listing of all of the indicators. **Civic indicators (5):** The first two provide sample questions: • *Community problem solving.* Have you ever worked together informally with someone or some group to solve a problem in the community where you live? If YES, was this in the last 12 months or not? • *Regular volunteering for a nonelectoral organization.* Have you ever spent time participating in any community service or volunteer activity, or haven't you had time to do this? Can you tell me if you have volunteered for this type of group or organization within the last 12 months? ○ An environmental organization ○ A civic or community organization involved in health or social services ○ An organization involved with youth, children, or education ○ Any other type of group • Active membership in a group or association • Participation in fund-raising run/walk/ride • Other fund raising for charity **Electoral indicators (5):** The first two provide sample questions: • *Regular voting.* We know that most people don't vote in all elections. Usually between one-quarter to one-half of those eligible actually come out to vote. Can you tell me how often you vote in local and national elections? Always, sometimes, rarely, or never? • *Persuading others.* When there is an election taking place, do you generally talk to any people and try to show them why they should vote for or against one of the parties or candidates or not? • *Displaying buttons, signs, stickers* • *Campaign contributions* • *Volunteering for candidate or political organizations* **Indicators of political voice (9):** The first four provide sample questions: • *Contacting officials.* Now I'm going to read you a quick list of things that some people have done to express their views. For each one I read, please just tell me whether you have ever done it or not. (FOR EACH YES, PROBE: And have you done this is the last 12 months, or not?)] Contacted or visited a public official—at any level of government—to ask for assistance or to express your opinion? • *Contacting the print media.* Contacted a newspaper or magazine to express your opinion on an issue? • *Contacting the broadcast media.* Called in to a radio or television talk show to express your opinion on a political issue, even if you did not get on the air? • *Protesting.* Taken part in a protest, march, or demonstration? • *Email petitions.* Signed an email petition?

	• *Written petitions* • *Boycotting* • *Buycotting* • *Canvassing*
Sample	• Telephone survey: nationwide sample of 3246 youth and adults, 15 years of age and older, during the period April 4 through May 20, 2002. Because of a special interest in youth, the two youngest cohorts were oversampled (DotNet, *N* = 1001 Generation X = 1000). A total of 604 Baby Boomers and 602 Matures completed the sample. • Internet survey: 15- to 25-year-olds, conducted between January 29, 2002, and February 25, 2002, 1166 who met the age requirements for inclusion completed the study. The sample was stratified by education, with one group consisting of those currently enrolled in high school (*N* = 312), a second group comprised of college graduates and those with some history of college attendance (*N* = 336), and a final group of individuals who did not meet the criteria for inclusion in the two previous groups (*N* = 518).
Scoring	See questions for scoring.
Assessment	No information is provided on reliability.
Related Reference	Adler, P., & Goggin, J. (2005). What do you we mean by "Civic Engagement"? *Journal of Transformative Education, 3*(3), 236–253.
Language	English
Contact	Krista Jenkins Rutgers University Eagleton Institute of Politics 191 Ryders Lane New Brunswick, New Jersey 08901 kristaj@eden.rutgers.edu
Website	Study website: https://civicyouth.org/the-civic-and-political-health-of-the-nation-national-civic-engagement-survey-i-spring-2002/ Publication: http://www.civicyouth.org/research/products/Civic_Political_Health.pdf

TABLE 7.15 ■ Civic Engagement Scale (CES)	
Primary Reference	Doolittle, A., & Faul, A. C. (2013, July–September). Civic engagement scale: A validation study. *SAGE Open* 1–7.
Purpose	The purpose of this study was to develop and validate the Civic Engagement Scale (CES). This scale is developed to be easily administered and useful to educators who are seeking to measure the attitudes and behaviors of students affected by a service-learning experience.
Description	The respondents were asked to indicate their level of agreement or disagreement with the 14 items regarding attitudes and to rate their level of participation as never to always regarding behaviors. Their level of agreement was measured on a 7-point Likert scale (1 = *disagree* to 7 = *agree*), and their level of participation was also measured on a 7-point Likert-type scale (1 = *never* to 7 = *always*). Please see the primary reference for all of the items. **Attitudes (8 items):** Sample items include • I believe I should make a difference in my community • I am committed to serve in my community • I believe that it is important to be informed of community issues • I believe that it is important to volunteer **Behaviors (6 items):** Sample items include • When working with others, I make positive changes in the community • I help members of my community • I participate in discussions that raise issues of social responsibility
Sample	• 513 surveys were administered as a purposive sample with a return of 354 (69%). • Sample characteristics: majority female (83.1%) and White (88.1%); the age ranged from 17 to 63 years (*M* = 28.42); single, never married (53.9%), and married (38.1%). • Education: undergraduate (59%), education majors (50.6%); graduate students were all social work majors (40.4%); the mean years of education completed ranged between 12 and 25 with a mean of 17.18. • Previous volunteer experience (83.9%), no previous volunteer experience (12.1%).
Scoring	Mean scores are calculated.
Assessment	• Attitudes: α = .91 • Behaviors: α = .85
Language	English
Contact	Amy Doolittle Social Work Department, Dept. 3133 University of Tennessee, Chattanooga 615 McCallie Avenue, Chattanooga, TN 37403 Email: Amy-Doolittle@utc.edu

TABLE 7.16 ■ Civic Identity/Civic Engagement Instrument for Youth (CICE)	
Primary Reference	Bobek, D., Zaff, J., Li, Y., & Lerner, R. M. (2009). Cognitive, emotional, and behavioral components of civic action: Towards an integrated measure of civic engagement. *Journal of Applied Developmental Psychology, 30*(2009), 615–627.
Purpose	Uses data from 8th-grade participants in the 4-H Positive Youth Development and factor analytics procedures to explore a model of active, engaged citizenship (civic identity/civic engagement).
Description	The measure has 42 items with six factors. **Civic duty (12 items):** Participants were asked to respond on a 5-point Likert scale (from 1 = *not important* to 5 = *extremely important*) for items 1 to 5. Sample items include • How important is helping to reduce hunger and poverty in the world? • How important is helping to make the world a better place to live in? • How important is helping to make sure all people are treated fairly? Participants were asked to respond on a 5-point Likert scale (from 1 = *strongly disagree* to 5 = *strongly agree*) for items six to 12. Sample items included • I believe I can make a difference in my community. • It is important for me to contribute to my community and society. • I often think about doing things so that people in the future can have things better. **Civic skill (6 items):** asked respondents to indicate the extent to which they can do six things, on a 5-point Likert scale (from 1 = "*I definitely can't*" to 5 = "*I definitely can*"). Sample items include • What is your ability to contact a newspaper, radio, or TV talk show to express your opinion on an issue? • What is your ability to contact or visit someone in government who represents your community? • What is your ability to sign an email or written petition? **Neighborhood social skills (6 items):** asked respondents about six skills on a 5-point Likert scale (from 1 = *strongly disagree* to 5 = *strongly agree*). Sample items include • Adults in my town or city listen to what I have to say. • In my town or city, I feel like I matter to people. • In my neighborhood, there are lots of people who care about me. **Peer social connection (6 items):** asked respondents about six skills, on a 5-point Likert scale (from 1 = *strongly disagree* to 5 = *strongly agree*). Sample items include • My friends are there when I need them. • I feel that my friends are good friends. • My friends care about me. **Civic participation (9 items):** • How often do you spend time volunteering? • How often do you help make your city or town a better place for people to live? • How often do you help a neighborhood? • How often do you help out at your church, synagogue, or other place of worship?

(*Continued*)

TABLE 7.16 ■ (Continued)	
	Adult social connection (3 items): • Not including your parents or teachers, how many adults have you known for one or more years who you look forward to spending time with? • Other than your parents, is there at least one other adult you would feel able to talk to if you were having problems in your life?
Sample	• 1,890 eighth-grade participants of Wave 4 of the 4-H study. 1072 had previously participated in at least one prior wave and 818 were new. Youth were from 35 schools, nine 4-H sites in 24 states. • Sampling provided regional rural–urban, racial/ethnic, and religious diversity. • The survey was distributed by trained staff in school and 4-H sites, or students received survey by mail or competed online. Data collection took about two hours (including one to two short breaks).
Scoring	Mean scores are calculated.
Assessment	**Overall scale**: $\alpha = 0.75$ (across six factors) • Adult social connection (3 items): $\alpha = 0.71$ • Civic participation (9 items): $\alpha = 0.73$ • Civic duty (12 items): $\alpha = 0.80$ • Peer social connection (6 items): $\alpha = 0.84$ • Neighborhood social connection (6 items): $\alpha = 0.86$ • Civic skills (6 items): $\alpha = 0.91$
Related Reference	Zaff, J., Boyd, M., Li, Y., Lerner, J. V., & Lerner, R. M. (2010). Active and engaged citizenship: Multi-group and longitudinal factorial analysis of an integrated construct of civic engagement. *Journal of Youth and Adolescence, 39*(7), 736–750.
Language	English
Contact	Richard Lerner Bergstrom Chair Director of Institute for Applied Research in Youth Development Eliot Pearson Department of Child Study and Human Development 105 College Avenue Tufts University, Medford MA 02155 Email: Richard.lerner@tufts.edu

TABLE 7.17 ■ Active and Engaged Citizenship (ACE) for Youth

Primary Reference	Zaff, J., Boyd, M., Li, Y., Lerner, J. V., & Lerner, R. M. (2010). Active and engaged citizenship: Multi-group and longitudinal factorial analysis of an integrated construct of civic engagement. *Journal of Youth and Adolescence, 39*(7), 736–750.
Purpose	This study aimed to evaluate the goodness-of-fit between a hypothesized model of active and engaged citizenship and empirical data. The second purpose was to examine this model for measurement invariance across time and between boys and girls. This study builds off of Bobek et al., 2009. The goal of this study was to refine the measurement model and test the factor structure and validity of the refined model across three years of adolescence for boys and girl.
Description	The measure includes 32 items across four factors. **Civic duty: (12 items)** Derived from the social responsibility scale of the teen assessment project survey question bank (SRS; Greenberger & Bond, 1984; Small & Rogers, 1995), political efficacy and participatory citizen constructs of student voice measure (Flanagan et al., 2007), and the Search Institute's Profiles of Student Life-Attitudes and Beliefs questionnaire (Leffert et al., 1998). Responses were rated on a 5-point Likert scale (from 1 = *not important* to 5 = *extremely important*) for items 1 to 5. Sample items included • Helping to reduce hunger and poverty in the world • Helping to make sure all people are treated fairly • Speaking up for equality (everyone should have the same rights and opportunities) Responses were rated on a 5-point Likert scale (from 1 = *strongly disagree* to 5 = *strongly agree* for items 6 to 12. Sample items included • It's not really my problem if my neighbors are in trouble and I need help • When I see someone being taken advantage of, I want to help them • It is important to me to contribute to my community and society **Civic skills: (6 items)** Adapted from the political voice and competence for civic action constructs of the student voices measure (Flanagan et al., 2007). Asked respondents to indicate the extent to which they can do several things, on a scale from 1 to 5 (from "I definitely can't" to "I definitely can"). Sample items included • Contact or visit someone in government who represents your community • Write an opinion letter to a local newspaper • Express your views in front of a group of people **Neighborhood social connection: (6 items)** From the Search Institute's PSL-AB questionnaire (Leffert et al., 1998). Asked respondents about several statements, on a 5-point Likert scale (from 1 = *strongly disagree* to 5 = *strongly agree*). Sample items include • Adults in my town or city listen to what I have to say • In my neighborhood, there are lots of people who care about me • If one of my neighbors saw me do something wrong, he or she would tell one of my parents

(Continued)

TABLE 7.17 ■ (Continued)	
	Civic participation: (8 items) Created specifically for the 4-H Study; drawn from the Search Institute's PSL-AB questionnaire (Leffert et al., 1998). Asked respondents: "How often do you . . . " The first three items are measured on a 5-point Likert scale (from 1 = *never* to 5 = *very often*): • Help make your city or town a better place for people to live • Help a neighbor Then next 5 items are measured on a 6-point Likert scale (from 1 = *never* to 6 = *every day*): • Volunteering your time (at a hospital, day care center, food bank, youth program, community service agency) • During the last 12 months, how many times have you been a leader in a group or organization? • Help out at your school
Sample	Grade 8, 9, and 10 waves of data of the longitudinal 4-H Study of Positive Youth Development. • Grade 8 data was collected from a total of 1,990 youth from 35 schools and 12 4-H sites in 17 states. • Grade 9 data was collected from a total of 1,203 youth from 40 schools and 24 4-H sites in 18 states. • Grade 10 data was collected from a total of 2,371 youth and 18 schools and 82 4-H sites in 32 states. The longitudinal sample, comprised of individuals who participated in at least two waves of data, consisted of 909 individuals. • Overall, the sample was 62.4% female; mean ages were 14.17 in Grade 8, 14.97 in Grade 9, and 16.03 in Grade 10 for females and 14.22, 15.16, and 16.08 for males; most were European American and less than 10% African American Youth and Hispanic. • The youth could have completed the survey at school or 4-H sites by paper or computer, or they were contacted if they were absent from school and were asked to complete the survey and return it. Beginning in Grade 9, youth could complete the survey online.
Scoring	Mean scores are calculated.
Assessment	Grade 8 (Wave 4) • Overall AEC measure: $\alpha = 0.72$ • Civic duty: $\alpha = 0.86$ • Neighborhood connection: $\alpha = 0.87$ • Civic skills: $\alpha = 0.92$ • Civic participation: $\alpha = 0.76$ Grade 9 (Wave 5) • Overall AEC measure: $\alpha = 0.73$ • Civic duty: $\alpha = 0.87$ • Neighborhood connection: $\alpha = 0.89$ • Civic skills: $\alpha = 0.92$ • Civic participation: $\alpha = 0.78$

	Grade 10 (Wave 6) • Overall AEC measure: $\alpha = 0.70$ • Civic duty: $\alpha = 0.87$ • Neighborhood connection: $\alpha = 0.89$ • Civic skills: $\alpha = 0.91$ • Civic participation: $\alpha = 0.77$
Related Reference	Bobek, D., Zaff, J., Li, Y., & Lerner, R. M. (2009). Cognitive, emotional, and behavioral components of civic action: Towards an integrated measure of civic engagement. *Journal of Applied Developmental Psychology, 30*(2009), 615–627.
Language	English
Contact	Jonathan Zaff, PhD America's Promise Alliance 1110 Vermont Avenue NW, Suite 900, Washington, DC 20005 Email: jonz@americaspromie.org

REFERENCES

Adler, P., & Goggin, J. (2005). What do you we mean by "Civic Engagement"? *Journal of Transformative Education, 3*(3), 236–253.

Bandura, A. (1982). Self-efficacy mechanism in human agency. *American Psychologist, 37*, 122–147.

Bobek, D., Zaff, J., Li, Y., & Lerner, R. M. (2009). Cognitive, emotional, and behavioral components of civic action: Towards an integrated measure of civic engagement. *Journal of Applied Developmental Psychology, 30*, 615–627.

Christens, B. D., Peterson, N. A., & Speer, P. W. (2011). Community participation and psychological empowerment: Testing reciprocal causality using a cross-lagged panel design and latent constructs. *Health Education & Behavior, 38*(4), 339–347.

Developmental Studies Center. (2000). *Middle school student questionnaire measures*. Oakland, CA: Author.

Doolittle, A., & Faul, A. C. (2013, July–September). Civic engagement scale: A validation study. *SAGE Open*, 1–7.

Eisman, A. B., Zimmerman, M. A., Kruger, D., Reischl, T. M., Miller, A. L., Franzen, S. P., & Morrell-Samuels, S. (2016). Psychological empowerment among urban youth: Measurement model and associations with youth outcomes. *American Journal of Community Psychology, 58*, 410–421.

Foster-Fishman, P. G., Cantillon, D., Pierce, S. J., & Van Egeren, L. A. (2007). Building an active citizenry: The role of neighborhood problems, readiness, and capacity for change. *American Journal of Community Psychology, 39*, 91–106.

Foster-Fishman, P. G., Pierce, S. J., & Van Egeren, L. A. (2009). Who participates and why: Building a process model of citizen participation. *Health Education & Behavior, 36*(3), 550–569.

Gutierrez, L. M. (1990). Working with women of color: An empowerment perspective. *Social Work, 35*, 149–153.

Holden, D. J., Crankshaw, E., Nimsch, C., Hinnant, L. W., & Hund, L. (2004). Quantifying the impact of participation in local tobacco control groups on the psychological empowerment of involved youth. *Health Education & Behavior, 31*, 615–628.

Holden, D. J., Evans, W. D., Hinnant, L. W., & Messeri, P. (2005). Modeling psychological empowerment among youth involved in local tobacco control efforts. *Health Education & Behavior, 32*, 264–278.

Israel, B. A., Checkoway, B., Schulz, A., & Zimmerman, M. (1994). Health education and community empowerment: Conceptualizing and measuring perceptions of individual, organizational, and community control. *Health Education Quarterly, 21*(2), 149–170.

Keeter, S., Zukin, C., Andolina, M., & Jenkins, M. (2002). *The civic and political health of the nation: A generational portrait*. College Park, MD: Center for Information and Research on Civic Learning and Engagement (CIRCLE), School of Public Policy, University of Maryland.

Laverack, G., & Wallerstein, N. (2001). Measuring community empowerment: A fresh look at organizational domains. *Health Promotion International, 16*(2), 179–185.

Lenzi, M., Vieno, A., Perkins, D. D., Santinello, M., Elgar, F. J., Morgan, A., Mazzardis, S. (2012). Family affluence, school and neighborhood contexts and adolescents' civic engagement: A cross-national study. *American Journal of Community Psychology*. doi: 10.1007/s10464-012-9489-7

Lippman, S. A., Neilands, T. B., Leslie, H. H., Maman, S., MacPhail, C., Twine, R., . . . Pettifor, A. (2016). Development, validation, and performance of a scale to measure community mobilization. *Social Science & Medicine, 157*, 127–137.

Ohmer, M. L. (2007). Citizen participation in neighborhood organizations and its relationship to volunteers' self- and collective efficacy and sense of community. *Social Work Research, 31*(2), 109–120.

Ozer, E. J., & Schotland, M. (2011). Psychological empowerment among urban youth: Measure development and relationship to psychological functioning. *Health Education & Behavior, 38*(4), 348–356.

Perkins, D. D., & Long, D. A. (2002). Neighborhood sense of community and social capital: A multi-level analysis. In A. Fisher, C. Sonn, & B. Bishop (Eds.), *Psychological sense of community: Research, applications, and implications* (pp. 291–318). New York: Plenum.

Perkins, D., Florin, P., Rich, R., Wandersman A., & Chavis, D. (1990). Participation and the social and physical environment of residential blocks: Crime and community context. *American Journal of Community Psychology, 18,* 83–115.

Peterson, N. A, Peterson, C. H., Agre, L., Christens, B. D., & Morton, C. M. (2011). Measuring youth empowerment: Validation of a sociopolitical control scale for youth in an urban context. *Journal of Community Psychology, 39*(5), 592–605.

Peterson, N. S., Lowe, J. B., Hughey, J., Reid, R. J., Zimmerman, M. A., & Speer, P. W. (2006). Measuring the intrapersonal component of psychological empowerment: Confirmatory factor analysis of the sociopolitical control scale. *American Journal of Community Psychology, 38,* 287–297.

Sampson, R. J., & Graif, C. (2009). Neighborhood social capital as differential social organization resident and leadership dimensions. *American Behavioral Scientist, 52*(11), 1579–1605.

Smallwood, S. W., Freedman, D. A., Pitner, R. O., Sharpe, P. A., Cole, J. A., Hastie, S., & Hunter, B. (2015). Implementing a community empowerment center to build capacity for developing, implementing, and sustaining interventions to promote community health. *Journal of Community Health, 40*(6), 1122–1129.

Smith, P. D., & Propst, D. B. (2001). Are topic-specific measures of socio-political control justified? Exploring the realm of citizen participation in natural resource decision making. *Journal of Community Psychology, 29,* 179–187.

Speer, P. W., & Peterson, N. A. (2000). Psychometric properties of an empowerment scale: Testing cognitive, emotional and behavioral domains. *Social Work Research, 24*(2), 109–119.

Wandersman, A., & Florin, P. (2000). Citizen participation and community organizations. In J. Rappaport & E. Seidman (Eds.), *Handbook of community psychology*. New York: Kluwer Academic/Plenum Publishers.

Zaff, J., Boyd, M., Li, Y., Lerner, J. V., & Lerner, R. M. (2010). Active and engaged citizenship: Multi-group and longitudinal factorial analysis of an integrated construct of civic engagement. *Journal of Youth and Adolescence, 39*(7), 736–750.

Zimmerman, M. A. (1995). Psychological empowerment: Issues and illustrations. *American Journal of Community Psychology, 23,* 581–599.

Zimmerman, M. A. (2000). Empowerment theory: Psychological, organizational and community levels of analysis. In J. Rappaport & E. Seidman (Eds.), *Handbook of community psychology*. New York: Kluwer Academic/Plenum Publishers.

Zimmerman, M. A., & Rappaport, J. (1988). Citizen participation, perceived control, and psychological empowerment. *American Journal of Community Psychology, 16*(5), 725–750.

Zimmerman, M. A., & Zahniser, J. H. (1991). Refinements of sphere-specific measures of perceived control: Development of a sociopolitical control scale. *Journal of Community Psychology, 19*(2), 189–204.

8 COMMUNITY RESOURCES AND RESIDENT SATISFACTION

Measuring community resources and satisfaction with community and its public services is instrumental to taking a strengths-based approach to understanding and working with neighborhoods. Resources and community satisfaction impact residents' well-being and are important targets for community practitioners conducting asset-based community development (ABCD) in neighborhoods. Additionally, researchers are often interested in documenting disparities in resources or examining how policies and programs affect their quality and availability. Resources in neighborhoods allow residents to meet basic needs and foster community stability, social control, and collective efficacy (Curley, 2010). Similarly, satisfaction with community and public services is crucial to overall life satisfaction and encourages individuals to continue living in their existing neighborhood, creating stability and contributing to the overall health of the neighborhood (Bruin & Cook, 1997). Several chapters in this book have discussed measures that assess specific aspects of the resource or service environment, such as recreational centers or parks. In this chapter, we focus on global measures of community resources, community satisfaction, and satisfaction with public services that could be utilized in the assessment of neighborhood/community assets. In this chapter, we will define and discuss the importance of measuring community resources and satisfaction with community and public services, outline the general trends in the measurement of these domains, and discuss specific measurement tools that have been developed and tested to measure them in the neighborhood/community context.

DEFINING COMMUNITY RESOURCES AND SATISFACTION

Community Resources

Generally, resources are defined as a supply of something (money, staff, time, skills, etc.) that someone, in this case a neighborhood, has and can use when needed. When discussed in the neighborhood context, community resources may include individuals, associations and organization, and/or local institutions (Kretzman & McKnight, 1993). Although individuals are an important aspect of resources found in neighborhoods, most measures of individual resources are either measured at the individual level (rather than the neighborhood) or are aggregates of measures of social capital or efficacy, domains covered extensively in other chapters of this book. This chapter focuses on the measurement of community associations/organizations and institutions.

A neighborhood institution is "any organization with a physical establishment, located in a neighborhood, and having a clientele composed primarily of neighborhood residents" (Small, 2006, p. 276). These institutions can be nonprofit or for profit and/or privately or public funded. Under this definition, businesses and restaurants in addition to social service agencies are considered neighborhood institutions. When defining organizations and associations, Swaroop and Morenoff (2006) make a distinction between instrumental organizations/associations (organized to make improvements to the neighborhood) and expressive organizations/associations (formed to increase social ties and interaction). Instrumental formal organizations/associations include neighborhood watches, block groups or tenant associations, and local political organizations; expressive formal organizations/associations include religious groups, ethnic or nationality groups, and civic groups. Although there is considerable variation in the level of structure in formal organizations and associations, some structure does exist. These definitions will be used throughout this chapter to discuss measures that assess resources in communities.

Community Satisfaction

Community satisfaction is one way to gauge one's sense of residence. It taps into a psychological construct that residents perceive in relation to their community-at-large and is often used in research as a measure of quality of life in a community (Campbell, Converse, & Rogers, 1976; Sirgy, Rahtz, Cicic, & Underwood, 2000). Community satisfaction typically is considered a person's subjective evaluation of their location as a place to live, based on various social, environmental, physical, and other aspects of that locality (Auh & Cook, 2009; Crowe, 2010; Filkins, Allen, & Cordes, 2000; Goudy, 1977; Low & Altman, 1992; Marans & Rodgers, 1975; Payne & Schaumleffel, 2008). It includes a person's assessment of the quality of their physical environment, housing quality, availability of community services, interactive networks, feelings of belongingness and acceptance, norm and value systems (Grillo, Teixeira, & Wilson, 2010; James, Carswell, & Sweaney, 2009; Sirgy & Cornwell, 2002). For our purposes, we have included community satisfaction measures that reflect the subjective evaluation of a community as a whole.

Satisfaction With Public Services

As a concept, satisfaction with services reveals an intensity of preferences, a subjective impression of what individuals think of the services provided in their community. Like many measures, satisfaction with services is multidimensional (Ware, Snyder, & Wright, 1977). It can assess general satisfaction with public services or it can be tailored to assess satisfaction with specific services among current consumers. Residents' satisfaction with services can vary. For example, one may be satisfied with the services of local businesses but dissatisfied with government services. We also know that differences in satisfaction exist among individuals living in the same communities, which presents challenges with reconciliation and interpretation.

The Relationship Between Community Satisfaction and Satisfaction With Public Services

Community satisfaction is linked to a person's assessment of public services in a community (Bruin & Cook, 1997; Vrbka & Combs, 1993). If school services, for example, are perceived to be of low quality, then these feelings of dissatisfaction translate into an overall general perception of the quality of their community and may contribute to low housing values and diminishing population. Thus, community satisfaction is driven by lower-order domain of satisfaction with services provided by government, business, and nonprofit services as well as other constructs including community commitment and satisfaction with community conditions (Grzeskowiak et al., 2003).

To understand the relationship between satisfaction with community and satisfaction with public services, Sirgy (2012) used a bottom-up, spillover theory established in the quality-of-life research (Andrews & Withey, 1976; Campbell et al., 1976; Diener, 1984), which posits that individual feelings about specific services in a community also impact overall perceptions of community satisfaction, residents' commitment to the community, and overall life satisfaction. In a hierarchical model, life satisfaction is swayed by satisfaction with life domains, such as community, family, health, and so forth. Satisfaction with one, community for example, is in turn influenced by other levels of satisfaction in that domain (e.g., satisfaction with nonprofits, government, and businesses). The bottom-up spillover theory suggests that, as residents' experience or perceive greater satisfaction with government services, retail or business services, or nonprofit resources, the more satisfied they are with their communities and in turn, more satisfied with life in general.

WHY MEASURE COMMUNITY RESOURCES AND SATISFACTION?

Neighborhood/community resources may influence an individual's ability to meet basic needs, such as sustenance or employment, especially when transportation (i.e., owning a car) is not readily available (Curley, 2010). Neighborhood/community resources might also provide pro-social structured activities outside of schools, fostering positive youth development (Byrd & Chavous, 2009). As discussed in Chapter 7, the disproportionate lack of access to resources in disadvantaged neighborhoods (Allard, Tolman, & Rosen, 2003; McKenzie et al., 2013; Macintyre, Macdonald, & Ellaway, 2008) perpetuates social inequality and exclusion by limiting access to resources necessary to meet basic needs and achieve upward mobility. Beyond their utility, neighborhood resources, like neighborhood issues, also communicate information to residents about the level of investment, stability, and collective identity present in their neighborhood (Wen et al., 2006). Despite the relative lack of access to resources such as employment (covered extensively in Chapter 7 and excluded from this discussion) in disadvantaged neighborhoods, some studies have suggested that strong organizations and institutions can coexist within disadvantaged neighborhoods (Small, 2006). While early neighborhood researchers focused on deficits, such as crime and disorder, there has been growing acknowledgment that building on or increasing resources may be a viable approach to improving outcomes in disadvantaged neighborhoods. Identifying crucial resources and gaps in what is currently available not only provides insight into the effect of resources on residents but also indicates important areas for neighborhood-level intervention.

Over the past 25 years, asset-based or resource-based development has been an essential strategy for community change. Asset-based community development (ABCD), introduced in 1993 by Kretzman and McKnight, argued that problem-based organizing was ineffective and forced communities to over emphasize deficits in order to attract resources, often isolating rather than integrating the most marginal residents of a community. They argue that ABCD is a bottom-up or inside-out strategy that is more organic and grassroots than to outside organizations attempting to address needs. The use of asset-based development strategies necessitates a systematic approach to the measurement of community resources. Community asset mapping is one method used in ABCD to build community capacity, mobilize residents, and collect data about resources in the neighborhood. Community assets maps note the gifts and capacities of individuals, organizations and associations, and local institutions. This method has been primarily used as a community organizing tool rather than a research method but may utilize one or a combination of the measurement methods discussed in this chapter. While the asset mapping method of assessment will not be discussed at length here, the following validated measures may be used to better understand the resources available in the community that can be leveraged for ABCD approaches to organizing.

The role of neighborhood resources has also been emphasized in models of community resilience to disasters. Community resilience is a complex process in which a community responds positively to stress or change (Wickes, Zahnow, & Mazerolle, 2010). In this model, organizational resources, in additional to human and social capital, are one of the most central factors influencing a community's capacity to respond (Magis, 2010). In these models of resilience, a major focus is on the presence of economic resources and the ability of the community to mobilize them when necessary (Wickes, Zahnow, & Mazerolle, 2010). Resource development can be used as a strategy to increase the viability of a neighborhood in the present and increase its ability to respond to crises or stress in the future. Empirically measuring the landscape of resources in a neighborhood may be essential to planning for and responding to disasters.

The measures of community satisfaction as well as satisfaction with public services remains important and timely. As we seek to understand migration patterns in and out of communities and measure the desirability of a community, knowing what drives the reasons to stay can provide direction or expand our thinking about the relationship between residents and the place they live. This type of information can lead to developing better ways for measuring and linking concepts important for community attachment or developing a sense of community, as discussed in Chapter 6. Measuring resident satisfaction or dissatisfaction can also provide actionable evidence for community practitioners, city planners, and others who have a stake in directing efforts to retain and attract residents. Public policies continue to be used in communities to incentivize economic development, improve housing options, and create structural improvements for designated neighborhoods or cities as ways to increase community satisfaction.

Measures of satisfaction also may benefit researchers. First, there is value in getting a baseline measure so that we can compare subsequent measures to know just how satisfied people are in a community over time. Communities grow and contract according to outside indicators, but resident perceptions may not follow those objective measures.

Community satisfaction may also be a function of belonging to a subgroup. Do people become more or less content with their communities as they age? Are there pockets of residents more satisfied with the resurgence in their areas than other groups in their neighborhood? Some research shows that newly arrived residents are more concerned with physical issues like housing whereas long-term residents are more concerned with how the community could improve it services (Potter & Cantarero, 2006). Understanding how different subgroups feel about their community will allow for more specific tailoring of messages, action, and strategies for community development.

Relatedly, the diversity in one's community may also be associated with satisfaction. Many communities, including municipalities, college campuses, and the workplaces, implement programs and policies that seek to advance the diversity of the population based on the hypothesized benefits. However, the research on patterns of residential satisfaction in multiethnic contexts is complicated. For example, in a Chicago-area study on neighborhood satisfaction, Whites were found to report less satisfaction in neighborhoods with more minority residents, some of which is related to socioeconomic status (Swaroop & Krysan, 2011). Latinos, however, living in integrated neighborhoods, were more satisfied with their neighborhood because these places were perceived to have better socioeconomic conditions and fewer social problems than predominately minority communities. African Americans were more satisfied in moderately integrated neighborhoods because of the fact that these neighborhoods have better living conditions than predominately Black neighborhoods. The authors conclude that both social characteristics and race/ethnicity are important in shaping neighborhood satisfaction across racial/ethnic groups.

Third, by assessing the satisfaction or quality of public services, practitioners and policy makers can identify strengths or gaps, pinpointing potential areas for action. Indeed, there are state laws that require institutions such as health and human services to conduct community satisfactions surveys. For example, Texas law requires the Texas Department of Family and Protective Services to conduct community satisfaction surveys about adult protective services in terms of their capacity, effectiveness, and professionalism. (For more information see https://www.dfps.state.tx.us/adult_protection/about_adult_protective_services/survey.asp.) They use the results to develop strategies for sustaining community support, augmenting local community networks, strengthening volunteer programs, and improving community resources. Improving the quality of services can enhance resident perceptions and also place the community in a "more strategically advantageous position in the external marketplace" (Sirgy et al., 2000, p. 281).

Finally, there is value in understanding how people combine their feelings of their social network, attachment to neighborhood, and quality of services in assessing a broader measure, such as community satisfaction. The structure and independence of these related concepts needs to be examined to better understand the complex emotion of being "satisfied" with one's neighborhood or community.

METHODS USED TO MEASURE COMMUNITY RESOURCES AND SATISFACTION

Neighborhood resources have been measured using two approaches to data collection: observations, considered more objective measures, or surveys, which are considered subjective. Both of these methods typically rely on counts that are then summarized to a defined geographical level, similar to the "container approach" discussed in Chapter 9. As we will see when discussing individual measures, survey methods typically assess the presence or absence of a resource in a large geographical area, such as a census tract or "my neighborhood." Survey items may also ask participants how long it takes them to walk to a given resource, drawing a radius around a point of origin (10 min walk) and measuring the presence or absence of the resource within the given boundary. This approach is similar to the "travel cost" or "minimum distance" approach discussed in Chapter 9 but relies solely on participant self-report rather than geographical data. Observational data, on the other hand, is most frequently measured at smaller geographical levels, such as streets, blocks, or block faces, allowing researchers to consider the density of resources in a given space (Mastrofski, Parks, & McCluskey, 2010).

Administrative data collected by the government and private business have been used to objectively measure neighborhood resources. In this method, existing data are collected and typically joined with other data sources based on geographical location. When the data is accessed, it may already be aggregated to a certain geographical level, such as a census tract, or may be provided as geographical points (addresses) that need to be mapped and aggregated by the researcher or community practitioner. Several sources of administrative data may be used to measure community resources, including records of tax-exempt organizations, community referral services and directories, public transit records, and data on community development block grant programs (Coulton, 2008). Some of these are more difficult to obtain than others. For example, the Urban Institute maintains databases of IRS tax records that are available for a fee, but data from HUD-funded community development projects can vary significantly from project to project (Coulton, 2008). Allard and colleagues (2003) used a list of service providers compiled by The United Way and the Substance Abuse and Mental Health administration to measure resources in a neighborhood. Some studies have used databases such as Dunn and Bradstreet data to extract data on the number of business, which may be considered resources (Galster, Hayes, & Johnson, 2005). Although efficient, because of the limited cost associated with access, data obtained from these sources are often measured at differing geographical levels, making them difficult to combine with other data sources. The use of administrative data to understand resources in a neighborhood is also significantly hindered by the limitation of reliable measures that are publicly available (Nicotera, 2007). Both of these limitations of administrative data frequently result in the use of proxy measures for the main constructs that the researcher and practitioners are interested in assessing, necessitating other data collection methods for more precise measurement.

Observations go beyond administrative data by measuring the physical properties of the neighborhood (Raudenbush & Sampson, 1999). The methods used to collect observational data include direct observation and using technology such as Google Maps or video recordings of neighborhood assets. Regardless of the method, the measurement tools are similar; raters are asked to move physically or virtually around a defined space and count the number of defined resources in that given location. Although theoretically objective and therefore preferred over survey methods that rely on subjective self-report, these methods are not without their limitations. Measurement error may be introduced to observations when the observer is biased or the phenomena being observed vary significantly based on the time of observation (Nicotera, 2007). Measurement error produced by the time of observation is less important when observing resources because institutions are typically observed as buildings, which do not change over the course of a day (Mastrofski, Parks, & McCluskey, 2010). Observer bias is more of a concern when measuring resources. Observers can introduce error by intentionally marking something that is not observed, to save time, or unintentionally due to stereotypes, prejudice, or misinformation (Mastrofski et al., 2010). In these studies, observers are rarely from the neighborhood that they are observing and therefore may misinterpret physical cues based on their own experience. Again, observational bias may be more salient when observing behavior or interactions but less so when observing organizations or institutions because the observer is not required to make subjective judgment about what is being observed and the object of observation (resources) will not react to being observed, two of the most common sources of observational bias (Mastrofski et al., 2010). We do, however, see that bias is still present when measuring some resources (Zenk et al., 2007). Many methods have been used to increase the reliability of systematic social observation studies, such as extensive training, including members of the neighborhood on the research team, using multiple observers and test of inter-rater reliability, or the extent to which observers agree (Raudenbush & Sampson, 1999; Zenk et al., 2007).

Using surveys to measure resources may be a more cost-effective approach but can produce results that are biased and difficult to generalize to the neighborhood level (Evans, 1999). Survey items that ask participants to report the presence or absence of an organization or institution in their neighborhood assume that the respondent has interacted with these spaces and are able to provide a reasonable report. This reliance on participant self-report may provide unreliable estimates of the actual resource environment. Despite the lack of objectivity, in some cases, subjective measures of neighborhood resources are preferable because perceptions are more central to the research/practice question than the actual presence or absence of the resource in the neighborhood. If, for example, a study is interested in understanding the relationship between older adults' access to parks and their physical activity, their perception of the time it takes them to reach the park may be more important than the parks' objective presence or distance. If the park is present but the older adult does not know it is there or perceives it to be farther from their home then it actually is, then the parks' presence may have no impact on their physical activity. Additionally, different residents may value different resources as being helpful to their functioning, differences that may be explained by life stage or access to transportation (Wen et al., 2006), again necessitating residents' self-report rather than objective measures of neighborhood resources.

Historically satisfaction has been measured through surveys or interviews administered in a community that began with a single global item such as "are you satisfied with your community?" or "are you satisfied with government services in general?" These early single item measures lacked reliability. However, the structure of community satisfaction measures has been enhanced with the widespread acceptance of its multidimensionality (Brown, Dorius, & Krannich, 2005; Carro, Valera, & Vidal, 2010; Galster & Hesser, 1981; Hughey & Bardo, 1984). Thus, survey questions assessing community satisfaction contain multiple items assessing satisfaction with various community structures and services but also perceptions of conditions in the social environment such as safety, relations among neighbors, and whether the community is good place to raise families. Measuring community satisfaction takes a territorial approach whereby participants are asked to rate selected features of their local environment using Likert scale-type responses. Data can be collected through a random selection of residents who are interviewed or surveyed either in person, by telephone, mail/email, or through web-based surveys offering a link to a survey for everyone who visits a community's official website. The latter method provides the least rigorous approach as a convenience sample but can be used as a starting point to understand perceptions of community and public services. As described previously, the selection of the best method is determined by the purpose of the survey and the resources available to support the inquiry.

Satisfaction measures, like other measures, have limitations. The biggest criticism of service satisfaction measures is that they generate high favorable rates (Royce, Thayer, Padgett, & Logan, 2001). Social desirability, fear of reprisal, and lack of specificity with items contribute to these high rates. The order of items has also been found to impact scores. With a large community sample, Van de Walle and Van Ryzin (2011) measured satisfaction with government services. They found that satisfaction levels change, depending on question order; specific service rating, when asked first, resulted in lower overall satisfaction. In addition, most satisfaction with service tools assess generalized satisfaction within an overall domain (e.g., police protection) rather than an assessment of specific quality of police services (e.g., response times, interaction). Pascoe and Attkisson (1983) sought to determine if respondents could discriminate and independently assess the various dimensions that represent distinct characteristics of the services and settings. The results indicate that consumers can distinguish between the various dimensions, leading to a more precise tool for assessing satisfaction with community services.

MEASURES OF COMMUNITY RESOURCES

Observation-Based Measures of Resources

Objective measures of neighborhood environments have primarily focused on assessing disorder and disorganization, measuring environmental characteristics like vacant lots, graffiti, and/or litter (note: these types of measures are included in Chapter 9). Some of the studies that have conducted social observations have included resources such as churches or recreational centers, but these have been included far less often in published research (House et al., 2011). Both the Project of Human Development conducted in 1995 and the follow-up study, the Chicago Community Adult Health Study (CCHAS), collected systematic social observations of community resources (House et al., 2011). This was achieved by sending two raters to a given geographical location with a tool that asked them to indicate whether or not a variety of neighborhood characteristics was present on each of the block faces observed, including the presence of neighborhood resources such as recreation centers, pharmacies, churches, community houses, and banks (see **Table 8.1 Observed Chicago Neighborhood Characteristics**). During data collection, each rater walked around each block twice while coding. In addition to individual observation, blocks were also videotaped and randomly selected tape was coded to assess for measurement reliability. In this study, inter-rater reliability ranged from .78 to 1.00 and was higher for items that were objective, such as the presence of a high rise, and lower for items that were subjective such as the quality of the sidewalk (Clarke, Ailshire, Melendez, Bader, & Morenoff, 2010).

- A study compared the systematic social observations data collected as part of the CCAHS and observations of the same blocks using the same instrument conducted with Google Street View and found that items such as recreational facilities, parks, churches, and stores were reliably assessed using the virtual method.
- In this study there was considerable agreement between the systematic social observations and observations using Google Street View.
- The agreement was higher for measures of the presence of recreational facilities and characteristics of the local food environment and lower for observations of less common features of the neighborhood, such as supermarkets and drug stores or pharmacies (Clark et al., 2010).

Using the CCHAS observational tool as a starting point, the **Neighborhood Observational Checklist (NOC)** (see **Table 8.2**) was created with the input of residents living in the community being assessed and implemented by a community partner (Zenk et al., 2007). The tool was designed to test the hypothesis that residential racial/ethnic composition influenced the availability and effectiveness of municipal and other services. NOC is a 140-item tool designed to assess a variety of domains, including neighborhood social relations, services, material resources, stressors, and behaviors. For the purposes of this chapter, we will focus on the items that measure services and resources. This measure was not only developed with community input but was implemented by community members and tested for inter-rater reliability. In the first iteration of this tool, seven out of the 15 of community members that had been trained to use this tool were able to achieve a kappa of at least .75. To improve the inter-rater reliability, many items were clarified based on the feedback of the residents. After the modification, 61% of items in the tool had perfect test–retest reliability, 29% had moderate test–retest reliability, and 5% had poor test–retest reliability. Similar to findings in the previous study, large stable items, such as recreation centers, had the strongest test–retest reliability. This measure is unique because, in addition to listing "establishments," such as banks, community-based organizations, and medical care facilities, it also included "ethnic symbols and services," which included "business or institutions with African or Caribbean product or services" and "business or institutions with Spanish name or surname." The inclusion of race-based resources is significant contribution that has not be replicated in other measures.

Survey-Based Measures of Resources

Similar to the systematic social observations, the most basic assessment of resources in a survey includes a list of institutions and/or organizations and asks participates to indicate if they are present in their neighborhood. Byrd and Chavous (2009) (see **Table 8.3 Institutional Resources**) offer one example of this type of measure asking participants if a list of four community services (i.e., scouting troops, after school programs) are present in their neighborhood. In a similar instrument, Molnar, Cerda, Roberts, and Buka (2008) (see **Table 8.4 Organizations and Services**) used a list of 14 items, eight of which were general items—such as neighborhood watch programs, family planning clinics, and substance abuse treatment facilities—and the other six were youth-orientated services that included items like youth centers, mental health services, and so forth. Respondents were asked to indicate if they were or were not present. Similarly Sooman and Macintyre (1995) (see **Table 8.5 Local Amenities)** asked respondents if any of the following "amenities" were within walking distance for their home: GP surgery, a dental surgery, a chemist, a post office, a public telephone, public sports facilities, a public park, a grocery store, a launderette, a public house, and a bank. In this study, amenities were not related to health outcomes but were significantly related to area satisfaction and the participants' overall assessment of their neighborhood, which in turn was related to anxiety and overall self-rated health. In all of these studies a simple count was created to summarize the items in the construct. Internal consistency reliability measures (e.g., Cronbach's alpha) were not reported because it was not expected that these items were necessarily related to each other. While these measures do give us a sense of the overall resource environment, they represent a count rather than a concept because there is no a priori reason to suspect that one facility's presence would be related to another's (e.g., a public sporting facility may not be related to the presence of a grocery store). In all three of these studies neighborhood resources were associated with positive outcomes: student GPA (Byrd & Chavous, 2009), less aggressive behavior among youth (Molnar et al., 2008), and area satisfaction (Sooman & Macintyre, 1995). Both Byrd and Chavous (2009) and Molnar and colleagues (2008) also found that the amount of neighborhood resources interacted with other individual level processes such as racial identity and interaction with pro-social peers to impact youth outcomes.

In addition to asking about the presence of resources, Richard, Gauvin, Gosselin, and Laforest (2008) (see **Table 8.6 Perceived Accessibility to Key Resources**) asked respondents to rate the ease/difficulty of accessing resources in the neighborhoods with resources including "1) good quality affordable food, 2) a good range of businesses and services, and 3) leisure activities of interest." In this study perceived accessibility of resources predicted social participation (Richard et al., 2008). Similarly, Van der Pas et al. (2016) (see **Table 8.7 Home and Community Environmental Instrument**) asked respondents to indicate if any of the facilities (parks, places to sit, public transportation) are found in their neighborhood, with responses ranging from "a lot" to "not at all"; in the analysis, however, these items where dichotomized similar to the other measures discussed. Notably, this study included a question about the participant's use of the facility when the participant indicated that a resource was present. This addition was notable because it took into account both the presence of the resource and the resident interaction with that resource. All items in these scales were treated as independent and not aggregated. In the study, the response to the questions about the use of resources was used as the dependent variable, testing the relationship between having lower limb osteoarthritis and the use the resources. In this study participants with lower-limb osteoarthritis (LLOA) made more use of places to sit in the United Kingdom and less use of parks and walking areas compared to participants without LLOA, particularly in countries with high availability of resources (Van der Pas et al., 2016).

Combining Observations and Survey Methods to Measure Community Resources

Few studies have incorporated both survey and observational measures. In one study that utilized both methods, Boehmer et al. (2007) (see **Table 8.8 Environmental Indicators**) measures resources across four domains: recreational facilities, land use, transportation, and aesthetics. In this study, the two forms of data were linked using geographic information systems software. A comprehensive audit tool was created, and GPS technology was utilized to record the positioning of the observations. In this study, the observational street segment data was aggregated to 400-m radius surrounding each participant's residence, what the authors estimated was within a five-minute walk. Similarly, the survey items asked respondents how long it took them to walk to the resources that they indicated were present in their neighborhood. In this study being obese was significantly associated with perceived indicators of nearby nonresidential destinations, absence of sidewalks, unpleasant community, and lack of interesting sites and observed indicators of poor sidewalk quality, physical disorder, and presence of garbage (Boehmer et al., 2007). While the goal of this study was to assess the relationship between these resources and obesity, this measure could be used to gain a more comprehensive understanding of a neighborhood's resources, such as access to public transportation, recreational facilities, nonresidential destinations (including supermarkets, restaurants, post office), and "interesting things to look at." This study also assessed two nontraditional definitions of neighborhoods, with stronger associations found between fewer perceived nonresidential destinations (less mixed-land use) and obesity, with a one-km radius compared to a 400-m radius of an individual's residence.

MEASURES OF COMMUNITY SATISFACTION

Much of the early research on community satisfaction began with instruments assessing resident's general sense of satisfaction with their neighborhood, town, city, or larger community context. Residents rated various features like courteousness, cultural interests, and recreation (Fessler, 1952). In an attempt to validate the idea that a general measure of community satisfaction is needed for use in comparative studies, Vreugdenhil and Rigby (1987) tested a **General Community Satisfaction Scale (GCSS)** in two different communities in southern Australia (see **Table 8.9**). The GCSS contains 24 items with an equal number of positively stated items (e.g., this suburb is a good place for children to grow up in, people should be proud to say that they live in this suburb) and negatively stated items (e.g., it is dangerous to live in this suburb, the quality of life in this suburb is low). Factor analyses showed that each of the 24 GCSS items loaded on the first factor, accounting for 40.1% of the total variance in one community and 31.2% in the second community. The internal consistency of the

GCSSs was high along with high concurrent validity. The authors acknowledged that there were minor differences in the factors that were extracted, noting that the factorial structure of community satisfaction may differ from one community to the next.

More recently, satisfaction with community is understood to include other dimensions, including a person's perception of their social life, physical environment, and the extent and availability of services. Wen, Hawkley, and Cacioppo (2006) investigated the links between health and the objective environment and subjective perceptions of local neighborhoods. These researchers used three subjective measures to assess residents' **perceptions of neighborhood quality** (see **Table 8.10**). Assessing physical environment perceptions, residents were asked to describe their neighborhood with regard to affordable and comfortable housing, public parks, noise, crowdedness, and air quality. Perceived social environment is a six-item scale that asked residents, for example, to rate the friendliness of neighbors, morale of residents, personal safety, and opportunity to participate in local government. Finally, to measure perceptions of local services, residents were asked to evaluate the quality of a number of neighborhood's institutions, like schools, hospitals, and city services, such as lighting and garbage pick-up. Factor analysis showed items loading on three separate factors (see Table 8.10 for reported reliabilities). The researchers also created a composite scale of perceived general neighborhood quality consisting of the three subscales, which demonstrated high internal reliability.

- The study results showed that perceived neighborhood quality had an important and unique impact on self-rated health controlling for other factors.
- Specifically, perceived physical environment was stronger than perceptions of social and service environments in contributing to the link between neighborhood and health (Wen et al., 2006).

Using a national sample of communities, researchers examined individual and community contributors to community satisfaction (Fitz, Lyon, & Driskell, 2015). Overall community satisfaction was measured with items such as likelihood of recommending community to others and able to say that you are proud to live in the community (see **Table 8.11 Community Satisfaction**). This general measure allowed the researchers to make initial comparisons across 26 cities. To understand the potential variation in residents' sense of satisfaction, however, a factor analysis of satisfaction-related items was conducted. The analysis yielded two other separate measures of community satisfaction: social life and infrastructure. Social life was rated using questions, for example, pertaining to the availability of arts and cultural opportunities, the beauty or physical setting, or how much people care about each other. The other domain asked respondents about their satisfaction related to the community's infrastructure. Researchers, for example, included items asking about satisfaction with the highway and freeway system, quality of colleges and universities, and the effectiveness of the local police. This study also included several indicators of human capital, individual level social/capital networks, and community-level human capital and social capita/networks to identify individual- and community-level factors that influence community satisfaction.

- In general Fitz and colleagues (2015) found that factors that contribute to satisfaction with social life and community infrastructure looked similar to patterns found for overall community satisfaction; however, two human capital variables were consistent; being female and being an older adult were positively related to overall community satisfaction and social and infrastructure satisfaction.

- Living in large communities with dense populations was found to be negatively associated with all three domains of community satisfaction.
- However, living among active participants in various civic organizations contributes significantly to individual satisfaction with the community.
- Other findings suggest the importance of distinguishing between domains of satisfaction, individual and community levels, and types of capital (Fitz et al., 2015).

One study examined how community sentiment is affected by one's personal ties to the community compared with the organizational network structure of the community, using an interesting approach to measure the community environment. Crowe (2010) asked respondents to assess their community using five word pairs (see **Table 8.12 Community Attachment and Satisfaction**). Respondents were asked to imagine a scale that ranged from 1 to 7 and to rate each of the following word pairs: friendly/unfriendly, indifferent/supportive, not trusting/trusting, prejudiced/tolerant, rejecting of new ideas/open to new ideas. A second set of four questions, using a 5-point scale, were used to evaluate community spaces including senior centers, meeting space in city offices, and formal meeting space in local restaurants or other businesses. Researchers examined how community sentiment is affected by one's personal ties to the community compared with the organizational network structure of the community. Researchers found that living in a community characterized by a complete or coalitional network structure significantly influences an individual's favorable evaluation of the community. While the internal consistencies were modest, the measure offers a brief tool to evaluate the community environment on issues of value to residents.

Building on prior studies (Sirgy et al., 2000; Sirgy & Cornwell, 2002), researchers tested a comprehensive model of community satisfaction and satisfaction with community services (Grzeskowiak, Sirgy, & Widgery, 2003). There were 57 items measuring satisfaction with various aspects of community life; five constructs related to this chapter are included here (see **Table 8.13 Multidimensional Measure of Community Satisfaction and Services**). Satisfaction with community was assessed using four items, ranging from a general question about overall satisfaction to one rating the community as a desirable place to live. A second construct measured satisfaction with community conditions such as race relations, community leaders, condition of streets, availability of parks, and so forth. Satisfaction with community services was asked in relation to features such as recreational facilities, public schools and medical services, crime prevention, and so forth. Another construct used to understand community satisfaction was neighborhood satisfaction. This is logical because a neighborhood is the closest psychological representation of community. One general question asked about satisfaction with the quality of life in the neighborhood. This was followed by questions about neighborhood conditions. Residents were asked how satisfied they were with neighbors, number of children, racial mix, appearances of homes, traffic, and so forth. The authors noted that most of these measures were developed for formative purposes and thus they only reported Cronbach's alpha = .67 for the satisfaction with community scale. However, they did report a reliability coefficient for all tested items at .80. In the study researchers found that:

- Satisfaction with community services is directly influenced by residents' satisfaction with community conditions and residents' satisfaction with their neighborhood.
- Satisfaction with other life domains (social, family, work) is linked to satisfaction with community services.

- Confidence in local institutions strongly influenced residents' satisfaction with community services, community satisfaction, and community commitment (Grzeskowiak et al., 2003).

MEASURES OF SATISFACTION WITH PUBLIC SERVICES

One of the important dimensions of community satisfaction is the availability of and satisfaction with services or resources. As mentioned earlier in this chapter, the availability of resources relies upon an observation or survey-based measure or counts of a community's parks, libraries, local police, and so forth. It also has a subjective dimension: asking residents their perceptions of availability regardless of whether or not they use those services.

Residents form opinions about the quality of services or assess their satisfaction with services based on their experience but also through the experiences and information from families, friends, coworkers, social media, advertising, and marketing. For example, residents may be influenced by recent media reports about corrupt government officials and form a negative opinion about government services in general. Even if respondents have no experience, it appears that many have opinions about specific services. Thus, satisfaction with services is influenced by a range of factors.

Surveys of resident or consumer satisfaction with services have emerged in the last half century, and measures have evolved, because of their widespread use by nonprofits, business, and government. Satisfaction with services is often used as an outcome measure when program administrators are faced with requirements of measurement by funding, regulatory, and certification agencies. In these cases, consumer feedback is valued and can easily be collected and summarized. A more competitive global marketplace has served to ignite interest in customer satisfaction, as businesses seek competitive advantages. State and local government use satisfaction surveys to reorganize services, allocate budgets, and hold bureaucrats accountable. The availability of services is also used by researchers to explain disparities in health, economic well-being, violence, and stability of communities.

Sirgy and colleagues (2000) developed a measure for assessing resident's **satisfaction with community-based services** (see **Table 8.14**). Rather than assessing residents' satisfaction with services in general, these researchers developed a tool to measure specific government, business, and nonprofit services that can be used for internal evaluation and corrective action. Their assessment procedure involved two parts. First, respondents were asked to rate three specific domains of service: government, business, and nonprofit. Within each domain there were lists of services; for example, in government services, respondents were asked about services such as voter registration, economic development, and public education. Individual business services were also listed such as healthcare, transportation, and investment services. Lists of services such as support groups, senior services, and food/shelter services made up the individual nonprofit services. Respondents used an 8-point Delighted–Terrible scale to evaluate each item. A second step required respondents to rate how important or unimportant each of these services were in their community. Composite index scores were computed as average satisfaction scores, weighted by perceived importance of each service. The results supported their model that consumer satisfaction with individual government services, business services, and nonprofit services affect broader community satisfaction.

Many local governments and municipalities conduct satisfaction surveys on a regular basis to assess citizen quality ratings of public services (Miller & Kobayashi, 2000). Using a random sample of New York City residents, Van Ryzin, Muzzio,

Immerwahr, Gulick, and Martinez (2004) examined the drivers and consequences of citizen satisfaction. These researchers asked a series of questions about local government services (see **Table 8.15 Customer Satisfaction With Local Government Services**). For example, they asked respondents to rate library services in general, police force, city bus services, fire protection services, recreation services, cleanliness of the streets, and public schools. Rather than use the data to determine which services were rated higher, they looked at factors that explain the variation in satisfaction. They found that the highest-rated services (fire protection, library services, and parks) were not significant drivers in explaining overall judgments of quality and satisfaction with city services. Rather, the lowest-rated services, including road surfaces, public schools, and subway services, were important predictors of overall quality and satisfaction. Thus, interpreting the results from individual satisfaction items is not sufficient when there is such variability in their relationship to predicting overall satisfaction.

For many individuals, accessing services and resources is paramount to addressing the physical or health needs of family members or other vulnerable populations. Services may not operate as scheduled or be provided in ways that reflect common standards of care. Community planners and others measure access to resources as a sub domain of satisfaction with services in order to determine if some groups have lesser access to services. For example, Montes, Halterman, and Magyar (2009) used a nationally representative sample of over 40,000 children to assess access to and satisfaction with school and community health services among U.S. children with autism spectrum disorder (ASD) (see **Table 8.16**). Satisfaction is measured with one question, but this measure also looks at difficulties in using services. This measure is included because it provides a checklist of 12 follow-up options to record the reason for the lack of access and therefore satisfaction or dissatisfaction with services.

- The study found that parents of children with ASDs were three times more likely to report difficulties accessing community and health services compared to other parents.
- Also, parents of children with ASD were more likely to identify lack of supply of qualified providers and available service as a problem than other parents.
- By assessing access and satisfaction among parents of children with ASD, researchers used the information to make public policy recommendations in areas of short provider supply and for training and more services for these children (Montes et al., 2009).

Finally, Gareis and Barnett (2008) proposed that a good community resource fit, such as the areas of work and school, may act as a safety buffer from the stress working parents might experience as they try to meet the obligations associated with work and family. The authors developed a measure of "resource fit" (see **Table 8.17 Community Resource Fit**) to assess community members' perceptions of how well resources in their community meet their needs. Community resource fit was measured with 36 items that addressed six resource areas, including work, public transportation, school, school transportation, after-school, and after-school transportation. Internal consistency was good for mothers and fathers. The results indicate that good community resource fit may act as a buffer protecting parents of school-age children from the stress they experience associated with work and family obligations. While the tool is specific to families of school-aged children, the authors suggest that it can be adapted to assess resources critical for other types of families, such as those with eldercare responsibilities.

CONCLUSION

Measuring community resources and satisfaction are essential to taking a strength-based approach to community development, can be important for identifying deficits, and may lead to more precise community-level interventions. Although the measures of community resources are typically crude, involving counts that are aggregated to some level of geography, their inclusion in the assessment of the overall neighborhood environment provides a more nuanced picture of neighborhoods. While evidence does suggest that neighborhoods with more economic disadvantage have less resources, some studies have shown that this is not necessarily the case (Small, 2006). Identifying and improving crucial resources in disadvantaged neighborhoods, as suggested by Asset Based Community Development strategies, may be essential to addressing the negative impacts of living in disadvantaged neighborhoods. In addition to resources, measuring community satisfaction with existing resources also provides important information to researchers and community practitioners about targets of community intervention. In addition to the direct benefit of engaging with quality social services, community satisfaction is related to neighborhood retention, which in turn is related to lower rates of disorder and improved overall neighborhood well-being. Capitalizing on the objectivity provided by social observations and the valuable information provided by residents about their subjective experiences with resources, the combination of these measures and approaches may help neighborhood researcher and practitioners create neighborhoods that are optimal for resident well-being.

LIST OF MEASURES AND TABLE NUMBERS

TABLE 8.1 ■ Observed Chicago Neighborhood Characteristics

Primary Reference	Clarke, P. Ailshire, J., Melendez, R., Bader, M., & Morenoff, J. (2010). Using Google Earth to conduct a neighborhood audit: reliability of a virtual audit instrument. *Health & Place, 16*(6), 1224–1229. House, J. S., Kaplan, G. A., Morenoff, J., Raudenbush, S. W., Williams, D. R., & Young, E. A. (2011, June 7). *Chicago Community Adult Health Study, 2001–2003.* (ICPSR31142-v1). Ann Arbor, MI: Inter-university Consortium for Political and Social Research [distributor]. http://doi.org/10.3886/ICPSR31142.v1
Purpose	The study was designed to measure the relationship between neighborhood factors and health outcomes.
Description	This data was collected using a survey instrument that depicted a city block. In this measure raters were asked to indicate the presence or absence of 11 items including • Recreational facilities (i.e., any park) • Food environment (i.e., any convenience store) • General land use (i.e., any high-rise housing) • Commercial land use (i.e., any bank) • Community house • Store-front church For all items, see the survey instrument publically available on ICPR.
Sample	• The data come from the Chicago Community Adult Health Study (CCAHS). • 3,105 adults were sampled in 343 neighborhood clusters. • Data was collected using systematic social observations conducted on blocks where survey participants lived.
Scoring	This information was not available.
Assessment	Inter-rater reliability was established with a subsample of 80 blocks. The observed agreement ranged from .78 to 1. The agreement was higher for objective measures and lower for measure that required judgment.
Language	English
Contact	Philippa Clarke Institute for Social Research University of Michigan 426 Thompson Street Ann Arbor, MI, 48104 Tel: 734-647-9611, Fax: 734-936-0548 Email: pjclarke@umich.edu

TABLE 8.2 ■	Neighborhood Observational Checklist: Establishments, Ethnic Symbols, and Services
Primary Reference	Zenk, S. N., Schulz, A. J., Mentz, G., House, J. S., Gravlee, C. C., Miranda, P. Y., & Kannan, S. (2007). Inter-rater and test-retest reliability: methods and results for the neighborhood observational checklist. *Health & Place, 13*(2), 452–465.
Purpose	• Develop an observation tool that had adequate test-retest reliability when used with community members • Test the relationship between neighborhood resources and health disparities
Description	This tool included two observational measures of resources: (1) establishments and (2) ethnic symbols and service. This measure used the audit tool developed as part of the Chicago Community Adult Health Study and was modified based on the feedback of residents in the study neighborhoods. **Establishments** was an 11-item scale that included • Bank • Bar/cocktail lounge • Community-based organization, social service agency, or community center • Medical care facility • Pawn shop/second hand store • Restaurant The 9 items of the **ethnic, symbols, and services** scale included • Saying, symbol, or mural of African, African American, or Black identity pride • Religious saying, symbol, or mural • Business or institutions with African or Caribbean products or services for African Americans • Business or institutions with Latino symbols • Business or institutions with *se habla espanol* sign • Business or institutions with Spanish name or surname
Sample	• Eleven observers conducted observations on 551 blocks in three communities. • The blocks included blocks where participants in a survey-based study were living as wells as block that shared a common border with these blocks. • The median number of minutes to collect data on one block was 78.
Scoring	This information was not available.
Assessment	• Most items on both scales had substantial or almost perfect test-retest reliability (Kappa 0.60–1.00). • "Saying, symbol, or mural of Latino or Mexican identity or pride" and "Religious saying, symbol, or mural" had moderate kappas of .57 and .50, respectively. • Inter-rater reliability sores for each item on the establishments scale fell between .63 and .54. • All items on the ethnic symbols and services scale had inter-rater reliability scores between .82 and .67 except for "Saying, symbol, or mural of Latino or Mexican identity or pride" and "Religious saying, symbol, or mural" demonstrated poor test-retest reliability," which fell far below the acceptable range.
Language	English.

Contact	Department of Public Health, Mental Health, and Administrative Nursing University of Illinois at Chicago College of Nursing 845 S Damen Ave, M/C 802 Chicago, IL 60608 Tel.: 312-355-2790 Fax: 312-996-8066. Email: szenk@uic.edu (S.N. Zenk)

TABLE 8.3 ■	**Institutional Resources**
Primary Reference	Byrd, C. M., & Chavous, T. M. (2009). Racial identity and academic achievement in the neighborhood context: A multilevel analysis. *Journal of Youth and Adolescence, 38*(4), 544–59.
Purpose	• Used to test the interaction between racial identity and community-level factors, in this case resources on African American youth's academic outcomes. • Tested the hypothesis that institutional resources aided youth identity development.
Description	In this study, institutional resources were defined as the "quality and availability of organizations and services that improve the resident's lives" (p. 545). In this study, the institutional resources is a neighborhood-level variable measured by two scales. The first 4-item scale included • After school recreation programs for children • Organized summer recreational programs for children The second 4-item scale asked respondents to rate the quality of services in their neighborhood. Some of the services include • The schools in this neighborhood are . . . • The parks and playgrounds in this neighborhood are . . .
Sample	• 564 African American eighth graders (56% male) who were parts of the Maryland Adolescent Development in Context Study (MADICS) (http://www.rcgd.isr.umich.edu/pgc/) • The sample included a range of neighborhood types and income levels, and the majority of the county where the data collection took place was African American.
Scoring	The article indicated that "responses were aggregated to the census tract level" but the method of aggregation was not specified.
Assessment	No assessment of reliability was included.
Language	English
Contact	C. M. Byrd and T. M. Chavous Combined Program in Education & Psychology University of Michigan 610 E. University Ave. Ann Arbor, MI 48109-1259 Email: tchavous@umich.edu

TABLE 8.4 ■	Organizations and Services
Primary Reference	Molnar, B. E., Cerda, M., Roberts, A. L., & Buka, S. L. (2008). Effects of neighborhood resources on aggressive and delinquent behaviors among urban youths. *American Journal of Public Health, 98*(6), 1086–93.
Purpose	This measure was used to test the relationship between neighborhood-level resources and aggression and delinquency among youth.
Description	Organizations and services were measured using 14-item scale that assessed the presence of local organizations, resources, and programs. Two subscales were outlined, one that measured organization and services generally and the other that measured organizations and services focused on meeting the needs of youth. The general 8-item subscale that was used to measure **general resources** included • Parks and playgrounds • Community newsletters • Family health services • Block groups and tenant associations • Substance abuse treatment centers The 6-item subscale that focused on **youth services** included • Youth centers • Recreational programs • Mentoring and counseling programs • Crisis intervention services
Sample	• This data comes from the Project on Human Development in Chicago Neighborhoods (PHDCN). • The measure of community resources was derived from 2226 survey respondents in 80 neighborhood clusters in Chicago (this analysis only included youth participants who were enrolled at baseline and their caregivers). • Demographics of the sample were not provided.
Scoring	• The scales were summed creating a continuous count variable and then mean centered. • These items were then aggregated up to the census-tract level, but the method of aggregation was not specified.
Assessment	Reliability and validity of this measure was not provided.
Results	• This study found that living in a neighborhood where organizations and services were available was associated with less aggressive behavior. • There was also significant cross-level interaction found between the concentration of organizations and services and prosocial peers such that, when both were high, they resulted in lower odds of aggressive behavior, with organizations and services effectively amplifying the protective effect of pro social peers.
Language	English
Contact	Beth E. Molnar Department of Society, Human Development and Health Harvard School of Public Health 677 Huntington Ave, Sixth Floor Boston, MA 02115 Email: bmolnar@hsph.harvard.edu

TABLE 8.5 ■ Local Amenities	
Primary Reference	Sooman, A., & Macintyre, S. (1995). Health and perceptions of the local environment in socially contrasting neighbourhoods in Glasgow. *Health & Place, 1*(1), 15–26.
Purpose	This measure was used to assess differences in amenities across neighborhoods and if these differences were associated with mental health and self-rated health outcomes.
Description	The 11-item measure of amenities located within walking distance (or half a mile) of the respondent's home included • A post office • A public telephone • A public sports facilities • A public park • Bank • Public house
Sample	• The data used in this study was collected in 1992 as part of The West of Scotland Twenty-07 Study: Health in the community. • The sample included 318 forty-year-olds and 373 sixty-year-olds. • Respondents were sampled from two social contrasting (advantaged and disadvantaged) areas in Glasgow, in four neighborhoods.
Scoring	• A summary variable (range 0–11) was constructed from a simple count of the presence of these 11 amenities.
Assessment	Measures of reliability do not apply to this scale.
Language	English
Contact	Anne Sooman MRC Medical Sociology Unit 6 Lilybank Gardens Glasgow G12 8QQ, UK

TABLE 8.6 ■	Perceived Accessibility to Key Resources
Primary Reference	Richard L., Gauvin, L., Gosselin, C., & Laforest, S. (2009). Staying connected: Neighbourhood correlates of social participation among older adults living in an urban environment in Montreal, Quebec. *Health Promotion International, 24*(1), 46–57.
Purpose	Test the relationship between perceived accessibility of key resources to examine the relationship between resources and social participation among older adults.
Description	This measure included two scales. The first was composed of 8 items assessing the ease/difficulty of **accessing resources** including • Good quality, affordable food • Leisure activities of interest • Facilities to engage in preferred physical activities or sports • Pleasant and welcoming restaurants or cafés • A library or cultural center The second scale measured the **proportion of services/amenities** located within a 5-min walk of the respondent's residents. Respondent were asked how many minutes it would take to walk from their residence to 11 different services. Some of these include • Grocery/food store • Pharmacy • Library/cultural center • Bank • Restaurant/bistro/café • Church/place of worship
Sample	• 282 older adults recruited through community organizations located in high-, average-, and low-income neighborhood in Montreal, Quebec, with the goal of recruiting 100 participants from each designation. • The majority of the sample was female (73.8%), the average age was 71.5, 27.9% had attended 7 years of less of high school, 42.5% had attended high school, and 29.6% attended more than high school.
Scoring	Details of how the measure was scored were not included.
Assessment	The first scale had a Cronbach's α of 0.70 and the second scale had a Cronbach's α of 0.94.
Language	English
Contact	Lucie Richard Faculty of Nursing Pavillon Marguerite d'Youville 2375 Cote-Ste-Catherine Montreal, Quebec H3T 1 A8 Email: Lucie.richard@umontreal.ca

TABLE 8.7 ■	The Home and Community Environment (HACE) Instrument
Primary Reference	Van der Pas, S., Schaap, L. A., Castell, M. V., Cooper, C., Denkinger, M., Edwards, M. H., & Peter, R. (2016). Availability and use of neighborhood resources by older people with osteoarthritis: Results from the European Project on OsteoArthritis. *Health & Place*, *37*, 1–7.
Purpose	To assess differences in access and use of neighborhood resources among older adults who were diagnosed with clinical lower limb osteoarthritis (LLOA) and those who were not and if they were available, if the resource was related to its frequency of use
Description	This measure was based on the original HACE developed by Keysor, Jette, and Haley (2005) that was concerned with measuring all aspects of the environment that impacted an older adult's mobility. The original measure included multiple domains that are considered out of the scope of this chapter. The modified 3-item measure was designed to assess that aide with mobility and transportation and include • Places to sit and rest at bus stops, in parks, or in other places where people walk • Public transportation close to home Use of the resource was assessed if they indicated that they had the resource in their neighborhood by asking the participant "Do you make use of these facilities?"
Sample	• 2757 participants whose ages ranged from 65–85 years in six European counties. • The average age of the sample was 73.8 years, the majority were female (56.7%), and 33.5% were single. • The majority lived in urban settings and 51% reported that they were experiencing a functional impairment.
Scoring	Response categories for the first set of questions included "a lot," "some," and "not at all." Items in the scale were dichotomized to reflect the presence of the resource ("a lot" and "some" were coded to 1 and "not at all" was coded to 0). Possible response for the follow up question included yes (1) and no (0). These items were not aggregated, they were modeled separately.
Assessment	Measures of reliability do not apply to this scale.
Language	English
Contact	Suzan Van der Pas Department of Epidemiology and Biostatistics EMGO Institute for Health and Care Research, VU University Medical Center Boelelaan 1089a, 1081HV Amsterdam, The Netherlands Email: s.vanderpas@vumc.nl

TABLE 8.8 ■	Environmental Indicators
Primary Reference	Boehmer, T. K., Hoehner, C. M., Deshpande, A. D., Brennan Ramirez, L. K., & Brownson, R. C. (2007). Perceived and observed neighborhood indicators of obesity among urban adults. *International Journal of Obesity, 31*(6), 968–77. doi: http://dx.doi.org/10.1038/sj.ijo.0803531
Purpose	The purpose of this study was to test the relationship between both perceived and observed aspects of the environment and obesity.
Description	This measure used two data collection methods: survey items and an environmental audit. Both surveys and the environmental audit measured neighborhood characteristics in four domains: recreational facilities, land use, transportation, and athletics. In the **survey**, these domains were measured using the following scales: The 4-item **recreational facilities** measure includes • There is equipment available for physical activity in my community • Number of recreational facilities with a 5-min walk from home The 3-item **land use** measure includes • Number of nonresidential destinations within a five-min walk from home • There are many destinations to go within easy walking distance from home The 3-item **transportation** measure includes • It is easy to walk to a bus stop, train, or subway station from my home • How safe from traffic do you feel while walking or riding your bike in your neighborhood The 4-item **aesthetics** measure includes • There are my interesting things to look at while walking in my neighborhood • My neighborhood is well maintained In the **environmental audit** these domains were measured using the following items: The single-item **recreational facilities** measure assessed the number of recreational facilities. The single-item **land use** measure asses the number of nonresidential destinations. The 3-item **transportation** measure included • Segments with a bus or other transit stop • Segments of the sidewalks with no or little unevenness The 4-item **aesthetics** measure included • Segments with some or a lot of attractive features • Segments with some or a lot of comfort features
Sample	1032 randomly selected urban residents (20% obese, 32% black, 65% female)
Scoring	• The perceived number (count) of recreational facility types and destination types within 5-min walk of home (400 m) were categorized into quartiles. • Two other measures were created: distance to the nearest recreational facility and no nonresidential destination within a 10-min walk. Each item was tested separately, not aggregated in any way. • Street segment audit data within each respondent's 400m buffer was aggregated using counts, proportions, and averages and then quartiles were created based on the distribution of the total sample. Counts included the total number of recreational facilities and nonresidential facilities within the buffer.
Assessment	Measures of reliability do not apply to this scale.
Language	English
Contact	T. Boehmer 724 S. Washington Street Denver, CO 80209, USA Email: tkboehmer@gmail.com

TABLE 8.9 ■	General Community Satisfaction Scale (GCSS)
Primary Reference	Vreugdenhil, A., & Rigby, K. (1987). Assessing generalized community satisfaction. *The Journal of Social Psychology, 127*(4), 367–374.
Purpose	The purpose is to measure general community satisfaction.
Description	**General Community Satisfaction Scale** consists of 24 items, half with positive statements and half with negative statements to form a Likert scale. Each item had five response categories ranging from *agree strongly* to *disagree strongly*. For a description of all items, please see the primary reference. Sample items include • This suburb is a wonderful place in which to live. • This suburb is good place for children to grow up in. • This suburb is a boring place. • There is a feeling of pride in this community. • The environment in this suburb is bleak and depressing. • This suburb has a lot of good things going for it. • There just isn't enough privacy in this area. • Life is really dreary in this suburb. • This suburb is a very clean place. • This area has a good feeling about it. • Living in this suburb is unpleasant.
Sample	• Random sample of residents living in two areas of South Australia (Adelaide and Munno Para) • 1007 residents completed questionnaires with an average response rate of 35%
Scoring	• Factor analyses were conducted for each community separately. Factors that loaded the highest and substantially (> .50) were extracted using a Varimax rotation and are comprised of the items above.
Assessment	• Internal consistency was assessed with $\alpha = .97$ for both areas sampled.
Language	English
Contact	Ken Rigby University of South Australia 101 Currie St., Adelaide SA, 5001 South Australia, Australia Email: Ken.rigby@unisa.edu.au

TABLE 8.10 ■	Perceived Neighborhood Quality
Primary Reference	Wen, M., Hawkley, L. C., & Cacioppo, J. T. (2006). Objective and perceived neighborhood environment, individual SES and psychosocial factors, and self-rated health: An analysis of older adults in Cook County, Illinois. *Social Science & Medicine, 63*(10), 2575–2590.
Purpose	The purpose is to measure perceptions of neighborhood quality.
Description	Perceived neighborhood context tapped into three subjective assessments of the physical environment, social environment, and perceived local services. Respondents rated each item on a 4-point scale of excellent, good, fair, and poor. **Perceived physical environment** is a five-item scale that asks residents to describe their neighborhood with regard to • Affordable and comfortable housing • Noise • Air quality **Perceived social environment** is a six-item measure that asked residents to rate • Friendliness/helpfulness of neighbors • Self-esteem and morale of the residents • Opportunity to participate in local government **Perceived local services** is a six-item measure that asked residents to evaluate their neighborhood's quality of • Policing • Hospital/medical care • Garbage pick-up/snow removal Other measures on social network, social support, loneliness, depressive symptoms, hostility, perceived stress, optimism, and psychosocial status are also described in the primary reference.
Sample	• Population-based sample of 229 residents between ages of 50 to 67 years from Cook County, Illinois.
Scoring	• Responses were aggregated into composite indices for each of the three subscales. • Overall perceived general neighborhood quality factor score was calculated based on the three subscales as a composite score. Higher scores indicate better-perceived physical condition, social environment, and service environment.
Assessment	• Physical environment: $\alpha = .80$ • Perceived social environment: $\alpha = .88$ • Perceived local services: $\alpha = .85$ (excluding public transportation) • Perceived general neighborhood quality: $\alpha = .84$
Related References	Cacioppo, J. T., Hughes, M. E., Waite, L. J., & Thisted, R. A. (2006). Loneliness as a specific factor for depressive symptoms: Cross sectional and longitudinal analyses. *Psychology and Aging, 21*, 140–151. Hughes, M. E., Waite, L. J., Hawkley, L. C., & Cacioppo, J. T. (2004). A short scale for measuring loneliness in large surveys: Results from two population-based studies. *Research on Aging, 26*(6), 633–672.
Language	English
Contact	Ming Wen Department of Sociology, University of Utah, Salt Lake City, UT 84112-0250 Email: Ming.wen@soc.utah.edu

TABLE 8.11 ■	Community Satisfaction
Primary Reference	Fitz, B. M., Lyon, L., & Driskell, R. (2015). Why people like where they live: Individual and community-level contributors to community satisfaction. *Social Indicators Research, 126*, 1209–1224.
Purpose	This measure was designed to assess satisfaction with community and determine if any of those factors exist at the community level. It seeks to answer the question, why do people live where they live?
Description	Community satisfaction measure includes three domains: **Overall community satisfaction: (4 items)** • Taking everything into account, how satisfied are you with this community as a place to live? • I am proud to say I live in this community. Respondents rated each item on a 4-point scale with lowest indicating less satisfaction and higher value indicating greater satisfaction. **Satisfaction with community life: (6 items)** • The availability of social community events, such as festivals, picnics, parades, and street fairs • Being a good place to meet people and make friends • How much people in this community care about each other Respondents rated each item on a 5-point scale ranging from very bad to very good. **Satisfaction with community infrastructure: (6 items)** • The highway and freeway system • The overall quality of public schools in your community • The leadership of elected officials in your city Respondents rated each item on a 5-point scale.
Sample	• Nationally random representative sample of 26 communities with a total of 15,200 participants (Knight Soul of the Community Survey—Gallup)
Scoring	• Responses from overall satisfaction were combined into an additive index. • Means were calculated for community comparisons. • A factor analysis of the other 15 items yielded two separate measures: social life and community infrastructure.
Assessment	• Community satisfaction: $\alpha = .92$ • Social life satisfaction index: $\alpha = .83$ • Community infrastructure satisfaction: $\alpha = .79$
Language	English and Spanish
Contact	B.M. Fitz Department of Sociology Baylor University One Bear Place #97326 Waco, TX 76798 Email: Brittany_Fitz@Baylor.edu

TABLE 8.12 ■	Community Attachment and Satisfaction
Primary Reference	Crowe, J. (2010) Community attachment and satisfaction. The role of a community's social network structure. *Journal of Community Psychology, 38*(5), 622–644.
Purpose	This measure was designed to evaluate community satisfaction as a component of understanding community sentiment.
Description	Community satisfaction is comprised of two subscales: **Evaluation of the social environment**: Respondents were asked to imagine a scale that ranged from 1 to 7 for five word pairs: • Friendly/unfriendly (1 = *friendly* and 7 = *unfriendly*) • Not trusting/trusting • Prejudiced/tolerant **Evaluation of the physical environment:** Respondents rated the quality of four community spaces on a scale of 1 = *not available* to 5 = *very good*: • Senior center • Formal meeting space in local restaurants or other businesses Measures of community attachment and community network can be found in the primary reference.
Sample	• 150 participants in six rural communities in Washington
Scoring	• An additive index of social environment was created by coding all of the questions in the same direction and summing the responses to the five-word pairs. • Confirmatory factor analysis confirmed one factor for the physical environment; an additive index was created by summing the responses to the four statements.
Assessment	• Social environment: $\alpha = .69$ • Physical environment: $\alpha = .71$
Language	English
Contact	Jessica Crowe 18952 E. Fisher Road St. Mary's City, Maryland, 20686 Email: acrow@smcm.edu

TABLE 8.13 ■	Multidimensional Measure of Community Satisfaction and Services
Primary Reference	Grzeskowiak, S., Sirgy, M. J., & Widgery, R. (2003). Residents' satisfaction with community services: Predictors and outcomes. *The Journal of Regional Analysis and Policy, 33*(2), 1–36.
Purpose	This measure was designed to assess multiple constructs that predict satisfaction with community services.
Description	**Satisfaction with the community: (4 items)** • Overall, how satisfied are you with the quality of life in _____ County? (6-point scale from 1 = *strongly dissatisfied* to 6 = *strongly satisfied*) • In years to come do you believe that conditions in ________ County will be: (3-point scale from 1 = *worse than today* to 3 = *better than today*) **Satisfaction with community conditions** Respondents rated their satisfaction using a 6-point scale from 1 = *strongly dissatisfied* to 6 = *strongly satisfied.* For a description of all of the items, please see the primary reference. Sample items include • Race relations in ____ County • Your personal safety in public places • The condition of streets in the community generally • Job opportunities available in the area • Property taxes in the area **Satisfaction with community services** Respondents were asked the degree of satisfaction or dissatisfaction with 19 community services using a 6-point scale from 1 = *strongly dissatisfied* to 6 = *strongly satisfied.* For a description of all of the items, please see the primary reference. Sample items include • Entertainment facilities • Local colleges and universities • Local township or city government • Police protection for your neighborhood • Public transportation in the community • Hospitals in the community **Satisfaction with the neighborhood** Respondents rated their satisfaction with the quality of life in the neighborhood using a 6-point scale from 1 = *strongly dissatisfied* to 6 = *strongly satisfied.* **Satisfaction with neighborhood conditions** Respondents rated their satisfaction with nine neighborhood conditions using a 6-point scale from *strongly dissatisfied* to *strongly satisfied.* For a description of all of the items, please see the primary reference. Sample items include: • the number of children in your neighborhood • the racial mix of your neighborhood • the number of trees in your neighborhood • the amount of traffic on your own street
Sample	• 8,412 randomly selected households in Flint, MI.
Scoring	• Individual items measuring each construct was combined into a single indicator measure.

Assessment	• Satisfaction with the community: $\alpha = .67$ • Authors report reliability coefficient for all tested items was $\alpha = .801$; standard item $\alpha = .804$ • Other scales were used as formative measures.
Contact	M. Joseph Sirgy Virginia Polytechnic Institute and State University Department of Marketing, Pamplin College of Business Blacksburg, VA 24061-0236 Email: sirgy@vt.edu

TABLE 8.14 ■ Satisfaction With Community-Based Services	
Primary Reference	Sirgy, M. J., Rahtz, D. R., Cicic, M., & Underwood, R. (2000). A method for assessing residents' satisfaction with community-based services: A quality-of-life perspective. *Social Indicators Research, 49*(3), 279–316.
Purpose	This measure was designed to assess the degree of personal importance and satisfaction on specific services in an area.
Description	This measure is comprised of three types of services. Respondents were asked how they felt about services using a "Delighted–Terrible Scale" with 8 = *never thought about it or don't have an opinion or doesn't apply*, 7 = *delighted*, 6 = *pleased*, 5 = *mostly satisfied*, 4 = *mixed feelings*, 3 = *mostly dissatisfied*, 2 = *unhappy*, 1 = *terrible*. For a description of all of the items, please see the primary reference. Sample items include • **Individual government services** ○ Public education, fire, sanitation, water, postal, public health services, planning for land use, parks and recreation, employment/job assistance, beautification, cost of utilities, public education • **Individual business services** ○ Banking/savings, insurance, taxi/private transportation, drug stores/supermarkets, healthcare, electricity services, day care, nursing homes/retirement, spectator sports, automobile care services • **Individual nonprofit services** ○ Alcohol/drug abuse, adoption/foster care, family planning, religious services, legal aid services, mental health services, senior citizen services, adult education, disability services, youth services A second component asked about the importance of government, business, and nonprofit services using a response options scale: +3 (*of utmost importance*), +2 (*very important*), +1 (*somewhat important*), 0 (*so/so*), –1 (*somewhat unimportant*), –2 (*very unimportant*), and –3 (*of no importance whatsoever*). A measure of global satisfaction with life domains is also included in the primary reference.
Sample	• Two convenience samples drawn from the United States (n = 681) and two convenience samples drawn from Australia (n = 310). • Samples were characterized as having more males, mostly living in households with 1 to 2 people, mostly married.
Scoring	• Composite indices of satisfaction were developed for each area of services; sum and average satisfaction were used to predict global life satisfaction. • Composite scores were computed as the average satisfaction scores weighted by perceived importance of each service.
Assessment	Measures of reliability do not apply to this scale.
Related Reference	Sirgy, M., & Cornwell, T. (2002). How neighborhood features affect quality of life. *Social Indicators Research, 59*(1), 79–114.
Language	English
Contact	M. Joseph Sirgy Virginia Polytechnic Institute and State University Department of Marketing, Pamplin College of Business Blacksburg, VA 24061-0236 Email: sirgy@vt.edu

TABLE 8.15 ■	Customer Satisfaction With Local Government Services
Primary Reference	Van Ryzin, G. G., Muzzio, D., Immerwahr, M., Gulick, L., & Martinez, E. (2004). Drivers and consequences of citizen satisfaction: An application of the American customer satisfaction index model to New York City. *Public Administration Review, 64*(3), 331–341.
Purpose	The purpose is to assess customer satisfaction with city services.
Description	**Customer satisfaction: (9 services)** assessed using a 4-point scale of *excellent, good, only fair,* or *poor*. For a description of all of the items, please see the primary reference. Sample items include • Would you say the fire protection service provided to you and your household by the NY city fire department over the past 12 months was . . . • In general would you rate the public library services available to you and members of your household in the past 12 months as . . . • Rate the cleanliness of the streets in your neighborhood. • Based on your overall experience in the last 12 months, how would you rate the NY city public schools would you say . . . Other measures on expectations of services, overall government services, moving out, and trust in government are described in primary reference.
Sample	• Purposive sample of 1500 residents drawn from five boroughs of New York City.
Scoring	• Mean scores of customer satisfaction were calculated for each of the specific services.
Assessment	Measures of reliability do not apply to this scale.
Language	English
Contact	Gregg Van Ryzin School of Public Affairs and Administration Rutgers University-Newark, New Jersey Email: vanryzin@rutgers.edu

TABLE 8.16 ■	Access to and Satisfaction With School and Community Health Services
Primary Reference	Montes, G., Halterman, J. S., & Magyar, C. I. (2009). Access to and satisfaction with school and community health services for US children with ASD. *Pediatrics, 124* (Supplement 4), S407-S413.
Purpose	The purpose is to measure access to and satisfaction with school and community health resources.
Description	Satisfaction was measured with one question: "Thinking about (child's health needs and the services he/she received), how satisfied or dissatisfied are you with services?" Response options include *very dissatisfied, somewhat dissatisfied, somewhat satisfied,* and *very satisfied*. Yes or no response options. If yes, respondents were asked to indicate the reason for the lack of access from a list of 12 options. For a description of all of the items, please see the primary reference. Sample items include • Could not get information needed • Too much paperwork required • Couldn't get services when needed • Problem in communication with service provider • Services were available but he/she had used up all eligible benefits
Sample	• 40,256 children (National Survey of Children with Special Health Care Needs)
Scoring	• Satisfaction was measured with a dichotomous variable that grouped those who answered "very dissatisfied" and "somewhat dissatisfied" versus those who responded "somewhat satisfied" and "very satisfied."
Assessment	Measures of reliability do not apply to this scale.
Related Reference	Kogan, M. D., Strickland B. B., & Newacheck P. W. (2009). Building systems of care: Findings from the National Survey of Children with Special Health Care Needs [Supplemental material]. *Pediatrics, 124*(4), S333–S336.
Language	English
Contact	Guillermo Montes Department of Research, Children's Institute 271 N Goodman St, Suite D103 Rochester New York 14607 Email: gmontes@childrensinstitute.net

TABLE 8.17 ■	Community Resource Fit
Primary Reference	Gareis, K. C., & Chait Barnett, R. (2008). The development of a new measure for work-family research: Community resource fit. *Community, Work & Family, 11*(3), 273–282.
Purpose	The purpose is to assess resource fit in the areas of work, public transportation, school, school transportation, after-school programs, and after-school transportation resources.
Description	This measure consists of 36 aspects of community resources. Respondents were asked to rate their level of satisfaction on a scale from 1 (*completely dissatisfied*) to 7 (*completely satisfied*) with six categories of resources. For a description of all of the items, please see the primary reference. Sample items include • **Work resources** (e.g., the flexibility available at your workplace to handle emergencies, your ability to work at home) • **Public transportation resources** (e.g., the convenience of your own access to public transportation, the way that the public transportation schedule fits with your own travel needs) • **School resources** (e.g., the times our children's school starts in the morning, the scheduling of school meetings, parent conferences, and events) • **School transportation resources** (e.g., where the children wait to be picked up by the school bus in the morning, the reliability of school bus transportation to and from school) • **After-school program resources** (e.g., the availability of after-school programs, the scheduling of after-school programs) • **After-school transportation** (e.g., the availability of transportation between school and after-school activities, the cost of transportation to and/or from after-school activities).
Sample	• Random sample of 145 residents in city of Boston • Mean age was 42 years, majority employed parents, median family income was $77,500, and an average of two children in home
Scoring	• Individual subscales and an overall scale for community resource fit was calculated.
Assessment	• Overall Cronbach's alpha for mothers = .86 and .90 for fathers. • Internal consistency for the subscales ranged from .69 to .95.
Language	English
Contact	Karen Gareis Brandeis University—Community, Families, and Work Program Women's Studies Research Center Mailstop 079, 515 South Street Waltham, MA 02453 Email: gareis@brandeis.edu
Other comments	The components of the measure focus on community resources that relate to families of school-aged children; the authors suggest that it can be modified and tailored to assess resources that are important to different types of families (those with elder-care responsibilities).

REFERENCES

Allard, S. W., Tolman, R. M., & Rosen, D. (2003). The geography of need: Spatial distribution of barriers to employment in metropolitan Detroit. *Policy Studies Journal, 31*(3), 293–307.

Andrews, F. M., & Withey, S. B. (1976). *Social indicators of well-being: America's perceptions of life quality.* New York: Plenum Press.

Auh, S., & Cook, C. C. (2009). Quality of community life among rural residents: An integrated model. *Social Indicators Research, 94*(3), 377–389.

Boehmer, T. K., Hoehner, C. M., Deshpande, A. D., Brennan Ramirez, L. K., & Brownson, R. C. (2007). Perceived and observed neighborhood indicators of obesity among urban adults. *International Journal of Obesity, 31*(6), 968–977. doi: http://dx.doi.org/10.1038/sj.ijo.0803531

Brown, R., Dorius, S., & Krannich, R. (2005). The boom-bust-recovery cycle: Dynamics of change in community satisfaction and social integration in Delta, Utah. *Rural Sociology, 70*(1), 28–49.

Bruin, M. J., & Cook., C. C. (1997). Understanding constraints and residential satisfaction among low-income single-parent families. *Environment and Behavior, 29*(4), 532–553.

Byrd, C. M., & Chavous, T. M. (2009). Racial identity and academic achievement in the neighborhood context: A multilevel analysis. *Journal of Youth and Adolescence, 38*(4), 544–59.

Cacioppo, J. T., Hughes, M. E., Waite, L. J., & Thisted, R. A. (2006). Loneliness as a specific factor for depressive symptoms: Cross sectional and longitudinal analyses. *Psychology and Aging, 21*, 140–151.

Campbell, A., Converse, P. E., & Rogers, W. J. (1976). *The quality of American life: Perceptions, evaluations, and satisfaction.* New York: Russell Sage Foundation.

Carro, D., Valera, S., & Vidal, T. (2010). Perceived insecurity in the public space: Personal, social and environmental variables. *Quality & Quantity: International Journal of Methodology, 44*(2), 303–314.

Clarke, P., Ailshire, J., Melendez, R., Bader, M., & Morenoff, J. (2010). Using Google Earth to conduct a neighborhood audit: Reliability of a virtual audit instrument. *Health & Place, 16*(6), 1224–1229.

Coulton, C. J. (2008). *Catalog of administrative data sources for neighborhood indicators. A National Neighborhood Indicators Partnership Guide.* Washington, DC: The Urban Institute.

Crowe, J. (2010). Community attachment and satisfaction. The role of a community's social network structure. *Journal of Community Psychology, 38*(5), 622–644.

Curley, A. M. (2010). Neighborhood institutions, facilities, and public space: A missing link for HOPE VI residents' development of social capital? *A Journal of Policy Development and Research, 12*(1), 33.

Diener, E. (1984). Subjective well-being. *Psychology Bulletin, 95*(3), 542–575.

Fessler, D. R. (1952). The development of a scale for measuring community solidarity. *Rural Sociology, 42*(3), 144–152.

Filkins, R., Allen, J., & Cordes, S. (2000). Predicting community satisfaction among rural residents: An integrative model. *Rural Sociology, 65*(1), 72–86.

Fitz, B. M., Lyon, L., & Driskell, R. (2015). Why people like where they live: Individual and community-level contributors to community satisfaction. *Social Indicators Research, 126*, 1209–1224.

Galster, G., Hayes, C., & Johnson, J. (2005). Identifying robust, parsimonious neighborhood indicators. *Journal of Planning Education and Research, 24*(3), 265–280.

Galster, G., & Hesser, G. (1981). Residential satisfaction: Compositional and contextual correlates. *Environment and Behavior, 13*(6), 735–758.

Gareis, K. C., & Chait Barnett, R. (2008). The development of a new measure for work-family research: Community resource fit. *Community, Work & Family, 11*(3), 273–282.

Goudy, W. J. (1977). Evaluations of local attributes and community satisfaction in small towns. *Rural Sociology, 42*(3), 371–382.

Grillo, M., Teixeira, M., & Wilson, D. (2010). Residential satisfaction and civic engagement: Understanding the causes of community participation. *Social Indicators Research, 97*(3), 451–466.

Grzeskowiak, S., Sirgy, M. J., & Widgery, R. (2003). Residents' satisfaction with community services: Predictors and outcomes. *The Journal of Regional Analysis and Policy, 33*, 2–36. http://extension.usu.edu/files/uploads/surveyguide.pdf

House, J. S., Kaplan, G. A , Morenoff, J., Raudenbush, S. W., Williams D. R., & Young, E. A. (2011, June 7). *Chicago community adult health study*, 2001–2003 (ICPSR31142-v1). Ann Arbor, MI: Inter-university Consortium for Political and Social Research [distributor]. http://doi.org/10.3886/ICPSR31142.v1

Hughes, M. E., Waite, L. J., Hawkley, L. C., & Cacioppo, J. T. (2004). A short scale for measuring loneliness in large surveys: Results from two population-based studies. *Research on Aging, 26*(6), 633–672.

Hughey, J. B., & Bardo, J. W. (1984). The structure of community satisfaction in a southeastern American city. *Journal of Social Psychology, 123*, 91–99.

James, R., III, Carswell, A., & Sweaney, A. (2009). Sources of discontent: Residential satisfaction of tenants from an internet ratings site. *Environment and Behavior, 41*(1), 43–59.

Keysor, J., Jette, A., & Haley, S. (2005). Development of the home and community environment (HACE) instrument. *Journal of Rehabilitative Medicine, 37*(1), 37–44.

Kogan, M. D., Strickland, B. B., & Newacheck, P. W. (2009). Building systems of care: Findings from the National Survey of Children with Special Health Care Needs [Supplement 4]. *Pediatrics, 124*(4), S333–S336

Kretzman, J. P., & McKnight, J. L. (1993). *Building communities from the inside out: A path toward finding and mobilizing a community's assets.* Evanston, IL: Asset-Based Community Development Institute for Policy Research.

Low, S. M., & Altman, I. (1992). Place attachment: A conceptual inquiry. In I. Altman & S. M. Low (Eds.), *Place attachment* (pp. 1–12). New York: Plenum Press.

Macintyre, S., Macdonald, L., & Ellaway, A. (2008). Do poorer people have poorer access to local resources and facilities? The distribution of local resources by area deprivation in Glasgow, Scotland. *Social Science & Medicine, 67*(6), 900–914.

Magis, K. (2010). Community resilience: An indicator of social sustainability. *Society and Natural Resources, 23*(5), 401–416.

Marans, R., & Rodgers, W. (1975). Toward an understanding of community satisfaction. In A. Hawley & V. Rock (Eds.), *Metropolitan American in contemporary perspective* (pp. 311–377). New York: Sage.

Mastrofski, S. D., Parks, R. B., & McCluskey, J. D. (2010). Systematic social observation in criminology. In *Handbook of quantitative criminology* (pp. 225–247). New York: Springer.

McKenzie, T. L., Moody, J. S., Carlson, J. A., Lopez, N. V., & Elder, J. P. (2013). Neighborhood income matters: Disparities in community recreation facilities, amenities, and programs. *Journal of Park and Recreation Administration, 31*(4), 12.

Miller, T. I., & Kobayashi, M. M. (2000). *City surveys: How to do them, how to use them, what they mean* (2nd ed.) Washington, DC: International City/County Management Association.

Molnar, B. E., Cerda, M., Roberts, A. L., & Buka, S. L. (2008). Effects of neighborhood resources on aggressive and delinquent behaviors among urban youths. *American Journal of Public Health, 98*(6), 1086–1093.

Montes, G., Halterman, J. S., & Magyar, C. I. (2009). Access to and satisfaction with school and community health services for US children with ASD [Supplement 4]. *Pediatrics, 124*, S407–S413.

Nicotera, N. (2007). Measuring neighborhood: A conundrum for human services researchers and practitioners. *American Journal of Community Psychology, 40*(1–2), 26–51.

Pascoe, G. C., & Attkisson, C. C. (1983). The evaluation ranking scale: A new methodology for assessing satisfaction. *Evaluation and Program Planning, 6*, 335–347.

Payne, L., & Schaumleffel, N. (2008). Relationship between attitudes toward rural community parks and recreation and rural community satisfaction. *Journal of Park and Recreation Administration, 26*(3), 116–135.

Potter, J., & Cantarero, R. (2006). How does increasing population and diversity affect resident satisfaction? A small community case study. *Environment and Behavior, 38*(5), 605–625.

Raudenbush, S. W., & Sampson, R. J. (1999). Ecometrics: Toward a science of assessing ecological settings, with application to the systematic social observation of neighborhoods. *Sociological Methodology, 29*(1), 1–41.

Richard, L., Gauvin, L., Gosselin, C., & Laforest, S. (2009). Staying connected: Neighbourhood correlates of social participation among older adults living in an urban environment in Montreal, Quebec. *Health Promotion International, 24*(1), 46–57.

Sirgy, M. (2012). *The psychology of quality of life: Hedonic well-Being, life satisfaction and eudaimonia* (2nd ed.). Springer: New York.

Sirgy, M., & Cornwell, T. (2002). How neighborhood features affect quality of life. *Social Indicators Research, 59*(1), 79–114.

Sirgy, M., Rahtz, D., Cicic, M., & Underwood, R. (2000). A method for assessing residents' satisfaction with community-based services: A quality-of-life perspective. *Social Indictors Research, 49*(3), 279–316.

Small, M. L. (2006). Neighborhood institutions as resource brokers: Childcare centers, interorganizational ties, and resource access among the poor. *Social Problems, 53*(2), 274–292.

Sooman, A., & Macintyre, S. (1995). Health and perceptions of the local environment in socially contrasting neighbourhoods in Glasgow. *Health & Place, 1*(1), 15–26.

Swaroop, S., & Krysan, M. (2011). The determinants of neighborhood satisfaction: Racial proxy revisited. *Demography, 48*(3), 1203–1229.

Swaroop, S., & Morenoff, J. D. (2006). Building community: The neighborhood context of social organization. *Social Forces, 84*(3), 1665–1695.

Van der Pas, S., Schaap, L. A., Castell, M. V., Cooper, C., Denkinger, M., Edwards, M. H., & Peter, R. (2016). Availability and use of neighborhood resources by older people with osteoarthritis: Results from the European Project on OsteoArthritis. *Health & Place, 37*, 1–7.

Van de Walle, S., & Van Ryzin, G. G. (2011). The order of questions in a survey on citizen satisfaction with public services: Lessons from a split-ballot experiment. *Public Administration, 89*, 1436–1450.

Van Ryzin, G. G., Muzzio, D., Immerwahr, S., Gulick, L., & Martinez, E. (2004). Drivers and consequences of citizen satisfaction: An application of the American customer satisfaction index model to New York City. *Public Administration Review, 64*(3) 331–341.

Vrbka, S. J., & E. R. Combs. (1993). Predictors of neighborhood and community satisfactions in rural communities. *Housing and Society, 20*(1), 41–49.

Vreugdenhil, A., & Rigby, K. (1987). Assessing generalized community satisfaction. *The Journal of Social Psychology, 127*(4), 367–374.

Ware, J. E., Snyder, M. K., & Wright, W. R. (1977). *Some issues in the measurement of patient satisfaction with health care services* (p. 6021). Santa Monica CA: The Rand Corporation.

Wen, M., Hawkley, L. C., & Cacioppo, J. T. (2006). Objective and perceived neighborhood environment, individual SES and psychosocial factors, and self-rated health: An analysis of older adults in Cook County, Illinois. *Social Science & Medicine, 63*(10), 2575–2590.

Wickes, R., Zahnow, R., & Mazerolle, L. (2010). Community resilience research: Current approaches, challenges and opportunities. In *2010 National Security Science and Innovation Conference* (pp. 62–78). Australian Security Research Centre.

Zenk, S. N., Schulz, A. J., Mentz, G., House, J. S., Gravlee, C. C., Miranda, P. Y., & Kannan, S. (2007). Inter-rater and test–retest reliability: Methods and results for the neighborhood observational checklist. *Health & Place, 13*(2), 452–465.

9 THE BUILT ENVIRONMENT INFLUENCING HEALTHY LIVING

There is increasing attention among researchers and practitioners working in different sectors ranging from health to urban planning to community development on neighborhood factors that may have an impact on the health and well-being of populations. This resulted in the development and use of measures to assess features of healthy living, the focus of this chapter. The measures included in this chapter will narrow in on the "built environment" within a neighborhood, defined as the "human-made space in which people live, work, and recreate on a day-to-day basis" (Roof & Oleru, 2008, p. 24). Measures of the built environment influencing healthy living focus on access to healthy foods, walkability, and spaces for recreation in neighborhoods.

WHY IS IT IMPORTANT TO MEASURE THE BUILT ENVIRONMENT?

As a result of a paradigm shift within the health sciences (Warnecke et al., 2008), there is now greater emphasis on measuring healthy and sustainable built environments and their influences on health and well-being. This shift in thinking is exemplified in research and practice focused on obesity and was motivated because obesity rates have been on the rise over the past 50 years despite numerous efforts to curtail trends (Flegal, Carroll, Kit & Ogden, 2012; Flegal, Carroll, Kuczmarski, & Johnson, 1998; Ogden, Carroll, Curtin, Lamb, & Flegal, 2010; Ogden et al., 2006). During the latter part of the 20th century, obesity prevention efforts were individually oriented and focused on shifting personal knowledge, attitudes, beliefs, and behaviors. When these interventions were showing little or no effect on population levels of obesity (Kamath et al., 2008; Lemmens, Oenema, Klepp, Henriksen, & Brug, 2008), there was a call to move upstream to address neighborhood influences that may be contributing to risk.

Moreover, careful analysis of obesity trends revealed disparities by race and class (i.e., higher rates of obesity among low-income populations and racial and ethnic minorities) that mapped onto neighborhoods such that communities of color and low-income communities became hotspots for obesity (Bailey-Davis, Horst, Hillemeier, & Lauter, 2012; Flegal et al., 2012). In addition to obesity, low-income neighborhoods are hotspots for other health issues such as childhood lead poisoning, infectious disease, injury, and premature mortality (Krieger, Chen, Waterman, Rehkopf, & Subramanian, 2005). What many communities have known through lived experience was becoming known to researchers and practitioners: It is difficult to choose to engage in healthy behaviors, such as eating more fruits and vegetables, in what some researchers are calling "obesogenic environments" (Kirk, Penney, & McHugh, 2010).

HOW IS THE BUILT ENVIRONMENT MEASURED?

Since 2000, there has been a surge in research focused on measuring healthy and sustainable built environments. One approach to measuring the built environment is systematic observation of features of the neighborhood (e.g., food stores available). This information is then geocoded and converted into maps that allow for visualization of variability in the built environment. Figure 9.1 provides one example of this type of research. This map depicts access to full-service supermarkets. The gray census tracts signify areas where most residents in the tract live at least one-half mile from a full-service supermarket. These types of maps are often used to identify gaps in healthy food access (i.e., food deserts) in communities. Maps produced through this approach to measurement serve as powerful tools for unleashing neighborhood-level data to build momentum for addressing concerns related to the built environment.

Systematically measuring features of the built environment has both strengths and challenges. For relatively small geographic areas, capturing this information may be possible through a "ground truthing" approach wherein observations are made at each targeted space (e.g., each food store or park). However, as geographic scope increases, it becomes more difficult to conduct these types of assessments. This results in the use of existing or secondary databases about the built environment, including free resources such as Google Maps or commercial databases such as InfoUSA, but measurement error is more likely when using these secondary sources (Han et al., 2012). Additionally, there is risk for interpretation error during the process of systematic observation such that outside observers may interpret features of the built environment differently than residents living in the neighborhood. Steps

FIGURE 9.1 ■ Map of low-income census tracts in Cleveland, Ohio with most residents living more than one-half mile from a full-service supermarket.

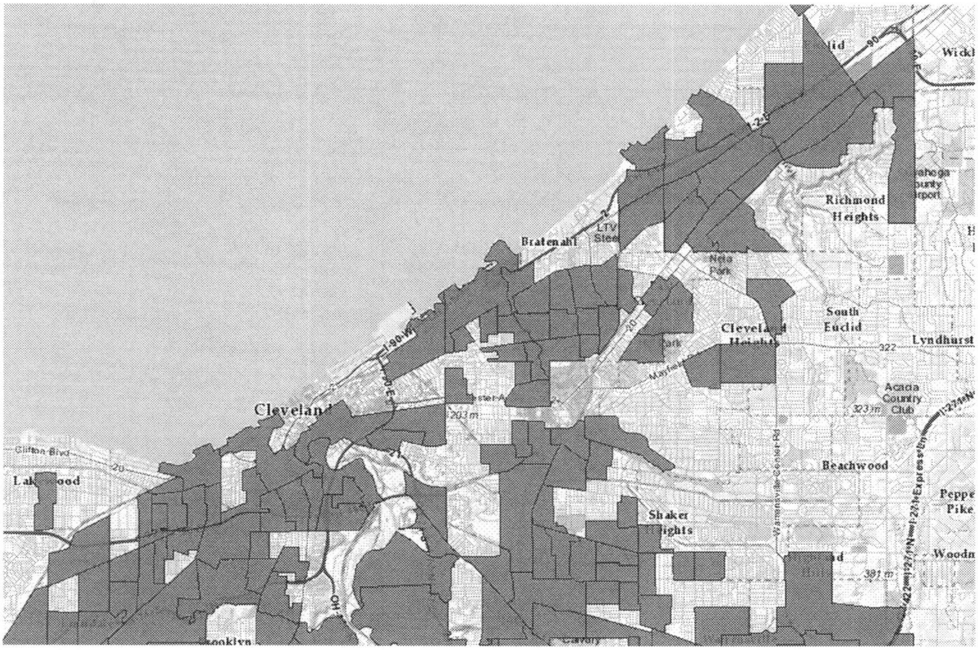

Source: U.S. Department of Agriculture Food Access Research Atlas available at http://www.ers.usda.gov/data-products/food-access-research-atlas/.

are often taken to promote reliability of the observation data, such as the use of two raters of the same facility (Glanz, Sallis, Saelens, & Frank, 2007). Another approach is to include community members in the mapping process to capture local interpretations of the built environment (Hill, Chau, Luebbering, Kolivras, & Zoellner, 2012).

A second method for measuring the built environment is to examine perceptions of the neighborhood based on individual feedback. An individual's perceptions of access to healthy features in the neighborhood—regardless of whether these features are actually there—may be more important to one's health than their objective presence. Research suggests individual perceptions of the neighborhood food environment, for instance, align with systematic observations of the same context (Freedman & Bell, 2009). These types of assessments may more accurately capture local perspectives about the built environment. Measuring perceptions of the built environment requires careful attention to the psychometric properties of the measurement tool. Chapter 3 provides more information about measurement methodology.

OVERVIEW OF MEASURES

The measures included in this chapter are focused on three domains of healthy environments, including (a) neighborhood food environment, (b) walkability of neighborhoods, and (c) spaces for recreation. For each domain, measures include both systematic observation tools and measures of perceptions of the built environment. A brief history of the measures in each domain as well as a summary of the variety and focus of existing measures is provided.

Neighborhood Food Environment

Measures of the neighborhood food environment focus on food stores and restaurants. Food stores include grocery stores, supermarkets, convenience or corner stores, specialty stores, farmers' markets, and food pantries while restaurants include fast-food and full-service restaurants (McKinnon, Reedy, Morrissette, Lytle, & Yaroch, 2009). The number of measures designed to assess the neighborhood food environment has grown substantially over the past 20 years—however, most have not included assessment of psychometric properties of the measures (McKinnon et al., 2009; Ohri-Vachaspati & Leviton, 2010). For instance, McKinnon and colleagues (2009) found that less than 10% of all measures of food stores assessed psychometric properties of the instruments. Given the proliferation of measures of the neighborhood food environment, this chapter describes in detail only those that include assessment of reliability and/or validity.

Measuring the Physical Food Environment. In an effort to quantify the quality of the food environment of a particular area, Truong and colleagues (2010) developed the **Physical Food Environment Indicator (PFEI)** (**Table 9.1**). The PFEI is designed to assess the overall quality of the food environment. An innovation of the PFEI is its inclusion of smaller food retail venues, such as corner stores, in the index score. The PFEI is calculated as the proportion of small food retail venues over the sum of all retail food venues. Truong and colleagues (2010) used the PFEI scores to observe the relationship between PFEI score and overall obesity trends within specific geographic units (e.g., census tracts and counties within the state of California).

- The researchers found that PFEI scores among counties in California ranged from 0.735 to 0.855. The tool was validated by assessing its ability to predict obesity among participants from the California Health Interview Survey (CHIS). The data used in the validation analysis included 43,020 participants representative of the population in California. All participants include measures of their county and census tract.

- After controlling for covariates, PFEI at the tract level was predictive of greater risk for high BMI ($p < 0.001$) and obesity ($p < 0.01$). However, relationships between county-level PFEI and BMI ($p = 0.07$) and obesity ($p = 0.05$) were somewhat weaker.
- Using simulation modeling, when county-level PFEI was increased from the 25th percentile to the median level and the 75th percentile, the predicted obesity prevalence among women changed from 19.99% to 20.2% and 20.05%, respectively.
- Similar results were found for changes in tract-level estimates. In multivariate analysis, the PFEI added minimal explanation to variation in obesity prevalence at the county or tract level. This small effect may be related to limited variability in PFEI scores across counties, a threshold effect (i.e., above a certain PFEI score it is not predictive of obesity), or the risk that the PFEI captures elements of context that are already accounted for when individual- and geographic-level measures of sociodemographics are included in the model (Truong et al., 2010).

Measuring Food Availability in the Retail Food Environment. There are numerous tools used to capture food options that are available at retail food stores located in a neighborhood. These measures range along a spectrum of simple to complex, depending on the particular items of interest. Simple measures tend to be brief tools that focus on specific components of the retail food environment, such as the availability of vegetables or low-fat milk. Complex measures, on the other hand, are intended to capture multiple components of the retail food environment, like the availability of a variety of different foods, prices of these foods, and quality of the foods.

Glanz and colleagues (2007) developed the **Nutrition Environment Measures Survey in Stores (NEMS-S)**, which is a complex tool designed to measure a variety of features of the food retail environment (**Table 9.2**). The NEMS-S tool collects data on availability, quality, and price of 10 indicator food categories. Observations collected by the NEMS-S tool are used to calculate a "food environment quality score." Higher scores indicate greater availability, better quality, and lower prices for healthy options compared to their regular counterpart. Since corner stores are more prevalent in many communities, the NEMS-S was adapted to form the NEMS for Corner Stores (i.e., NEMS-CS) to more effectively capture healthy food access in these settings (Cavanaugh, Mallya, Brensinger, Tierney, & Glanz, 2013). The NEMS-CS includes smaller package sizes typically available in smaller stores. The tool was developed based on a review of the literature, consultation with experts in the field, pretesting proposed measures in two neighborhoods, and developing detailed protocols for training. Nutrition-related variables included in the NEMS-S were selected based on the types of food products that contribute the most fat and calories to the U.S. diet and those that are most recommend for healthful eating based on federal and professional guidelines. Reliability and inter-rater reliability were examined, and results showed that the scale performed very well with high reliability scores.

- The researchers found that the composite food environment quality differentiated grocery stores versus convenience stores.
- Grocery stores had mean composite scores that were statistically significantly higher than convenience stores (22.58 v. 5.85).
- The composite scores also significantly differed by the socioeconomic status of the neighborhood, with high-income neighborhoods having higher scores versus low-income neighborhoods (13.14 v. 7.83) (Glanz et al., 2007).

The **Bridging the Gap: Food Store Observation Form (BTG-FSOF)**, developed by Rimkus and colleagues (2013), includes the same food and beverage categories as the NEMS-S (**Table 9.3**). However, the BTG-FSOF extends the NEMS-S to include a focus on exterior advertisements as well as interior and exterior store characteristics—such as product placement and promotion—as well as enhances the measurement of price to include regular, sales, or member (e.g., store loyalty card) prices at the time of observation. The BTG-FSOF was informed by three existing instruments and input from researchers, practitioners, and advocates with expertise in nutrition, measurement of the food environment, and food policy. The form was pilot tested in four communities in 2008 before reliability testing in 2010. Inter-rater reliability was very high overall.

- The researchers found that only three of the 14 restaurants included labeling on their menus. However, healthy food options, such as fruit or vegetable choices, were available in all of the restaurants. In contrast, very few restaurants included low-fat options on the menu (Rimkus et al., 2013).

Another complex tool intended to assess multiple components of the food retail environment is the **Food Environment Audit for Diverse Neighborhoods (FEAD-N)**, developed by Izumi and colleagues (2012) (**Table 9.4**). The FEAD-N assesses the availability of eight food categories but also examines the physical and social features of the store. The physical features include infrastructure, services, products, marketing, and government assistance participation. The social features of the store include security features, disorder, behaviors of the owner or employees, and race and ethnicity of the employees and owners. Inter-rater reliability was also very high for this measure.

The simple measures of availability, developed prior to the more complex measures, are limited in scope. For example, Horowitz and colleagues (Horowitz, Colson, Hebert, & Lancaster, 2004) developed the **Availability and Costs of Foods Recommended for People With Diabetes Audit (Table 9.5)**. They categorized a store as desirable only when stores had at least one item from each of the five specified indicator categories. The tool was developed based on expert advice from dieticians, health professionals, and outreach workers who provided guidance about the types of foods to be included in the tool. The foods selected for the tool were commonly recommended by clinicians for people with diabetes, considered to be relatively affordable and culturally acceptable for Whites, African Americans, and Latinos, and were quickly and accurately identifiable on store shelves by data collectors.

- The researchers found a gradient in store desirability, with small stores being much less likely to be rated as desirable while > 90% of large stores were found to be desirable. The number of desirable stores per 100,000 residents was greater for the Upper East Side compared to East Harlem (36 v. 26). A greater proportion of residents in East Harlem were living in census blocks with more undesirable stores than desirable stores (42.2% v. 18.9%) (Horowitz et al., 2004).

Two other more limited measures are included here. Wechsler and colleagues (Wechsler, Basch, Zybert, Lantigua, & Shea, 1995) created the **Availability of Low-Fat Milk in Food Stores Audit (Table 9.6)**.

- The research team found that availability of milk remained stable over the course of the month. The milk availability and shelf-space measures differentiated neighborhoods in the area with different racial and ethnic make-up (Wechsler et al., 1995).

Edmonds and colleagues (Edmonds, Baranowski, Baranowski, Cullen, & Myres, 2001) developed the **Fruit, Juice, and Vegetable Availability Assessment** to document availability of fruits, juices, and vegetables in a store or on a restaurant menu (**Table 9.7**).

- Findings were aggregated for all store types (e.g., grocery, convenience) and for restaurants. Shelf space filled with fruits, juice, and vegetables was highest for vegetables (184.8 inches), yet the standard deviation was very large (SD = 242.2) indicating wide variability.
- Restaurant availability (controlling for SES of the census tract) was the only store-level factor significantly correlated with dietary patterns among the boys participating in the study.
- Specifically, restaurant availability was correlated with vegetable consumption (r = 0.72) and fruit juice consumption (r = 0.70) (Edmonds et al., 2001).

Measuring Perception of Food Access. Perception of food access is assessed using self-reported measures. Dibsdall and colleagues (Dibsdall, Lambert, Bobbin, & Frewer, 2003) asked participants to rate their perceptions of the availability of fresh vegetables, motivation and satisfaction with their food retail venue, and affordability of fruit using Likert scales using the **Choice in Food Store Access** tool (**Table 9.8**) The items were developed based on qualitative research related to the topic and on current beliefs and attitudes found in studies with low-income populations. The items were designed to assess both attitudes and behaviors. The readability of the items was assessed by having residents from the housing associate review the questions before they were finalized. Principal components factor and reliability analyses were conducted on this scale (see table for findings).

- The study team found that participants were more likely to agree with the statements about choice in food store access, with strongest agreement (88.3% agreed) related to the statement: "Where I shop has a wide choice of fresh fruit/ vegetables."
- The item with the greatest level of disagreement (29.5% disagreed) was the statement: "Lack of money prevents me from eating healthily."
- Participants who reported zero to two portions of fruit and vegetables eaten in a day had statistically significantly higher mean scores (i.e., less agreement) on the choice in food stores measure compared to those reporting five plus portions eaten each day (Dibsdall et al., 2003).

Echeverria and colleagues (Echeverria, Diez-Roux, Link, 2004) created the **Perceptions of Access to Healthy Foods in the Neighborhood** scale to assess ease of purchasing and availability of low-fat options and high-quality produce using Likert scales and found associations with these perceptions with other neighborhood characteristics, such as safety, social cohesion, neighborhood problems, and general neighborhood quality (**Table 9.9**). The items were developed based on a review of the literature to assess how prior studies measured self-reports of the neighborhood environment. Scale development was focused on neighborhood characteristics relevant to cardiovascular health. Items for each domain (e.g., access to healthy foods) were developed and scrutinized to eliminate redundancy and promote clarity. Problematic items were reworded. Preliminary testing of the items was conducted with a sample of 20 participants. Test–retest reliability was high as well as the Cronbach's alpha reliability scores.

- The research team found that perceptions of access to healthy foods in the neighborhood scale were associated with other measures of the neighborhood environment.
- Using Spearman's correlations, there were statistically significant associations between the perceptions of access to healthy foods measure and self-reports on the following neighborhood characteristics: safety from crime (0.33), neighborhood violence (0.43), social cohesion (0.46), neighborhood problems index (0.59), and general neighborhood quality (0.50) (Echeverria et al., 2004).

In contrast with usage of Likert scales, Giskes and colleagues (2007) used the **Perceptions of Food Availability and Price** tool to assess perceptions of the availability of different foods based on "yes," "no," or "not sure" response choices and perceptions of price based on "recommended choice perceived more expensive," "regular choice perceived more expensive," "perceived about the same price," or "not sure" response choices (**Table 9.10**).

- The research team compared perceptions of food availability and price scale to "objective" measures of the food environment.
- Food audits were conducted within 2.5 kilometers of the centroid of each small area used in the first stage of the cluster sampling design. Of these, 58 stores were identified as places where participants shopped. Nearly all of the 14 recommended foods were available in the food stores based on the objective assessments (range: 91.2%–100%), while participants perceived these items were less available.
- Perceptions of availability ranged from 83.3% to 97.9%. The majority of the participants did not perceive price differences between the recommended healthy choices and the regular food choices; however, based on objective assessment, the recommended choices were more expensive than the regular choices for most food groups (Giskes et al., 2007).

Measuring the Restaurant Environment. Restaurants represent a different but important realm of the food retail environment. They are retail spaces for accessing ready-to-eat foods prepared outside of the home. Menus are the most common way to assess food availability at a restaurant.

Assessing restaurants often proves problematic because of varied methods for labeling food items on the menu and limited access to ingredient lists and recipes for preparation. This was the case for Cassady, Housemann, and Dagher (2004), who developed the **Menu Checklist** that examines labeling and cues for healthy eating and the quantity of healthy options available in entrees, side dishes, appetizers, and nonalcoholic beverages (**Table 9.11**). Community researchers ($n = 18$) received a three-hour training focused on the Menu Checklist. Discrepancies in coding the restaurant menus using the checklist existed. This resulted in selection of community members with at least high school-level education to complete the audits. Additionally, coders were selected because of demonstrated attention to detail in their auditing process. This resulted in selection of three community researchers to complete data collection. Inter-rater reliability was moderate to high.

- The researchers found that only three of the 14 restaurants included labeling on their menus. However, healthy food options, such as fruit or vegetable choices, were available in all of the restaurants. In contrast, very few restaurants included low-fat options on the menu (Cassady et al., 2004).

Saelens and colleagues (Saelens, Glanz, Sallis, & Frank, 2007) developed the **Neighborhood Environment Measures Survey in Restaurants (NEMS-R)** tool, which assesses a restaurant based on examination of menu items and marketing focused on facilitators and barriers of healthy eating (**Table 9.12**). The NEMS-R was developed based on a conceptual model of nutrition environments, literature on the factors related to food choice, and input from nutrition and public health researchers. The NEMS-R assessed the relative healthfulness of foods and beverages available on the main menu and children's menus, with a focus on availability, facilitators, and supports for healthful eating, barriers to healthful eating, pricing, and signage/promotion. Inter-rater reliability ranged from low to high, while test-retest reliability was high.

- The researchers made comparisons between sit-down and fast-food restaurants. Twenty-two of the 33 items on the scale had the ability to discriminate between these two restaurant types. The high test–retest reliability indicated the observed variables were relatively stable over a one-month timeframe (Saelens et al., 2007).

Walkability of Neighborhoods

In addition to evaluating access to healthy foods in neighborhoods, there is growing interest in examining the layout of the neighborhood, which has been found to be associated with physical activity behaviors like walking that are critical for health promotion (Saelens & Handy, 2008). Moreover, neighborhoods that promote recreational walking may also be supportive of utilitarian walking for residents without access to a personal vehicle. Specifically, there is interest in investigating the walkability of the neighborhood by examining the ease of active transportation (e.g., walking, biking) between residential and nonresidential destinations. Walkability measures take into account the density of people and places, diversity of amenities, and design of neighborhoods and streets, which combine to either promote active or vehicle-based transportation (Frank et al., 2010). Researchers, practitioners, and government officials are investigating the walkability of neighborhoods using a number of measures and tools focused on macroscale (e.g., neighborhood characteristics) and microscale (e.g., pedestrian environment) elements (Toker, 2015).

Measuring Macroscale Elements of Walkability. The macroscale elements influencing walkability focus on land use mix, street connectivity, and residential density (Toker, 2015). These neighborhood-level features may be assessed and then mapped using geographic information systems (GIS) to better visualize the built environment. The **Walk Score®** (2011) assesses walkability by examining the density of amenities available within walking distance of homes and workplaces (**Table 9.13**). The premise here is that when a person is surrounded by food and retail amenities that are nearby, they will be more likely to walk to these locations. The Walk Score methodology is relatively simple method for describing the built environment. It is computed by capturing addresses of amenity types, plotting them within a GIS platform, and then calculating how many clusters of amenities fall within a one-mile radius of the home or work address. However, it does not include critical microscale elements that allow for a greater degree of granularity in understanding the built environment. Reliability was examined using test–retest analyses. The Walk Score® can be used to estimate areas with high densities of walkable amenities.

Measuring Microscale Elements of Walkability. The vast majority of tools and methods intended to measure the built environment surrounding walking behaviors focus on microscale or street-level elements, such as pedestrian infrastructure, safety, and aesthetics. These tools lie along a spectrum of simple to more complex. One of the first reliable tools developed was the **Systematic Pedestrian and Cycling Environmental Scan (SPACES)** (**Table 9.14**). SPACES consists of 37 different factors categorized into four major groups including functional features (walking/cycling surface, streets, traffic, permeability), safety (personal, traffic), aesthetics (streetscapes, views), destination (facilities), and a subjective assessment aimed at determining attractiveness and difficulty for walking/cycling (Pikora et al., 2002). Both inter-rater reliability and intra-rater reliability were examined; the results demonstrated that there was very high agreement among all of the observers, except for one item. The SPACES tool is useful in assessing the safety of the physical environment detailed at the street-level.

SPACES laid the foundation for a variety of other researchers to develop additional tools. Most notably are the **St. Louis Analytic Audit and Checklist** and the **Irvine-Minnesota Inventory (IMI)**. The St. Louis Analytic Audit expands the four main groups of factors included in SPACES into eight different categorizations (Brownson et al., 2004) (**Table 9.15**). Audits were carried out in pairs with each observer assigned either the analytic or the checklist audit tool. The results showed that overall the reliability was higher for the checklist tool than for the analytic tool. These tools can be reliably used to obtain information regarding the street-level environment influencing walkability.

The IMI further builds upon these tools by synthesizing 162 different indicators into four broad domains focused on accessibility, pleasurability, perceived safety from traffic, and perceived safety from crime (Boarnet, Day, Alfonzo, Forsyth, & Oakes, 2006) (**Table 9.16**). Independent audits of the segments of the measure were conducted in California and Minnesota. Overall, there were high levels of agreement among the raters, and the scale was revised based on their findings. This tool gives an in-depth view on a variety of factors that can be used to assess the physical attributes of residential areas that may influence walking behaviors.

Similar to the IMI, the **Microscale Audit of Pedestrian Streetscapes (MAPS)** synthesizes over 150 items into four domains focused on overall route, street segments/area between crossings, crossings, and cul-de-sacs (Millstein et al., 2013) (**Table 9.17**). Two raters independently conducted audits of the routes. The results showed that for most of the items, there was moderate to excellent inter-rater reliability. These tools are based on similar scoring scales using ascending and Likert scales or dichotomies to aggregate topic scores for each domain. This tool can provide data beyond the macroscale environment to look at features that have an impact on walkability.

Other tools provide simpler methods to calculate walkability scores based on presence and absence of various features. This is the case with the St. Louis Checklist tool as well as the **Pedestrian Environmental Data Scan (PEDS)** (**Table 9.18**). PEDS differs from the aforementioned tools in that it includes measures of the macroscale environment (e.g., pedestrian facilities and road attributes) in addition to the microscale elements (Clifton, Smith, & Rodriguez, 2007). PEDS audits were conducted in pairs. The results showed that overall, the inter-rater reliability was very high. This tool can capture features that are most commonly thought to be associated with walking behavior.

Many of these tools have been developed and tested in urban environments, limiting applicability in rural areas that differ greatly in built environment infrastructure. The **Rural Pedestrian Environmental Audit Instrument** addresses this limitation by adapting existing tools for the rural context, which includes five domains:

destinations, street characteristics, quality of the pedestrian facility, aesthetics/quality of environment, and social/dynamic environment (Scanlin, Haardoerfer, Kegler, & Glanz, 2014) (**Table 9.19**). Independent audits were conducted by two raters. The results showed that the inter-rater agreement for each domain was high. The Rural Pedestrian Environment Audit Instrument expands upon other tools and adapts them for use in a rural context.

Measuring Perceptions of Walkability. The **Neighborhood Environment Walkability Scale (NEWS)** is perhaps the most commonly used tool to measure residents' perceptions of walkability in their neighborhoods (**Table 9.20**). This questionnaire examines perceived density and proximity to resources, street connectivity, walking/cycling facilities (e.g., sidewalks), and two items regarding perceived safety and crime safety (Saelens et al., 2003). This tool has been adapted into a short version and for use by youth and translated into several other languages. Test–retest reliability of the NEWS subscales were moderate to high.

- The results showed that the ideal high-walkability neighborhood had higher NEWS scores versus the low-walkability neighborhood.
- The researchers found that the only physical activity difference between neighborhoods was walking for errands, in which the high-walkability neighborhood had a greater proportion of residents who walked for errands.
- The authors suggest the use of the NEWS-CFA version of the scale (Saelens et al., 2003).

Recreation in Neighborhoods

As the previous section highlighted, the built environment can foster active transportation, such as walking or cycling. In addition, there is evidence that the built environment can be structured in ways to promote or hinder moderate-to-vigorous forms of physical activity (Committee on Physical Activity, Health, Transportation, and Land Use, 2005). The final set of measures included in Chapter 9 focus on assessing features of the neighborhood that are supportive of physical activity, which may include walking but also other activities, such as field sports, swimming, and strength exercises. The measures included in this section are an extension of those described in the section on walkability since many of the built environment attributes that support walking also are supportive of other forms of physical activity. These measures assess both perceptions and objective observations of the neighborhood environment.

Perceptions of Physical Activity Environment. There are more measures of perceptions of the physical activity environment compared to tools for objective observations. Interestingly, many of the perceptions measures were developed based on youth samples, though they may be used with adult populations. The **Neighborhood Physical Activity Environment Scale and Convenient Facilities Scale** was one of the first measures of perceptions of the physical activity environment, which was developed by Sallis and colleagues (Sallis, Johnson, Calfas, Caparosa, & Nichols, 1997) (**Table 9.21**). This measure includes features measured in many of the walkability assessments, such as perceptions of safety and land use, yet extends these measures by also assessing convenience to facilities for physical activity, such as basketball courts or a gym, on the route to or from work or home. Participants who reported higher levels of convenience to these types of facilities were more likely to report higher levels of vigorous exercise (Sallis et al., 1997). One-week, one-way model, intra-class test–retest reliabilities for the two scales were assessed. The results showed moderate to high reliabilities for the two scales. Construct validity was also assessed by computing Pearson correlations between the environmental variables and three physical activity variables.

Hume and colleagues (Hume, Ball, & Salmon, 2006) extend the measurement field in the **Children's Perceptions of the Physical Activity Environment in Their Neighborhood** tool (**Table 9.22**). This tool assesses perceptions of the neighborhood social environment (e.g., number of friends in the area where you live) that may influence physical activity behaviors in addition to measuring access to physical activity facilities, neighborhood aesthetics, and perceptions of safety. Most of the items on the scale showed at least moderate reliability in the test–retest analysis. Internal consistency was low for the aesthetics scale and somewhat higher for the safety and social environment scales. Umstattd and colleagues (2012) added to the field by developing the **Rural Active Living Perceived Environment Support Scale (RALPESS)** to assess perceptions of the physical activity environment in rural settings (**Table 9.23**). Internal consistency was acceptable for all seven factors and the overall scale. The development of this instrument included feedback from other researchers, students, and parents to assess face, content, and construct validity.

- Principal component analysis found the 33-items resulted in seven factors that accounted for 71.6% of the variance. (Umstattd et al., 2012)

Observations of Physical Activity Environment. The **System for Observing Physical Activity and Recreation in Communities** (**SOPARC**) is a widely used tool for assessing contextual factors influencing physical activity and leisure behaviors (McKenzie, Cohen, Sehgal, Williamson, & Golinelli, 2006). SOPARC involves data collection using the Planned Activity Check method wherein segments of the target area (e.g., the wading pool of a park) are observed during a specified period of time during which both physical activity behaviors and contextual characteristics are observed (**Table 9.24**). Contextual characteristics assessed include accessibility and usability as well as whether or not supervision, organized activities, and equipment are provided.

- The researchers found that most parks were identified as usable and accessible, while less than half (42.7%) were occupied at time of assessment. Park areas with the highest proportion of users engaging in vigorous physical activity were fields, volleyball, tennis, basketball, gym equipment, and playgrounds (McKenzie et al., 2006).

SOPARC has been adapted for use via technology (e.g., IPAD) to facilitate data collection and analysis.

CONCLUSION

As this chapter highlights, the field of measurement is burgeoning when it comes to tools for assessing features of the built environment influencing healthy living. This chapter highlights 24 different measures related to food access, walkability, and the physical activity environment in neighborhood settings. This does not include the long list of measures that currently lack research on their psychometric properties. However, given the growth of this field, it is likely that existing untested measures may be tested, tested measures will be refined, and new measures will be developed.

As this field of measurement evolves, online resources are being developed to facilitate identification and analysis of measures of the built environment. The National Collaborative on Childhood Obesity Research developed a measures registry that includes hundreds of indicators of the built environment (https://tools.nccor.org/measures/). The Healthy Food Access Portal (http://www.healthyfoodaccess.org/) includes an interactive mapping function to quickly identify indicators of a specific geographic context such as retailers accepting federal food assistance benefits, layered on poverty rates of the targeted census tract. This portal aggregates publicly available data sources into a user-friendly platform to further community planning and action. Similarly, the Food Environment Atlas sponsored by the U.S. Department of Agriculture aggregates publically available data into an analytic platform to identify gaps in healthy food access to target interventions (https://www.ers.usda.gov/data-products/food-environment-atlas/). These online resources should be reviewed in conjunction with this chapter to inform measurement selection.

A benefit of this chapter is the inclusion of a range of measures such as those that are rather simple as well as tools that are more complex. Additionally, the chapter features measurement tools that rely on secondary analysis of existing data versus primary data collection. Some of the tools, such as the app available for using the SOPARC assessment for evaluating the physical activity environment, have already innovated methods to facilitate utilization (McKenzie et al., 2006). This technology-oriented trend will likely be mirrored in the future to facilitate real-time data collection and analysis.

The growth in measurement within this field of study is reflective of the surge of interest in environmental factors influencing health. This field of measurement is largely driven by researchers and practitioners focused on obesity and other diet-related health conditions. Existing measures may be less sensitive for studying other health conditions that are influenced by the built environment (e.g., infant mortality). While it is a strength to see a rise in the development of measures focused on built environment factors influencing healthy living, this also creates challenges. Given the range of measures available, it may be difficult to compare findings across studies because the built environment is measured differently. Moreover, the diversity of measures available may create confusion for practitioners. Selecting the best measure requires careful analysis of the questions one intends to investigate as well as the resources available to carry out data collection.

LIST OF MEASURES AND TABLE NUMBERS

TABLE 9.1 ■ Physical Food Environment Indicator (PFEI)	
Primary Reference	Truong, K., Fernandes, M., An, R., Shier, V., & Sturm, R. (2010). Measuring the physical food environment and its relationship with obesity: Evidence from California. *Public Health, 124*(2), 115–118.
Purpose	Method for measuring the ratio of healthy to unhealthy food stores in a census tract
Description	• The PFEI is designed to assess the overall quality of the food environment and its relationship with obesity trends in specific geographic units of analysis (either census tracts or counties). • The tool builds on an existing tool, the Retail Food Environment Index, which had limitations in geographic areas without access to a supermarket or produce vendor.
Data	• Food stores in California included in the study were selected from Info USA (a commercial database). • Stores were selected based on North American Industry Classification System (NAICS) codes for fast food, supermarkets and grocery stores (annual sales $1 million or more), and small stores.
Measurement	PFEI = ____________ F + C + S / F + C + S + L + P Where F = fast-food restaurants C = convenience stores S = small food stores L = supermarkets P = produce vendors PFEI was bounded between 0 and 1 with lower scores indicating more balanced access between healthy and unhealthy choices.
Assessment	Not provided.
Language	English
Contact	Khoa Truong, PhD Clemson University Department of Public Health Sciences 505 Edwards Hall Clemson, SC 29634-0745 Email: ktruong@clemson.edu

TABLE 9.2 ■	Nutrition Environment Measures Survey in Stores (NEMS-S)
Primary Reference	Glanz, K., Sallis, J. F., Saelens, B. E., & Frank, L. D. (2007). Nutrition environment measures survey in stores (NEMS-S): Development and evaluation. *American Journal of Preventive Medicine, 32*(4), 282–289.
Purpose	Designed to measure features of the food store environment based on observation of food retail outlets.
Description	The NEMS-S assesses the availability, quality, and price of 10 indicator food categories: • Fruit • Vegetables • Milk • Ground beef • Hot dogs • Frozen dinners • Baked goods • Beverages (soda/juice) • Whole grain bread • Baked chips The tool focuses on the availability of these products in general as well as the more healthful or recommended choices (e.g., low-fat milk versus whole, lean ground beef versus regular). • The produce specified in the tool focused on the top 10 most consumed fruits and vegetables consumed in the United States at the time of the study (excluding potatoes). • The quality indicator was only used to assess fruits and vegetables by asking raters to report if the produce was "acceptable" or "unacceptable," with unacceptable used for foods that were clearly bruised, old looking, overripe, or spotted. • The price indicator was assessed using the posted non-sale prices of the food items. In addition, the number of cash registers at the store was assessed to estimate store size. Data collectors were college educated but with no prior experience in nutrition research. • All data collectors completed a two-day training on the tool, including didactic and field-based components. • During the training, assessments of pilot stores were conducted by two raters and monitored for reliability (> 90% agreement). • Feedback from the training experience was used to inform future data collection. • On average, it took 42 minutes to conduct the NEMS-S in a grocery store and 14 minutes in a convenience store.
Sample	• The study took place in four neighborhoods in Atlanta, GA, USA, with one of the targeted neighborhoods defined as a food desert. • Within each neighborhood, grocery stores and convenience stores (including food marts within gas stations) were sampled. • The study did not include specialty stores (e.g., bakeries). A total of 85 stores (24 grocery, 61 convenience) were included in the sample.

(Continued)

TABLE 9.2 ■ (Continued)	
Scoring	A "food environment quality score" was calculated for each store, synthesizing information collected related to availability, price, and quality. • The availability score assigned two points per indicator for the availability of healthier options and an extra point for more varieties (e.g., two extra points for three or more varieties of lean meats). • The price score assigned two points for a lower-priced, healthier option and -1 for a higher-priced, healthier option. • Up to three points were assigned for having more produce of acceptable quality. The food environment quality score ranged from -8 to 50, with a higher score indicating greater availability and better quality and lower prices for healthful options compared to "regular" choices.
Assessment	• Inter-rater reliability was assessed by having two raters independently visit the food outlets to complete the same set of assessments on the same day. • Rates of agreement and kappa statistics for inter-rater reliability were consistently high, ranging from 92% to 100% and 0.83 and 1.00. • Test–retest reliability was assessment within one month of the initial observation by one of the original raters. Test–retest reliability was high, with the lowest repeatability for 100% whole grain bread at 90% and 0.75.
Related Reference	Cavanaugh, E., Mallya, G., Brensinger, C., Tierney, A., & Glanz, K. (2013). Nutrition environments in corner stores in Philadelphia. *Preventive Medicine, 56*(2),149–151.
Language	English
Contact	Karen Glanz, PhD, MPH University of Pennsylvania School of Nursing Room 321 Fagin Hall 418 Curie Blvd. Philadelphia, PA, USA 19104-4217 Email: kglanz@upenn.edu
Website	A website dedicated to provide information, resources, and training related to the NEMS-S is available at http://www.med.upenn.edu/nems/measures.shtml.

TABLE 9.3 ■	Bridging the Gap: Food Store Observation Form (BTG-FSOF)
Primary Reference	Rimkus, L., Powell, L. M., Zenk, S. N., Han, E., Ohri-Vachaspati, P., Pugach, O., . . . Chaloupka, F. J. (2013). Development and reliability testing of a food store observation form. *Journal of Nutrition Education and Behavior, 45*(6), 540–548.
Purpose	Instrument to measure the availability, pricing, and marketing of both healthy and unhealthy foods and beverages in diverse types of food stores
Description	The form assessed the following major topics: • Food and beverage product availability • Product pricing • Price type • Number of fruit and vegetable options • Number of exterior advertisements • Interior and exterior store characteristics including product placement and promotion Foods and beverages included in the assessment were those on the NEMS-S (Glanz et al., 2007) and/or the American Chamber of Commerce Research Association Cost of Living Index. The form focused on sugar-sweetened beverages because these contribute to increased caloric intake. Any time the price of the food or beverage item was not posted, it was coded as "unknown." Additionally, prices were denoted as regular, sale, or member (store loyalty card) prices at the time of observation. Counts of fruits and vegetables were assessed with a maximum of 21 items. Counts of advertisements were conducted with separate categorization for food ads, beverage ads, combination (food/beverage) ads, ads with price promotions, and ads with fresh produce. All data collectors participated in a three-day training involving lectures, presentations, and field practice. • All data collectors had a bachelor's degree but did not necessarily have training in research. Two researchers independently audited each store using the form. All data collectors received identification badges worn during data collection. • Observation time was an average of 97 minutes in a supermarket and 44 minutes in smaller stores. • The reliability study for BTG-FOSF was conducted in the Chicago area. Food retail store data from the Dun and Bradstreet commercial database were extracted and augmented using web-based searches and were then mapped.
Sample	• Census tracts were selected for inclusion in the study if they had at least one of the following: one supermarket, two grocery stores, or four stores of any type. Ultimately, a convenience sample of stores was selected based on geographic clustering of stores. • Stores were selected in census tracts that were predominantly White and non-White and tracts within and outside the city limits of Chicago. • The study focused on 120 food stores (26 supermarkets, 34 grocery stores, 54 gas/convenience stores, and six mass merchandise stores).
Scoring	All items analyzed individually.

(Continued)

TABLE 9.3 ■ (Continued)	
Assessment	Inter-rater reliability was assessed for measures of product availability and price. • There was high agreement for product availability (kappa = 0.84, average proportion agreement = 0.96). • Lower agreement was found in the beverages and snacks sections. • For product pricing, inter-rater reliability was very high (kappa = 0.82). • Likewise, agreement on the availability of fruit and vegetable options was high (ICC = 0.87–0.95). • Agreement for advertising was also high with a few exceptions (e.g., at least one candy-free checkout lane (k= 0.27), candy available at checkout (k = 0.34).
Language	English
Contact	Leah Rimkus, MPH, RD Institute for Health Policy and Research University of Illinois at Chicago (MC 275) 445 Westside Research Office Building 1747 West Roosevelt Road Chicago, IL 60608 Email: lrimkus@uic.edu
Website	The Bridging the Gap team has developed a series of resources to assess the food environment, including measures of fast-food restaurants available on their website: http://www.bridgingthegapresearch.org/research/community_data/.

TABLE 9.4 ■	Food Environment Audit for Diverse Neighborhoods (FEAD-N)
Primary Reference	Izumi, B. T., Zenk, S. N., Schulz, A. J., Mentz, G. B., Sand, S. L., de Majo, R. F., . . . Odoms-Young, A. (2011). Inter-rater reliability of the food environment audit for diverse neighborhoods (FEAD-N). *Journal of Urban Health, 89*(3), 486–499.
Purpose	Instrument assesses multiple components of the food retail environment in diverse neighborhoods, including physical and social elements and availability of culturally specific foods.
Description	The tool assesses **availability of eight categories of foods:** • Fruits • Vegetables • Meats • Beans • Grains • Dairy • Fats • Added sugars For each item, healthy and less healthy options were assessed (e.g., skim milk and whole milk). Additionally, culturally relevant foods for African Americans (e.g., collard greens, okra) and Hispanics (e.g., tomatillos, mango) were assessed. In all, a total of 130 fresh fruits and vegetables and 83 other food items were included in the assessment. Price of the food item was assessed, when available. The FEAD-N also assesses the **physical and social features of the food store**. Physical features (n = 34 items) included • Infrastructure • Services • Products • Marketing • Government assistance participation Social features of the food store (n = 20 items) included • Security features • Disorder inside or outside of the store • Behaviors of owner or employees • Race/ethnicity of employees and owners Data were collected by neighborhood residents (n = 5) who received 25 hours of training on the tool, including classroom and field-based training. • After completing training, all observers audited five practice stores as a group, in pairs, and individually. This informed refinement of the data collection tool. • Observers were hired to complete the audits if at the end of the training their inter-rater reliability (against the gold standard of a postdoctoral fellow's audits) had an agreement rate of 80% or higher. • Four of the five residents were certified for the food retail audit team. • On average, audits were completed in 26.6 minutes with a range of 15 for small stores and 60 minutes for large stores. Audits were conducted over a 10-week timeframe.

(Continued)

TABLE 9.4 ■ (Continued)	
Sample	• The study occurred in three diverse communities in Detroit, Michigan, including two majority African American communities and one majority Hispanic community. All communities had lower levels of household income. • Stores were selected from a list of stores provided by the Michigan Department of Agriculture. The stores located in the targeted zip codes received a letter about the store auditing study. Additionally, the team ground truthed the data by driving up and down all streets in the targeted areas to identify stores from the original list that were permanently closed or identify new stores. In all, a total of 167 stores were audited from the original list of 170 stores. Three stores refused an audit.
Scoring	Availability is defined as the presence of the food item in the store.
Assessment	• Four trained observers each visited about 55 stores. Two observers independently coded a random subset of 44 stores on the same day (not necessarily at the same time). • Inter-rater reliability was assessed on these 44 stores using kappa statistics and for those items with low levels of availability, percentage agreement. • For 75% of the food items, inter-rater reliability was between 0.81 and 1.00 (i.e., very high). • More than 50% of the physical features and 47% of the social features assessed had almost perfect inter-rater reliability. • Features with the lowest inter-rater reliability were candy or gum in the checkout aisle, foul odor in the store, and bulletproof or thick glass at checkout.
Language	English
Contact	Betty Izumi, PhD Portland State University School of Community Health 506 SW Mill Street, Suite 450 Portland, Oregon 97201

TABLE 9.5 ■	Availability and Costs of Foods Recommended for People With Diabetes Audit
Primary Reference	Horowitz, C. R., Colson, K. A., Hebert, P. L., & Lancaster, K. (2004). Barriers to buying healthy foods for people with diabetes: Evidence of environmental disparities. *American Journal of Public Health, 94*, 1549–1554.
Purpose	Measure and compare the availability and cost of foods recommended for people with diabetes between two neighborhoods with different racial and socioeconomic composition
Description	The **food items** in this measure included • Diet soda • 1% or skim milk • High-fiber bread or low-carbohydrate bread (or both) • Fresh fruits • Fresh green vegetables or tomatoes **Stores** selected for assessment using the tool were selected from a database of stores inspected and licensed to sell food. Stores were categorized based on the number of cash registers at the store as follows: • 1 register = bodega • 2–4 registers = medium-sized store • 5+ registers = large store **Store audits** were collected by dietetic interns and local outreach workers who volunteered to complete the assessments. • All data collectors received six hours of training in conducting the survey, including didactic and field-based training. • Data collectors went to all stores in pairs, provided managers with a letter about the study, and gave managers a T-shirt with messages about diabetes that were designed by a local artist. • Data collectors assessed the presence of each food and beverage item and the lowest price available. • They did not collect prices for fruits or vegetables. If prices were not available, they asked the store manager for the price.
Sample	• The study took place in East Harlem, New York City, and an adjacent neighborhood (Upper East Side). • The neighborhoods had different racial and socioeconomic compositions. East Harlem was 6% White with the lowest median household income while the Upper East Side was 84% White with the highest median household income.
Scoring	A store was scored as "desirable" if they had at least one item from each of the five food and beverage groups. All other stores were scored as "undesirable."
Assessment	• Two independent data collectors assessed each store. At the end of the audit, data collectors compared observations, recorded discrepancies, and resolved them together while at the store. • Inter-rater reliability (based on initial observations before discrepancies were addressed) was high with a kappa score ranging from 0.94 to 1.0.

(Continued)

TABLE 9.5 ■ (Continued)	
Language	English
Contact	Carol Horowitz, MD, MPH Mount Sinai Hospital 17 East 102nd Street New York, NY 1002 Email: Carol.horowitz@mountsinai.org

TABLE 9.6 ■	Availability of Low-Fat Milk in Food Stores Audit
Primary Reference	Wechsler, H., Basch, C. E., Zybert, P., Lantigua, R., & Shea, S. (1995). The availability of low-fat milk in an inner-city Latino community: Implications for nutrition education. *American Journal of Public Health, 85*, 1690–1692.
Purpose	Measure availability of low-fat milk in small grocery stores (bodegas) and supermarkets
Description	• The tool examines both availability and the proportion of store shelves of all milk that was low fat. • In each store, the number of containers of four different types of milk (whole, 2% fat, 1% fat, and skim) in each of three different sizes (quart, half-gallon, gallon) were assessed.
Sample	• The study took place in Washington Heights-Inwood neighborhood in New York City. • The context was defined as low-income, inner-city community with approximately 40% of its residents living below the poverty level. Most residents in the area identified as Latino (67%). • The study focused on bodegas (food stores that sell milk and have only one cash register) and supermarkets. A total of 257 bodegas were identified for the study, and of these, 251 agreed to have their store audited. A total of 25 supermarkets were identified and observed.
Scoring	• Milk counts were aggregated into "total quarts" for each of the four milk types by adding up the total number of quarts, the total number of half-gallons divided by two, and the total number of gallons divided by four. • The proportion of milk shelf space occupied by low-fat milk was summarized by the proportion of total quarts of all milk that was 2%, 1%, or skim.
Assessment	• To assess inter-rater reliability, two independent raters assessed milk access at the same time in the same store in a total of 15 bodegas. Internal consistency was high (r = 0.99) for the proportion of shelf space occupied by low-fat milk. • To assess test–retest reliability, one rater observed 14 of the 15 bodegas 17 days after the initial observations. Low-fat milk availability was the same at all stores, and repeated measures of the proportion of milk shelf space occupied by low-fat milk were highly correlated (r = 0.92).
Language	English
Contact	Howell Wechsler, EdD, MPH Chief Executive Officer Alliance for a Healthier Generation 606 SE 9th Ave Portland, OR 97214

TABLE 9.7 ■ Fruit, Juice, and Vegetable Availability Assessment

Primary Reference	Edmonds, J., Baranowski, T., Baranowski, J., Cullen, K. W., & Myres, D. (2001). Ecological and socioeconomic correlates of fruit, juice, and vegetable consumption among African-American boys. *Preventive Medicine, 32,* 476–481.
Purpose	Assess the availability of fruits, juices, and vegetables in census stores and restaurants.
Description	Inventories were conducted after 9:00 a.m. because inventories were often stocked during the early morning hours. Availability was defined as the following present in store or on a restaurant menu: • Fruit • Juice • Vegetables The grocery store audit focused on 10 fruits, 12 vegetables, and three 100% juices. Items were separated into four categories: • Fresh • Frozen • Bottled/canned • Dried For restaurants, menus were assessed using a checklist that was pretested by the team. The checklist focused on the number of fruit, juice, and vegetable offerings at breakfast, lunch, and dinner.
Sample	• The study took place in Houston, Texas. The store audits focused on 11 census tracts where study participants (Boy Scouts) resided. Boy Scout troops with 80% or more African American boys participating were the target population for the broader study. • All convenience stores, convenience and gas stores, and restaurants (sit down, fast food) in each selected census tract were audited. One small grocery store and one supermarket per census tract were randomly selected to be inventoried for fruit, juice, and vegetable availability. • A small grocery store was defined as an independently owned "mom and pop" establishment carrying some produce and a limited variety of brand names and sizes. • A supermarket was defined as a grocery store that was part of a national or regional chain and carried a large variety of fresh produce, brand names, and sizes. • In all, 34 stores and 61 restaurants were audited.
Scoring	• Availability of fruit, juice, or vegetables was assessed "yes/no" and in grocery stores, shelf space occupied was assessed using a measuring tape. • Once store-level data were analyzed, then stores within the same census tract were aggregated and averaged to create a composite score for the census tract.
Assessment	In restaurants, two raters reviewed the menu items. There was high inter-rater reliability for identifying the number of fruits, juices, and vegetables on the menus (r = 0.79).
Language	English
Contact	Tom Baranowski, PhD Children's Nutrition Research Center Department of Pediatrics Baylor College of Medicine 1100 Bates, Suite 2038 Houston, TX 77030

TABLE 9.8 ■ Choice in Food Store Access	
Primary Reference	Dibsdall, L. A., Lambert, N., Bobbin, R. F., & Frewer, L. J. (2003). Low-income consumers' attitudes and behaviour towards access, availability and motivation to eat fruits and vegetables. *Public Health Nutrition, 6*(2), 159–168.
Purpose	Designed to measure perceptions of choice in access to shopping facilities and availability and choice of fresh, frozen, or tinned fruits and vegetables.
Description	Choice in food store access is a 10-item self-report scale consisting of items related to food store access, affordability, and motivation to shop at stores. The scale asks participants to rate their level of agreement using a 7-point Likert scale (1 = *strongly agree*, 2 = *moderately agree*, 3= *slightly agree*, 4 = *neither agree nor disagree*, 5 = *slightly disagree*, 6 = *moderately disagree*, 7 = *strongly disagree*) with items such as the following: • Where I shop has a wide choice of fresh vegetables (access). • I am satisfied with the shop where I buy most of my food (motivation). • I think fruit is affordable to me in the shop where I buy most of my food (affordability).
Sample	• The sample included 680 low-income men and women residing in homes owned by a large housing association in the United Kingdom. • The researchers had a 23% response rate to the mail survey that included the scale. Most participants (78%) were women living in urban (64%) settings.
Scoring	• A mean score was calculated for the 10 items. • Mean scores greater than four indicated respondents tended to disagree with the statements. • Mean scores less than four indicated respondents tended to agree with the statements.
Assessment	• Principle components analysis with varimax rotation was conducted on a 30-item scale. • The choice in food store access items hung together with factor loadings of 0.35 to 0.85. • Reliability analysis of the 10 items was conducted using Cronbach's alpha as a measure of internal consistency resulting in a reliability measure of $\alpha = 0.87$.
Language	English
Contact	Louise Dibsdall, PhD Institute of Food Research Norwich, United Kingdom Email: Louise.Dibsdall@bbsrc.ac.uk

TABLE 9.9 ■ Perceptions of Access to Healthy Foods in the Neighborhood

Primary Reference	Echeverria, S. E., Diez-Roux, A. V., & Link, B. G. (2004). Reliability of self-reported neighborhood characteristics. *Journal of Urban Health, 81*(4), 682–700.
Purpose	Designed to measure perceptions of access to healthy foods in the neighborhood as a part of a broader assessment of the neighborhood environment.
Description	Perceptions of access to healthy foods in the neighborhood included a 6-item self-report scale. In this survey, "neighborhood" was defined as the area within a 20-minute walk or about a mile from a participant's home. The scale asks participants to rate their level of agreement using a 5-point Likert scale (1 = *strongly agree*, 2= *agree*, 3 = *neutral, neither agree nor disagree*, 4 = *disagree*, 5 = *strongly disagree*), with items such as the following: • It is easy to purchase fresh fruits and vegetables in my neighborhood. • There is a large selection of low-fat milk products in my neighborhood. • The produce in my neighborhood is of high quality.
Sample	• The sample included 48 people, most identified as African American or Latino. • Participants were recruited through fliers distributed in public housing complexes in the Washington Heights area of New York City. • The mean age of participants was 38 years and 75% were women.
Scoring	Mean score was calculated for the six items. Standard deviations were also calculated. Scores ranged from 6 to 30, with a mean score at Time 1 of 15.1 (*SD*: 5.3) and at Time 2 of 15.4 (*SD*: 5.6).
Assessment	• Test-retest reliability was assessed using intraclass correlation coefficients, variant ICC. Test-retest reliability ICC of the 6-item scale was 0.88 (95% confidence interval: 0.79–0.83). • Reliability analysis of the six items was conducted using Cronbach's alpha for the scale was high at Time 1 (α = 0.91) and Time 2 (α = 0.94).
Related Reference	For updated analyses related to the measure, see Mujahid, M. S., Diez Roux, A. V., Morenoff, J. D., & Raghunathan, T. (2007). Assessing the measurement properties of neighborhood scales: From psychometrics to ecometrics. *American Journal of Epidemiology, 165*(8), 858–867.
Language	English
Contact	Ana Diez Roux, PhD, MPH Drexel University Dornsife School of Public Health Philadelphia, PA Email: avd37@drexel.edu

TABLE 9.10 ■	Perceptions of Food Availability and Price
Primary Reference	Giskes, K., Van Lenthe, F. J., Brug, J., Mackenbach, J. P., & Turrell, G. (2007). Socioeconomic inequalities in food purchasing: The contribution of respondent-perceived and actual (objectively measured) price and availability of foods. *Preventive Medicine, 45*, 41–48.
Purpose	Designed to measure perceptions of food availability and food prices in the neighborhood environment.
Description	Perceptions of food availability and price were measured using a 28-item scale that was completed via self-report. The scale assessed perceptions of both availability and price of 14 recommended food choices (e.g., whole meal bread, lean chicken). • For each food item, availability was assessed using the question: "Is [name of recommended food] available where you usually shop (even if you do not buy it)?" Response choices were "yes," "no," or "not sure." • To assess perceptions of price, participants were presented with the recommended choice for a given food group and its complementary regular choice and asked to nominate which choice was more expensive. For example, for the bread food group, both whole meal and white bread were presented. Response options were: "recommended choice perceived more expensive," "regular choice perceived more expensive," "perceived about the same price," or "not sure."
Sample	• The study took place in Brisbane, Australia. The sample was selected using a two-stage cluster design to select households within 50 small areas within the city. • Within these 50 areas, 1003 private dwellings were selected via simple random sampling. • The person primarily responsible for the household's food shopping was selected to take part. Interview response rate was 66.4%.
Scoring	Each item was treated as a single variable for analysis. Frequencies were calculated for each recommended food choice perceived to be available in the supermarket (% yes) and perceived to be more expensive than the regular option (% recommended choice perceived more expensive).
Assessment	None
Language	English
Contact	K. Giskes Queensland University of Technology Australia Email: k.giskes@qut.edu.au

TABLE 9.11 ■ Menu Checklist	
Primary Reference	Cassady, D., Housemann, R., & Dagher, C. (2004). Measuring cues for healthy choices on restaurant menus: Development and testing of a measurement instrument. *American Journal of Health Promotion, 18*(6), 444–449.
Purpose	Instrument used by community members to assess cues for healthy food choices and quantity of healthy food options on restaurant menus
Description	The Menu Checklist is based on environmental indicators for behaviors related to cardiovascular diseases (e.g., physical inactivity, smoking, poor nutrition). The checklist was modified from an existing tool that was validated in rural and urban settings. The checklist examines • Labeling and cues for healthy eating (such as, Does the menu indicate that all frying is done in 100% vegetable oil) • Quantity of healthy options (such as, number of healthy or low-fat entrees) in four contents of the menu: entrees, side dishes, appetizers, and non-alcoholic beverages
Sample	• The study took place in nine zip codes in predominantly African American neighborhoods in South Central Los Angeles, California. This included 14 restaurants. • Restaurants were selected for inclusion in the study based on popularity among residents and if they were locally owned since it was believed by the team that it was unlikely that an intervention could be implemented in a regionally or nationally run restaurant. • Selection of restaurants was guided by a community coalition. Ten restaurants specialized in soul, Caribbean, or Cajun food, and the remaining four were diners or "fast casual" restaurants that included soul food on the menu or catered to an African American clientele.
Scoring	All items were analyzed individually.
Assessment	Inter-rater reliability was high of the labeling or cues for healthy eating indicators (0.929–1.0) and moderate to high for the quantity of options (0.794–1.0).
Related Reference	Rimkus, L., Ohri-Vachaspati, P., Powell, L. M., Zenk, S. N., Quinn, C. M., Barker, D. C., . . . Chaloupka, F.J. (2015) Development and reliability testing of a fast-food restaurant observation form. *American Journal of Health Promotion, 30*(1), 9–18.
Language	English
Contact	Diane Cassady, DrPH Department of Public Health Sciences University of California, Davis One Shields Avenue, Med-Sci 1C Davis, CA 95616 Email: dlcassady@ucdavis.edu

TABLE 9.12 ■ Neighborhood Environment Measures Survey in Restaurants (NEMS-R)

Primary Reference	Saelens, B. E., Glanz, K., Sallis, J. F., & Frank, L. (2007). Nutrition environment measures study in restaurants (NEMS-R): Development and evaluation. *American Journal of Preventive Medicine, 32*(4), 273–281.
Purpose	Designed to measure features of the restaurant food environment using observation methods.

Description	Availability of menu items were assessed in multiple categories, including entrées, main dish salads, side dishes, and beverages.
	• Menu items were not assumed to be "unhealthy," unless specific information to the contrary was provided or if the nature of the item was healthful (e.g., raw fruit).
	  ○ Healthy entrees were defined as ≤ 800 calories, ≤ 30% calories from fat, ≤ 10% calories from saturated fat for non-burger/sandwich entrees, or regulated healthy designation (e.g., light, low-fat) was provided for the entrée.
	  ○ Specific criteria for defining "healthy" for different menu items are available in the manuscript.
	• In addition, availability of the following items was assessed at all restaurants:
	  ○ Fruit without added sugar
	  ○ Non-fried vegetables without sauce or toppings
	  ○ Baked chips
	  ○ Whole grain bread
	  ○ Diet soda
	  ○ 100% fruit juice
	  ○ 1% fat or nonfat milk
	• Children's menu items included assessment of availability of non-fried foods (e.g., grilled chicken v. fried chicken), 100% fruit juice, and 1% fat or nonfat milk.
	Five items assessed "facilitators" of healthy eating:
	• Any nutrition information provided on the menu
	• Any entrees labeled as being healthier (e.g., low-fat)
	• Reduced sized portions available (e.g., ½ portion)
	• Special request for modifying entrees encouraged on the menu (e.g., can substitute fresh fruit instead of French fries)
	• Salad bar available
	Additionally, five items assessed "barriers" to healthy eating:
	• Larger portion was encouraged on the menu (e.g., get 50% more for $0.25)
	• Over-eating was encouraged on the menu (e.g., we keep bringing the food until you say stop)
	• Special request were either prohibited or charged (e.g., no substitutions)
	• There was a low-carbohydrate promotion
	• "All-you-can-eat" or "unlimited" portions of any food (not beverage)
	Additionally, five items assessed healthy and unhealthy food non-menu marketing within the restaurant, such as nutrition information provided at point of purchase, signs displaying health menu options, and sign encouraging healthy eating.
	Data collectors were college-educated but with no prior experience in nutrition research. All data collectors completed 10 to 20 hours of training on the tool including didactic and field-based components. Assessment of stores include in-store audits and review of online menus. On average, it took 28.1 minutes to conduct the NEMS-R in the restaurant and complete the menu evaluation.

(Continued)

TABLE 9.12 ■ (Continued)	
Sample	• The study took place in four neighborhoods in Atlanta, Georgia, with one of the targeted neighborhoods defined as a food desert. Restaurants had to be open to the public to be included in the assessment (e.g., worksite cafeteria excluded). • Restaurants were classified as either fast food or sit down. Fast food included restaurants having limited service where patrons order and pay before eating. Sit down restaurants were characterized as having table ordering and service. A total of 217 restaurants were included in the sample (102 fast food, 115 sit down).
Scoring	Items were examined individually. No scale scores were computed.
Assessment	• Inter-rater reliability was assessed by having two raters independently visit the restaurants to complete the same set of assessments on the same day. • Rates of agreement and kappa statistics for inter-rater reliability varied, ranging from 77.6% to 100% and 0.33 and 1.00, respectively. • Test–retest reliability was assessed within one month of the initial observation by one of the original raters. Test–retest reliability was high, with the lowest repeatability of 80.0% for availability of reduced portion sized items on the menu (kappa = 0.64).
Language	English
Contact	Brian Saelens, PhD Seattle Children's Hospital Center for Child Health Behavior and Development 2001 8th Avenue, Suite 400 Seattle, Washington Email: bsaelens@u.washington.edu
Website	A website dedicated to provide information, resources, and training related to the NEMS-R is available at http://www.med.upenn.edu/nems/measures.shtml.

TABLE 9.13 ■ Walk Score®	
Primary Reference	Carr, L. J., Dunsiger, S. I., & Marcus, B. H. (2011). Validation of Walk Score for estimating access to walkable amenities. *British Journal of Sports Medicine, 45*(14), 1144–1148.
Purpose	Estimate neighborhood walkability using density of walkable amenities
Description	This tool evaluates the distance of various amenities to residences and workplaces utilizing GIS data. The amenities include • Grocery stores • Restaurants • Coffee shops • Bars • Movie theaters • Schools • Parks • Libraries • Bookstores • Fitness facilities • Drug stores • Hardware stores • Clothing stores • Music stores
Sample	• A total of 379 residential (n = 232) and nonresidential/work addresses (n =147) in Providence, Rhode Island, were matched to RIGIS Tiger Shapefiles. • Other GIS data regarding amenities was provided by the Rhode Island Department of Health and included all food vendors and retail services (n = 4,194), which were also geocoded and matched.
Scoring	A one-mile radius buffer was inserted over each point address within the GIS software to see if the buffer intersected with amenities. All the points or amenities lying within the buffer were summed and normalized to yield a score from 0 to 100 where • 0–24 = car-dependent (driving only; nothing within walking range) • 24–49 = car-dependent (only a few destinations are within easy walking range and for most errands, driving or public transportation is a must) • 50–69 = somewhat walkable (some stores and amenities are within walking distance but many may still require a bike, public transportation, or car) • 70–89 = very walkable (possible to get by without owning a car) • 90–100 = walkers' paradise (most errands can be accomplished on foot and many people get by without owning a car)
Assessment	Test–retest reliability analysis was conducted on two different occasions with the correlation coefficient of a subsample of 100 addresses being equal to 1.0.

(Continued)

TABLE 9.13 ■ (Continued)	
Related Reference	Duncan, D. T., Aldstadt, J., Whalen, J., Melly, S. J., & Gortmaker, S. L. (2011). Validation of Walk Score® for estimating neighborhood walkability: An analysis of four US metropolitan areas. *International Journal of Environmental Research and Public Health, 8*(11), 4160–4179.
Language	English
Contact	Lucas J. Carr, PhD University of Iowa 225 S. Grand Avenue, Field House E118 Iowa City, IA 52242 Email: Lucas-Carr@uiowa.edu

TABLE 9.14 ■	Systematic Pedestrian and Cycling Environmental Scan (SPACES)
Primary Reference	Pikora, T. J., Bull, F. C., Jamrozik, K., Knuiman, M., Giles-Corti, B., & Donovan, R. J. (2002). Developing a reliable audit instrument to measure the physical environment for physical activity. *American Journal of Preventive Medicine*, *23*(3), 187–194.
Purpose	Measures of the physical environment that influence participation in walking
Description	This audit tool examines 37 factors believed to influence walking and cycling in neighborhoods as categorized into the following groups: • Functional features (walking/cycling surface, streets, traffic, permeability) • Safety (personal, traffic) • Aesthetics (streetscapes, views) • Destination (facilities) • A subjective assessment aimed at determining attractiveness and difficulty for walking/cycling
Sample	Researchers surveyed a total of 1,987 km of streets that were audited by 16 observers within 408 km^2 of Perth, Western Australia.
Scoring	• Each variable coded to provide a score between 0 and 1 based on whether the item was present as the ideal = 1, have it all = 0.5, and anything extra is a bonus to 1. • Scores were added to give a raw aggregate score for that neighborhood, which was then multiplied by the weight assigned by the Delphi expert panel (weighted with a number between 0 and 1).
Assessment	• Both inter-rater reliability and intra-rater reliability were calculated. • Inter-rater reliability was calculated by taking 27 randomly selected segments that were re-audited by four observers. • A total of 83 randomly selected segments were re-audited by the same observer to calculate intra-rater reliability. • There was greater than 70% agreement among all four observers for all but one item.
Related Reference	Pikora, T. J., Giles-Corti, B., Knuiman, M. W., Bull, F. C., Jamrozik, K., & Donovan, R. J. (2006). Neighborhood environmental factors correlated with walking near home: Using SPACES. *Medicine and Science in Sports and Exercise*, *38*(4), 708–714.
Language	English
Contact	Terri J. Pikora Adjunct Senior Research Fellow School of Population Health The University of Western Australia (MM431) 35 Stirling Highway Crawley WA 6009 Australia Email: Terri.pikora@uwa.edu.au

TABLE 9.15 ■	St. Louis Analytic Audit Tool and Checklist Tool
Primary Reference	Brownson, R. C, Hoehner, C. M., Brennan, L. K., Cook, R. A., Elliott, M. B., & McCullen, K. M. (2004). Reliability of two instruments for auditing the environment for physical activity. *Journal of Physical Activity and Health, 1,* 191–208.
Purpose	Establish a method to broadly capture the street-scale environment
Description	Two tools, the analytic audit tool and checklist tool, were adapted from current literature. Both tools span across eight broad categories, which span over a number of street-scale environment factors in an effort to measure the street-scale environment, with the defining characteristics being the ways in which constructs are scored. The seven categories include • Community indicators • Transportation environment • Land-use environment • Recreational facilities • Physical disorder • Signage • The social environment
Sample	In St. Louis, a total of 475 street segments were identified (193 in higher income areas and 282 in lower income areas) to conduct audits using the analytic and the checklist tools.
Scoring	Responses in the analytic audit tool are assigned points based on a Likert or ordinal scale while responses in the checklist tool are coded as 0 = *not visible* or 1 = *visible.*
Assessment	• Audits were carried out in pairs, with each observer assigned either the analytic or the checklist audit tool. • A random sample of 150 street segments was re-audited by different observer pairs using the same instruments. • Inter-rater agreement was calculated along with a kappa statistic reported separately for each measure within the eight broad categories. • More than 50% of indicators have an inter-rater reliability of greater than 50% and kappa value greater than 0.41 for each individual measure. • Overall, researchers stated that reliability was higher for the checklist tool than for the analytic tool.
Related Reference	Scanlin, K., Haardoerfer, R., Kegler, M. C., & Glanz, K. (2014). Development of a pedestrian audit tool to assess rural neighborhood walkability. *Journal of Physical Activity and Health, 11*(6), 1085–1096.
Language	English
Contact	Robert Brownson, PhD Prevention Research Center School of Public Health St. Louis University St. Louis, MO 63104 Email: rbrownson@wustl.edu

TABLE 9.16 ■	Irvine-Minnesota Inventory (IMI)
Primary Reference	Boarnet, M. G., Day, K., Alfonzo, M., Forsyth, A., & Oakes, M. (2006). The Irvine-Minnesota inventory to measure built environments: Reliability tests. *American Journal of Preventive Medicine, 30*(2), 153–159.
Purpose	Assessing the relationship between the physical features of residential areas and walking behaviors
Description	The IMI builds upon SPACES and the St. Louis tools. The IMI broadens the scope of built environment by including 162 items under the four domains: • Accessibility **(62 items)** • Pleasurability **(56 items)** • Perceived safety from traffic **(31 items)** • Perceived safety from crime **(15 items)**
Sample	• The California-Irvine team tested the IMI tool in residential and nonresidential areas of walkable size in Southern California (1/4 mile radius areas) • The Minnesota team focused on areas comprised of 1/2 mile geographic districts in the Minneapolis—St. Paul metropolitan area. • The IMI was applied to 1.0 mile areas that surround the focus areas. • Segments assessed are represented by street block faces. • In California, observers sampled 27 study areas with 15 to 20 segments per area while Minnesota had a total of 891 segments.
Scoring	• Each variable coded to provide a score between 0 and 1 based on whether the item was present as the ideal = 1, have it all = 0.5, and anything extra is a bonus to 1. • Scores were added to give a raw aggregate score for that neighborhood, which was then multiplied by the weight assigned by the Delphi expert panel (weighted with a number between 0 and 1).
Assessment	• At eight of 27 settings in California, a team of three observers conducted independent audits of the segments. • In Minnesota, two independent observers conducted the audit on 147 randomly selected segments until there was near perfect agreement, after which the observers had split up. • There was greater than 80% of agreement among 76.8% of topics for tests conducted at California-Irvine and among 99.2% of topics observed at the University of Minnesota. • Items that scored less than that were eliminated from the inventory. Items with low reliability were removed from the tool—there were greater than 241 items measured and 162 remained after low-reliability items were removed.
Related Reference	Boarnet, M. G., Forsyth, A., Day, K., & Oakes, J. M. (2011). The street level built environment and physical activity and walking: Results of a predictive validity study for the Irvine Minnesota Inventory. *Environment and Behavior, 43*(6), 735–755.
Language	English
Contact	Marlon G. Boarnet, PhD University of Southern California Ralph and Goldy Lewis Hall 301C Los Angeles, CA 90089-0626 Email: boarnet@usc.edu

TABLE 9.17 ■	Microscale Audit of Pedestrian Streetscapes
Primary Reference	Millstein, R. A., Cain, K. L., Sallis, J. F., Conway, T. L., Geremia, C., Frank, L. D., & Saelens, B. E. (2013). Development, scoring, and reliability of the Microscale Audit of Pedestrian Streetscapes (MAPS). *BMC Public Health, 13*(1), 403.
Purpose	Assess relationship between microscale features of the neighborhood environment and perceptions of walkability
Description	This tool is comprised of 160 items and 26 specific subscales split across four sections of the microscale environment: • Overall route (land use, destinations, transit stops, street amenities, traffic calming, hardscape and softscape aesthetics, social environment) • Street segments/area between crossings (sidewalks, street buffers, sidewalk slope, bicycle facilities, shortcuts, building visibility, building aesthetics, trees, setbacks, building height) • Crossings (crosswalks, slopes, width of crossings, crossing signals, pedestrian protection) • Cul-de-sacs (condition of the surface area, slope, surveillance from surrounding homes, and amenities)
Sample	The sample came from three different studies that looked at San Diego County, Seattle/King County, and Maryland-DC. A total of 2,117 routes were selected along a quarter mile route starting at a participant's home and then walking to the nearest cluster of three or more destinations.
Scoring	Items were scored as a dichotomy (0 = no/1 = yes), frequency items (0, 1, 2+), or dichotomized or trichotomized based on characteristics.
Assessment	Two raters independently conducted audits for 13.7% of the routes. For 75.6% of the items, there was moderate to excellent inter-reliability (kappa > 0.41).
Related Reference	Cain, K. L., Millstein, R. A., Sallis, J. F., Conway, T. L., Gavand, K. A., Frank, L. D., . . . King, A.C. (2014). Contribution of streetscape audits to explanation of physical activity in four age groups based on the Microscale Audit of Pedestrian Streetscapes (MAPS). *Social Science & Medicine, 116*, 82–92.
Language	English
Contact	Kelli L Cain, MA University of California, San Diego 3900 5th Avenue, Suite 310 San Diego, CA 92103 Email: kcain@ucsd.edu

TABLE 9.18 ■	Pedestrian Environmental Data Scan (PEDS)
Primary Reference	Clifton, K. J., Smith, A. D. L., & Rodriguez, D. (2007). The development and testing of an audit for the pedestrian environment. *Landscape and Urban Planning, 80*(1), 95–110.
Purpose	Assess the availability of a range of elements of the built and natural environment to determine "walkability"
Description	PEDS is built off of the SPACES and IMI tools developed in the early 2000s. The PEDS tool looks at 83 measures within 40 questions focused on factors of the macroscale environment: • Pedestrian facilities • Road attributes • Microscale features (walking/cycling environment, subjective measures)
Sample	Researchers evaluated 71.5 miles (995 street segments) in College Park, Maryland, which is located near the University of Maryland.
Scoring	Each measure has an assigned value based on whether or not it is present. Scoring can be done by aggregating the number of measures that are present.
Assessment	• PEDS audits were conducted in pairs. • Raters looked at about 100 segments each day. • One day per week was dedicated to reliability testing where raters discussed any problems to improve and update protocol. • Overall, the inter-rater reliability was 80%. Those items with lower inter-rater agreement tended to be more subjective but were not excised from the tool.
Related Reference	Scanlin, K., Haardoerfer, R., Kegler, M. C., & Glanz, K. (2014). Development of a pedestrian audit tool to assess rural neighborhood walkability. *Journal of Physical Activity and Health, 11*(6), 1085–96.
Language	English
Contact	Kelly J. Clifton, PhD Portland State University PO Box 751 Portland, OR 97207-0751 Email: kclifton@pdx.edu
Website	http://kellyjclifton.com/products/peds/ http://planningandactivity.unc.edu/RP1.htm

TABLE 9.19 ■	Rural Pedestrian Environmental Audit Instrument
Primary Reference	Scanlin, K., Haardoerfer, R., Kegler, M. C., & Glanz, K. (2014). Development of a pedestrian audit tool to assess rural neighborhood walkability. *Journal of Physical Activity and Health, 11*(6), 1085–1096.
Purpose	Examine the relationship between objective features of the pedestrian environment, perception of walkability, and walking behaviors among rural populations
Description	This tool was adapted from the St. Louis Analytic Audit Tool, the Active Neighborhood Checklist (ANC), the Healthy Aging Network (HAN) tool, and the Pedestrian Environmental Data Scan (PEDS) and spans five domains: • Destinations (from the HAN, ANC, and St. Louis) • Street characteristics (from the ANC and HAN) • Quality of pedestrian facility (from the St. Louis, ANC, and PEDS) • Aesthetics/quality of environment (from the ANC and PEDS) • Social/dynamic environment (from St. Louis)
Sample	• The audit covered a county in southwest Georgia with a population of less than 35,000 in 2010 and a population density of less than 70 persons per square mile. • "Neighborhood environment," defined as 1/4 mile to 1/2 mile, was observed for 23 participants from the Healthy Rural Communities 2 (HRC2) study. • There were a total sample of 116 surrounding segments selected from areas surrounding the subset of participants—36 from out-of-town and 80 from in-town.
Scoring	• The Neighborhood Walkability Index is calculated from three types of variables: dichotomized (absent/present), rated into three or more categories (highest scores for ideal conditions versus partial scores when conditions not ideal), and the number of food-related destinations (up to two). • Scores within all domains were summed and then transformed into percentage scores. Overall walkability score is determined by averaging the five percentage scores with each domain receiving equal weighting of 20%.
Assessment	Of the 116 total segments assessed, 42 were independently audited by two raters. The percentage of inter-rater agreement for each domain was above 80%, and all Cohen's kappa values were greater than 0.40.
Related References	Clifton, K. J., Smith, A. D. L., & Rodriguez, D. (2007). The development and testing of an audit for the pedestrian environment. *Landscape and Urban Planning, 80*(1), 95–110. Brownson, R. C, Hoehner, C. M., Brennan, L. K., Cook, R. A., Elliott, M. B., & McCullen, K. M. (2004). Reliability of two instruments for auditing the environment for physical activity. *Journal of Physical Activity and Health, 1,* 191–208.
Language	English
Contact	Karen Glanz, PhD, MPH University of Pennsylvania School of Nursing Room 321 Fagin Hall 418 Curie Blvd. Philadelphia, PA, USA 19104-4217 kglanz@upenn.edu

TABLE 9.20 ■ Neighborhood Environment Walkability Scale (NEWS)	
Primary Reference	Saelens, B. E., Sallis, J. F., Black, J. B., & Chen, D. (2003). Neighborhood-based differences in physical activity: An environment scale evaluation. *American Journal of Public Health, 936*(9), 1552–1558.
Purpose	Measure the perception of walkability based on land use and community design
Description	NEWS is a survey tool that engages residents to gather information about seven environmental characteristics: • Residential density • Proximity to nonresidential land uses (e.g., restaurants and retail stores) • Street connectivity • Walking/cycling facilities (e.g., sidewalks and pedestrian/bike trails) • Aesthetics • Traffic safety • Crime safety
Sample	• Residents from two non-adjacent census tracts in San Diego, California, were selected to represent the ideal high-walkability neighborhoods and low-walkability neighborhoods. • A total of 54 residents from the high-walkability neighborhood and 53 residents in the low-walkability neighborhood provided data on physical activity (e.g., completed a survey and wore an activity monitor).
Scoring	• Items are scaled 1 = *strongly disagree* to 4 = *strongly agree*, with higher scores indicating a more favorable type of environmental characteristic. • Residential density is scaled with a range of 1 = *none* to 5 = *all* and are weighted relative to the average density of single-family detached residences.
Assessment	Test–retest reliability of the NEWS subscales were all greater than or equal to 0.58, and the majority of test–retest values were greater than or equal to 0.75.
Related References	Cerin, E., Conway, T., Saelens, B., Frank, L., & Sallis, J. (2009). Cross-validation of the factorial structure of the Neighborhood Environment Walkability Scale (NEWS) and its abbreviated form (NEWS-A). *International Journal of Behavioral Nutrition and Physical Activity, 6*(1), 32. Cerin, E., Saelens, B. E., Sallis, J. F., & Frank, L. D. (2006). Neighborhood environment walkability scale: Validity and development of a short form. *Medicine and Science in Sports and Exercise, 38,* 1682–1691. Sallis, J. F., Kerr, J., Carlson, J. A., Norman, G. J., Saelens, B. E., Durant, N., & Ainsworth, B. E. (2010). Evaluating a brief self-report measure of neighborhood environments for physical activity research and surveillance: Physical activity neighborhood environment scale (PANES). *Journal of Physical Activity and Health, 7,* 533–540.
Language	English, Japanese, Chinese, Maltese
Contact	Brian E. Saelens, PhD Division of Psychology, Cincinnati Children's Hospital Medical Center 3333 Burnet Avenue, MLC 3015 Cincinnati, OH 45229 Email: Brian.saelens@cchmc.org
Website	http://sallis.ucsd.edu/measure_news.html

TABLE 9.21 ■	Neighborhood Physical Activity Environment Scale and Convenient Facilities Scale
Primary Reference	Sallis, J. F., Johnson, M. F., Calfas, K. J., Caparosa, S., & Nichols, J. (1997). Assessing perceived physical environmental variables that may influence physical activity. *Research Quarterly for Exercise and Sport, 68*(4), 345–351.
Purpose	Measure perceptions of the environment that may have an influence on physical activity behaviors
Description	The **neighborhood physical activity environment** scale included three scales focused on • Neighborhood features • Perceived safety • Neighborhood character (e.g., whether neighborhood was perceived to be residential, mixed commercial and residential, or mainly commercial) The **convenient facilities** scale includes assessments of 18 facilities that can be used for physical activity. For each facility, participants were asked, "For each of these places where you can exercise, please indicate if it is on a frequently traveled route (e.g., to and from work) or within a 5-minute walk from work or home." • Basketball court • Health spa or gym • Bike lane
Sample	Students from a large urban university (n = 110) completed the survey. Most were women (n = 83) with a mean age of 20.6 years, and most identified as European American (43%).
Scoring	• The neighborhood physical activity environment scale was the sum of the three sub-scales (neighborhood features, perceived safety, neighborhood character), with more positive scores reflecting greater facilitation of physical activity (mean = 12.1). • The convenient facilities scale was the sum of the items selected (mean = 10.7).
Assessment	One-week, one-way model, intra-class test–retest reliabilities for the two scales were assessed. Intra-class reliabilities were 0.68 for neighborhood physical activity and 0.80 for convenient facilities.
Related Reference	Erwin, H. E. (2008). Test-retest reliability of a preadolescent environmental access to physical activity questionnaire [Supplement 1]. *Journal of Physical Activity & Health, 5,* S62–S72.
Language	English
Contact	James Sallis, PhD Active Living Research Department of Family and Preventive Medicine University of California, San Diego 3900 5th Avenue, Suite 310 San Diego, CA 92103

TABLE 9.22 ■ Children's Perceptions of the Physical Activity Environment in Their Neighborhood

Primary Reference	Hume, C., Ball, K., & Salmon, J. (2006). Development and reliability of a self-report questionnaire to examine children's perceptions of the physical activity environment at home and in the neighbourhood. *International Journal of Behavioral Nutrition and Physical Activity, 3*(16). doi: 10.1186/1479-5868-3-16
Purpose	Measure children's perceptions of the environment that may have an influence on physical activity behaviors
Description	Children's perceptions of the neighborhood physical environment was assessed, with 29 items related to access to specific facilities accessible by active transport, aesthetics of the neighborhood, and safety. The neighborhood social environment was assessed to evaluate children's social connections in the neighborhood.
Sample	A convenience sample of children (n = 39) attending public schools in Melbourne, Australia. Mean age was 11.1 years.
Scoring	**Access to specific facilities sub-scale (15 items)** Sum of total destinations accessible by active transport (range 0–15). **Neighborhood aesthetics sub-scale (5 items)** Reverse coding negatively worded questions and summing the yes responses (range 0–5). **Perceptions of safety sub-scale (9 items)** Reverse coding negatively worded questions and summing the yes responses (range 0–9). **Neighborhood social environment sub-scale (7 items)** Sum of responses with an answer of "yes" with a higher scoring indicating more positive perceptions of the social environment.
Assessment	• Surveys were administered at two time points up to nine days apart. • Most of the 29 items on the scale showed at least moderate reliability in the test–retest analysis. • All items showed at least 75% agreement in the test–retest analysis. Internal consistency was low for the aesthetics scale (α = 0.43) and somewhat higher for the safety (α = 0.65) and social environment (α = 0.77) scales. • Cronbach's alpha was not provided for the access to specific facilities sub-scale.
Related Reference	Gattshall, M. L., Shoup, J. A., Marshall, J. A., Crane, L. A., & Estabrooks, P.A. (2007). Validation of a survey instrument to assess home environments for physical activity and healthy eating in overweight children. *International Journal of Behavioral Nutrition and Physical Activity, 5*(3). doi: 10.1186/1479-5868-5-3
Language	English
Contact	Clare Hume, PhD Senior Research Fellow Deakin University Australia

TABLE 9.23 ■ Rural Active Living Perceived Environment Support Scale (RALPESS)	
Primary Reference	Umstattd, M. R., Baller, S. L., Hennessy, E., Hartley, D., Economos, C. D., Hyatt, D. R., . . . Hallam, J. S. (2012). Development of the Rural Active Living Perceived Environment Support Scale (RALPESS). *Journal of Physical Activity and Health, 9,* 724–730.
Purpose	Measure perceptions of the rural environment supportive of physical activity among youth.
Description	A 33-item self-report questionnaire focused on assessing opportunities for physical activity in rural settings (e.g., at church, town center, indoor areas).
Sample	High school students (grades 9–12) were recruited through two public school systems in two rural counties in the Alabama-Mississippi delta region. One county was majority White and the other was majority African American. A total of 1500 surveys were distributed and 592 were completed. Analysis for this study was based on 542 surveys with complete data.
Scoring	The overall score was calculated by summing all 33 items. Higher scores indicate greater perceived support for physical activity in the rural area.
Assessment	Internal consistency was acceptable for all seven factors (α = 0.82–0.94) and the overall scale (0.94).
Language	English
Contact	M. Renee Umstattd, PhD, MCHES Baylor University One Bear Place #97313 Waco, Texas 76798-7313 Email: renee_umstattd@baylor.edu
Website	http://activelivingresearch.org/rural-active-living-perceived-environment-support-scale-ralpess
Other comments	Perceptions of physical activity environment in neighborhood

TABLE 9.24 ■	System for Observing Physical Activity and Recreation in Communities (SOPARC)
Primary Reference	McKenzie, T. L., Cohen, D. A., Sehgal, A., Williamson, S., & Golinelli, D. (2006). System for observing play and recreation in communities (SOPARC): Reliability and feasibility measures [Supplement 1]. *Journal of Physical Activity and Health, 3,* S208–S222.
Purpose	Objective tool for assessing contextual factors influencing physical activity and leisure behaviors
Description	SOPARC is an observation tool for recording community environments that facilitate or impede physical activity and leisure behaviors. All data collectors received one day of training to familiarize themselves with the tool, practice vignettes, and practice field-based data collection.
Sample	Data were collected at eight parks in Los Angeles, California, in urban neighborhoods with high percentages of people of color (African American, Latino) and household poverty. Within each park, areas were targeted for observation (e.g., picnic areas, playgrounds, wading pools), resulting in a total of 127 target areas.
Scoring	Data are collected using a Planned Activity Check (Placheck) utilizing momentary time sampling to assess physical activity behaviors of people in the target area (sedentary, walking, or vigorous) as well as contextual characteristics of the target area related to accessibility (e.g., not locked), usability, and whether or not supervision, organized activities, and equipment are provided.
Assessment	There was strong inter-observer agreement for contextual variables ranging from 94% to 99%.
Related References	McKenzie, T., L., Marshall, S. J., Sallis, S. F., & Conway, T. L. (2000). Leisure-time physical activity in school environments: An observational study. *Preventive Medicine, 30,* 70–77. Mckenzie, T. L., & Cohen, D. A. (2006). SOPARC: System for Observing Play and Active Recreation in Communities. Protocols, mapping strategies, forms. Available at https://activelivingresearch.org/soparc-system-observing-play-and-recreation-communities. Available at http://activelivingresearch.org/node/10654 Bocarro, J. N., Floyd, M., Moore, R., Baran, P., Danninger, T., Smith, W., & Cosco, N. (2009). Adaptation of the System for Observing Physical Activity and Recreation in Communities (SOPARC) to assess age groupings of children. *Human Kinetics, 6,* 699–707.
Language	English
Contact	Thomas L. McKenzie, PhD, FACSM San Diego State University 5127 Walsh Way, San Diego, CA 92115 Email: tmckenzie@sdsu.edu

REFERENCES

Bailey-Davis, L., Horst, M., Hillemeier, M. M., & Lauter, A. (2012). Obesity disparities among elementary-aged children: Data from school-based BMI surveillance. *Pediatrics, 130*(6), 1102–1109. doi: 10.1542/peds.2012-0192

Boarnet, M. G., Day, K., Alfonzo, M., Forsyth, A., & Oakes, M. (2006). The Irvine-Minnesota inventory to measure built environments: reliability tests. *American Journal of Preventive Medicine, 30*(2), 153–159. doi: 10.1016/j.amepre.2005.09.018

Boarnet, M. G., Forsyth, A., Day, K., & Oakes, J. M. (2011). The street level built environment and physical activity and walking: Results of a predictive validity study for the Irvine Minnesota Inventory. *Environment and Behavior, 43*(6), 735–755.

Bocarro, J. N., Floyd, M., Moore, R., Baran, P., Danninger, T., Smith, W., & Cosco, N. (2009). Adaptation of the System for Observing Physical Activity and Recreation in Communities (SOPARC) to assess age groupings of children. *Human Kinetics, 6,* 699–707.

Brownson, R. C, Hoehner, C. M., Brennan, L. K., Cook, R. A., Elliott, M. B., & McCullen, K. M. (2004). Reliability of two instruments for auditing the environment for physical activity. *Journal of Physical Activity and Health, 1,* 191–208.

Carr, L. J., Dunsiger, S. I., & Marcus, B. H. (2011). Validation of Walk Score for estimating access to walkable amenities. *British Journal of Sports Medicine, 45*(14), 1144–1148. doi: 10.1136/bjsm.2009.069609

Cassady, D., Housemann, R., & Dagher, C. (2004). Measuring cues for healthy choices on restaurant menus: Development and testing of a measurement instrument. *American Journal of Health Promotion, 18*(6), 444–449.

Cavanaugh, E., Mallya, G., Brensinger, C., Tierney, A., & Glanz, K. (2013). Nutrition environments in corner stores in Philadelphia. *Preventive Medicine, 56*(2), 149–151.

Cerin, E., Conway, T., Saelens, B., Frank, L., & Sallis, J. (2009). Cross-validation of the factorial structure of the Neighborhood Environment Walkability Scale (NEWS) and its abbreviated form (NEWS-A). *International Journal of Behavioral Nutrition and Physical Activity, 6*(1), 32.

Cerin, E., Saelens, B. E., Sallis, J. F., & Frank, L. D. (2006). Neighborhood environment walkability scale: Validity and development of a short form. *Medicine and Science in Sports and Exercise, 38,* 1682–1691.

Clifton, K. J., Smith, A. D. L., & Rodriguez, D. (2007). The development and testing of an audit for the pedestrian environment. *Landscape and Urban Planning, 80*(1), 95–110.

Committee on Physical Activity, H., Transportation, and Land Use. (2005). *Does the built environment influence physical activity? Examining the evidence* [Special report 282]. Washington, DC: Transportation Research Board, Institute of Medicine.

Dibsdall, L. A., Lambert, N., Bobbin, R. F., & Frewer, L. J. (2003). Low-income consumers' attitudes and behaviour towards access, availability and motivation to eat fruit and vegetables. *Public Health Nutrition, 6*(2), 159–168. doi: 10.1079/phn2002412

Duncan, D. T., Aldstadt, J., Whalen, J., Melly, S. J., & Gortmaker, S. L. (2011). Validation of Walk Score® for estimating neighborhood walkability: An analysis of four US metropolitan areas. *International Journal of Environmental Research and Public Health, 8*(11), 4160–4179.

Echeverria, S. E., Diez-Roux, A. V., & Link, B. G. (2004). Reliability of self-reported neighborhood characteristics. *Journal of Urban Health, 81*(4), 682–701. doi: 10.1093/jurban/jth151

Edmonds, J., Baranowski, T., Baranowski, J., Cullen, K. W., & Myres, D. (2001). Ecological and socioeconomic correlates of fruit, juice, and vegetable consumption among African-American boys. *Preventive Medicine, 32*(6), 476–481. doi: 10.1006/pmed.2001.0831

Erwin, H. E. (2008). Test-retest reliability of a preadolescent environmental access to physical activity questionnaire [Supplement 1]. *Journal of Physical Activity & Health, 5,* S62–S72.

Flegal, K. M., Carroll, M. D., Kit, B. K., & Ogden, C. L. (2012). Prevalence of obesity and trends in the distribution of body mass index among US adults, 1999–2010. *JAMA, 307*(5), 491–497. doi: 10.1001/jama.2012.39

Flegal, K. M., Carroll, M. D., Kuczmarski, R. J., & Johnson, C. L. (1998). Overweight and obesity in the United States: Prevalence and trends, 1960–1994. *International Journal of Obesity and Related Metabolic Disorders, 22*(1), 39–47.

Frank, L. D., Sallis, J. F., Saelens, B. E., Leary, L., Cain, K., Conway, T. L., & Hess, P. M. (2010). The development of a walkability index: Application to the Neighborhood Quality of Life Study. *British Journal of Sports Medicine, 44*(13), 924–933. doi: 10.1136/bjsm.2009.058701

Freedman, D. A., & Bell, B. A. (2009). Access to healthful foods among an urban food insecure population: Perceptions versus reality. *Journal of Urban Health, 86*(6), 825–838.

Gattshall, M. L., Shoup, J. A., Marshall, J. A., Crane, L. A., & Estabrooks, P.A. (2007). Validation of a survey instrument to assess home environments for physical activity and healthy eating in overweight children. *International Journal of Behavioral Nutrition and Physical Activity, 5*(3). doi: 10.1186/1479-5868-5-3.

Giskes, K., Van Lenthe, F. J., Brug, J., Mackenbach, J. P., & Turrell, G. (2007). Socioeconomic inequalities in food purchasing: The contribution of respondent-perceived and actual (objectively measured) price and availability of foods. *Preventive Medicine, 45*, 41–48.

Glanz, K., Sallis, J. F., Saelens, B. E., & Frank, L. D. (2007). Nutrition environment measures survey in stores (NEMS-S): Development and evaluation. *American Journal of Preventive Medicine, 32*(4), 282–289.

Han, E., Powell, L. M., Zenk, S. N., Rimkus, L., Ohri-Vachaspati, P., & Chaloupka, F. J. (2012). Classification bias in commercial business lists for retail food stores in the U.S. *International Journal of Behavioral Nutrition and Physical Activity, 9*, 46–46. doi: 10.1186/1479-5868-9-46

Hill, J. L., Chau, C., Luebbering, C. R., Kolivras, K. K., & Zoellner, J. (2012). Does availability of physical activity and food outlets differ by race and income? Findings from an enumeration study in a health disparate region. *International Journal of Behavioral Nutrition and Physical Activity, 9*, 105. doi: 10.1186/1479-5868-9-105

Horowitz, C. R., Colson, K. A., Hebert, P. L., & Lancaster, K. (2004). Barriers to buying healthy foods for people with diabetes: Evidence of environmental disparities. *American Journal of Public Health, 94*(9), 1549–1554.

Hume, C., Ball, K., & Salmon, J. (2006). Development and reliability of a self-report questionnaire to examine children's perceptions of the physical activity environment at home and in the neighbourhood. *International Journal of Behavioral Nutrition and Physical Activity, 3*, 16. doi: 10.1186/1479-5868-3-16

Izumi, B. T., Zenk, S. N., Schulz, A. J., Mentz, G. B., Sand, S. L., de Majo, R. F., . . . Odoms-Young, A. (2012). Inter-rater reliability of the food environment audit for diverse neighborhoods (FEAD-N). *Journal of Urban Health, 89*(3), 486–499. doi: 10.1007/s11524-011-9657-3

Kamath, C. C., Vickers, K. S., Ehrlich, A., McGovern, L., Johnson, J., Singhal, V., . . . Montori, V. M. (2008). Behavioral interventions to prevent childhood obesity: A systematic review and metaanalyses of randomized trials. *The Journal of Clinical Endocrinology & Metabolism, 93*(12), 4606–4615. doi:10.1210/jc.2006-2411

Kirk, S. F. L., Penney, T. L., & McHugh, T. L. F. (2010). Characterizing the obesogenic environment: The state of the evidence with directions for future research. *Obesity Reviews, 11*, 109–117.

Krieger, N., Chen, J. T., Waterman, P. D., Rehkopf, D. H., & Subramanian, S. V. (2005). Painting a Truer Picture of US Socioeconomic and Racial/Ethnic Health Inequalities: The Public Health Disparities Geocoding Project. *American Journal of Public Health, 95*(2), 312–323. doi: 10.2105/AJPH.2003.032482

Lemmens, V. E. P. P., Oenema, A., Klepp, K. I., Henriksen, H. B., & Brug, J. (2008). A systematic review of the evidence regarding efficacy of obesity prevention interventions among adults. *Obesity Reviews, 9*, 446–455.

Mckenzie, T. L., & Cohen, D.A. (2006). SOPARC: System for Observing Play and Active Recreation in Communities. Protocols, mapping strategies, forms. *Active Living Research.* Retrieved from https://activelivingresearch.org/soparc-system-observing-play-and-recreation-communities

McKenzie, T. L., Cohen, D. A., Sehgal, A., Williamson, S., & Golinelli, D. (2006). System for Observing Play and Recreation in Communities

(SOPARC): Reliability and feasibility measures [Supplement 1]. *Journal of Physical Activity and Health, 3,* S208–S222.

McKenzie, T., L., Marshall, S. J., Sallis, S. F., & Conway, T. L. (2000). Leisure-time physical activity in school environments: An observational study. *Preventive Medicine, 30,* 70–77. Available at http://activelivingresearch.org/node/10654

McKinnon, R. A., Reedy, J., Morrissette, M. A., Lytle, L. A., & Yaroch, A. L. (2009). Measure of the food environment: A compilation of the literature, 1990–2007. *American Journal of Preventive Medicine, 36*(4S), S124–S133.

Millstein, R. A., Cain, K. L., Sallis, J. F., Conway, T. L., Geremia, C., Frank, L. D., . . . Saelens, B. E. (2013). Development, scoring, and reliability of the Microscale Audit of Pedestrian Streetscapes (MAPS). *BMC Public Health, 13,* 403. doi: 10.1186/1471-2458-13-403

Mujahid, M. S., Diez Roux, A. V., Morenoff, J. D., Raghunathan, T. (2007). Assessing the measurement properties of neighborhood scales: From psychometrics to ecometrics. *American Journal of Epidemiology, 165*(8), 858–867.

Ogden, C. L., Carroll, M. D., Curtin, L. R., Lamb, M. M., & Flegal, K. M. (2010). Prevalence of high body mass index in US children and adolescents, 2007–2008. *Journal of the American Medical Association, 303*(3), 242–249.

Ogden, C. L., Carroll, M. D., Curtin, L. R., McDowell, M. A., Tabak, C. J., & Flegal, K. M. (2006). Prevalence of overweight and obesity in the United States, 1999–2004. *JAMA, 295*(13), 1549–1555. doi: 10.1001/jama.295.13.1549

Ohri-Vachaspati, P., & Leviton, L. (2010). Measuring food environments: A guide to available instruments. *American Journal of Health Promotion, 24*(6), 410–426.

Pikora, T. J., Bull, F. C., Jamrozik, K., Knuiman, M., Giles-Corti, B., & Donovan, R. J. (2002). Developing a reliable audit instrument to measure the physical environment for physical activity. *American Journal of Preventive Medicine, 23*(3), 187–194.

Pikora, T. J., Giles-Corti, B., Knuiman, M. W., Bull, F. C., Jamrozik, K., & Donovan, R. J. (2006). Neighborhood environmental factors correlated with walking near home: Using SPACES. *Medicine and Science in Sports and Exercise, 38*(4); 708–714.

Rimkus, L., Ohri-Vachaspati, P., Powell, L. M., Zenk, S. N., Quinn, C. M., Barker, D. C., . . . Chaloupka, F. J. (2015) Development and reliability testing of a fast-food restaurant observation form. *American Journal of Health Promotion, 30*(1), 9–18.

Rimkus, L., Powell, L. M., Zenk, S. N., Han, E., Ohri-Vachaspati, P., Pugach, O., . . . Chaloupka, F. J. (2013). Development and reliability testing of a Food Store Observation Form. *Journal of Nutrition Education and Behavior, 45*(6), 540–548. doi: http://dx.doi.org/10.1016/j.jneb.2013.02.005

Roof, K., & Oleru, N. (2008). Public health: Seattle and King County's push for the built environment. *Journal of Environmental Health, 71*(1), 24–27.

Saelens, B. E., Glanz, K., Sallis, J. F., & Frank, L. D. (2007). Nutrition environment measures study in restaurants (NEMS-R): Development and evaluation. *American Journal of Preventive Medicine, 32*(4), 273–281. doi: http://dx.doi.org/10.1016/j.amepre.2006.12.022

Saelens, B. E., & Handy, S. L. (2008). Built environment correlates of walking: A review [Supplement]. *Medicine and Science in Sports and Exercise, 40*(7), S550–566. doi: 10.1249/MSS.0b013e31817c67a4

Saelens, B. E., Sallis, J. F., Black, J. B., & Chen, D. (2003). Neighborhood-based differences in physical activity: An environment scale evaluation. *American Journal of Public Health, 936(9),* 1552–1558.

Sallis, J. F., Johnson, M. F., Calfas, K. J., Caparosa, S., & Nichols, J. F. (1997). Assessing perceived physical environmental variables that may influence physical activity. *Research Quarterly for Exercise and Sport, 68*(4), 345–351. doi: 10.1080/02701367.1997.10608015

Sallis, J. F., Kerr, J., Carlson, J. A., Norman, G. J., Saelens, B. E., Durant, N., & Ainsworth, B. E. (2010). Evaluating a brief self-report measure of neighborhood environments for physical activity research and surveillance: Physical activity neighborhood environment scale (PANES). *Journal of Physical Activity and Health, 7,* 533–540.

Scanlin, K., Haardoerfer, R., Kegler, M. C., & Glanz, K. (2014). Development of a pedestrian audit tool to assess rural neighborhood walkability. *Journal of Physical Activity and Health, 11*(6), 1085–1096. doi: 10.1123/jpah.2012-0224

Toker, Z. (2015). Walking beyond the socioeconomic status in an objectively and perceptually walkable pedestrian environment. *Urban Studies Research, 2015*, 15. doi: 10.1155/2015/919874

Truong, K., Fernandes, M., An, R., Shier, V., & Sturm, R. (2010). Measuring the physical food environment and its relationship with obesity: Evidence from California. *Public Health, 124*(2), 115–118. doi: 10.1016/j.puhe.2009.12.004

Umstattd, M. R., Baller, S. L., Hennessy, E., Hartley, D., Economos, C. D., Hyatt, R. R., . . . Hallam, J. S. (2012). Development of the Rural Active Living Perceived Environmental Support Scale (RALPESS). *Journal of Physical Activity and Health, 9*(5), 724–730.

Warnecke, R. B., Oh, A., Breen, N., Gehlert, S., Paskett, E., Tucker, K. L., . . . Hiatt, R. A. (2008). Approaching health disparities from a population perspective: The National Institutes of Health Centers for Population Health and Health Disparities. *American Journal of Public Health, 98*(9), 1608–1615.

Wechsler, H., Basch, C. E., Zybert, P., Lantigua, R., & Shea, S. (1995). The availability of low-fat milk in an inner-city Latino community: implications for nutrition education. *American Journal of Public Health, 85*(12), 1690–1692.

10 HOUSING AND NEIGHBORHOOD CHANGE

There is longstanding research interest in the dynamics of neighborhood development and how the built environment can be maintained and improved by residents, institutions, and various systems of governance. Housing units and real estate markets are fundamental elements of neighborhood quality and viability. Moreover, the character, upkeep, and appeal of its housing stock helps shape the socioeconomic composition of the population and the trajectory of neighborhood change. Whether because of market dynamics, institutional decisions, forces of nature, or geographic factors, neighborhoods are in constant flux, making measurement of the elements a moving target. Nevertheless, in this chapter we discuss some of the more commonly assessed aspects—such as housing quality, affordability, and market strength; vacancy, abandonment and blight; residential mobility and instability; and neighborhood decline, upgrading, and gentrification.

WHY ARE MEASURES RELATED TO HOUSING AND NEIGHBORHOOD CHANGE IMPORTANT?

The physical capital of a neighborhood has a strong bearing on other aspects of community life. The housing stock, commercial buildings, land use, and physical infrastructure are relatively fixed assets. They help to shape characteristics of the residential population, types of activities that take place, decisions about financial investments in the area, and how inhabitants and outsiders view the place. None of these factors are static, however. In general, there is a dynamic relationship between the physical assets of a community, population change, the flow of investment, and perceptions of neighborhood viability. A particular concern is when these dynamics lead to a downward trajectory of housing deterioration and neighborhood decline, which has negative effects on people and places.

Researchers are interested in methods of measuring these phenomena for a variety of reasons. In interdisciplinary fields such as urban and housing studies, investigators often want to examine the causes of neighborhood change or evaluate the effectiveness of policies that address housing problems and neighborhood decline. Researchers in public health, social work, and behavioral sciences are interested in how housing and neighborhood deterioration affect the health and development of the individuals that are exposed to these conditions. At a more practical level, community development professionals, residents, and community advocates utilize such measures to target their interventions and evaluate progress toward their goals.

HOUSING MEASURES

Measures of Housing Quality

The adequacy and physical conditions of housing are of concern to researchers, practitioners, and policy makers from a variety of perspectives. Within housing policy studies, there has been a longstanding focus on evaluating the housing experiences of low-income households and the implications for the design of housing programs (Newman, 2008). Housing conditions have also been of fundamental interest within public health, especially as related to acute and chronic medical conditions that are exacerbated by residential environments (Jacobs, Wilson, Dixon, Smith, & Evens, 2009; Wu & Takaro, 2007). Studies of human well-being have often examined the influence of housing conditions on individuals at various life stages. Numerous aspects of housing quality have been associated with child development outcomes (Evans, 2006; Leventhal & Newman, 2010) and psychological distress in adult and elderly populations (Evans, Kantrowitz, & Eshelman, 2002; Evans, Wells, Chan, & Saltzman, 2000).

Although research interest in housing quality is high, there is surprisingly little methodological work on its measurement (Newman, 2008). There does not seem to be any general agreement among researchers about what aspects of the housing unit should be assessed, how those elements should be weighted, or how to demarcate housing that is physically adequate from units that are below that standard. One distinction among housing quality measures is whether they rely on self-reports of residents, ratings by professionally trained observers, or combine both perspectives. Measures also differ in their relative emphasis on the structural conditions of the dwelling, the exterior or interior of the home, and housekeeping and upkeep. An additional complication in evaluating housing quality measures is that regional and historical context may need to be taken into account in determining the particular aspects of housing that are important standards for adequacy.

In this section, we cover measures that have been used by researchers to assess the adequacy, safety, and material quality of occupied dwelling units.[1] Although these measures are designed to evaluate specific housing units, results from a representative sample can be aggregated to evaluate housing quality for a community or neighborhood. We begin with **measures of housing quality** based on items from the American Housing Survey (AHS) (see **Table 10.1**). AHS is conducted by the U.S. Census Bureau biannually in even-numbered years and covers both national and metropolitan area samples of housing units. In occupied units, field representatives from the U.S. Census Bureau conduct interviews in person or by telephone with a designated household member. Among the core questions in AHS, a number pertain to housing quality, such as plumbing and electrical problems, lack of adequate heat, leaks and cracks in the house, and so forth. **The Physical Adequacy Index** incorporates markers from AHS of moderate and severe deficits in housing units (Holupka & Newman, 2011; Newman & Garboden, 2013). The **Poor Quality Index** is a weighted combination of housing problems in the dwelling (Eggers & Moumen, 2013). Both of these measures have shown correlations

[1] Building inspectors manuals and municipal ordinances contain detailed information defining housing inadequacies and housing code violations. We do not evaluate those tools in this book.

between inadequate housing and socio-economic disadvantage of households. More specifically:

- Results of multivariate analyses showed that renting instead of owning, larger household size, and low-income were significantly associated with inadequate housing. In addition, physical adequacy was the strongest predictor of the house rating (i.e., having physical adequacy problems reduced the respondent's subjective rating of their house).
- Results showed that between 1985 and 1995, all units that were judged by ZADEQ in the AHS to be severely inadequate have positive PQI scores. Also, compared with ZADEQ, the PQI recognizes a broader range of deficiencies and has greater stability on the problem side between survey waves (Holupka & Newman, 2011; Eggers & Moumen, 2013).

A second set of housing quality measures have been adapted from a larger instrument, the Early Childhood version of the Home Observation Measurement Environment (EC-HOME) Inventory (Bradley & Caldwell, 1979). The original instrument was developed to assess environments for young children at various stages of development. The items having to do with housing quality are ascertained through mothers' self-reports and interviewer observations. These housing quality items have been used as scales in several studies of children's home environments (Han, Leventhal, & Linver, 2004; Leventhal, Martin, & Brooks-Gunn, 2004; Totsika & Sylva, 2004). The **Physical Quality Subscales EC-HOME** are covered in **Table 10.2**. Generally, the results show that:

- Scores on the EC-HOME are associated with better children's behavior and cognitive development.
- Both interior of home and exterior of home scales were significantly related to child outcomes. That is, higher scores on HOME physical subscales (i.e., better environment) were associated with better children' cognitive scores and fewer child behavioral problems (Leventhal et al., 2004).

Several measures of housing quality have been developed specifically to relate to mental health and psychological well-being. In contrast to the previous housing quality measures that are based on self-report, the **Housing Quality Instrument** (see **Table 10.3**) exclusively relies on trained observers to rate housing along multiple dimensions. Low scores on the quality ratings have been shown to be related to mental health problems among mothers with children at home (Evans et al., 2000). A related housing quality observation measure showed a correlation with psychological well-being of elderly individuals living independently in the community (Evans et al., 2002).

- These associations persisted after controlling for measures of socio-economic status.
- Regarding discriminate validity, principal-components factor analysis produced six coherent housing quality factors.
- With the exception of indoor climatic conditions, all of the interior housing subscales successfully discriminated between poor- and high-quality houses.
- Comparison between the overall housing quality score and the subscale scores before and after residential relocation showed significant improvement except for child resources (Evans et al., 2002).

Housing quality measures have also been designed for specialized populations. The **Observer-Rated Housing Quality Scale** (see **Table 10.4**) was developed for observers to rate housing quality for individuals in a multi-site program for homeless individuals with mental illness. Studies using this instrument have shown correlations between the elements of housing quality and outcomes for populations participating in homelessness services programs (Adair et al., 2014). Scores on this scale were also found to be positively related to housing stability of residents (Adair, et al., 2016).

- According to Adair et al. (2016), validity of the unit/building subscale of the OHQS was supported by (1) a high correlation between the OHQS and Perceived Housing Quality (PHQ) scores ($r = 0.51$) and (2) a lower unit/building score for participants who reported a perceived need for major repairs.
- Unit/building scores were positively related to housing stability after adjusting for site, housing characteristics, ethno-cultural status, community functioning, and social support.

Measures of Housing Affordability

Housing is generally the largest single expenditure in a household's budget, and shelter is a basic human need. Many low- and moderate-income households have difficulty finding decent housing at a price they can afford. Communities also face challenges in maintaining an adequate supply of affordable housing units for low- to moderate-income populations. Although there are numerous government programs that support the development of affordable housing or provide subsidies to help tenants pay their rents, these programs fall well short of meeting the needs in most communities (Joint Center for Housing Studies of Harvard, 2016).

While the problem of housing affordability is widely recognized, its measurement is not straightforward. In this chapter, we focus on those methods that have been used by researchers to assess whether households face an excessive housing cost burden or to examine the supply of affordable housing in communities. It should be noted that trade associations and government agencies have developed affordability indices and rubrics tailored to particular programs (e.g., public housing) or business decisions (e.g., mortgage underwriting). We do not discuss these tools here because, although they have practical value, they are less useful for community research because of problems with comparability and completeness (Jewkes & Delgadillo, 2010).

We begin with percentage of income measures of housing affordability. The most common approach is to calculate housing cost burden as the ratio of gross housing expenses to pretax income. If this ratio exceeds 30%, the household is considered to have a housing cost burden. The 30% of income threshold was established as the federal standard for housing programs in 1981 and since then has been utilized in numerous studies and reports. Researchers can calculate the percentage of income measure for households by determining their gross housing expenditures and pretax income using this information to calculate their housing cost burden ratio. Households with ratios above 50% are classified as having a severe housing cost burden. The American Community Survey (ACS) is a data source that can be used to measure the number of households that have a **housing cost burden** in a community (see **Table 10.5** for details on calculation). Housing cost burden is found to be higher for younger renters, elderly households with limited income and for racial and ethnic minority groups (Schwartz & Wilson, 2008).

- Mortgaged households comprised the highest overall share of housing cost burden.

- Hispanic, younger (under 25), and older households (with social security as the only source of income) had a higher share of housing-cost burden than other groups (Schwartz & Wilson, 2008).
- Wardrip and Pelletiere (2008) suggested that the housing cost-to-income ratios (HCIRs) should be used with caution because of the 3.2 million households in the 2006 ACS for which the U.S. Census Bureau did not calculate an HCRI, although there were useful housing cost and income data for them. Additionally, they identified 2.8 million homeowners for which the HCIR was underestimated because mobile home fees were not included in their calculation of monthly costs.

It should be noted that ACS estimates for small areas, such as communities, are a five-year estimate rather than a point in time and may have a large margin of error if populations are small (Spielman, Folch, & Nagle, 2014).

Critics have noted that the 30% threshold used in the standard measure of housing cost burden is arbitrary and can underestimate the hardship faced by families with very low incomes and overestimate the deprivation for affluent households that choose costly properties. They have suggested an alternative approach referred to as residual income; that is, the absolute amount that a household has left to spend after housing expenses have been taken into account (Stone, 2006). If this residual income is too low to meet basic needs, the household is considered to be "shelter poor" (Stone, 2004) or to experience "shelter induced poverty" (Kutty, 2005). The housing induced poverty rate has been shown to be higher than the official poverty rate (Kutty, 2005). (See **Table 10.6** for a description of such **residual measures of housing affordability**.)

- Results demonstrated that 3.8 million households that were above the official poverty line could not afford the poverty basket of non-housing goods in 1999 after paying for their housing costs.
- The housing-induced poverty rate was 2.7 percentage points higher than the official poverty rate.
- Regional and locational variables significantly predicted the probability of housing-induced poverty (Kutty, 2005).

The previous measures focus on households and whether they can afford the housing units they occupy. Researchers are also interested in gauging the size of the affordable housing stock and whether it is commensurate with the number of low- and moderate-income households in need of housing. A simple indicator of affordable rental housing is to count the units that rent below the fair market rent (FMR) in an area. FMR is set by Department of Housing and Urban Development (HUD) and is currently at approximately the 40th percentile of rents in the region.[2] This is by definition the rent that is allowable for households with government assistance (such as housing choice vouchers). However, this measure does not take into account the fact that most low-income households do not receive subsidies, and for many of them, the FMR represents a housing cost burden that is well above the 30% of income standard discussed above.

---

[2] Changes in the definition of fair market rent have been proposed. See Establishing a more effective fair market rent (FMR) system; using small area fair market rents (SAFMRs) in housing choice voucher program instead of the current 50th percentile FMRs, 81 *Fed. Reg.* 39218 (proposed June 16, 2016) (to be codified at 45 C.F.R. pts. 888, 982, 983, and 985).

The **Rental Housing Affordability Mismatch Ratio** (see **Table 10.7**) uses the 30% standard for housing costs and takes the level of potential demand into account (Bogdon & Can, 1997). The ratio compares the number of units available in various price ranges to the number of households in commensurate income categories and applies the 30% standard. Ratios of less than one indicate that there are too few affordable units for the population in need. This ratio is more readily applied to rental units and renter households but has also been extended to impute affordable owner occupied units as well (Harkness & Newman, 2005). Using these methods, it has been shown that poor children have better health and educational outcomes when they live in areas with more affordable housing.

- In Onondaga County, housing units affordable to extremely low-income households were in short supply. That is, there was only about one housing unit available at an affordable rent for every two extremely low-income households.
- "Extremely low-income" is defined as households whose incomes do not exceed 30 percent of the HUD-adjusted median family income (HAMFI) thresholds for the given area (Bogdon & Can, 1997).

Harkness and Newman (2005) found that poor children who lived in areas with more affordable housing fared better than their counterparts in terms of perceived health, school engagement, and grade retention.

- They also suggested that affordable housing has a stronger impact on older children than on young ones.
- Affordability seems to affect childrens' well-being mainly through the material consumption of basic necessities when they are young.

Measures of Housing Market Strength

Housing market trends are of considerable interest in studies of neighborhood decline and revitalization. Such information is often used to target programs or evaluate whether community development efforts are showing signs of successfully stabilizing neighborhood-housing values. Additionally, researchers have been interested in how housing market conditions in neighborhoods affect asset accumulation for low-income households and future neighborhood trajectories.

One of the most common ways to evaluate housing market strength has been to look at housing price appreciation (or depreciation) in neighborhoods over time or relative to metropolitan-wide trends. Sales prices are typically ascertained from public records of property transfers, with a focus on arms-length sales (for example, excluding transfers at foreclosure auctions or between family members). The simplest housing market index for neighborhoods is to calculate the median sales price for a given time period. This index is often standardized as a percentile rank for all neighborhoods within a metropolitan area. Appreciation is calculated as the inflation adjusted difference between median sales prices at two points in time. This index can be unreliable, especially if there are too few transactions during the period that is being examined. Moreover, the median difference in sales price index does not control for the characteristics of the housing units that are sold in each period. If the mix of quality is not similar, a change may be misinterpreted as housing appreciation or depreciation, when in reality, the properties that were sold are not of comparable quality.

Many housing market studies rely on hedonic price models to control for quality in their analysis of housing values. Hedonic models adjust for numerous characteristics of housing units that are theorized to determine price. For example, a statistical model is estimated as $SP = f(C + O + T)$, where sales price (SP) is a function of a set of housing characteristics (C) assumed to affect price (e.g., age, size, rooms, amenities) and other (O) factors (e.g., location). Appreciation is the effect of time (T)—that is, the difference between a base year (0) and other year (1). T is a dummy variable that can be interpreted as the average housing price change adjusted for the housing characteristics and other factors. However, hedonic modeling can yield biased estimates of housing market trends if explanatory variables are incomplete or the functional form of the model is incorrectly specified (Case, Pollakowski, & Wachter, 1991). These limitations are particularly problematic when applied to the problem of estimating small-area housing market trends. First, there may be unrecognized spatial heterogeneity or in the hedonic models, making their application in specific neighborhoods less valid than the overall model would suggest. Second, the data sources available for small geographic areas often have limited information about housing quality. Finally, in weak market areas, there may be a problem of small samples because of a dearth of arms-length sales.

Repeat sales indexes of housing markets addresses overcome some of these problems by comparing sales prices for houses that have sold twice during a selected period to calculate appreciation or depreciation (McMillen & Dombrow, 2001). This eliminates the need to statistically adjust for housing characteristics because the property is compared only with itself. The repeat sales approach, however, introduces a few other sources of potential error. One is a problem of missing data because houses that sell more than once in a period are not necessarily representative of all of the properties in a community. An additional drawback is that some properties may undergo significant change (i.e., improvements or damage) that is not measured. Since such occurrences are more likely when sales are far apart in time, some models give higher weight to repeat sales where the gap is of shorter duration (Han, 2014). The feasibility of the repeat sales approach for estimating neighborhood housing market trends is illustrated in a neighborhood taxonomy project in Chicago. A spatially and temporarily smoothed repeat sales index was calculated for census tracts and found to be correlated with other markers of housing market vitality, suggesting its usefulness in combination with other metrics (Bodini, 2014).

Housing sales price trends are not the only indicator of housing market strength in communities. Changes in sales volume and access to mortgage lending are also important markers of whether the housing market is viable. The **Neighborhood Housing Market Index** (see **Table 10.8**) is a weighted average score for each neighborhood that combines information about sales volume, prices, and mortgage characteristics. The underlying data for this index are readily available to researchers through a file of all mortgages processed by lenders known as HMDA (Housing Mortgage Disclosure Act). This data file identifies the census tract for each loan application and is available from the Federal Financial Institutions Examination Council (FFIEC). This index has been used to compare market strength of neighborhoods over time and within metropolitan areas. The index is correlated in the expected direction with other markers of housing market distress such as tax delinquency and foreclosure rates. It is negatively related to new construction and the number of building permits issued in an area (Walker & Winston, 2010).

- Results showed that the Housing Market Index was strongly associated with the percentage of residential parcels with new construction or modeling building permits.

- The Housing Market Index was significantly related to both foreclosure rate and remodeling permit rate in Minneapolis.
- The index was only moderately associated with foreclosure rate but strongly associated with tax delinquency (Walker & Winston, 2010).

NEIGHBORHOOD CHANGE MEASURES

Measures of Vacancy, Abandonment, and Blight

Vacant, abandoned, and blighted properties are among the foremost concerns to communities facing disinvestment (Accordino & Johnson, 2000; Vacant Properties Campaign, 2005). These distressed buildings can have a negative impact on housing values of nearby properties, spreading disinvestment and further decline (Han, 2014; Mikelbank, 2008; Shlay & Whitman, 2006). Moreover, deteriorating structures are associated with other indicators of social disorganization and crime incidents (Raleigh & Galster, 2015). Living in or near these properties can also affect the health of residents, especially of children (Coulton, Richter, Kim, Fischer, & Cho, 2016).

There are various signs that properties are at risk of becoming distressed, such as foreclosure, prolonged vacancy, tax delinquency, unresolved housing code violations, abandonment, and being declared blighted (Hillier, Culhane, Smith, & Tomlin, 2003). Researchers have found it difficult to track and quantify these markers of property deterioration because they change over time. Foreclosed homes may transition to vacancy and then abandonment. But eventually, they may become candidates for demolition or rehabilitation, with the potential to reduce the downward spiral. Capturing the timing of these events is crucial to evaluating their magnitude and impact on housing markets (Griswold, Calnin, Schramm, Anselin, & Boehnlein, 2014) and on the vitality of neighborhoods.

Vacant housing is a key concept in this line of research, but whether or not a vacant unit should be counted as a problem depends on why the house is unoccupied. For example, houses may be temporarily vacant when the occupants are on vacation or units are turning over from previous to new tenants or owners. Units that have been unoccupied for an extended period are more problematic because they are often improperly maintained or vandalized. It is these types of long-term vacancies that are typically of interest to researchers assessing the problem of vacant housing.

There are several possible sources of data on vacant housing in communities. Some cities maintain vacant housing registries, but these sources may be incomplete and not useful for precise measurement because of spotty reporting. Vacancy surveys using an observational instrument are another potential data source. However, such point-in-time observations are typically recorded by volunteers or city employees that have not been evaluated as measures for research, and these volunteers or employees cannot distinguish between short-term or long-term vacant units. The ACS (five-year estimates) provides counts of vacant units based on interviews with sampled households. The ACS count reflects a kind of average over a five-year period that may be too imprecise for many research questions. For smaller communities, such as neighborhoods, the ACS margin of error also may be prohibitively wide because of small sample size.

The U.S. Postal Service (USPS) vacancy data has proven more valuable to researchers for measuring problematic housing vacancy in communities. This data set is created from records generated by mail carriers who report when an address has been vacant for at least 90 days. The records are updated quarterly, and HUD makes these data available to researchers for census tracts in the United States. This makes it possible to distinguish properties that have been vacant for long periods from those that are just temporarily unoccupied. The USPS vacancy ratio can be calculated for census tracts or aggregations of census tracts to create larger units of geography. Immergluck (2015) used this data source to calculate **long-term vacancy** rates as a percentage of residential addresses for the 50 largest metropolitan areas (see **Table 10.9**). He found that long-term vacancy rates were correlated in the expected direction with a number of measures of neighborhood socioeconomic distress. Moreover, neighborhoods with new immigrants decreased their long-term vacancy rates over time.

- Results from negative binomial regression of long-term vacancies showed that demographic and housing market variables were predictive of vacancy rates in the expected direction.
- For example, high neighborhood vacancy rates persisted in high-poverty neighborhoods, while neighborhoods with more Hispanic and Asian residents experienced larger declines in long-term vacancy rates (Immurgluck, 2015).

Abandonment is a marker of severe housing distress that contributes to the cycle of neighborhood decline. It occurs through a process of disinvestment, as owners stop taking physical, financial, and functional responsibility for their property (Bartlett, 1998). Efforts to measure abandonment have been hampered by the fact that the owner decisions and behaviors signaling abandonment are difficult to observe. Abandonment is only confirmed at the end of the process when there is government action that recognizes the property as a nuisance, an eminent danger, or as long-term tax delinquent. City registries have been used to measure the abandonment problem for properties at this advanced stage (e.g., Han, 2014; Mikelbank, 2008), but this arguably leaves out those housing units that are seriously neglected or dysfunctional but have not yet come to city attention.

A study in Buffalo combined several indicators, including the USPS data described above, to identify neighborhoods that were plagued with what they referred to as **zombie properties** (Silverman, Yin, & Patterson, 2013). These properties were defined not only by their vacancy and abandonment status but by their location within an area of profound demographic and economic decline. They reasoned that, unlike vacant properties in areas on the rebound, these structures had no useful life remaining and were likely to be toxic influences on what remained in the area (see **Table 10.10**). The combination of multiple indicators showed high correlations with poverty rates, renters receiving rental assistance and long term vacancies at the census tract level.

- This study conducted four separate multiple regression analyses (i.e., four models using the above four neighborhood-level variables as separate dependent variables)
- Results showed that the percentage of vacant residential properties was higher in census tracts with elevated poverty rates, higher percentages of renters receiving rental assistance, and long-term vacancies.
- Higher percentages of Black populations, increased poverty rates, long-term vacancies, and higher percentages of business addresses were significantly associated with higher percentages of abandoned residential properties in census tracts (Silverman et al., 2013).

An alternative way of gauging properties in the process of abandonment is to derive a measure based on various signs that abandonment is taking place. In

Philadelphia, researchers evaluated numerous variables as predictors of properties later being classified as "eminently dangerous," a local standard consistent with abandonment. Outstanding housing code violations, long-term vacancy information, tax delinquency status, and water shutoffs strongly contributed to the accuracy of vacancy prediction in a linear probability model (Hillier et al., 2003). These same indicators are likely to be useful proxies for determining abandonment in other cities but would first need to be evaluated with local data.

Blight is a contentious term, imbued with legalities, politics, and power dynamics (Gordon, 2004; Shlay & Whitman, 2006). Although the term may be used casually to include property that is severely deteriorated, there are often very real consequences of such an official designation. For example, governments may use blight designation to take land from low-income landowners, including communities of color, and offer it for redevelopment (Bowen, 2015). Officially, blight is defined as real property deterioration as indicated by noncompliance with building codes. These blighted properties that are in distress by definition must have a damaging effect on the economic viability of communities and on the well-being of residents. Weaver and Bagchi-Sen (2013) use open housing code violations on file with the city building department to calculate the **blight per unit (BPU)** measure to study patterns of blight in Buffalo (see **Table 10.11**). Their analyses show that BPU was spatially clustered in areas with other markers of urban decline.

- Results from spatial methods of cluster detection demonstrated that blight measured in BPU was positively associated with urban decline in time and space.
- Blight in one census tract in a city was significantly related to poor socioeconomic conditions in adjacent neighborhoods (Weaver & Bagchi-Sen, 2013).

Measures of Residential Mobility and Housing Unit Turnover

Residential mobility is often viewed as a destabilizing factor for communities because it may undercut established social networks and reduce social control (Sampson, Raudenbush, & Earls, 1997; Taylor, 1996). Although there are also concerns about households that may be stuck in distressed areas because of racial and economic segregation (Sharkey, 2013), high levels of residential instability have been found to be detrimental to individual and community well-being.

A simple measure of a community's residential mobility rates can be obtained directly from the ACS. Specifically, the yearly mobility rate is calculated based on the survey item that asks, for each of the individuals in the sampled households, whether they lived in the current housing unit for at least one year. The yearly residential mobility rate for the neighborhood is calculated as the percentage of the population that moved into their housing unit in the previous year. For small areas such as census tracts, the yearly individual residential mobility rates must be derived from the ACS five-year sample estimates, so they reflect a five-year average.

Several multi-item indexes of **residential stability and instability** provide a somewhat broader perspective on the concept than the single-year mobility rate described above. These census-based indexes typically include home ownership rate and other indicators of residential duration beyond the one-year threshold (see **Table 10.12**). It should be noted that because of changes in census residential mobility questions between 2000 and 2010, there are slight differences in the variables used in earlier versions of these indexes.

- Residential stability at the neighborhood level has been found to be positively associated with perceived collective efficacy and negatively correlated with perceived violence (Sampson, Raudenbush & Earls, 1997).
- However, for neighborhoods that started out high in crime, neighborhood instability was associated with a decrease in their crime rates over time (Hipp, 2010).
- At the neighborhood level, residential stability was significantly positively related to collective efficacy, after controlling for personal background characteristics. Also, residential stability was significantly negatively associated with perceived neighborhood violence and violent victimization, although the coefficients were reduced when collective efficacy was entered into the models as a mediator. Lastly, residential stability was weakly associated with homicide.
- This study found no evidence that residential instability increased crime rates ten years later. A striking finding was that neighborhoods with higher levels of instability experienced greater decrease in crime over the following decade, while this effect was accentuated further in neighborhoods with greater concentrated disadvantage. The results suggest that highly disadvantaged neighborhood, in which the residents lack ability to leave, can be more vulnerable to increases in violence over time (Hipp, 2010).

Selective residential mobility in which newcomers differ from out movers, along with incumbent processes whereby stayers change their economic status, can produce a gradual shift in a neighborhood's socioeconomic mix (Ellen & O'Regan, 2011). Once begun, the direction of neighborhood change can be reinforcing over time as individual and institutional investment decisions are influenced by expectations of the economic future of the community (Temkin & Rohe, 1996).

Housing unit turnover is a useful approach to measuring how residential mobility contributes to neighborhood change. The dynamic movement of households into and out of housing units can change the socioeconomic composition of a community if in-movers differ from out-movers. The investigation of these "stocks" and "flows" requires longitudinal data on housing units and their household occupants. By comparing the characteristics of in-movers, out-movers, and stayers that remain in place, the researcher can characterize the processes of change in the community.

The AHS tracks a panel of housing units in selected cities over multiple years. The survey notes whether the housing unit has changed occupants between waves and provides information on the socioeconomic characteristics of the households. This panel has been used to measure change in average income of occupants over time, distinguishing between units that changed occupants and those where occupants remained the same but changed their income (Ellen & O'Regan, 2011). Other studies based on AHS have measured the degree to which housing units transition between households of similar or different racial or ethnic backgrounds (Ellen, 2000; Hipp, 2010; Marullo, 1985; Spain, 1980), thus capturing the duration and pace of neighborhood socioeconomic change because of residential mobility.

The Making Connections survey is another example of a survey design that can be used to evaluate the process of neighborhood socioeconomic change in selected communities. The study tracked a representative sample of housing units and their occupants over time within designated neighborhoods in ten cities. The investigators were able to classify the housing units into those that turned over to new occupants and those that were occupied by the same households across waves. By comparing occupants' socioeconomic status at each wave, the overall economic change in the neighborhoods could be decomposed into that due to incumbent upgrading and that due to differences in economic status of newcomers to the area (Coulton, Theodos, & Turner, 2012). Additionally, it was possible to identify the unique characteristics of housing and neighborhood units that were conducive to economic upgrading through turnover (Theodos, Coulton, & Pitingolo, 2015).

Measures of Gentrification and Displacement

Gentrification is a pattern of neighborhood change that has received considerable attention in the popular media and urban policy literature. In particular, it raises a number of concerns about whether low-income individuals are becoming priced out of the housing market and displaced from their traditional communities as a result. The *Encyclopedia of Housing* defines gentrification as "the process by which central urban neighborhoods that have undergone disinvestments and economic decline experience a reversal, reinvestment and in-migration of a relatively well-off middle and upper-middle class population" (Smith, 1998, p. 198). Displacement is not a component of this definition, but researchers often are interested in evaluating whether there are signs of displacement within areas classified as gentrifying.

Determining whether areas are undergoing gentrification is not an easy task. Wyly and Hammel (1998) used block-by-block field surveys in five cities to qualitatively classify areas as gentrifying or not gentrifying based on their observations. Then they evaluated a number of readily available census variables to determine which combination could statistically discriminate between these two types of areas. Using similar census variables, Bostic and Martin (2003) developed a scoring algorithm that they applied across a number of metropolitan areas to classify census tracts that were gentrifying and those that were not (see **Table 10.13** for a description of the **Gentrification Score**).

- Results indicated that Black home owners were a gentrifying influence in the 1970s but not in the 1980s.
- The authors suggested that by the 1980s, fair lending and anti-discrimination efforts began to have a measureable impact and Black home owners were increasingly drawn to non-gentrification neighborhoods, which might lead to a decline in their importance as a gentrifying force (Bostic & Martin, 2003).

Freeman (2005) used a two-step process and census data to classify neighborhoods as gentrifying or not. First, he identified markers of whether a neighborhood was gentrifiable, such as whether it was in an inner city, was populated by low-income households, and had experienced disinvestment. Second, he determined which of the gentrifiable neighborhoods showed signs that they were actually gentrifying by looking at whether there was a recent influx of affluent households and an increase in investment. He classified census tracts meeting all five of his criteria as gentrifying (see **Table 10.14 Gentrifying Neighborhoods**).

- Results suggested that displacement (captured by higher mobility rates) was not significantly associated with gentrification.
- Rental inflation was modestly associated with displacement in gentrifying neighborhoods.

- Freeman argued that displacement may not be the engine of neighborhood change in gentrifying neighborhoods, and demographic change in gentrifying neighborhoods may be a consequence of lower rates of intra-neighborhood mobility and the relative affluence of in-movers (Freeman, 2005).

Barton (2016) applied Bostic and Martin's (2003) and Freeman's (2005) gentrification measures to neighborhoods in New York City. He found that the former method classified fewer areas as gentrified than did the later. In this study, Barton also classified neighborhoods as gentrified based on a content analysis of the *New York Times* (*NYT*). He found that the Bostic and Martin classification method showed higher agreement with the results of the *NYT* analysis than was found using the Freeman method.

An alternative to census-based measures of gentrification are methods that use outward signs of gentrification to classify areas. Field surveys have been used in the past to assess blocks for signs of gentrification (Hammel & Wyly, 1996), but these have been difficult to replicate. More recently, Google Street View images have proven useful in this regard. Hwang and Sampson (2014) developed methods to code these images for blocks in Chicago along a number of dimensions and compared the results to previously conducted field surveys. (See **Table 10.15** for a description of the **Google Street View Gentrification Observations Instrument**.) They used this information to calculate gentrification scores for census tracts. Combined with socioeconomic census variables, these assessments achieved a fuller assessment of gentrification than either source of data alone. The GGO score had greater explanatory power than traditional census-based measures in predicting the development of businesses and amenities perceived to be signs of gentrification.

- Results showed that the pace of gentrification in Chicago was negatively related to the concentration of Blacks and Latinos in neighborhoods.
- Gentrification was attenuated when the percentage of Blacks in a neighborhood was greater than 40% (Hwang & Sampson, 2014).

Although progress is being made on measuring gentrification, there is little agreement in the literature on how to evaluate the degree to which displacement has occurred. Several studies have assessed displacement indirectly by comparing gentrified and nongentrified neighborhoods on the relative move-out rates for households at different levels of income. Such studies of housing unit transitions show little evidence of wholesale displacement of the poor in gentrifying neighborhoods and suggest some signs of their benefiting from slower residential turnover in upgrading areas (Ellen & O'Regan, 2011; Freeman & Braconi, 2004; Vigdor, 2002). However, as pressure on property values in gentrifying areas mounts, a growing number of low-income renters have been found to face prohibitive rent burdens and have needed to resort to housing assistance programs, which are in short supply (Newman & Wyly, 2006). These mixed results point to the need to develop more refined measures of displacement that can identify moves that are caused by gentrification along with gentrification-induced housing cost burdens on those who do not move. Currently, most available data sources, such as the AHS or ACS, do not ask about households' reasons for moving or how changing housing values have affected them, leaving researchers to infer displacement from comparing patterns of who moves and who stays in gentrifying neighborhoods.

CONCLUSION

The built environment, especially housing, is an important context for individual and community well-being. Deteriorated or substandard housing can have a negative effect on health and contributes to household and social instability. Having difficulty affording housing can drive households into substandard conditions or place considerable financial and psychological stress on them as the struggle to pay for their housing and other necessities. Measuring how these aspects of housing are affecting residents is fundamental to understanding how problems with meeting these basic needs is affecting populations.

Housing and other aspects of local infrastructure are physical and economic drivers that shape the character of neighborhoods. Changes in housing quality, affordability, and market strength are driven by economic forces and the choices that residents make to move in, move out, or stay in place. Government policies, institutional decisions, and community action can affect that balance. Indeed, organizations and groups interested in community development or preservation are often working to tilt the trajectory of neighborhoods upward through their actions and investments. As this happens, many aspects of the neighborhood change, and the population that can or wants to live in that place is also likely to change. Finding that balance between achieving upgrades and improvements while retaining mixed-income and mixed-use communities can be elusive. Careful measurement of these related processes can be crucial to keeping strategies on track, evaluating their impact, and informing public policies related to housing and community.

LIST OF MEASURES AND TABLE NUMBERS

TABLE 10.1 ■ Housing Quality Measures From the American Housing Survey

Primary References	Holupka, C. S., & Newman, S. J. (2011). The housing and neighborhood conditions of America's children: Patterns and trends over four decades. *Housing Policy Debate, 21*(2), 215–245. Eggers, F. J., & Moumen, F. (2013). American Housing Survey: A measure of (poor) housing quality. Retrieved from https://www.huduser.gov/publications/pdf/ahs_hsg.pdf
Purpose	• The purpose of physical adequacy (PA) is to measure whether dwellings contain either moderate or severe defects. • The purpose of the Poor Quality Index (PQI) is to measure the level of physical deficiencies in American Housing Survey (AHS) sample housing units.

Description	This measure has the following two components. Both measures are calculated from data that are self-reported in the American Household Survey (AHS).
	
	Physical adequacy (PA) is a categorical measure that classifies housing units as moderately or severely defective based on whether or not they have any of a list of key physical defects. Occupied units that have at least one "moderate" or one "severe" defect are classified as "physically inadequate" (see Holupka & Newman, 2011, p. 224, for details).
	
	• **"Severely defective"** units include at least one of five problems, such as
	  ○ Lacking complete plumbing facilities
	  ○ Had three or more heating breakdowns last winter
	  ○ Has at least five of these six possible maintenance problems
	• **"Moderately defective"** includes units that are not severely defective but have any of five problems, such as
	  ○ At least three toilet breakdowns in the past 90 days
	  ○ An unvented heater
	  ○ At least three of the maintenance problems mentioned under severely defective
	
	Poor Quality Index (PQI) focuses more on quality than adequacy by recognizing a wide range of deficiencies. The PQI is numerical, not categorical, with higher scores on the PQI representing greater deficiencies. **PQI** has eight components with 35 items (each item has a different weight). The eight components include (see Eggers & Moumen, 2013, p. 5, for details)
	
	• Electricity problems (**4 items**, 15 points)
	• Heating problems (**7 items**, 32 points)
	• Inside structural or other problems (**11 items**, 22 points)
	• Bathroom problems (**2 items**, 16 point)
	• Kitchen problems (**1 item**, 10 points)
	• Outside structural problems (**7 items**, 35 points)
	• Water and sewer problems (**2 items**, 32 points)
	• Elevator problems (**1 item**, 4 points)

Sample/Data	• Data sources were from the national American Housing Surveys 1975 (n = 55,527), 1985 (n = 27,283), 1995 (n = 32,740), and 2005 (n = 28,489). Data included all children 18 years of age or younger living in an AHS housing unit. • This study used the 14 AHS surveys from 1985 to 2011, because AHS has interviewed the residents of the same units every two years during that period. Sample units size (N) varied from 33,000 to 39,622.

Scoring	• **PA** The items are counted to determine PA based on the criteria mentioned above. • **PQI:** The weighted items are summed. The maximum possible PQI score is 166 points.
Related Reference	Newman, S. J., & Garboden, P. M. (2013). Psychometrics of housing quality measurement in the American Housing Survey. *Cityscape*, 293–306.
Language	English
Contacts	Scott Holupk 624 N. Broadway Hampton House 345 Baltimore, Maryland 21205, USA Email: scott.holupka@jhu.edu Frederick J. Eggers Econometrica, Inc. 4416 E West Hwy # 215 Bethesda, MD 20814, USA Email: fje@sagecomputing.com

TABLE 10.2 ■ Physical Quality Subscales EC-HOME (Early Childhood Home Observation for Measurement of the Environment Inventory)

Primary Reference	Leventhal, T., Martin, A., & Brooks-Gunn, J. (2004). The EC-HOME across five national data sets in the 3rd to 5th year of life. *Parenting: Science and Practice*, 4(2–3), 161–188.
Purpose	The purpose of EC-HOME physical subscales is to measure physical environment including interior and exterior of home.
Description	The EC-HOME is a single inventory comprising 55 items gathered through mothers' report and interviewers' observation. From this original inventory, two physical subscales assess Interior of Home and Exterior of Home. Each scale item was coded as yes = 1 (good environment) or no = 0 (poor environment). The two scales are (see primary and related references for information on all of the items) **Interior of home: (8 items)** such as • All visible rooms of the house are reasonably clean and minimally cluttered • The interior of the home is not dark or perceptually monotonous • In terms of available space, the rooms are not overcrowded with furniture • Building has no potentially dangerous structural or health defects (e.g., plaster coming down from the ceiling, rodents, etc.) **Exterior of home: (4 items)** such as • No garbage/broken glass in street/sidewalk • Buildings in face block in good condition
Sample/Data	This study used five large-scale data sets of children: IHDP (N = 743), NLSY-CS (7,402), NICHD-SECC (1,128), PHDCN (511), and PSID-CDS (N = 384)
Scoring	The item ratings are summed for each subscale. Higher scores indicate more enriched home environment.
Assessment	• Physical subscales demonstrated moderate to high reliability. • Across the five data sets, Cronbach's alpha ranged from 0.52 to 0.73 for the interior of home items, and from 0.54 to 0.78 for the exterior of home items (all $\alpha > 0.5$). • Item-to-scale correlations (r) for both subscales were greater than 0.25 across data sets.
Related References	Han, W. J., Leventhal, T., & Linver, M. R. (2004). The home observation for measurement of the environment (home) in middle childhood: A study of three large-scale data sets. *Parenting: Science and Practice*, 4(2–3), 189–210. Totsika, V., & Sylva, K. (2004). The home observation for measurement of the environment revisited. *Child and Adolescent Mental Health*, 9(1), 25–35.
Language	English
Contact	Tama Leventhal Tufts University Eliot-Pearson Department of Child Study and Human Development 105 College Avenue Medford, MA 02155, USA Email: tama.leventhal@tufts.edu

TABLE 10.3 ■ Housing Quality Instrument (HQI)

Primary Reference	Evans, G. W., Wells, N. M., Chan, H. Y. E., & Saltzman, H. (2000). Housing quality and mental health. *Journal of Consulting and Clinical Psychology, 68*(3), 526–530.
Purpose	The purpose of this observer-based instrument is to measure physical housing quality that is conceptually relevant to mental health and psychometrically sound.
Description	The Housing Quality Instrument (HQI) is based on an observer rating scale (score: 0 to 2) consisting of 88 items. This instrument consists of the following six subscales (see Evans et al., 2002, for details): • **Child resources**: "Toys are accessible to the child" (0 = *no toys clearly accessible to the child*, 1 = *in one room*, 2 = *in more than one room*) • **Cleanliness/clutter**: "How much clutter is in the kitchen?" (0 = *chaos*, 1 = *some clutter*, 2 = *little or none*) • **Indoor climatic conditions**: "Heat has broken down" (0 = *once a month or more*, 1 = *once in the past three months or last winter*, 2 = *not in a year*) • **Privacy**: "Do you have to walk through the bedroom to get to another room?" (0 = *more than one other room*, 1 = *one other room*, 2 = *no other rooms*) • **Hazards**: "Stairs are . . . " (0 = *potentially dangerous [e.g., no risers to individual steps, loose or no handrails, nails sticking out]*, 1 = *structurally sound but cracked, discolored, paint peeling*, 2 = *in good condition*) • **Structural quality**: "Rate the worst ceiling/wall surface in the room" (0 = *more than 1 square foot [.30 m²] loose or missing*, 1 = *less than 1 square foot (.30 m2) loose or missing*, 2 = *good*) Also, there is a 45-item scale version, which is focused on elderly residents. This revised version incorporates 3-point rating scales of (see related references below): • Infrastructure • Amenities • Support for mobility impairment • Spatial requirement
Sample	Data were from two samples: (1) cross-sectional data from rural women living with at least one child ($n = 207$) and (2) a longitudinal, urban sample ($n = 31$) who relocated into a residence financed and constructed cooperatively with Habitat for Humanity.
Scoring	The Housing Quality Scale was built by using factor analysis and item-scaling techniques. Three-point ratings of housing quality were assessed for items on 6 housing quality subscales: structural quality, privacy, indoor climatic conditions, hazards, cleanliness/clutter, and child resources. The values on the subscales are summed. Higher scores on HQI represent better physical housing quality.
Assessment	**Reliability analysis** • Reliability coefficient (α) for the HQI was 0.78 (moderate internal consistency for overall instrument). • Reliability coefficient (α) for the six subclasses ranged from .71 to .89. • Overall inter-observer reliability (r) from 23 randomly selected homes was .72, and subscale inter-observer reliability (r) ranged from .61 to .81. **Factor analysis** • Based on a large number of initial items from a variety of sources (e.g., existing housing indices, literature, and interviews with specialists), the final version of Housing Quality Scale was built by using factor analysis and item-scaling techniques.

(Continued)

TABLE 10.3 ■ (Continued)

	• Three-point ratings of housing quality were assessed for items composing the six housing quality subscales: structural quality, privacy, indoor climatic conditions, hazards, cleanliness/clutter, and child resources.
Related References	Evans, G. W., Kantrowitz, E., & Eshelman, P. (2002). Housing quality and psychological well-being among the elderly population. *The Journals of Gerontology Series B: Psychological Sciences and Social Sciences*, *57*(4), 381–383. Evans, G. W., Saltzman, H., & Cooperman, J. L. (2001). Housing quality and children's socioemotional health. *Environment and Behavior*, *33*(3), 389–399.
Language	English
Contact	Gary W. Evans Departments of Design and Environmental Analysis and of Human Development College of Human Ecology Cornell University Ithaca, NY 14853-4401 USA Email: gwe1@cornell.edu

TABLE 10.4 ■	Observer-Rated Housing Quality Scale (OHQS)
Primary Reference	Adair, C. E., Kopp, B., Lavoie, J., Distasio, J., Hwang, S. W., Watson, A., . . . & Ahmed, N. (2014). Development and initial validation of the observer-rated housing quality scale (OHQS) in a multisite trial of housing first. *Journal of Urban Health*, *91*(2), 242–255.
Purpose	The purpose of this scale is to measure observed physical quality of the built environment including the housing unit, building, and neighborhood.
Description	Observer-Rated Housing Quality Scale (OHQS) is an observer-based rating scale consisting of 25 items. Higher scores on OHQS indicate better-observed housing quality. This instrument consists of two primary subscales (see above source for a description of all of the items): **Housing unit (18 items)** • Safety/security • Natural light • Utilities—heating/cooling • Utilities—plumbing • Structural condition • Kitchen appliances • Bedroom/sleeping space • Noise • Overall design **Building (7 items)** • Security/safety • Access/visitability • Outside condition (property and building) A neighborhood quality **(9 items)** was also developed through this research; however, the items are not discussed in this article.
Sample	The sample consisted of 55 housing units in Toronto and Winnipeg, Canada.
Scoring	• From an initial attribute pool of 76 items in three domains, the final OHQS was built through attribute reduction, formatting and scaling, and instrument refinement. • With respect to the 18 unit and 7 building items, the response scale ranges from 0.5 to 5 in half-point increments with a total possible score (unit and building) ranging from 12.5 to 125. • High scores indicate better housing quality.
Assessment	• Internal consistency of the OHQS was good: $\alpha = 0.90$ for the unit items, 0.80 for the building items, and 0.92 total. • Inter-rater reliability was also good: Intra-class correlation coefficients were 0.87 for the unit, 0.85 for the building, and 0.93 for the total scale.
Related Reference	Adair, C. E., Kopp, B., Distasio, J., Hwang, S. W., Lavoie, J., Veldhuizen, S., . . . & Cote, S. (2016). Housing quality in a randomized controlled trial of housing first for homeless individuals with mental illness: Correlates and associations with outcomes. *Journal of Urban Health*, 1–16.
Language	English
Contact	Carol E. Adair Mental Health Commission of Canada 100 Sparks Street, Suite 600 Ottawa, Ontario, Canada, K1P 5B7 Email: ceadair@ucalgary.ca

TABLE 10.5 ■ Housing Cost Burden Using ACS	
Primary Reference	Schwartz, M., & Wilson, E. (2008). Who can afford to live in a home?: A look at data from the 2006 American Community Survey. *US Census Bureau.*
Purpose	The purpose of housing cost burden is to measure the extent to which households can afford to pay for their renter or owner related costs.
Description	Housing cost burden assesses affordability of suitable housing by looking at the monthly housing costs as a percentage of monthly household income (pre-tax). • For owners, housing costs come from questions in the census about the following: mortgage, second mortgage or home equity loans, real estate taxes, homeowners insurance, condo fee, mobile home cost, and utilities. • For renters, housing costs come from questions in the census about the following: contract rent and utilities.
Sample	This study used data from the 2006 American Community Survey (ACS), which is a nationwide survey carried out by the Census Bureau to measure socioeconomic and housing characteristics of the population.
Scoring	A household (owners or renters) are considered to be burdened if they pay 30% or more of their income for housing costs (i.e., housing cost-to-income ratios or HCIRs ≥ 30%).
Related Reference	Wardrip, K. E., & Pelletiere, D. (2008). Fully utilizing housing cost data in the American Community Survey PUMS data: Identifying issues and proposing solutions. *Cityscape,* 331–339.
Language	English
Contact	Mary B. Schwartz Housing and Household Economic Statistics (HHES) Division of the Census Bureau. Washington, DC 20233-8500, USA Email: mary.b.schwartz@ccmail.census.gov

TABLE 10.6 ■ Housing-Induced Poverty	
Primary Reference	Kutty, N. K. (2005). A new measure of housing affordability: Estimates and analytical results. *Housing Policy Debate, 16*(1), 113–142.
Purpose	The purpose of housing-induced poverty measure is to assess a severe form of the housing affordability problem.
Description	• A household is considered to be in housing-induced poverty when it cannot afford the poverty basket of non-housing goods, after paying for housing costs. • The poverty basket is assumed to be two-thirds of the official poverty line. • A household at the poverty line is considered to be in housing-induced poverty when its housing costs exceeds one-third of household income. • A household above the poverty line would enter housing-induced poverty if housing expenditures were so high that their remaining income is below two-thirds of the poverty line.
Sample/Data	This study used data from the Public Use Files of the 1999 American Housing Survey (AHS), national sample.
Scoring	See above in Table 10.5
Related References	Stone, M. E. (2004). Shelter poverty: The chronic crisis of housing affordability. *New England Journal of Public Policy, 20*(1), 107–119. Stone, M. E. (2006). What is housing affordability? The case for the residual income approach. *Housing Policy Debate, 17*(1), 151–184.
Language	English
Contact	Nandinee K. Kutty 1040 N Quincy St., Apt. 411 Arlington, VA 22201, USA Email: NndKutty@aol.com

TABLE 10.7 ■	Rental Housing Affordability Mismatch Ratio (RHAMR)
Primary Reference	Bogdon, A. S., & Can, A. (1997). Indicators of local housing affordability: Comparative and spatial approaches. *Real Estate Economics, 25*(1), 43–80.
Purpose	The purpose of rental housing affordability mismatch ratio is to measure the gap in local housing that is affordable.
Description	• The rental housing affordability mismatch ratio (RHAMR) combines supply (housing cost burden) and demand (affordable housing stock) by comparing actual rents with the rents that households in different income groups can afford. • The RHAMR refers to the ratio of housing units affordable to households in a given income group to the number of households in the income group.
Sample/Data	This study used the Comprehensive Housing Affordability Strategy Database (CHAS) 1993 and the 1990 Census STF 3C file in order to apply the indicators to a selected area, Onondaga County, New York.
Measurement	Mismatch ratio = (R + H)/N, Where • R = the number of units renting for less than 30 percent of the poverty level • H = the number of owner-occupied units valued at below three times of the poverty level • N = the number of households with incomes below the poverty level (Harkness & Newman, 2005, p. 234)
Related Reference	Harkness, J., & Newman, S. J. (2005). Housing affordability and children's well-being: Evidence from the national survey of America's families. *Housing Policy Debate, 16*(2), 223–255.
Language	English
Contact	Amy S. Bogdon Fannie Mae Foundation Washington DC 20016-8111, USA

TABLE 10.8 ■ Housing Market Index	
Primary Reference	Walker, C., & Winston, F. (2010). *A HMDA-based housing market index to track neighborhood change.* Washington, DC: The Local Initiatives Support Corporation.
Purpose	The purpose of Housing Market Index is to measure the relative housing market strength for each neighborhood within a metropolitan area.
Description	Housing Market Index assesses aspects of the housing market that include • Relatively high housing values • An active market for investor and owner-occupied purchases • Investments in the renovation or upgrade of the housing stock • Expectation of returns on investment from owner-occupied and rental housing (Walker & Winston, 2010, p. 2) Higher scores indicate greater housing market strength.
Sample	This study used 20 data components from the 2004–2008 Home Mortgage Disclosure Act (HMDA) data files that contain all metropolitan areas in the United States. It also used two data components from the 2000 U.S. Census (see Walker & Winston, 2010, pp. 28–29 for the details).
Measurement	**Housing Market Index** = .6 * VALUE–.4 * HIGHCOST + .3 * OWNELOC + .1 * INVESTVELOC + .2 * OWNPCT **Where** • VALUE = median value of first lien home • HIGHCOST = percent of all first-lien mortgages that are high-cost • OWNELOC = velocity of home purchase mortgages transactions to owner-occupants, measured as the number of first-lien owner-occupant mortgages/the number of owner-occupied units • INVESTVELOC = velocity of home purchase mortgage transactions to investors, measured as the number of first lien investor mortgages/the number of single-family rental units • OWNPCT = the percentage of first lien mortgages to owner occupants, measured as the number of owner-occupant mortgages/(owner-occupant mortgages + investor mortgages) These variables are converted to common units (i.e., standardized variables) through a *z*-score transformation.
Related Reference	Kingsley, G. T., Hendey, L., & Price, D. (2011). Setting priorities for neighborhood stabilization: Guide to using foreclosure-response.org indexes. Washington, DC: Urban Institute.
Language	English
Contact	Chris Walker Local Initiatives Support Corporation 501 Seventh Avenue New York, 10018, USA Email: cwalker@lisc.org

TABLE 10.9 ■ HUD-USPS Vacancy Ratio

Primary Reference	Immergluck, D. (2015). Examining changes in long-term neighborhood housing vacancy during the 2011 to 2014 U.S. national recovery. *Journal of Urban Affairs, 38*(5), 607–622.
Purpose	The purpose of HUD-USPS Vacancy Ratio is to measure the neighborhood-level vacancy rate.
Description	• The HUD-USPS Vacancy Ratio uses data from the U.S. Postal Service (USPS) on residential addresses that are gathered from the administration of mail delivery. • Using these data, U.S. Department of Housing and Urban Development (HUD) creates census-tract-level aggregates, which are broken out by type of property and duration of vacancy.
Sample/Data	This study used the HUD-USPS vacancy data (Q2, 2010–Q2, 2014) and 2008–2012 American Community Survey. The sample consisted of 36,905 census tracts across the 50 largest metropolitan areas.
Measurement	• The HUD-USPS data reported vacant residential addresses of three months and going up to a period of 36 months or longer. • Immergluck (2015, p.6) defined the long-term vacancy rate as the share of residential addresses that have been vacant for at least six months in a census tract.
Related References	Newman, G., Gu, D., Kim, J. H., & Li, W. (2016). Elasticity and urban vacancy: A longitudinal comparison of U.S. cities. *Cities, 58*, 143–151. Silverman, R., Yin, L., & Patterson, K. L. (2013). Dawn of the dead city: An exploratory analysis of vacant addresses in Buffalo, NY 2008–2010. *Journal of Urban Affairs, 35*(2), 131–152.
Language	English
Contact	Dan Immergluck School of City and Regional Planning Georgia Institute of Technology 245 4th Street NW, Suite 204 Atlanta, GA 30322-0155, USA Email: Dan.immergluck@coa.gatech.edu

TABLE 10.10 ■ Zombie Properties

Primary Reference	Silverman, R., Yin, L., & Patterson, K. L. (2013). Dawn of the dead city: An exploratory analysis of vacant addresses in Buffalo, NY 2008–2010. *Journal of Urban Affairs, 35*(2), 131–152.
Purpose	The purpose of zombie properties is to identify neighborhoods that struggle with a distinct type of long-term vacant and abandoned structures or properties.
Description	• Zombie properties are a specific type of abandoned structure. • They are found in shrinking cities where demographic and economic decline make abandonment an enduring fixture of the urban milieu (Silverman, Yin, & Patterson, 2013, p. 4).
Sample/Data	This study used four data sources to examine residential vacancy patterns in a total of 89 census tracts in the city of Buffalo: (1) HUD Aggregate USPS Administrative Data on Address Vacancies for 2008-2010, (2) the American Community Survey (ACS) five-year estimates for 2005–2009, (3) housing choice voucher (HCV) records of local public housing agencies, and (4) municipal in rem property records.
Measurement	Four neighborhood-level variables were used as measures of vacancy and abandonment: • Percentage of housing units vacant, estimate 2009; percentage of all housing units vacant, 2009 estimate (source: 2005–09 ACS) • Percentage of residential addresses vacant 2010; percentage of all residential addresses vacant in the third quarter of 2010 (source: HUD Aggregated USPS Administrative Data on Address Vacancies) • Percentage of vacant housing units "other," estimate 2009; percentage of vacant units not being offered for rent or sale, being held for future occupancy, or limited to seasonal or occasional use, 2009 estimate (source: 2005–09 ACS) • Percentage of all addresses in rem, estimate 2010; percentage of addresses that were in rem, estimate 2010 (source: HUD Aggregated USPS Administrative Data on Address Vacancies and City of Buffalo property files)
Language	English
Contact	Robert Mark Silverman, School of Architecture and Planning 114, Diefendorf Hall University at Buffalo, South Campus Buffalo, NY 14214 Email: rms35@buffalo.edu

TABLE 10.11 ■ Blight Per Unit (BPU)	
Primary Reference	Weaver, R. C., & Bagchi-Sen, S. (2013). Spatial analysis of urban decline: The geography of blight. *Applied Geography, 40*, 61–70.
Purpose	The purpose of *blight per unit of housing* (BPU) is to quantify the concept of *blight* by using the neighborhood-level code violation rates.
Description	• The BPU measure assumes that code violations can effectively capture the concept of "blight" because they are physical manifestations of urban decline. • "Blight" can be quantified as noncompliance with real property regulations. • Thus, BPU is defined as the percentage of properties with code violations within a census tract.
Sample/Data	• This study used data from the City of Buffalo Department of Management Information Systems, which contained 21,032 open property code violations between October 1, 1999, and June 30, 2009. • All property addresses were geocoded. This resulted in 20,082 of the property violations. Additionally, they used the 5-Year U.S. American Community Survey (ACS, 2005–2009) for relevant socioeconomic status indicators.
Measurement	**BPU = number of code violations/total housing units** Point locations of the property code violations were aggregated to the census tract level to obtain values for the following: • Total open code violations accumulated over the entire range of dates • Violations observed during each quarter-year interval of the time series (January–March, April–June, July–September, October–December) • For each of these quantities, the number of violations in a census tract is weighted by the reciprocal of the given tract's estimated stock of housing units at the end of the time series (Weaver & Bagchi-Sen, 2013, p. 63).
Language	English
Contact	Russell Weaver University of Redlands MS GIS Program 1200 E. Colton Ave, Box 3080 Redlands, CA 92373, USA Email: russell_weaver@redlands.edu

TABLE 10.12 ■ Residential Stability Index and Residential Instability Index

Primary References	(1) Sampson, R. J., Raudenbush, S. W., & Earls, F. (1997). Neighborhoods and violent crime: A multilevel study of collective efficacy. *Science, 277*(5328), 918–924. (2) Hipp, J. R. (2010). A dynamic view of neighborhoods: The reciprocal relationship between crime and neighborhood structural characteristics. *Social Problems, 57*(2), 205–230.
Purpose	(1) The purpose of Residential Stability Index is to measure neighborhood differences in residential mobility. (2) Residential Instability Index also measures neighborhood-level residential mobility, but in an opposite direction.
Description	(1) Two characteristics of census tracts are used to define a measure of **Residential Stability**: • Living in the same house as five years earlier • Owner-occupied house A value of this index is calculated using a weighted factor score. Higher scores represent higher levels of neighborhood residential stability. (2) To create the **Residential Instability** Index, three census-tract level characteristics were used: • Home ownership • Living in the same house five years previously • Length of residence A higher score indicates greater instability.
Sample/Data	(1) This study used two data sources: (a) data from the Project on Human Development in Chicago Neighborhoods (PHDCN, N = 8,782 residents), and (b) 847 census tracts (data from the 1990 Census) in the city of Chicago, which were combined to create 343 "neighborhood clusters" (NCs). (2) This study used crime data for 2,534 census tracts in 13 U.S. cities between 1990 and 2000 and data from the 1990 and 2000 Census.
Measurement	(1) First, a factor analysis was conducted to confirm the emergence of a factor of residential stability by using the alpha-scoring method to maximize the reliability of measures and the oblique factor rotation to allow the extracted dimensions to covary. Second, to represent this dimension parsimoniously, they calculate a factor regression score that weights each variable by its factor loading. (2) First, the instability index is created using a principal components analysis that combines the percentage of tract households who own their residence, the percentage of households in the same housing unit five years previously, and the average length of residence in the tract. The factor scores are then created using regression scoring. Second, the scores are multiplied by −1 to make it a measure of instability.
Assessment	(1) The factor analysis of residential stability was dominated by two variables with high (> 0.75) loadings: 0.77 for living in the same house as in 1985 and 0.86 for owner-occupied house. That is, consistent with previous research, a residential stability factor clearly emerged. (2) The Cronbach's alpha for the residential instability index was: α = .78. The largest Eigenvalue was 2.4 and 80% of the variance was explained. The factor loadings ranged from 0.82 to 0.95.

(Continued)

TABLE 10.12 ■ (Continued)

Related Reference	Krivo, L. J., Byron, R. A., Calder, C. A., Peterson, R. D., Browning, C. R., Kwan, M. P., & Lee, J. Y. (2015). Patterns of local segregation: Do they matter for neighborhood crime? *Social Science Research, 54*, 303–318.
Language	English
Contacts	Robert J. Sampson Department of Sociology William James Hall Harvard University 33 Kirkland Street Cambridge, MA 02138, USA Email: rsampson@wjh.harvard.edu John R. Hipp Department of Criminology, Law & Society Department of Sociology University of California 3311 Social Ecology II Irvine, CA 92697, USA Email: john.hipp@uci.edu

TABLE 10.13 ■ Gentrification Score	
Primary Reference	Bostic, R. W., & Martin, R. W. (2003). Black home-owners as a gentrifying force? Neighbourhood dynamics in the context of minority home-ownership. *Urban Studies, 40*(12), 2427–2449.
Purpose	The purpose of gentrification score is to identify gentrifying neighborhoods using census data.
Description	The gentrification score is a census-based strategy that is used to assess neighborhood gentrification across metropolitan areas. To overcome the limitation of previous work that has identified gentrified tracts with a single variable, the gentrifications score utilizes the nine census indicators highlighted by Hammel and Wyly (1996) to develop a multivariate strategy for identifying gentrified tracts. • Share of persons 25 or older with a college degree at t + 1 • Ratio of average family income at t + 1 and average family income at t • The home-ownership rate at t + 1 • The change in population share of the cohort that is aged between 30 and 44 at t to that at t + 1 • The t + 1 poverty rate • The t + 1 population share of White non-family households • The t + 1 Black population share • Managerial and administrative workers as share of the total workforce at t + 1 • The t + 1 population share of persons 25 and older with some college education
Sample	This study used census tract data from the 50 largest metropolitan areas, measured by central-city population between 1970 and 1990. The final data-set included information on over 27,000 tracts.
Measurement	• The first step was to identify neighborhoods that are gentrifiable. A tract is gentrifiable if its median income is less than 50 percent of the median income for the Metropolitan Statistical Area (MSA). In Step 2, nine census variables are used to classify the gentrifiable neighborhoods into those that have gentrified between year t and year t + 1 and those that have not (Bostic & Martin, 2003, p. 2431). The nine census indicators listed above are used. • To identify gentrified neighborhoods, all of the gentrifiable tracts for a given year are ranked according to each of the nine variables above. Then the average rank of the tracts across the nine measures is used as a score, and the tracts with the lowest average rank are identified as gentrifying.
Related References	Barton, M. (2016). An exploration of the importance of the strategy used to identify gentrification. *Urban Studies, 53*(1), 92–111. Hammel, D. J., & Wyly, E. K. (1996). A model for identifying gentrified areas with census data. *Urban Geography, 17*(3), 248–268. Wyly, E. K., & Hammel, D. J. (1998). Modeling the context and contingency of gentrification. *Journal of Urban Affairs, 20*(3), 303–326.
Language	English
Contact	Raphael W. Bostic Ralph and Goldy Lewis Hall 326 School of Policy, Planning, and Development University of Southern California Los Angeles, CA 90089-0626, USA Email: bostic@usc.edu

TABLE 10.14 ■ Gentrifying Neighborhoods	
Primary Reference	Freeman, L. (2005). Displacement or succession? Residential mobility in gentrifying neighborhoods. *Urban Affairs Review, 40*(4), 463–491.
Purpose	The purpose of this measure is to identify gentrifying neighborhoods (census tracts) by taking into account the potential to be gentrified as well as the actual process of gentrification.
Description	Freeman (2005) used several dimensions to define gentrifying neighborhoods. First, he considers the types of neighborhoods with the potential to be gentrified (e.g., central city neighborhoods, populated by low-income households, disinvestment). Second, he considers the actual process of gentrification (e.g., influx of the relatively affluent of gentry, an increase in investment). **A neighborhood must meet the following criteria to be considered gentrifying** (Freeman, 2005, pp. 471–472): • Be located in the central city at the beginning of the intercensal period • Have a median income less than the median (40th percentile) for that metropolitan area at the beginning of the intercensal period • Have a proportion of housing built within the past 20 years lower than the proportion found at the median (40th percentile) for the respective metropolitan area • Have a percentage increase in educational attainment greater than the median increase in educational attainment for that metropolitan area • Have an increase in real housing prices during the intercensal period
Sample/Data	This study used the geocoded version of the Panel Study of Income Dynamics (PSID) from 1986 to 1999, which were linked to tract and metropolitan level data from the decennial census 1980 and 1990 (N = 45,108 person years).
Measurement	"Potentially gentrifying" = meeting the first three criteria "Nongentrifying" = meeting the first three but not last two criteria "Gentrifying" = meeting all five criteria
Related Reference	Barton, M. (2016). An exploration of the importance of the strategy used to identify gentrification. *Urban Studies, 53*(1), 92–111.
Language	English
Contact	Lance Freeman Columbia University 400 Avery Hall New York, NY 10027, USA Email: lf182@columbia.edu

TABLE 10.15 ■ Google Street View Gentrification Observations (GGO) Instrument

Primary Reference	Hwang, J., & Sampson, R. J. (2014). Divergent pathways of gentrification: Racial inequality and the social order of renewal in Chicago neighborhoods. *American Sociological Review, 79*(4), 726–751.
Purpose	The purpose of GGO instrument is to assess the visible aspects of gentrification (e.g., reinvestment, renewal, and in-migration of middle- and upper-middle-class residents) and to identify a neighborhood's degree of gentrification by using a systematic social observational of street blocks that draws on Google Street View.

Description	GGO instrument combines three main characteristics to define a neighborhood's stage of gentrification:
	• **The "structural mix" of an area**—the combined condition of older structures (i.e., an area's preexisting socioeconomic status; **1 item**), and the degree of new structures and rehabilitation **(5 items)**. This measure focuses on various aspects of new construction and rehabilitation, capturing both public and private reinvestment and small- and large-scale development:
	  ○ The amount of new or rehabilitated building structures
	  ○ New traffic signs/structures
	  ○ New large developments
	• **Visible beautification efforts (3 items):** Beautification efforts are visible cues of the presence of community investment that, in turn, attract further reinvestment. Items such as those below were combined to capture beautification:
	  ○ Efforts discouraging disorder (e.g., painting over graffiti)
	  ○ Personal frontage beautification
	• **Lack of disorder and decay (3 items):** Physical signs of disorder and decay, such as trash and unkempt vacant lots, are visible cues that signal neighborhood disinvestment and deter reinvestment. Items such as the following were combined to measure the lack of disorder and decay in a neighborhood:
	  ○ Lack of physical disorder
	  ○ Lack of unkempt vacant/public space
	Higher values indicate higher stages of gentrification.

Sample/Data	• This study used systematically observed and coded street-level images from 2007 to 2009 in a random sample of blocks stratified by 140 Chicago census tracts that were selected to match the 66 core and fringe gentrified tracts and the 74 "gentrifiable" tracts. • For supplementary analyses, they also used the 2005 to 2009 American Community Survey, in addition to 1990 and 2000 census data.
Measurement	• First, all indicators are originally recorded at the block-face level. For each block face, the relevant indicators are combined to calculate a summary score for each of the three measures. • Then, they define the overall gentrification stage score for a block face as the average of the three summary measures. • The block-level score for each indicator is the average of its block-face scores, and each tract-level score is the average of its randomly sampled blocks' scores (Hwang & Sampson, 2014, p. 733).

(Continued)

TABLE 10.15 ■ (Continued)

Assessment	• Reliability coefficients were relatively strong, and GGO-stage scores detected variance between blocks and tracts. • Intraclass correlations were high compared to prior studies using systematic social observation, indicating GGO instruments properly detected block- and tract-level differences.
Related Reference	Hwang, J. (2015). Gentrification in changing cities immigration, new diversity, and racial inequality in neighborhood renewal. *The ANNALS of the American Academy of Political and Social Science, 660*(1), 319–340.
Language	English
Contact	Jackelyn Hwang Princeton University Office of Population Research 261 Wallace Hall Princeton, NJ 08544, USA Email: jihwang@princeton.edu

REFERENCES

Accordino, J., & Johnson, G. T. (2000). Addressing the vacant and abandoned property problem. *Journal of Urban Affairs, 22*(3), 301–315.

Adair, C. E., Kopp, B., Distasio, J., Hwang, S. W., Lavoie, J., Veldhuizen, S., . . . & Cote, S. (2016). Housing quality in a randomized controlled trial of housing first for homeless individuals with mental illness: Correlates and associations with outcomes. *Journal of Urban Health*, 1–16.

Adair, C. E., Kopp, B., Lavoie, J., Distasio, J., Hwang, S. W., Watson, A., . . . & Ahmed, N. (2014). Development and initial validation of the observer-rated housing quality scale (OHQS) in a multisite trial of housing first. *Journal of Urban Health, 91*(2), 242–255.

Bartlett, D. (1998). Abandonment. In W. van Vliet (Ed.), *Encyclopedia of housing* (pp. 21–22). Thousand Oaks, CA: Sage.

Barton, M. (2016). An exploration of the importance of the strategy used to identify gentrification. *Urban Studies, 53*(1), 92–111.

Bodini, R. (2014). The dynamic neighborhood taxonomy: An innovative typology for community and economic development. In G. T. Kingsley, C. J. Coulton, & K. L. S. Pettit (Eds.), *Strengthening communities with neighborhood data* (pp. 317–339). Washington, DC: Urban Institute.

Bogdon, A. S., & Can, A. (1997). Indicators of local housing affordability: Comparative and spatial approaches. *Real Estate Economics, 25*(1), 43–80.

Bostic, R. W., & Martin, R. W. (2003). Black home-owners as a gentrifying force? Neighbourhood dynamics in the context of minority home-ownership. *Urban Studies, 40*(12), 2427–2449.

Bowen, E. A. (2015). Community practice in the bulldozer's shadow: The history and legacy of social work in urban renewal. *Journal of Community Practice, 23*(2), 164–181.

Bradley, R. H., & Caldwell, B. M. (1979). Home observation for measurement of the environment: A revision of the preschool scale. *American Journal of Mental Deficiency, 84*(3), 235–244.

Case, B., Pollakowski, H. O., & Wachter, S. M. (1991). On choosing among house price index methodologies. *Real Estate Economics, 19*(3), 286–307.

Coulton, C. J., Richter, F., Kim, S. J., Fischer, R., & Cho, Y. (2016). Temporal effects of distressed housing on early childhood risk factors and kindergarten readiness. *Children and Youth Services Review, 68*, 59–72.

Coulton, C. J., Theodos, B., & Turner, M. A. (2012). Residential mobility and neighborhood change: Real neighborhoods under the microscope. *Cityscape*, 55–89.

Eggers, F. J., & Moumen, F. (2013). *American Housing Survey: A measure of (poor) housing quality.* Retrieved from https://www.huduser.gov/publications/pdf/ahs_hsg.pdf

Ellen, I. G. (2000). Race-based neighbourhood projection: A proposed framework for understanding new data on racial integration. *Urban Studies, 37*(9), 1513–1533.

Ellen, I. G., & O'Regan, K. M. (2011). How low income neighborhoods change: Entry, exit, and enhancement. *Regional Science and Urban Economics, 41*(2), 89–97.

Evans, G. W. (2006). Child development and the physical environment. *Annual Review of Psychology, 57*(1), 423–451.

Evans, G. W., Kantrowitz, E., & Eshelman, P. (2002). Housing quality and psychological well-being among the elderly population. *The Journals of Gerontology Series B: Psychological Sciences and Social Sciences, 57*(4), 381–383.

Evans, G. W., Saltzman, H., & Cooperman, J. L. (2001). Housing quality and children's socioemotional health. *Environment and Behavior, 33*(3), 389–399.

Evans, G. W., Wells, N. M., Chan, H. Y. E., & Saltzman, H. (2000). Housing quality and mental health. *Journal of Consulting and Clinical Psychology, 68*(3), 526–530.

Freeman, L. (2005). Displacement or succession? Residential mobility in gentrifying neighborhoods. *Urban Affairs Review, 40*(4), 463–491.

Freeman, L., & Braconi, F. (2004). Gentrification and displacement New York City in the 1990s. *Journal of the American Planning Association, 70*(1), 39–52.

Gordon, C. (2004). Blighting the way: Urban renewal, economic development, and the elusive definition of blight. *Fordham Urban Law Journal, 31*, 305–337.

Griswold, N., Calnin, B., Schramm, M., Anselin, L., & Boehnlein, P. (2014). *Estimating the effect of demolishing distressed structures in Cleveland, OH, 2009–2013: Impacts on real estate equity and mortgage-foreclosure.* The Center on Urban Poverty and Community Development, Case Western Reserve University.

Hammel, D. J., & Wyly, E. K. (1996). A model for identifying gentrified areas with census data. *Urban Geography, 17*(3), 248–268.

Han, H. S. (2014). The impact of abandoned properties on nearby property values. *Housing Policy Debate, 24*(2), 311–334.

Han, W. J., Leventhal, T., & Linver, M. R. (2004). The home observation for measurement of the environment (HOME) in middle childhood: A study of three large-scale data sets. *Parenting, 4*(2–3), 189–210.

Harkness, J., & Newman, S. J. (2005). Housing affordability and children's well-being: Evidence from the national survey of America's families. *Housing Policy Debate, 16*(2), 223–255.

Hillier, A. E., Culhane, D. P., Smith, T. E., & Tomlin, C. D. (2003). Predicting housing abandonment with the Philadelphia neighborhood information system. *Journal of Urban Affairs, 25*(1), 91–106.

Hipp, J. R. (2010). A dynamic view of neighborhoods: The reciprocal relationship between crime and neighborhood structural characteristics. *Social Problems, 57*(2), 205–230.

Holupka, C. S., & Newman, S. J. (2011). The housing and neighborhood conditions of America's children: Patterns and trends over four decades. *Housing Policy Debate, 21*(2), 215–245.

Hwang, J. (2015). Gentrification in changing cities immigration, new diversity, and racial inequality in neighborhood renewal. *The ANNALS of the American Academy of Political and Social Science, 660*(1), 319–340.

Hwang, J., & Sampson, R. J. (2014). Divergent pathways of gentrification racial inequality and the social order of renewal in Chicago neighborhoods. *American Sociological Review, 79*(4), 726–751.

Immergluck, D. (2015). Examining changes in long-term neighborhood housing vacancy during the 2011 to 2014 U.S. national recovery. *Journal of Urban Affairs, 38*(5), 607–622.

Jacobs, D. E., Wilson, J., Dixon, S. L., Smith, J., & Evens, A. (2009). The relationship of housing and population health: A 30-year retrospective analysis. *Environmental Health Perspectives, 117*(4), 597–604.

Jewkes, M. D., & Delgadillo, L. M. (2010). Weaknesses of housing affordability indices used by practitioners. *Journal of Financial Counseling and Planning, 21*(1), 43–52.

Joint Center for Housing Studies of Harvard University. (2016). *The state of the nation's housing 2016.* Boston, MA: Harvard University. Retrieved from http://www.jchs.harvard.edu/research/state_nations_housing

Kingsley, G. T., Hendey, L., & Price, D. (2011). *Setting priorities for neighborhood stabilization: Guide to using foreclosure-response.org indexes.* Washington, DC: Urban Institute.

Krivo, L. J., Byron, R. A., Calder, C. A., Peterson, R. D., Browning, C. R., Kwan, M. P., & Lee, J. Y. (2015). Patterns of local segregation: Do they matter for neighborhood crime? *Social Science Research, 54*, 303–318.

Kutty, N. K. (2005). A new measure of housing affordability: Estimates and analytical results. *Housing Policy Debate, 16*(1), 113–142.

Leventhal, T., Martin, A., & Brooks-Gunn, J. (2004). The EC-HOME across five national data sets in the 3rd to 5th year of life. *Parenting, 4*(2–3), 161–188.

Leventhal, T., & Newman, S. (2010). Housing and child development. *Children and Youth Services Review, 32*(9), 1165–1174.

Marullo, S. (1985). Targets for racial invasion and reinvasion: Housing units where racial turnovers occurred, 1974–1977. *Social Forces, 63*(3), 748–774.

McMillen, D. P., & Dombrow, J. (2001). A flexible Fourier approach to repeat sales price indexes. *Real Estate Economics, 29*(2), 207–225.

Mikelbank, B. A. (2008). *Spatial analysis of the impact of vacant, abandoned, and foreclosed properties.* Retrieved from https://www.clevelandfed.org/newsroom-and-events/publications/special-reports/sr-200811-spatial-analysis-of-impact-of-vacant-abandoned-foreclosed-properties.aspx

Newman, G., Gu, D., Kim, J. H., & Li, W. (2016). Elasticity and urban vacancy: A longitudinal comparison of US cities. *Cities, 58*, 143–151.

Newman, K., & Wyly, E. K. (2006). The right to stay put, revisited: Gentrification and resistance to displacement in New York City. *Urban Studies, 43*(1), 23–57.

Newman, S. J. (2008). Does housing matter for poor families? A critical summary of research and issues still to be resolved. *Journal of Policy Analysis and Management, 27*(4), 895–925.

Newman, S. J., & Garboden, P. M. (2013). Psychometrics of housing quality measurement in the American Housing Survey. *Cityscape*, 293–306.

Raleigh, E., & Galster, G. (2015). Neighborhood disinvestment, abandonment, and crime dynamics. *Journal of Urban Affairs, 37*(4), 367–396.

Sampson, R. J., Raudenbush, S. W., & Earls, F. (1997). Neighborhoods and violent crime: A multilevel study of collective efficacy. *Science, 277*(5328), 918–924.

Schwartz, M., & Wilson, E. (2008). *Who can afford to live in a home?: A look at data from the 2006 American Community Survey*. US Census Bureau.

Sharkey, P. (2013). *Stuck in place: Urban neighborhoods and the end of progress toward racial equality*. Chicago: University of Chicago Press.

Shlay, A. B., & Whitman, G. (2006). Research for democracy: Linking community organizing and research to leverage blight policy. *City & Community, 5*(2), 153–171.

Silverman, R., Yin, L., & Patterson, K. L. (2013). Dawn of the dead city: An exploratory analysis of vacant addresses in Buffalo, NY 2008–2010. *Journal of Urban Affairs, 35*(2), 131–152.

Smith, N. (1998) Gentrification. In W. van Vliet (Ed.), *Encyclopedia of housing* (pp. 107–123). Thousand Oaks, CA: Sage.

Spain, D. (1980). Black-To-White successions in central-city housing limited evidence of urban revitalization. *Urban Affairs Review, 15*(4), 381–396.

Spielman, S. E., Folch, D., & Nagle, N. (2014). Patterns and causes of uncertainty in the American Community Survey. *Applied Geography, 46*, 147–157.

Stone, M. E. (2004). Shelter poverty: The chronic crisis of housing affordability. *New England Journal of Public Policy, 20*(1), 107–119.

Stone, M. E. (2006). What is housing affordability? The case for the residual income approach. *Housing Policy Debate, 17*(1), 151-184.

Taylor, R. B. (1996). Neighborhood responses to disorder and local attachments: The systemic model of attachment, social disorganization, and neighborhood use value. *Sociological Forum, 11*, 41–74.

Temkin, K., & Rohe, W. (1996). Neighborhood change and urban policy. *Journal of Planning Education and Research, 15*(3), 159–170.

Theodos, B., Coulton, C. J., & Pitingolo, R. (2015). Housing unit turnover and the socioeconomic mix of low-income neighborhoods. *The ANNALS of the American Academy of Political and Social Science, 660*(1), 117–135.

Totsika, V., & Sylva, K. (2004). The home observation for measurement of the environment revisited. *Child and Adolescent Mental Health, 9*(1), 25–35.

Vacant Properties Campaign. (2005). *Vacant properties: The true costs to communities*. Washington DC: National Vacant Properties Campaign.

Vigdor, J. L. (2002). Does gentrification hurt the poor? *Brookings–Wharton Papers on Urban Affairs*, 133–182.

Walker, C., & Winston, F. (2010). *A HMDA-based housing market index to track neighborhood change*. Washington, DC: The Local Initiatives Support Corporation.

Wardrip, K. E., & Pelletiere, D. (2008). Fully utilizing housing cost data in the American Community Survey PUMS data: Identifying issues and proposing solutions. *Cityscape*, 331–339.

Weaver, R. C., & Bagchi-Sen, S. (2013). Spatial analysis of urban decline: The geography of blight. *Applied Geography, 40*, 61–70.

Wu, F., & Takaro, T. K. (2007). Childhood asthma and environmental interventions. *Environmental Health Perspectives, 115*(6), 971–975.

Wyly, E. K., & Hammel, D. J. (1998). Modeling the context and contingency of gentrification. *Journal of Urban Affairs, 20*(3), 303–326.

11 COMMUNITY DISORDER, CRIME, AND VIOLENCE

The chapter presents measures related to community order and disorder, fear of crime, and exposure to community violence. This chapter also discusses methods currently used to examine crime and violence data. The importance of safety in communities is paramount to the overall well-being of residents and their quality of life. Researchers have attempted to measure factors in communities that affect actual crime as well as perceptions of safety, including the physical and social characteristics that represent order or disorder, residents' perceptions of crime and safety, and the exposure of residents to violence.

WHY IS IT IMPORTANT TO MEASURE DISORDER, CRIME, AND VIOLENCE?

Shaw and McKay (1942/1969) were among the first scholars to discuss the concept of social disorganization in communities in their research on juvenile delinquency. They referred to social disorganization as weakened social control in neighborhoods, including the lack of support and cooperation among institutions and organizations and the weakening of social norms and values that support safety. More recently, Sampson and Raudenbush (1999) argued that community disorder and the symbolism attached to it are "fundamental to the understanding of urban neighborhoods" (p. 604). The concept of disorder can be traced back to several scholars (Goffman, 1963; Hunter, 1985; Jacobs, 1961; Lofland, 1973 [all of these as cited by Sampson & Raudenbush, 1999]), who theorized that visible signs of disorder were associated with "incivilities" that disrupted the public life of communities. Perkins and Taylor (1996) argued that conditions of disorder or "incivility" symbolize to residents and visitors "a superficial neglect of the community [and] also an underlying breakdown in both local norms of behavior and formal and informal social controls" (pp. 66–67). Community disorder can signify residents' unwillingness to intervene to address neighborhood problems, including confronting strangers or calling the police when witnessing a crime (Greenberg & Rohe, 1986; Skogan, 1990). The "broken windows" theory, which is related to the concept of disorder, posits that public incivilities may attract predatory crime because potential offenders assume that residents are indifferent to what goes on in their neighborhood (Wilson & Kelling, 1982).

Prior research has demonstrated a connection between community disorder, fear of crime, and actual crime rates as well as other neighborhood structural characteristics, including unemployment, neighborhood disinvestment, and decline (Kelling & Coles, 1996; Perkins & Taylor, 1996, Skogan, 1990 as cited in Sampson & Raudenbush, 1999). However, broken windows theory can be used as a rationale for law enforcement to use more aggressive tactics, such as stop and frisk laws, as well as an acceleration of police-involved shootings. The labeling of communities as disorderly can also lead to stigmatization and blaming the victim, so researchers must be careful in how they use the measures in this book to identify factors contributing to crime and violence.

Several scholars, including Sampson and Raudenbush (1999), have challenged the broken windows theory, arguing that disorder is "part and parcel of crime" rather than a direct cause of crime. For example, a lack of social controls or norms may explain "both graffiti and robbery," thus researchers should examine the causal mechanisms rather than "inferring lack of order from graffiti and using it to explain robbery" (Sampson & Raudenbush, 1999, p. 608). Sampson and Raudenbush (1999) introduce the idea of "collective efficacy" (e.g., social cohesion among residents, along with a willingness to intervene to prevent crime) as a causal mechanism for explaining the incidence of crime and disorder in public spaces (note: measures of collective efficacy are included in Chapter 6 of this book). In fact, Shaw and McKay (1942/1969) also argued that prosocial shared values and informal social control could mediate the negative effects of social disorganization. Structural characteristics, such as poverty and residential instability, can undermine collective efficacy and informal social control, which can lead to increased crime and further disorder (Sampson & Raudenbush, 1999; Shaw & McKay, 1942/1969). Fear of crime and avoidance behaviors contribute to weakened informal social control and collective efficacy, as incivilities increase and potential offenders are emboldened (Skogan, 1990, as cited in Perkins & Taylor, 1996). Skogan (2015) argued that disorder independently and in tandem with conventional crime undermines neighborhood stability and undercuts the natural process of informal social control, discouraging community stability and stimulating fear of crime (pp. 480–481). Moreover, living in a neighborhood with high levels of disorder may adversely affect individual well-being, including increasing isolation, perceived powerlessness, stress, anxiety, depression, and poor health (Mooney et al., 2014; Ross, 1993; Ross & Mirowsky, 1999; Skogan, 2015). While fear of crime can be protective, signaling potential crime victims to use caution and avoid victimization, it can become a concern when excessive behaviors dramatically alter or change one's everyday life (Henson & Reyns, 2015).

Finally, exposure to crime and violence is a significant public health problem that can have detrimental effects, particularly among individuals living in urban neighborhoods, minorities, and youth. Neighborhood disadvantage, including residential instability and concentrated poverty, has been consistently linked to higher rates of violence (David-Ferdon & Simon, 2014; Peterson, Krivo, & Harris, 2000; Sampson, Raudenbush, & Earls, 1997). The link between violence and neighborhood disadvantage may be due to higher rates of disorganization and lower rates of informal social control (Peterson et al., 2000). Violence in disadvantaged communities can also be a deterrent to economic and social development, creating a cycle of disinvestment and violence (Rosenfeld, Messner, & Baumer, 2001). A lack of positive relationships among residents and views that violence is acceptable can also perpetuate youth violence (David-Ferdon & Simon, 2014).

A National Survey of Adolescents (Kilpatrick et al., 2000, as cited in Thompson et al., 2007, p. 454) showed that 39% of 12- to 17-year-olds reported having directly observed someone being shot, stabbed, sexually assaulted, mugged, robbed, or threatened with a weapon. The rate of adult exposure to community violence is also high in at-risk communities (DeCou & Lynch, 2017). In one study conducted in an urban high-risk neighborhood, 79% of adults reported direct exposure to community violence (Walling, Eriksson, Putman, & Foy, 2011). Prior research also demonstrates that children living in lower socioeconomic urban neighborhoods experience and witness community violence at high rates (Campbell & Schwarz, 1996, as cited in Suglia, Ryan, & Wright, 2008; Schubiner, Scott, & Tzelepis, 1993, as cited Suglia et al., 2008,

p. 479). Most youth living in urban areas have witnessed violent events, and a third or more report being a direct victim (Osofsky, Wewers, Hann, & Fick, 1993; Sheehan, DiCara, LeBaily, & Christoffel, 1997). Moreover, there are strong links between exposure to community violence and a range of health and mental health outcomes. Exposure to community violence among children and youth can lead to adverse cognitive (lowered educational outcomes), behavioral (substance abuse, poor peer relationships, higher rates of juvenile justice involvement, aggression), and poor health and mental health outcomes (obesity, morbidity, cardiac problems, stress, anxiety, and depression) (Cooley, Turner, & Beidel, 1995; Suglia et al., 2008; Thompson et al., 2007). Among adults, several studies have found a connection between exposure to community violence and PTSD (post-traumatic stress disorder), depression, and anxiety (DeCou & Lynch, 2017). Given the negative impact from exposure to community violence, it is critical to have valid and reliable measures for children, youth, and adults.

COMMUNITY DISORDER AND ORDER MEASURES

One of the first measures of community disorder was developed by Perkins and Taylor (1996) using three ecological methods: resident perceptions reported in surveys; on-site observations; and content analysis of crime and disorder-related newspaper articles. Through their study of Chicago neighborhoods, scholars Sampson and Raudenbush (1999) defined and develop measures of physical and social disorder at the neighborhood level. At around the same time, Ross and Mirowsky (1999) introduced a measure of perceived neighborhood disorder that also included both physical and social order and disorder. While Sampson and Raudenbush utilized systematic social observation to measure disorder, Ross and Mirowsky used survey methods to examine residents' perceptions of disorder.

Defining Community Disorder and Order

Perkins and Taylor (1996) defined community disorder as "social and physical conditions and events in a locale beyond the serious crimes that may be occurring there" (p. 64). Ross and Mirowsky (1999) defined perceived neighborhood disorder as "visible cues indicating a lack of order and social control in the community" (p. 413). On the other hand, "order is a state of peace, safety, and observance of the law, and control is an act of maintaining this order" (Ross & Mirowksy, 1999, p. 413). Social disorder involves signs and behaviors indicating "a lack of social control that involves people" (Ross & Mirowsky, 1999, p. 413), including behavior involving strangers that is considered threatening, such as "verbal harassment on the street, open solicitation for prostitution, public intoxication, and rowdy groups of young males in public" (Sampson & Raudenbush, 1999, pp. 603–604). Physical disorder refers to visible deterioration or signs of disorder in the overall physical appearance of a neighborhood (Ross & Mirowsky, 1999). Examples include deteriorated urban landscapes, such as "graffiti on buildings, abandoned cars, broken windows, and garbage in the streets" (Sampson & Raudenbush, 1999, p. 604), as well as vacant and dilapidated housing and unkempt lots (Perkins & Taylor, 1996). On the other hand, "visible signs of order include a clean, safe, quiet neighborhood where buildings are in good repair, police protection is good, crime is low, neighbors watch out for one another, and not a lot of young people are hanging out" (Ross & Mirowsky, 1999, p. 413). Skogan (2015) recently reviewed the state of research on disorder and decline, including the definitions discussed above as well as the British government's 1998 codification of antisocial behaviors that can be considered characteristics of social disorder. Skogan (2015) provides a detailed list of indicators of social disorder (see Skogan, 2015, Table I on p. 466) and physical disorder (see Skogan, 2015, Table II on p. 467) that have been used in the discussion and measurement of disorder. These indicators can be considered violations of health and safety codes, misdemeanors, or the consequences of neglect, underinvestment, economic distress, or lack of regard for others (Skogan, 2015). Skogan (2015) also provides an analysis of the various methods used to measure disorder (see Skogan, 2015, Table III on p. 476), including 911 data, systematic observation, resident surveys, and administrative records. Administrative and 911 data are more accessible and can be used to characterize small areas over time, including prior to, during, and after interventions. Surveys and systematic observation methods can be tailored to more closely match the theoretical and/or conceptual framework of one's study but can be more time consuming and expensive. Skogan (2015) also discussed validity issues, including whether or not conventional crime and disorder indicators load on separate factors. The results have been mixed; however, physical and social indicators of disorder typically form separate factors. The community order and disorder measures discussed below include survey and systematic social observation methods that have been used most frequently in the literature.

Measures of Community Disorder and Order

Perkins and Taylor's (1996) measures of **community disorder** are summarized in **Table 11.1.** The purpose of their study was to examine the relationship between three measures of disorder and residents' fear of crime. Their measure of fear of crime is also included in Table 11.1 (note: additional measures of fear of crime are discussed later in this chapter). The majority of disorder measures were based solely on residents' perceptions drawn from survey questions, with a few studies also examining observations of disorder (Taylor, Shumaker, & Gottfredson, 1985). Perkins and Taylor's (1996) study used three ecological measurement methods including (a) resident perceptions reported in surveys; (b) on-site observations by trained raters aggregated to the street-block level; and (c) content analysis of crime and disorder-related newspaper articles aggregated to the neighborhood level. These measures were based on several prior measures and studies conducted by Perkins and colleagues (Perkins, Meeks, & Taylor, 1992; Perkins, Wandersman, Rich, & Taylor, 1993).

The researchers argued that examining disorder at the block level was more relevant because disorder and fear may increase as the level of analysis gets smaller and "closer to home" (Perkins & Taylor, 1996, p. 69). Street blocks were used in the current study, defined as both sides of a street bounded by cross streets or a cross street and a dead end. The study included 50 street blocks in 50 different neighborhoods in Baltimore City, Maryland, which were randomly selected to participate in two waves of panel surveys to examine changes in sampled individuals and neighborhoods over time. Eight residents on each study block were interviewed. Data were also collected by trained, independent raters at the beginning of the study on the crime and fear-related physical environment of each block and from almost 70% of the respondent households. The third source of data was a 15-month archive of content-analyzed crime and disorder related articles from the city's major daily newspaper and a minority community newspaper (Perkins & Taylor, 1996, p. 72).

The researchers used correlational and hierarchical linear modeling to examine their results (Perkins & Taylor, 1996, pp. 96–97), with the key findings including the following:

- Resident perceptions of disorder contribute to fear at the individual and aggregate levels.

- Perceived disorder and observed disorder on fear are significant one year later.
- Social and physical disorder correlate with fear but physical disorder had higher block-level and individual level HLM coefficients than social disorder, and this effect was triangulated in all three assessment methods.
- Nonresidential physical disorder may contribute more to fear of crime.
- All three different ecological methods of assessing community disorder perform about the same, yielding comparably sized coefficients. There are no major differences in the proportions of Level II variance explained. Each explained about 6% to 8% of the total variation in estimated "true" fear scores.

In summary, the results demonstrated that all three methods produced reliable and valid measures of disorder. Criterion-related validity of the three measurement methods was "demonstrated by their roughly equal ability to predict subsequent fear of crime, even after controlling for the influence of variables that have been linked with fear in the research literature (race, sex, age, and victimization)" (Perkins & Taylor, 1996, p. 94). Furthermore, the results showed that gender and age were related to fear of crime. The proportion of non-White respondents on the block was also related, but when disorder was controlled, the relationship weakened.

Table 11.2 presents Sampson and Raudenbush's (1999) measure of **public disorder**, which used a data collection method called **systematic social observation**. The purpose of their study was to assess the causes and consequences of public disorder and to test the theory of collective efficacy and structural constraints on crime and disorder at the neighborhood level (Sampson & Raudenbush, 1999, p. 603). The researchers used "novel systematic procedures for collecting observational assessments of public spaces using videotaping procedures that produce a permanent visual record amenable to later coding and reinterpretation based on emergent insights" (Sampson & Raudenbush, 1999, p. 605). They also formulated "a hierarchical item-response model that identifies sources of error in aggregating across observed disorder items within block faces and in aggregating across block faces within some 200 census tracts" (Sampson & Raudenbush, 1999, p. 605). They argue that these methods result in high tract-level reliabilities for assessing social and physical disorder. The study also examined the sources and consequences of disorder by testing the association between systematically observed disorder and official measures of recorded and survey-reported crime, sociodemographic data from the census, and a survey measure of residents' perceived collective efficacy.

Table 11.2 includes Sampson and Raudenbush's (1999) observed measure of physical and social disorder as well as the other survey and administrative measures of crime used in their study. For their measure of observed disorder, "trained observers drove a sport utility vehicle (SUV) at a rate of five miles per hour down every street in 196 Chicago census tracts." Observations were made on face blocks, which are the block segments on one side of a street, so that "buildings across the street from one another on any city block comprised two separate units of observation" (Samson & Raudenbush, 1999, p. 616). As the SUV drove down the street, a pair of video recorders, one located on each side of the SUV, captured social activities and physical features of both face blocks simultaneously, and two trained observers, one on each side of the SUV, recorded their observations onto an observer log for each block face. The hours of observation were between 7 a.m. and 7 p.m. The data collected on the logs focused on land use, traffic, the physical condition of buildings, and evidence of disorder. A random sample of video recordings were viewed and then coded (Sampson &

Raudenbush, 1999, pp. 617–618). The results of the study demonstrated that their systematically observed measures of physical and social public disorder were robust ecological constructs that were reliably measured at the neighborhood level (Sampson & Raudenbush, 1999, p. 637).

- Structural characteristics, particularly mixed land use and concentrated poverty, were strongly related to social and physical disorder; collective efficacy predicted lower observed disorder, perceived disorder, and predatory crime, after controlling for sociodemographic and land use characteristics. Collective efficacy maintained a significant relationship with violent crime.
- However, the broken windows theory was not supported because disorder was not related to crime in four of five tests when controlling for neighborhood characteristics; thus predatory crime and public disorder are explained by the same constructs at the neighborhood level, particularly concentrated disadvantage and lower collective efficacy (Sampson & Raudenbush, 1999, p. 637).

In a separate article, Raudenbush and Sampson (1999) describe the science of "ecometrics" as a method for assessing ecological settings, including examining bias and random error in neighborhood assessments. They argue that ecological assessments are conceptually distinct from individual-level assessments that aggregate individual constructs and use psychometric methods for evaluating their reliability and validity. Raudenbush and Sampson (1999) describe the value of the ecometric assessment of ecological measures to assess measurement reliability and validity. The article describes in detail the science of ecometrics and presents a three-level hierarchical model that identifies "sources of error in aggregating across items within face blocks and in aggregating across face blocks to larger geographic units such as census tracts" (Raudenbush & Sampson, 1999, p. 2). More information on ecometrics is included in Chapter 3.

More recently, Conley and colleagues (Conley, Stein, & Davis, 2014) adapted Sampson and Raudenbush's public disorder measure in their study of observed and residential perceptions of public disorder. The purpose of their study was to identify the scale of resident-defined neighborhoods (bespoke neighborhoods) and their impact on the correlation between systematic observations of disorder and residents' perceptions of disorder. Bespoke neighborhoods are defined as circular areas or regions around residents' homes, including the nearest individuals to their home (Conley et al., 2014). The researchers argue that community policing efforts and efforts to facilitate collective efficacy can be more successful if they focus on residents' perceptions of their neighborhood, including neighborhood boundaries. Their study assessed neighborhood size by using measures of perceived and observed disorder as proxies to configure neighborhood boundaries. **Table 11.3** describes their measures of **observed and perceived physical disorder** at the neighborhood level. The measure of observed disorder in the Conley and colleagues study is derived from Sampson and Raudenbush's (1999) measure described in Table 11.2, utilizing several of their items. However, Conley and colleagues (2014) add other items to their measure, incorporate the type of land use, and the index for each street segment was a weighted sum of each of the disorder items. Objective measures of disorder were collected through systematic social observations (SSOs). Observations were collected by the original research team for each block segment within the defined area. A one-page instrument was used to collect information as they traveled each street by foot. Information was recorded by two researchers on each block to ensure inter-rater reliability.

The observed disorder scale in Conley and colleagues' (2014) study had acceptable inter-rater reliabilities. The researchers evaluated the relationship between residents' perceptions of disorder and the SSO measures of disorder using a series of concentric circles as different definitions of the local neighborhood in order to identify which neighborhood size most strongly correlated with its observed and perceived disorder.

- The results demonstrated an increasing correlation between residents' perceptions of disorder and observed disorder as the radius of the residents' bespoke neighborhoods increased in size (Conley et al., 2014, p. 194). However, the relationship between perceived and objective disorder was weak.
- Perceptions of the neighborhood were interpreted by respondents as encompassing a larger area beyond their street block.
- Larger areas constitute neighborhoods in terms of matching residents' perceptions of disorder and observations of disorder. Residents may also see disorder as a problem in the area surrounding their residence but not on their immediate street block (Conley et al., 2014).

Prior research suggests that residents may become desensitized to the physical disorder in their neighborhoods through daily exposure to it, so residents' perceptions may not align with observations of disorder (Perkins et al., 1993, as cited in Conley et al., 2014, p. 198). It is possible that residents may become more aware of disorder as new or increased incidents of disorder occur (Conley et al., 2014, p. 198).

Ross and Mirowsky (1999) also developed measures of perceived **physical and social disorder (Table 11.4)** around the same time as Sampson and Raudenbush (1999). The goal of Ross and Mirowsky's study (1999) was to systematically define the concept of disorder, and measure and empirically assess the relationships between perceptions of crime and disorder, order and disorder, and physical and social disorder (p. 413). Similar to other disorder measures discussed so far, Ross and Mirowsky's (1999) measure includes both physical and social disorder; however, their conceptualization also includes reports of crime in the area and both ends of the continuum from order to disorder. The appendix of their article also contains items of social and physical disorder that were used in prior studies. The results of their study showed that the perceived neighborhood disorder scale had high reliability, external validity, and demonstrated distinctions as well as overlaps between physical and social disorder (Ross & Mirowsky, 1999, p. 425).

- An exploratory factor analysis was conducted that indicated that physical and social order and disorder loaded on one factor.
- Construct validity was assessed using a covariance structure model using EQS. The results from this assessment showed that most indicators loaded on the disorder factor, four indicators loaded on both the disorder factor and a decay factor, and two indicators loaded on the decay factor alone (pp. 418–419). Disorder included both social and physical cues that social order is weak, and physical decay included physical problems with buildings. Reports of crime in the neighborhood loaded highly and significantly on disorder.
- The final results demonstrated a high correlation between disorder and decay and that they share many indicators. The presence of graffiti, noise, and vandalism, along with reports that a neighborhood is not "clean" indicate both social disorder and physical decay. The physical aspects of

> a neighborhood (such as graffiti, noise, vandalism, dirt, and grime) are important indicators of the breakdown of social control, clear cues to residents that people are not involved (Ross & Mirowsky, 1999, p. 419).

The authors argue that order and disorder form two ends of a single continuum. They suggest that researchers can combine disorder and decay and use all 15 items in one scale or separate the two items that are pure physical decay (abandoned buildings and well-maintained houses and apartments), depending on their purposes. A related study is O'Brien and Kauffman's (2013) study of adolescent prosociality that used Ross and Mirowsky's (1999) four items of neighborhood physical decay and Sampson and Raudenbush's (1999) measure of collective efficacy. The results showed that adolescent prosociality was lower in neighborhoods with greater physical disorder; however, objective and perceived disorder had no significant relationship with prosociality when controlling for collective efficacy, demonstrating that levels of disorder and lower prosociality were co-symptoms of a neighborhood weak in collective efficacy (O'Brien & Kauffman, 2013, p. 366).

Finally, Mooney and colleagues (2014) developed an ecometric measure of **neighborhood physical disorder** constructed by using **virtual street audit (Table 11.5).** The researchers used indicators of physical disorder from Sampson and Raudenbush's study (1999) of Chicago neighborhoods as well as two other indicators from prior research. They trained eleven auditors to assess nine disorder items on 1,826 block faces using *Google Street View Imagery* in four cities (Mooney et al., 2014, p. 626). The results of their study demonstrated a novel and cost effective approach for measuring disorder that was reliable and valid.

- Census measures were generally correlated as expected, with the average estimated level of neighborhood physical disorder within a census tract across 10 conditional realizations.
- Results showed that U.S. Census data on unemployment and housing vacancy were positively correlated with their measure of disorder, while owner-occupied housing was negatively correlated with disorder.
- Geospatial techniques used in this study demonstrated the convergent and divergent validity of the disorder measure (Mooney et al., 2014, p. 630).

The authors argue that "combining ecometric measures with spatial interpolations offers more flexibility to define neighborhood boundaries. Spatial interpolation predicts the level of disorder on streets not sampled based on the spatial correlation of disorder ecometrically measured on a sample of streets, allowing researchers to estimate the level of physical disorder and confidence bounds around the estimate for all streets in a city" (Mooney et al., 2014, p. 627).

FEAR OF CRIME

Fear of crime is associated with residents' emotional response and vulnerable feelings when faced with dangerous conditions or the possibility of victimization that can influence how freely people move about in the places where they live (Perkins & Taylor, 1996). Research on the fear of crime goes back to the creation of the Commission on Law Enforcement and Administration of Justice by President Lyndon B. Johnson in 1964 (Henson & Reyns, 2015). The Commission conducted research on social and crime issues, including reports about crime and victimization in the United States. The results showed that crime had "a major impact on individuals' daily lives, even if they had never been victimized, a finding which had previously been dismissed" (Henson & Reyns, 2015, p. 91). A more recent study found that "40 percent of Americans admit to being afraid of crime, and that fear has a negative impact on their lives" (Saad, 2010, as cited in Henson & Reyns, 2015, p. 91). More recent studies have also examined relationships between fear of crime and other neighborhood indicators. For example, Ferguson and Mindel (2007) found that several forms of social capital lowered fear of crime, including police presence in the neighborhood, social support networks, neighborhood satisfaction, and collective efficacy. Scarborough and colleagues (Scarborough, Like-Haislip, Novak, Lucas, & Alarid, 2012) found that the structure of a neighborhood predicted fear of crime, even after controlling for several demographic characteristics, and that disorder was strongly associated with fear of crime.

Defining Fear of Crime

One of the earliest substantive reviews of fear of crime measurement was conducted by Ferraro and LaGrange in 1987, who argued that one of the major problems in conceptualizing and measuring fear of crime is when researchers confound fear of crime with crime risk or vulnerability. Ferraro and LaGrange (1987) argued that fear of crime is emotional rather than values or judgments about crime, risk of crime, or safety concerns. They argue that fear of crime is one's emotional reaction to crime or the symbols associated with crime or potential victimization that involves changes in bodily functions alerting individuals to potential danger (Ferraro & LaGrange, 1987, p. 72). Fear of crime can be both an effect and a cause related to one's judgments about risk. However, measuring judgments about risk of crime is not the same as measuring fear of crime; fear of crime is conceptually distinct from judgments (risk) and concerns (values) about crime (Ferraro & LaGrange, 1987, p. 73). For example, asking residents about how safe they feel walking alone at night in their neighborhood more accurately assesses risk to self rather than fear of crime because it does not examine an emotional reaction (Ferraro & LaGrange, 1987, p. 76). Ferraro and LaGrange (1987) also argue that the fear of crime or victimization varies widely by the type of crime, with violent personal crimes (e.g., assault, robbery, rape) being the most feared types of crime (p. 74). Therefore, the most valid and reliable measures of fear of crime specify the type of crime to the respondent but also differentiate emotional reactions from judgments. Ferraro and LaGrange (1987) provided suggestions for measuring fear of crime including: (a) ask respondents about their fears, using statements such as "how afraid are you . . .?" (b) make an explicit reference to crime; (c) reference specific crimes or types of victimization (e.g., how afraid are you of being a victim of robbery on your block at night?); and (d) ask respondents how they feel in everyday situations not hypothetical situations (e.g., "in your everyday life") (p. 78). Ferraro and LaGrange's (1987) review of 46 measures of fear of crime demonstrated that 44 were single item measures and the majority did not meet all of their criteria. In fact, two of the most commonly used measures of fear of crime developed in the early 1970s asked people about their fears associated with walking alone or being out alone at night (Henson & Reyns, 2015). Measures in the 1980s incorporated some of the criteria suggested by Ferraro and LaGrange, including specifying the potential crime threat; and Likert scales were used increasingly in the 1990s (Henson & Reyns, 2015). However, there has been little agreement or research on the appropriate range for measuring the intensity of fear of crime (Henson & Reyns, 2015).

While Ferraro and LaGrange's (1987) definition of fear of crime is one of the more frequently used, there continues to be no universally accepted definition of fear of crime (Henson & Reyns, 2015). However, Lane and colleagues (Lane, Rader, Henson,

Fisher, & May, 2014) argued that most definitions share several key elements, including the following: (a) fear of crime is a negative emotional response; (b) the response is the result of a threat or potential threat of victimization or of being harmed; and (c) the fear occurs because of the immediacy or potential imminence of the threat or potential threat. Thus, fear of crime can be more concisely defined as "an emotional response to a danger or threat of an actual or potential criminal incident" (Henson & Reyns, 2015, p. 92). Despite substantial research on the fear of crime, there is limited research examining current measurement tools. Moreover, these various definitions have led to different ways to measure fear of crime.

Measures of Fear of Crime

A recent review of fear of crime measurement was conducted by Farrall and colleagues (Farrall, Bannister, Ditton, & Gillchrist, 1997), which examined research methodologies used to evaluate fear of crime. Several criticisms were examined, including the possibility that fear of crime was significantly misrepresented, including the limited range of responses to crime and inaccurately portraying fear of crime. In their review, Farrall and colleagues (1997) argued that several issues need to be addressed in future attempts to measure fear of crime, including (a) validating fear of crime measures; (b) measuring fear of crime as a multi-faceted phenomenon; (c) examining changes in the level of fear and emotional responses to particular victimization events at different times; (d) using questions to ask about crime experiences in ways other than the usual "last 12 months"; (e) examining why individuals may feel fearful after asking general questions about fear; and (f) asking about the social, temporal, and geographical aspects of fear of crime, including specific areas in which they feel unsafe. **Table 11.6** describes measures for examining **fear of crime** that were suggested by Farrall and colleagues (1997) from their research in Great Britian. A qualitative interview with residents informed the development of their quantitative measure of fear of crime. The qualitative interview had questions about worry about crime, the safety of their area, safety-related behaviors, prior victimization, and other related questions. The quantitative fear of crime measure also includes questions about worry, victimization, safety, and worry about other things.

Table 11.7 describes a later study by Farrall and Ditton (1999) that assessed the validity of questions used to examine **fear of crime**. It is important to note that Farrall and colleagues (1997, 1999) incorporate the recommendations for fear of crime measures suggested by Ferraro and LaGrange (1987), which are described above. Farrall and colleagues' (1997) fear of crime measure consisted of three emotional and cognitive elements: (a) thinking or being aware of crime; (b) fearing, being afraid, or feeling anxious about crime; and (c) feeling anger, outrage or annoyance about crime (p. 58). The sample in their study consisted of four areas, two inner-city areas and two outlying areas near Glasgow, Scotland (Farrall & Ditton, 1999). Two of the areas were poor and two considered as more affluent areas. The researchers measured fear of crime using a quantitative survey; however, they also conducted follow-up qualitative interviews with a subsample of residents to address conceptualization of the questions in their quantitative measure. The follow-up validity interviews focused on the respondents' understanding of the questions asked of them, the design of the questions, and general issues surrounding whether the respondent had given answers for themselves or "general" answers (not concerned with their own anxiety levels but with how much of a problem they thought crime was for other groups). The researchers examined the extent to which respondents interpreted the questions and the social contexts and meanings that they inferred from the question. Farrall and Ditton (1999) also examined the reliability of the data they generated, including the extent to which respondents reported similar answers to the same question when repeatedly asked. The consistency between the survey interviews and the validity interviews was also examined. Respondents were asked to complete the new fear of crime questions three times: once during the survey interview and twice during the validity interview (once without seeing the codes at the start of the interview, and once again at the very end of the interview, this time seeing the codes) (Farrall & Ditton, 1999, p. 63). By repeatedly asking the same question, the researchers examined consistency: (a) over *time* for the same question procedure (by comparing the closed-ended questions); (b) over *format* between interviews (by comparing the survey questions and the open-ended validity questions) and (c) over *format* during the *same* interview (by comparing open and closed-ended questions during the validity interview). The results of their study demonstrated that validity assessments have some value, even when small numbers of follow-ups are undertaken.

- Factor analyses were later conducted by Farrell et al.; demonstrating that the 12 quantitative questions formed a distinct pattern: All of the "angry" questions loaded together on one factor, and all of the "think" and "afraid" questions formed another factor. This finding suggests the usefulness in asking respondents about their different emotional responses to various crimes (Farrall & Ditton, 1999, p. 65).
- In other research conducted by the authors, they also found that more people reported being very angry than very afraid (see Ditton et al. 1999) and respondent's levels of anger were greater than their levels of being afraid and that this was consistently the case across age groups, gender, victims, and nonvictims and offence type (Farrall & Ditton, 1999, p. 67).

Table 11.8 describes Jackson's (2005) validated measure of **fear of crime** from his research in England and Wales. Contrary to prior research and theory, Jackson's (2005) definition of fear of crime combines several constructs into a multi-dimensional measure, including "worry events, subjective risk perceptions and assessments and interpretations of the social and physical environment that shape the social meaning of risk and sense of possibility" (p. 300). Jackson argued that prior measures of fear of crime fail to capture its richness and complexity and result in a lack of reliability and validity. Jackson (2005) stated that his fear of crime measure consisted of "empirically distinct but related constructions that combine emotion, risk perception and vulnerability, and environmental perception" (pp. 300–301). The emotional component focuses on worry versus anxiety or fear; worry is conceptualized as an emotional evaluation as well as a mental state. Jackson's appraisal of threat or risk includes feelings of control over, severity of consequences, and the likelihood of victimization. Jackson (2005) also argued that environmental perceptions of the social and physical environment shape one's appraisal of potential threats, including attitudes toward community cohesion and perceptions of incivilities. The purpose of the study was to assess whether particular survey questions scaled to form adequate measures of the fear of crime constructs, whether the constructs were empirically distinct, and how the constructs formed a process explanation of the fear of crime (Jackson, 2005, p. 303). Confirmatory factor analyses were used to test a priori theoretical explanations of Jackson's fear of crime constructs.

- The results demonstrated that "when respondents were asked about worry, risk perceptions and beliefs about crime prevalence, their responses indicated that they thought about crime in two domains: personal crime in public spaces and burglary. The measures of the five constructs that involved these offence categories had good scaling properties. Furthermore, respondents treated worry, perceived likelihood, perceived control, perceived consequences and beliefs about crime as separate things" (Jackson, 2005, p. 306).

- The results suggest that "perceptions of the environment" (incivilities and community cohesion) are shaped by respondents' assessments of the incidence of crime and of one's personal threat and vulnerability (including control and likelihood).
- Control and consequences predicted perceptions of the likelihood of being a victim; all aspects of threat predicted worry.
- Different levels of worry of respondents in the two areas were mediated by environmental perceptions and threat appraisal (Jackson, 2005, p. 307).

Alper and Chappell (2012) examined the predictive power of three theoretical models on offense type-specific, emotionally based fear of violent and property crime in the United States: the vulnerability and disorder models, which focus on facilitators of fear, and the social integration model, which focuses on inhibitors of fear. According to the vulnerability model "those who feel unable to defend themselves, either physically or socially, will experience more fear," including women, the elderly, those with low SES, and victims of crime (Alper & Chappell, 2012, p. 349). The disorder model is based on Shaw and McKay's (1972) research and broken windows theory, which argues that neighborhood incivilities influence perceptions of crime. As unresolved physical deterioration and social disorder grow progressively worse, "escalating into more serious crime and less social control," residents may withdraw from social life and become more fearful of crime (Alper & Chappell, 2012, p. 349). The social integration model argues that fear can be reduced when residents collectively respond and address neighborhood problems, which increases social capital, social cohesion, and collective efficacy. These social processes, in turn, mediate the relationship between fear of crime and neighborhood structural characteristics that are often associated with increased crime and violence, such as poverty and ethnic heterogeneity (Alper & Chappell, 2012, p. 349). Alper and Chappell's (2012) measure of fear of crime (Table 11.9) is included in this chapter because it is one of the more recent studies that theoretically examined predictors of violent and property-related measures of fear of crime. **Table 11.9** describes the **fear of crime** measure used in their study, as well as measures examining the three predictive models.

- The predictors consistently explained more of the variation in the fear of property crime.
- The strongest model predicting fear of violent crime was the social integration model.
- The strongest model predicting fear of property crime was the disorder model.
- The social integration model was the weakest model in predicting this fear of property crime.
- Trusting one's neighbors has more of an effect on fear of violent crime than perceptions of disorder or prior victimization.
- Trust has less of an effect on fear of property crime than perceptions of disorder or prior victimization.

- The vulnerability model was less consistent. When the variables from the other theoretical models were added, the effects of victimization on fear of violent crime disappeared. While those who have been victimized are more fearful of violent crime, that variation is explained away by the level of perceived disorder and perceived trust.
- Race and education were better predictors of fear of property crime than fear of violent crime Alper & Chappel, 2012, p. 359–360.

In summary, the results demonstrated that multiple processes explain predictors of fear of crime and that no one theoretical model accounts for all of the variation. The researchers found that "all three theoretical models helped to explain fear of crime, with aspects of vulnerability, disorder, and social integration" significantly predicting fear of property crime and fear of violent crime (Alper & Chappell, 2012, p. 360). Their analysis also supports prior research by demonstrating the importance of using crime-specific fear of crime measures and separating the type of crimes (e.g., violent and property).

EXPOSURE TO COMMUNITY VIOLENCE

While prior research on the measurement of exposure to community violence among children and youth is fairly extensive, there is very little research on how to measure exposure to community violence among adults. DeCou and Lynch (2017) conducted a systematic review of the literature on the definition and assessment of community violence exposure among adults to identify studies that "(1) included a self-report of community violence exposure, (2) included primarily adult respondents, and (3) reported psychometric data" (p. 51). The results showed that only 17 studies fit their criteria. Moreover, with the exception of one study, the 17 studies in their review used measures that were initially developed for children and adolescents. Because their use is more widespread, this section focuses mainly on measures of exposure to community violence among children and youth. We also include a few measures noted by DeCou and Lynch (2017) as more widely used assessments of adult exposure to community violence.

Defining Exposure to Community Violence

DeCou and Lynch (2017) note that there is very little consensus about how to define exposure to community violence. However, several conceptual considerations have emerged out of the research on exposure to community violence among children, including the need to distinguish between "the community" and other settings, such as the home, school, and so forth, as well as the difference between direct and indirect exposure to community violence (e.g., witnessing versus victimization). While clear conceptualizations of other forms of violence (e.g., domestic violence, intimate partner violence, family violence) exist, clear definition of community violence is lacking, which makes it difficult to compare results across studies. DeCou and Lynch (2017) argue that "community violence be assessed as a distinct construct concerning one's public sense of safety and distinct from other forms of violence within the context of specific familial, romantic, or other intimate relationships" (p. 52). They offer the following definition: "community violence refers to the ubiquitous exposure (i.e., witnessing and victimization) to public acts of violence via threatened, witnessed, or completed victimization over time that is not perpetrated by an intimate partner or family member" (DeCou & Lynch, 2017, p. 52).

Measures of Exposure to Community Violence Among Children and Adolescents

Researchers argue that child reports of exposure to community violence are needed because parents often underestimate the amount and type of their children's exposure to violence (Richters & Martinez, 1992; Thompson et al., 2007). This may be because parents are not aware of their children's activities and/or companions or they underreport violence in the home and their children's exposure to it. Children's perceptions of exposure to violence are also important because violent events impact child development, health, and mental health (Thompson et al., 2007). While DeCou and Lynch (2017) argue that community violence measurement should focus exclusively on the public sphere, the measurement of children's exposure to violence has historically included measures of exposure to community or neighborhood violence as well as violence in the home.

One of the first measures was created by Cooley, Turner, and Beidel (1995), focusing on exposure to community violence outside of the home as well as exposure among three victims, including the child, strangers, and those familiar to the child (**Children's Report of Exposure to Violence or CREV**; see **Table 11.10**). The researchers developed an operational definition of community violence as "deliberate acts intended to cause physical harm against a person or persons in the community" (Cooley et al., 1995, p. 202). Their definition excluded accidental harm or injury, self-inflicted, or indirect acts of violence. The items generated by the authors were consistent with their definition and included items from other available instruments measuring children's exposure to community violence. The instrument was administered to schoolchildren between the ages of nine and 15 years. Test–retest reliability was examined with a small subsample two weeks later, and the reliability and factor structure of the scale were also examined.

- Results show that the CREV has good test–retest reliability and that the reliability of total scores is higher for males than females. The factor analysis indicated that 42.9% of the variance was accounted for in a two-factor model (Cooley et al., 1995, p. 206). The results showed that fit best into a two-factor model: 21 items loaded on to one factor, which was named "Direct Exposure," which included the "reported" and "witnessed" modes, and the other items related to fictional community violence loaded onto another factor named "Media Exposure." None of the "victim" content areas loaded on either factor (Cooley et al., 1995, p. 203).
- Results also showed that the CREV has good internal consistency reliability as well as construct validity, and no differences by race or gender were found in frequency of exposure to community violence. There were no demographic differences between girls and boys, and there were no significant gender differences in level of exposure to community violence. Results also suggest that exposure to violence may be an issue of socioeconomic status and setting, not race (Cooley et al., 1995, p. 207).
- Test–retest reliability: a small sample of the 228 were retested two weeks later ($n = 42$; 18.4%).
- The results demonstrated good test–retest reliability; there was no significant difference on any of the parameters assessed (Cooley et al., 1995, p. 204).

The researchers state that the measure may be useful to assess children's exposure to community violence in clinical settings, especially in cases where traumatic events may not be reported. The CREV may also be useful as a prompt when interviewing children to get more information (Cooley et al., 1995).

The earliest and most common measure to assess violence exposure in children, in its original and adapted forms, was developed by Richters and Martinez (1992) (see **Table 11.11: Things I Have Seen and Heard: Children's Exposure to Violence Scale**). The original measure included items related to children's exposure to violence in the community. The 1992 version also measured exposure to violence-related activities (drugs, arrests), exposure to violence within the home, direct experience of violence, and feelings of safety at home, school, and with adults in general. The measure was developed for children in Grades 1 and 2 and used a pictorial format for responses. The scale was examined for reliability and validity and compared to parental reports of exposure to violence. Overall, the results demonstrated that the scale had good short-term test–retest reliability (Richters & Martinez, 1992).

- The results from the first sample showed that the first- and second-grade children were two to six times more likely than their parents to report having witnessed violence.
- Agreement between boys and their parents on a summary measure of witnessed community violence was moderate.
- Agreement between girls and their parents was non-significant.
- Children who reported witnessing drugs and/or guns in their homes reported significantly higher levels of feeling threatened or victimized than the other children . . . but did not report higher levels of witnessing violence to others. These children also reported higher levels of fear in their homes (Richters & Martinez, 1992).

Thompson and colleagues (2007) used a modified version of Richters and Martinez's (1992) exposure scale (e.g., Things I Have Seen and Heard) in the Longitudinal Studies on Child Abuse and Neglect (LONGSCAN) (see **Table 11.12; Children's Exposure to Community Violence Scale**). Thompson and colleagues' (2007) study attempted to address several prior measurement issues, including lack of clarity around the conceptualization of violence exposure and how the measure was summed or scored. Thompson and colleagues (2007) argued that "exposure to violence is a heterogeneous phenomenon; unless this heterogeneity is acknowledged, limits will remain to understanding the nature of the events witnessed/experienced, the context in which they were experienced, and how traumatic the experiences are for the child or youth" (p. 455). In addition, there is little evidence or rationale that all types of violence are equally serious, thus summing all of the items and not acknowledging this issue can be a problem. There has also been a lack of a standardized approach to assessment. These measurement challenges have also been noted by other researchers (e.g., see the measure by Selner-O'Hagan and colleagues [1998] in the next section).

Thompson and colleagues' (2007) modified version of the Richter and Martinez's (1992) scale excluded items referring to victimization in response to ethical issues regarding mandated reporting of child maltreatment (Farrell & Bruce, 1997). Thus, six items were removed and replaced by five items associated with witnessing violent family and neighborhood behaviors. The purpose of Thompson and colleagues' (2007) study was to examine two different approaches to the Things I Have Seen and Heard Scale (Richter & Martinez, 1992): as an item-level list of experiences and as a multifactor index of violence exposure (p. 456). Their results suggested a two-factor solution: one on global/community violence and the other on violence in the home, confirming DeCou and Lynch's (2017) argument that these settings are distinct and should be analyzed separately. The results of Thompson and colleagues' study (2007) showed strong validity for their community violence subscale.

- Study One focused on item-level analysis of Things I Have Seen and Heard Scale and examined the validity of the individual items and cumulative change over time.
- Study Two focused on whether the Things I Have Seen and Heard Scale could be treated as a multi-item scale.
    - The results from the item-level analysis showed that there was modest support for the validity of the use of the scale as a single-item measure.
    - The factor structure suggested two subscales: Global/Community Violence and Violence in the Home.
    - There was a decrease in lifetime exposure to violence between ages 6 and 8. This raises questions relating to the utility of using the individual items as separate indicators of lifetime prevalence in young children. Change in individual item scores between ages 6 and 8 exhibited a weak relationship to other indicators of violence exposure and demographic/clinical variables.
    - White ethnicity was associated with a decrease in reports of lifetime exposure to one type of violence, and a Southwestern site was associated with a decrease in three types of violence.
    - Results of these analyses indicate issues associated with the use of the simple sum of all items on the Things I Have Seen and Heard Scale. Substantial support was demonstrated for the validity of the Global/Community Violence scale, especially at age 8 (Thompson et al., 2007, pp. 463–464).

The results also demonstrated the limitations to the use of self-reports of violence exposure in very young children, as well as the use of the measure as a single scale in high-risk samples. The community violence measure (from the Things I Have Seen and Heard Scale) is likely to be useful when a brief assessment of children's general exposure to violence is needed for research or clinical purpose (Thompson et al., 2007, p. 464).

Suglia, Ryan, and Wright (2008) also examined the Things I Have Seen and Heard Scale using the Rasch model, creating a scale that included event circumstance information previously shown to modify the impact of experienced events. Suglia and colleagues (2008) created a continuous scale from Richters and Martinez's (1992) measure to test the creation of a single latent construct of **Children's Exposure to Violence (ETV: Table 11.13)**. They also compared the Rasch ETC scale to a simpler sum ETV score and examined the effects of the ETV on post-traumatic stress symptoms among children in their study. The results showed that the Rasch model created a more parsimonious scale that was better at discriminating between children with low and high exposure to violence and more clearly associated with children's post-traumatic stress symptoms. The Rasch model demonstrated that increased levels of violence were related to higher post-traumatic stress symptoms, even after controlling for potential confounders (socioeconomic and demographic indicators as well as risk factors) (Suglia et al., 2008, pp. 483–484).

- Data were treated as repeated measurement data and the models were implemented using logistic nonlinear mixed models. These results were compared using the Rasch ETC score to this sum. Bivariate and multivariate regression analyses were completed, estimating the effect of the ETV scores on the child's post-traumatic stress symptoms, adjusting for confounder variables.

- The Rasch model incorporated the event circumstance information, created a more parsimonious and fit scale, discriminating between children with low- and high-violence exposure using all available information, including information that is conditional on other survey questions.
- The Rasch model produced a more adequate spread of items along the linear measurement summary scale, enhancing the power to detect differences in the effects across the scale (Suglia et al. 2008, p. 483–485).

More recently, Martin, Revington, and Seedat (2013) examined the psychometric properties of an adapted version of the Things I Have Seen and Heard Scale using a sample of trauma-exposed youth in South Africa **(Child Exposure to Community Violence [CECV]; Table 11.14).** The researchers sampled young children and teenagers, and examined the relationship between the CECV and PTSD. The factor analysis revealed that 29 of the 39 items created a more psychometrically adequate measure that consisted of three distinct subscales or factors.

- A Spearman rank order correlation test was used to assess the relationship between the Child PTSD Checklist (CPC) and the CECV. An independent samples Mann-Whitney U test was used to assess difference in mean rank scores on both the CECV and CPC and to assess differences in mean rank scores on the CECV in those with and without a formal diagnosis with PTSD. Missing data for the CECV and CPC were replaced by means of the k-nearest neighbor imputation method (Martin et al., 2013, p. 602).
- The examination of the factor structure of the 39-item CECV showed that there were three distinct factors consisting of 29 of the original 39 items:
  - Witnessing general violent/criminal acts
  - Directly experiencing and witnessing family and non-family violence and threats of physical harm
  - Directly experiencing non-family sexual abuse and general feelings of unsafety
- The briefer 29-item measure is more psychometrically adequate (Martin et al., 2013, pp. 604–606).

In summary, the results showed a highly significant, positive association between exposure to community violence and PTSD; significantly higher exposure to community violence was found among adolescents in high school compared with primary school children. However, no significant differences were found by ethnicity or gender (Martin et al., 2013, p. 606).

Measures of Exposure to Community Violence Among Adults

Several adult measures on exposure to community violence have adapted some of the child measures included above. The measure most commonly used to assess adult exposure to community violence was adapted from the **Survey of Exposure to Community Violence (SECV)** that was originally developed for children and youth (Richters & Saltzman, 1990). The full measure includes 54 items that assess both direct and indirect violence in the home, school, and community. Nine of the 17 studies reviewed by DeCou and Lynch (2017) used the SECV or a modified version of this scale. The SECV measure was developed by Richters and Saltzman (1990), which is related to a similar measure of exposure to community violence among children (Richters & Martinez, 1992) described above (e.g., Table 11.11, Things I Have Seen and Heard). The original SECV contains 54 items; however, most studies on adults modify the scale and reduce the number of items to between nine and 27. Several studies are discussed in this chapter, one focusing on low-income residents and the other that more rigorously tested the SECV on college students. Scarpa and/or Scarpa and colleagues (for example, please see Scarpa et al., 2002; Scarpa, Hurley, Shumate, & Haden, 2006) conducted a series of nine studies testing the SECV among young adults, mainly college students. The Scarpa and colleagues' (2002) study replicating and extending the findings from a study by Scarpa (2001) on community violence exposure among low-risk college students is described here. The purpose of Scarpa and colleagues' (2002) study was to validate the **SECV (see Table 11.15)**, including examining lifetime community violence exposure among college students, and assessing the psychological impact of violence exposure among witnesses and victims. The results of the study demonstrated the validity of the SECV by showing that a majority of the participants experienced some violence during their lifetime and that a higher level of violence exposure was associated with higher levels of depression, anxiety, interpersonal personality problems, and PTSD (Scarpa et al., 2002). The extent of exposure was examined through the following methods:

- Prevalence was considered as the percentage of respondents who reported experiencing any of the violent items at least once.
- For the significance of exposure, prevalence was considered as the percentage of respondents who reported (a) exposure to any item at least three times in their lifetime and (b) exposure to three or more different forms of violence in their lifetime.
- Overall, 92.7% of respondents reported witnessing and 75.7% being victimized by some form of violence at least once in their lifetime (Scarpa et al., 2002, p. 260).

The researchers also assessed the construct validity of the SECV by comparing it to a self-report of violent trauma and to groups with and without PTSD (Scarpa et al., 2002). The results showed that as violent trauma reports increased, so did reports of community violence exposure, showing that the SECV yielded similar results that were consistent with those related to interpersonal violence (Scarpa et al., 2002).

- To validate the SECV, a chi-square analysis examined the relationship between the three levels of SECV victimization (low, moderate, and high) and violent traumatic events (Vrana & Lauterbach, 1994). Results of the chi-square were significant, suggesting that scores on the SECV may accurately reflect exposure to violence in the community.
- To further validate the SECV, Mann-Whitney U analyses were conducted to compare the PTSD and non-PTSD groups on victimization and witnessing scores from the SECV. The results showed that individuals who met criteria for PTSD reported higher levels of both violence victimization and witnessing (Scarpa et al., 2002, pp. 263–265).
- One-way analyses of variance (ANOVAs) were conducted to assess the relationship between exposure to violence and difficulties in psychological adjustment in both victims and witnesses. Results indicated significant

group differences for depression, aggression, interpersonal problems associated with personality disorder, and PTSD symptomatology, but not for trait anxiety (Scarpa et al., 2002, pp. 265–266).

Mitchell and colleagues (2009) examined community violence exposure among African American mothers living in violence-prone neighborhoods in Washington, D.C., using the SECV. Their study examined the link between mothers' exposure to community violence, mothers' discipline, and child behavior as well as the interplay between maternal and child violence exposure (Mitchell et al., 2009). Mitchell and colleagues' study found that African American mothers with high levels of exposure to community violence were more likely to use harsh disciplinary practices. The results of most studies on the SECV demonstrate that it is a reliable measure (DeCou & Lynch, 2017).

The final study of adult exposure to community violence comes out of the Project on Human Development in Chicago Neighborhoods (which is discussed in several other chapters in this book). Selner-O'Hagan, Kindlon, Buka, Raudenbush and Earls (1998) utilized the **My ETV (Exposure to Violence)** structured-interview scale that assesses lifetime and past-year exposure to 18 types of community violence (**Table 11.16**). This is an adapted version of the scale examined by Suglia et al. (2008) to assess exposure to violence among children and youth (see Table 11.13). Similar to the SECV, the My ETV consists of witnessing and victimization subscales; however, it does not distinguish between public or at home or exclude sexual violence. The My ETV measure is included in this chapter because it is one of the few measures of adult exposure to community violence that has been rigorously examined for its psychometric properties and its validity. Selner-O'Hagan and colleagues (1998) examined the My ETV among an ethnically diverse and stratified sample of residents in 80 Chicago neighborhoods. While this study included children under age 18, the majority (55%) of the respondents were older than 18 years old. Selner-O'Hagan and colleagues (1998) state that one of the "primary challenges in the area of measure development is to create an instrument that contains items covering a broad range of events in terms of severity and that addresses victimization and witnessed violence separately" (p. 216). Another issue is how the ETV is scored, using equal intervals between the ordinal scale points that are quite different, such as between 0 (no exposure) and 1 (exposed once), and between 7 (exposed once a week) to 8 (exposed every day). Moreover, giving equal weight to all types of exposure is a problem when there are clear qualitative differences between being a victim of a knife attack versus hearing gunshots; however, both are scored the same on most versions of the ETV.

Selner-O'Hagan and colleagues' (1998) study represents the third phase in the development of a new ETV measure that attempts to address several of the challenges mentioned above. Prior attempts using the Rausch method (also used by Suglia and colleagues to examine the ETV with children, see Table 11.13) demonstrated that the ETV was a latent construct, so the initial ETV was expanded to cover a wider range of violence events and renamed the My ETV. The current study tested the hypothesis that the responses to questions on My ETV depended on a single latent variable and also examined the reliability (internal consistency and test–retest) and construct validity of the scale. The results demonstrated that the My ETV was a reliable and valid instrument. The data from the scale were fit into a Rasch model that generated interval-level measures and allowed the characterization of both acute and chronic exposure to community violence.

- The fit statistics for the six scales that covered lifetime and past-year victimization, witnessing, or both were all good. Construct validity was demonstrated through item analysis and bivariate associations.

- Validity was initially examined using item analysis, which revealed a theoretically sensible ordering of item extremity. Bivariate analysis showed that the ETV predicted age, gender, race/ethnicity, violent offending and neighborhood crime.
- The results showed that younger participants in the study reported less exposure than the older participants, males reported more exposure than females, and African Americans reported higher levels than Whites (Selner O'Hagan et al., 1998, p. 222).
- Furthermore, violent offenders reported more exposure than non-offenders, and those living in high-crime areas reported more exposure than those living in low-crime areas.
- Construct validity was also examined using Rasch modeling. Results indicated that the response data fit the Rasch model well and that the psychometric soundness of the scale was supported (Selner O'Hagan et al., 1998).

The authors suggest that future research examine the association between the My ETV and antisocial behaviors as well as mental health (e.g., PTSD).

CRIME, VIOLENCE, AND RELATED DATA

Finally, researchers can access a variety of administrative data sources to examine actual crime and related incidents at the neighborhood level, including surveillance data, police records, mortality, juvenile justice and school data, and health records from emergency departments, ambulance records, and the chief medical examiner (Azrael et al., 2009; Farrell, Henry, Bradshaw, & Reischl, 2016; Masho, Schoeny, Webster, & Sigel, 2016). Crime incident data can be collected from local police and law enforcement agencies, including the violent crime rate, the number of violent crimes, and the number of violent crimes with youth or adults involved. For youth or adult-involved crimes, researchers can examine homicides, shootings, aggravated or sexual assaults, theft, and arrest data (Farrell et al., 2016; Masho et al., 2016). The Uniform Crime Reporting system classifies Part I and Part II crimes. Part I crimes include homicide/murder, rape, robbery, aggravated assault, burglary, theft, vehicle theft, arson, violent crimes, and property crimes (UCR Statistics, n.d.). Part II crimes include but are not limited to misdemeanor assault, vandalism, prostitution, child abuse, criminal trespass, embezzlement, forgery, and drug offenses. Crime data can be examined at the block, census tract, or community level, along with other spatial and demographic data. Crime data also has high face validity and can be analyzed over time to examine trends, but it may be biased toward racial stereotyping and specific neighborhoods (Masho et al., 2016). Moreover, sexual assault data is often underreported and the data are affected by reporting practices.

Data on death rates can be accessed from the National Violent Death Reporting System (NVDRS), including homicide and suicide, unintentional firearm, legal intervention, and child abuse and maltreatment fatalities (Masho et al., 2016). This data can be examined in detail and is linked to other types of data, including crime data. This data also includes rates by different demographic and geographic characteristics; however, this data is not nationally representative and is only available for 17 states. Mortality data can be accessed from state vital statistics data, including death by homicide or suicide, and this data can also be analyzed spatially (Masho et al., 2016).

Other sources of data from health and youth-related agencies can also provide crime and violence-related data that researchers and practitioners can examine. Emergency departments collect data on patients' demographic characteristics, diagnosis, and procedure codes. ER data is classified by external cause of injury codes that can be used to determine injury groupings, such as assaults, child abuse, suicide, or firearm injury (Masho et al., 2016). Ambulance service data includes data on violence-related traumatic incidents that required an ambulance pick-up, and include rates of assault, firearm-related injuries, rape, stabbings, or fights. Data from the chief medical examiner includes violence-related mortality data, such as rates of homicide related to child maltreatment and abuse, firearms, and suicide. Data from the juvenile justice system and local school districts provide individual-level data on the number and proportion of youth referred for violence-related activities, including fighting, weapons possession, rape, threat, gang-related activity, theft, disorderly conduct, and substance abuse possession (Masho et al., 2016).

There are multiple ways to utilize crime and violence-related data to examine the actual crime and violence rates in neighborhoods and to link crime and violence data to other neighborhood outcomes. Armstead, Wilkins, and Doreson (2018) conducted a review of the literature on indicators for evaluating community- and societal-level risk and protective factors for violence prevention. The goal of their review was to identify indicators that are accessible and measured at the community level, based on the Centers for Disease Control and Prevention's (CDC) framework that examines the links among multiple forms of violence (Wilkins, Tsao, Hertz, Davis, & Klevens, 2014). Armstead and colleagues (2018) define "risk factors as the conditions that increase the likelihood that a community will experience violence (e.g., diminished economic opportunities, social norms that supportive aggression); while protective factors are the conditions that help increase communities' resilience and lower the likelihood of violence (e.g., community support, cohesion, and connectedness)" (p. S42). Their review identified more than 150 indicators (e.g., measurable and observable metrics) that represent shared risk and protective factors for multiple forms of violence, including diminished economic opportunity, societal-level factors such as norms, income inequality, community violence, community connectedness and support, and physical and social disorder.

The majority of the constructs Armstead and colleagues (2018) discuss are derived from publicly available data sources, including the U.S. Census. For example, U.S. Census data are used as indicators for risk and protective factors, such as income, poverty, education, employment, and housing tenure (Masho et al., 2016). Administrative data can be quite useful and easy to access. U.S. Census data can also be combined and mapped using GIS or other geographic information systems. Researchers can use administrative data and GIS to map "hot spots," grouping together high-crime density areas and related neighborhood characteristics in areas where the crimes frequently occur (Masho et al., 2016). This and other chapters in this book include measures or indicators that are reflective of these and other constructs related to crime and violence. Armstead and colleagues' (2018) review also provides links to eight tables that describe the indicators included in their assessment, broken down into the key risk and protective factors identified by the CDC.

While data can be examined at the individual level and is often aggregated to varying geographic units ranging from block groups to census tracks (Masho et al., 2016), there are several challenges to using this approach (Armstead et al., 2018). Aggregating individual-level survey responses can introduce measurement bias, conflating, for example, residents' fear of crime with their perceptions of disorder (Armstead et al., 2018). However, "indicators for community level risk and protective factors that are measured at the community level (versus aggregated individual level surveys or interviews) have been historically underrepresented in the research literature" (Armstead et al., 2018, p. S43). Several methods to address this issue have been discussed in this chapter and others (see Chapter 3), including using hierarchal linear modeling and other techniques to assess nested, environmental, and community-level constructs (Armstead et al., 2018). For example, the science of ecometrics (see Chapter 3) is a method used to examine community or societal-level phenomena as conceptually distinct and observable constructs (Sampson & Raudenbush, 1999).

CONCLUSION

The measures in this chapter provide researchers and practitioners with the tools to examine the factors that may contribute to crime and violence, including measures of community disorder, and indicators representing the risk and protective factors related to crime and violence. These measures are important for understanding the context in which crime and violence occur, and the community- and societal-level factors that alleviate and/or contribute to crime and violence at the community level. This chapter also describes measures to examine residents' current perceptions of crime in their own communities, including fear and risk of crime and violence as well as the exposure to crime and violence among children and adults. The science behind understanding violence and how it occurs has grown considerably over the last few decades, providing researchers and practitioners with sound theoretical frameworks and measures that can be used to better understand and examine community crime and violence and use more rigorous, valid, and reliable measures to assess the impact of prevention and other efforts to curb violence.

LIST OF MEASURES AND TABLE NUMBERS

TABLE 11.1 ■ Community Disorder and Fear of Crime

Primary Reference	Perkins D. D., & Taylor, R. B. (1996). Ecological assessments of community disorder: Their relationship to fear of crime and theoretical implications. *American Journal of Community Psychology, 24*(1), 63–107.
Purpose	The authors present three ecological methods for measuring community disorder: resident perceptions reported in surveys; on-site observations by trained raters aggregated to the street-block level; and content analysis of crime- and disorder-related newspaper articles aggregated to the neighborhood level. They examine the relationship between these disorder measures and fear of crime.
Description	**Community Disorder Measures** **Block environmental inventory:** This measure includes direct observational measurement of crime and the fear-related physical environment of urban residential blocks (p. 75). Three teams of two raters each were sent to separate blocks. Raters were not allowed to discuss a particular rule or rating as they conducted a block observation; however, they could discuss the interpretation of a rule between blocks (p. 75). The inventory was divided into four sections (as outlined in Table 1 in the article, p. 77): ***Section I: Block-level characteristics (8 indicators):*** This section covers the number of young men and women (approximately 10–35 years old), children, and adults outdoors at any given point in time and their general activities as well as other block characteristics. Data were collected between 5 and 8 p.m. weeknights and noon to 8 p.m. on weekends. Indicators included • Males, 10–35, observed outdoors hanging out • Total males, 10–35 • Unused vacant lots as estimated percentage of block • Number of abandoned cars on street For the next three sections, raters started over at the beginning of the block, walked down one side of the street at a time, keeping a count of the number of occupied residential units. Each nonresidential and mixed-use building was rated (see Section III), and the eight primary survey sample households were selected and rated for the items in Section IV below. ***Section II: All properties (per block)*** • Total abandoned buildings ***Section III: All nonresidential properties (4 indicators)*** • Total vacant nonresidential units • Litter on/in front of nonresidential property ***Section IV: Sample homes*** ***Physical disorder subscale (3 indicators)*** • Vandalism/graffiti • Dilapidated exterior **Newspaper measures:** 73.5% of the articles were taken from the *Baltimore Sun* and the remainder were taken from the *Baltimore African American* newspaper. Four research assistants were trained to skim and identify relevant articles. The types of articles which were abstracted covered two general topics (p. 79): • Eighty percent were reports of events expected to influence crime-related attitudes in or adjacent to one or more study neighborhoods. They examined three areas including specific crimes, social or physical disorder problems, or the immediate community response to specific crime-related problems.

- Twenty percent were news stories about the criminal justice system, community development programs, or policy changes.

From the archive, the researchers created the following variables (p. 82):

- ***Serious crime:*** combined all stories about five types of crimes, including homicides and burglaries (Neighborhood M = 14.04)
- ***Disorder crime news:*** combined all stories that mentioned five other non-traffic offences, such as carrying a weapon, drug abuse, and vandalism (Neighborhood M = 4.72)
- ***Disorder news:*** stories on four areas, including the physical deterioration of housing or other property and racial unrest (Neighborhood M = 0.26)

Resident survey: measured residents' perceptions of the quality of the surrounding social and physical environment using the following scales (pp. 77–78).

Crime and fear-related block problems were rated on a 3-point scale (a big problem, somewhat of a problem, or not a problem) (Perkins et al., 1990).

- ***Perceived physical disorder (5 indicators)***
    - Vandalism, like people breaking windows or spray painting buildings
    - Vacant housing
    - People who don't keep up their property or yards
- ***Perceived social disorder (4 indicators)***
    - People who say insulting things or bother other people when they walk down the street
    - Groups of teenagers hanging out in the street

Emotional fear of crime measure: (6 items)

This scale used a series of questions on felt and perceived safety of self and household members, in the neighborhood and on the block (adapted from several other studies, including Greenberg, Rohe, & Williams, 1982). **Sample** items included

- How safe would you feel being out alone on your block during the day? At night? Elsewhere in the neighborhood at day? At night?
- Would you be afraid if a stranger stopped you at night in your neighborhood to ask for directions?
- Would you feel uneasy if you heard footsteps behind you at night in your neighborhood?

Sample

- Neighborhoods were systematically selected using a probability proportionate to size (PPS) procedure.
- Blocks were randomly selected using block household listings from a city address directory.
- For the survey and environmental measures, a field household enumeration on each selected block provided a complete and up-to-date listing of households (p. 73).
- The survey sample for Time 1 was 412 (65% female; 52.4% African American; 46.3% White; 58.5% were homeowners; average residency was 14.6 years), the sample at Time 2 one year later was 305, with similar characteristics; however, there were more homeowners and long-term residents (pp. 74–75).

Scoring

- Mean scores were calculated for each of the items observed in the block environmental inventory.
- Mean scores were calculated for the survey as well as the newspaper scales.
- For the newspaper scales, all three variables were aggregated to the neighborhood level (sum of stories) and each story was weighted according to whether the event or problem took place near (= 1) or in (= 2) the target neighborhood.

(Continued)

TABLE 11.1 ■ (Continued)

Assessment	***Block environmental inventory:*** Block level alpha = .76 for Section III non-residential properties; block level alpha = .73 for Section IV household sample. Inter-rater agreement for block-level observations was high (mean intraclass correlation: IC_r = .78), property observations (IC_r = .92), Section III nonresidential property (IC_r = .86), and Section IV (IC_r = .81) (p. 76). ***Survey:*** physical disorder (individual level alpha = .75; block level alpha = .87), social disorder (individual level alpha = .80; block level alpha = .89). Fear of crime (individual level alpha = .82; block level alpha = .77) (p. 78).
Related References	Perkins, D. D., Florin, P., Rich, R. C., Wandersman, A., & Chavis, D. M. (1990). Participation and the social and physical environment of residential blocks: Crime and community context. *American Journal of Community Psychology, 18,* 83–115. Perkins, D. D., Meeks, J. W., & Taylor, R. B. (1992). The physical environment of street blocks and residential perceptions of crime and disorder: Implications for theory and measurement. *Journal of Environmental Psychology, 12,* 21–34. Perkins, D. D., Wandersman, A., Rich, R. C., & Taylor, R. B. (1993). The Physical environment of street crime: Defensible space, territoriality, and incivilities. *Journal of Environmental Psychology, 13,* 29–49.
Language	English
Contact	Douglas D. Perkins Department of Human and Organizational Development Box 90 Peabody College, Vanderbilt University Nashville, TN 37203 Email: douglas.d.perkins@vanderbilt.edu

TABLE 11.2 ■ Systematic Social Observation of Public Disorder

Primary Reference	Sampson, R. J., & Raudenbush, S. W. (1999). Systematic social observation of public spaces: A new look at disorder in urban neighborhoods. *American Journal of Sociology, 105*(3), 603–651.
Purpose	The purpose of the study was to assess the sources and consequences of public disorder. The authors develop and test a measurement method called systematic social observation to examine physical and social disorder, which is based on videotaping and systematic rating of more than 23,000 street segments in Chicago. The study also used census data, police records, and an independent survey of 3,500 residents to test a theory of collective efficacy and structural constraints.
Description	<u>**Systematic Social Observation Measures**</u> The observations were coded for analysis as 1 = presence and 0 = absence of the indicator of disorder. The following scales were created (pp. 617–618): • **Physical disorder (10 items taken from the observer logs)** ○ Cigarettes or cigars in the street or gutter ○ Garbage or litter on the street or sidewalk ○ Empty beer bottles visible in the street ○ Graffiti painted over ○ Abandoned cars • **Social disorder (7 items coded from the videotapes)** ○ Adults loitering or congregating ○ Peer group with gang indicators present ○ Adults fighting or arguing in a hostile manner ○ People selling drugs <u>**Survey measures**</u> The study also included a multi-item disorder scale in their survey of residents. This scale tapped how much a problem ("a big problem," "somewhat of a problem," or "not a problem") residents rated the presence of incivilities in their neighborhood (p. 620): • **Social incivilities (3 indicators)** ○ Drinking in public ○ Teenagers causing a disturbance • **Physical incivilities (3 indicators)** ○ Litter ○ Vacant housing The survey also examined residents' perceptions of **collective efficacy** (described in Chapter 6); and experiences with **predatory crime:** Residents were asked whether they (or any member of their household) had experienced within the past 6 months: • A violent victimization in the neighborhood • A household burglary or theft victimization

(Continued)

TABLE 11.2 ■ (Continued)	

	Administrative data measures (p. 621)
	• **Reported incidents (not arrests) of homicide, robbery, and burglary:** Chicago Police Department records, aggregated to the census tracts
	• **Census data at the tract level**
	  ○ **Concentrated disadvantage (5 indicators):** such as poverty, female headed households, percentage black
	  ○ **Concentrated immigration (3 indicators):** such as percentage Latino, density of children
	  ○ **Residential stability (2 indicators):** percentage living in the same house as five years earlier, percentage of owner-occupied homes

Sample	• 196 Chicago census tracts "were selected from a stratified probability sample to maximize variation by race/ethnicity and SES." • As part of a larger study, 343 "neighborhood clusters" (NC) representing combinations of all 865 census tracts in Chicago were first stratified by seven categories of race/ethnic mix and three levels of SES. • Within strata, "80 NCs were then sampled for intensive study with the aim of obtaining a near balanced design, eliminating confounding between ethnic mix and SES" (p. 615).
Assessment	• The physical disorder scale would behave better as an ecological measure than the social disorder scale because it had more items and the items ranged widely, with several occurring with large frequency and others with modest frequency. • The social disorder scale indicators occurred with less frequency or rarely, leading to a lack of between-neighborhood reliability. • The appendix in the article describes the three-level statistical model and measurement properties of both the physical and social disorder scales (see pp. 641–643). • The results of these models showed that the disorder scales were highly reliable at the ecological level. The reliability of combined survey measure of disorder was .83 at the tract level.
Related Reference	Sampson, R. J., Raudenbush, S. W., & Earls, F. (1997). Neighborhoods and violent crime: A study of collective efficacy. *Science, 277*, 918–924.
Language	English
Contact	Robert J. Sampson, PhD Professor and Chair, Department of Sociology Harvard University William James Hall 33 Kirkland St. Cambridge, MA 02138 Email: rsampson@wjh.harvard.edu
Website	For more information on this research, see the study website: Project on Human Development in Chicago Neighborhoods: http://www.icpsr.umich.edu/icpsrweb/PHDCN/instruments.jsp.

TABLE 11.3 ■ Observed and Perceived Physical Disorder	
Primary Reference	Conley, J., Stein, R. E., & Davis, C. (2014). A spatial analysis of the neighborhood scale of residential perceptions of physical disorder. *Applied Spatial Analysis and Policy, 7,* 183–201
Purpose	The goal of this study was to examine the impact of the size of bespoke neighborhoods on the correlation between observations of disorder and survey measures of residents' perceptions of disorder.
Description	**Observed Physical Disorder (SSO Index)** The measure of physical disorder was derived from Sampson and Raudenbush (1999). If a factor was present it was coded as 1, and absent factors were coded as 0. This SSO index in the current study incorporated the type of land use. The SSO index for each street segment was a weighted sum of **14 factors** (weight listed in parenthesis). Factors included • Single family residential land use (1) • Vacant block (3) • Commercial land use (3) • Mixed use: apartments and commercial use (5) • Excessive trash (2) • Dilapidated houses (3) • Abandoned cars (5) **Perceived Physical Disorder (Resident Survey)** This scale consisted of **five items**. The researchers did not define neighborhood for the residents but let them use their own definition. Respondents were asked: "For each item please indicate if it is a big problem (2), somewhat of a problem (1) or not a problem (0)": Sample items included • Vandalism (breaking windows or spray painting buildings) • Vacant houses • People who don't keep up their properties or yards
Sample	• Data for this study were collected in 2009 through research focused on situational policing (Nolan et al., 2013). The full data set includes information from 16 neighborhoods across four U.S. cities. • This study focused on information from two adjacent neighborhoods in an eastern city. The analysis measured effects at the subtract level. The two neighborhoods represented an area of about .45 square miles with a combined population of 5,900 (p. 188). • Survey data were collected by a research team who went door to door to a randomly selected sample of households in each neighborhood. • The sample consisted of SSOs from 306 faceblocks and 105 survey respondents living in the study area, distributed across 76 faceblocks. • Faceblocks are defined as the block segment on one side of the street. SSOs of physical data were recorded for each faceblock in the neighborhoods.
Scoring	A local average of all SSO physical disorder values within a series of threshold distances around each survey location was computed. A mean was computed for an average score for the survey variables.

(Continued)

TABLE 11.3 ■ (Continued)

Assessment	SSO: The inter-rater reliability scales ranged from 0.700–1.00 and were acceptable across all variables.
Related Reference	Sampson, R. J., & Raudenbush, S. (1999). Systematic social observation of public spaces: A new look at disorder in urban neighborhoods. *American Journal of Sociology, 105,* 603–651.
Language	English
Contact	Jamison Conley Department of Geology & Geography West Virginia University PO Box 6300 Morgantown, WV 26506 Email: Jamison.conley@mail.wvu.edu

TABLE 11.4 ■ Perceived Physical and Social Order and Disorder

Reference	Ross, C. E., & Mirowsky, J. (1999). Disorder and decay: The concept and measurement of perceived neighborhood disorder. *Urban Affairs Review, 34*(3), 412–432.
Purpose	Provide a systematic definition of the concept of neighborhood disorder and assess the relationships between perceptions of crime and disorder, order and disorder, and physical and social disorder.
Description	**The Perceived Neighborhood Disorder Scale** includes four subscales. All subscales are rated on a 4-point scale. For the disorder items, 1 means "strongly disagree," 2 means "disagree," 3 means "agree," and 4 means "strongly agree." The order items are reversely scored: 1 means "strongly agree," 2 means "agree," 3 means "disagree," and 4 means "strongly disagree" (p. 417). **Physical disorder (4 items)** • Vandalism is common in my neighborhood. • There are a lot of abandoned buildings in my neighborhood. **Physical order (2 items)** • My neighborhood is clean. **Social disorder (5 items)** • There are too many people hanging around on the streets near my home. • I'm always having trouble with my neighbors. • There is a lot of crime in my neighborhood. **Social order (4 items)** • In my neighborhood, people watch out for each other. • The police protection in my neighborhood is adequate.
Sample	• Participants were taken from the 1995 Survey of Community, Crime and Health (CCH), which was a probability sample of Illinois households. • The respondents (English speaking adults) were selected through a random-digit dialing method and were interviewed via phone. • Interviews were completed with 73.1% of eligible persons contacted. The final sample was comprised of 2,482 adults, with an average age of 45; 41% were male, 84% were White, and 56% were married (pp. 415–416).
Scoring	Mean scores were calculated. A higher score indicates more disorder.
Assessment	Alpha reliability for the entire scale = .921.
Related Reference	Obrien, R. T., & Kauffmann, R. A. (2013). Broken windows and low adolescent prosociality: Not cause and consequence, but co-symptoms of low collective efficacy. *American Journal of Community Psychology, 51*, 359–369.
Language	English
Contact	Catherine Ross University of Texas Population Research Center 305 E. 23rd Street, Stop G1800 Austin, TX 78712-1699 512.232.7064 Email: cross@prc.utexas.edu

TABLE 11.5 ■ Ecometric Measure of Neighborhood Physical Disorder	
Primary Reference	Mooney, S. J., Bader, M. D. M., Lovasi, G. S., Neckerman, K. M., Teitler, J. O., & Rundle, A.G. (2014). Validity of an ecometric neighborhood physical disorder measure constructed by virtual street audit. *American Journal of Epidemiology, 180*(6), 626–635.
Purpose	The study aims to create a valid measure of physical disorder at the neighborhood level using virtual street audit, which uses Google Street View imagery as an alternative to systematic field audits, which can be expensive and time consuming.
Description	Nine virtual audit items designed to assess neighborhood physical disorder were developed from pre-existing and validated scales. Items were coded as 1 = yes or 0 = no, except where noted below (p. 626). **Project on Human Development in Chicago Neighborhoods (7 items):** • Is there garbage, litter, or broken glass in the street or on the sidewalks? • Are there abandoned cars? • Do you see boarded-up or abandoned buildings in the block face? • How would you rate the condition of most of the buildings on the block face? [Fair condition or poor/badly deteriorated condition (1) versus very well kept/good condition or moderately well-kept condition (0)] **Pedestrian Environment Scan tool (1 item):** • Is there vacant or undeveloped land? **Irvine MN Inventory to measure Built Environments (1 item):** • Do any buildings have windows with bars? [Yes (1) vs. no or not applicable (0)] To assess for imagery limitations that could undermine street audit reliability, 2 measures were used: • An indication of camera quality problems: dark versus bright; where 4 instances of "other" were recorded as bright after manual verification of the imagery by data analyst. • The proportion of Street View vantage points along the block face that were obscured; obstructions were primarily parked cars.
Sample	• The "Computer Assisted Neighborhood Visual Assessment System (CANVAS) with Google Street View imagery was used to virtually audit block faces within 4 U.S. cities with varied spatial and economic profiles": New York, Philadelphia, Detroit, and San Jose (p. 627). • Subjects in the Fragile Families and Child Wellbeing Study resided in the sampled areas. The sample included 1,826 block faces with Google Street View imagery across all four sites. Eleven auditors were trained and engaged in auditing. • Approximately 5% of the sampled block faces in each city were randomly selected to be part of reliability subsample to be audited by all auditors in that city: 109 block faces each audited by an average of 3.9 auditors. The remaining 95% of block faces were audited by one auditor (p. 627).
Scoring	The frequency of response indicating disorder in the overall sample was calculated as a percentage.
Assessment	• Inter-rater reliability scores for each item were computed. The final analytical subsample included about 600 pairs of observations for each item in the disorder scale. Reliabilities ranged from .34 ("fair agreement") to .80 ("substantial agreement"). • The internal consistency of the item set for the physical disorder items was assessed using Cronbach's alpha; values ranged from .86 to .89 in each of the cities examined. Internal consistency for the scale pooling from all cities was .93 (p. 629).

Language	English
Contact	Dr. Andrew G. Rundle Department of Epidemiology Mailman School of Public Health Columbia University 722 West 168th Street New York, NY 10032 Email: agr3@columbia.edu

TABLE 11.6 ■ Qualitative and Quantitative Fear of Crime Measures

Primary Reference	Farrall, S., Bannister, J., Ditton, J., & Gillchrist, E. (1997). Questioning the measurement of fear of crime: Findings from a major methodological study. *British Journal of Criminology, 37*(4), 658–679.
Purpose	This study used data to improve the conceptualization and measurement of the fear of crime and discusses how assessments regarding the validity of fear of crime questions can be incorporated into crime surveys.
Description	Farrall and Ditton (1999) describes the *Qualitative interview* that informed the development of their quantitative fear of crime measure. The following interview questions from Farrall and Ditton (1999) are included in the appendix of Farrall et al. (1997) on p. 677. **Worry about crime (4 items)** • You said that you did/did not worry about— • How often do you worry? Constant? Intermittent? **Area (3 items)** • What is it like? • Safe or not? Why? (Relate to R and to specific crime) **Behavior (5 items)** • What types of things do you do? Not do? • Where do you go? How get there? • Avoidance strategies **Victimization (5 items)** • What happened? • How did you feel before? and after? • Who/what helped? (formal and informal forms of help) **Other questions (6 items)** • Culpability for victimization? • Domestic violence location of danger • Concern—corporate crime? Health and safety issues—ferry disasters, Kings Cross **Fear of crime measure (p. 676 in the appendix)** **Worry about crime (4 items):** Respondents were asked, on a scale of 1 to 5 (with 1 representing *not being worried at all ever* and 5 meaning *worrying a lot all the time*) about how worried they are that somebody might • Break into your house (or try to break in) and steal things, or try to, or damage things? • Rob you or assault you or threaten to do either? **Victimization:** How many times have you been a victim of any of these crimes in the last five years? **Likelihood of victimization:** How likely (with 1 representing *very unlikely* and 5 *almost certain to happen*) is it, do you think, that you will be a victim of any of these crimes in the next year? **Safety:** How safe do you feel walking alone in this area after dark? (1 = *very safe*; 2 = *fairly safe*; 3 = *a bit unsafe*; 4 = *very unsafe*)

	Worry about other things (9 items): Respondents were asked, on a scale from 1 to 5 (1 = *a lot*, 2 = *a bit*, 3 = *not much*, 4 = *very little*, 5 = *not at all*), how much do you worry about • Losing your job or being unable to find a job? • Another member of your family losing their job? • Being a victim of any crime? • Having a fire in your home?
Sample	• Researchers used the "random walk method" to select individuals for the first set of interviews, calling on every fifth house and asking the first person over age 16 to be interviewed. In one area the café was used to sample from. • Approximately 40 people were interviewed in each area (*N* = 167) and were asked if they would be prepared to take part in a longer interview if selected. The response rate for agreeing to be contacted for the longer interview was 90%. • Each individual interviewed at the first stage was classified according to their fear and risk ratings. Four groups were produced: high fear/low risk, low fear/low risk, high fear/high risk, and low fear/high risk. • In each area, a total of 16 people were re-interviewed (four from each fear/risk group). Within each fear/risk group, there was an equal gender split and, where possible, a range of ages. The qualitative data set contains 64 interviews.
Related Reference	Farrall, S., & Ditton, J. (1999). Improving the measurement of attitudinal responses: An example from a crime survey. *International Journal of Social Research Methodology, 2*(1), 55–68.
Language	English
Contact	Dr. Stephen Farrall Deputy Head of School Professor of Criminology School of Law University of Sheffield Email: S.Farrall@sheffield.ac.uk Telephone: +44 (0)114 222 6718

TABLE 11.7 ■ Examining the Validity of a Fear of Crime Measure	
Primary Reference	Farrall, S., & Ditton, J. (1999). Improving the measurement of attitudinal responses: An example from a crime survey. *International Journal of Social Research Methodology, 2*(1), 55–68.
Purpose	This study used data to improve the conceptualization and measurement of the fear of crime and discusses how assessments regarding the validity of fear of crime questions can be incorporated into crime surveys.
Description	**Quantitative Fear of Crime Measure** Respondents were asked on a scale from 1 to 5 (*not at all* = 1; *hardly ever* = 2; *don't know* = 3; *some of the time* = 4; and *all the time* = 5) to 5 questions, including • In your everyday life, do you *think* about (e.g. someone breaking into your home)? • In your everyday life, does the thought of someone (e.g. breaking into your home) make you *angry*? • Car crime (i.e., someone stealing your car, van, motorcycle, or other road vehicle) • Vandalism (i.e., someone vandalizing your home) Each question had the same codes and for each question the codes were shown to the respondents on cards. These questions appeared toward the start of the questionnaire. Each of the questions outlined above had been tested prior to the fieldwork to assess their acceptability and interpretation. **Follow-up qualitative interviews with a subsample of respondents (R) were aimed to address the conceptualization of the questions in the fear of crime measure. This interview consisted of 11 questions, such as** • What did R **have in mind** when answering the question (i.e., any particular situational contexts)? • What did the **words** *(think, afraid, angry)* mean to R? **Their design of the questions** • What did the expression *"in your **everyday life** . . . "* mean to R? • What did the expression *"someone **breaking into your home** . . ."* mean to R? **Generally** • Did R **interpret** the question as we intended, or did they assume any unique factors? • If so, why, which and how **does this alter** Rs' answers?
Sample	• Data were collected from 64 respondents in the Strathclyde area. • Follow-up interviews were conducted with a small sample of respondents who had completed the questionnaire with the aim of validating the quantitative questions.
Scoring	No information is available on scoring.
Assessment	• Reliability coefficients were calculated using Cronbach's alpha. • The reliability for the "think" questions ranged from 0.57 to 0.76. • The reliability for the "afraid" questions ranged from 0.51 to 0.90. • The reliability for the "angry" questions ranged from 0.40 to 0.89.
Related Reference	Farrall, S., Bannister, J., Ditton, J., & Gillchrist, E. (1997). Questioning the measurement of fear of crime: Findings from a major methodological study. *British Journal of Criminology, 37*(4), 658–679.

Language	English
Contact	Dr. Stephen Farrall Deputy Head of School Professor of Criminology School of Law University of Sheffield Email: S.Farrall@sheffield.ac.uk Telephone: +44 (0)114 222 6718

TABLE 11.8 ■ Fear of Crime: Emotions, Risk Perception, and Environmental Perception	
Primary Reference	Jackson, J. (2005). Validating new measures of the fear of crime. *International Journal of Social Research Methodology, 8*(4), 297–315.
Purpose	This study assessed the scaling properties of several measures of fear of crime, including several constructs that constitute the fear of crime (e.g., emotions, risk perception, and environmental perception).

Description	The **Fear of Crime Measure** consists of the following subscales (p. 315):
	Worry (emotional construct): asked respondents about the frequency with which they have worried about becoming a victim of any of **5 classes of victimization** in their neighborhood during the past month using the following scale: "not once in the last month," "once or twice in the past month," "once or twice in the past week," and "every day."
	• Personal crimes (3) such as
	  ○ Being attacked by a stranger in the street
	  ○ Being harassed, threatened, or verbally abused in the street
	• Property crimes (2) such as
	  ○ Having someone break into your home whilst the inhabitants were there
	Likelihood (risk): asked respondents how likely they thought it was that they would fall victim during the next 12 months to the crimes listed above, using the following scale: 1 = *definitely not going to happen*, to 7 = *certain to happen*.
	Seriousness of the consequences: asked respondents the extent to which an experience of a typical instance of each of the above crimes would affect their lives, using the following scale: 1 = *not at all* to 7 = *to a very great extent*.
	Perceived control: asked respondents the extent to which they felt able to control whether or not they became a victim of the above crimes, using the following scale: from 1 = *not at all* to 7 = *to a very great extent*.
	Incivilities (note: these are similar to the measures of disorder discussed in the first section of this chapter): Asked respondents if **seven incivilities** were present in their neighborhoods, such as
	• Vandalism/graffiti
	• Rubbish in the streets
	• Drug-taking in the open
	• Teenagers hanging around
	Community cohesion (note: these are similar to measures of collective efficacy discussed in Chapter 6): Residents were asked to respond to two related constructs, on a scale from 1 = *very strongly agree* to 5 = *very strongly disagree*.
	• The extent to which respondents thought they lived in a friendly, supportive, and trusting community **(3 items)**, such as
	  ○ This area has a close, tight-knit community.
	  ○ Most people who live in this area trust one another.
	• The levels of informal social control **(3 items)**, such as
	  ○ People who live here can be relied on to call the police if someone is acting suspiciously

Sample	• Data were gathered from a mail survey of a pure random probability sample of 1,800 adult residents of two socioeconomically contrasting areas of London. The sampling frame was drawn from the Electoral Register. • The response rate was 26.6%, with an *N* of 479. • One area was a wealthy, well-kept suburb with predominantly White and middle-class residents, with low personal crime rates and a relatively high rate of burglary and car thefts. • The other area was a high-rise, high-density, public housing estate, with residents who were predominantly low income and ethnically diverse, and relatively high levels of personal crime and significant social and physical incivilities.
Scoring	Mean scores were calculated for Likert scale items; for yes/no items (incivilities), a total was calculated.
Assessment	The reliability of the measures was not assessed. Confirmatory factor analyses were conducted.
Language	English
Contact	Dr. Jonathan Jackson Methodology Institute London School of Economics and Political Science Houghton Street London WC2A, UK Phone: +44(0)20-7955-7652 Email: j.p.jackson@lse.ac.uk

TABLE 11.9 ■ Three Models Predicting Fear of Crime	
Primary Reference	Alper, M., & Chappell, A. T. (2012). Untangling fear of crime: A multi-theoretical approach to examining the causes of crime-specific fear. *Sociological Spectrum, 32*, 346–363.
Purpose	This study assessed the predictive power of three theoretical models—vulnerability, disorder, and social integration—on offense type-specific, emotionally-based fear of violent and property crime.
Description	**Fear of Crime (dependent variable in the study):** Two dependent variables were created from a four-part question. Respondents were asked how often they worried about the following things, on a scale from 1 to 4 (1 = *never*; 2 = *rarely*; 3 = *sometimes*; and 4 = *often*) (pp. 351–352): **Fear of personal crime (3 items)** • Having someone break into your home **Fear of violent crime (1 item)** • Having yourself or family assaulted or harmed **Victimization:** Respondents were asked: "'During the past six months, have any of the following things happened to you?" If the respondent answered that he or she had been a victim of one or more of the crimes, victimization was coded as 1. There were 6 options, including • Something belonging to YOU was stolen, such as a wallet, clothing, jewelry, or other personal property. • Someone stole or ATTEMPTED to steal one of your motor vehicles (motorcycle or car). • Someone threatened you with a weapon (gun, knife, or club). **Disorder (10 physical and social disorder items):** Respondents were asked "How often do you encounter or see the following problems in your neighborhood? On a scale from 1 to 4 (1 = *almost never*; 2 = *sometimes*; 3 = *usually*; and 4 = *almost always*)." Sample items included • Abandoned/vacant buildings • Public drinking/intoxication • Abandoned/inoperable vehicles • People hanging out in the street (loitering) • Drug dealing or activities that look like drug dealing **Neighborhood trust:** Respondents were asked "How much do you trust people in your neighborhood?" The options were 4 = *a lot*, 3 = *somewhat*, 2 = *a little bit*, or 1 = *not at all*. **Participation in neighborhood organizations:** Respondents were asked "Do you participate in any neighborhood associations or activities?" The options were yes = 1 or no = 0.
Sample	• The data were collected from a phone survey. The sample included residents living in a medium-sized southeastern U.S. city with a population of approximately 220,000. • The sampling method began with a pool of telephone numbers provided by a commercial sampling company. The phone numbers were stratified by police precinct population and included a sample of randomly generated telephone numbers supplemented by listed telephone numbers. • The refusal rate was 40%, resulting in a total of 628 successfully completed interviews and a response rate of 22.5%. • The majority of the respondents were female (64.2%); 53.5% were age 50 or older; and 32.5% were non-White, and 67.5% were White (pp. 351–352).

Scoring	For the fear of crime measures, a mean was calculated so that a lower score indicated a lower level of worry. Due to the low number of victimizations (9.7%), all types of victimizations were combined (the majority of the victimizations were property victimizations).
Assessment	• The fear of crime measure had high reliability (Cronbach's alpha = .824). • A mean score was calculated for the disorder scale; a factor analysis showed that all types of disorder loaded into one factor, which explained 42.96% of the variance; and the reliability of this scale was .787.
Language	English
Contact	Dr. Mariel Alper Department of Criminology and Criminal Justice University of Maryland College Park, MD 20742-8235 Email: malper@umd.edu

TABLE 11.10 ■ Children's Report of Exposure to Violence (CREV)	
Primary Reference	Cooley, M. R., Turner, S. M., & Beidel, D. C. (1995). Assessing community violence: The children's report of exposure to violence. *Journal of the American Academy of Child & Adolescent Psychiatry, 34*(2), 201–208.
Purpose	The purpose of this study was to examine the psychometric properties of the Children's Report of Exposure to Violence (CREV).
Description	The CREV is a self-report questionnaire developed to serve as a screening instrument for children (aged 9 to 15 years). A background questionnaire and the CREV were administered during school hours in small groups by the research team. The instructions and items were read aloud and the children determined their pace. The CREV assesses exposure to community violence through four modes: • Media (TV or film exposure; "media" content area) • Other people's reports of occurrence ("reported" content area) • Violence that is directly witnessed ("witnessed" content area) • Violence that is directly experienced ("victim" content area). There are three categories of victims (strangers, familiar persons, and self). The four content areas have different numbers of items because the types of acts and victims vary in appropriateness for each area. The instrument contains 32 items, 29 ask children to rate the frequency of their lifetime exposure to various types of community violence. The items are evaluated on a 5-point Likert scale (*no/never, one time, a few times, many times*, or *every day*). **The CREV is divided into sections that identify and define the victim of the violence.** The victim of the violence is specified for each act corresponding with the four different modes/areas. • "These questions ask about violence against a *stranger.* A *stranger* is somebody you do not know." • "These questions ask about violence against *familiar people. Familiar people* are people you know, like friends, classmates, relatives, cousins, sisters, brothers, and parents." • "These questions ask about violence that has happened to *you.*" **Each item also specifies the method of exposure:** • For the Media content area the items ask, "Have you ever *watched* on TV or in the movies?" • For the Reported area, the items ask, "Has anyone ever *told* you that?" • For the Witnessed area, the items ask, "Have you ever *seen*?" • And for the Victim area, the items ask, "Have *YOU* ever been?" **The types of violent situations surveyed include** • Being chased or threatened with bodily harm • Beaten up, robbed or mugged, shot, stabbed or killed The CREV was not designed to detect child abuse.
Sample/ Data	• The sample was composed of 228 children who attended public elementary and middle schools in urban and rural communities in South Carolina. All of the children in the sample were enrolled in the same school district (fourth through seventh grades). • Sample characteristics: 50.9% females and 49.1% males; 74.1% African American, 19.7% Caucasian, 1.8% Hispanic, 1.3% Native American, 1.8% biracial, and 1.3% Asian (p. 203).

Scoring	• Each category in the CREV has a corresponding score of 0, 1, 2, 3, and 4. • The final three items are not scored because they are open-ended questions for the children to indicate other violent experiences that were not specifically assessed in the previous questions. • To obtain the score, all 29 items from the four content areas are summed.
Assessment	**Internal consistency** • Direct exposure: $\alpha = .93$ • Media exposure: $\alpha = .75$ • Total score: $\alpha = .78$
Language	English
Contact	Michele Cooley, PhD NPI-Semel Institute for Neuroscience 760 Westwood Plaza, Box 62 Los Angeles, CA 90024 Email: mcooley@mednet.ucla.edu

TABLE 11.11 ■ Things I Have Seen and Heard: Children's Exposure to Violence Scale	
Primary Reference	Richters, J. E., & Martinez, P. (1992). *Things I Have Seen and Heard.* Unpublished manuscript.
Purpose	The purpose of the study was to assess the frequency, through child self-report, of exposure to violence and violence-related activities at home and in the community.
Description	• The original version developed in 1990 had **15 items**; the 1992 version expanded the form to include items related to violence in the home. • A pictorial format was used to facilitate child comprehension of the response options: On the response form, five stacks of balls are depicted below each description of violence, each with a different number of balls, ranging from no balls (an empty circle representing never) to four balls (representing many times). • The instrument was administered through an interview. Interviewers introduced the measure with statement that helped the child to focus on events in real life versus on TV or the movies and also teach the child how to use the visual scale. The scale consists of the following **20 items**, including ○ Heard gun shots ○ Seen somebody arrested ○ Feel safe at home ○ Seen someone get stabbed ○ Seen somebody get shot ○ Seen grownups hitting each other ○ Feel safe outside in neighborhood ○ Seen gangs in neighborhood ○ Seen gun pulled on someone ○ House has been broken into
Sample	• The first sample consisted of 152 first- and second-grade students from a low-income, moderately violent neighborhood in Southeast Washington, DC; 47% reported that they had witnessed shootings; 31% had witnessed stabbings; and 37% has seen a dead body outside (Richters & Martinez, 1993). • Additional samples were also tested, including children ages 6 (N = 1128) and 8 (N = 992) (see Richters & Martinez, 1992).
Scoring	Responses are summed. Higher scores reflect greater exposure to violence.
Assessment	• One week test-retest reliability of the composite variable reflecting the sum of all instances of child reported exposure was r = .81 for a random sample of 21 children (Richters & Martinez, 1993). • The Cronbach's alpha for the total scale was .76.
Related References	Richters, J. E., & Martinez, P. (1993). The NIMH community violence project: I. Children as victims of and witnesses to violence. *Psychiatry, 56*, 7–21. Richters, J. E., & Martinez, P. (1993). Violent communities, family choices, and children's chances: An algorithm for improving the odds. *Development and Psychopathology, 5*, 609–627.

Language	English
Contact	John Richters, PhD University of Maryland Department of Human Development and Institute for Child Study Benjamin Building, Room 4104 College Park, MD 20742 Phone: (301) 405-7354 Email: jrichter@nih.gov

TABLE 11.12 ■ Children's Exposure to Community Violence Scale: Adapted From Richters & Martinez	
Primary Reference	Thompson, R., Proctor, L. J., Weisbart, C., Lewis, T. L., English, D. J., Hussey, J. M.,& Runyan, D. K. (2007). Children's self-reports about violence exposure: An examination of the things I have seen and heard scale. *American Journal of Orthopsychiatry, 77*(3), 454–466.
Purpose	• The purpose of this study was to examine a modified version of the Things I Have Seen and Heard Scale that was used in the Longitudinal Studies on Child Abuse and Neglect (LONGSCAN). • The LONGSCAN version excludes items that refer to victimization and has been treated as a single summed scale indicator of witnessed violence exposure. • The focus of the analysis was to examine the psychometric properties of two different approaches to the LONGSCAN modified scale: item-level list of experiences and as a multifactor scale index of violence exposure.
Description	**Modified Things I Have Seen and Heard Scale** The LONGSCAN study used a modified version of the expanded Things I Have Seen and Heard Scale that consisted of **16 items**. Respondents were asked to rate each question on a 5-point Likert scale assessing how frequently they had witnessed a given form of violence in their life, on a scale from 0 to 4 (0 = *never*, 1 = *one time*, 2 = *twice*, 3 = *three times*, 4 = *more than three times*). **Six items** were deleted from Richters and Martinez (1992, 1993) original scale for human subject concerns. The deleted items focused on violence directed at children and other experiences that could be considered abuse or neglect. Sample items include • Heard gun shot • Seen somebody beaten up • Heard grownups in home yell at each other • Seen somebody get stabbed • Seen somebody get shot • Seen a gun in my home • Seen grownups in home hit each other • Seen gangs in neighborhood **Parent reports** • **Neighborhood Short Form** (Hunter et al., 2003): Elicited parents' ratings of several characteristics of the neighborhood (safety, support available in the community, and pride or morale in the community) • **The Child Life Events Scale** (Coddington, 1972): Provided information about major life events that occurred in the child's life during the past year **Reports to Child Protective Services (CPS)**: CPS data was reviewed to determine presence and nature of allegations of maltreatment of children in their samples. **Demographic variables**: Demographic information was collected from parents/caregivers during interview. This included child race, child gender, family income, whether there was an adult male living in the home, and whether the child's biological mother was living in the home.

Sample	• The current analysis used pooled data from the LONGSCAN studies. LONGSCAN is a consortium of studies located at five different regions of the United States (South, Eastern, Midwest, Northwest, and Southwest regions). • At each of the five sites, a sample of children were recruited who had been maltreated or were at risk of maltreatment when the children were 4 years or younger. The data used in this study focused on children ages 6 to 8. • Of the 1,354 caregiver-child dyads in the baseline sample, 1,230 completed either an age 6 or an age 8 interview. Of these, 784 (63.7%) completed the Things I Have Seen and Heard Scale at both age six and age eight and comprise the analysis sample used in the current study (p. 457).
Scoring	Responses are summed. Higher scores reflect greater exposure to violence.
Assessment	**Study One:** data from 8-year-old respondents Community violence: $\alpha = 0.74$ Domestic violence: $\alpha = 0.58$ **Study Two:** data from 6-year-old respondents Community violence: $\alpha = 0.78$ Domestic violence: $\alpha = 0.49$
Related References	Richters, J. E., & Martinez, P. (1990). Things I Have Seen and Heard: An interview for young children about exposure to violence (Unpublished manuscript). Richters, J. E., & Martinez, P. (1992). Things I Have Seen and Heard: A structured interview for assessing young children's violence exposure. National Institute of Mental Health.
Language	English
Contact	Richard Thompson, PhD Juvenile Protective Associates 1333 N. Kingsbury, Suite 306 Chicago, IL 60622 Email: rthompson@juvenile.org

TABLE 11.13 ■ Exposure to Violence Scale (ETV)	
Primary Reference	Suglia, S. F., Ryan, L., & Wright, R. J. (2008). Creation of a community violence exposure scale: Accounting for what, who, where, and how often. *Journal of Traumatic Stress, 21*(5), 479–486.
Purpose	This study builds on previous research that has used the Rasch model, a method for obtaining a continuous scale from dichotomous survey items measuring a single construct, to create a scale of community violence exposure. The authors describe the Rausch model method to create an exposure to community violence scale that includes event circumstance information.
Description	**Children's Exposure to Community Violence** Violence was assessed using the Children's Exposure to Violence (Richters & Martinez, 1993), which was structured to measure lifetime exposure to community violence. Children who were 8 years old or older reported on their own violence experiences. Respondents were asked to rate each question on a 5-point Likert scale assessing how frequently they had witnessed a given form of violence in their life, on a scale from 0 to 4 (0 = *never*, 1 = *one time*, 2 = *twice*, 3 = *three times*, 4 = *more than three times*). The scale assesses witnessing and direct victimization in five areas and accounts for event circumstance information by asking a series of four follow-up questions if the child experienced the event for the first three events below: If so • Seen more than once • Know the victim • Know the perpetrator • Event happened at home **Ever witness someone being shoved/kicked/punched** Followed by If so questions above, then: Ever been a victim of a shove/kick/punch **Ever witnessed a knife attack** Followed by If so questions above, then: Ever been a victim of a knife attack **Ever witnessed someone being shot** Followed by If so questions above, then: Ever been a victim of a shooting **Ever heard gunshots** • Heard gunshots more than once • Event happened at home **Witnessed verbal abuse of caregiver** **Checklist of Children's Distress Symptoms (CCDS)**, American Psychiatric Association, 1987; Richters & Martinez, 1993 (p. 484). This scale is based on the diagnostic criteria in the *DSM III*. The 28-item scale assessed children's distress symptoms in the past 6 months related to their reported community violence experiences. Participants respond on a 5-point Likert scale, ranging from 1 = *never* to 5 = *most of the time*.

	Confounder variables were also examined: • Demographics, socioeconomic status, child's age, race/ethnicity, gender, maternal education level and marital status • Prenatal alcohol and tobacco exposure • Maternal depression—assessed using the depression subscale from the Brief Symptom Inventory. Responses range from 1 to 5 with a higher score indicating more symptoms.
Sample	• This study includes women and their children who were already enrolled in a cohort designed to study the effects of prenatal tobacco smoke exposure on childhood respiratory health. • Sample: 412 women continued in the follow-up study and completed a violence exposure assessment, and 171 children who were 8 years or older completed the self-report violence assessment. • Analysis was completed on 162 with complete data; mean age was 9.3 years old; 51% were male; 57.4% were White, and 42.6% were Hispanic/other race/ethnicity; 61% reported witnessing shoving; 20% heard gunshots; and 26% witnessed caregiver verbal abuse (pp. 480–481).
Scoring	• Using the Rasch modeling technique, a continuous exposure to violence (ETV) measure was obtained. • This model is generalized to account for salient features of each event. • A continuation ratio model is used to compare three groups distinguished (e.g., 0 = *I have not seen shoving*, 1 = *Yes, I have seen it and I did not know the person who did it*, and 2 = *Yes, I have seen it and I knew the person who did it*).
Assessment	• Children's exposure to community violence: Acceptable internal consistency, test-retest reliability and validity have been described for this scale (Selner-O'Hagan et al., 1998; Thompson, Roberts, Curran, Ryan, & Wright, 2002). • Checklist of Children's Distress Symptoms: $\alpha = 0.88$
Related References	Richters, J. E., & Martinez, P. (1993). The NIMH community violence project: I. Children as victims of and witnesses to violence. *Psychiatry, 56*, 7–21.
Language	English
Contact	Shakira Franco Suglia, MS, ScD Mailman School of Public Health Columbia University 722 West 168th St Room 508 NY, NY 10032 Email: sfs2150@cumc.columbia.edu

TABLE 11.14 ■ Child Exposure to Community Violence (CECV)	
Primary Reference	Martin, L., Revington, N., & Seedat, S. (2013). The 39-item child exposure to community violence (CECV) scale: Exploratory factor analysis and relationship to PTSD symptomatology in trauma-exposed children and adolescents. *International Journal of Behavioral Medicine, 20,* 599–608.
Purpose	The purpose of this study was to examine the psychometric properties of an adapted version of the CECV in a South African sample of trauma-exposed youth. The study also assessed the relationship between exposure to community violence and PTSD symptomatology.
Description	**Child Exposure to Community Violence Scale Item Checklist:** contains 39 items integrating the hearing about, witnessing, or experiencing violence; adapted from Richters and Martinez (1992, 1993) to more accurately capture the experience of South African youth. The Checklist is coded on a 5-point Likert scale, with responses ranging from 0 = *never* to 4 = *more than 10 times*, and also a response for "don't know." Sample items include • Heard gunshots • Seen someone arrested • Felt unsafe at home • Seen drug deals • Seen someone beaten up • Heard grown-ups yell at each other • Felt unsafe at home • Seen adults at home hit each other • Felt unsafe outside neighborhood • Seen dead body in neighborhood • Seen someone steal from another's house/store • Been beaten by non-family member • Threatened to be killed • Been shot or stabbed • Family member touched/kissed uncomfortably • Pinched, kicked, or locked up by non-family member • Other situation that was frightening or made you think that you would die
Sample	• The sample used was composed of 231 school children and adolescents aged 8 through 19 who had experienced a PTSD qualifying traumatic event, defined by the *DSM-IV* criteria. • They were referred by either primary and high school teachers or social workers to a trauma research team based in the Department of Psychiatry, University of Stellenbosch. Inclusion criteria: participants had to have been exposed to at least one life-threatening traumatic event, defined by *DSM-IV* criteria; participants had to be proficient in English or Afrikaans and be a resident in the Cape Town metropolitan area. • Exclusionary criteria: known mental retardation; current use of sedative psychotropic medication; visual or auditory impairment; traumatic brain injury with loss of consciousness; any major medical illness or current illicit substance abuse (p. 601). • The sample included 49.8% who met the criteria for a formal diagnosis of PTSD; mean age was 13.91; 32% were between 8 and 12 years old and 68% were between 13 and 19 years old; 57.1% were female; 81.5% were mixed race; median grade was eighth grade, ranging from second to 12th grade (p. 601).

Scoring	Mean scores were calculated, with higher scores meaning higher exposure to violence.
Assessment	The reliability of the CECV was Cronbach's alpha = 0.896.
Related References	Amaya-Jackson L. (1998). Child's exposure to violence checklist. Adopted from Richter's Things I've Seen and Heard. *Trauma evaluation, treatment and research program.* Durham, NC: Center for Child and Family Health.
Language	English
Contact	Lindi Martin Department of Psychiatry University of Stellenbosch PO Box 19063, Tygerberg 7505, Cape Town, South Africa Email: lmartin@sun.ac.za

TABLE 11.15 ■ Survey of Exposure to Community Violence (SECV): Self-Report Version	
Primary Reference	Scarpa, A., Fikretoglu, D., Bowser, F., Hurley, J. D., Pappert, C. A., Romero, N., & Van Voorhees, E. (2002). Community violence exposure in university students. *Journal of Interpersonal Violence, 17,* 253–272.
Purpose	This study examined community violence exposure among college students, in order to validate the SECV measure.
Description	The SECV contains 27 items in which the respondent reports the frequency of having directly experienced (e.g., been a victim of) or witnessed violence-related events. Respondents are asked how many times "you yourself" have experienced each violent event and how many times they had seen someone else experience the event. Each item was rated according to the following scale to reflect increasing frequency: 0 = *never,* 1 = *one time,* 2 = *two times,* 3 = *three to four times,* 4 = *five to six times,* 5 = *seven to eight times,* 6 = *once per month,* 7 = *once per week,* 8 = *almost every day.* Respondents were also asked to report the perpetrator (i.e., adult or youth stranger, adult or youth family member, adult or youth acquaintance, and other) and the location (i.e., near home, in home, near school, in school, and other) of the event. **Witnessing (17 items), such as** • Break in, others home • Gunfire outside, in/near home • Sexually assaulted • Punched or hit by a non-family member • Exposed to a weapon • Someone seriously wounded by violence • Someone killed • Stabbed **Victimization (10 items), such as** • Chased by gangs or individuals • Break in, home • Threatened with serious physical harm • Punched or hit by a family member • Beaten/mugged
Sample	• Participants were 518 psychology students (351 women and 160 men; 7 participants did not indicate gender). • Of these, 81% were Caucasian, 4.9% were African American, 8% were Asian, and 2.9% were Hispanic. • About 92.6% of the participants were between the ages of 17 and 22; 7.4% were 22 or older.
Scoring	• To categorize groups, a victimization score was calculated by summing the nine items referring to "you yourself." • A witnessing score was calculated by summing the 14 items referring to having seen someone else in such circumstances plus three items referring to hearing gunfire. • Respondents who scored in the top 25%, middle 50%, or bottom 25% of the distribution of victimization or witnessing scores were placed in the high, moderate, or low victim or witness groups, respectively, based on the method used in Cooley-Quille and Lorion (1999).

Assessment	Witnessing: coefficient alpha = .72 Victimization: coefficient alpha = .55
Related References	Richters, J. E., & Saltzman, W. (1990). *Survey of exposure to community violence: Self-report version.* Rockville, MD: National Institute of Mental Health. Scarpa, A. (2001). Community violence exposure in a young adult sample. *Journal of Interpersonal Violence, 16,* 36–53. Scarpa, A., Haden, S. C., & Hurley, J. (2006). Community violence victimization and symptoms of posttraumatic stress disorder. *Journal of Interpersonal Violence, 21,* 446–469. Scarpa, A., Hurley, J. D., Shumate, H. W., & Haden, S. C. (2006). Lifetime prevalence and socioemotional effects of hearing about community violence. *Journal of Interpersonal Violence, 21,* 5–23.
Language	English
Contact	Angela Scarpa Department of Psychology 109 Williams Hall Virginia Polytechnic Institute and State University Blacksburg, VA 24061-0436 E-mail: ascarpa@vt.edu

TABLE 11.16 ■ My ETV (Exposure to Violence)	
Primary Reference	Selner-O'Hagan, M. B., Kindlon, D. J., Buka, S. L., Raudenbush, S. W., & Earls, F. J. (1998). Assessing exposure to violence in urban youth. *Journal of Child Psychology and Psychiatry, 39,* 215–224.
Purpose	The purpose of the study was to examine the development of the My ETV structured interview scale for violence exposure, testing its psychometric properties, reliability, and validity.
Description	The scale is a highly structured interviewer administered instrument that covers a subject's lifetime and past-year exposure to 18 different violence events that have either been witnessed or personally experienced. The wording of the questions are specified and the interview structure is explicit. Frequency of exposure during the past year and lifetime is measured on a six point scale (never, once, two or three times, four to 10 times, 11 to 50 times, more than 50 times). **Witnessed (10 items)** • Sexual assault • Shooting • Someone chased • Weapon attack • Heard gunfire **Victimization (8 items)** • Home during break in • Shot at • Seriously threatened • Chased
Sample	• 80 persons between 9 and 24 participated in the study; 55% were over 18 • 61% were male; 47% African American, 38% White, 10% Latino, 5% other • 50% resided in low crime areas, 17% moderate crime areas, and 33% high
Scoring	• Three forms of exposure are assessed: Witnessing, Victimization or Total Exposure. Scores are also obtained for past year and lifetime exposure. • This data is then fit into a Rausch model for rating scales, specified using person exposure and extremity of event.
Assessment	**Internal consistency reliability** **Lifetime** • Total ETV: $\alpha = .93$ • Victimization: $\alpha = .79$ • Witnessing: $\alpha = .92$ **Past year** • Total ETV: $\alpha = .89$ • Victimization: $\alpha = .68$ • Witnessing: $\alpha = .91$

	Test-retest reliability **Lifetime** • Total ETV: $r = .88$ • Victimization: $r = .75$ • Witnessing: $r = .85$ **Past year** • Total ETV: $r = .81$ • Victimization: $r = .94$ • Witnessing: $r = .75$
Language	English
Contact	Mary Beth Selner O'Hagan Harvard School of Public Health Dept. of Maternal and Child Health 677 Huntington Ave Boston, MA 02115 Email: mohagan@phdcn.harvard.edu

REFERENCES

Alper, M., & Chappell, A. T. (2012). Untangling fear of crime: A multi-theoretical approach to examining the causes of crime-specific fear. *Sociological Spectrum, 32*, 346–363.

Amaya-Jackson L. (1998). Child's exposure to violence checklist. Adopted from Richter's Things I've Seen and Heard. *Trauma evaluation, treatment and research program*. Durham, NC: Center for Child and Family Health.

Armstead, T. L., Wilkins, N., & Doreson, A. (2018). Indicators for evaluating community-and societal-level risk and protective factors for violence prevention: Findings from a review of the literature. *Journal of Public Health Management Practice, 24*(1), S42–S50.

Azrael, D., Johnson, R. M., Molnar, B., Vriniotis, M., Dunn, E. C., Duncan, D. T., & Hemenway, D. (2016). Creating a youth violence data system for Boston, Massachusetts. *The Australian and New Zealand Journal of Criminology, 42*(3), 406–421.

Conley, J., Stein, R. E., & Davis, C. (2014). A spatial analysis of the neighborhood scale of residential perceptions of physical disorder. *Applied Spatial Analysis and Policy, 7*, 183–201.

Cooley, M. R., Turner, S. M., & Beidel, D. C. (1995). Assessing community violence: The children's report of exposure to violence. *Journal of the American Academy of Child & Adolescent Psychiatry, 34*(2), 201–208.

David-Ferdon, C., & Simon, T. R. (2014). *Preventing youth violence: Opportunities for Action*. Atlanta, GA: Centers for Disease Control and Prevention, National Center for Injury Prevention and Control, Division of Youth Violence Prevention.

DeCou, C.R., & Lynch, S. M. (2017). Assessing adult exposure to community violence: A Review of definition and measures. *Trauma, violence and abuse, 18*(1), 51-61.

Farrall, S., Bannister, J., Ditton, J., & Gillchrist, E. (1997). Questioning the measurement of fear of crime: Findings from a major methodological study. *British Journal of Criminology, 37*(4), 658–679.

Farrall, S., & Ditton, J. (1999). Improving the measurement of attitudinal responses: An example from a crime survey. *International Journal of Social Research Methodology, 2*(1), 55–68.

Farrell, A. D., & Bruce, S. E. (1997). Impact of exposure to community violence on violent behavior and emotional distress among urban adolescents. *Journal of Clinical Child Psychology, 26*, 2–14.

Farrell, A. D., Henry, D., Bradshaw, C., & Reischl, T. (2016). Designs for evaluating the community-level impact of comprehensive prevention programs: Examples from the CDC Centers of Excellence in youth violence prevention. *Journal of Primary Prevention, 37*, 165–188. doi: 10.1007/s10935-016-0425-8

Ferguson, K. M., & Mindel, C. H. (2007). Modeling fear of crime in Dallas neighborhoods: A test of social capital theory. *Crime and Delinquency, 53*(2), 322–49.

Ferraro, K. F., & LaGrange, R. (1987). The measurement of fear of crime. *Sociological Inquiry, 57*(1), 70–97.

Greenberg, S. W., Rohe, W. M., & Williams, J. R. (1982). *Safe and secure neighborhoods: Physical characteristics and informal territorial control in high and low crime neighborhoods*. Washington, DC: Community Crime Prevention Division, National Institute of Justice, U.S. Department of Justice.

Henson, B., & Reyns, B. W. (2015). The only thing we have to fear is fear itself . . . and crime: The current state of crime literature and where it should go next. *Sociology Compass, 9*(2), 91–103.

Jackson, J. (2005). Validating new measures of the fear of crime. *International Journal of Social Research Methodology, 8*(4), 297–315.

Kelling, G., & Coles, C. (1996). *Fixing broken windows: Restoring order and reducing crime in our communities*. New York: Free Press.

Lane, J., Rader, N., Henson, B., Fisher, B., & May, D. (2014). *Fear of crime in the United States: Causes, consequences, and contradictions*. Durham, NC: Carolina Academic Press.

Martin, L., Revington, N., & Seedat, S. (2013). The 39-item child exposure to community violence (CECV) scale: Exploratory factor analysis and relationship to PTSD symptomatology in trauma-exposed children and adolescents. *International Journal of Behavioral Medicine, 20,* 599–608.

Masho, S. W., Schoeny, M. E., Webster, D., & Sigel, E. (2016). Outcomes, data, and indicators of violence at the community level. *Journal of primary prevention, 37,* 121–139.

Mitchell, S. J., Lewin, A., Horn, I. B., Rasmussen, A., Sanders-Phillips, K., Valentine, D., & Joseph, J. G. (2009). Violence exposure and the association between young African American mothers' discipline and child problem behavior. *Academic Pediatrics, 9*(3), 157–163.

Mooney, S. J., Bader, M. D. M., Lovasi, G. S., Neckerman, K. M., Teitler, J. O., & Rundle, A. G. (2014). Validity of an ecometric neighborhood physical disorder measure constructed by virtual street audit. *American Journal of Epidemiology, 180*(6), 626–635.

O'Brien, D. T., & Kauffman, R. (2013). Broken windows and low adolescent prosociality: Not cause and consequence, but co-symptoms of low collective efficacy. *American Journal of Community Psychology, 51,* 359–369.

Osofsky, J., Wewers, S., Hann, D., & Fick, A. (1993). Chronic community violence: What is happening to our children? *Psychiatry, 56,* 36–45.

Perkins, D. D., Florin, P., Rich, R. C., Wandersman, A., & Chavis, D. M. (1990). Participation and the social and physical environment of residential blocks: Crime and community context. *American Journal of Community Psychology, 18,* 83–115.

Perkins, D. D., Meeks, J. W., & Taylor, R. B. (1992). The physical environment of street blocks and residential perceptions of crime and disorder: Implications for theory and measurement. *Journal of Environmental Psychology, 12,* 21–34.

Perkins D. D., & Taylor, R. B. (1996). Ecological assessments of community disorder: Their relationship to fear of crime and theoretical implications. *American Journal of Community Psychology, 24*(1), 63–107.

Perkins, D. D., Wandersman, A., Rich, R. C., & Taylor, R. B. (1993). The physical environment of street crime: Defensible space, territoriality, and incivilities. *Journal of Environmental Psychology, 13,* 29–49.

Peterson, R. D., Krivo, L. J., & Harris, M. A. (2000). Disadvantage and neighborhood violent crime: Do local institutions matter? *Journal of Research in Crime and Delinquency, 37*(1), 31–63.

Raudenbush, S. W., & Sampson, R. J. (1999). 'Ecometrics': Toward a science of assessing ecological settings, with application to the systematic social observation of neighborhoods. *Sociological Methodology, 29,* 1–41.

Richters, J. E., & Martinez, P. (1990). *Things I have seen and heard: An interview for young children about exposure to violence* (Unpublished manuscript).

Richters, J. E., & Martinez, P. (1992). *Things I have seen and heard* (Unpublished manuscript).

Richters, J. E., & Saltzman, W. (1990). *Survey of exposure to community violence: Self-report version.* Rockville, MD: National Institute of Mental Health.

Rosenfeld, R., Messner, S., & Baumer, E. (2001). Social capital and homicide. *Social Forces, 80(1),* 283–309.

Ross, C. E. (1993). Fear of victimization and health. *Journal of Quantitative Criminology, 9*(2), 159–75.

Ross, C. E., & Mirowsky, J. (1999). Disorder and decay: The concept and measurement of perceived neighborhood disorder. *Urban Affairs Review, 34*(3), 412–432.

Sampson, R. J., & Raudenbush, S. W. (1999). Systematic social observation of public spaces: A new look at disorder in urban neighborhoods. *American Journal of Sociology, 105*(3), 603–651.

Sampson, R. J., Raudenbush, S. W., & Earls, F. (1997). Neighborhoods and violent crime: A study of collective efficacy. *Science, 277,* 918–924.

Scarborough, B. K., Like-Haislip, T. Z., Novak, K. J., Lucas, W. L., & Alarid, L. F. (2010). Assessing the relationship between individual characteristics, neighborhood context, and fear of crime. *Journal of Criminal Justice, 38*(4), 819–26.

Scarpa, A. (2001). Community violence exposure in a young adult sample. *Journal of Interpersonal Violence, 16*, 36–53.

Scarpa, A., Fikretoglu, D., Bowser, F., Hurley, J. D., Pappert, C. A., Romero, N., & Van Voorhees, E. (2002). Community violence exposure in university students. *Journal of Interpersonal Violence, 17*, 253–272.

Scarpa, A., Haden, S. C., & Hurley, J. (2006). Community violence victimization and symptoms of posttraumatic stress disorder. *Journal of Interpersonal Violence*, 21, 446–469.

Scarpa, A., Hurley, J. D., Shumate, H. W., & Haden, S. C. (2006). Lifetime prevalence and socioemotional effects of hearing about community violence. *Journal of Interpersonal Violence, 21*, 5–23.

Selner-O'Hagan, M. B., Kindlon, D. J., Buka, S. L., Raudenbush, S. W., & Earls, F. J. (1998). Assessing exposure to violence in urban youth. *Journal of Child Psychology and Psychiatry, 39*, 215–224.

Shaw, C., & McKay, H. (1942/1969). *Juvenile delinquency and urban areas*. Chicago, IL: University of Chicago Press.

Shaw, C. R., & McKay, H. D. (1972). *Juvenile delinquency and urban areas* (Rev. ed.). Chicago: The University of Chicago Press.

Sheehan, K., DiCara, J., LeBaily, S., & Christoffel, K. (1997). Children's exposure to violence in an urban setting. *Archives of Pediatrics and Adolescent-Medicine, 151*, 502–504.

Skogan, W. (1990). *Disorder and decline: Crime and the spiral of decay in American cities*. Berkeley: University of California Press.

Skogan, W. (2015). Disorder and decline: The state of research. *Journal of Research in Crime and Delinquency, 52*(4), 464–485.

Suglia, S. F., Ryan, L., & Wright, R. J. (2008). Creation of a community violence exposure scale: Accounting for what, who, where, and how often. *Journal of Traumatic Stress, 21*(5), 479–486.

Taylor, R. B., Shumaker, S. A., & Gottfredson, S.D. (1985). Neighborhood-level links between physical features and local sentiments. *Journal of Architectural and Planning Research, 2*, 261–275.

Thompson, R., Proctor, L. J., Weisbart, C., Lewis, T. L., English, D. J., Hussey, J. M., & Runyan, D. K. (2007). Children's self-reports about violence exposure: An examination of the things I have seen and heard scale. *American Journal of Orthopsychiatry, 77*(3), 454–466.

Uniform Crime Reporting Statistics (UCR Statistics). (n.d.). UCR offense definitions. Retrieved from https://www.ucrdatatool.gov/offenses.cfm

Walling, S. M., Eriksson, C. B., Putman, K. M., & Foy, D. W. (2011). Community violence exposure, adverse childhood experiences, and post-traumatic stress distress among urban development workers. *Psychological trauma: Theory, research, practice and policy, 3*, 42–49.

Wilkins, N., Tsao, B., Hertz, M., Davis, R., & Klevens, J. (2014). *Connecting the dots: An overview of the links among multiple forms of violence*. Atlanta, GA: National Center for Injury Prevention and Control, Centers for Disease Control and Prevention.

Wilson, J. Q., & Kelling, G. (1982). The police and neighborhood safety: Broken windows. *Atlantic, 127*, 29–38.

12 PLACE-BASED SOCIAL EXCLUSION AND INEQUITY

The concept of social exclusion recognizes that the marginalization and disadvantage experienced by individuals and groups are embedded in systems and structures of society. Social exclusion at the community level is often manifest as inequality among places or groups in their living conditions and opportunities. Many researchers are interested in studying the origins and patterns of these place-based disparities. Other investigators endeavor to describe the effects of these exclusionary processes and disparate conditions on individuals and communities. Practitioners and policy makers may be concerned with finding out how place-based social exclusion is affecting their constituents or assessing whether their programs or policies are effective in reducing place-based disparities or ameliorating their negative effects. All of these purposes require methods of measuring some aspect of place-based social exclusion.

This chapter covers commonly used measures in several domains of place-based inequalities and exclusionary processes. We begin by examining measures that quantify the degree of social deprivation or socioeconomic disadvantage experienced in communities. Next, we focus on ways of evaluating the residential sorting processes that affect where particular groups reside. These include measures of exclusionary processes, such as racial and economic segregation, as well as indicators of inclusiveness in the form of ethnic and income diversity. Finally, the chapter examines place-based disparities in access to opportunities and resources. The focus here is on measuring disparities in communities' access to jobs, services, and amenities.

MEASURING COMMUNITY SOCIAL DISADVANTAGE

There is a vast literature that associates the level of socioeconomic disadvantage in residential neighborhoods with adverse health and developmental outcomes for the individuals that live there (Ellen, Mijanovich, & Dillman, 2001; Ellen & Turner 1997; Leventhal & Brooks-Gunn, 2000). Researchers have used indicators of neighborhood socioeconomic deprivation in numerous studies that attempt to estimate neighborhood effects on children and adults (Sellström & Bremberg, 2006) and to uncover mechanisms that are responsible for the association between residential contexts and individual well-being (Galster, 2012; Sampson, Morenoff, & Gannon-Rowley, 2002). Although distinguishing the causal effect of neighborhood disadvantage from the process of neighborhood selection has proven challenging (Oakes, 2004), concerns about the deleterious effects of distressed areas have driven efforts to measure this continuum of community disadvantage in all of its complexity. Moreover, on a practical level, measures of neighborhood disadvantage are commonly used to describe communities and to locate studies in contexts where there is high risk (e.g., Elliott et al., 2006) or to complement measures of individual socioeconomic deprivation in studies of disparities (Shavers, 2007).

A widely used measure of neighborhood disadvantage, grounded in social disorganization theory, was first put forward in a seminal study of social structure, collective efficacy, and crime in Chicago neighborhoods (Sampson, Raudenbush, & Earls, 1997). That research identified three dimensions of social structure that related neighborhoods' collective efficacy (please refer to Chapter 6 of this book for more details on the collective efficacy measure), which in turn explained violent crime levels. The most consistently influential factor was labeled **concentrated disadvantage**. This six-item factor, based on census data, reflects the degree to which households holding disadvantaged positions in the social structure are concentrated in particular neighborhoods (see **Table 12.1** for details on this index). The emergence and stability of this concentrated disadvantage factor is consistent with other evidence on the persistent geographic concentration of social problems and the long-standing segregation of urban populations by race and class (Sharkey, 2013). Although the original work on the concentrated disadvantage factor was carried out on Chicago neighborhoods, the approach has been replicated in many other locales. The factor loadings tend to differ somewhat across metropolitan areas because of historical and current variation in the structure of social disadvantage, but the items in the index have generally loaded on a single factor and proven to be reliable measures of the concentrated disadvantage construct (Sharkey, 2013).

- Results of the neighborhood-level analysis showed that concentrated disadvantage was significantly negatively associated with collective efficacy (please refer to Chapter 6 of this book for more details of the collective efficacy measure), which in turn led to higher levels of violence (e.g., homicide), when controlling for personal background effects.
- These findings are consistent with a theoretical expectation that collective efficacy would mediate the effects of neighborhood disadvantage on violence (Sharkey, 2013).

There are three other area disadvantage measures that have grown out of efforts to investigate place-based disparities in health status. Specially, we cover the **Townsend Index** (see **Table 12.2**), the **Index of Socioeconomic Position** (see **Table 12.3**), and the **Area Deprivation Index** (see **Table 12.4**). These indexes all rely on census indicators of material deprivation and socioeconomic status, but they vary in the specific items that are included and in the way the items are weighted and combined. Nevertheless, all three of these indexes of community disadvantage have been associated with gradients of health status measures, with a greater frequency of health problems observed in areas with higher levels of disadvantage according to these measures. The following summarizes studies examining the Townsend Index:

- Results showed that there is a statistically significant relationship between poor health and material deprivation, with a correlation of 82% between the Overall Health Index (combination of mortality, disablement, and delayed development) and the Townsend Index.
- In addition, four components of the Townsend Index are highly intercorrelated and make a significant contribution to explaining the variation in overall health.
- These findings suggest that the explanatory power of the four deprivation variables is strong enough to justify their initial choice of variables (Townsend et al., 1988).

Studies examining the Index of Socioeconomic Position found that:

- Block group and tract socioeconomic measures (including the SEP index and Townsend Index) performed comparably within and across both states in detecting the socioeconomic gradients in health.
- However, zip code measures failed to detect gradients observed with the block group and tract measures (Krieger et al., 2002).

Studies examining the Area Deprivation Index found that:

- Comparison of a census-based ADI to county mortality data, area deprivation gradients in mortality increased substantially between 1969 and 1998.
- Area gradients were more pronounced for men than women in each age group, with higher mortality rates observed in more deprived areas (Singh, 2003).

QUANTIFYING PLACE-BASED SEGREGATION BY RACE, ETHNICITY, AND INCOME

Decades of research documents the spatial concentration, separation, and isolation of oppressed racial and ethnic groups (Iceland, 2004a; Massey & Denton, 1993), immigrants (Iceland & Scopilliti, 2008) and low-income households (Jargowsky, 1997; Reardon & Bischoff, 2011). The evidence points to the negative effects that this spatial isolation has on the well-being of the individuals (Kramer & Hogue, 2009; LaVeist, 2003; Massey, Condron, & Denton, 1987) and the vitality of communities, cities, and regions (Li, Campbell, & Fernandez, 2013). Left unabated, the forces that sort households into neighborhoods based on race and income can contribute to the intergenerational transmission of disadvantage and the reproduction of social exclusion (Sampson & Sharkey, 2008; Sampson, Sharkey, & Raudenbush, 2008; Sharkey, 2008).

Measures of segregation and other indices of place-based inequality have been fundamental to documenting and understanding the causes and consequences of these residential patterns (Charles, 2003; Massey & Denton, 1993). Many different indices for quantifying patterns of population sorting have been proposed over the years (e.g., Massey & Denton, 1988; Massey, White, & Phua, 1996), and work to refine these measures and expand application continues to evolve (Iceland, 2004a). In this section, we cover commonly used methods to measure residential segregation[1] of minority groups from majority groups in the population. We also cover the extension of these methods to multi-group segregation indexes, ordinal measures of segregation, and spatially calibrated measures of segregation.

Minority–Majority Group Measures of Segregation

Numerous approaches have been used to measure the degree of two-group segregation, between a minority and a majority group. The focus has been on measuring the degree of segregation in various jurisdictions (e.g., cities, counties, metropolitan areas) by examining the distribution of groups across smaller units within these

[1] These are place-based measures consistent with the community focus of this handbook. However, there is a growing literature that evaluates segregation at the person level through examining individuals travel patterns and activity spaces (see for example Kwan, 2013).

jurisdictions (e.g., neighborhoods, subdivisions, or localized communities). In principle, these measures can be calculated for any set of larger units that have smaller units nested within. Massey and Denton (1988) conducted an exhaustive review of the indexes of segregation that were in use at that time and classified them into five dimensions. *Evenness* measures referred to the "differential distribution of two social groups among residential units in a city" (p. 283). *Exposure* measures reflected the chances that minority group members would encounter majority group members within their residential areas (p. 287). *Concentration* indexes measure the proportion of space occupied by minority group members (p. 289). *Centralization* captures the degree to which the minority population is located in the center of the jurisdiction (p. 291). *Clustering* is the extent to which the residential units with minority population are contiguous to one another (p. 293). Results of a factor analysis confirmed these five dimensions. **Table 12.5 (Dimensions of Residential Segregation [two-group minority-majority group segregation])** delineates the most commonly used methods for measuring segregation along the above dimensions. This study also found the following results:

- Based on a systematic methodological evaluation of 20 different indices, one index was chosen to represent each of the five key dimensions of residential segregation: D for evenness, P* for exposure, RCO for concentration, ACE for centralization, and SP for clustering.
- Results of a final factor analysis—a principal components analysis with both orthogonal (varimax) and oblique (promax) rotations—also confirmed these selections.
- In particular, the oblique rotation provided the cleanest and most realistic solution in that each measure loads highly on one and only one factor.
- These finding are consistent with a theoretical expectation that urban spatial structure is inherently multidimensional (Massey & Denton, 1988).

In their landmark book entitled *American Apartheid: Segregation and the Making of the Underclass,* Massey and Denton (1993) rank metropolitan areas on the five dimensions of segregation. The dimensions were found to be correlated with each other, and the metropolitan areas that ranked highly on all dimensions were considered to be hyper-segregated. Segregation as measured along these dimensions has been shown to adversely affect some health outcomes for minority group members (McFarland & Smith, 2011; Subramanian, Chen, Rehkopf, Waterman, & Krieger, 2005), but the strength of the effects of each dimension may differ depending on the health condition studied and the race or ethnicity of the individual (Kramer & Hogue, 2009).

Multiple Group Segregation Measures

These earlier measures of segregation focused on comparing two groups, typically a majority group to a minority group. As society has become more racially and ethnically diverse, attention has turned to developing multi-group indexes of segregation. Reardon and Firebaugh (2002) evaluated several methods of measuring multiple-group segregation. They concluded that an information theory index (H) is the preferred method for quantifying multiple group segregation because of its mathematical properties and its consistency with conceptual aspects of segregation. The multi-group H index builds on the entropy index originally proposed by

Theil (1972). The entropy index is the difference between a units' proportions of race and ethnic groups and a larger system's proportions. The multi-group H index is calculated by comparing each areal unit's population distribution across mutually exclusive race and ethnic categories to the distribution of the population of the metropolitan area across the same categories. The average of the deviations for all areal units yields the H index for the metropolitan area. It varies from 0 where all areal units have the same composition as the entire metropolitan area to 1 where all areal units have only one group (for further information about the **Multiple Group H index** see **Table 12.6**).

- Compared to other five multi-group segregation indices, the multi-group H index alone obeys the principle of "transfer" in the multi-group case (i.e., the index declines when an individual of group m moves from unit i to unit j, where the proportion of persons of group m is higher in unit i than in unit j).
- Also, it is the only index that can be decomposed into a sum of between- and within-group components (Reardon & Firebaugh, 2002).

Economic Segregation Measures

Economic segregation refers to the unequal distribution of income groups across residential areas. While there is a long history of development of racial segregation measures, there has been less work on income segregation. However, concerns about the growing concentration of poverty led to an interest in measuring income segregation (Massey & Eggers, 1990). Several researchers have applied the same measurement techniques to income segregation that have been used for racial segregation between minority and majority groups. For example, the segregation between poor and affluent households has been measured using an exposure measure such as P* (interaction index) and an evenness measure such as D (dissimilarity index) indexes (Coulton, Chow, Wang & Su, 1996; Massey & Fischer, 2003). (These indexes are described in **Table 12.5.**) However, income itself is typically measured as a set of ordered categories, but these categorical segregation measures such as P* and D throw away this valuable information.

Several indexes of economic segregation make use of the ordered categories of income that are available from census data. Jargowsky (1996) proposed the **Neighborhood Sorting Index** (NSI) as an improvement over categorical measures of income segregation. NSI is based on the correlation ratio, in essence comparing the variation on household income between neighborhoods to the total variation in household income in the metropolitan area. It provides an index of the homogeneity of income distribution across neighborhoods within a larger metropolitan area, varying from 0, where there is no economic segregation, to 1, where there is complete economic segregation (See **Table 12.7** for details on this index). Results from the analysis of U.S. metropolitan areas using this index showed a steady trend of increasing economic segregation (Jargowsky, 1996). More specifically:

- Results from an analysis of all U.S. metropolitan areas from 1970 to 1990 showed a steady trend toward increasing economic segregation.
- The increases were particularly large and widespread for African American and Hispanics in the 1980s.
- Similar to previous studies that documented relatively low levels of economic segregation (regardless of the measures employed), values of the NSI were relatively modest, though increasing (Jargowksy, 1996).

Reardon and Bischoff (2011) demonstrate the use of the **rank-order information theory index** to measure income segregation. Their index utilizes income percentile ranks of the population within a metropolitan area as a basis for calculating H^R (rank-order information theory index). They argue that, by using income percentile ranks rather than raw income ranges, their measure is independent of the household income distribution within the metropolitan area. This avoids distortions of the index that can occur because of inflation or change in income inequality over time. The rank-order information theory index varies from 0 when there is no income segregation to 1 where there is complete income segregation (see **Table 12.8** for more information). In a study of 100 metropolitan areas, Bischoff and Reardon (2013) found that income inequality affected income segregation, largely through increasing segregation of the affluent population rather then further concentrating the poor.

- Analysis of data from the 100 largest metropolitan areas showed that there is a robust relationship between income inequality and income segregation.
- They also found that income inequality affects income segregation primarily through its effect on the large-scale spatial segregation of affluence rather than by affecting the segregation of poverty.
- These findings reproduce the results in previous literature linking income inequality to income segregation (Reardon & Bischoff, 2011).

Spatial Segregation Measures

The measures of segregation discussed thus far treat residential units as buckets without regard to their geographic location, size, or density. Commonly used segregation measures such as the D (Dissimilarity) index do not distinguish whether the predominant racial makeup of units follows a checkerboard pattern or whether there are large contiguous groupings of units that are of one race (Massey & Denton, 1988). Another drawback of fixed units is that the value of segregation indices can differ depending on the sizes and density of the areal units (e.g., blocks, census tracts, zip codes) that are utilized (Wong, 2004). The advent of GIS tools and spatial statistics have made it more feasible for researchers to overcome these limitations to conventional methods of measuring segregation and to suggest alternatives that take space into account.

Reardon and O'Sullivan (2004) propose a general framework for measuring spatial segregation that considers individuals to reside in individualized local environments that can be characterized on the distribution of the population according to race or income. The definition of the local environment can be flexibly determined and represented as spatial weights consistent with theory or research objectives. After reviewing various possible indices of spatial segregation, they conclude that the information theory index, symbolized as H and discussed above, has desirable properties for use as a multi-group spatial segregation measure. Reardon et al. (2008) apply these principles to studying spatial segregation in 40 metropolitan areas. They use block-level race and ethnic counts to compute the spatial information theory (H) index using a biweight kernel proximity function at 500m, 1,000m, 2,000m, and 4,000m (p. 497). Further information on the **spatial information theory index H** is in **Table 12.9.** The results reveal interesting differences among metropolitan areas in the geographic scale of segregation.

- The spatial information index is the most satisfactory (compared to a general spatial exposure isolation index, a spatial relative diversity index, and a spatial dissimilarity index), because it satisfies the exchange criteria in the widest range of case.

- It is also the only index that has both a meaningful spatial and grouping decomposition (Reardon & O'Sullivan, 2004).

Östh, Clark, and Malmberg (2015) propose a measure of spatial segregation that uses population as a gradient rather than distance. They calculate an index of exposure for two groups to one another, conceptually similar to the commonly used P* (Interaction) index. However, rather than using fixed units, the index is calculated for the k-nearest neighbors (using varying values of k) of each individual. They demonstrate that the probability of exposure of racial and ethnic groups to one another varies by group but increases as the scale gets larger. Moreover, the authors suggest that segregation measures based on neighborhood units that are equal in population size may be superior to the use of census tracts or other variable size units for comparing segregation across metropolitan areas. Further information on their **spatial isolation index** is in **Table 12.10**. Results from this study are summarized below.

- Using individualized scalable neighborhoods with fixed population size to measure residential segregation, they found that the scale of segregation is associated with the population size in the neighborhood for which the population composition is estimated.
- Consistent with previous studies, results showed that segregation (i.e., the probability of encountering a same-group individual in the neighborhood) decreased with increasing neighborhood scale.
- Their findings supported the idea that segregation in large metropolitan areas is more likely to be macroscale (i.e., large-scale segregation that occurs at community- and city-wide scales) than in smaller metropolitan areas.
- They concluded that segregation measures based on individualized neighborhoods with the same population count can be useful in comparing levels of segregation across metropolitan areas and across countries (Osth et al., 2015).

Cities that have the same values on segregation indices that are nonspatial or do not take varying scales into account may in reality have quite different patterns with respect to the location and size of segregated sections. However, these differences in spatial patterns can be revealed by comparing profiles of macro–micro segregation ratios. For example, combined with density maps, these measures have been successful in distinguishing cities where the segregated spaces are contiguous and expansive (e.g., Atlanta) from those where the segregated areas are more scattered and localized (e.g., Pittsburgh) (Lee et al., 2008; Reardon et al., 2008). Although these metrics begin with census block population counts by race, they utilize several spatial statistical methods to weight distance and density. Most importantly, they vary the size of the geographic units rather than relying on singular definitions such as census tracts. This allows segregation measures to be calculated for multiple geographic scales and then compared. One of the important findings of this line of research is that segregation declines as scale increases—in other words, larger spaces incorporate more diverse populations (Lee et al., 2008). However, this is tempered by the fact that for African Americans, as compared to Hispanics or Asian Americans, their segregation from Whites operates over larger distances, suggesting the possibility of more profound isolation.

COMMUNITY DIVERSITY MEASURES

In this section, we cover several measures that might be considered the converse of segregation, such as the degree to which communities are racially and ethnically diverse and whether they have a mix of income levels. Even within metropolitan areas that on the whole are segregated, there may be some communities that are more or less integrated or inclusive. Researchers are often interested in studying such communities and in examining the processes of change through which residential areas become more or less diverse. Examples can be seen in studies of mixed income communities (Joseph, Chaskin, & Webber, 2007), racially and ethnically integrated neighborhoods (Ellen, Horn, & O'Regan, 2012), and economically upgrading communities (Ellen & O'Regan, 2011).

Measurement of Neighborhood Racial and Ethnic Diversity

A diverse community can be thought of as one that is made up of many groups. Unlike the segregation indexes described above, which provide a score for the entire city or metropolitan area, diversity indexes tend to be calculated for each neighborhood that make up the larger geography. White (1986) defines diversity as the relative heterogeneity of the population. He argues that an index of diversity should summarize the distribution of the population among a set of categories. A diverse community has more groups and more equal representation of those groups.

The entropy index (White, 1986) forms the basis for measuring ethnic diversity in several studies of neighborhoods in the United States. The entropy index has no defined limit, as its maximum is related to the number of groups in the population. Since there is no fixed upper bound, a population consisting of more equal-sized groups will produce a higher E (entropy) score than one consisting of fewer equal-sized groups.

Lee, Iceland, and Sharp (2012) standardize the entropy index in their analysis of trends in ethnic diversity across census tracts. Specifically, they divide the entropy score for each census tract by its maximum value and multiply by 100. The resulting Entropy Index for Multi-Group Diversity has a value of 0 when a tract is made up of only one group and a value of 100 when the community has equal representation of all groups. They find that their entropy index reliably detects change in neighborhood diversity over a ten-year period.

- Although racial and ethnic diversity has increased in all types of communities since 1980, diversity rankings have remained stable over time.
- An increasing number of Hispanic and Asian populations have contributed to an increase in diversity.
- This finding is consistent with the expectation that sustained immigration from minority groups would spur community diversity (Lee et al., 2012).

(See **Table 12.11** for more information on their **Entropy Index of Multi-Group Diversity**). Modarres (2004) also evaluates the entropy index as a tool for measuring neighborhood ethnic diversity in Los Angeles. He demonstrates that it yields patterns that were consistent with other evidence of changing diversity in the region.

Another approach to measuring diversity is based on the interaction index. This index reflects the probability that two members of the population chosen at random will be of different ethnic groups (White, 1986). The interaction index is also known as Simpson's index in biology and the Herfindahl index in economics. Talen (2006) demonstrates the use of the interaction index in her study of social diversity in Chicago neighborhoods along four dimensions: race/ethnicity, age of population, household income, and household type. She finds that the four types of social diversity are correlated with one another and that various predictors correlate with diversity in the expected direction, suggesting the construct validity of the measure. Population density is positively associated with social diversity, but only up to a point, consistent with other research documenting this non-linear association. (See **Table 12.12** for details on the **Interaction Index of Multi-Group Diversity**). A summary of the results is presented below.

- Comparison of the Interaction Index of Multi-Group Diversity across block groups shows that income and racial diversity have different spatial patterns.
- Population density is positively associated with social diversity but only up to a point. This finding is consistent with other research documenting a nonlinear association between population density and social segregation.
- The most diverse areas are in inner-ring suburbs, which is also consistent with previous research that has shown that middle-income, first-tier suburbs have the highest social diversity.
- Residential areas are changing over time and half of the block groups in Cook County lost diversity between 1990 and 2000 (Talen, 2006).

The **Location Quotient for Racial Residential Segregation (LQRRS)** is another index that characterizes the racial or ethnic composition of neighborhoods. However, unlike the interaction indexes that quantify the racial or ethnic mix, it focuses on the degree to which a minority group is concentrated in each neighborhood (see **Table 12.13** for details). The LQRRS has been applied in studies of population health to investigate whether health status is affected by living in a neighborhood that is highly segregated relative to the surrounding region. Findings suggest that health status is negatively affected by living in areas that are higher on the LQRRS (Sudano, Perzynski, Wong, Colabianchi, & Litaker, 2013).

- The distribution of respondents by LQRRS showed that 50.1% of the respondents lived in minimal, 33.7% in low, 8.4% in moderate, and 7.8% in high LQRRS tracts in 1992.
- Results of a logit analysis documented that living in low, moderate, and high LQRRS tracts was associated with higher likelihood of major declines in health and mortality compared to minimal LQRRS when adjusting for demographic characteristics.
- Controlling for all covariates, only residence in moderate LQRRS census tract was associated with major declines in health and mortality (Sudano et al., 2013).

Measuring Income Diversity in Neighborhoods

In recent decades there has been growing concern about the isolation of low-income populations and affluent populations in separate communities. This has given rise to significant policy interest in mixed income development (Joseph et al., 2007) and efforts to promote stably mixed income communities. At the same time, affordable neighborhoods seem to be disappearing in some cities as high-income newcomers upgrade properties and price lower income households out of the market (Wyly, Newman, Schafran, & Lee, 2010). Researchers that study these topics require measures that capture the degree to which neighborhoods can be considered economically diverse or stably mixed income and characterize the extent and direction of economic change that is occurring in communities.

Galster, Booza, and Cutsinger (2008) adapt the entropy index discussed in the previous section to study neighborhood income diversity. They calculate the entropy index for five income ranges defined as very low income, moderate income, high-moderate income, high income, and very high income. To test the usefulness of the index, they specify ranges on the entropy score that they then use to classify census tracts as having high diversity, moderate diversity, low diversity, and not diverse. Applying these methods in various cities, they provide evidence for criterion-related validity for an entropy index on diversity of income categories.

Such overall indexes of income diversity have not proven particularly useful in assessing the specific goal of policies directed at changing high poverty areas into mixed income communities. Mixed income by design encourages neighborhoods that are neither extremely poor nor extremely affluent but have a share of low-income households along with middle- and upper-middle income households. Recognizing this focus, Sampson, Mare, and Perkins (2015) developed the **Index of Concentration at the Extremes (ICE)** to quantify the degree to which neighborhoods departed from the ideal mix in either direction toward concentrated poverty or affluence (for further information on ICE, see **Table 12.14**). They used this index to study stability and change in mixed income communities in Chicago. They found that neighborhoods at the extremes of concentrated affluence or poverty changed little over time. There was more change in ICE scores over time for those neighborhoods that started out with mixed income populations.

- Comparison of ICE scores over time show that high scores and low scores persist suggesting that neighborhood poverty and affluence are sticky.
- Persistence is greatest for those tracts that are at the two ends of the ICE range—that is, with concentrated affluence or poverty.
- Mixed-income neighborhoods showed more transitions in both directions, also consistent with other research on neighborhood decline and gentrification (Sampson et al., 2015).

MEASURING ACCESS TO OPPORTUNITY

In the previous section, we focused on measuring place-based social exclusion because of the disproportionate distribution of the population along race, ethnic, and class lines. A related concern is how places vary in whether they provide residents with access to the resources they need to succeed. In fact, along a number of dimensions, it is minority and low-income neighborhoods that suffer the poorest access to resources (Squires & Kubrin, 2005). A number of literature reviews have concluded that lack of access to employment opportunities, high-quality services, and amenities are important mechanisms that are responsible for the negative effects that living in disadvantaged neighborhoods have on children and adults (Ellen & Turner, 1997; Galster, 2012; Sampson et al., 2002; Shinn & Toohey, 2003). Moreover, many scholars of urban affairs consider both population diversity and access to opportunity to be hallmarks of livable neighborhoods and sustainable cities (Talen, 2012).

Characterizing communities in terms of their proximity to opportunity is, therefore, of longstanding interest in the field. As a result, there has been considerable investment in developing measures of access to various resources at the neighborhood level. In this chapter, we focus on two types of important resources, measures of access to employment opportunities and access to services and amenities. Measures of the availability of healthy living resources are discussed in Chapter 9.

Measures of Job Access

The lack of access to employment is potentially an important component of what constitutes place-based social exclusion. Researchers' interest in studying job access has grown since Kain (1968, 2004) put forward the spatial mismatch hypothesis, which shined a light on how the geography of racial segregation posed barriers for employment in minority populations. A key component of his argument was that job opportunities for minority populations were increasingly moving to the outskirts of cities, while the forces responsible for segregation trapped workers in inner-city locations that were increasingly far away from these jobs. He argued that these distances posed social, economic, and physical obstacles to getting and keeping jobs. The connection between the suburbanization of industries and declining rates of employment and earnings in minority neighborhoods were well documented by Wilson (1987, 1996). To varying degrees, studies have demonstrated that greater distances between employment opportunities and residential locations undermine individuals' employment success (Allard, 2002; Allard & Danziger, 2002; Holzer & Ihlanfeldt, 1996; Ihlanfeldt, 1994; Pan, Jensen, Fuller, & Mohanty, 2006; Vartanian, 1999).

Researchers have examined job access across numerous populations and multiple metropolitan areas and have measured job availability and accessibility in varied ways (e.g., Allard & Danziger, 2002; Bania, Leete, & Coulton, 2008; Gurley & Bruce, 2005; Gurmu & Smith, 2006; Gurmu, Ihlanfeldt, & Smith, 2008; Lens, 2014; Ong & Blumenberg, 1998; Sanchez, Shen, & Peng, 2004). Nevertheless, there are some essential components of a useful job access measure that can be specified. They include job proximity, job availability, and local job competition (Bunel & Tovar, 2013). When they are combined into one index, the result can be used to quantify job accessibility for individuals and communities.

Conceptually, job proximity reflects the distance between residential locations and employment opportunities. In practice, distance can be measured categorically (e.g., all jobs within 5 miles or not), as a straight line (e.g., Euclidean distance to jobs), or by travel time to jobs. Researchers sometimes differentiate between automobile and public transit travel times (Bania et al., 2008; Sanchez et al., 2004; Shen, 1998). Many investigators employ a distance-decay function, typically used in transportation analysis, to give greater weight to opportunities that are close by rather than those at considerable distance (e.g., Parks, 2004; Raphael, 1998).

Job availability acknowledges that not all jobs can be considered available to particular populations. For example, in studies of low-skill workers, some researchers have focused their measurement on low-skill jobs rather than all jobs in the region (e.g., Bania et al., 2008; Hu, 2014). Another aspect of availability is to estimate job openings rather than all existing jobs, since these are presumably jobs that new job seekers could get. Several studies have used job growth as a proxy for job openings (e.g., Gurmu et al., 2008; Shen, 2001).

A final aspect of job access measurement is to take into account the level of competition from other potential job seekers in the area. Competitors are typically defined as individuals in the same areas who are similar to the population for whom job access is being calculated. For example, all adults of working age in a study of overall job access or all individuals that have low levels of education in a study of a low-skill population job access (Bania et al., 2008). The same distance weighting functions are applied to competitors as to job opportunities.

As pointed out by Bunel and Tovar (2013), a problem with the literature is that studies tend to rely on slightly different ways of measuring local job accessibility, making their results difficult to compare. They demonstrate, for example, that conclusions are sensitive to whether proximity is represented by travel time or distance to jobs. They also note that findings are affected by the various ways in which job availability may be defined (e.g., all jobs or only vacancies). Finally, they raise concerns about frontier effects that occur when data sources are limited to a particular administrative jurisdiction. Job access for individuals and communities near the border are likely to be poorly estimated because of missing data.

Nevertheless, there is enough commonality across studies to specify a basic approach to measurement of local job accessibility. **Table 12.15** provides the key elements of a **local job accessibility (LJA)** index that is made up of three weighted components. These elements can be customized to fit particular populations and research purposes (Raphael, 1998).

- African American male youths in the Bay Area are at a significant accessibility disadvantage compared to White male youths in the same area. Overall, accessibility to jobs (combined with the variable) explains 12% of the variance in neighborhood male youth employment rates. Differential accessibility (i.e., job accessibility and labor supply) explains 30–50% of the difference in neighborhood employment rates between White and African-American Bay Area male youths (when estimates are taken from separate regressions by race, differential accessibility explains 20% of the employment rate differential) (Raphael, 1998).
- With regards to validity, Raphael (1998) compares his index to previous studies. In particular, earlier studies of Chicago in 1970 and Los Angeles in 1980 did not find a substantial relationship between accessibility and youth employment or racial difference in youth employment rates (Ellwood, 1986; Leonard, 1985). Raphael runs regressions on the Bay Area data using Ellwood's measures, which yield quite different results than using Raphael's measures. This suggests the divergence from past results is down to the measures rather than the data.
- Additionally, Allard and Danziger (2002) found a relationship between accessibility and employment among welfare recipients in the Detroit metropolitan area using the same basic index as Raphael but specified for the welfare population. However, also using the same measures, Gurmu and colleagues (2008) found effect of local job access on employment rates for welfare recipients in Atlanta, and Bania and colleagues (2008) also found no such relationship for female welfare recipients in Cleveland.

Measures of Access to Services and Amenities

Unequal access to services and amenities is another dimension of social exclusion that has been of concern in the literature on neighborhoods and communities. Studies have documented place-based disparities in access to social services (Allard, 2009; Allard, Rosen, & Tolman, 2003), health care (Wang, 2003), public transit (McKenzie, 2013), businesses (e.g., banks) and amenities (e.g., health clubs) (Macintyre, Macdonald, & Ellaway, 2008).

Handy and Niemeier (1997) argue that accessibility is determined by the spatial distribution of potential destinations and the ease of reaching those destinations. In a model of measurement, these potential destinations may need to be weighted for their various attributes, such as size, quality, or attractiveness (Koenig, 1980). Travel costs or barriers (referred to as impedance) also need to be taken into account.

Talen and Anselin (1998) propose a general approach to the measurement of spatial equity in access to resources. They identify four alternative measures for calibrating the access to resources from residential locations. First is the "container approach," which counts the number of resources within a defined unit, such as a census tract or radius, from a given point. The second is a "gravity potential" method based on weighted distances between the origins and all destinations. The third index, based on "travel cost," is simply the average distance from each origin to all destinations. The fourth measure is referred to as "minimum distance." It reflects the distance from a residential location to the nearest facility. In their empirical demonstration of these measures, they use census tract population weighted centroids to proxy residential locations, street networks to specify distance, and the coordinates of facilities as the destination locations. Details on the four indexes are presented in **Table 12.16 (Accessibility Index [*Z*])**.

- Spatial analysis confirmed that the gravity measure is distinct from the other two. No significant spatial autocorrelation was found for the gravity measure, while travel and distance measures showed strong and positive spatial autocorrelation (Talen & Anselin, 1998).

CONCLUSION

There are several commonalities and limitations that seem to run through all of these measures of place-based social exclusion. First, they all focus on residential locations as the primary context that confers various advantages and disadvantages. However, there is growing recognition that people are mobile and that they may also be affected by places outside their residential communities (Sheller & Urry, 2006). For example, there is evidence that activity spaces—that is, areas where individuals tend to spend time—may also be segregated and vary in the kinds of resources they supply (Atkinson & Flint, 2004; Lee & Kwan, 2011). Researchers interested in place-based communities might also be interested in overlaying activity spaces (Golledge & Stimson, 1997) or individuals' unique or bespoke neighborhoods based on perceptions (Coulton, Jennings, & Chan, 2013) to determine whether measures of social exclusion differ across these alternative perspectives on community.

Second, recent literature suggests that the measurement of place-based social exclusion and access to resources is moving beyond static boundaries and two-group measures to take into account more fluid notions of space and the reality of an increasingly diverse population. Recent advances in GIS tools and more complex modeling have made these advances possible, and it is expected that we will continue to see new measures and methods evolving for this work.

A third feature of all of the measures covered in this chapter is that they tend to rely on available data from government or commercial sources. Census data, for example, feature prominently in the empirical work on these measures. Travel distances often come from commercial data products. Information on the location of resources is frequently limited to those organizations or firms that are in business and government databases. It is important that researchers depending on these data sources are familiar with their limitations. One concern, particularly with estimates that come from sample surveys such as the census, is that the margins of error around small area estimates can be quite large. Another issue that requires careful investigation is the amount of missing data that may occur in government records, service and business directories, or any other data resource that is originally put together for another purpose. Prior to using these data to craft measures, a careful evaluation of data quality is required.

Despite these limitations, the processes of social exclusion clearly confer advantages on some communities and disadvantages on others. It is crucial that research continue to document these disparities, determine how these conditions affect the wellbeing of individuals and groups and evaluate how policies, programs, and social action can reduce social exclusion in our communities. Continued attention to the measurement of these phenomena is important and should be supported.

LIST OF MEASURES AND TABLE NUMBERS

TABLE 12.1 ■	Concentrated Disadvantage
Primary Reference	Sampson, R. J., Raudenbush, S. W., & Earls, F. (1997). Neighborhoods and violent crime: A multilevel study of collective efficacy. *Science, 277*(5328), 918–924.
Purpose	The purpose of concentrated disadvantage is to measure neighborhood differences in poverty.
Description	Six characteristics of census tracts are used to define a measure of concentrated disadvantage: • Welfare receipt • Poverty • Unemployment • Female-headed households • Racial composition (percentage black) • Density of children (less than age 18) A value of this index is calculated as a weighted factor score, with higher scores representing higher levels of neighborhood disadvantage.
Sample/Data	To validate concentrated disadvantage, two data sources were utilized: • Data from the Project on Human Development in Chicago Neighborhoods (PHDCN, *N* = 8,782 residents) • 847 census tracts (data from the 1990 Census) in the city of Chicago, which were combined to create 343 "Neighborhood Clusters" (NCs)
Measurement	• First, a factor analysis is conducted to confirm the emergence of a single factor of concentrated disadvantage. To be specific, the alpha-scoring method was chosen to maximize the reliability of measures, and an oblique factor rotation was used to allow the extracted dimensions to covary. • Second, to represent this dimension, they calculate a factor regression score that weights each variable by its factor loading.
Assessment	• Consistent with theories and research on U.S. cities, the factor of concentrated disadvantage was dominated by high loadings (> 0.85) for poverty, public assistance, unemployment, female headed-families, and density of children. • An alternative method, a principal components analysis with varimax rotation, provided substantively identical results.
Related Reference	Sampson, R. J., Sharkey, P., & Raudenbush, S. W. (2008). Durable effects of concentrated disadvantage on verbal ability among African-American children. *Proceedings of the National Academy of Sciences, 105*(3), 845–852.
Language	English
Contact	Robert J. Sampson Department of Sociology William James Hall Harvard University 33 Kirkland Street Cambridge, MA 02138, USA Email: rsampson@wjh.harvard.edu
Web Site	For more information see: Project on Human Development in Chicago Neighborhoods: http://www.icpsr.umich.edu/icpsrweb/PHDCN/instruments.jsp.

TABLE 12.2 ■ Townsend Index of Concentrated Disadvantage

Primary Reference	Townsend, P., Phillimore, P., & Beattie, A. (1988). *Health and deprivation: Inequality and the North.* London: Croom Helm.
Purpose	The purpose of the Townsend Index is to measure economic deprivation within an area.
Description	The Townsend Index is an index of material deprivation measure that consists of a standardized *z* score combining four census variables: • Percentage of crowding • Percentage of unemployment • Percentage of no car ownership • Percentage of renters Equal weights are given to each measure, and a high score reflects high material deprivation.
Sample	Three data sources are used: • The 1981 Census Small Area Statistics • Postcoded death registration records • Postcoded birth registration records All of these data are provided by the Office of Population Censuses and Surveys. The populations of 678 wards throughout the Northern Region of England were used as a sample.
Measurement	Townsend Index = $\sum_{i=1}^{4} Z_i, Z_i = \frac{T_i - \mu_{Ti}}{S_{Ti}}$ Where $T_i = \log(X_i + 1)$ when $i = 1, 2$ (log transformed to normalize their distribution) or $T_i = X_i$ when $i = 3, 4$ X_1 and X_2 = percentage of unemployment and percentage of households with more than two people living in a room X_3 and X_4 = percentage of households without a car and percentage of house renter μ_{Ti} = average of T_i and S_{Ti} = standard deviation of T_i
Related Reference	Aggarwal, V. R., Macfarlane, T. V., & Macfarlane, G. J. (2003). Why is pain more common amongst people living in areas of low socio-economic status? A population-based cross-sectional study. *British Dental Journal, 194*(7), 383–387.
Language	English
Contact	Peter Phillimore, Sociology Claremont Bridge Building Newcastle University Newcastle upon Tyne, NE1 7RU, UK Email: peter.phillimore@ncl.ac.uk

TABLE 12.3 ■	Socioeconomic Position Index (SEP)
Primary Reference	Krieger, N., Chen, J. T., Waterman, P. D., Soobader, M. J , Subramanian, S. V., & Carson, R. (2002). Geocoding and monitoring of US socioeconomic inequalities in mortality and cancer incidence: Does the choice of area-based measure and geographic level matter? The public health disparities geocoding project. *American Journal of Epidemiology, 156*(5), 471–482.
Purpose	The purpose of SEP index is to assess the level of socioeconomic deprivation in neighborhood.
Description	SEP index is a summary deprivation measure consisting of standardized *z* scores combining data on six areas: • Occupational class • Income • Poverty • Wealth • Education • Crowding Higher values of the index indicate a higher degree of deprivation.
Sample/ Data	To validate the SEP index, two data sources are used: • Administrative data on mortality and cancer incidence from Massachusetts and Rhode Island • 1990 Census data for census tracts and block groups from U.S. Bureau of the Census Summary Tape File 3A and zip code data from Summary Tape File 3B
Measurement	$SEP = \sum_{i=1}^{6} Z_i,\ Z_i = \frac{T_i - \mu_{Ti}}{S_{Ti}}$ Where $T_i = X_i$ when i = 1, 2, 3, 4 or T_i = reverse-coded X_i when i = 5, 6 (to make a higher score on the SEP indicate a higher degree of deprivation) X_1, X_2, X_3, X_4 = % of working class, unemployment, % of below poverty line, and % of low education (less than high school) X_5 and X_6 = % of expensive homes and median household income μ_{Ti} = average of T_i and S_{Ti} = standard deviation of T_i
Related Reference	Krieger, N., Chen, J. T., Waterman, P. D., Rehkopf, D. H., & Subramanian, S. V. (2003). Race/ethnicity, gender, and monitoring socioeconomic gradients in health: A comparison of area-based socioeconomic measures-the public health disparities geocoding project. *American Journal of Public Health, 93*(10), 1655–1671.
Language	English
Contact	Nancy Krieger Department of Health and Social Behavior Harvard School of Public Health 677 Huntington Ave Boston, MA 02115, USA Email: nkrieger@hsph.harvard.edu

TABLE 12.4 ■ Area Deprivation Index

Primary Reference	Singh, G. K. (2003). Area deprivation and widening inequalities in US mortality, 1969-1998. *American Journal of Public Health, 93*(7), 1137–1143.
Purpose	The purpose of this index is to measure neighborhood socioeconomic disadvantage for the United States.
Description	Area Deprivation Index (ADI) is a factor-based deprivation index that consisted of census-based social indicators. This index uses 17 census indicators including • Educational attainment • Occupation • Employment • Income • Housing price • Household composition • Crowding • Automobile access • Telephone • Plumbing in a given county Communities with higher ADI scores have higher levels of deprivation.
Sample/ Data	The sample was made up of all census tracts in 3,097 U.S. counties in 1990. Census data were used for the study.
Scoring	• 17 U.S. census variables are weighted using factor score coefficients from Principal Component Analysis (PCA). • Poverty, income, and education have the largest relative weights among all the variables. • These variables are multiplied by their factor weights and then summed for each geographic unit. • The result is then transformed into a standardized index (the ADI) by arbitrarily setting the index mean at 100 and *SD* at 20.
Assessment	• The reliability coefficient (α) for the census tract index was 0.95, representing a high degree of internal consistency among the 17 indicators. • The factor structure matrix for the different random subsamples remained unchanged, indicating a high degree of index reliability. In addition, the factor loadings for the three geographic levels (census tract, zip code, and county levels) were similar in magnitude and relative importance. For county level, the weighted correlations of the ADI with health outcomes were in the expected direction, indicating predictive validity. • Singh and Kogan (2007) linked the ADI to county vital records data and showed that socioeconomic disparities persisted in both neonatal and post neonatal mortality in the United States from 1969 to 2001.
Related References	Kind, A. J., Jencks, S., Brock, J., Yu, M., Bartels, C., Ehlenbach, W., . . . & Smith, M. (2014). Neighborhood socioeconomic disadvantage and 30-day rehospitalization: A retrospective cohort study. *Annals of Internal Medicine, 161*(11), 765–774. Singh, G. K., & Kogan, M. D. (2007). Persistent socioeconomic disparities in infant, neonatal, and postneonatal mortality rates in the United States, 1969–2001. *Pediatrics, 119*(4), e928–e939.

Language	English
Contact	Gopal K. Singh Health Resources and Services Administration Maternal and Child Health Bureau US Department of Health and Human Services Rockville, MD, USA Email: gsingh@hrsa.gov

TABLE 12.5 ■ Dimensions of Residential Segregation (two-group minority–majority group segregation)

Primary Reference	Massey, D. S., & Denton, N. A. (1988). The dimensions of residential segregation. *Social Forces, 67*(2), 281–315.
Purpose	The purpose of this approach is to conceptualize residential segregation in terms of five distinct dimensions of spatial variation.
Description	The five dimensions of spatial variation include 1. **Evenness:** The dissimilarity index (D) measures departures from evenness by taking the weighted mean absolute deviation of every unit's minority proportion from the city's minority proportion (0 = no segregation; 1 = complete segregation). 2. **Exposure:** The interaction index (P*) measures the extent to which members of minority group X are exposed to members of majority group Y. The index varies from 0 to 1.0 and can be interpreted as the probability that a randomly drawn X-member shares an area with a member of Y. 3. **Concentration:** The Relative Concentration Index (RCO) measures the geographic concentration of minority group X in an absolute sense, regardless of how majority group Y is distributed (0 = the minority and majority groups are equally concentrated; −1 = Y's concentration exceeds X's to the maximum extent possible; 1 = the reverse of −1). 4. **Centralization:** The Absolute Centralization Index (ACE) measures a group's spatial distribution compared to the distribution of land area around the city center (negative ACE values = a tendency for minority group members to reside close to the city center; positive ACE values = a tendency to live in outlying areas; ACE is 0 = a group has a uniform distribution throughout the metropolitan area). 5. **Clustering:** The Spatial Proximity Index (SP) quantifies the degree of spatial clustering exhibited by a minority group, and it is calculated by using the average of intragroup proximities, weighted by the fraction of each group in the population (SP greater than 1 = members of each group live nearer to one another than to members of the other group; SP less than 1 = minority and majority members live nearer to members of the other group than to members of their own group; SP is 1 = no difference).
Sample/ Data	The data were a part of a larger study of Hispanic, African American, and Asian segregation in the 50 largest SMSAS in the United States plus 10 others with sizeable concentrations of Hispanics. They were obtained from the Census 1980 STF4 data tapes.
Measurement	1. $D=\sum_{i=1}^{n}[t_i \mid p_i - P \mid / 2TP(1-P)]$ Where n = the number of areas (tracts), t_i and p_i = the total population and minority proportion of areal unit i; T and P = the population size and minority proportion of the whole city, which is subdivided into n areal units. 2. ${}_xP^*_y = \sum_{i=1}^{n}\left[x_i/X\right]\left[y_i/t_i\right]$ Where x_i, y_i, and t_i = the numbers of X members, Y members, and the total population of unit i, respectively; X = the number of X members citywide (the sum of all x_i)

	3. $RCC = \{[\sum_{i=1}^{n}(x_i a_i / X)]/[\sum_{i=1}^{n}(y_i a_i / Y)] - 1\} - \{[\sum_{i=1}^{n_1}(t_i a_i / T_1)]/[\sum_{i=n_2}^{n} t_i a_i / T_2)] - 1\}$ Where geographic units are ordered from smallest to largest in areal size; a_i = the land area of unit i; n_1 = rank of the tract where the cumulative total population of areal units equals the total minority population of the city, summing from the smallest unit up; n_2 = rank of the tract where the cumulative total population of areal units equals the minority population totaling from the largest unit down; T_1 = the total population of tracts from 1 to n_1; T_2 = the total population of tracts from n_2 to n. t_i = the total population of area i; X = the number of group X members in the city. 4. $ACE = (\sum_{i=1}^{n} x_{i-1} A_i) - (\sum_{i=1}^{n} X_i A_{i-1})$ Where the areal units are ordered as smallest to largest in areal size; A_i = the cumulative proportion of land area through unit i; X_i = the cumulative proportions of X's population in tract i. 5. $SP = (XP_{xx} + YP_{yy}) / TP_{tt}$ Where P_{xx} = the average proximity between group X members; P_{yy} = the average proximity between group Y members; P_{tt} = the average proximity between all members of population.
Related References	Kramer, M. R., & Hogue, C. R. (2009). Is segregation bad for your health? *Epidemiologic Reviews, 31*(1), 178–194. Iceland, J. (2002). Appendix B: *Measures of residential segregation. Housing patterns.* U.S. Census Bureau. Available at: http://www.census.gov/hhes/www/housing/housing_patterns/app_b.html
Language	English
Contact	Douglas S. Massey Office of Population Research Princeton University Wallace Hall Princeton, NJ 08544, USA Email: dmassey@princeton.edu

TABLE 12.6 ■ Multi-Group H Index (or multi-group entropy index)	
Primary Reference	Reardon, S. F., & Firebaugh, G. (2002). Measures of multi-group segregation. *Sociological Methodology, 32*(1), 33–67.
Purpose	The purpose of multi-group H index is to measure the distribution of groups across neighborhoods (i.e., "evenness").
Description	• The multi-group H index is a measure of the average difference between a census tract's group proportions of ethnic and racial groups and that of the metropolitan area as a whole. • This index is measured as the weighted average deviation of each tract's entropy from metropolitan-wide entropy, with possible values ranging from 0 (maximum integration) to 1 (maximum segregation). • The index is also known as "multi-group entropy index," "multi-group version of Theil's H," or "multi-group information theory index."
Sample/ Data	An example of the distribution of members of three groups among three organizational units were used for proofs of transfer and exchange properties. No actual data was utilized.
Measurement	A metropolitan area's entropy score is calculated as: $E = \sum_{r=1}^{r} (\Pi_r) \ln [1/\Pi_r]$ Where Π_r = a particular racial/ethnic group's proportion of the whole metropolitan area population. The higher the number E, the more diverse an area. A census tract's entropy score (or diversity) is defined as $E_i = \sum_{r=1}^{r} (\Pi_{ri}) \ln [1/\Pi_{ri}]$ Where Π_{ri} = a particular racial/ethnic group's proportion of population in tract i. Then, the multi-group H index is expressed as a fraction of the metropolitan area's total entropy: $H = \sum_{i=1}^{n} \left[\sum_{n=1}^{N} \frac{t_i(E - E_i)}{H} \right]$ Where t_i = the total population of tract i, T = the metropolitan area population, n = number of tracts, E_i and E = tract i's diversity (entropy) and metropolitan area diversity, respectively.
Related Reference	Iceland, J. (2004b). The multigroup entropy index (also known as Theil's H or the information theory index). *US Census Bureau.*
Language	English
Contact	Sean F. Reardon 520 Galvez mall, #526 Stanford University School of Education Stanford, CA 94305-3084, USA Email: sean.reardon@stanford.edu

TABLE 12.7 ■	Neighborhood Sorting Index (NSI)
Primary Reference	Jargowsky, P. A. (1996). Take the money and run: Economic segregation in US metropolitan areas. *American Sociological Review, 61*(6), 984–998.
Purpose	The purpose of the NSI is to measure neighborhood (e.g., census tract) income segregation within metropolitan areas, adjusting for the average income level and the total amount of income inequality.
Description	• The NSI is a measure of overall income segregation across census tracts. This measure is a correlation-based index that employs a continuous measure of income. • Technically, it is the square root of the ratio of the between-tract income variance over the total variance of household income, treating income as truly continuous and not a set of categories. • The index ranges from 0 (no economic segregation) to 1 (complete segregation).
Sample/Data	The data were drawn from multiple sources: 1970 Fourth Count File A, 1980 Summary Tape File 4A, and 1990 Summary Tape File 3A.
Measurement	$NSI = \frac{\sigma_N}{\sigma_H} = \frac{\sqrt{\frac{\sum_{n=1}^{N} h_n(\bar{y}_n - \bar{y})^2}{H}}}{\sqrt{\frac{\sum_{i=1}^{N} (y_i - \bar{y})^2}{H}}}$ Where y = household income, i = households, n = neighborhood (census tracts), h_n = the number of households in neighborhood n, H and N = the total number of households and neighborhoods respectively
Assessment	Unlike the index of dissimilarity, the NSI is not sensitive to changes in the parameters of the income distribution, only to movements of households from one neighborhood to another.
Related Reference	Costa, D. L., & Kahn, M. E. (2001). *Understanding the decline in social capital, 1952–1998* (No. w8295). National Bureau of Economic Research.
Language	English
Contact	Paul Jargowsky Rutgers University–Camden Center for Urban Research and Education 321 Cooper St. Camden NJ 08102, USA Email: paul.jargowsky@rutgers.edu

TABLE 12.8 ■ Rank-Order Information Theory Index	
Primary Reference	Reardon, S. F., & Bischoff, K. (2011). Income inequality and income segregation. *American Journal of Sociology, 116*(4), 1092–1153.
Purpose	The purpose of the rank-order information theory index is to measure the ratio of within-unit (tract) income rank variation to overall (metropolitan area) income rank variation.
Description	• The measure compares the variation in household incomes within census tracts to the variation in household incomes in the metropolitan area. It ranges from 0 (no income segregation) to 1 (complete income segregation). • The measure is independent of the income distribution because it uses only information on the rank ordering of household incomes within a metropolitan area. This allows meaningful comparisons across time, metropolitan areas, and population subgroups (e.g., racial groups).
Sample/Data	U.S. Census data from the 1970 summary Tape Files 3A, the 1980 Summary Tape Files 3A, the 1990 Summary Tape Files 4a and the 2000 Summary Files 3A were used to validate the index.
Measurement	$E(p) = p \log_2 \frac{1}{p} + (1-p) \log_2 \frac{1}{(1-p)}$ Where, E(p) = the entropy of the population when divided into two groups (cut-off = p), p = income percentile ranks (range from 0 to 1) in a given income distribution $H(p) = 1 - \sum_j \frac{t_j E_j(p)}{TE(p)}$ Where, H(p) = the value of the traditional information theory index, T = the population of the metropolitan area, t_j = the population of neighborhood j Then the rank-order information theory index can be written as, $H^R = 2\ln(2) \int_0^1 E(p)\, H(p)\, dp$
Related Reference	Bischoff, K., & Reardon, S. F. (2013). Residential segregation by income, 1970–2009. In J. R. Logan (Ed.), *The lost decade? Social change in the US after 2000.* New York, NY: Russell Sage.
Language	English
Contact	Sean F. Reardon 520 Galvez mall, 526 Stanford University School of Education Stanford, CA 94305-3084, USA Email: sean.reardon@stanford.edu

TABLE 12.9 ■	Spatial Information H Index
Primary Reference	Reardon, S. F., & O'Sullivan, D. (2004). Measures of spatial segregation. *Sociological Methodology, 34*(1), 121–162.
Purpose	The purpose of spatial information H index is to measure the extent to which the local environments of individuals differ in their racial or socioeconomic composition.
Description	• This index measures the variation across a region in the local spatially weighted average racial composition, where a proximity function defining the proximity of any two locations in space is used as a spatial weight. • The index is a measure of how much less diverse individuals' local environments are, on average, than the total population of region R. • The index has a minimum value of 0, which is obtained if and only if each subarea has the same group composition (the minimum possible segregation). • A maximum value of 1 is obtained if and only if each subarea is comprised of a single group (the maximum possible segregation).
Sample/ Data	N/A
Measurement	$\tilde{H} = 1 - \frac{1}{TE} \int_{p \in R} T_p \tilde{E}_p \, dp$ Where T = total population in the study region R E = overall regional entropy, given by $E = -\sum_{m=1}^{M} (\pi_{pm}) \log_M(\pi_{pm})$ where π_{pm} = proportion in group m at point p, and M = number of mutually exclusive population subgroups (e.g., racial groups), indexed by m T_p = population density in the local environment of point p $\tilde{E}_p$ = spatial entropy at p, given by $\tilde{E}_p = -\sum_{m-1}^{M} (\tilde{\pi}_{pm}) \log_M(\tilde{\pi}_{pm})$ Where $\tilde{\pi}_{pm}$ = proportion in group m in the local environment of point p p = subarea (e.g., census tract) and R = study region (e.g., metropolitan region)
Related Reference	Reardon, S. F., Matthews, S. A., O'Sullivan, D., Lee, B. A., Firebaugh, G., Farrell, C. R., & Bischoff, K. (2008). The geographic scale of metropolitan racial segregation. *Demography, 45*(3), 489–514.
Language	English
Contact	Sean F. Reardon 520 Galvez mall, #526 Stanford University School of Education Stanford, CA 94305-3084, USA Email: sean.reardon@stanford.edu
Web Site	https://cran.r-project.org/web/packages/seg/seg.pdf

TABLE 12.10 ■ Spatial Isolation (SI) Index	
Primary Reference	Östh, J., Clark, W. A., & Malmberg, B. (2015). Measuring the scale of segregation using k-nearest neighbor aggregates. *Geographical Analysis, 47*(1), 34–49.
Purpose	The purpose of spatial isolation index is to measure aggregate segregation across neighborhoods based on behavioral considerations by using population count-based definitions of neighborhood scale.
Description	• The spatial isolation index is an aggregate measure that captures the probability of encountering people belonging to different subpopulation (ethnic group). • This index uses individualized scalable neighborhoods with fixed population size to assess spatial variations in population composition, and it does not require administrative units. • Higher scores indicate lower levels of segregation.
Sample/Data	Block-level population data from Los Angeles (U.S. Census 2010 data) and gridded register data from Sweden's three largest city regions comprise the sample for validation of spatial isolation index.
Measurement	$\text{Spatial isolation } k = \dfrac{\sum_{i=1}\left(x_i * \dfrac{x_{i,k}}{k}\right)}{\sum_{i=1}(x_i)}$ Where k = a predetermined count of nearest neighbors X_i = the size of the minority population in block i $X_{i,k}/k$ = the share of the minority population among the k-nearest neighbors of individuals living in block i
Related Reference	Clark, W., Anderson, E., Malmberg, B., & Östh, J. (2014). Segregation and de-segregation in metropolitan contexts: Los Angeles as a paradigm for a changing ethnic world.
Language	English
Contact	John Östh Department of Social and Economic Geography Uppsala University Box 513, SE-751 20 Uppsala, Sweden Email: john.osth@kultgeog.uu.se
Web Site	http://equipop.kultgeog.uu.se/

TABLE 12.11 ■	Entropy Index of Multi-Group Neighborhood Diversity
Primary Reference	Lee, B. A., Iceland, J., & Sharp, G. (2012). Racial and ethnic diversity goes local: Charting change in American communities over three decades. *USA2010 Project*.
Purpose	The purpose of this measure is to assess the level of multi-group diversity in neighborhoods. The measure focuses on how uniformly members of a population are spread.
Description	• The entropy index captures the magnitude of multi-group diversity in neighborhood. • The value ranges from 0 (complete homogeneity or no diversity) to 1 (maximum heterogeneity), which is often multiplied by 100 to set its range of possible values from 0 to 100. • This index satisfies the decomposition criterion, which allows comparison of variables with different numbers of categories.
Sample/Data	The 1980 through 2010 decennial censuses and the 2006–2010 American Community Survey (ACS) comprise the sample for validation of the entropy index. Two classes of census geographic units were defined: • Areas = metropolitan, metropolitan and rural (by 2008 U.S. Office of Management and Budget geographic definitions). The index ranges from 23.9 to 89.3 in 2010. • Places: communities that have at least 1,000 residents in given years. The index ranges from 3.8 to 95.4 in 2010.
Measurement	$E = \sum_{r=1}^{n} P_r \ln\left(\frac{1}{P_r}\right)$ where P_r = racial-ethnic group r's proportion of the population in a geographic unit n = the number of groups under consideration
Assessment	• A comparison of the entropy index across time points show that the magnitude of racial-ethnic diversity (or diversity rank) was highly stable. • Spearman correlation was 0.92 between 2000 and 2010 and 0.80 between 1980 and 2010.
Related References	Farrell, C. R., & Lee, B. A. (2011). Racial diversity and change in metropolitan neighborhoods. *Social Science Research*, *40*(4), 1108–1123. Modarres, A. (2004). Neighborhood integration: Temporality and social fracture. *Journal of Urban Affairs*, *26*(3), 351–377.
Language	English
Contact	Barrett A. Lee Department of Sociology Penn State University 614 Oswald Tower University Park, PA 16802, USA Email: bal6@psu.edu
Web Site	https://cran.r-project.org/web/packages/entropy/entropy.pdf

TABLE 12.12 ■ Interaction Index of Multi-Group Diversity

Primary Reference	Talen, E. (2006). Neighborhood-level social diversity: Insights from Chicago. *Journal of the American Planning Association, 72*(4), 431–446.
Purpose	This index measures the probability that two individuals randomly selected from an area will belong the same subpopulations. The measure is commonly used in the biological literature to measure biological diversity and can be viewed as the average differentness between two randomly chosen individuals.
Description	This measure focuses on social diversity using census variables: • Resident diversity: race, age, family income, and family type • Housing diversity: units in structure, housing tenure, year built, number of bedrooms, value, and rent The inverse (reciprocal) form of the Simpson Index is used to allow a more intuitive interpretation of values. The value can range from 1 (no diversity) to the number of categories (maximum value). The higher the value, the greater the diversity.
Sample/ Data	The block groups in Cook County, Illinois, are the sample for validation of the interaction index. The data used were Census Summary Tape File 3 data, which are spatially adjusted to allow comparisons between block groups over time.
Measurement	Simpson's Reciprocal Index (1/D): $A = \frac{N(N-1)}{\sum_i n_i(n_i-1)}$ Simpson's index: $D = \frac{\sum_i n_i(n_i-1)}{N(N-1)}$ where n_i = the number of individuals in the ith category N = the total number of individuals of all categories
Related Reference	White, M. J. (1986). Segregation and diversity measures in population distribution. *Population Index, 52*(2), 198–221.
Language	English
Contact	Emily Talen School of Geographical Sciences and Urban Planning Arizona State University PO Box 875302 Tempe, Arizona, 85287-5302, USA Email: etalen@asu.edu.
Web Site	https://cran.r-project.org/web/packages/vegan/vignettes/diversity-vegan.pdf

TABLE 12.13 ■ Location Quotient for Racial Residential Segregation (LQRRS)

Primary Reference	Sudano, J. J., Perzynski, A., Wong, D. W., Colabianchi, N., & Litaker, D. (2013). Neighborhood racial residential segregation and changes in health or death among older adults. *Health & Place, 19*, 80–88
Purpose	The purpose of LQRRS is to measure racial residential segregation in local areas.
Description	• The LQRRS is a local (small area) measure of the relative racial homogeneity of each neighborhood within an MSA. • Higher values indicate higher racial segregation. • This index can be calculated for any two groups (or two characteristics), so researchers have to choose which groups to use in their measure of LQRRS.
Sample/Data	Two data sources were used to compute and validate the LQRRS: • Wave 1 (1992) and Wave 5 (2000) of the Health and Retirement Study (HRS, $N = 7{,}608$ households and 12,652 individuals) • The 1990 U.S. Decennial Census to obtain the population values at the Metropolitan Statistical Area (MSA) and census tract levels
Measurement	$LQ_{im} = (x_{im}/X^i)/(X_m/X)$ where $LQim$ = the value for the *ith* unit or tract in a region or MSA for minority group *m* x_{im} = the number of individuals from minority group m living in the *ith* tract X_i = the total number of residents in the *ith* tract of the MSA X_m = the total number of individuals from minority group m in the MSA X = the total number of residents in the MSA
Related Reference	Pruitt, S. L., Lee, S. J. C., Tiro, J. A., Xuan, L., Ruiz, J. M., & Inrig, S. (2015). Residential racial segregation and mortality among black, white, and Hispanic urban breast cancer patients in Texas, 1995 to 2009. *Cancer, 121*(11), 1845–1855.
Language	English
Contact	Joseph J. Sudano Center for Health Care Research and Policy Case Western Reserve University at The MetroHealth System 2500 MetroHealth Drive, Rammelkamp 236a Cleveland, OH 44109, USA Email: jsudano@metrohealth.org

TABLE 12.14 ■ Index of Concentration at the Extremes (ICE)

Primary Reference	Sampson, R. J., Mare, R. D., & Perkins, K. L. (2015). Achieving middle ground in an age of concentrated extremes: Mixed middle-income neighborhoods and emerging adulthood. *ANNALS of the American Academy of Political and Social Science, 660*(1), 156–174.
Purpose	The purpose of this measure is to quantify the degree to which a neighborhood is a mixed income neighborhood. The measure speaks to the concern about both the concentration of poverty and the process of gentrification.
Description	• This measure places each neighborhood along a relative continuum of concentrated affluence and poverty. • Neighborhoods with neither a disproportionate number of affluent or poor households score zero on the measure. • Positive values are indicative of departure from equality in the direction of affluence and negative values in the direction of poverty.
Sample/ Data	The Census tracts in Cook County Illinois comprise the sample for validation of the ICE. The data used were from the American Community Survey 2008–2012. The ICE values ranged from −0.85 to 0.70. Of all the tracts in Cook County, 18% were in the mixed-income range.
Measurement	The ICE uses census data to obtain the counts of affluent, poor, and total family households in each neighborhood at a point in time. The income cut points for affluent and poor households are based on cut points for the top and lowest quintile of income distribution in the nation at that point in time. For each neighborhood, the ICE is calculated as $$\text{ICE} = \frac{A_i - P_i}{T_i}$$ where *A* is the number of affluent households or individuals *P* is the number of poor households or individuals and *T* is the total population in neighborhood *i*.
Assessment	The correlation in ICE scores between two time points was .77 for tracts in Chicago and .87 for Cook County tracts outside Chicago.
Related Reference	The ICE was originally proposed by Massey, D. S. (2001). The prodigal paradigm returns: Ecology comes back to sociology. In A. Booth & A. C. Crouter (Eds.), *Does it take a village? Community effects on children, adolescents, and families* (pp. 41–48). Mahwah, NJ: Lawrence Erlbaum Associates.
Language	English
Contact	Robert J. Sampson Harvard University 33 Kirkland St. Cambridge, MA 02138, USA Email: rsampson@wjh.harvard.edu

TABLE 12.15 ■ Local Job Accessibility Index

Primary Reference	Raphael, S. (1998). The spatial mismatch hypothesis and black youth joblessness: Evidence from the San Francisco Bay Area. *Journal of Urban Economics, 43*(1), 79–111.
Purpose	This index measures the accessibility of job opportunities for the residents of a locale. Since job opportunities depend both on the number of jobs and local competitors for these jobs, this index is comprised of two components. The first component of the index is the number of accessible employment opportunities in neighborhood *i*. The second component controls for spatial differences in labor supply in a given area.
Description	• There are two component measures that combine to create the local job accessibility index. • The first component captures the demand side of labor (accessible jobs), while the second captures the supply side of labor (the number of competing job-seekers in a given area). • A distance-decay function is used to give lesser weight to jobs located at further distance.
Sample/ Data	Samples came from census tracts in the San Francisco Metropolitan Area. The study focuses on youth commute flows and employment statuses of males 16–19 years old. It also uses data from the Bay Area Metropolitan Transportation Commission on peak-period travel times and Association of Bay Area Governments on employment counts by broad industrial groupings. Since this particular study focused on job accessibility for youth, Raphael restricted his count of jobs to new openings for which youth might compete and his count of competitors for those jobs to youth 16–19.
Measurement	$$\text{JOBACCESS}_i = \sum_{j=1}^{j=J} \text{JOBS} * \exp(-\bar{r}d_{ij})$$ where Jobs = total employment opportunities in neighborhood *j*, *i* = origin neighborhood, *j* = destination neighborhood, d_{ij} = distance between neighborhoods *i* and *j*, and *r* is a decay parameter that weights job distances (i.e., farther job opportunities are given less weight). $$\text{COMPETING LABOR SUPPLY}_i = \sum_{j=1}^{j=J} \text{SUPPLY}_j * \exp(-\bar{r}d_{ij})$$ where SUPPLY_j = the sum of competitors for jobs residing in neighborhood *j*
Related References	Gurmu, S., Ihlanfeldt, K. R., & Smith, W. J. (2008). Does residential location matter to the employment of TANF recipients? Evidence from a dynamic discrete choice model with unobserved effects. *Journal of Urban Economics, 63*(1), 325–351. Allard, S. W., & Danziger, S. (2002). Proximity and opportunity: How residence and race affect the employment of welfare recipients. *Housing Policy Debate, 13*(4), 675–700. Bania, N., Leete, L., & Coulton, C. (2008). Job access, employment and earnings: Outcomes for welfare leavers in a US urban labour market. *Urban Studies, 45*(11), 2179–2202.

(Continued)

TABLE 12.15 ■ (Continued)	
Language	English
Contact	Steven Raphael Goldman School of Public Policy UC Berkeley 2607 Hearst Avenue Berkeley, CA 94720-7320, USA Email: stevenraphael@berkeley.edu

TABLE 12.16 ■ Accessibility Index (Z)	
Primary Reference	Talen, E., & Anselin, L. (1998). Assessing spatial equity: An evaluation of measures of accessibility to public playgrounds. *Environment and Planning A, 30*(4), 595–613.
Purpose	The purpose of this index is to quantify the degree to which any land-use activity (service or facility) can be reached from a residential location.
Description	1. **Container approach:** Number of facilities or services contained within a given unit (e.g., census tract or political precinct). 2. **Gravity potential**: Facilities are weighted by their size and adjusted for the "friction of distance." A higher score represents better access. 3. **Travel cost:** A measure of the total or average distance between each origin (census tract) and all destinations (public facilities). A lower score reflects better access. 4. **Minimum distance:** The distance from a residential location (census tract) to the closest facility. A lower score represents better access.
Sample/Data	• Data on the number and location of playgrounds (n = 88 playgrounds) in Tulsa, Oklahoma, were used. This data were obtained from the Tulsa Metropolitan Area Planning Commission's Park, Recreation and Open Space Plan 2005. • The boundary files for census tracts and for the street network of Tulsa were extracted from the census tiger files. • The tract level socioeconomic data were extracted from the 1990 census files (n = 94 census tracts).
Measurement	1. Container approach: $Z_i^c = \sum_j S_j, \ \forall j \in I$ where the number or aggregate size, S_j, is summed for those facilities located within the boundaries I of i 2. Gravity potential: $Z_i^G = \sum_j \frac{S_j}{d_{ij}^a}$ where S_j = the number of facilities or their size at each facility location j, d_{ij}^a = distance decay factor, with distance d_{ij} between tract i and facility j, and friction parameter α 3. Travel cost: $Z_i^T = \sum_j d_{ij}$ or $\bar{Z}_i^T = \sum_j \frac{d_{ij}}{N}$ where d_{ij} = distance between a residential location (tract) i and facility j, N = the total number of facilities 4. Minimum distance: $Z_i^E = \min \| d_{ij} \|$ The same notation as before
Related Reference	Koenig, J. G. (1980). Indicators of urban accessibility: Theory and application. *Transportation, 9*(2), 145–172.
Language	English
Contact	Emily Talen School of Geographical Sciences and Urban Planning Arizona State University 975 S Myrtle Avenue Tempe, AZ 85287-5302, USA Email: etalen@asu.edu
Web Sites	http://www.arcgis.com/home/item.html? id=6b0072199afb457baefb1672fea7e900 http://www.crwr.utexas.edu/gis/gishydro03/Classroom/trmproj/Okola/feedback.htm#Accessibility

REFERENCES

Aggarwal, V. R., Macfarlane, T. V., & Macfarlane, G. J. (2003). Why is pain more common amongst people living in areas of low socio-economic status? A population-based cross-sectional study. *British Dental Journal, 194*(7), 383–387.

Allard, S. W. (2002). The urban geography of welfare reform: Spatial patterns of caseload dynamics in Detroit. *Social Science Quarterly, 83*(4), 1044–1062.

Allard, S. W. (2009). Mismatches and unmet needs: Access to social services in urban and rural America. In J. P. Ziliak (Ed.), *Welfare reform and its long-term consequence for America's poor.* Cambridge, UK: Cambridge University Press.

Allard, S. W., & Danziger, S. (2002). Proximity and opportunity: How residence and race affect the employment of welfare recipients. *Housing Policy Debate, 13*(4), 675–700.

Allard, S. W., Rosen, D., & Tolman, R. M. (2003). Access to mental health and substance abuse services among women receiving welfare in Detroit. *Urban Affairs Review, 38*(6), 787–807.

Atkinson, R., & Flint, J. (2004). Fortress UK? Gated communities, the spatial revolt of the elites and time–space trajectories of segregation. *Housing Studies, 19*(6), 875–892.

Bania, N., Leete, L., & Coulton, C. (2008). Job access, employment and earnings: Outcomes for welfare leavers in a US urban labour market. *Urban Studies, 45*(11), 2179–2202.

Bischoff, K., & Reardon, S. F. (2013). Residential segregation by income, 1970–2009. In J. R. Logan (Ed.), *The lost decade? Social change in the US after 2000.* New York, NY: Russell Sage.

Bunel, M., & Tovar, E. (2013). Key issues in local accessibility measurement. *Urban Studies*, 1–17.

Charles, C. Z. (2003). The dynamics of racial residential segregation. *Annual Review of Sociology, 29*, 167–207.

Clark, W., Anderson, E., Malmberg, B., & Östh, J. (2014). *Segregation and de-segregation in metropolitan contexts: Los Angeles as a paradigm for a changing ethnic world.*

Costa, D. L., & Kahn, M. E. (2001). *Understanding the decline in social capital, 1952–1998* (Working paper no. w8295). National Bureau of Economic Research.

Coulton, C. J., Chow, J., Wang, E. C., & Su, M. (1996). Geographic concentration of affluence and poverty in 100 metropolitan areas, 1990. *Urban Affairs Review, 32*(2), 186–216.

Coulton, C. J., Jennings, M. Z., & Chan, T. (2013). How big is my neighborhood? Individual and contextual effects on perceptions of neighborhood scale. *American Journal of Community Psychology, 51*(1–2), 140–150.

Ellen, I. G., Horn, K., & O'Regan, K. (2012). Pathways to integration: Examining changes in the prevalence of racially integrated neighborhoods. *Cityscape, 14*(3), 33–53.

Ellen, I. G., Mijanovich, T., & Dillman, K. N. (2001). Neighborhood effects on health: Exploring the links and assessing the evidence. *Journal of Urban Affairs, 23*(3–4), 391–408.

Ellen, I. G., & O'Regan, K. M. (2011). How low income neighborhoods change: Entry, exit, and enhancement. *Regional Science and Urban Economics, 41*(2), 89–97.

Ellen, I. G., & Turner, M. A. (1997). Does neighborhood matter? Assessing recent evidence. *Housing Policy Debate, 8*(4), 833–866.

Elliott, D. S., Menard, S., Rankin, B., Elliott, A., Wilson, W. J., & Huizinga, D. (2006). *Good kids from bad neighborhoods: Successful development in social context.* Cambridge: Cambridge University Press.

Ellwood, D. T. (1986). *Targeting would-be long-term recipients of AFDC.* Princeton, NJ: Mathematica Policy Research.

Farrell, C. R., & Lee, B. A. (2011). Racial diversity and change in metropolitan neighborhoods. *Social Science Research, 40*(4), 1108–1123.

Galster, G. (2012). The mechanism(s) of neighbourhood effects: Theory, evidence, and policy implications. In M. van Ham, D. Manley, N. Bailey, L. Simpson, D. Maclennan (Eds.), *Neighbourhood effects research: New perspectives* (pp. 23–56). Dordrecht, NL: Springer.

Galster, G. C., Booza, J. C., & Cutsinger, J. M. (2008). Income diversity within neighborhoods and very low-income families. *Cityscape, 10*(2), 257–300.

Golledge, R., & Stimson, R. (1997). *Spatial behavior: A geographic perspective.* New York: Guilford Press.

Gurley, T., & Bruce, D. (2005). The effects of car access on employment outcomes for welfare recipients. *Journal of Urban Economics, 58*(2), 250–272.

Gurmu, S., Ihlanfeldt, K. R., & Smith, W. J. (2008). Does residential location matter to the employment of TANF recipients? Evidence from a dynamic discrete choice model with unobserved effects. *Journal of Urban Economics, 63*(1), 325–351.

Gurmu, S., & Smith, W. J. (2006). Recidivism among welfare recipients: The role of neighborhood and access to employment. *Atlantic Economic Journal, 34*(4), 405–419.

Handy, S. L., & Niemeier, D. A. (1997). Measuring accessibility: An exploration of issues and alternatives. *Environment and Planning A, 29*(7), 1175–1194.

Holzer, H. J., & Ihlanfeldt, K. R. (1996). *Spatial factors and the employment of blacks at the firm level.* Madison, WI: Institute for Research on Poverty, University of Wisconsin.

Hu, L. (2014). Changing job access of the poor: Effects of spatial and socioeconomic transformations in Chicago, 1990–2010. *Urban Studies, 51*(4), 675–692.

Iceland, J. (2002). Appendix B: *Measures of residential segregation. Housing patterns.* U.S. Census Bureau. Available at http://www.census.gov/hhes/www/housing/housing_patterns/app_b.html

Iceland, J. (2004a). Beyond black and white: Metropolitan residential segregation in multi-ethnic America. *Social Science Research, 33*(2), 248–271.

Iceland, J. (2004b). The multigroup entropy index (also known as Theil's H or the information theory index). *US Census Bureau.*

Iceland, J., & Scopilliti, M. (2008). Immigrant residential segregation in US metropolitan areas, 1990–2000. *Demography, 45*(1), 79–94.

Ihlanfeldt, K. (1994). The spatial mismatch between jobs and residential locations within urban areas. *Cityscape, 1*(1), 219–244.

Jargowsky, P. A. (1996). Take the money and run: Economic segregation in US metropolitan areas. *American Sociological Review, 61*(6), 984–998.

Jargowsky, P. A. (1997). *Poverty and place: Ghettos, barrios, and the American city.* New York: Russell Sage Foundation.

Joseph, M. L., Chaskin, R. J., & Webber, H. S. (2007). The theoretical basis for addressing poverty through mixed-income development. *Urban Affairs Review, 42*(3), 369–409.

Kain, J. F. (1968). Housing segregation, Negro employment, and metropolitan decentralization. *The Quarterly Journal of Economics, 82*(2), 175–197.

Kain, J. F. (2004). A pioneer's perspective on the spatial mismatch literature. *Urban Studies, 41*(1), 7–32.

Kind, A. J., Jencks, S., Brock, J., Yu, M., Bartels, C., Ehlenbach, W., . . . & Smith, M. (2014). Neighborhood socioeconomic disadvantage and 30-day rehospitalization: A retrospective cohort study. *Annals of Internal Medicine, 161*(11), 765–774.

Koenig, J. G. (1980). Indicators of urban accessibility: theory and application. *Transportation, 9*(2), 145–172.

Kramer, M. R., & Hogue, C. R. (2009). Is segregation bad for your health? *Epidemiologic Reviews, 31*(1), 178–194.

Krieger, N., Chen, J. T., Waterman, P. D., Rehkopf, D. H., & Subramanian, S. V. (2003). Race/ethnicity, gender, and monitoring socioeconomic gradients in health: A comparison of area-based socioeconomic measures-the public health disparities geocoding project. *American Journal of Public Health, 93*(10), 1655–1671

Krieger, N., Chen, J. T., Waterman, P. D., Soobader, M. J., Subramanian, S. V., & Carson, R. (2002). Geocoding and monitoring of US socioeconomic inequalities in mortality and cancer incidence: Does the choice of area-based measure and geographic level matter? The public health disparities geocoding project. *American Journal of Epidemiology, 156*(5), 471–482.

Kwan, M.-P. (2013). Beyond space (as we know it): Toward temporally integrated geographies of segregation, health and accessibility. *Annals of the Association of American Geographers, 103*(5), 1078–1086.

LaVeist, T. A. (2003). Racial segregation and longevity among African Americans: An individual-level analysis. *Health Services Research, 38*(6p2), 1719–1734.

Lee, B. A., Iceland, J., & Sharp, G. (2012). Racial and ethnic diversity goes local: Charting change in American communities over three decades. *USA2010 Project.*

Lee, B. A., Reardon, S. F., Firebaugh, G., Farrell, C. R., Matthews, S. A., & O'Sullivan, D. (2008). Beyond the census tract: Patterns and determinants of racial segregation at multiple geographic scales. *American Sociological Review, 73*(5), 766–791.

Lee, J. Y., & Kwan, M. P. (2011). Visualisation of socio-spatial isolation based on human activity patterns and social networks in space-time. *Tijdschrift voor Economische en Sociale Geografie, 102*(4), 468–485.

Lens, M. (2014). Employment accessibility among housing subsidy recipients. *Housing Policy Debate, 24*(4), 671–691.

Leonard, J. (1985). *Space, time, and unemployment* (unpublished manuscript). Berkley, CA: University of California.

Leventhal, T., & Brooks-Gunn, J. (2000). The neighborhoods they live in: The effects of neighborhood residence on child and adolescent outcomes. *Psychological Bulletin, 126*(2), 309–337.

Li, H., Campbell, H., & Fernandez, S. (2013). Residential segregation, spatial mismatch and economic growth across US metropolitan areas. *Urban Studies, 50*(13), 2642–2660.

Macintyre, S., Macdonald, L., & Ellaway, A. (2008). Do poorer people have poorer access to local resources and facilities? The distribution of local resources by area deprivation in Glasgow, Scotland. *Social Science & Medicine, 67*(6), 900–914.

Massey, D. S. (2001). The prodigal paradigm returns: ecology comes back to sociology. In A. Booth & A. C. Crouter (Eds.), *Does it take a village? Community effects on children, adolescents, and families* (pp. 41–48). Mahwah, NJ: Lawrence Erlbaum Associates.

Massey, D. S., Condron, G. A., & Denton, N. A. (1987). The effects of residential segregation on black social and economic mobility. *Social Forces, 66*(1), 29–56.

Massey, D. S., & Denton, N. A. (1988). The dimensions of residential segregation. *Social Forces, 67*(2), 281–315.

Massey, D. S., & Denton, N. A. (1993). *American apartheid: Segregation and the making of the underclass.* Cambridge, MA: Harvard University Press.

Massey, D. S., & Eggers, M. L. (1990). The ecology of inequality: Minorities and the concentration of poverty, 1970–1980. *American Journal of Sociology, 95*(5), 1153–1188.

Massey, D. S., & Fischer, M. J. (2003). The geography of inequality in the United States, 1950–2000. *Brookings-Wharton Papers on Urban Affairs*, 2003, 1–39

Massey, D. S., White, M. J., & Phua, V. C. (1996). The dimensions of segregation revisited. *Sociological Methods & Research, 25*(2), 172–206.

McFarland, M., & Smith, C. A. (2011). Segregation, race, and infant well-being. *Population Research and Policy Review, 30*(3), 467–493.

McKenzie, B. S. (2013). Neighborhood access to transit by race, ethnicity, and poverty in Portland, OR. *City & Community, 12*(2), 134–155.

Modarres, A. (2004). Neighborhood integration: Temporality and social fracture. *Journal of Urban Affairs, 26*(3), 351–377.

Oakes, J. M. (2004). The (mis) estimation of neighborhood effects: Causal inference for a practicable social epidemiology. *Social Science & Medicine, 58*(10), 1929–1952.

Ong, P., & Blumenberg, E. (1998). Job access, commute and travel burden among welfare recipients. *Urban Studies, 35*(1), 77–93.

Östh, J., Clark, W. A., & Malmberg, B. (2015). Measuring the scale of segregation using k-nearest neighbor aggregates. *Geographical Analysis, 47*(1), 34–49.

Pan, S., Jensen, H. H., Fuller, W. A., & Mohanty, S. (2006). The effects of local labour market conditions on welfare programme participation. *Applied Economics, 38*(6), 649–659.

Parks, V. (2004). Access to work: The effects of spatial and social accessibility on unemployment for native-born black and immigrant women in Los Angeles. *Economic Geography, 80*(2), 141–172.

Pruitt, S. L., Lee, S. J. C., Tiro, J. A., Xuan, L., Ruiz, J. M., & Inrig, S. (2015). Residential racial segregation and mortality among Black, White, and Hispanic urban breast cancer patients in Texas, 1995 to 2009. *Cancer, 121*(11), 1845–1855.

Raphael, S. (1998). The spatial mismatch hypothesis and black youth joblessness: Evidence from the San Francisco Bay Area. *Journal of Urban Economics, 43*(1), 79–111.

Reardon, S. F., & Bischoff, K. (2011). Income inequality and income segregation. *American Journal of Sociology, 116*(4), 1092–1153.

Reardon, S. F., & Firebaugh, G. (2002). Measures of multigroup segregation. *Sociological Methodology, 32*(1), 33–67.

Reardon, S. F., Matthews, S. A., O'Sullivan, D., Lee, B. A., Firebaugh, G., Farrell, C. R., & Bischoff, K. (2008). The geographic scale of metropolitan racial segregation. *Demography, 45*(3), 489–514.

Reardon, S. F., & O'Sullivan, D. (2004). Measures of spatial segregation. *Sociological Methodology, 34*(1), 121–162.

Sampson, R. J., Mare, R. D., & Perkins, K. L. (2015). Achieving the Middle Ground in an Age of Concentrated Extremes Mixed Middle-Income Neighborhoods and Emerging Adulthood. *The ANNALS of the American Academy of Political and Social Science, 660*(1), 156–174.

Sampson, R. J., Morenoff, J. D., & Gannon-Rowley, T. (2002). Assessing "neighborhood effects": Social processes and new directions in research. *Annual Review of Sociology, 28*, 443–478.

Sampson, R. J., Raudenbush, S. W., & Earls, F. (1997). Neighborhoods and violent crime: A multilevel study of collective efficacy. *Science, 277*(5328), 918–924.

Sampson, R. J., & Sharkey, P. (2008). Neighborhood selection and the social reproduction of concentrated racial inequality. *Demography, 45*(1), 1–29.

Sampson, R. J., Sharkey, P., & Raudenbush, S. W. (2008). Durable effects of concentrated disadvantage on verbal ability among African-American children. *Proceedings of the National Academy of Sciences, 105*(3), 845–852.

Sanchez, T. W., Shen, Q., & Peng, Z. R. (2004). Transit mobility, jobs access and low-income labour participation in US metropolitan areas. *Urban Studies, 41*(7), 1313–1331.

Sellström, E., & Bremberg, S. (2006). Review article: The significance of neighbourhood context to child and adolescent health and well-being: A systematic review of multilevel studies. *Scandinavian Journal of Public Health, 34*(5), 544–554.

Sharkey, P. (2008). The intergenerational transmission of Context1. *American Journal of Sociology, 113*(4), 931–969.

Sharkey, P. (2013). *Stuck in place: Urban neighborhoods and the end of progress toward racial equality.* Chicago: University of Chicago Press.

Shavers, V. L. (2007). Measurement of socioeconomic status in health disparities research. *Journal of the National Medical Association, 99*(9), 1013–1023.

Sheller, M., & Urry, J. (2006). The new mobilities paradigm. *Environment and Planning A, 38*(2), 207–226.

Shen, Q. (1998). Location characteristics of inner-city neighborhoods and employment accessibility of low-wage workers. *Environment and Planning B: Planning and Design, 25*(3), 345–365.

Shen, Q. (2001). A spatial analysis of job openings and access in a US metropolitan area. *Journal of the American Planning Association, 67*(1), 53–68.

Shinn, M., & Toohey, S. M. (2003). Community contexts of human welfare. *Annual Review of Psychology, 54*(1), 427–459.

Singh, G. K. (2003). Area deprivation and widening inequalities in US mortality, 1969–1998. *American Journal of Public Health, 93*(7), 1137–1143.

Singh, G. K., & Kogan, M. D. (2007). Persistent socioeconomic disparities in infant, neonatal, and postneonatal mortality rates in the United States, 1969–2001. *Pediatrics, 119*(4), e928–e939.

Squires, G. D., & Kubrin, C. E. (2005). Privileged places: Race, uneven development and the geography of opportunity in urban America. *Urban Studies, 42*(1), 47–68.

Subramanian, S. V., Chen, J. T., Rehkopf, D. H., Waterman, P. D., & Krieger, N. (2005). Racial disparities in context: A multilevel analysis of neighborhood variations in poverty and excess mortality among Black populations in Massachusetts. *American Journal of Public Health, 95*(2), 260–265.

Sudano, J. J., Perzynski, A., Wong, D. W., Colabianchi, N., & Litaker, D. (2013). Neighborhood racial residential segregation and changes in health or death among older adults. *Health & Place, 19*, 80–88.

Talen, E. (2006). Design that enables diversity: The complications of a planning ideal. *Journal of Planning Literature, 20*(3), 233–249.

Talen, E. (2012). *Design for diversity.* New York: Routledge.

Talen, E., & Anselin, L. (1998). Assessing spatial equity: An evaluation of measures of accessibility to public playgrounds. *Environment and Planning A, 30*(4), 595–613.

Theil, H. (1972). *Statistical decomposition analysis.* Amsterdam: North-Holland Publishing Company.

Townsend, P., Phillimore, P., & Beattie, A. (1988). *Health and deprivation: Inequality and the North.* London: Croom Helm.

Vartanian, T. P. (1999). Adolescent neighborhood effects on labor market and economic outcomes. *Social Service Review, 73*(2), 142–167.

Wang, L. (2003). Determinants of child mortality in LDCs: Empirical findings from demographic and health surveys. *Health Policy, 65*(3), 277–299.

White, M. J. (1986). Segregation and diversity measures in population distribution. *Population Index, 52*(2), 198–221.

Wilson, W.J. (1987). *The truly disadvantaged.* Chicago, IL: University of Chicago Press.

Wilson, W.J. (1996). *When work disappears: The world of the new urban poor.* Chicago, IL: University of Chicago Press.

Wong, D. W. (2004). Comparing traditional and spatial segregation measures: A spatial scale perspective1. *Urban Geography, 25*(1), 66–82.

Wyly, E., Newman, K., Schafran, A., & Lee, E. (2010). Displacing New York. *Environment and Planning. A, 42*(11), 2602–2623.

13 COMMUNITY WELL-BEING AND QUALITY OF LIFE

It is generally agreed that promoting well-being is a worthwhile goal, but there is little agreement in how well-being is defined and what factors are necessary to achieve it. Aristotle defined the good life as goods of the body (i.e., physical health), goods of the mind (wisdom and moral virtue), and external goods (wealth, good friends, good communities) and concluded that if you enjoy these things that you have good well-being (Topcu, 2014). Despite this early understanding that there are many facets of well-being, the term *well-being* has often been used to refer to economic wealth or the absence of disease. Increasingly these definitions are being expanded to encompass our more comprehensive understanding of what is necessary for humans to have well-being, one of which is a healthy and functioning neighborhood or community. In addition to being acknowledged as an essential component of global well-being measurements, measures have also been developed to measure community well-being specifically. While it could be argued that all the measures that are included in this book are essential for community/neighborhood well-being, this chapter will focus on measures that consider community and/or neighborhoods as a crucial part of overall well-being and are being used to characterize a larger geographical area or measures that attempt to define and measure community/neighborhood well-being as a construct separate from individual well-being. Because of the current lack of U.S.-based community/neighborhood level measures of well-being, we include measures that have been developed internationally and are used to characterize larger geographical units. We begin by defining well-being, discuss why it is important to measure community/neighborhood well-being, summarize some examples of community/neighborhood well-being measures, and discuss the limitations of current measures.

DEFINING WELL-BEING/QUALITY OF LIFE

Despite decades of research, there is no universally accepted definition of well-being or quality of life (Topcu, 2014). Some of the discrepancies may be because of the fact that our understanding of well-being is culturally bound and has changed over time (Manderson, 2005). The other challenge when defining neighborhood or community-level well-being is its relationship to individual well-being; is it a construct that exists separate from the individuals that live in a geographic space, or is it simply an aggregation of individual well-being? Hagerty et al. (2001) use systems theory of subjective well-being to discuss well-being as a collection of throughputs or inputs that lead to the output of well-being. Within this theory they identify two types of throughputs: (a) endogenous or individual factors, such as mental and emotional reactions, and (b) exogenous factors that include structural, cultural, and social influences. It has been argued that both endogenous and exogenous factors interact to influence the outcome of well-being. In this chapter, we are concerned with measures that attempt to capture exogenous factors that contribute to individual well-being or characterize the well-being of a community, the output. It has to be remembered, as we discuss these measures, that community/neighborhood well-being does not exist separate from the overall goal of achieving optimum individual well-being. For this reason, we begin with a brief discussion of definition of individual, social, and neighborhood well-being and the conceptual connection between the three levels.

Individual Well-Being

While assessing individual well-being is not the purpose of the measures discussed in this chapter, understanding definitions of individual well-being is essential to understanding how community/neighborhood well-being is conceptualized and why questions about the neighborhood or community are included in more global measures of well-being. Individual well-being has been defined, at the most basic level, as the absences of pathology or illness. This definition centers on physical health as the main determinant of well-being and/or the defining feature of well-being but does not account for multiple domains that may be impacting health-related outcomes or acknowledge that physical health is not the only defining feature of well-being. This definition has been critiqued for being too narrow, and an expanding body of research has defined and measured individual well-being along several domains, including but not limited to physical health. Denier (2006), for example, defines subjective well-being as "an umbrella term for the different valuations people make regarding their lives, the events that happen to them, their bodies and minds, and the circumstances in which they live" (p. 153). Under this much broader definition, several important aspects of well-being have been identified, such as positive and negative affect (Denier, 2006) and life satisfaction (Chamberlain, 1988). Life satisfaction typically focuses on a individual's subjective evaluation of their life—however, some have argued that there are objective standards of living—that is, adequate food, shelter, work that can be used to assess well-being. This perspective argues that well-being is a reaction to a given set of life circumstances or environmental factors (Manderson, 2004). The acknowledgment that social and environmental factors impact individual well-being has led to the development of theory and measures to assess these connections.

Social Well-Being

The conception of social well-being stems from the assumption that individuals are essentially social and that the formation of self and sense of well-being is derived from their interaction with the social world (Keyes, 1998). Social well-being, therefore, includes social integration, social acceptance, social contribution, social actualization, and social coherence (Keyes, 1998), all of which are dependent on supportive relationships, efficacy, trust, and belonging (Michaelson, Abdallah, Steuer, Thompson, & Marks, 2009). These humanistic theories of well-being argue that there are several universal psychological needs essentially social in nature, including competence, relatedness, and self-acceptance (Diener et al., 2010). Generally, social well-being evaluates the social aspects of well-being that have been found to be essential to individual well-being. Therefore, the context for social interaction within communities and neighborhoods is central to this conception of well-being, and figures prominently in its measurement (an example of a measure of social well-being is described below).

Community or Neighborhood Well-Being

Similar to social well-being, scholars have argued that being a member of a neighborhood or community is essential to well-being (Cramm & Nieboer, 2015), serving as an antidote to isolation (O'Brien, McClendon, Ahmed, 1989; Kearns, Whitley, Tannahill, & Ellaway, 2015). Classical urban ecologists linked neighborhood characteristics to psychological distress (Park, Burgess, & McKenzie, 1984). More recently, studies have shown that neighborhoods contribute significantly to overall variations in well-being (Dong & Qin, 2017). Similar to individual well-being, neighborhood well-being can cover objective conditions as well as subjective assessment of domains of one's life.

The study of the ecology of well-being is essential to understanding what features of a neighborhood or community may be impacting individual well-being. The "ecology of well-being" is an attempt to integrate social, bio-physical, and urban predictors in the observed variation in well-being at the neighborhood level (Townshend, 2001, p. 179). Davies and Herbert (1993) identified the following aspects of place-based variation in well-being: areal content, experiential features, behaviors/interaction, and perception. The areal content was defined as objective traits within a community, such as size, environmental qualities and attributes, presence or absence of facilities/structures, aspects of built environment (see Chapters 8 and 9 for more details), and demographic characteristics. Experiential features included behaviors and interactions, such as facility use, informal interaction, mutual cooperative behaviors, organizational involvement, political participation, and economic capital flows. Perceptions included both cognitive characteristics, place identity and cognitive mapping, and affective characteristics, symbolism of place, sentiment and attachment, safety and security, empowerment, place appearance, aesthetics and empathy, and belonging. All of these constructs have been included in conceptions of community/neighborhood well-being because of their known relationship with individual well-being as well as their inclusion in an overall conception of community or neighborhood well-being. While the measurement of most of these concepts has been covered in previous chapters of this book, this chapter will cover measures of well-being that includes community/neighborhood components as central to their global measurement of well-being or that attempt to provide a comprehensive measure of neighborhood well-being by integrating multiple aspects of the community/neighborhood that may contribute to overall well-being.

WHY MEASURE NEIGHBORHOOD WELL-BEING/QUALITY OF LIFE?

Policy priorities are influenced by the overall goal or outcomes being measured. Increasingly, social democracies are using measures of well-being rather than gross domestic product (GDP) or even disability adjusted life years lost (DALY) as the metric for evaluating the success or failure of policy. The use of well-being as a more appropriate yardstick by which policies are measured has been advanced more widely in countries that have more robust social policies, such as the United Kingdom and the Netherlands (Christakopoulou, Dowson, & Gari, 2001). This alternative conceptualization of successful social policy promotes policy priorities that not only protect the economy or the health of a necessary labor force but rather facilitate the well-being of the population. The motivation for using well-being measures as an alternative to economic (GDP) and health (DALY) outcomes will be discussed in the following section.

As an Alternative to GDP

Neighborhood well-being has received increased attention lately as an important metric for the evaluation of public policy. The assumption that economic prosperity would necessarily lead to more well-being and less ill-being (defined as depression, anxiety, and decreases in social connectedness) has generally been acknowledged as untrue (Michalos, 2014). In fact, studies have found that there is a relationship between increases in GDP and increases in depression and anxiety or ill-being (Michalos, 2014). A focus on well-being rather than GDP shifts policy focus from economic growth to the distribution of wealth, health care, and education (Tiliouine, Cummins, & Davern, 2006). Rather than being evaluated for their economic impact, policies are evaluated for how they will impact a wide variety of aspects of human life that have been found to be essential to well-being (Michalos, 2014). This shift, though subtle, may impact how society evaluates policy. It is, therefore, necessary to develop reliable tools to measure well-being, not only at the national or state level but also at the neighborhood/community level. One very common metric of national well-being is the international well-being index (IWI), which comprises both personal well-being and national well-being. The Human Development Index (HDI) is another metric that has been developed to provide an alternative to GDP that considers not only wealth but education and health as well. Although most frequently used as the country level, this measure will be briefly discussed for its utility at the community or neighborhood level.

As an Alternative to DALY

The World Bank has primarily relied on a measure of disability-adjusted life years lost or DALY as their indicator of well-being (Manderson, 2004). This measure has been criticized for several reasons. Some argue that it is problematic because it makes being able bodied the ideal, leading to an attitude of ableism. Defining well-being as the absences of sickness or disability is a reflection of society that privileges perfection and does not recognize the fact that being able-bodied is a transitory state (Manderson, 2004). Focusing on health generally has been criticized as a narrow conception of well-being based on the medical paradigm, a definition that is reflective of larger western social and cultural norms.

As an alternative to a medical conception of well-being, the capabilities approach to well-being argues that society should be structured in such a way that everyone can reach their highest potential based on their ability status. Rather than arguing that being able bodied is the mark of well-being, well-being is measured based on the societies ability to facilitate every individual ability to achieve their maximum potential (Nussbaum, 2001). In line with this approach international decelerations have argued for a global society that agrees to provide for essentials to well-being regardless of cultural, social, political, and economic difference (Manderson, 2004). These statements are essentially moral and provide an outline of what "institutions, structures and services are necessary to create and sustain the kinds of societies in which we would like to live and the way in which we would like to be cared for by others" (Manderson, 2004, p. 10). The task, then, is to develop a set of policies around areas of education, law and justice, environmental protection, health care, and social welfare that allows individuals to achieve optimal well-being, if they chose, regardless of their ability status (Manderson, 2004). This theoretical perspective undergirds the use of both subjective and objective facet based measures of community/neighborhood well-being or those that assess several community/neighborhood domains believed to be essential to all people being able to achieve their optimal level well-being given their ability.

WELL-BEING MEASURES

Measures of well-being have generally fallen into two categories, global and facet based. In this chapter we will provide examples of (a) facet-based measures of individual well-being that included significant community/neighborhood components and are used to understand a geographical area, (b) global measures of community/neighborhood well-being, and (c) facet-based measures of community/neighborhood well-being. The facet-based measures of community/neighborhood well-being typically fall into two categories, subjective measures of satisfaction with community functions and/or objective measures of resources or characteristics (material living conditions) thought to be essential to overall community well-being (Topcu, 2014). While the categories vary, they generally include domains such as school/education, employment, social inclusion, housing, safety, and personal and community health. It should be noted that because of the limited number of measures that assess neighborhood/community-level well-being, we include measures of well-being assessed at larger geographical areas, such as towns or counties. Likewise, because of the increased popularity of assessing well-being as a crucial social indicator internationally, many of the measures discussed were not developed or tested in the United States. While these examples are useful to consider given the limited number neighborhood/community-level well-being measures, it is important to remember that additional tests of validity and reliability maybe required when they are being used to make inferences about neighborhood/community well-being in the U.S. context.

Facet-Based Measures of Individual Well-Being That Include Community/Neighborhood Components

Zumbo and Michalos (2000) (**Table 13.1**) provide an example of a facet-based measure of individual well-being that includes both neighborhood/community items theorized to be essential to well-being. The goal of the measures was to assess the **quality of life** of residents from Jasper, Alberta, Canada—made up of 1669 households—and was used to compare this over time. Originally the measure assessed resident's general satisfaction with 95 aspects of life and reduced them into 15 indices. Factor analytic tests initially employed failed to produce conceptually coherent factors. The authors then constructed the indices based on the domains of quality of life that they seemed to represent and then tested the Cronbach's alpha for each scale. Nine of the 15 identified domains could be considered measures of neighborhood/community-level phenomena, including elderly and disabled services and health, hospitals, and clinics (see Table 13.1 for a full list). In these measures, there are also domains measuring either larger processes at the city, state, or federal level, such as taxes or individual process, such as finances, personal worth, and interpersonal relations. All of the indices had alpha coefficients grater then .65. While this measure is not strictly measuring neighborhood-level characteristics, all of the domains included are being used to assess community-level well-being—in this case, the well-being of the town of Jasper over time—and to understand how the domains relate to a global measures of happiness, life satisfaction, and quality of life. Although the study is based out of Canada and is used to understand a small town rather than a neighborhood per se, it provides a decent example of one of the early facet-based measures that have been used to understand community-level well-being.

Keyes (1998) (**Table 13.2**) developed a facet-based measure of **social well-being** based on aspects of social relationships that have been found in social psychology to be important for individual well-being. This measure assesses five domains of social well-being: social integration, social acceptance, social contribution, social actualization, and social coherence. Like the previous measure, this measure includes items that pertain directly to communities/neighborhood and others that assess aspect of well-being that fall outside of realm of community/neighborhood measurement. More specifically, social integration and social contribution are assessed in relation to a "community," whereas the questions included in the domain of social acceptance ask the respondents to make judgments about "people," and the questions assessing social actualization and social coherence are referring to the respondent's perception of "society" or the "world." After the proposed items were trimmed based on set criteria for item to scale correlations, the study provides a final 33-item version of the five constructs as well as a shortened version that includes three items per construct. Before finalizing the scales, the author estimated a confirmatory factor analysis and assessed the indicator to scale overlap of all five construct, cutting items that had conceptual overlap. The exact wordings of final questions used in both scales as well as the Cronbach alphas and factor loadings are included in the appendix of the paper (Keyes, 1998). The final measures were further validated by correlating them with standard measures of anomie, psychosocial well-being, perceived-neighborhood health, and depression (Keyes, 1998). More specifically in Study 1, the new scales correlate in the direction expected with anomie and community involvement (Keyes, 1998). In the second study, the new scales correlated in the expected direction with generativity, neighborhood health, and perceived constrains (Keyes, 1998). In both studies, the scales correlated in the expected direction with life satisfaction, happiness, and dysphoria (Keyes, 1998). The authors conclude that they link but do not overlap with measures of mental health that represent psychological well-being. There was also a relatively strong association between social well-being and prosocial community involvement (Keyes, 1998). This measure of social well-being is theoretically driven and its psychometric properties are rigorously tested, but it does not provide a definition of what is meant by "community" or test the ecometric properties of the measure when used to assess a community/neighborhood. The reliability of this measure as a neighborhood-level construct would need to be assessed before it is used to assess neighborhood level well-being. The following are the results from the studies examining this measure:

- In Study 1, the new scales correlate in the direction expected with anomie and community involvement.
- In the second study, the new scales correlated in the expected direction with generativity, neighborhood health, and perceived constraints.
- In both studies, the scales correlated in the expected direction with life satisfaction, happiness, and dysphoria. The authors conclude that they link but do not overlap with measures of mental health that represent psychological well-being.
- They also found that social well-being is graded by education and age, much the same way that social well-being is.
- There was also a relatively strong association between social well-being and prosocial community involvement (Keyes, 1998).

Global Measures of Community/Neighborhood Well-Being

Global measures of neighborhood/community well-being are used to assess overall well-being without making assumptions about what is contributing to this evaluation (Sirgy, Widgery, Lee, & Yu, 2010). As discussed previously, at times it is assumed that well-being is simply the absence of diseases, and therefore community/neighborhood well-being is understood as the aggregation of some individual health indicator. This, however, assesses a very narrow conceptualization of well-being and is not considered a neighborhood-level measure. Global indicators of community/neighborhood well-being in contrast may ask, in general, how satisfied a person is with their community or how they perceive the overall quality of life or well-being in the community. Although frequently single item measures, some scales have been developed and tested for reliability. Sirgy and colleagues (2010) (**Table 13.3**), for example, created a **global community well-being index** (in the original measure, the items referred to Flint; this has been replaced with "the community" to make them more widely applicable) that asked participants, (a) Overall, how satisfied are you with the quality of life in the community? (b) To what extent do you enjoy living in the community? (c) When thinking about the conditions in the community, are they getting worse/the same/better? (d) In years to come, do you think the conditions in the community are getting worse/about the same/better? (e) How would you rate the community as a desirable place to live? The measure was then calculated by taking the average of the five items. The measure was found to be highly reliable with a Cronbach's alpha = .723, an average variance extracted (AVE) = .574, and a composite reliability = .741. It should be noted that, in this study, this variable was not modeled or tested at the neighborhood level, although it does provide a nice example of a geographically based global community well-being measure.

Global measures of community well-being are typically used by researchers who are not interested in understanding what characteristics of a community/neighborhood are contributing to an individual's assessment of community/neighborhood well-being, community planners that are attempting to compare global well-being levels across neighborhoods or over time, and/or those who have limited time and/or space to assess multiple domains (Sirgy et al., 2010). Although these global measures are widely used, it has been argued that facet-based indictors of community well-being are both more accurate and more useful because they assess a variety of domains that are believed to be essential to community/neighborhood well-being.

Facet-Based Indicators of Community/Neighborhood Well-Being

Community researchers may want more information about specific domains that are believed to comprise community/neighborhood well-being in order to target areas that need to be addressed. Measuring several domains that are necessary for optimal well-being has been argued to provide a more accurate assessment of well-being at the community/neighborhood level. For this reason, facet-based measures of community well-being have been developed. Facet-based measures of community well-being are based on the bottom-up spillover theory of well-being that states that communities will have well-being when the essential aspects of well-being are provided in the community context (Andrews & Withey, 1976). The challenge with these measures is determining what facets of the community/neighborhood should be included to create a measure that accurately reflects well-being. As previously discussed, models of well-being have suggested several domains that are essential to well-being (deductive measures); however, more often than not, these measures are developed inductively, relying on previous studies to identify what aspects of the community are related to global measures of well-being (Sirgy et al., 2010). We will first review some examples of facet-based measures of well-being that assess various domains using surveys, a couple that have attempted to assess multiple domains using administrative data, and one that uses both survey and administrative data to understand community/neighborhood-level well-being.

Measures Used in Surveys

Sirgy and colleagues (2010) (**Table 13.4**) argue that a facet-based measure of **community well-being** will more accurately represent community well-being then a global measure. Based on this argument, they developed a theoretically based, subjective, facet-based measure of community/neighborhood-level well-being. While all facet-based measures of community well-being are loosely based on the spillover theory of well-being, Sirgy et al. (2010) argues that they developed a measures of community well-being by considering all community systems that have been proposed within the theory to have an impact on well-being. In this theory, all of the following domains are conceptualized as being an important part of well-being that are impacted by community systems: social, leisure, health, safety, family and home, political, spiritual, neighborhood, environmental, transportation, education, work, financial, and consumer well-being. Each domain was measured using several items with alpha coefficients ranging from .56 (community systems impacting financial well-being) to .90 (community systems affecting leisure well-being). A detailed description of each item that comprises each domain and their overall alpha coefficient is included in the appendix of the article presenting this measure (Sirgy et al., 2010). The overall facet-based measure of community well-being was constructed by averaging the scores in each domain and then averaging the averages of all domains for each participant. This facet-based measure demonstrated good predicative validity, being significantly positively related to a global measure of well-being, community commitment, and overall life satisfaction. The community well-being composite index was significantly associated with the global measure of community well-being (discussed in Table 13.3) and community commitment in all four data sets and pooled (Sirgy et al., 2010). The community well-being composite index was significantly associated with overall life satisfaction in the 2001 and 2006 data sets; the life satisfaction variable was not available for the other data sets (Sirgy et al., 2010). Despite asking geographically specific questions, this measure was not assessed or modeled as a neighborhood-level measure. Sirgy and colleagues (2010) studies on both measures of community wellbeing (Table 13.3 and 13.4) found the following results:

- The community well-being composite index was significantly associated with the global measure of community well-being and community commitment in all four data sets and pooled.
- The community well-being composite index was significantly associated with overall life satisfaction in the 2001 and 2006 data sets; the life satisfaction variable was not available for the other data sets.

Christakopoulou et al. (2001) **(Table 13.5)** also created a facet-based measure of **community/neighborhood well-being**. Rather than using theory to identify the important facets to include, Christakopoulou et al. (2001) used the literature and input from key informants in the community to identify six dimensions essential to community well-being, including a good place to live, a social community, an economic community, a political community, a community that provides individuals with personal space, and a community that is attached to a larger community. The final questionnaire examined the community as (a) a place to live, including a measure of satisfaction with the build environment, environmental quality, services and facilities, and personal safety; (b) a social community, including a measure of informal interaction scale and community spirit scale; (c) an economic community, including a measure of income sufficiency scale; (d) the area as a political community, including a measure of the decision-making process scale; and (e) The area as personal space, including a measure of place attachment scale. This community well-being questionnaire was pilot tested in three neighborhoods in Greece, two neighborhoods in Ireland, and one neighborhood in the United Kingdom. Internal consistency of all scales was measured using Cronbach's alpha. Alphas were presented for the total sample and by each data collection site, and all alphas higher than .70 were considered acceptable (see Table 13.5 for details). Factor analysis of each scale was also conducted using the a priori groupings identified. All correlations among the nine factors were less than .30 except for two. When all items were entered in to the measurement model the eigenvalue criteria suggested that an eight-factor solution was the best fit; however, the nine factors were retained because each factor was conceptually meaningful. The nine factors explained 55% of the overall variance. Full factor loading and the correlations between all the scales are presented in the source article. Correlations between each of the scales and related constructs were also conducted to establish construct validity. A subsample was also used to test the test–retest reliability of the items, and high correlations were found across all constructs. Again, while this measure provides an excellent example of a subjective facet-based measure whose psychometric properties have been thoroughly tested, this study did not test if this measure reliably measures neighborhood-level well-being, and it was developed internationally.

Measures That Use Administrative Data

When administrative data is used, well-being indexes are typically limited to the availability of data in each given domain. Several indices of community well-being have been developed and are generally applied at the city, county, state, and national levels because of the limitation of administrative data. A few of these will be discussed in this section because of their possible utility at the neighborhood level where data is available. The indices generally have similar domains that are then measured in various ways dependent on available data.

In one attempt to use administrative data to understand geographically based well-being, Burd-Sharps, Guyer, Lechterman, and Lewis (2011) **(Table 13.6)** applied the **Human Development Index (HDI),** developed to measure country-level well-being at the county level to understand within state and between state differences. While this is not a neighborhood-level measure per se, it is an important measure of well-being that could be applied to the neighborhood level if the administrative data became available. The HDI is a simple formula in which health, education, and income are weighted equally. In this application of the HDI, *health* was measured using life expectancy at birth, calculated from mortality data from vital statistics collected by the state health department and population data from the National Center for Health Statistics of the CDC; *education* was measured using combined gross enrollment in all levels of education and educational-degree attainment of all adults over the age of 25; and *income* was measured using median earnings of individuals 16 years old and above. Sub-indexes were created for each item—health, education, and income—by setting minimum and maximum values for each underlying indicator. The goal posts were determined by examine the maximum and minimum in different populations and considering how these might change over time. These were then adjusted to achieve balance in the final index. The index was designed to vary from 0 to 10, with 10 being the highest level of well-being. In this study, Mississippi had a considerably lower HD index than most of the country. Differences were found by county group, and large disparities were found by the racial makeup of the county. The same analysis was done at the parish level in Louisiana. In Louisiana, two extreme

HD indices were found in the same city, Baton Rouge, and similar racial disparities were found. This index was able to detect differences in well-being at the county or parish level allowing for comparisons. While this was not applied at the neighborhood level, this formula could effectively be used to asses between neighborhood differences in well-being if the administrative data was available at the neighborhood level.

Cook and Te Linde (2009) **(Table 13.7)** assessed **community/neighborhood-level well-being** by examining administrative data in Canada. In this study, authors present a neighborhood-based measure of well-being that the city of Calgary has developed to aid the local government in the planning and distribution of social services. This index has been used since 1985. The authors acknowledge that the indicators are not based on theory but rather the availability of data. The measures are split into three large subsections: economic well-being, social well-being, physical well-being. Economic well-being includes poverty and employment. Social well-being includes family stability (lone parent) and social inclusion (i.e., recent immigrants, recent movers, knowledge of official language). Physical well-being includes personal health (hospital inpatients) and personal safety (emergency room visits, person and property crimes). In this study, two indices are created, the Index of Volume (INV)—the number of individuals in a community that experience a particular indicator—and Index of Risk (INR)—the percentage of total population in the community experiencing a given indicator. None of the indicators were weighted and therefore count equally to the overall index. These neighborhoods were then ranked and divided into quintiles, providing a typology, such as high-risk, low-volume. This study provides some innovative methods for using administrative data to understand neighborhood level well-being; however, no assessment of reliability or validity was conducted. The authors also note that their analysis was limited by the administrative data that was available to them. Lastly, the specific indicators used in this study may not be available in the United States, but the calculations employed maybe useful to U.S.-based practitioners and researchers.

Measures That Combine Survey Items and Administrative Data

Townshend (2001) **(Table 13.8)** attempted to construct a measure of **community well-being** by assessing the aspect of the community that is the most essential to individual well-being outcomes. This measure includes 55 subjective items that assessed behavioral, cognitive, and affective measures of community well-being in a survey. This study also included forty-one census items to characterize the community's social structure. Subjective items were aggregated to the neighborhood level. Both sets of data were subjected to principle component analysis (PCA). Based on this analysis, 11 social structural dimensions were identified using the administrative data accounting for 82% of the variance, and 16 experiential community structures were identified using the survey data accounting for 70% of the variance. The social structural components identified included family and age, young adult renters, socioeconomic status, housing and age, mobility, immigrants, family unemployment, migrant versus not a migrant, female single parent versus female clerical, charter versus non-charter, and male unemployment. Behavioral constructs identified included informal interaction, mutual informal cooperation, formal organizations, political participation and the supportive milieu, cognitive dimensions including individual's cognitive map, and affective dimensions including common values, safety and security, empowerment, and status symbols. A detailed list of items and factor loading is included in the paper outlining the measures. The authors then examined the amount of variance in neighborhood-level well-being that each of these factors explained. The experiential or subjective measures of community well-being examined more of the neighborhood-level variation in individual well-being than the social structural factors. The five significant experiential (survey based) factors that predicted community-level well-being included

- Activity and facility use (behavioral) was significantly associated with neighborhood-level variation in well-being. This was however a negative relationship. Common values and latent involvement (affective), moral similarity in values, and beliefs, a belief that leads to latent involvement or potential interaction or non-obligatory mutual aid (+association) was significantly associated with neighborhood-level variation in well-being.
- People similarity (cognitive), including ethnicity, age, and appearance (+association).
- Safety and security (affective), feelings of safety after dark, personal safety, and personal property safety (+association) was significantly associated with neighborhood-level variation in well-being.
- Empowerment (affective), informal collective power, and formal collective power (+association) was significantly associated with neighborhood-level variation in well-being (Townshend, 2001).

Again this study was conducted in Canada but provided a fairly comprehensive characterization of community/neighborhood well-being that is used to understand neighborhood-level variation in individual well-being. The use of both survey and administrative data also provides a rare opportunity to assess the relative relationship between objective and subjective measures of neighborhood.

CONCLUSION

Well-being is being increasingly used as an indicator of successful social policy rather than GDP and disability-adjusted life years lost. It is generally agreed that aspects of the community/neighborhood are essential for optimal well-being, but few measures have been developed to comprehensively assess well-being at the neighborhood level. The development of community/neighborhood-level measures of well-being is challenging because the definition of well-being is dependent on the social, cultural, and economic conditions of a place and an individual's life circumstances and choices (Manderson, 2004). If, for example, a researcher defines community/neighborhood well-being as strong social connections, then they may select a measure for that, or if they argue that community/neighborhood well-being is the absence of crime, then they will select a measure to assess that construct. While a substantial amount of work has been to create conceptual models of the different aspect of individual well-being, such as positive and negative affect, less has been done to understand community/neighborhood well-being separate from the individuals that comprise the geographical space. Most of the measures in this chapter have attempted to identify a multitude of neighborhood-level features that determine individual-level well-being and argue that the combination of these factors can be used to understand neighborhood-level well-being. Neighborhood researchers may only be interested in how communities/neighborhoods impact individual well-being, but it may be the case that neighborhood researchers and practitioners wish to conceptualize a construct of neighborhood well-being that is separate from our understanding of well-being at the individual level. If this is the case, more work needs to be done to theorize and test which elements of the community/neighborhood are essential to well-being. Based on the current state of development of community/neighborhood-level measures of well-being, this chapter presented facet-based measures of individual well-being that included significant community/neighborhood components and are used to understand a geographical area, global measures of community/neighborhood well-being, and facet-based measures of community/neighborhood well-being. Despite a general consensus that neighborhood/community-level well-being is an important outcome, more needs to be done to define the essential components of community well-being and validate their measurement at the neighborhood level.

LIST OF MEASURES AND TABLE NUMBERS

TABLE 13.1 ■ Quality of Life

Primary Reference	Zumbo, B. D., & Michalos, A. C. (2000). Quality of life in Jasper, Alberta. *Social Indicators Research*, *49*(2), 121–145.
Purpose	Create a community satisfaction measure that reflects the quality of life in Jasper, Alberta
Description	Questionnaires were distributed to all residents of Jasper, and they were given a plastic bag that could be picked up or dropped off. The questionnaire asked the residents about their level of satisfaction with a variety of services and their overall level of happiness, all of which were measured on Likert scales. This survey asked about the respondent's level of satisfaction on 95 aspects of life, including personal qualities (i.e., your self-esteem), employment (i.e., your work schedule), relationships (i.e., your friendships), institutions (i.e., police protection services), and the neighborhood/community (i.e., your neighborhood as a place to live), with possible responses ranging from 1, *very dissatisfied*, to 7, *very satisfied*. Questions were reduced to residents general satisfaction in the following 15 domains: **Community/neighborhood** • Child care services • Elderly and disabled services • Health, hospitals, and clinics • Recreation opportunities • Human services • Shopping facilities • Sanitation and waste removal services • House and neighborhood • Educational opportunities **City/state/federal** • Taxes • Government **Individual/interpersonal** • Personal worth • Finances • Job • Interpersonal relations
Sample	• 447 questionnaires were returned • 55% of the respondents were females, 61% were married, the average age was 44, 67% owned or were in the process of buying their own home, 37% had come high school education, and 54% were educated full time
Scoring	• The authors originally used factor-analytic techniques to construct indices but were unable to identify a factor structure that was theoretically or conceptually meaningful. • They then constructed indices that were conceptually coherent and had acceptable Cronbach alpha values. • The items in each of the indices were then averaged to create a score.

(Continued)

TABLE 13.1 ■ (Continued)

Assessment	• The alpha coefficient was calculated for each of the 15 indices: • Taxes (α = .89) • Child care services (α = .89) • Elderly and disabled services (α = .91) • Health, hospitals, and clinics (α = .88) • Recreation opportunities (α = .85) • Human services (α = .84) • Shopping facilities (α = .80) • Personal worth (α = .79) • Sanitation and waste removal services (α = .78) • Finances (α = .76) • House and neighborhood (α = .74) • Job (α = .73) • Government (α = .71) • Educational opportunities (α = .68) • Interpersonal relations (α = .67)
Language	English
Contact	Bruno D. Zumbo The University of British Columbia Measurement, Evaluation, and Research Methodology Paragon UBC Professor of Psychometrics and Measurement Institute of Applied Mathematics Email: bruno.zumbo@ubc.ca Tel.: 604-822-1931

TABLE 13.2 ■ Social Well-Being	
Primary Reference	Keyes, C. L. M. (1998). Social well-being. *Social Psychology Quarterly*, 121–140.
Purpose	Create a theoretically valid measure of social well-being
Description	The following aspects of social wellness identified in sociological literature are discussed: social integration, social acceptance, social contribution, social actualization, and social coherence. Structural determinants of these different domains are discussed. In order to construct the measure, two studies were conducted. Responses to all items ranged from 1 = *strongly disagree* to 7 = *strongly agree*. In the first study, each construct was measured with 6- to 7-item scale; in the second study, each construct was measured with a 3-item scale. The second studies scale was a subset of items used in the first and smaller study. **Social integration (5 items):** • You don't feel you belong to anything you'd call a community (–) • You feel close to other people in your community (+) • You feel like you're an important part of your community (+) **Social acceptance (7 items):** • I think that other people are unreliable (–) • You feel that people are not trustworthy (–) • You think people care about other people's problems (+) • You believe that people are kind (+) **Social contribution (7 items):** • Your behavior have some impact on other people in the community (+) • Your daily activities do not produce anything worthwhile for your community (–) • You don't have the time or energy to give anything to your community (–) • You think that your work provides an important product for society (–) **Social actualization (6 items):** • You believe that society has stopped making progress (–) • The world is becoming a better place for everyone (+) • Society isn't improving for people like you (–) **Social coherence (5 items):** • The world is too complex for me (–) • You cannot make sense of what's going on in the world (–) • You think that it is worthwhile to understand the world you live in (–) Although this measure is designed to measure aspects of community that are theoretically important for well-being, no explicit definition was provided for "community" in this study, and this measure is not validated or modeled at the neighborhood level.
Sample	• In the first, 373 adults were sampled using random digit dialing in Dane County, Wisconsin, and in the second, 3,032 adults between the ages of 25 and 74 living in the 48 contiguous states were sampled.

(Continued)

TABLE 13.2 ■ (Continued)	
	• In the first study (N = 373), 58.8% of the sample was female, 51.5% was married, 92.2% was Caucasian, 39.4% reported completing 16 or more years of education, and 36.6% of the sample reported earning more than 50k a year. • In the second sample (N = 3,032), 56.5% of the sample was female, 68.1% was married, 83.8% was Caucasian, 51.5% reported completing up to 12 years of education, and 33.6% of the sample reported earning more than 50k a year.
Scoring	The items in each construct were averaged and modeled separately.
Assessment	A confirmatory factor analysis was conducted and a five-factor solution was found to be the best fitting model in both samples. Factor loading are provided in the appendix of the article. In the first sample, the scales had the following Cronbach alpha coefficient: • Social coherence (α = .57) • Social actualization (α = .69) • Social integration (α = .81) • Social contribution (α = .75) • Social acceptance (α = .77) In the second sample, the Cronbach alphas were as follows: • Social coherence (α = .64) • Social actualization (α = .64) • Social integration (α = .73) • Social contribution (α = .66) • Social acceptance (α = .41)
Language	English
Contact	Corey Lee M. Keyes Emory University Department of Sociology 1555 Pierce Drive Tarbutton Hall Atlanta, GA 30322

TABLE 13.3 ■ Overall Community Well-Being

Primary Reference	Sirgy, M. J., Widgery, R. N., Lee, D. J., & Yu, G. (2010). Developing a measure of community well-being based on perceptions of impact in various life domains. *Social Indicators Research, 96*(2), 295–311.
Purpose	The purpose of the study is to develop a facet-based community well-being assessment tool.
Description	The author's goal was to develop a facet-based subjective measure. In the course of developing the facet-base measure, they present a global measure of community well-being. This composite index includes residents'... • Satisfaction with the overall quality of life in the community • The degree to which one enjoys living in the community • The degree to which the community is getting better • The overall evaluation of the community as being a desirable place to live
Sample	• The sample comes from four data sets from Flint, Michigan, collected in 1978 (n = 6,915), 1990 (n = 397), 2001 (n = 1,100), and 2006 (n = 846). • The majority of all samples were female: 44%, 59%, 66%, and 62%, respectively. The majority of all samples were White: 78%, 88%, 74%, 70%, respectively. • The majority of all samples owned their own home: 81%, 71%, 69%, 70%. • The majority of all samples earned less than 50K, but the samples collected in 1990 and 2001 had more individuals making more than 50K: 33.6% and 30.5%.
Scoring	This composite index was scored by averaging the responses across all four items.
Assessment	• Models were estimated separately for each data set, and then a model of the pooled data was estimated. • The measure was found to be highly reliable (α = .723) • Average variance extracted (AVE) = .574 • Composite reliability = .741.
Language	English
Contact	M. J. Sirgy Department of Marketing Pamplin College of Business Virginia Polytechnic Institute and State University Blacksburg, VA 24061-0236 Email: sirgy@vt.edu

TABLE 13.4 ■ Community Well-Being Composite Index	
Primary Reference	Sirgy, M. J., Widgery, R. N., Lee, D. J., & Yu, G. (2010). Developing a measure of community well-being based on perceptions of impact in various life domains. *Social Indicators Research, 96*(2), 295–311.
Purpose	Develop a facet-based measure of community well-being based on resident's perceived quality of life across multiple domains.
Description	The author's goal is to develop a facet-based subjective measure of community well-being based on the bottom-up spillover theory. The bottom-up spillover theory states that overall well-being is based on satisfaction in multiple domains of life and when satisfaction in these domains is achieved that it will create a net effect of overall well-being. Allied to the community context, they argue that the residents' perception of community systems on the following life domain should be assessed: • **Social well-being (4 items):** ○ Your neighbors ○ The racial mix of your neighborhood • **Leisure well-being (5 items):** ○ Entertainment facilities ○ Recreation facilities ○ Parks available in and near Flint • **Health well-being (5 items):** ○ Medical doctor services available in the Flint area ○ Dental services available in the Flint area • **Safety well-being (8 items):** ○ Race relations in the Flint area ○ Your personal safety in your neighborhood ○ Fire protection in your neighborhood ○ Crime prevention efforts in the Flint area • **Family and home well-being (6 items):** ○ The number of children in your neighborhood ○ Your own family life ○ The interior of your home • **Political well-being (7 items):** ○ Community leaders ○ Local government services generally ○ Property taxes in Flint • **Spiritual well-being (4 items):** ○ Church-related activities ○ Are you a member of a local church

	• **Neighborhood well-being (14 items):** ○ Your neighbors ○ The personal safety of your neighborhood ○ The number of trees in your neighborhood ○ The appearance of trees in your neighborhood ○ Police protection in your neighborhood ○ Grocery stores in your neighborhood • **Environmental well-being (12 items):** ○ The appearance of commercial and business area ○ The conditions of the street in the Flint area ○ The climate in the Flint area ○ Parks available in and near Flint • **Transportation well-being (4 items):** ○ The amount of traffic on your own street ○ Traffic conditions generally in the Flint area • **Education well-being (8 items):** ○ Local college and university ○ Public schools in your neighborhood ○ Libraries in the Flint area • **Work well-being (5 items):** ○ Job opportunities in the Flint area ○ Your husband's (wife's) job • **Financial well-being (4 items):** ○ Your family's income ○ The cost of living in the Flint area • **Consumer well-being (1 item)**
Sample	• The sample comes from four data sets from Flint, Michigan, collected in 1978 (n = 6,915), 1990 (n = 397), 2001 (n = 1,100), and 2006 (n = 846). • The majority of all samples were White and owned their own home. • There was variation in the number of respondents that lived in Flint within the data set collected in 1978 having the highest percentage at 55% and the data collected in 1990 having the lowest at 37%. • The majority of all samples earned less than 50K, but the samples collected in 1990 and 2001 had more individuals making more than 50K: 33.6% and 30.5%. • Models were estimated separately for each data set, and then a model of the pooled data was estimated.
Scoring	• Averaged individual's items within each life domain to create a composite score for each domain. • They then calculated a community well-being composite by averaging the composite scores across all individuals' life domains.

(Continued)

TABLE 13.4 ■ (Continued)

Assessment	Alpha reliability tests were conducted on all domains: • Safety well-being (α = .72) • Social well-being (α = .58) • Leisure well-being (α = .90) • Family and home well-being (α = .64) • Political well-being (α = .83) • Spiritual well-being (α = .79) • Neighborhood well-being (α = .84) • Environmental well-being (α = .80) • Transportation well-being (α = .57) • Educational well-being (α = .68) • Health and well-being (α = .73) • Work well-being (α = .60) • Financial well-being (α = .56) • Consumer well-being (α = N/A)
Language	English
Contact	M. J. Sirgy Department of Marketing Pamplin College of Business Virginia Polytechnic Institute and State University Blacksburg, VA 24061-0236 Email: sirgy@vt.edu

TABLE 13.5 ■ Community Well-Being Questionnaire

Primary Reference	Christakopoulou, S., Dawson, J., & Gari, A. (2001). The community well-being questionnaire: Theoretical context and initial assessment of its reliability and validity. *Social 'ndicators Research, 56*(3), 319–349.
Purpose	Create a theoretically grounded comprehensive measure of community well-being
Description	The authors began by doing a comprehensive literature review of five dimensions of community well-being. After discussion with key informants, a pilot questionnaire was created that examined the community as the following: **The community as a place to live:** • **Satisfaction with specific aspects of living conditions** ○ **Services and facilities (10 items):** • Public transport • Access to cultural facilities • Access to medical facilities • Quality of schools • Places of worship ○ **Environmental quality (5 items):** • Amount of traffic • Quality of air • Level of noise ○ **Build environment (6 items):** • Cleanliness • Greenery and parks • General appearance • **Personal safety (5 items):** ○ Safe to be at home alone during the day ○ Safe to leave the car in the street at night ○ Safe to walk alone in the street at night **The area as a social community:** • **Informal interaction scale (4 items):** ○ Speak on the phone ○ Talk outdoors • **Community spirit scale (3 items):** ○ People can rely upon one another for help ○ People could collaborate in case of a serious problem **The area as an economic community:** • **Income sufficiency scale (3 items):** ○ Income enough for the lifestyle we enjoy ○ Easy to afford unexpectedly large bills **The area as a political community:** • **Decision-making process scale (4 items):** ○ Council takes notice of residents' requests ○ Residents able to be involved in decisions

(Continued)

TABLE 13.5 ■ (Continued)

	The area as personal space:
	• **Place attachment scale (5 items):**
	  ○ Emotionally attached to the area
	  ○ Pleased to come back to the area
	  ○ Would like to be living in the area in three years' time

Sample	• The questionnaire was piloted in Greece, Ireland, and the United Kingdom. • The areas selected represented a range of environmental and socioeconomic characteristics. • Households were selected using random selection. • 706 interviews were completed with a 68% response rate. • Ages of respondents ranged from 18 to 80, with a mean of 43 years of age.
Scoring	The items in each construct were averaged and modeled separately.
Assessment	Internal consistency of all scales was measured using Cronbach's alpha. Alphas were presented for the total sample and by data collection site. Alphas of the total sample are as follows: • Satisfaction built environment (α = .79) • Satisfaction environmental quality (α = .78) • Satisfaction services and facilities (α = .82) • Personal safety (α = .75) • Informal interaction scale (α = .78) • Community spirit scale (α = .80) • Income sufficiency scale (α = .82) • Decision-making process scale (α = .84) • Place attachment scale (α = .91)
Language	English and Greek
Contact	Sophia Christakopoulou Jon Dawson and Associates Urban Consultants Chester, UK Email: jdassoc@cwcom.net

TABLE 13.6 ■ American Human Development Index

Primary Reference	Burd-Sharps, S., Guyer, P. N., Lechterman, T., & Lewis, K. (2011). The American Human Development Index: Results from Mississippi and Louisiana. In J. Sirgy, R. Phillips, & D. Rahtz (Eds.), *Community quality-of-life indicators: Best cases V* (pp. 113–136). Springer: Netherlands.
Purpose	Applies the Human Development Index, which was developed to compare countries, to communities in Mississippi and Louisiana to understand disparities.
Description	Proposed as an alternative measure to GDP, the Human Development index has been used to gauge counties' development from a more humanistic perspective. The items consist of • **Health** ○ Life expectancy at birth, calculated from mortality data from vital statistics collected by the state health department and population data from the National Center for Health Statistics of the CDC • **Education** ○ Combined gross enrollment in all levels of education and educational degree attainment of all adults over the age of 25. Both of these measures came from the American Community Survey. • **Income** ○ Median earnings of individuals 16 years old and above
Sample	The index in this study uses county-level statistics in Mississippi and Louisiana.
Scoring	• Sub-indexes are created for each item—health, education, and income—by setting minimum and maximum values for each underlying indicator. • The goalpost are determined by examining the maximum and minimum in different populations and considering how these might change over time. These are then adjusted to achieve balance in the final index. All three dimensions are weighted equally. • HD index$_i$ = (health index$_i$ + education index$_i$ + income index$_i$) /3 • The index is designed to vary from 0 to 10, with 10 being the highest level of well-being.
Language	NA
Contact	Kristen Lewis American Human Development Project Social Science Research Council Brooklyn, NY US Kristen@measureofamerica.org

TABLE 13.7 ■ Indices of Community Well-Being

Primary Reference	Cook, D., & Te Linde, J. (2009). The indices of community well-being for Calgary community districts: A neighborhood-based approach to quality of life reporting. In J. Sirgy, R. Phillips, & D. Rahtz (Eds.), *Community quality-of-life indicators: Best cases III* (pp. 165–179). Springer Netherlands.
Purpose	Develop a municipal-based well-being index that can be used to compare neighborhood well-being over time and between neighborhoods.
Description	The city of Calgary has developed a neighborhood-based measure of well-being to help in the planning and distribution of social services. Measures were converted to index values that represent the neighborhoods' value in relation to the rest of the city. The measure is split into three large subsections: • **Economic well-being** ○ Poverty ○ Employment • **Social well-being** ○ Family stability (lone parent) ○ Social inclusion (e.g.,. recent immigrants, recent movers, knowledge of official language) • **Physical well-being** ○ Personal health (hospital inpatients) ○ Personal safety (emergency room visits, person and property crimes)
Sample	The data is a mix of census data and service data.
Measurement	In this study, two indices are created, the Index of Volume (INV), and Index of Risk (INR). None of the indicators are weighted and therefore count equally in overall index. INV is the prevalence of individuals that experience a particular problem in the community. First, the number of people on average experiencing the problem for the city is calculated by totaling the total number and dividing by the total number of communities. Each community prevalence is compared to the mean where the mean equals "0." $INV = (n/a) - 1$ Where n = the number of indicator experiences for each community and a = the average for all communities. INR is the percentage of individual experiencing the problem in a particular community. This is done by calculating the percent of individuals experiencing the problem in the community and the whole city. Individual community INR scores are adjusted so that the average is "0." $INR = ((n/p)*100/r) - 1$ Where n = the number of cases for each community, p = the population for each community, and r = the rate for all communities. A community variability rating is then calculated by summing both variables. Communities are then divided into quintiles. These quintiles are then used to make policy decisions.
Assessment	No assessments of psychometric properties were done.
Language	English
Contact	Derek Cook City of Calgary, Community and Neighborhood Services, Policy and Planning Division (8116), Alberta, Canada Email: dcook@calgary.ca

TABLE 13.8 ■ Ecology of Well-Being	
Primary Reference	Townshend, I. (2001). The contribution of social and experiential community structures to the intra-urban ecology of well-being. *Canadian Journal of Urban Research, 10*(2), 175.
Purpose	This study attempts to understand what neighborhood factors are associated with the geographical distribution of well-being in order to create a measure of community level well-being.
Description	This is a case study of Lethbridge, Alberta. This study attempts to understand the ecology of well-being in an entire city. This city is the third largest in Alberta with a population of 68K. The authors used an ecological valid definition of neighborhood that is smaller than census tracts, allowing for enough variation between to make neighborhood-level inferences (*N* = 71). This study contained measures of individual experiences of community (subjective measures) and measures of the objective environment. Fifty-five items were used to measure individual-level indicators of community well-being. These items were designed to measure behavioral, cognitive, and affective aspects of the community experience. The factors identified using the individual-level experience of neighborhood include the following: **Behavioral Dimensions:** • **Informal interaction (neighboring) (8 items):** ○ Number of 20 nearest neighbors recognized on the street ○ Percentage of friends living within 3 or 4 blocks ○ Number of neighbors who have become close friends ○ Number of 20 nearest neighbors know by first name • **Mutual informal cooperation (4 items):** ○ Frequency of borrowing from neighbors ○ Frequency of requesting information/advice from neighbors in past month • **Facility use (3 items):** ○ Maximum frequency of use of any one community facility in a month ○ Total number of facilities (shops etc.) known in the area • **Formal organizations (2 items):** ○ Membership in local voluntary organizations: number of organizations • **Political participation (2 items):** ○ Extent of support of local government agencies for the needs of the community • **Supportive milieu (2 items):** ○ Extent of support of local government agencies for the needs of the community **Cognitive Dimensions:** • **People identity (4 items):** ○ Perceived similarity of age, appearance, wealth, and behavior of 20 nearest neighbors ○ Perceived ethic similarity of 20 nearest neighbors • **Cognitive mapping (4 items):** ○ Perceived ability to map main 4 or 5 streets in neighborhood ○ Perceived ability to locate nearest transit stop on a map

(Continued)

TABLE 13.8 ■ (Continued)

	Affective Dimensions:
	• **Neighborhood evaluation (2 items):**
	  ○ Relative satisfaction with present community compared to other lived in
	• **Common values and latent involvement (6 items):**
	  ○ Expected willingness of neighbors to collect mail and check house if away
	  ○ Degree to which resident are perceived to be always willing to help
	  ○ Perceived commonality with neighbors of social and moral behavior
	• **Safety and security (4 items):**
	  ○ Perceived safety in the community after dark
	  ○ Perceived fear of personal safety if alone in the community
	• **Empowerment (3 items):**
	  ○ Personal power/influence in opposing unwanted development in the area
	• **Place symbolism (3 items):**
	  ○ Degree to which residence in area signifies financial success
	  ○ Degree to which residence in area signifies status enhancement
	• **Local nuisances and appearance (3 items):**
	  ○ Degree of nuisances occurring within neighborhood
	  ○ Rating the tidiness/maintenance of the neighborhood
	• **Empathy and belonging (3 items):**
	  ○ Feeling that respondents truly "belong" in the neighborhood
	  ○ Extent to which the neighborhood provides a sense of community
	41 social structure features were subjected to a principle component analysis. **Social structure** components identified include:
	• Family and age
	• Young adult renters
	• Socioeconomic status
	• Housing and age
	• Mobility
	• Immigrants
	• Family unemployment
	• Migrant vs. no migrant
	• Female single parent vs. female clerical
	• Charter vs. non charter
	• Male unemployment

Sample	• Data was collected in Lethbridge, Alberta, using enumeration areas ($N = 71$) as the neighborhood level unit of analysis. • Social indicators were measured in the 1996 Canadian census profile. • A 200-item survey was administered to a random selection of 1,000 residents. Residents were contacted by phone and then mailed surveys with return postage included, and 300 surveys were returned. • Respondents were geocoded and responses were aggregated to the neighborhood level. • The sample was spatially randomly distributed in the city and reflected the cities' composition of males and females. • The sample was older, was more educated, and had more married people than the general population.
Scoring	The mean of the items in each construct was used to test the relationship between the components and aggregate individual well-being scores.
Assessment	• A principle component analysis was conducted on the social structure variables, and axis Oblimin rotation provided an eleven-factor solution, eleven distinct social structure components. • A separate PCA was conducted with 55 experiential measures of community well-being using a Varimax rotation. Factor loading of each identified factor is provided.
Language	English
Contact	Ivan J. Townshend Department of Geography University of Lethbridge 4401 University Drive Lethbridege, Alberta, Canada T1K3M4 (403) 329-2226 Email: Towni0@uleth.ca

REFERENCES

Andrews, F. M., & Withey, F. B. (1976). *Social indicators of well-being in America: The development and measurement of perceptual indicators.* New York: Plenum.

Burd-Sharps, S., Guyer, P. N., Lechterman, T., & Lewis, K. (2011). The American human development index: Results from Mississippi and Louisiana. In *Community quality-of-life indicators: Best cases V* (pp. 113–136). Netherlands: Springer.

Chamberlain, K. (1988). On the structure of subjective well-being. *Social Indicators Research, 20*(6), 581–604.

Christakopoulou, S., Dawson, J., & Gari, A. (2001). The community well-being questionnaire: Theoretical context and initial assessment of its reliability and validity. *Social Indicators Research, 56*(3), 319–349.

Cook, D., & Te Linde, J. (2009). The indices of community well-being for Calgary community districts: A neighborhood-based approach to quality of life reporting. In J. Sirgy, R. Phillips, & D. Rahtz (Eds.), *Community quality-of-life indicators: Best cases III* (pp. 165–179). Netherlands: Springer Netherlands.

Cramm, J. M., & Nieboer, A. P. (2015). Social cohesion and belonging predict the well-being of community-dwelling older people. *BMC Geriatrics, 15*(1), 1–10.

Davies, W. K. D., & Herbert, D. (1993). *Communities within cities: An urban social geography.* London: Belhaven Press.

Denier, Y. (2006). Public health, well-being and reciprocity. *Ethical perspectives/Catholic University of Leuven; European Centre for Christian Ethics, 12*(1), 41–66.

Diener, E., Wirtz, D., Tov, W., Kim-Prieto, C., Choi, D. W., Oishi, S., & Biswas-Diener, R. (2010). New well-being measures: Short scales to assess flourishing and positive and negative feelings. *Social Indicators Research, 97*(2), 143–156.

Dong, H., & Qin, B. (2017). Exploring the link between neighborhood environment and mental well-being: A case study in Beijing, China. *Landscape and Urban Planning, 164*, 71–80.

Hagerty, M. R., Cummins, R., Ferriss, A. L., Land, K., Michalos, A. C., Peterson, M., . . . & Vogel, J. (2001). Quality of life indexes for national policy: Review and agenda for research. *Bulletin of Sociological Methodology/Bulletin de Méthodologie Sociologique, 71*(1), 58–78.

Kearns, A., Whitley, E., Tannahill, C., & Ellaway, A. (2015). Loneliness, social relations and health and well-being in deprived communities. *Psychology, Health & Medicine, 20*(3), 332–344.

Keyes, C. L. M. (1998). Social well-being. *Social Psychology Quarterly*, 121–140.

Manderson, L. (2004). Disability, global legislation and human rights. *Development, 47*(2), 29–35.

Manderson, L. (2005). Introduction: The social context of well-being. *Rethinking well-being* (pp. 1–25). Perth: Australia Research Institute.

Michalos, A. C. (2014). *Encyclopedia of quality of life and well-being research.* Vienna: Springer.

Michaelson, J., Abdallah, S., Steuer, N., Thompson, S., & Marks, N. (2009). *National accounts of well-being: Bringing real wealth onto the balance sheet.* London: New Economics Foundation.

Nussbaum, M. C. (2001). *Women and human development: The capabilities approach* (Vol. 3). Cambridge University Press.

O'Brien, D. J., McClendon, M. J., & Ahmed, A. (1989). Neighborhood community and quality of life. *Community Development, 20*(2), 59–71.

Park, R. E., Burgess, E. W., & McKenzie, R. D. (1984). *The city.* Chicago: University of Chicago Press.

Sirgy, M. J., Widgery, R. N., Lee, D. J., & Yu, G. (2010). Developing a measure of community well-being based on perceptions of impact in various life domains. *Social Indicators Research, 96*(2), 295–311.

Tiliouine, H., Cummins, R. A., & Davern, M. (2006). Measuring well-being in developing countries: The case of Algeria. *Social Indicators Research, 75*(1), 1–30.

Topcu, U. (2014). Neighborhood well-being. In *Encyclopedia of quality of life and well-being research* (pp. 4337–4340). Springer Netherlands.

Townshend, I. (2001). The contribution of social and experiential community structures to the intra-urban ecology of well-being. *Canadian Journal of Urban Research, 10*(2), 175.

Zumbo, B. D., & Michalos, A. C. (2000). Quality of life in Jasper, Alberta. *Social Indicators Research, 49*(2), 121–145.

INDEX

Made in the USA
Columbia, SC
08 January 2022

53863822R00267